**FORD** | CRO...
1989-...

Covers U.S. and Canadian models of
**Ford Crown Victoria and Mercury Grand Marquis**

*Does not include Mercury Marauder, 5.8L V8 engine information or
information specific to natural gas-fueled models*

**by Eric Michael Mihalyi,** A.S.E., S.A.E., S.T.S.
**and Mark Ryan**

PUBLISHED BY **HAYNES NORTH AMERICA. Inc.**

Manufactured in USA
©2000, 2007, 2010 Haynes North America, Inc.
ISBN-13: 978-1-56392-904-5
ISBN-10: 1-56392-904-X
Library of Congress Control Number 2010943144

**Haynes Publishing Group**
Sparkford Nr Yeovil
Somerset BA22 7JJ England

**Haynes North America, Inc**
861 Lawrence Drive
Newbury Park
California 91320 USA

ABCDE
F

7R5-2

# Contents

**Mechanic, author and photographer with a Crown Victoria**

## ACKNOWLEDGEMENTS

Technical writers who contributed to this project include Rob Maddox, Mike Stubblefield and Larry Warren.

While every attempt is made to ensure that the information in this manual is correct, no liability can be accepted by the authors or publishers for loss, damage or injury caused by any errors in, or omissions from, the information given.

"Ford" and the Ford logo are registered trademarks of Ford Motor Company. Ford Motor Company is not a sponsor or affiliate of Haynes Publishing Group or Haynes North America, Inc. and is not a contributor to the content of this manual.

## About this manual

### ITS PURPOSE

The purpose of this manual is to help you get the best value from your vehicle. It can do so in several ways. It can help you decide what work must be done, even if you choose to have it done by a dealer service department or a repair shop; it provides information and procedures for routine maintenance and servicing; and it offers diagnostic and repair procedures to follow when trouble occurs.

We hope you use the manual to tackle the work yourself. For many simpler jobs, doing it yourself may be quicker than arranging an appointment to get the vehicle into a shop and making the trips to leave it and pick it up. More importantly, a lot of money can be saved by avoiding the expense the shop must pass on to you to cover its labor and overhead costs. An added benefit is the sense of satisfaction and accomplishment that you feel after doing the job yourself.

### USING THE MANUAL

The manual is divided into Chapters. Each Chapter is divided into numbered Sections. Each Section consists of consecutively numbered paragraphs.

At the beginning of each numbered Section you will be referred to any illustrations which apply to the procedures in that Section. The reference numbers used in illustration captions pinpoint the pertinent Section and the Step within that Section. That is, illustration 3.2 means the illustration refers to Section 3 and Step (or paragraph) 2 within that Section.

Procedures, once described in the text, are not normally repeated. When it's necessary to refer to another Chapter, the reference will be given as Chapter and Section number. Cross references given without use of the word "Chapter" apply to Sections and/or paragraphs in the same Chapter. For example, "see Section 8" means in the same Chapter.

References to the left or right side of the vehicle assume you are sitting in the driver's seat, facing forward.

Even though we have prepared this manual with extreme care, neither the publisher nor the author can accept responsibility for any errors in, or omissions from, the information given.

➡**NOTE**

**A *Note* provides information necessary to properly complete a procedure or information which will make the procedure easier to understand.**

✳ **CAUTION**

**A *Caution* provides a special procedure or special steps which must be taken while completing the procedure where the Caution is found. Not heeding a Caution can result in damage to the assembly being worked on.**

✳ **WARNING**

**A *Warning* provides a special procedure or special steps which must be taken while completing the procedure where the Warning is found. Not heeding a Warning can result in personal injury.**

## Introduction

These models are available in four-door sedan and station wagon body styles.

The Crown Victoria and Grand Marquis have the conventional front engine/rear-wheel drive layout. All models covered by this manual are equipped with a fuel-injected V8 engine.

Power from the engine is transferred through an automatic transmission to the differential mounted in the solid rear axle assembly by a tubular driveshaft incorporating universal joints. Axles inside the assembly carry power from the differential to the rear wheels.

Suspension is independent in the front, with upper and lower control arms used to locate the knuckle assembly at each wheel. The front and rear suspension features coil springs and shock absorbers. Some models are equipped with air suspension.

2002 and earlier models are equipped with a recirculating ball-type steering gearbox. 2003 and later models use rack-and-pinion steering gear.

The brakes are disc at the front and drum or disc (later models) at the rear with vacuum assist standard. Some models are equipped an Anti-lock Braking System (ABS).

## VEHICLE IDENTIFICATION NUMBERS

Modifications are a continuing and unpublicized process in vehicle manufacturing. Since spare parts lists and manuals are compiled on a numerical basis, the individual vehicle numbers are necessary to correctly identify the component required.

### VEHICLE IDENTIFICATION NUMBER (VIN)

This very important identification number is stamped on a plate attached to the dashboard inside the windshield on the driver's side of the vehicle (see illustration). The VIN also appears on the Vehicle Certificate of Title and Registration. It contains information such as where and when the vehicle was manufactured, the model year and the body style.

### VIN ENGINE AND MODEL YEAR CODES

Two particularly important pieces of information found in the VIN are the engine code and the model year code. Counting from the left, the engine code letter designation is the 8th digit and the model year code letter designation is the 10th digit.

On the models covered by this manual the engine codes are:

| | |
|---|---|
| F | 5.0L OHV V8 |
| W | 4.6L OHC V8 |

On the models covered by this manual the model year codes are:

| | |
|---|---|
| K | 1989 |
| L | 1990 |
| M | 1991 |
| N | 1992 |
| P | 1993 |
| R | 1994 |
| S | 1995 |
| T | 1996 |
| V | 1997 |
| W | 1998 |
| X | 1999 |
| Y | 2000 |
| 1 | 2001 |
| 2 | 2002 |
| 3 | 2003 |
| 4 | 2004 |
| 5 | 2005 |
| 6 | 2006 |
| 7 | 2007 |
| 8 | 2008 |
| 9 | 2009 |
| A | 2010 |

### VEHICLE CERTIFICATION LABEL

The Vehicle Certification Label is attached to the driver's side door. Information on this label includes the name of the manufacturer, the month and year of production, the Gross Vehicle Weight Rating (GVWR), the Gross Axle Weight Rating (GAWR) and the certification statement.

### ENGINE NUMBERS

Labels containing the engine code, engine number and build date can be found on the valve cover. The engine number is also stamped onto a machined pad on the external surface of the engine block.

**The VIN number is visible through the driver's side windshield**

## Buying parts

Replacement parts are available from many sources, which generally fall into one of two categories - authorized dealer parts departments and independent retail auto parts stores. Our advice concerning these parts is as follows:

**Retail auto parts stores:** Good auto parts stores will stock frequently needed components which wear out relatively fast, such as clutch components, exhaust systems, brake parts, tune-up parts, etc. These stores often supply new or reconditioned parts on an exchange basis, which can save a considerable amount of money. Discount auto parts stores are often very good places to buy materials and parts needed for general vehicle maintenance such as oil, grease, filters, spark plugs, belts, touch-up paint, bulbs, etc. They also usually sell

tools and general accessories, have convenient hours, charge lower prices and can often be found not far from home.

**Authorized dealer parts department:** This is the best source for parts which are unique to the vehicle and not generally available elsewhere (such as major engine parts, transmission parts, trim pieces, etc.).

**Warranty information:** If the vehicle is still covered under warranty, be sure that any replacement parts purchased - regardless of the source - do not invalidate the warranty!

To be sure of obtaining the correct parts, have engine and chassis numbers available and, if possible, take the old parts along for positive identification.

## Maintenance techniques, tools and working facilities

## MAINTENANCE TECHNIQUES

There are a number of techniques involved in maintenance and repair that will be referred to throughout this manual. Application of these techniques will enable the home mechanic to be more efficient, better organized and capable of performing the various tasks properly, which will ensure that the repair job is thorough and complete.

### Fasteners

Fasteners are nuts, bolts, studs and screws used to hold two or more parts together. There are a few things to keep in mind when working with fasteners. Almost all of them use a locking device of some type, either a lockwasher, locknut, locking tab or thread adhesive. All threaded fasteners should be clean and straight, with undamaged threads and undamaged corners on the hex head where the wrench fits. Develop the habit of replacing all damaged nuts and bolts with new ones. Special locknuts with nylon or fiber inserts can only be used once. If they are removed, they lose their locking ability and must be replaced with new ones.

Rusted nuts and bolts should be treated with a penetrating fluid to ease removal and prevent breakage. Some mechanics use turpentine in a spout-type oil can, which works quite well. After applying the rust penetrant, let it work for a few minutes before trying to loosen the nut or bolt. Badly rusted fasteners may have to be chiseled or sawed off or removed with a special nut breaker, available at tool stores.

If a bolt or stud breaks off in an assembly, it can be drilled and removed with a special tool commonly available for this purpose. Most automotive machine shops can perform this task, as well as other

repair procedures, such as the repair of threaded holes that have been stripped out.

Flat washers and lockwashers, when removed from an assembly, should always be replaced exactly as removed. Replace any damaged washers with new ones. Never use a lockwasher on any soft metal surface (such as aluminum), thin sheet metal or plastic.

### Fastener sizes

For a number of reasons, automobile manufacturers are making wider and wider use of metric fasteners. Therefore, it is important to be able to tell the difference between standard (sometimes called U.S. or SAE) and metric hardware, since they cannot be interchanged.

All bolts, whether standard or metric, are sized according to diameter, thread pitch and length. For example, a standard 1/2 - 13 x 1 bolt is 1/2 inch in diameter, has 13 threads per inch and is 1 inch long. An M12 - 1.75 x 25 metric bolt is 12 mm in diameter, has a thread pitch of 1.75 mm (the distance between threads) and is 25 mm long. The two bolts are nearly identical, and easily confused, but they are not interchangeable.

In addition to the differences in diameter, thread pitch and length, metric and standard bolts can also be distinguished by examining the bolt heads. To begin with, the distance across the flats on a standard bolt head is measured in inches, while the same dimension on a metric bolt is sized in millimeters (the same is true for nuts). As a result, a standard wrench should not be used on a metric bolt and a metric wrench should not be used on a standard bolt. Also, most standard bolts have slashes radiating out from the center of the head to denote the grade or strength of the bolt, which is an indication of the amount of torque that

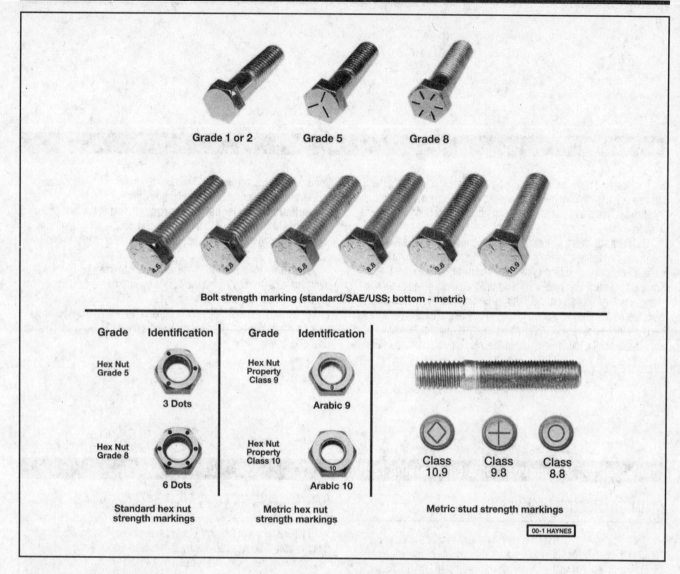

Grade 1 or 2      Grade 5      Grade 8

Bolt strength marking (standard/SAE/USS; bottom - metric)

| Grade | Identification | Grade | Identification |
|---|---|---|---|
| Hex Nut Grade 5 | 3 Dots | Hex Nut Property Class 9 | Arabic 9 |
| Hex Nut Grade 8 | 6 Dots | Hex Nut Property Class 10 | Arabic 10 |

Standard hex nut strength markings

Metric hex nut strength markings

Class 10.9      Class 9.8      Class 8.8

Metric stud strength markings

00-1 HAYNES

can be applied to it. The greater the number of slashes, the greater the strength of the bolt. Grades 0 through 5 are commonly used on automobiles. Metric bolts have a property class (grade) number, rather than a slash, molded into their heads to indicate bolt strength. In this case, the higher the number, the stronger the bolt. Property class numbers 8.8, 9.8 and 10.9 are commonly used on automobiles.

Strength markings can also be used to distinguish standard hex nuts from metric hex nuts. Many standard nuts have dots stamped into one side, while metric nuts are marked with a number. The greater the number of dots, or the higher the number, the greater the strength of the nut.

Metric studs are also marked on their ends according to property class (grade). Larger studs are numbered (the same as metric bolts), while smaller studs carry a geometric code to denote grade.

It should be noted that many fasteners, especially Grades 0 through 2, have no distinguishing marks on them. When such is the case, the only way to determine whether it is standard or metric is to measure the thread pitch or compare it to a known fastener of the same size.

Standard fasteners are often referred to as SAE, as opposed to metric. However, it should be noted that SAE technically refers to a non-metric fine thread fastener only. Coarse thread non-metric fasteners are referred to as USS sizes.

Since fasteners of the same size (both standard and metric) may have different strength ratings, be sure to reinstall any bolts, studs or nuts removed from your vehicle in their original locations. Also, when replacing a fastener with a new one, make sure that the new one has a strength rating equal to or greater than the original.

## Tightening sequences and procedures

Most threaded fasteners should be tightened to a specific torque value (torque is the twisting force applied to a threaded component such as a nut or bolt). Overtightening the fastener can weaken it and cause it to break, while undertightening can cause it to eventually come loose. Bolts, screws and studs, depending on the material they are made of and their thread diameters, have specific torque values, many of which are noted in the Specifications at the end of each Chapter. Be sure to follow the torque recommendations closely. For fasteners not assigned a specific torque, a general torque value chart is presented here as a guide. These torque values are for dry (unlubricated) fasteners threaded into steel or cast iron (not aluminum). As was previously mentioned, the size and grade of a fastener determine the amount of torque that can safely be applied to it. The figures listed here are approximate for Grade 2 and Grade 3 fasteners. Higher grades can tolerate higher torque values.

Fasteners laid out in a pattern, such as cylinder head bolts, oil pan

| Metric thread sizes | Ft-lbs | Nm |
|---|---|---|
| M-6 | 6 to 9 | 9 to 12 |
| M-8 | 14 to 21 | 19 to 28 |
| M-10 | 28 to 40 | 38 to 54 |
| M-12 | 50 to 71 | 68 to 96 |
| M-14 | 80 to 140 | 109 to 154 |

| Pipe thread sizes | | |
|---|---|---|
| 1/8 | 5 to 8 | 7 to 10 |
| 1/4 | 12 to 18 | 17 to 24 |
| 3/8 | 22 to 33 | 30 to 44 |
| 1/2 | 25 to 35 | 34 to 47 |

| U.S. thread sizes | | |
|---|---|---|
| 1/4 - 20 | 6 to 9 | 9 to 12 |
| 5/16 - 18 | 12 to 18 | 17 to 24 |
| 5/16 - 24 | 14 to 20 | 19 to 27 |
| 3/8 - 16 | 22 to 32 | 30 to 43 |
| 3/8 - 24 | 27 to 38 | 37 to 51 |
| 7/16 - 14 | 40 to 55 | 55 to 74 |
| 7/16 - 20 | 40 to 60 | 55 to 81 |
| 1/2 - 13 | 55 to 80 | 75 to 108 |

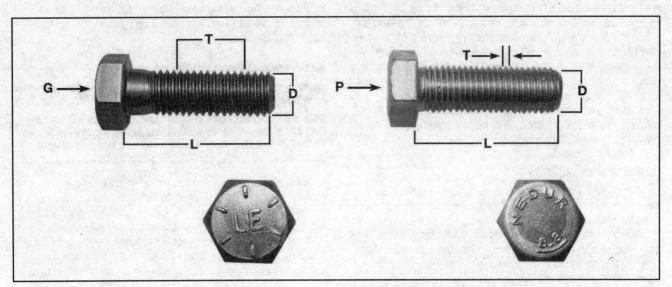

**Standard (SAE and USS) bolt dimensions/grade marks**

G   Grade marks (bolt strength)
L   Length (in inches)
T   Thread pitch (number of threads per inch)
D   Nominal diameter (in inches)

**Metric bolt dimensions/grade marks**

P   Property class (bolt strength)
L   Length (in millimeters)
T   Thread pitch (distance between threads in millimeters)
D   Diameter

bolts, differential cover bolts, etc., must be loosened or tightened in sequence to avoid warping the component. This sequence will normally be shown in the appropriate Chapter. If a specific pattern is not given, the following procedures can be used to prevent warping.

Initially, the bolts or nuts should be assembled finger-tight only. Next, they should be tightened one full turn each, in a criss-cross or diagonal pattern. After each one has been tightened one full turn, return to the first one and tighten them all one-half turn, following the same pattern. Finally, tighten each of them one-quarter turn at a time until each fastener has been tightened to the proper torque. To loosen and remove the fasteners, the procedure would be reversed.

## Component disassembly

Component disassembly should be done with care and purpose to help ensure that the parts go back together properly. Always keep track of the sequence in which parts are removed. Make note of special characteristics or marks on parts that can be installed more than one way, such as a grooved thrust washer on a shaft. It is a good idea to lay the disassembled parts out on a clean surface in the order that they were removed. It may also be helpful to make sketches or take instant photos of components before removal.

When removing fasteners from a component, keep track of their locations. Sometimes threading a bolt back in a part, or putting the

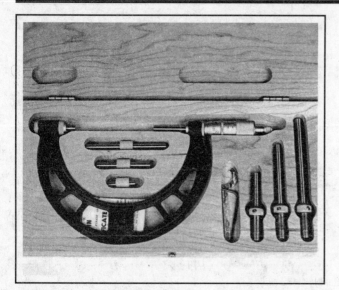

**Micrometer set**

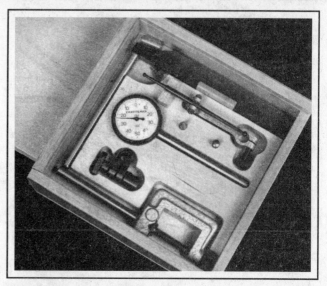

**Dial indicator set**

washers and nut back on a stud, can prevent mix-ups later. If nuts and bolts cannot be returned to their original locations, they should be kept in a compartmented box or a series of small boxes. A cupcake or muffin tin is ideal for this purpose, since each cavity can hold the bolts and nuts from a particular area (i.e. oil pan bolts, valve cover bolts, engine mount bolts, etc.). A pan of this type is especially helpful when working on assemblies with very small parts, such as the carburetor, alternator, valve train or interior dash and trim pieces. The cavities can be marked with paint or tape to identify the contents.

Whenever wiring looms, harnesses or connectors are separated, it is a good idea to identify the two halves with numbered pieces of masking tape so they can be easily reconnected.

### Gasket sealing surfaces

Throughout any vehicle, gaskets are used to seal the mating surfaces between two parts and keep lubricants, fluids, vacuum or pressure contained in an assembly.

Many times these gaskets are coated with a liquid or paste-type gasket sealing compound before assembly. Age, heat and pressure can sometimes cause the two parts to stick together so tightly that they are very difficult to separate. Often, the assembly can be loosened by striking it with a soft-face hammer near the mating surfaces. A regular hammer can be used if a block of wood is placed between the hammer and the part. Do not hammer on cast parts or parts that could be easily damaged. With any particularly stubborn part, always recheck to make sure that every fastener has been removed.

Avoid using a screwdriver or bar to pry apart an assembly, as they can easily mar the gasket sealing surfaces of the parts, which must remain smooth. If prying is absolutely necessary, use an old broom handle, but keep in mind that extra clean up will be necessary if the wood splinters.

After the parts are separated, the old gasket must be carefully scraped off and the gasket surfaces cleaned. Stubborn gasket material can be soaked with rust penetrant or treated with a special chemical to soften it so it can be easily scraped off. A scraper can be fashioned from a piece of copper tubing by flattening and sharpening one end. Copper is recommended because it is usually softer than the surfaces to be scraped, which reduces the chance of gouging the part. Some gaskets can be removed with a wire brush, but regardless of the method

used, the mating surfaces must be left clean and smooth. If for some reason the gasket surface is gouged, then a gasket sealer thick enough to fill scratches will have to be used during reassembly of the components. For most applications, a non-drying (or semi-drying) gasket sealer should be used.

### Hose removal tips

> **✳✳ WARNING:**
>
> **If the vehicle is equipped with air conditioning, do not disconnect any of the A/C hoses without first having the system depressurized by a dealer service department or a service station.**

Hose removal precautions closely parallel gasket removal precautions. Avoid scratching or gouging the surface that the hose mates against or the connection may leak. This is especially true for radiator hoses. Because of various chemical reactions, the rubber in hoses can bond itself to the metal spigot that the hose fits over. To remove a hose, first loosen the hose clamps that secure it to the spigot. Then, with slip-joint pliers, grab the hose at the clamp and rotate it around the spigot. Work it back and forth until it is completely free, then pull it off. Silicone or other lubricants will ease removal if they can be applied between the hose and the outside of the spigot. Apply the same lubricant to the inside of the hose and the outside of the spigot to simplify installation.

As a last resort (and if the hose is to be replaced with a new one anyway), the rubber can be slit with a knife and the hose peeled from the spigot. If this must be done, be careful that the metal connection is not damaged.

If a hose clamp is broken or damaged, do not reuse it. Wire-type clamps usually weaken with age, so it is a good idea to replace them with screw-type clamps whenever a hose is removed.

## TOOLS

A selection of good tools is a basic requirement for anyone who plans to maintain and repair his or her own vehicle. For the owner who has few tools, the initial investment might seem high, but when

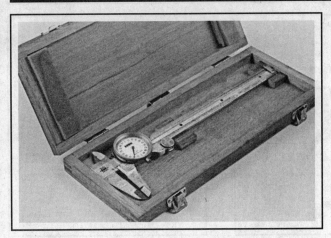

**Dial caliper**

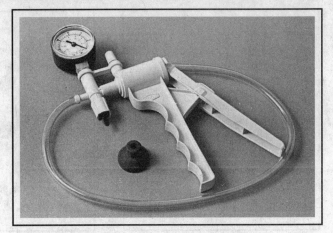

**Hand-operated vacuum pump**

**Timing light**

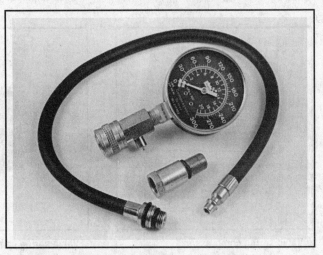

**Compression gauge with spark plug hole adapter**

compared to the spiraling costs of professional auto maintenance and repair, it is a wise one.

To help the owner decide which tools are needed to perform the tasks detailed in this manual, the following tool lists are offered: *Maintenance and minor repair, Repair/overhaul* and *Special.*

The newcomer to practical mechanics should start off with the *maintenance and minor repair* tool kit, which is adequate for the simpler jobs performed on a vehicle. Then, as confidence and experience grow, the owner can tackle more difficult tasks, buying additional tools as they are needed. Eventually the basic kit will be expanded into the *repair and overhaul* tool set. Over a period of time, the experienced do-it-yourselfer will assemble a tool set complete enough for most repair and overhaul procedures and will add tools from the special category when it is felt that the expense is justified by the frequency of use.

## Maintenance and minor repair tool kit

The tools in this list should be considered the minimum required for performance of routine maintenance, servicing and minor repair work. We recommend the purchase of combination wrenches (box-end and open-end combined in one wrench). While more expensive than open end wrenches, they offer the advantages of both types of wrench.

*Combination wrench set (1/4-inch to 1 inch or 6 mm to 19 mm)*
*Adjustable wrench, 8 inch*
*Spark plug wrench with rubber insert*

*Spark plug gap adjusting tool*
*Feeler gauge set*
*Brake bleeder wrench*
*Standard screwdriver (5/16-inch x 6 inch)*
*Phillips screwdriver (No. 2 x 6 inch)*
*Combination pliers - 6 inch*
*Hacksaw and assortment of blades*
*Tire pressure gauge*
*Grease gun*
*Oil can*
*Fine emery cloth*
*Wire brush*
*Battery post and cable cleaning tool*
*Oil filter wrench*
*Funnel (medium size)*
*Safety goggles*
*Jackstands (2)*
*Drain pan*

➡**Note: If basic tune-ups are going to be part of routine maintenance, it will be necessary to purchase a good quality stroboscopic timing light and combination tachometer/dwell meter. Although they are included in the list of special tools, it is mentioned here because they are absolutely necessary for tuning most vehicles properly.**

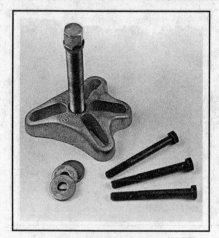

**Damper/steering wheel puller**

**General purpose puller**

**Hydraulic lifter removal tool**

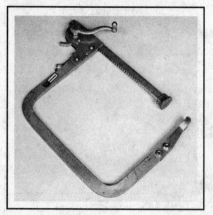

**Valve spring compressor**

**Valve spring compressor**

**Ridge reamer**

## Repair and overhaul tool set

These tools are essential for anyone who plans to perform major repairs and are in addition to those in the maintenance and minor repair tool kit. Included is a comprehensive set of sockets which, though expensive, are invaluable because of their versatility, especially when various extensions and drives are available. We recommend the 1/2-inch drive over the 3/8-inch drive. Although the larger drive is bulky and more expensive, it has the capacity of accepting a very wide range of large sockets. Ideally, however, the mechanic should have a 3/8-inch drive set and a 1/2-inch drive set.

*Socket set(s)*
*Reversible ratchet*
*Extension - 10 inch*
*Universal joint*
*Torque wrench (same size drive as sockets)*
*Ball peen hammer - 8 ounce*
*Soft-face hammer (plastic/rubber)*
*Standard screwdriver (1/4-inch x 6 inch)*
*Standard screwdriver (stubby - 5/16-inch)*
*Phillips screwdriver (No. 3 x 8 inch)*
*Phillips screwdriver (stubby - No. 2)*
*Pliers - vise grip*
*Pliers - lineman's*
*Pliers - needle nose*
*Pliers - snap-ring (internal and external)*

*Cold chisel - 1/2-inch*
*Scribe*
*Scraper (made from flattened copper tubing)*
*Centerpunch*
*Pin punches (1/16, 1/8, 3/16-inch)*
*Steel rule/straightedge - 12 inch*
*Allen wrench set (1/8 to 3/8-inch or 4 mm to 10 mm)*
*A selection of files*
*Wire brush (large)*
*Jackstands (second set)*
*Jack (scissor or hydraulic type)*

➡ **Note: Another tool which is often useful is an electric drill with a chuck capacity of 3/8-inch and a set of good quality drill bits.**

## Special tools

The tools in this list include those which are not used regularly, are expensive to buy, or which need to be used in accordance with their manufacturer's instructions. Unless these tools will be used frequently, it is not very economical to purchase many of them. A consideration would be to split the cost and use between yourself and a friend or friends. In addition, most of these tools can be obtained from a tool rental shop on a temporary basis.

This list primarily contains only those tools and instruments widely available to the public, and not those special tools produced by the vehicle manufacturer for distribution to dealer service depart-

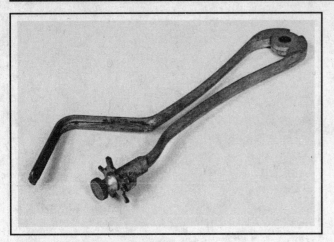

**Piston ring groove cleaning tool**

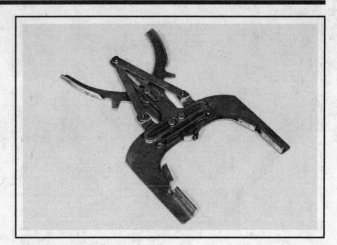

**Ring removal/installation tool**

**Ring compressor**

**Cylinder hone**

**Brake hold-down spring tool**

ments. Occasionally, references to the manufacturer's special tools are included in the text of this manual. Generally, an alternative method of doing the job without the special tool is offered. However, sometimes there is no alternative to their use. Where this is the case, and the tool cannot be purchased or borrowed, the work should be turned over to the dealer service department or an automotive repair shop.

*Valve spring compressor*
*Piston ring groove cleaning tool*
*Piston ring compressor*
*Piston ring installation tool*
*Cylinder compression gauge*
*Cylinder ridge reamer*
*Cylinder surfacing hone*
*Cylinder bore gauge*
*Micrometers and/or dial calipers*
*Hydraulic lifter removal tool*
*Balljoint separator*
*Universal-type puller*
*Impact screwdriver*
*Dial indicator set*
*Stroboscopic timing light (inductive pick-up)*
*Hand operated vacuum/pressure pump*
*Tachometer/dwell meter*
*Universal electrical multimeter*
*Cable hoist*
*Brake spring removal and installation tools*
*Floor jack*

## Buying tools

For the do-it-yourselfer who is just starting to get involved in vehicle maintenance and repair, there are a number of options available when purchasing tools. If maintenance and minor repair is the extent of the work to be done, the purchase of individual tools is satisfactory. If, on the other hand, extensive work is planned, it would be a good idea to purchase a modest tool set from one of the large retail chain stores. A set can usually be bought at a substantial savings over the individual tool prices, and they often come with a tool box. As additional tools are needed, add-on sets, individual tools and a larger tool box can be purchased to expand the tool selection. Building a tool set gradually allows the cost of the tools to be spread over a longer period of time and gives the mechanic the freedom to choose only those tools that will actually be used.

Tool stores will often be the only source of some of the special tools that are needed, but regardless of where tools are bought, try to avoid cheap ones, especially when buying screwdrivers and sockets, because they won't last very long. The expense involved in replacing cheap tools will eventually be greater than the initial cost of quality tools.

## Care and maintenance of tools

Good tools are expensive, so it makes sense to treat them with respect. Keep them clean and in usable condition and store them properly when not in use. Always wipe off any dirt, grease or metal chips before putting them away. Never leave tools lying around in the work area. Upon completion of a job, always check closely under the hood

**Torque angle gauge**

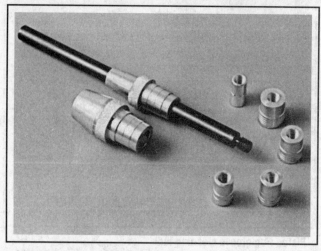

**Clutch plate alignment tool**

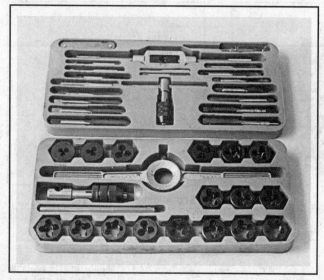

**Tap and die set**

for tools that may have been left there so they won't get lost during a test drive.

Some tools, such as screwdrivers, pliers, wrenches and sockets, can be hung on a panel mounted on the garage or workshop wall, while others should be kept in a tool box or tray. Measuring instruments, gauges, meters, etc. must be carefully stored where they cannot be damaged by weather or impact from other tools.

When tools are used with care and stored properly, they will last a very long time. Even with the best of care, though, tools will wear out if used frequently. When a tool is damaged or worn out, replace it. Subsequent jobs will be safer and more enjoyable if you do.

## HOW TO REPAIR DAMAGED THREADS

Sometimes, the internal threads of a nut or bolt hole can become stripped, usually from overtightening. Stripping threads is an all-too-common occurrence, especially when working with aluminum parts, because aluminum is so soft that it easily strips out.

Usually, external or internal threads are only partially stripped. After

they've been cleaned up with a tap or die, they'll still work. Sometimes, however, threads are badly damaged. When this happens, you've got three choices:

1) Drill and tap the hole to the next suitable oversize and install a larger diameter bolt, screw or stud.
2) Drill and tap the hole to accept a threaded plug, then drill and tap the plug to the original screw size. You can also buy a plug already threaded to the original size. Then you simply drill a hole to the specified size, then run the threaded plug into the hole with a bolt and jam nut. Once the plug is fully seated, remove the jam nut and bolt.
3) The third method uses a patented thread repair kit like Heli-Coil or Slimsert. These easy-to-use kits are designed to repair damaged threads in straight-through holes and blind holes. Both are available as kits which can handle a variety of sizes and thread patterns. Drill the hole, then tap it with the special included tap. Install the Heli-Coil and the hole is back to its original diameter and thread pitch.

Regardless of which method you use, be sure to proceed calmly and carefully. A little impatience or carelessness during one of these relatively simple procedures can ruin your whole day's work and cost you a bundle if you wreck an expensive part.

## WORKING FACILITIES

Not to be overlooked when discussing tools is the workshop. If anything more than routine maintenance is to be carried out, some sort of suitable work area is essential.

It is understood, and appreciated, that many home mechanics do not have a good workshop or garage available, and end up removing an engine or doing major repairs outside. It is recommended, however, that the overhaul or repair be completed under the cover of a roof.

A clean, flat workbench or table of comfortable working height is an absolute necessity. The workbench should be equipped with a vise that has a jaw opening of at least four inches.

As mentioned previously, some clean, dry storage space is also required for tools, as well as the lubricants, fluids, cleaning solvents, etc. which soon become necessary.

Sometimes waste oil and fluids, drained from the engine or cooling system during normal maintenance or repairs, present a disposal problem. To avoid pouring them on the ground or into a sewage system, pour the used fluids into large containers, seal them with caps and take them to an authorized disposal site or recycling center. Plastic jugs, such as old antifreeze containers, are ideal for this purpose.

Always keep a supply of old newspapers and clean rags available. Old towels are excellent for mopping up spills. Many mechanics use rolls of paper towels for most work because they are readily available

and disposable. To help keep the area under the vehicle clean, a large cardboard box can be cut open and flattened to protect the garage or shop floor.

Whenever working over a painted surface, such as when leaning over a fender to service something under the hood, always cover it with an old blanket or bedspread to protect the finish. Vinyl covered pads, made especially for this purpose, are available at auto parts stores.

## Booster battery (jump) starting

Observe these precautions when using a booster battery to start a vehicle:

a) *Before connecting the booster battery, make sure the ignition switch is in the Off position.*

b) *Turn off the lights, heater and other electrical loads.*

c) *Your eyes should be shielded. Safety goggles are a good idea.*

d) *Make sure the booster battery is the same voltage as the dead one in the vehicle.*

e) *The two vehicles MUST NOT TOUCH each other!*

f) *Make sure the transmission is in Neutral (manual) or Park (automatic).*

g) *If the booster battery is not a maintenance-free type, remove the vent caps and lay a cloth over the vent holes.*

Connect the red jumper cable to the positive (+) terminals of each battery.

Connect one end of the black jumper cable to the negative (-) terminal of the booster battery. The other end of this cable should be connected to a good ground on the vehicle to be started, such as a bolt or bracket on the body (see illustration).

Start the engine using the booster battery, then, with the engine running at idle speed, disconnect the jumper cables in the reverse order of connection.

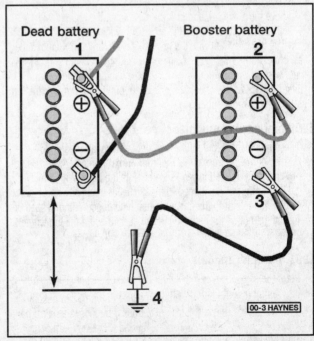

**Make the booster battery cable connections in the numerical order shown (note that the negative cable of the booster battery is NOT attached to the negative terminal of the dead battery)**

## Jacking and towing

## JACKING

### ✳✳ WARNING 1:

**The jack supplied with the vehicle should only be used for changing a tire or placing jackstands under the frame. Never work under the vehicle or start the engine while this jack is being used as the only means of support.**

### ✳✳ WARNING 2:

**On models with air suspension, turn the air suspension switch to Off before raising the vehicle.**

### ✳✳ WARNING 3:

**On models with a fire suppression system, disable the system before raising the rear of the vehicle by disconnecting the cable from the negative battery terminal and waiting at least three minutes.**

➡Note: The air suspension switch (if equipped) is located in the trunk, on the left side.

The vehicle should be located on level ground. Place the shift lever in Park. Block the wheel diagonally opposite the wheel being changed. Set the parking brake. On air suspension equipped models, turn off the air suspension switch before raising the vehicle.

Remove the spare tire and jack from stowage. If equipped with anti-theft wheel covers, pry off the ornament and remove the bolt with the special key provided with the vehicle (see illustration). Remove the wheel cover and trim ring (if so equipped) with the tapered end of the lug nut wrench by inserting and twisting the handle and then prying against the back of the wheel cover. Loosen, but do not remove, the lug nuts (one-half turn is sufficient).

### 1990 and earlier models

These models are equipped with a ratchet-type jack designed to lift one corner of the car from either the front or rear bumper. Assemble the jack by inserting the bottom end securely into the base. With the lever on the jack in the UP position, pull the ratchet assembly up and insert the hook into the slot in the under side of the bumper. With the base of the jack angled in slightly toward the vehicle and using the lug wrench as a handle, raise the vehicle enough to remove the wheel.

### 1991 and later models

Place the scissors-type jack under the side of the vehicle and adjust the jack height until it fits between the notches in the vertical rocker panel flange nearest the wheel being changed. There is a front and rear jacking point on each side of the vehicle (see illustration).

Turn the jack handle clockwise until the tire clears the ground. Remove the lug nuts and pull the wheel off. Replace it with the spare.

Install the lug nuts with the beveled edges facing in. Tighten them snugly. Don't attempt to tighten them completely until the vehicle is lowered or it could slip off the jack. Lower the vehicle. Remove the jack and tighten the lug nuts in a criss-cross pattern.

Install the cover (and trim ring, if used) and be sure it's snapped into place all the way around.

Stow the tire, jack and wrench. Unblock the wheels.

## TOWING

As a general rule, the vehicle should be towed with the rear wheels off the ground. If they can't be raised, either place them on a dolly or disconnect the driveshaft from the differential. When a vehicle is towed with the rear wheels raised, the steering wheel must be clamped in the straight ahead position with a special device designed for use during towing The ignition key must be in the OFF position, since the steering lock mechanism isn't strong enough to hold the front wheels straight while towing.

Vehicles equipped with an automatic transmission can be towed from the front only with all four wheels on the ground, provided that speeds don't exceed 35 mph and the distance is not over 50 miles. Before towing, check the transmission fluid level (see Chapter 1). If the level is below the HOT line on the dipstick, add fluid or use a towing dolly. Release the parking brake, put the transmission in Neutral and place the ignition key in the OFF position. There's no distance limitation when towing with either the rear wheels off the ground or the driveshaft disconnected, but don't exceed 50 mph.

Equipment specifically designed for towing should be used. It should be attached to the main structural members of the vehicle, not the bumpers or brackets.

Safety is a major consideration when towing and all applicable state and local laws must be obeyed. A safety chain system must be used at all times. Remember that power steering and power brakes will not work with the engine off.

**Place the jack so it engages in the notch in the rocker panel nearest the wheel to be raised**

## Automotive chemicals and lubricants

A number of automotive chemicals and lubricants are available for use during vehicle maintenance and repair. They include a wide variety of products ranging from cleaning solvents and degreasers to lubricants and protective sprays for rubber, plastic and vinyl.

## CLEANERS

*Carburetor cleaner and choke cleaner* is a strong solvent for gum, varnish and carbon. Most carburetor cleaners leave a dry-type lubricant film which will not harden or gum up. Because of this film it is not recommended for use on electrical components.

*Brake system cleaner* is used to remove brake dust, grease and brake fluid from the brake system, where clean surfaces are absolutely necessary. It leaves no residue and often eliminates brake squeal caused by contaminants.

*Electrical cleaner* removes oxidation, corrosion and carbon deposits from electrical contacts, restoring full current flow. It can also be used to clean spark plugs, carburetor jets, voltage regulators and other parts where an oil-free surface is desired.

*Demoisturants* remove water and moisture from electrical components such as alternators, voltage regulators, electrical connectors and fuse blocks. They are non-conductive and non-corrosive.

*Degreasers* are heavy-duty solvents used to remove grease from the outside of the engine and from chassis components. They can be sprayed or brushed on and, depending on the type, are rinsed off either with water or solvent.

## LUBRICANTS

*Motor oil* is the lubricant formulated for use in engines. It normally contains a wide variety of additives to prevent corrosion and reduce foaming and wear. Motor oil comes in various weights (viscosity ratings) from 0 to 50. The recommended weight of the oil depends on the season, temperature and the demands on the engine. Light oil is used in cold climates and under light load conditions. Heavy oil is used in hot climates and where high loads are encountered. Multi-viscosity oils are designed to have characteristics of both light and heavy oils and are available in a number of weights from 0W-20 to 20W-50.

*Gear oil* is designed to be used in differentials, manual transmissions and other areas where high-temperature lubrication is required.

*Chassis and wheel bearing grease* is a heavy grease used where increased loads and friction are encountered, such as for wheel bearings, ball-joints, tie-rod ends and universal joints.

*High-temperature wheel bearing grease* is designed to withstand the extreme temperatures encountered by wheel bearings in disc brake equipped vehicles. It usually contains molybdenum disulfide (moly), which is a dry-type lubricant.

*White grease* is a heavy grease for metal-to-metal applications where water is a problem. White grease stays soft under both low and high temperatures (usually from -100 to +190-degrees F), and will not wash off or dilute in the presence of water.

*Assembly lube* is a special extreme pressure lubricant, usually containing moly, used to lubricate high-load parts (such as main and rod bearings and cam lobes) for initial start-up of a new engine. The assembly lube lubricates the parts without being squeezed out or washed away until the engine oiling system begins to function.

*Silicone lubricants* are used to protect rubber, plastic, vinyl and nylon parts.

*Graphite lubricants* are used where oils cannot be used due to contamination problems, such as in locks. The dry graphite will lubricate metal parts while remaining uncontaminated by dirt, water, oil or acids. It is electrically conductive and will not foul electrical contacts in locks such as the ignition switch.

*Moly penetrants* loosen and lubricate frozen, rusted and corroded fasteners and prevent future rusting or freezing.

*Heat-sink grease* is a special electrically non-conductive grease that is used for mounting electronic ignition modules where it is essential that heat is transferred away from the module.

## SEALANTS

*RTV sealant* is one of the most widely used gasket compounds. Made from silicone, RTV is air curing, it seals, bonds, waterproofs, fills surface irregularities, remains flexible, doesn't shrink, is relatively easy to remove, and is used as a supplementary sealer with almost all low and medium temperature gaskets.

*Anaerobic sealant* is much like RTV in that it can be used either to seal gaskets or to form gaskets by itself. It remains flexible, is solvent resistant and fills surface imperfections. The difference between an anaerobic sealant and an RTV-type sealant is in the curing. RTV cures when exposed to air, while an anaerobic sealant cures only in the absence of air. This means that an anaerobic sealant cures only after the assembly of parts, sealing them together.

*Thread and pipe sealant* is used for sealing hydraulic and pneumatic fittings and vacuum lines. It is usually made from a Teflon compound, and comes in a spray, a paint-on liquid and as a wrap-around tape.

## CHEMICALS

*Anti-seize compound* prevents seizing, galling, cold welding, rust and corrosion in fasteners. High-temperature anti-seize, usually made with copper and graphite lubricants, is used for exhaust system and exhaust manifold bolts.

*Anaerobic locking compounds* are used to keep fasteners from vibrating or working loose and cure only after installation, in the absence of air. Medium strength locking compound is used for small nuts, bolts and screws that may be removed later. High-strength locking compound is for large nuts, bolts and studs which aren't removed on a regular basis.

*Oil additives* range from viscosity index improvers to chemical treatments that claim to reduce internal engine friction. It should be noted that most oil manufacturers caution against using additives with their oils.

*Gas additives* perform several functions, depending on their chemical makeup. They usually contain solvents that help dissolve gum and varnish that build up on carburetor, fuel injection and intake parts. They also serve to break down carbon deposits that form on the inside surfaces of the combustion chambers. Some additives contain upper cylinder lubricants for valves and piston rings, and others contain chemicals to remove condensation from the gas tank.

## MISCELLANEOUS

*Brake fluid* is specially formulated hydraulic fluid that can withstand the heat and pressure encountered in brake systems. Care must be taken so this fluid does not come in contact with painted surfaces or plastics. An opened container should always be resealed to prevent contamination by water or dirt.

*Weatherstrip adhesive* is used to bond weatherstripping around doors, windows and trunk lids. It is sometimes used to attach trim pieces.

*Undercoating* is a petroleum-based, tar-like substance that is designed to protect metal surfaces on the underside of the vehicle from corrosion. It also acts as a sound-deadening agent by insulating the bottom of the vehicle.

*Waxes and polishes* are used to help protect painted and plated surfaces from the weather. Different types of paint may require the use of different types of wax and polish. Some polishes utilize a chemical or abrasive cleaner to help remove the top layer of oxidized (dull) paint on older vehicles. In recent years many non-wax polishes that contain a wide variety of chemicals such as polymers and silicones have been introduced. These non-wax polishes are usually easier to apply and last longer than conventional waxes and polishes.

## CONVERSION FACTORS

### LENGTH (distance)

| | | | | | |
|---|---|---|---|---|---|
| Inches (in) | X | 25.4 = Millimeters (mm) | X | 0.0394 | = Inches (in) |
| Feet (ft) | X | 0.305 = Meters (m) | X | 3.281 | = Feet (ft) |
| Miles | X | 1.609 = Kilometers (km) | X | 0.621 | = Miles |

### VOLUME (capacity)

| | | | | | |
|---|---|---|---|---|---|
| Cubic inches (cu in; in$^3$) | X | 16.387 = Cubic centimeters (cc; cm$^3$) | X | 0.061 | = Cubic inches (cu in; in$^3$) |
| Imperial pints (Imp pt) | X | 0.568 = Liters (l) | X | 1.76 | = Imperial pints (Imp pt) |
| Imperial quarts (Imp qt) | X | 1.137 = Liters (l) | X | 0.88 | = Imperial quarts (Imp qt) |
| Imperial quarts (Imp qt) | X | 1.201 = US quarts (US qt) | X | 0.833 | = Imperial quarts (Imp qt) |
| US quarts (US qt) | X | 0.946 = Liters (l) | X | 1.057 | = US quarts (US qt) |
| Imperial gallons (Imp gal) | X | 4.546 = Liters (l) | X | 0.22 | = Imperial gallons (Imp gal) |
| Imperial gallons (Imp gal) | X | 1.201 = US gallons (US gal) | X | 0.833 | = Imperial gallons (Imp gal) |
| US gallons (US gal) | X | 3.785 = Liters (l) | X | 0.264 | = US gallons (US gal) |

### MASS (weight)

| | | | | | |
|---|---|---|---|---|---|
| Ounces (oz) | X | 28.35 = Grams (g) | X | 0.035 | = Ounces (oz) |
| Pounds (lb) | X | 0.454 = Kilograms (kg) | X | 2.205 | = Pounds (lb) |

### FORCE

| | | | | | |
|---|---|---|---|---|---|
| Ounces-force (ozf; oz) | X | 0.278 = Newtons (N) | X | 3.6 | = Ounces-force (ozf; oz) |
| Pounds-force (lbf; lb) | X | 4.448 = Newtons (N) | X | 0.225 | = Pounds-force (lbf; lb) |
| Newtons (N) | X | 0.1 = Kilograms-force (kgf; kg) | X | 9.81 | = Newtons (N) |

### PRESSURE

| | | | | | |
|---|---|---|---|---|---|
| Pounds-force per square inch (psi; lbf/in$^2$; lb/in$^2$) | X | 0.070 = Kilograms-force per square centimeter (kgf/cm$^2$; kg/cm$^2$) | X | 14.223 | = Pounds-force per square inch (psi; lbf/in$^2$; lb/in$^2$) |
| Pounds-force per square inch (psi; lbf/in$^2$; lb/in$^2$) | X | 0.068 = Atmospheres (atm) | X | 14.696 | = Pounds-force per square inch (psi; lbf/in$^2$; lb/in$^2$) |
| Pounds-force per square inch (psi; lbf/in$^2$; lb/in$^2$) | X | 0.069 = Bars | X | 14.5 | = Pounds-force per square inch (psi; lbf/in$^2$; lb/in$^2$) |
| Pounds-force per square inch (psi; lbf/in$^2$; lb/in$^2$) | X | 6.895 = Kilopascals (kPa) | X | 0.145 | = Pounds-force per square inch (psi; lbf/in$^2$; lb/in$^2$) |
| Kilopascals (kPa) | X | 0.01 = Kilograms-force per square centimeter (kgf/cm$^2$; kg/cm$^2$) | X | 98.1 | = Kilopascals (kPa) |

### TORQUE (moment of force)

| | | | | | |
|---|---|---|---|---|---|
| Pounds-force inches (lbf in; lb in) | X | 1.152 = Kilograms-force centimeter (kgf cm; kg cm) | X | 0.868 | = Pounds-force inches (lbf in; lb in) |
| Pounds-force inches (lbf in; lb in) | X | 0.113 = Newton meters (Nm) | X | 8.85 | = Pounds-force inches (lbf in; lb in) |
| Pounds-force inches (lbf in; lb in) | X | 0.083 = Pounds-force feet (lbf ft; lb ft) | X | 12 | = Pounds-force inches (lbf in; lb in) |
| Pounds-force feet (lbf ft; lb ft) | X | 0.138 = Kilograms-force meters (kgf m; kg m) | X | 7.233 | = Pounds-force feet (lbf ft; lb ft) |
| Pounds-force feet (lbf ft; lb ft) | X | 1.356 = Newton meters (Nm) | X | 0.738 | = Pounds-force feet (lbf ft; lb ft) |
| Newton meters (Nm) | X | 0.102 = Kilograms-force meters (kgf m; kg m) | X | 9.804 | = Newton meters (Nm) |

### VACUUM

| | | | | | |
|---|---|---|---|---|---|
| Inches mercury (in. Hg) | X | 3.377 = Kilopascals (kPa) | X | 0.2961 | = Inches mercury |
| Inches mercury (in. Hg) | X | 25.4 = Millimeters mercury (mm Hg) | X | 0.0394 | = Inches mercury |

### POWER

| | | | | | |
|---|---|---|---|---|---|
| Horsepower (hp) | X | 745.7 = Watts (W) | X | 0.0013 | = Horsepower (hp) |

### VELOCITY (speed)

| | | | | | |
|---|---|---|---|---|---|
| Miles per hour (miles/hr; mph) | X | 1.609 = Kilometers per hour (km/hr; kph) | X | 0.621 | = Miles per hour (miles/hr; mph) |

### FUEL CONSUMPTION *

| | | | | | |
|---|---|---|---|---|---|
| Miles per gallon, Imperial (mpg) | X | 0.354 = Kilometers per liter (km/l) | X | 2.825 | = Miles per gallon, Imperial (mpg) |
| Miles per gallon, US (mpg) | X | 0.425 = Kilometers per liter (km/l) | X | 2.352 | = Miles per gallon, US (mpg) |

### TEMPERATURE

Degrees Fahrenheit = (°C x 1.8) + 32          Degrees Celsius (Degrees Centigrade; °C) = (°F - 32) x 0.56

*It is common practice to convert from miles per gallon (mpg) to liters/100 kilometers (l/100km), where mpg (Imperial) x l/100 km = 282 and mpg (US) x l/100 km = 235*

## FRACTION/DECIMAL/MILLIMETER EQUIVALENTS

### DECIMALS to MILLIMETERS

| Decimal | mm | Decimal | mm |
|---|---|---|---|
| 0.001 | 0.0254 | 0.500 | 12.7000 |
| 0.002 | 0.0508 | 0.510 | 12.9540 |
| 0.003 | 0.0762 | 0.520 | 13.2080 |
| 0.004 | 0.1016 | 0.530 | 13.4620 |
| 0.005 | 0.1270 | 0.540 | 13.7160 |
| 0.006 | 0.1524 | 0.550 | 13.9700 |
| 0.007 | 0.1778 | 0.560 | 14.2240 |
| 0.008 | 0.2032 | 0.570 | 14.4780 |
| 0.009 | 0.2286 | 0.580 | 14.7320 |
| | | 0.590 | 14.9860 |
| 0.010 | 0.2540 | | |
| 0.020 | 0.5080 | | |
| 0.030 | 0.7620 | | |
| 0.040 | 1.0160 | 0.600 | 15.2400 |
| 0.050 | 1.2700 | 0.610 | 15.4940 |
| 0.060 | 1.5240 | 0.620 | 15.7480 |
| 0.070 | 1.7780 | 0.630 | 16.0020 |
| 0.080 | 2.0320 | 0.640 | 16.2560 |
| 0.090 | 2.2860 | 0.650 | 16.5100 |
| | | 0.660 | 16.7640 |
| 0.100 | 2.5400 | 0.670 | 17.0180 |
| 0.110 | 2.7940 | 0.680 | 17.2720 |
| 0.120 | 3.0480 | 0.690 | 17.5260 |
| 0.130 | 3.3020 | | |
| 0.140 | 3.5560 | | |
| 0.150 | 3.8100 | | |
| 0.160 | 4.0640 | 0.700 | 17.7800 |
| 0.170 | 4.3180 | 0.710 | 18.0340 |
| 0.180 | 4.5720 | 0.720 | 18.2880 |
| 0.190 | 4.8260 | 0.730 | 18.5420 |
| | | 0.740 | 18.7960 |
| 0.200 | 5.0800 | 0.750 | 19.0500 |
| 0.210 | 5.3340 | 0.760 | 19.3040 |
| 0.220 | 5.5880 | 0.770 | 19.5580 |
| 0.230 | 5.8420 | 0.780 | 19.8120 |
| 0.240 | 6.0960 | 0.790 | 20.0660 |
| 0.250 | 6.3500 | | |
| 0.260 | 6.6040 | | |
| 0.270 | 6.8580 | 0.800 | 20.3200 |
| 0.280 | 7.1120 | 0.810 | 20.5740 |
| 0.290 | 7.3660 | 0.820 | 20.8280 |
| | | 0.830 | 21.0820 |
| 0.300 | 7.6200 | 0.840 | 21.3360 |
| 0.310 | 7.8740 | 0.850 | 21.5900 |
| 0.320 | 8.1280 | 0.860 | 21.8440 |
| 0.330 | 8.3820 | 0.870 | 22.0980 |
| 0.340 | 8.6360 | 0.880 | 22.3520 |
| 0.350 | 8.8900 | 0.890 | 22.6060 |
| 0.360 | 9.1440 | | |
| 0.370 | 9.3980 | | |
| 0.380 | 9.6520 | | |
| 0.390 | 9.9060 | 0.900 | 22.8600 |
| 0.400 | 10.1600 | 0.910 | 23.1140 |
| 0.410 | 10.4140 | 0.920 | 23.3680 |
| 0.420 | 10.6680 | 0.930 | 23.6220 |
| 0.430 | 10.9220 | 0.940 | 23.8760 |
| 0.440 | 11.1760 | 0.950 | 24.1300 |
| 0.450 | 11.4300 | 0.960 | 24.3840 |
| 0.460 | 11.6840 | 0.970 | 24.6380 |
| 0.470 | 11.9380 | 0.980 | 24.8920 |
| 0.480 | 12.1920 | 0.990 | 25.1460 |
| 0.490 | 12.4460 | 1.000 | 25.4000 |

### FRACTIONS to DECIMALS to MILLIMETERS

| Fraction | Decimal | mm | Fraction | Decimal | mm |
|---|---|---|---|---|---|
| 1/64 | 0.0156 | 0.3969 | 33/64 | 0.5156 | 13.0969 |
| 1/32 | 0.0312 | 0.7938 | 17/32 | 0.5312 | 13.4938 |
| 3/64 | 0.0469 | 1.1906 | 35/64 | 0.5469 | 13.8906 |
| 1/16 | 0.0625 | 1.5875 | 9/16 | 0.5625 | 14.2875 |
| 5/64 | 0.0781 | 1.9844 | 37/64 | 0.5781 | 14.6844 |
| 3/32 | 0.0938 | 2.3812 | 19/32 | 0.5938 | 15.0812 |
| 7/64 | 0.1094 | 2.7781 | 39/64 | 0.6094 | 15.4781 |
| 1/8 | 0.1250 | 3.1750 | 5/8 | 0.6250 | 15.8750 |
| 9/64 | 0.1406 | 3.5719 | 41/64 | 0.6406 | 16.2719 |
| 5/32 | 0.1562 | 3.9688 | 21/32 | 0.6562 | 16.6688 |
| 11/64 | 0.1719 | 4.3656 | 43/64 | 0.6719 | 17.0656 |
| 3/16 | 0.1875 | 4.7625 | 11/16 | 0.6875 | 17.4625 |
| 13/64 | 0.2031 | 5.1594 | 45/64 | 0.7031 | 17.8594 |
| 7/32 | 0.2188 | 5.5562 | 23/32 | 0.7188 | 18.2562 |
| 15/64 | 0.2344 | 5.9531 | 47/64 | 0.7344 | 18.6531 |
| 1/4 | 0.2500 | 6.3500 | 3/4 | 0.7500 | 19.0500 |
| 17/64 | 0.2656 | 6.7469 | 49/64 | 0.7656 | 19.4469 |
| 9/32 | 0.2812 | 7.1438 | 25/32 | 0.7812 | 19.8438 |
| 19/64 | 0.2969 | 7.5406 | 51/64 | 0.7969 | 20.2406 |
| 5/16 | 0.3125 | 7.9375 | 13/16 | 0.8125 | 20.6375 |
| 21/64 | 0.3281 | 8.3344 | 53/64 | 0.8281 | 21.0344 |
| 11/32 | 0.3438 | 8.7312 | 27/32 | 0.8438 | 21.4312 |
| 23/64 | 0.3594 | 9.1281 | 55/64 | 0.8594 | 21.8281 |
| 3/8 | 0.3750 | 9.5250 | 7/8 | 0.8750 | 22.2250 |
| 25/64 | 0.3906 | 9.9219 | 57/64 | 0.8906 | 22.6219 |
| 13/32 | 0.4062 | 10.3188 | 29/32 | 0.9062 | 23.0188 |
| 27/64 | 0.4219 | 10.7156 | 59/64 | 0.9219 | 23.4156 |
| 7/16 | 0.4375 | 11.1125 | 15/16 | 0.9375 | 23.8125 |
| 29/64 | 0.4531 | 11.5094 | 61/64 | 0.9531 | 24.2094 |
| 15/32 | 0.4688 | 11.9062 | 31/32 | 0.9688 | 24.6062 |
| 31/64 | 0.4844 | 12.3031 | 63/64 | 0.9844 | 25.0031 |
| 1/2 | 0.5000 | 12.7000 | 1 | 1.0000 | 25.4000 |

## Safety first!

Regardless of how enthusiastic you may be about getting on with the job at hand, take the time to ensure that your safety is not jeopardized. A moment's lack of attention can result in an accident, as can failure to observe certain simple safety precautions. The possibility of an accident will always exist, and the following points should not be considered a comprehensive list of all dangers. Rather, they are intended to make you aware of the risks and to encourage a safety conscious approach to all work you carry out on your vehicle.

## ESSENTIAL DOS AND DON'TS

**DON'T** rely on a jack when working under the vehicle. Always use approved jackstands to support the weight of the vehicle and place them under the recommended lift or support points.

**DON'T** attempt to loosen extremely tight fasteners (i.e. wheel lug nuts) while the vehicle is on a jack - it may fall.

**DON'T** start the engine without first making sure that the transmission is in Neutral (or Park where applicable) and the parking brake is set.

**DON'T** remove the radiator cap from a hot cooling system - let it cool or cover it with a cloth and release the pressure gradually.

**DON'T** attempt to drain the engine oil until you are sure it has cooled to the point that it will not burn you.

**DON'T** touch any part of the engine or exhaust system until it has cooled sufficiently to avoid burns.

**DON'T** siphon toxic liquids such as gasoline, antifreeze and brake fluid by mouth, or allow them to remain on your skin.

**DON'T** inhale brake lining dust - it is potentially hazardous (see Asbestos below).

**DON'T** allow spilled oil or grease to remain on the floor - wipe it up before someone slips on it.

**DON'T** use loose fitting wrenches or other tools which may slip and cause injury.

**DON'T** push on wrenches when loosening or tightening nuts or bolts. Always try to pull the wrench toward you. If the situation calls for pushing the wrench away, push with an open hand to avoid scraped knuckles if the wrench should slip.

**DON'T** attempt to lift a heavy component alone - get someone to help you.

**DON'T** rush or take unsafe shortcuts to finish a job.

**DON'T** allow children or animals in or around the vehicle while you are working on it.

**DO** wear eye protection when using power tools such as a drill, sander, bench grinder, etc. and when working under a vehicle.

**DO** keep loose clothing and long hair well out of the way of moving parts.

**DO** make sure that any hoist used has a safe working load rating adequate for the job.

**DO** get someone to check on you periodically when working alone on a vehicle.

**DO** carry out work in a logical sequence and make sure that everything is correctly assembled and tightened.

**DO** keep chemicals and fluids tightly capped and out of the reach of children and pets.

**DO** remember that your vehicle's safety affects that of yourself and others. If in doubt on any point, get professional advice.

## STEERING, SUSPENSION AND BRAKES

These systems are essential to driving safety, so make sure you have a qualified shop or individual check your work. Also, compressed suspension springs can cause injury if released suddenly - be sure to use a spring compressor.

## AIRBAGS

Airbags are explosive devices that can CAUSE injury if they deploy while you're working on the vehicle. Follow the manufacturer's instructions to disable the airbag whenever you're working in the vicinity of airbag components.

## ASBESTOS

Certain friction, insulating, sealing, and other products - such as brake linings, brake bands, clutch linings, torque converters, gaskets, etc. - may contain asbestos or other hazardous friction material. Extreme care must be taken to avoid inhalation of dust from such products, since it is hazardous to health. If in doubt, assume that they do contain asbestos.

## FIRE

Remember at all times that gasoline is highly flammable. Never smoke or have any kind of open flame around when working on a vehicle. But the risk does not end there. A spark caused by an electrical short circuit, by two metal surfaces contacting each other, or even by static electricity built up in your body under certain conditions, can ignite gasoline vapors, which in a confined space are highly explosive. Do not, under any circumstances, use gasoline for cleaning parts. Use an approved safety solvent.

Always disconnect the battery ground (-) cable at the battery before working on any part of the fuel system or electrical system. Never risk spilling fuel on a hot engine or exhaust component. It is strongly recommended that a fire extinguisher suitable for use on fuel and electrical fires be kept handy in the garage or workshop at all times. Never try to extinguish a fuel or electrical fire with water.

## FUMES

Certain fumes are highly toxic and can quickly cause unconsciousness and even death if inhaled to any extent. Gasoline vapor falls into this category, as do the vapors from some cleaning solvents. Any draining or pouring of such volatile fluids should be done in a well ventilated area.

When using cleaning fluids and solvents, read the instructions on the container carefully. Never use materials from unmarked containers.

Never run the engine in an enclosed space, such as a garage. Exhaust fumes contain carbon monoxide, which is extremely poisonous. If you need to run the engine, always do so in the open air, or at least have the rear of the vehicle outside the work area.

## THE BATTERY

Never create a spark or allow a bare light bulb near a battery. They normally give off a certain amount of hydrogen gas, which is highly explosive.

Always disconnect the battery ground (-) cable at the battery before working on the fuel or electrical systems.

If possible, loosen the filler caps or cover when charging the battery from an external source (this does not apply to sealed or maintenance-free batteries). Do not charge at an excessive rate or the battery may burst.

Take care when adding water to a non maintenance-free battery and when carrying a battery. The electrolyte, even when diluted, is very corrosive and should not be allowed to contact clothing or skin.

Always wear eye protection when cleaning the battery to prevent the caustic deposits from entering your eyes.

## HOUSEHOLD CURRENT

When using an electric power tool, inspection light, etc., which operates on household current, always make sure that the tool is correctly connected to its plug and that, where necessary, it is properly grounded. Do not use such items in damp conditions and, again, do not create a spark or apply excessive heat in the vicinity of fuel or fuel vapor.

## SECONDARY IGNITION SYSTEM VOLTAGE

A severe electric shock can result from touching certain parts of the ignition system (such as the spark plug wires) when the engine is running or being cranked, particularly if components are damp or the insulation is defective. In the case of an electronic ignition system, the secondary system voltage is much higher and could prove fatal.

## HYDROFLUORIC ACID

This extremely corrosive acid is formed when certain types of synthetic rubber, found in some O-rings, oil seals, fuel hoses, etc. are exposed to temperatures above 750-degrees F (400-degrees C). The rubber changes into a charred or sticky substance containing the acid. *Once formed, the acid remains dangerous for years. If it gets onto the skin, it may be necessary to amputate the limb concerned.*

When dealing with a vehicle which has suffered a fire, or with components salvaged from such a vehicle, wear protective gloves and discard them after use.

## Troubleshooting

## CONTENTS

This Section provides an easy reference guide to the more common problems that may occur during the operation of your vehicle. Various symptoms and their probable causes are grouped under headings denoting components or systems, such as Engine, Cooling system, etc. They also refer to the Chapter and/or Section that deals with the problem.

Remember that successful troubleshooting isn't a mysterious art practiced only by professional mechanics, it's simply the result of knowledge combined with an intelligent, systematic approach to a problem. Always use a process of elimination starting with the simplest solution and working through to the most complex - and never overlook the obvious. Anyone can run the gas tank dry or leave the lights on overnight, so don't assume that you're exempt from such oversights.

Finally, always establish a clear idea why a problem has occurred and take steps to ensure that it doesn't happen again. If the electrical system fails because of a poor connection, check all other connections in the system to make sure they don't fail as well. If a particular fuse continues to blow, find out why - don't just go on replacing fuses. Remember, failure of a small component can often be indicative of potential failure or incorrect functioning of a more important component or system.

## ENGINE

### 1  Engine will not rotate when attempting to start

1  Battery terminal connections loose or corroded. Check the cable terminals at the battery; tighten cable clamp and/or clean off corrosion as necessary (see Chapter 1).

2  Battery discharged or faulty. If the cable ends are clean and tight on the battery posts, turn the key to the On position and switch on the headlights or windshield wipers. If they won't run, the battery is discharged.

3  Automatic transmission not engaged in park (P) or Neutral (N).

4  Broken, loose or disconnected wires in the starting circuit. Inspect all wires and connectors at the battery, starter solenoid and ignition switch (on steering column).

5  Starter motor pinion jammed in driveplate ring gear. Remove starter (Chapter 5) and inspect pinion and driveplate (Chapter 2).

6  Starter solenoid faulty (Chapter 5).

7  Starter motor faulty (Chapter 5).

8  Ignition switch faulty (Chapter 12).

9  Engine seized. Try to turn the crankshaft with a large socket and breaker bar on the pulley bolt.

### 2  Engine rotates but will not start

1  Fuel tank empty.

2  Battery discharged (engine rotates slowly).

3  Battery terminal connections loose or corroded.

4  Fuel not reaching fuel injectors. Check for clogged fuel filter or lines and defective fuel pump. Also make sure the tank vent lines aren't clogged (Chapter 4).

5  Faulty distributor components (if equipped). Check the cap and rotor (Chapter 1).

6  Low cylinder compression. Check as described in Chapter 2.

7  Water in fuel. Drain tank and fill with new fuel.

8  Defective ignition coil(s) (Chapter 5).

9  Dirty or clogged fuel injector(s).(Chapter 4).

10  Wet or damaged ignition components (Chapters 1 and 5).

11  Worn, faulty or incorrectly gapped spark plugs (Chapter 1).

12  Broken, loose or disconnected wires in the starting circuit (see previous Section).

13  Loose distributor (if equipped). Turn the distributor body as necessary to start the engine, then adjust the ignition timing as soon as possible (Chapter 5).

14  Broken, loose or disconnected wires at the ignition coil or faulty coil (Chapter 5).

15  Timing chain failure or wear affecting valve timing (Chapter 2).

16  Fuel injection or engine control systems failure (Chapters 4 and 6).

### 3  Starter motor operates without turning engine

1  Starter pinion sticking. Remove the starter (Chapter 5) and inspect.

2  Starter pinion or driveplate teeth worn or broken. Remove the inspection cover and inspect.

### 4  Engine hard to start when cold

1  Battery discharged or low. Check as described in Chapter 1.

2  Fuel not reaching the fuel injectors. Check the fuel filter, lines and fuel pump (Chapters 1 and 4).

3  Defective spark plugs (Chapter 1).

4  Defective engine coolant temperature sensor (Chapter 6).

5  Fuel injection or engine control systems malfunction (Chapters 4 and 6).

### 5  Engine hard to start when hot

1  Air filter dirty (Chapter 1).

2  Fuel not reaching the fuel injection (see Section 4).

3  Bad engine ground connection.

4  Defective pick-up coil in distributor (Chapter 5).

5  Fuel injection or engine control systems malfunction (Chapters 4 and 6).

### 6  Starter motor noisy or engages roughly

1  Pinion or driveplate teeth worn or broken. Remove the inspection cover on the left side of the engine and inspect.

2  Starter motor mounting bolts loose or missing.

### 7  Engine starts but stops immediately

1  Loose or damaged wire harness connections at distributor, coil or alternator.

2  Intake manifold vacuum leaks. Make sure all mounting bolts/nuts are tight and all vacuum hoses connected to the manifold are attached properly and in good condition.

3  Insufficient fuel pressure (see Chapter 4).

4  Fuel injection or engine control systems malfunction (Chapters 4 and 6).

## 8 Engine 'lopes' while idling or idles erratically

1  Vacuum leaks. Check mounting bolts at the intake manifold for tightness. Make sure that all vacuum hoses are connected and in good condition. Use a stethoscope or a length of fuel hose held against your ear to listen for vacuum leaks while the engine is running. A hissing sound will be heard. A soapy water solution will also detect leaks. Check the intake manifold gasket surfaces.
2  Leaking EGR valve or plugged PCV valve (see Chapters 1 and 6).
3  Air filter clogged (Chapter 1).
4  Fuel pump not delivering sufficient fuel (Chapter 4).
5  Leaking head gasket. Perform a cylinder compression check (Chapter 2).
6  Timing chain(s) worn (Chapter 2).
7  Camshaft lobes worn (Chapter 2).
8  Valves burned or otherwise leaking (Chapter 2).
9  Ignition timing out of adjustment (Chapter 5).
10 Ignition system not operating properly (Chapters 1 and 5).
11 Fuel injection or engine control systems malfunction (Chapters 4 and 6).

## 9 Engine misses at idle speed

1  Spark plugs faulty or not gapped properly (Chapter 1).
2  Faulty spark plug wires (Chapter 1).
3  Wet or damaged distributor components (Chapter 1).
4  Short circuits in ignition, coil or spark plug wires.
5  Sticking or faulty emissions systems (see Chapter 6).
6  Clogged fuel filter and/or foreign matter in fuel. Remove the fuel filter (Chapter 1) and inspect.
7  Vacuum leaks at intake manifold or hose connections. Check as described in Section 8.
8  Incorrect idle speed (Chapter 4).
9  Low or uneven cylinder compression. Check as described in Chapter 2.
10 Fuel injection or engine control systems malfunction (Chapters 4 and 6).

## 10 Excessively high idle speed

1  Sticking throttle linkage (Chapter 4).
2  Vacuum leaks at intake manifold or hose connections. Check as described in Section 8.
3  Fuel injection or engine control systems malfunction (Chapters 4 and 6).

## 11 Battery will not hold a charge

1  Alternator drivebelt defective or not adjusted properly (Chapter 1).
2  Battery cables loose or corroded (Chapter 1).
3  Alternator not charging properly (Chapter 5).
4  Loose, broken or faulty wires in the charging circuit (Chapter 5).
5  Short circuit causing a continuous drain on the battery.
6  Battery defective internally.

## 12 Alternator light stays on

1  Fault in alternator or charging circuit (Chapter 5).
2  Alternator drivebelt defective or not properly adjusted (Chapter 1).

## 13 Alternator light fails to come on when key is turned on

1  Faulty bulb (Chapter 12).
2  Defective alternator (Chapter 5).
3  Fault in the printed circuit, dash wiring or bulb holder (Chapter 12).

## 14 Engine misses throughout driving speed range

1  Fuel filter clogged and/or impurities in the fuel system. Check fuel filter (Chapter 1) or clean system (Chapter 4).
2  Faulty or incorrectly gapped spark plugs (Chapter 1).
3  Incorrect ignition timing (Chapter 1).
4  Cracked distributor cap, disconnected distributor wires or damaged distributor components (Chapter 1).
5  Defective spark plug wires (Chapter 1).
6  Emissions system components faulty (Chapter 6).
7  Low or uneven cylinder compression pressures. Check as described in Chapter 2.
8  Weak or faulty ignition coil(s) (Chapter 5).
9  Weak or faulty ignition system (Chapter 5).
10 Vacuum leaks at intake manifold or vacuum hoses (see Section 8).
11 Dirty or clogged fuel injector(s) (Chapter 4).
12 Leaky EGR valve (Chapter 6).
13 Fuel injection or engine control systems malfunction (Chapters 4 and 6).

## 15 Hesitation or stumble during acceleration

1  Ignition system not operating properly (Chapter 5).
2  Dirty or clogged fuel injector(s) (Chapter 4).
3  Low fuel pressure. Check for proper operation of the fuel pump and for restrictions in the fuel filter and lines (Chapter 4).
4  Fuel injection or engine control systems malfunction (Chapters 4 and 6).

## 16 Engine stalls

1  Idle speed incorrect (Chapter 4).
2  Fuel filter clogged and/or water and impurities in the fuel system (Chapter 1).
3  Damaged or wet distributor cap and wires.
4  Emissions system components faulty (Chapter 6).
5  Faulty or incorrectly gapped spark plugs (Chapter 1). Also check the spark plug wires (Chapter 1).
6  Vacuum leak at the intake manifold or vacuum hoses. Check as described in Section 8.
7  Fuel injection or engine control systems malfunction (Chapters 4 and 6).

## 17 Engine lacks power

1  Incorrect ignition timing (Chapter 1).
2  Excessive play in distributor shaft (if equipped). At the same time check for faulty distributor cap, wires, etc. (Chapter 1).
3  Faulty or incorrectly gapped spark plugs (Chapter 1).
4  Air filter dirty (Chapter 1).
5  Faulty ignition coil(s) (Chapter 5).

6  Brakes binding (Chapters 1 and 10).

7  Automatic transmission fluid level incorrect, causing slippage (Chapter 1).

8  Fuel filter clogged and/or impurities in the fuel system (Chapters 1 and 4).

9  EGR system not functioning properly (Chapter 6).

10  Use of sub-standard fuel. Fill tank with proper octane fuel.

11  Low or uneven cylinder compression pressures. Check as described in Chapter 2.

12  Vacuum leak at intake manifold or vacuum hoses (check as described in Section 8).

13  Dirty or clogged fuel injector(s) (Chapters 1 and 4).

14  Fuel injection or engine control systems malfunction (Chapters 4 and 6).

15  Restricted exhaust system (Chapter 4).

### 18  Engine backfires

1  EGR system not functioning properly (Chapter 6).

2  Ignition timing incorrect (Chapter 5).

3  Vacuum leak (refer to Section 8).

4  Damaged valve springs or sticking valves (Chapter 2).

5  Vacuum leak at the intake manifold or vacuum hoses (see Section 8).

### 19  Engine surges while holding accelerator steady

1  Vacuum leak at the intake manifold or vacuum hoses (see Section 8).

2  Restricted air filter (Chapter 1).

3  Fuel pump or pressure regulator defective (Chapter 4).

4  Fuel injection or engine control systems malfunction (Chapters 4 and 6).

### 20  Pinging or knocking engine sounds when engine is under load

1  Incorrect grade of fuel. Fill tank with fuel of the proper octane rating.

2  Ignition timing incorrect (Chapter 1).

3  Carbon build-up in combustion chambers. Remove cylinder head(s) and clean combustion chambers (Chapter 2).

4  Incorrect spark plugs (Chapter 1).

5  Fuel injection or engine control systems malfunction (Chapters 4 and 6).

6  Restricted exhaust system (Chapter 4).

### 21  Engine diesels (continues to run) after being turned off

1  Idle speed too high (Chapter 4).

2  Ignition timing incorrect (Chapter 5).

3  Incorrect spark plug heat range (Chapter 1).

4  Vacuum leak at the intake manifold or vacuum hoses (see Section 8).

5  Carbon build-up in combustion chambers. Remove the cylinder head(s) and clean the combustion chambers (Chapter 2).

6  Valves sticking (Chapter 2).

7  EGR system not operating properly (Chapter 6).

8  Fuel injection or engine control systems malfunction (Chapters 4 and 6).

9  Check for causes of overheating (Section 27).

### 22  Low oil pressure

1  Incorrect oil level

2  Improper grade of oil.

3  Oil pump worn or damaged (Chapter 2).

4  Engine overheating (refer to Section 27).

5  Clogged oil filter (Chapter 1).

6  Clogged oil strainer (Chapter 2).

7  Oil pressure gauge not working properly (Chapter 2).

### 23  Excessive oil consumption

1  Loose oil drain plug.

2  Loose bolts or damaged oil pan gasket (Chapter 2).

3  Loose bolts or damaged front cover gasket (Chapter 2).

4  Front or rear crankshaft oil seal leaking (Chapter 2).

5  Loose bolts or damaged valve cover gasket (Chapter 2).

6  Loose oil filter (Chapter 1).

7  Loose or damaged oil pressure switch (Chapter 2).

8  Pistons and cylinders excessively worn (Chapter 2).

9  Piston rings not installed correctly on pistons (Chapter 2).

10  Worn or damaged piston rings (Chapter 2).

11  Intake and/or exhaust valve oil seals worn or damaged (Chapter 2).

12  Worn valve stems or guides.

13  Worn or damaged valves/guides (Chapter 2).

14  Faulty or incorrect PCV valve allowing too much crankcase airflow.

### 24  Excessive fuel consumption

1  Dirty or clogged air filter element (Chapter 1).

2  Incorrect ignition timing (Chapter 5).

3  Incorrect idle speed (Chapter 4).

4  Low tire pressure or incorrect tire size (Chapter 10).

5  Inspect for binding brakes.

6  Fuel leakage. Check all connections, lines and components in the fuel system (Chapter 4).

7  Dirty or clogged fuel injectors (Chapter 4).

8  Fuel injection or engine control systems malfunction (Chapters 4 and 6).

9  Thermostat stuck open or not installed.

10  Improperly operating transmission.

### 25  Fuel odor

1  Fuel leakage. Check all connections, lines and components in the fuel system (Chapter 4).

2  Fuel tank overfilled. Fill only to automatic shut-off.

3  Charcoal canister filter in Evaporative Emissions Control system clogged (Chapter 1).

4  Vapor leaks from Evaporative Emissions Control system lines (Chapter 6).

### 26  Miscellaneous engine noises

1  A strong dull noise that becomes more rapid as the engine accelerates indicates worn or damaged crankshaft bearings or an unevenly worn crankshaft. To pinpoint the trouble spot, remove the spark plug wire from one plug at a time and crank the engine over. If the noise stops, the cylinder with the removed plug wire indicates the problem

area. Replace the bearing and/or service or replace the crankshaft (Chapter 2).

2  A similar (yet slightly higher pitched) noise to the crankshaft knocking described in the previous paragraph, that becomes more rapid as the engine accelerates, indicates worn or damaged connecting rod bearings (Chapter 2). The procedure for locating the problem cylinder is the same as described in Paragraph 1.

3  An overlapping metallic noise that increases in intensity as the engine speed increases, yet diminishes as the engine warms up indicates abnormal piston and cylinder wear (Chapter 2). To locate the problem cylinder, use the procedure described in Paragraph 1.

4  A rapid clicking noise that becomes faster as the engine accelerates indicates a worn piston pin or piston pin hole. This sound will happen each time the piston hits the highest and lowest points in the stroke (Chapter 2). The procedure for locating the problem piston is described in Paragraph 1.

5  A metallic clicking noise coming from the water pump indicates worn or damaged water pump bearings or pump. Replace the water pump with a new one (Chapter 3).

6  A rapid tapping sound or clicking sound that becomes faster as the engine speed increases indicates "valve tapping." This can be identified by holding one end of a section of hose to your ear and placing the other end at different spots along the valve cover. The point where the sound is loudest indicates the problem valve. If the pushrod and rocker arm components are in good shape, you likely have a collapsed valve lifter. Changing the engine oil and adding a high viscosity oil treatment will sometimes cure a stuck lifter problem. If the problem persists, the lifters, pushrods and rocker arms must be removed for inspection (see Chapter 2).

7  A steady metallic rattling or rapping sound coming from the area of the timing chain cover indicates a worn, damaged or out-of-adjustment timing chain. Service or replace the chain and related components (Chapter 2).

# COOLING SYSTEM

## 27  Overheating

1  Insufficient coolant in system (Chapter 1).
2  Drivebelt defective or not adjusted properly (Chapter 1).
3  Radiator core blocked or radiator grille dirty and restricted (Chapter 3).
4  Thermostat faulty (Chapter 3).
5  Cooling fan not functioning properly (Chapter 3).
6  Radiator cap not maintaining proper pressure. Have cap pressure tested by gas station or repair shop.
7  Ignition timing incorrect (Chapter 5).
8  Defective water pump (Chapter 3).
9  Improper grade of engine oil.
10 Inaccurate temperature gauge (Chapter 12).

## 28  Overcooling

1  Thermostat faulty (Chapter 3).
2  Inaccurate temperature gauge (Chapter 12).

## 29  External coolant leakage

1  Deteriorated or damaged hoses. Loose clamps at hose connections (Chapter 1).
2  Water pump seals defective. If this is the case, water will drip from the weep hole in the water pump body (Chapter 3).
3  Leakage from radiator core or header tank. This will require the radiator to be professionally repaired (see Chapter 3 for removal procedures).
4  Leakage from the coolant expansion tank.
5  Engine drain plugs or water jacket freeze plugs leaking (see Chapters 1 and 2).
6  Leak from coolant temperature switch (Chapter 3).
7  Leak from damaged gaskets or small cracks (Chapter 2).

## 30  Internal coolant leakage

➡Note: Internal coolant leaks can usually be detected by examining the oil. Check the dipstick and inside the rocker arm cover for water deposits and an oil consistency like that of a milkshake.

1  Leaking cylinder head gasket. Have the system pressure tested or remove the cylinder head (Chapter 2) and inspect.
2  Cracked cylinder bore or cylinder head. Dismantle engine and inspect (Chapter 2).
3  Loose cylinder head bolts (tighten as described in Chapter 2).

## 31  Abnormal coolant loss

1  Overfilling system (Chapter 1).
2  Coolant boiling away due to overheating (see causes in Section 27).
3  Internal or external leakage (see Sections 29 and 30).
4  Faulty radiator cap. Have the cap pressure tested.
5  Cooling system being pressurized by engine compression. This could be due to a cracked head or block or leaking head gasket(s).

## 32  Poor coolant circulation

1  Inoperative water pump. A quick test is to pinch the top radiator hose closed with your hand while the engine is idling, then release it. You should feel a surge of coolant if the pump is working properly (Chapter 3).
2  Restriction in cooling system. Drain, flush and refill the system (Chapter 1). If necessary, remove the radiator (Chapter 3) and have it reverse flushed or professionally cleaned.
3  Loose water pump drivebelt (Chapter 1).
4  Thermostat sticking (Chapter 3).
5  Insufficient coolant (Chapter 1).

## 33  Corrosion

1  Excessive impurities in the water. Soft, clean water is recommended. Distilled or rainwater is satisfactory.
2  Insufficient antifreeze solution (refer to Chapter 1 for the proper ratio of water to antifreeze).
3  Infrequent flushing and draining of system. Regular flushing of the cooling system should be carried out at the specified intervals as described in (Chapter 1).

## AUTOMATIC TRANSMISSION

➡ **Note: Due to the complexity of the automatic transmission, it's difficult for the home mechanic to properly diagnose and service. For problems other than the following, the vehicle should be taken to a reputable mechanic.**

### 34 Fluid leakage

1 Automatic transmission fluid is a deep red color, and fluid leaks should not be confused with engine oil which can easily be blown by air flow to the transmission.

2 To pinpoint a leak, first remove all built-up dirt and grime from the transmission. Degreasing agents and/or steam cleaning will achieve this. With the underside clean, drive the vehicle at low speeds so the air flow will not blow the leak far from its source. Raise the vehicle and determine where the leak is located. Common areas of leakage are:

a) *Fluid pan: tighten mounting bolts and/or replace pan gasket as necessary (Chapter 1).*

b) *Rear extension: tighten bolts and/or replace oil seal as necessary.*

c) *Filler pipe: replace the rubber oil seal where pipe enters transmission case.*

d) *Transmission oil lines: tighten fittings where lines enter transmission case and/or replace lines.*

e) *Vent pipe: transmission overfilled and/or water in fluid (see checking procedures, Chapter 1).*

f) *Speedometer connector: replace the O-ring where speedometer cable enters transmission case.*

### 35 General shift mechanism problems

Chapter 7 deals with checking and adjusting the shift linkage on automatic transmissions. Common problems which may be caused by out of adjustment linkage are:

a) *Engine starting in gears other than P (park) or N (Neutral).*

b) *Indicator pointing to a gear other than the one actually engaged.*

c) *Vehicle moves with transmission in P (Park) position.*

### 36 Transmission will not downshift with the accelerator pedal pressed to the floor

Chapter 7 deals with adjusting the throttle valve cable to enable the transmission to downshift properly.

### 37 Engine will start in gears other than Park or Neutral

Neutral start switch, Manual Lever Position (MLP) sensor or Transmission Range (TR) sensor out of adjustment or faulty (Chapter 7).

### 38 Transmission slips, shifts rough, is noisy or has no drive in forward or Reverse gears

1 There are many probable causes for the above problems, but the home mechanic should concern himself only with one possibility; fluid level.

2 Before taking the vehicle to a shop, check the fluid level and condition as described in Chapter 1. Add fluid, if necessary, or change the fluid and filter if needed. If problems persist, have a professional diagnose the transmission.

## DRIVESHAFT

➡ **Note: Refer to Chapter 8, unless otherwise specified, for service information.**

### 39 Leaks at front of driveshaft

Defective transmission or transfer case seal. See Chapter 7 for replacement procedure. As this is done, check the splined yoke for burrs or roughness that could damage the new seal. Remove burrs with a fine file or whetstone.

### 40 Knock or clunk when transmission is under initial load (just after transmission is put into gear)

1 Loose or disconnected rear suspension components. Check all mounting bolts and bushings (Chapters 7 and 10).

2 Loose driveshaft bolts. Inspect all bolts and nuts and tighten them securely.

3 Worn or damaged universal joint bearings (Chapter 8).

4 Worn sleeve yoke and mainshaft spline.

### 41 Metallic grating sound consistent with vehicle speed

Pronounced wear in the universal joint bearings. Replace U-joints or driveshaft, as necessary.

### 42 Vibration

➡ **Note: Before blaming the driveshaft, make sure the tires are perfectly balanced and perform the following test.**

1 Install a tachometer inside the vehicle to monitor engine speed as the vehicle is driven. Drive the vehicle and note the engine speed at which the vibration (roughness) is most pronounced. Now shift the transmission to a different gear and bring the engine speed to the same point.

2 If the vibration occurs at the same engine speed (rpm) regardless of which gear the transmission is in, the driveshaft is NOT at fault since the driveshaft speed varies.

3 If the vibration decreases or is eliminated when the transmission is in a different gear at the same engine speed, refer to the following probable causes:

a) *Bent or dented driveshaft. Inspect and replace as necessary.*

b) *Undercoating or built-up dirt, etc. on the driveshaft. Clean the shaft thoroughly.*

c) *Worn universal joint bearings. Replace the U-joints or driveshaft as necessary.*

d) *Driveshaft and/or companion flange out of balance. Check for missing weights on the shaft. Remove driveshaft and reinstall 180-degrees from original position, then recheck. Have the driveshaft balanced if problem persists.*

e) *Loose driveshaft mounting bolts/nuts.*

f) *Worn transmission rear bushing (Chapter 7).*

### 43 Scraping noise

Make sure there is nothing, such as an exhaust heat shield, rubbing on the driveshaft.

## AXLE(S) AND DIFFERENTIAL(S)

➡Note: For differential servicing information, refer to Chapter 8, unless otherwise specified.

### 44  Noise - same when in drive as when vehicle is coasting

1  Road noise. No corrective action available.
2  Tire noise. Inspect tires and check tire pressures (Chapter 1).
3  Front wheel bearings loose, worn or damaged (Chapter 1).
4  Insufficient differential oil (Chapter 1).
5  Defective differential.

### 45  Knocking sound when starting or shifting gears

Defective or incorrectly adjusted differential.

### 46  Noise when turning

Defective differential.

### 47  Vibration

See probable causes under Driveshaft. Proceed under the guidelines listed for the driveshaft. If the problem persists, check the rear wheel bearings by raising the rear of the vehicle and spinning the wheels by hand. Listen for evidence of rough (noisy) bearings. Remove and inspect (Chapter 8).

### 48  Oil leaks

1  Pinion oil seal damaged (Chapter 8).
2  Axleshaft oil seals damaged (Chapter 8).
3  Differential cover leaking. Tighten mounting bolts or replace the gasket as required.
4  Loose filler plug on differential (Chapter 1).
5  Clogged or damaged breather on differential.

## BRAKES

➡Note: Before assuming a brake problem exists, make sure the tires are in good condition and inflated properly, the front end alignment is correct and the vehicle is not loaded with weight in an unequal manner. All service procedures for the brakes are included in Chapter 9, unless otherwise noted.

### 49  Vehicle pulls to one side during braking

1  Defective, damaged or oil contaminated brake pad or lining on one side. Inspect as described in Chapter 1. Refer to Chapter 9 if replacement is required.
2  Excessive wear of brake pad or lining material, disc or drum on one side. Inspect and repair as necessary.
3  Loose or disconnected front suspension components. Inspect and tighten all bolts securely (Chapters 1 and 10).
4  Defective front brake caliper assembly. Remove caliper and inspect for stuck piston or damage.

5  Brake lining adjustment needed. Inspect automatic adjusting mechanism for proper operation.
6  Scored or out of round disc or drum.
7  Loose front brake caliper mounting bolts.
8  Incorrect wheel bearing adjustment.

### 50  Noise (high-pitched squeal)

1  Front brake pads worn out. This noise comes from the wear sensor rubbing against the disc. Replace pads with new ones immediately!
2  Glazed or contaminated pads.
3  Dirty or scored rotor.
4  Bent support plate.

### 51  Excessive brake pedal travel

1  Partial brake system failure. Inspect entire system (Chapter 1) and correct as required.
2  Insufficient fluid in master cylinder. Check (Chapter 1) and add fluid - bleed system if necessary.
3  Air in system. Bleed system.
4  Excessive lateral rotor play.
5  Brakes out of adjustment. Check the operation of the automatic adjusters.
6  Defective proportioning valve. Replace valve and bleed system.
7  Defective master cylinder.

### 52  Brake pedal feels spongy when depressed

1  Air in brake lines. Bleed the brake system.
2  Deteriorated rubber brake hoses. Inspect all system hoses and lines. Replace parts as necessary.
3  Master cylinder mounting nuts loose. Inspect master cylinder bolts (nuts) and tighten them securely.
4  Master cylinder faulty.
5  Incorrect shoe or pad clearance.
6  Defective check valve. Replace valve and bleed system.
7  Clogged reservoir cap vent hole.
8  Deformed rubber brake lines.
9  Soft or swollen caliper seals.
10 Poor quality brake fluid. Bleed entire system and fill with new approved fluid.

### 53  Excessive effort required to stop vehicle

1  Power brake booster not operating properly.
2  Excessively worn linings or pads. Check and replace if necessary.
3  One or more caliper pistons seized or sticking. Inspect and rebuild as required.
4  Brake pads or linings contaminated with oil or grease. Inspect and replace as required.
5  Worn or damaged master cylinder or caliper assemblies. Check particularly for frozen pistons.

### 54  Pedal travels to the floor with little resistance

Little or no fluid in the master cylinder reservoir caused by leaking caliper piston(s) or loose, damaged or disconnected brake lines. Inspect entire system and repair as necessary.

## 55   Brake pedal pulsates during brake application

1  Wheel bearings damaged, worn or out of adjustment (Chapter 1).
2  Caliper not sliding properly due to improper installation or obstructions. Remove and inspect.
3  Rotor not within specifications. Remove the rotor and check for excessive lateral runout and parallelism. Have the rotors resurfaced or replace them with new ones. Also make sure that all rotors are the same thickness.
4  Out of round rear brake drums. Remove the drums and have them turned or replace them with new ones.

## 56   Brakes drag (indicated by sluggish engine performance or wheels being very hot after driving)

1  Pushrod adjustment incorrect at the brake pedal or power booster.
2  Obstructed master cylinder compensator. Disassemble master cylinder and clean.
3  Master cylinder piston seized in bore. Overhaul master cylinder.
4  Caliper assembly in need of overhaul.
5  Brake pads or shoes worn out.
6  Piston cups in master cylinder or caliper assembly deformed. Overhaul master cylinder.
7  Rotor not within specifications.
8  Parking brake assembly will not release.
9  Clogged brake lines.
10 Wheel bearings out of adjustment (Chapter 1).
11 Brake pedal height improperly adjusted.
12 Wheel cylinder needs overhaul.
13 Improper shoe to drum clearance. Adjust as necessary.

## 57   Rear brakes lock up under light brake application

1  Tire pressures too high.
2  Tires excessively worn (Chapter 1).
3  Defective power brake booster.
4  Rear axle seal(s) leaking contaminating brake lining(s) with rear axle lubricant (Chapter 8).

## 58   Rear brakes lock up under heavy brake application

1  Tire pressures too high.
2  Tires excessively worn (Chapter 1).
3  Front brake pads contaminated with oil, mud or water. Clean or replace the pads.
4  Front brake pads excessively worn.
5  Defective master cylinder or caliper assembly.

# SUSPENSION AND STEERING

➡Note: All service procedures for the suspension and steering systems are included in Chapter 10, unless otherwise noted.

## 59   Vehicle pulls to one side

1  Tire pressures uneven (Chapter 1).
2  Defective tire (Chapter 1).
3  Excessive wear in suspension or steering components (Chapter 1).

4  Front end alignment incorrect.
5  Front brakes dragging. Inspect as described in Section 71.
6  Wheel bearings improperly adjusted (Chapter 1).
7  Wheel lug nuts loose.

## 60   Shimmy, shake or vibration

1  Tire or wheel out of balance or out of round.
2  Loose, worn or out of adjustment wheel bearings (Chapter 1).
3  Shock absorbers and/or suspension components worn or damaged (see Chapter 10).

## 61   Excessive pitching and/or rolling around corners or during braking

1  Defective shock absorbers. Replace as a set.
2  Broken or weak leaf springs and/or suspension components.
3  Worn or damaged stabilizer bar or bushings.

## 62   Wandering or general instability

1  Improper tire pressures.
2  Incorrect front end alignment.
3  Worn or damaged steering linkage or suspension components.
4  Improperly adjusted steering gear.
5  Out-of-balance wheels.
6  Loose wheel lug nuts.
7  Worn rear shock absorbers.
8  Fatigued or damaged rear leaf springs.

## 63   Excessively stiff steering

1  Lack of fluid in the power steering fluid reservoir, where appropriate (Chapter 1).
2  Incorrect tire pressures (Chapter 1).
3  Lack of lubrication at balljoints (Chapter 1).
4  Front end out of alignment.
5  Steering gear out of adjustment or lacking lubrication.
6  Improperly adjusted wheel bearings.
7  Worn or damaged steering gear.
8  Interference of steering column with turn signal switch.
9  Low tire pressures.
10 Worn or damaged balljoints.
11 Worn or damaged steering linkage.

## 64   Excessive play in steering

1  Loose wheel bearings (Chapter 1).
2  Excessive wear in suspension bushings (Chapter 1).
3  Steering gear improperly adjusted.
4  Incorrect front end alignment.
5  Steering gear mounting bolts loose.
6  Worn steering linkage.

## 65   Lack of power assistance

1  Steering pump drivebelt faulty or not adjusted properly (Chapter 1).
2  Fluid level low (Chapter 1).

3  Hoses or pipes restricting the flow. Inspect and replace parts as necessary.
4  Air in power steering system. Bleed system.
5  Defective power steering pump.

## 66  Steering wheel fails to return to straight-ahead position

1  Incorrect front end alignment.
2  Tire pressures low.
3  Steering gears improperly engaged.
4  Steering column out of alignment.
5  Worn or damaged balljoint.
6  Worn or damaged steering linkage.
7  Improperly lubricated idler arm.
8  Insufficient oil in steering gear.
9  Lack of fluid in power steering pump.

## 67  Steering effort not the same in both directions (power system)

1  Leaks in steering gear.
2  Clogged fluid passage in steering gear.

## 68  Noisy power steering pump

1  Insufficient oil in pump.
2  Clogged hoses or oil filter in pump.
3  Loose pulley.
4  Improperly adjusted drivebelt (Chapter 1).
5  Defective pump.

## 69  Miscellaneous noises

1  Improper tire pressures.
2  Insufficiently lubricated balljoint or steering linkage.
3  Loose or worn steering gear, steering linkage or suspension components.

4  Defective shock absorber.
5  Defective wheel bearing.
6  Worn or damaged suspension bushings.
7  Damaged leaf spring.
8  Loose wheel lug nuts.
9  Worn or damaged rear axleshaft spline.
10  Worn or damaged rear shock absorber mounting bushing.
11  Incorrect rear axle endplay.
12  See also causes of noises at the rear axle and driveshaft.

## 70  Excessive tire wear (not specific to one area)

1  Incorrect tire pressures.
2  Tires out of balance.
3  Wheels damaged. Inspect and replace as necessary.
4  Suspension or steering components worn (Chapter 1).
5  Front end alignment incorrect.
6  Lack of proper tire rotation routine. See Routine Maintenance Schedule, Chapter 1.

## 71  Excessive tire wear on outside edge

1  Incorrect tire pressure.
2  Excessive speed in turns.
3  Front end alignment incorrect.

## 72  Excessive tire wear on inside edge

1  Incorrect tire pressure.
2  Front end alignment incorrect.
3  Loose or damaged steering components (Chapter 1).

## 73  Tire tread worn in one place

1  Tires out of balance.
2  Damaged or buckled wheel. Inspect and replace if necessary.
3  Defective tire.

**Notes**

## 1

## TUNE-UP AND ROUTINE MAINTENANCE

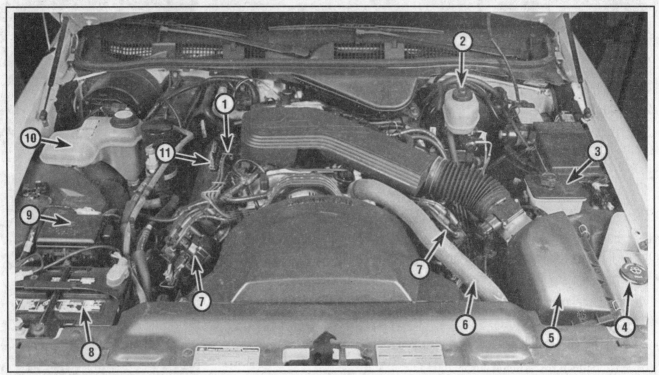

**Typical engine compartment components (4.6L engine) - early models**

| | | | | | |
|---|---|---|---|---|---|
| 1 | Spark plug wire | 5 | Air cleaner | 9 | Fuse block |
| 2 | Brake fluid reservoir | 6 | Upper radiator hose | 10 | Coolant expansion tank |
| 3 | Power steering fluid reservoir | 7 | Ignition coil | 11 | PCV valve |
| 4 | Windshield washer fluid reservoir | 8 | Battery | | |

**Typical engine compartment underside components - early models**

| | | | |
|---|---|---|---|
| 1 | Oil filter | 4 | Exhaust pipe |
| 2 | Lower suspension balljoint grease fitting | 5 | Tie-rod end grease fitting |
| 3 | Engine oil drain plug | | |

**Typical rear underside components - early models**

| 1 | Gas tank | 2 | Exhaust pipe | 3 | Parking brake cable | 4 | Fuel filter |
|---|---|---|---|---|---|---|---|

**Typical engine compartment components (4.6L engine) - late models**

| 1 | Brake fluid reservoir | 5 | Upper radiator hose | 9 | Oil filler cap |
|---|---|---|---|---|---|
| 2 | Windshield washer fluid reservoir | 6 | Coolant expansion tank | 10 | PCV valve |
| 3 | Air cleaner | 7 | Battery | 11 | Automatic transmission dipstick |
| 4 | Power steering fluid reservoir | 8 | Fuse/relay center | | |

**Typical engine compartment underside components - late models**

1   Tie rod end
2   Balljoint

3   Engine oil drain plug
4   Transmission fluid pan

**Typical rear underside components - late models**

1   Fuel tank
2   Rear differential

3   Fuel filter
4   Brake cable

## 1 Crown Victoria Maintenance schedule

The following maintenance intervals are based on the assumption that the vehicle owner will be doing the maintenance or service work, as opposed to having a dealer service department or other repair shop do the work. Although the time/mileage intervals are loosely based on factory recommendations, most have been shortened to ensure, for example, that such items as lubricants and fluids are checked/changed at intervals that promote maximum engine/driveline service life. Also, subject to the preference of the individual owner interested in keeping his or her vehicle in peak condition at all times, and with the vehicle's ultimate resale in mind, many of the maintenance procedures may be performed more often than recommended in the following schedule. We encourage such owner initiative.

When the vehicle is new it should be serviced initially by a factory authorized dealer service department to protect the factory warranty. In many cases the initial maintenance check is done at no cost to the owner (check with your dealer service department for more information).

### EVERY 250 MILES OR WEEKLY, WHICHEVER COMES FIRST

Check the engine oil level (Section 4)
Check the engine coolant level (Section 4)
Check the windshield washer fluid level (Section 4)
Check the brake fluid level (Section 4)
Check the tires and tire pressures (Section 5)

### EVERY 3000 MILES OR 3 MONTHS, WHICHEVER COMES FIRST

*All items listed above, plus:*
Check the power steering fluid level (Section 6)
Check the automatic transmission fluid level (Section 7)
Change the engine oil and oil filter (Section 8)

### EVERY 7500 MILES OR 6 MONTHS, WHICHEVER COMES FIRST

*All items listed above, plus:*
Inspect/replace the underhood hoses (Section 9)
Check the drivebelt(s) (Section 10)

Rotate the tires (Section 11)
Check the seat belt operation (Section 12)
Check/service the battery (Section 13)

### EVERY 15,000 MILES OR 12 MONTHS, WHICHEVER COMES FIRST

*All items listed above, plus:*
Inspect/replace the windshield wiper blades (Section 14)
Replace the air filter (Section 15)*
Check the PCV valve (Section 16)
Check the fuel system (Section 17)
Inspect the cooling system (Section 18)
Inspect the exhaust system (Section 19)
Inspect the steering and suspension components (Section 20)
Inspect the brakes (Section 21)
Lubricate the automatic transmission control linkage (Section 22)
Check the rear axle (differential) lubricant level (Section 23)

### EVERY 30,000 MILES OR 24 MONTHS, WHICHEVER COMES FIRST

Replace the spark plugs (1996 and earlier models) (Section 24)
Check/replace the spark plug wires, distributor cap and rotor (Section 25)
Change the automatic transmission fluid and filter (Section 26)**
Change the rear axle (differential) lubricant (Section 27)
Service the cooling system (drain, flush and refill) (Section 28)
Service the front wheel bearings (1991 and earlier models) (Section 29)
Lubricate the chassis components (Section 30)
Replace the fuel filter (Section 31)

   * Replace more often if is the vehicle is driven in dusty areas
   ** If the vehicle is operated in continuous stop-and-go driving or in mountainous areas, change at 15,000 miles

### ADDITIONAL SERVICE AT 100,000 MILES

Replace the PCV valve
Replace the spark plugs
Replace the orange-colored Dex-Cool antifreeze (used in some 1996 and later models)

## 2 Introduction

This Chapter is designed to help the home mechanic maintain the Crown Victoria/Grand Marquis with the goals of maximum performance, economy, safety and reliability in mind.

Included is a master maintenance schedule, followed by procedures dealing specifically with each item on the schedule. Visual checks, adjustments, component replacement and other helpful items are included. Refer to the accompanying illustrations of the engine compartment and the underside of the vehicle for the locations of various components.

Servicing the vehicle, in accordance with the mileage/time maintenance schedule and the step-by-step procedures will result in a planned maintenance program that should produce a long and reliable service life. Keep in mind that it is a comprehensive plan, so maintaining some items but not others at the specified intervals will not produce the same results.

As you service the vehicle, you will discover that many of the procedures can - and should - be grouped together because of the nature of the particular procedure you're performing or because of the close proximity of two otherwise unrelated components to one another.

For example, if the vehicle is raised for chassis lubrication, you should inspect the exhaust, suspension, steering and fuel systems while you're under the vehicle. When you're rotating the tires, it makes good sense to check the brakes since the wheels are already removed. Finally, let's suppose you have to borrow or rent a torque wrench. Even if you only need it to tighten the spark plugs, you might as well check the torque of as many critical fasteners as time allows.

The first step in this maintenance program is to prepare yourself

before the actual work begins. Read through all the procedures you're planning to do, then gather up all the parts and tools needed. If it looks like you might run into problems during a particular job, seek advice from a mechanic or an experienced do-it-yourselfer.

## 3  Tune-up general information

The term tune-up is used in this manual to represent a combination of individual operations rather than one specific procedure.

If, from the time the vehicle is new, the routine maintenance schedule is followed closely and frequent checks are made of fluid levels and high wear items, as suggested throughout this manual, the engine will be kept in relatively good running condition and the need for additional work will be minimized.

More likely than not, however, there will be times when the engine is running poorly due to lack of regular maintenance. This is even more likely if a used vehicle, which has not received regular and frequent maintenance checks, is purchased. In such cases, an engine tune-up will be needed outside of the regular routine maintenance intervals.

The first step in any tune-up or diagnostic procedure to help correct a poor running engine is a cylinder compression check. A compression check (see Chapter 2) will help determine the condition of internal engine components and should be used as a guide for tune-up and repair procedures. If, for instance, a compression check indicates serious internal engine wear, a conventional tune-up will not improve the performance of the engine and would be a waste of time and money. Because of its importance, the compression check should be done by someone with the right equipment and the knowledge to use it properly.

The following procedures are those most often needed to bring a generally poor running engine back into a proper state of tune.

### MINOR TUNE-UP

Check all engine related fluids (Section 4)
Check all underhood hoses (Section 9)
Check the drivebelt (Section 10)
Clean, inspect and test the battery (Section 13)
Check the air filter (Section 15)
Check the cooling system (Section 18)
Replace the spark plugs (1996 and earlier) (Section 24)
Inspect the spark plug and coil wires (Section 25)

### MAJOR TUNE-UP

*All items listed under Minor tune-up, plus . . .*
Check the charging system (Chapter 5)
Replace the air filter (Section 15)
Check the fuel system (Section 17)
Replace the spark plug and coil wires (Section 25)

## 4  Fluid level checks

1  Fluids are an essential part of the lubrication, cooling, brake and windshield washer systems. Because the fluids gradually become depleted and/or contaminated during normal operation of the vehicle, they must be periodically replenished. See *Recommended lubricants and fluids* at the end of this Chapter before adding fluid to any of the following components.

➡**Note: The vehicle must be on level ground when fluid levels are checked.**

### ENGINE OIL

◆ **Refer to illustrations 4.2, 4.4 and 4.6**

2  The oil level is checked with a dipstick, which is located on the left (driver's) side of the engine (see illustration). The dipstick extends through a metal tube down into the oil pan.

3  The oil level should be checked before the vehicle has been driven, or about 5 minutes after the engine has been shut off. If the oil is checked immediately after driving the vehicle, some of the oil will remain in the upper part of the engine, resulting in an inaccurate reading on the dipstick.

4  Pull the dipstick out of the tube and wipe all the oil from the end

4.2  The engine oil dipstick is located on the left side of the engine

4.4  The oil level should be at or near the upper hatched area on the dipstick - if it isn't, add enough oil to bring the level to near the upper mark (it takes one quart of oil to raise the level from the lower to the upper mark)

**4.6 The oil filler cap is located on the valve cover - always make sure the area around the opening is clean before unscrewing the cap to prevent dirt from contaminating the engine**

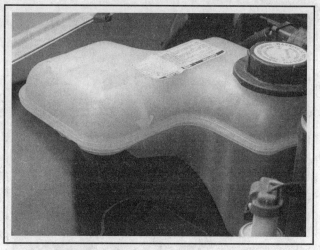

**4.9 Keep the coolant level near the arrow at the seam of the expansion tank**

with a clean rag or paper towel. Insert the clean dipstick all the way back into the tube and pull it out again. Note the oil at the end of the dipstick. At its highest point, the level should be above the ADD mark, within the hatched marked section of the dipstick (see illustration).

5   It takes one quart of oil to raise the level from the ADD mark to the FULL mark on the dipstick. Do not allow the level to drop below the ADD mark or oil starvation may cause engine damage. Conversely, overfilling the engine (adding oil above the FULL mark) may cause oil fouled spark plugs, oil leaks or oil seal failures.

6   To add oil, remove the filler cap located on valve cover (see illustration). After adding oil, wait a few minutes to allow the level to stabilize, then pull out the dipstick and check the level again. Add more oil if required. Install the filler cap and tighten it by hand only.

7   Checking the oil level is an important preventive maintenance step. A consistently low oil level indicates oil leakage through damaged seals, defective gaskets or past worn rings or valve guides. If the oil looks milky in color or has water droplets in it, the cylinder head gasket(s) may be blown or the head(s) or block may be cracked. The engine should be checked immediately. The condition of the oil should also be checked. Whenever you check the oil level, slide your thumb and index finger up the dipstick before wiping off the oil. If you see small dirt or metal particles clinging to the dipstick, the oil should be changed (see Section 8).

## ENGINE COOLANT

▶ **Refer to illustration 4.9**

**✳✳ WARNING:**

**Do not allow antifreeze to come in contact with your skin or painted surfaces of the vehicle. Flush contaminated areas immediately with plenty of water. Don't store new coolant or leave old coolant lying around where it's accessible to children or pets – they're attracted by its sweet smell. Ingestion of even a small amount of coolant can be fatal! Wipe up garage floor and drip pan spills immediately. Keep antifreeze containers covered and repair cooling system leaks as soon as they're noticed.**

**✳✳ CAUTION:**

**Some later models may have been factory-filled with orange-colored Dex-Cool coolant, with will normally be identified by a label near the radiator. Add only Dex-Cool-type coolant to Dex-Cool systems, and be sure to maintain a 50-50 mixture with water to avoid damaging the cooling system.**

8   All vehicles covered by this manual are equipped with a pressurized coolant recovery system. A white plastic expansion tank located at the front (1991 and earlier models) or side (1992 and later models) of the engine compartment is connected by a hose to the cooling system. As the engine heats up during operation, the expanding coolant fills the tank.

9   The coolant level in the tank should be checked regulary.

**✳✳ WARNING:**

**Do not remove the radiator cap (on models so equipped) or expansion tank cap to check the coolant level when the engine is warm! The level in the tank varies with the temperature of the engine. When the engine is cold, the coolant level should be at or slightly above the FULL COLD mark on the reservoir. Once the engine has warmed up, the level should be at or near the FULL HOT mark. If it isn't, allow the engine to cool, then remove the cap from the tank and add a 50/50 mixture of the recommended coolant and water (see illustration).**

10  Drive the vehicle and recheck the coolant level. Don't use rust inhibitors or additives. If only a small amount of coolant is required to bring the system up to the proper level, water can be used. However, repeated additions of water will dilute the antifreeze and water solution. In order to maintain the proper ratio of antifreeze and water, always top up the coolant level with the correct mixture. An empty plastic milk jug or bleach bottle makes an excellent container for mixing coolant.

11  If the coolant level drops consistently, there may be a leak in the system. Inspect the radiator, hoses, filler cap, drain plugs and water pump (see Section 18). If no leaks are noted, have the radiator cap or expansion tank cap pressure tested by a service station.

12  If you have to remove the radiator cap (1991 and earlier models)

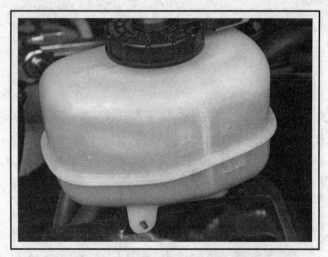

**4.15  The brake fluid level should be near the neck of the translucent plastic reservoir**

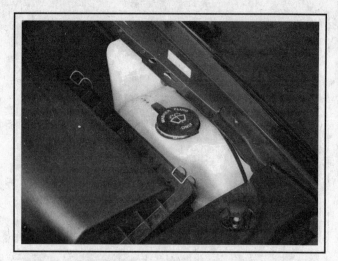

**4.22  The windshield washer reservoir is located at the left front corner of the engine compartment**

or expansion tank cap (1992 and later models), wait until the engine has cooled completely, then wrap a thick cloth around the cap and turn it to the first stop (if you're removing an expansion tank cap, unscrew it slowly, stopping if you hear a hissing noise). If coolant or steam escapes, let the engine cool down longer, then remove the cap.

13  Check the condition of the coolant as well. It should be relatively clear. If it's brown or rust colored, the system should be drained, flushed and refilled. Even if the coolant appears to be normal, the corrosion inhibitors wear out, so it must be replaced at the specified intervals.

## BRAKE FLUID

▶ **Refer to illustration 4.15**

14  The brake fluid level is checked by looking through the plastic reservoir mounted on the master cylinder. The master cylinder is mounted on the front of the power booster unit in the left (driver's side) rear corner of the engine compartment.

15  The fluid level should be between the MAX and MIN lines on the side of the reservoir (see illustration).

16  If the fluid level is low, wipe the top of the reservoir and the cap with a clean rag to prevent contamination of the system as the cap is unscrewed.

17  Add only the specified brake fluid to the reservoir (refer to *Recommended lubricants and fluids* at the end of this Chapter or your owner's manual). Mixing different types of brake fluid can damage the system. Fill the reservoir to the MAX line.

### ✳ WARNING:

**Brake fluid can harm your eyes and damage painted surfaces, so use extreme caution when handling or pouring it. Do not use brake fluid that has been standing open or is more than one year old. Brake fluid absorbs moisture from the air, which can cause a dangerous loss of braking effectiveness.**

18  While the reservoir cap is off, check the master cylinder reservoir for contamination. If rust deposits, dirt particles or water droplets are present, the system should be drained and refilled by a dealer service department or repair shop.

19  After filling the reservoir to the proper level, make sure the cap is seated to prevent fluid leakage and/or contamination.

20  The fluid level in the master cylinder will drop slightly as the brake shoes or pads at each wheel wear down during normal operation. If the brake fluid level drops consistently, check the entire system for leaks immediately. Examine all brake lines, hoses and connections, along with the calipers, wheel cylinders and master cylinder (see Section 21).

21  When checking the fluid level, if you discover one or both reservoirs empty or nearly empty, the brake system should be bled (see Chapter 9).

## WINDSHIELD WASHER FLUID

▶ **Refer to illustration 4.22**

22  Fluid for the windshield washer system is stored in a plastic reservoir located at the left (driver's) side of the engine compartment (see illustration).

23  In milder climates, plain water can be used in the reservoir, but it should be kept no more than 2/3 full to allow for expansion if the water freezes. In colder climates, use windshield washer system antifreeze, available at any auto parts store, to lower the freezing point of the fluid. Mix the antifreeze with water in accordance with the manufacturer's directions on the container.

### ✳ CAUTION:

**Do not use cooling system antifreeze - it will damage the vehicle's paint.**

## 5   Tire and tire pressure checks (every 250 miles or weekly)

▶ **Refer to illustrations 5.2, 5.3, 5.4a, 5.4b and 5.8**

1   Periodic inspection of the tires may spare you the inconvenience of being stranded with a flat tire. It can also provide you with vital information regarding possible problems in the steering and suspension systems before major damage occurs.

2   The original tires on this vehicle are equipped with 1/2-inch wide bands that will appear when tread depth reaches 1/16-inch, at which point the tires can be considered  worn out. Tread wear can be monitored with a simple, inexpensive device known as a tread depth indicator (see illustration).

3   Note any abnormal tread wear (see illustration). Tread pattern irregularities such as cupping, flat spots and more wear on one side than the other are indications of front end alignment and/or balance problems. If any of these conditions are noted, take the vehicle to a tire shop or service station to correct the problem.

4   Look closely for cuts, punctures and embedded nails or tacks. Sometimes a tire will hold air pressure for a short time or leak down very slowly after a nail has embedded itself in the tread. If a slow leak persists, check the valve stem core to make sure it is tight (see illustration). Examine the tread for an object that may have

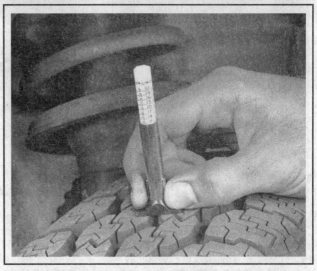

**5.2  Use a tire tread depth indicator to monitor tire wear - they are available at auto parts stores and service stations and cost very little**

**UNDERINFLATION**

**CUPPING**

**Cupping may be caused by:**
- Underinflation and/or mechanical irregularities such as out-of-balance condition of wheel and/or tire, and bent or damaged wheel.
- Loose or worn steering tie-rod or steering idler arm.
- Loose, damaged or worn front suspension parts.

**OVERINFLATION**

**INCORRECT TOE-IN OR EXTREME CAMBER**

**FEATHERING DUE TO MISALIGNMENT**

**5.3  This chart will help you determine the condition of the tires, the probable cause(s) of abnormal wear and the corrective action necessary**

**5.4a If a tire loses air on a steady basis, check the valve stem core first to make sure it's snug (special inexpensive wrenches are commonly available at auto parts stores)**

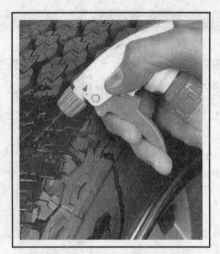

**5.4b If the valve stem core is tight, raise the corner of the vehicle with the low tire and spray a soapy water solution onto the tread as the tire is turned slowly - leaks will cause small bubbles to appear**

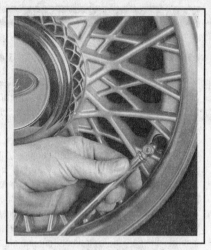

**5.8 To extend the life of the tires, check the air pressure at least once a week with an accurate gauge (don't forget the spare!)**

embedded itself in the tire or for a "plug" that may have begun to leak (radial tire punctures are repaired with a plug that is installed in a puncture). If a puncture is suspected, it can be easily verified by spraying a solution of soapy water onto the puncture area (see illustration). The soapy solution will bubble if there is a leak. Unless the puncture is unusually large, a tire shop or service station can usually repair the tire.

5   Carefully inspect the inner sidewall of each tire for evidence of brake fluid leakage. If you see any, inspect the brakes immediately.

6   Correct air pressure adds miles to the lifespan of the tires, improves mileage and enhances overall ride quality. Tire pressure cannot be accurately estimated by looking at a tire, especially if it's a radial. A tire pressure gauge is essential. Keep an accurate gauge in the glove compartment. The pressure gauges attached to the nozzles of air hoses at gas stations are often inaccurate.

7   Always check tire pressure when the tires are cold. Cold, in this case, means the vehicle has not been driven over a mile in the three hours preceding a tire pressure check. A pressure rise of four to eight pounds is not uncommon once the tires are warm.

8   Unscrew the valve cap protruding from the wheel or hubcap and push the gauge firmly onto the valve stem (see illustration). Note the reading on the gauge and compare the figure to the recommended tire pressure shown on the tire placard on the driver's side door. Be sure to reinstall the valve cap to keep dirt and moisture out of the valve stem mechanism. Check all four tires and, if necessary, add enough air to bring them up to the recommended pressure.

9   Don't forget to keep the spare tire inflated to the specified pressure (refer to your owner's manual or the decal attached to the right door pillar). Note that the pressure recommended for the temporary (mini) spare is higher than for the tires on the vehicle.

## 6   Power steering fluid level check (every 3000 miles or 3 months)

▶ **Refer to illustrations 6.5a, 6.5b, 6.5c and 6.9**

1   Check the power steering fluid level periodically to avoid steering system problems, such as damage to the pump.

### ❈❈ CAUTION:

**DO NOT hold the steering wheel against either stop (extreme left or right turn) for more than five seconds. If you do, the power steering pump could be damaged.**

### 1991 AND EARLIER MODELS

2   The power steering pump, located at the front corner of the engine, is equipped with a twist-off cap with an integral fluid level dipstick.

3   Park the vehicle on level ground and apply the parking brake.

4   Run the engine until it has reached normal operating temperature. With the engine at idle, turn the steering wheel back-and-forth several times to get any air out of the steering system. Shut the engine off, remove the cap by turning it counterclockwise, wipe the dipstick clean and reinstall the cap. (Make sure it is seated).

5   Remove the cap again and note the fluid level. It must be between the two lines designating the FULL HOT or FULL COLD range (see illustration). Be sure to use the proper temperature range on the dipstick when checking the fluid level - the FULL COLD lines on the reverse side of the dipstick are only usable when the engine is cold (see illustrations).

6   Add small amounts of fluid until the level is correct.

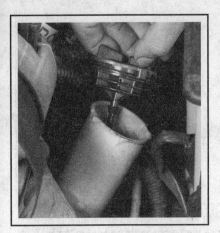

6.5a  A dipstick is used to check the power steering fluid level on earlier models

6.5b  The dipstick is marked on both sides so the fluid can be checked hot . . .

6.5c  . . . or cold

**✳✳ CAUTION:**

**Do not overfill the pump. If too much fluid is added, remove the excess with a clean syringe or suction pump.**

7   If additional fluid is required, pour the specified type directly into the reservoir, using a funnel to prevent spills.

### 1992 AND LATER MODELS

8   The fluid reservoir for the power steering pump is located on the inner fender panel near the front of the engine on the left (driver's) side of the engine compartment on early models or mounted on the left side (driver's side) of the radiator on later models.

9   On these models the reservoir is translucent plastic and the fluid level can be checked visually (see illustration).

10  The fluid level should be kept between the FULL and ADD marks on the reservoir.

11  Add small amounts of fluid until the level is correct.

**✳✳ CAUTION:**

**Do not overfill the reservoir. If too much fluid is added, remove the excess with a clean syringe or suction pump.**

6.9  The power steering fluid reservoir on later models is translucent so the fluid level can be checked without removing the cap - unscrew the cap to add fluid

### ALL MODELS

12  If the reservoir requires frequent fluid additions, all power steering hoses, hose connections, the power steering pump and the steering gear assembly should be carefully checked for leaks.

---

## 7   Automatic transmission fluid level check (every 3000 miles or 3 months)

▶ **Refer to illustrations 7.4 and 7.6**

1   The automatic transmission fluid level should be carefully maintained. Low fluid level can lead to slipping or loss of drive, while overfilling can cause foaming and loss of fluid. Either condition can cause transmission damage.

2   Since transmission fluid expands as it heats up, the fluid level should only be checked when the transmission is warm (at normal operating temperature). If the vehicle has just been driven over 20 miles (32 km), the transmission can be considered warm.

**✳✳ CAUTION:**

**If the vehicle has just been driven for a long time at high speed or in city traffic in hot weather, or if it has been pulling a trailer, an accurate fluid level reading cannot be obtained.**

Allow the transmission to cool down for about 30 minutes. You can also check the transmission fluid level when the transmission is cold. If the vehicle has not been driven for over five hours and the fluid is about room temperature (70 to 95-degrees F), the transmission is cold.

**7.4 The automatic transmission dipstick is located at the rear of the engine**

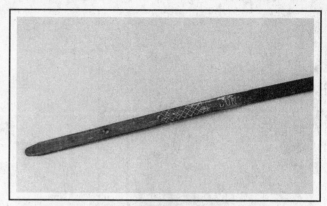

**7.6 Check the fluid with the transmission at normal operating temperature - the level should be kept in the HOT range in the cross-hatched area (don't add fluid if the level is anywhere in the cross-hatched area)**

However, the fluid level is normally checked with the transmission warm to ensure accurate results.

3   Immediately after driving the vehicle, park it on a level surface, set the parking brake and start the engine. While the engine is idling, depress the brake pedal and move the selector lever through all the gear ranges, beginning and ending in Park.

4   Locate the automatic transmission dipstick tube in the engine compartment (see illustration).

5   With the engine still idling, pull the dipstick from the tube, wipe it off with a clean rag, push it all the way back into the tube and withdraw it again, then note the fluid level.

6   If the transmission is cold, the level should be in the room temperature range on the dipstick (between the two holes); if it's warm, the fluid level should be in the operating temperature range (in the cross-hatched area) (see illustration). If the level is low, add the specified automatic transmission fluid through the dipstick tube - use a funnel to prevent spills.

7   Add just enough of the recommended fluid to fill the transmission to the proper level. It takes about one pint to raise the level from the low mark to the high mark when the fluid is hot, so add the fluid a little at a time and keep checking the level until it's correct.

8   The condition of the fluid should also be checked along with the level. If the fluid is black or a dark reddish-brown color, or if it smells burned, it should be changed (see Section 26). If you are in doubt about its condition, purchase some new fluid and compare the two for color and smell.

## 8   Engine oil and filter change (every 3000 miles or 3 months)

▶ Refer to illustrations 8.2, 8.7, 8.12 and 8.16

### ✳✳ WARNING:

**On models with air suspension, turn the air suspension switch to Off before raising the vehicle.**

1   Frequent oil changes are the most important preventive maintenance procedures that can be done by the home mechanic. As engine oil ages, in becomes diluted and contaminated, which leads to premature engine wear.

2   Make sure that you have all the necessary tools before you begin this procedure (see illustration). You should also have plenty of rags or newspapers handy for mopping up oil spills.

3   Access to the oil drain plug and filter will be improved if the vehicle can be lifted on a hoist, driven onto ramps or supported by jackstands.

### ✳✳ WARNING:

**Do not work under a vehicle supported only by a bumper, hydraulic or scissors-type jack - always use jackstands!**

4   If you haven't changed the oil on this vehicle before, get under it and locate the oil drain plug and the oil filter. The exhaust components will be warm as you work, so note how they are routed to avoid touching them when you are under the vehicle.

5   Start the engine and allow it to reach normal operating temperature - oil and sludge will flow out more easily when warm. If new oil, a filter or tools are needed, use the vehicle to go get them and warm up the engine/oil at the same time. Park on a level surface and shut off the engine when it's warmed up. Remove the oil filler cap from the valve cover.

6   Raise the vehicle and support it on jackstands. Make sure it is safely supported!

7   Being careful not to touch the hot exhaust components, position a drain pan under the plug in the bottom of the engine, then remove the plug (see illustration). It's a good idea to wear a rubber glove while unscrewing the plug the final few turns to avoid being scalded by hot oil.

8   It may be necessary to move the drain pan slightly as oil flow slows to a trickle. Inspect the old oil for the presence of metal particles.

9   After all the oil has drained, wipe off the drain plug with a clean rag. Any small metal particles clinging to the plug would immediately contaminate the new oil.

10   Clean the area around the drain plug opening, reinstall the plug and tighten it securely, but don't strip the threads.

11   Move the drain pan into position under the oil filter.

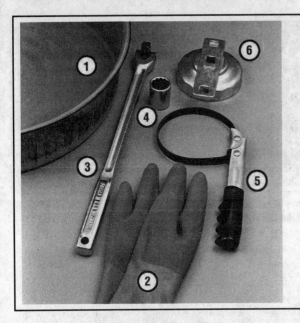

**8.2 These tools are required when changing the engine oil and filter**

1  **Drain pan** - It should be fairly shallow in depth, but wide to prevent spills
2  **Rubber gloves** - When removing the drain plug and filter, you will get oil on your hands (the gloves will prevent burns)
3  **Breaker bar** - Sometimes the oil drain plug is tight, and a long breaker bar is needed to loosen it
4  **Socket** – To be used with the breaker bar or a ratchet (must be the correct size to fit the drain plug - six-point preferred)
5  **Filter wrench** - This is a metal band-type wrench, which requires clearance around the filter to be effective
6  **Filter wrench** - This type fits on the bottom of the filter and can be turned with a ratchet or breaker bar (different-size wrenches are available for different types of filters)

12 Loosen the oil filter by turning it counterclockwise with a filter wrench (see illustration). Any standard filter wrench will work.

13 Sometimes the oil filter is screwed on so tightly that it can't be loosened. If it is, punch a metal bar or long screwdriver directly through it, as close to the engine as possible, and use it as a T-bar to turn the filter. Be prepared for oil to spurt out of the canister as it's punctured.

14 Once the filter is loose, use your hands to unscrew it from the block. Just as the filter is detached from the block, immediately tilt the open end up to prevent the oil inside the filter from spilling out.

15 Using a clean rag, wipe off the mounting surface on the block. Also, make sure that none of the old gasket remains stuck to the mounting surface. It can be removed with a scraper if necessary.

16 Compare the old filter with the new one to make sure they are the same type. Smear some engine oil on the rubber gasket of the new filter and screw it into place (see illustration). Overtightening the filter will damage the gasket, so don't use a filter wrench. Most filter manufacturers recommend tightening the filter by hand only. Normally they should be tightened 3/4-turn after the gasket contacts the block, but be sure to follow the directions on the filter or container.

17 Remove all tools and materials from under the vehicle, being

careful not to spill the oil in the drain pan, then lower the vehicle.

18 Add new oil to the engine through the oil filler cap in the valve cover. Use a funnel to prevent oil from spilling onto the top of the engine. Pour four quarts of fresh oil into the engine. Wait a few minutes to allow the oil to drain into the pan, then check the level on the dipstick (see Section 4 if necessary). If the oil level is in the SAFE range (hatched area), install the filler cap.

19 Start the engine and run it for about a minute. While the engine is running, look under the vehicle and check for leaks at the oil pan drain plug and around the oil filter. If either one is leaking, stop the engine and tighten the plug or filter slightly.

20 Wait a few minutes, then recheck the level on the dipstick. Add oil as necessary to bring the level into the SAFE range.

21 During the first few trips after an oil change, make it a point to check frequently for leaks and proper oil level.

22 The old oil drained from the engine cannot be reused in its present state and should be discarded. Oil reclamation centers, auto repair shops and gas stations will normally accept the oil, which can be recycled. After the oil has cooled, it can be drained into a container (plastic jugs, bottles, milk cartons, etc.) for transport to a disposal site.

**8.7  Use a proper size box-end wrench or socket to remove the oil drain plug and avoid rounding it off**

**8.12  Since the oil filter (accessible from below) is on very tight, you'll need a special wrench for removal - DO NOT use the wrench to tighten the new filter**

**8.16  Lubricate the oil filter gasket with clean engine oil before installing the filter on the engine**

**8.23a Press the SETUP button on the console to activate the on-screen message for start-up**

**8.23b Read the proper message at the console screen to initiate the Oil Life procedure**

## OIL LIFE AND OIL LIFE START VALUE ON DISPLAY FUNCTION - LATE MODELS

◆ **Refer to illustrations 8.23a and 8.23b**

➡**Note: The oil change intervals can be reset using the display function on the instrument panel. Maximum values for oil change intervals are 7,500 miles. The intervals can be changed to indicate oil change intervals of 6,000, 5,000, 3,000, etc. miles if necessary. The recommended oil change interval is 3,000 miles.**

23 Press the SETUP button on the display (see illustration). The display function will read PRESS SELECT TO BEGIN SYSTEM CHECK (see illustration).

24 Press the SELECT button to display OIL LIFE - PRESS RESET IF NEW OIL.

25 Press and hold the RESET button to display OIL LIFE START VALUE SET TO XXX%. This will set the oil life value or interval at 100% or 7,500 miles.

26 To change the interval or percentage, press the SETUP button until OIL LIFE START VALUE PRESS SELECT TO CHANGE is displayed on the instrument panel.

27 Press and release the SELECT button to change the percentage or the interval. Remember, 40% will adjust the interval to 3,000 miles.

---

**9   Underhood hose check and replacement (every 7500 miles or 6 months)**

---

❋❋ **WARNING:**

**Replacement of air conditioning hoses must be left to a dealer service department or air conditioning shop that has the equipment to depressurize the system safely. Never remove air conditioning components or hoses until the system has been depressurized.**

## GENERAL

1   High temperatures under the hood can cause deterioration of the rubber and plastic hoses used for engine, accessory and emission systems operation. Periodic inspection should be made for cracks, loose clamps, material hardening and leaks.

2   Information specific to the cooling system hoses can be found in Section 18.

3   Most (but not all) hoses are secured to the fittings with clamps. Where clamps are used, check to be sure they haven't lost their tension, allowing the hose to leak. If clamps aren't used, make sure the hose has not expanded and/or hardened where it slips over the fitting, allowing it to leak.

## PCV SYSTEM HOSE

4   To reduce hydrocarbon emissions, crankcase blow-by gas is vented through the PCV valve in the rocker arm cover to the intake manifold via a rubber hose on most models. The blow-by gases mix with incoming air in the intake manifold before being burned in the combustion chambers.

5   Check the PCV hose for cracks, leaks and other damage. Disconnect it from the valve cover and the intake manifold and check the inside for obstructions. If it's clogged, clean it out with solvent.

## VACUUM HOSES

6   It's quite common for vacuum hoses, especially those in the emissions system, to be color coded or identified by colored stripes molded into them. Various systems require hoses with different wall thicknesses, collapse resistance and temperature resistance. When replacing hoses, be sure the new ones are made of the same material.

7   Often the only effective way to check a hose is to remove it completely from the vehicle. If more than one hose is removed, be sure to label the hoses and fittings to ensure correct installation.

8   When checking vacuum hoses, be sure to include any plastic T-fittings in the check. Inspect the fittings for cracks and the hose where it fits over each fitting for distortion, which could cause leakage.

9   A small piece of vacuum hose (1/4-inch inside diameter) can be used as a stethoscope to detect vacuum leaks. Hold one end of the hose to your ear and probe around vacuum hoses and fittings, listening for the "hissing" sound characteristic of a vacuum leak.

❋❋ **WARNING:**

**When probing with the vacuum hose stethoscope, be careful not to come into contact with moving engine components such as drivebelts, the cooling fan, etc.**

## FUEL HOSE

### ✳✳ WARNING:

**Gasoline is extremely flammable, so take extra precautions when you work on any part of the fuel system. Don't smoke or allow open flames or bare light bulbs near the work area, and don't work in a garage where a gas-type appliance (such as a water heater or clothes dryer) is present. Since gasoline is carcinogenic, wear latex gloves when there's a possibility of being exposed to fuel, and, if you spill any fuel on your skin, rinse it off immediately with soap and water. Mop up any spills immediately and do not store fuel-soaked rags where they could ignite. The fuel system is under constant pressure, so, if any fuel lines are to be disconnected, the fuel pressure in the system must be relieved first (see Chapter 4 for more information). When you perform any kind of work on the fuel system, wear safety glasses and have a Class B type fire extinguisher on hand.**

10  The fuel lines are usually under pressure, so if any fuel lines are to be disconnected be prepared to catch spilled fuel.

### ✳✳ WARNING:

**Your vehicle is equipped with fuel injection and you must relieve the fuel system pressure before servicing the fuel lines. Refer to Chapter 4 for the fuel system pressure relief procedure.**

11  Check all flexible fuel lines for deterioration and chafing. Check especially for cracks in areas where the hose bends and just before fittings, such as where a hose attaches to the fuel pump, fuel filter and fuel injection unit.

12  When replacing a hose, use only hose that is specifically designed for your fuel injection system.

13  Spring-type clamps are sometimes used on fuel return or vapor lines. These clamps often lose their tension over a period of time, and can be "sprung" during removal. Replace all spring-type clamps with screw clamps whenever a hose is replaced. Some fuel lines use spring-lock type couplings, which require a special tool to disconnect. See Chapter 4 for more information on these type of couplings.

## METAL LINES

14  Sections of metal line are often used for fuel line between the fuel pump and the fuel injection unit. Check carefully to make sure the line isn't bent, crimped or cracked.

15  If a section of metal fuel line must be replaced, use seamless steel tubing only, since copper and aluminum tubing do not have the strength necessary to withstand vibration caused by the engine.

16  Check the metal brake lines where they enter the master cylinder and brake proportioning unit (if used) for cracks in the lines and loose fittings. Any sign of brake fluid leakage calls for an immediate thorough inspection of the brake system.

## 10  Drivebelt check and replacement/tensioner replacement (every 7500 miles or 6 months)

♦ **Refer to illustrations 10.4, 10.5, 10.6, 10.13 and 10.15**

1  The drivebelts are located at the front of the engine and play an important role in the overall operation of the vehicle and its components. Due to their function and material make-up, the drivebelts are prone to failure after a period of time and should be inspected and adjusted periodically to prevent major engine damage.

2  The number of belts used on a particular vehicle depends on the accessories installed. Drivebelts are used to turn the alternator, power steering pump, water pump and air-conditioning compressor. Depending on the pulley arrangement, more than one of these components may be driven by a single belt. On later models, a single self-adjusting serpentine drivebelt is used to drive all of the components.

### INSPECTION

3  With the engine off, open the hood and locate the various belts at the front of the engine. Using your fingers (and a flashlight, if necessary), move along the belts checking for cracks and separation of the belt plies. Also check for fraying and glazing, which gives the belt a shiny appearance. Both sides of each belt should be inspected, which means you will have to twist the belt to check the underside.

4  Check the ribs on the underside of the belt. They should all be the same depth, with none of the surface uneven (see illustration).

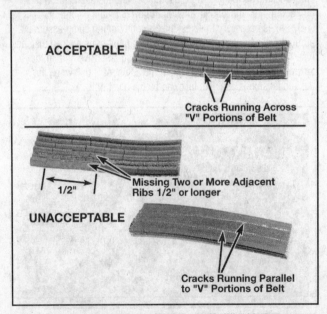

**10.4  Small cracks in the underside of a V-ribbed belt are acceptable - lengthwise cracks, or missing pieces that cause the belt to make noise, are cause for replacement**

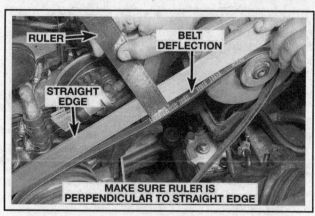

**10.5 Measuring drivebelt deflection with a straightedge and ruler**

5   The tension of each belt on models without an automatic tensioner is checked by pushing on the belt at a distance halfway between the pulleys. Push firmly with your thumb and see how much the belt moves (deflects) (see illustration). A rule of thumb is that if the distance from pulley center-to-pulley center is between 7 and 11 inches, the belt should deflect 1/4-inch. If the belt travels between pulleys spaced 12 to 16 inches apart, the belt should deflect 1/2-inch.

6   The tension of the belt on models with an automatic tensioner is checked visually. Locate the belt tensioner at the front of the engine on the right (passenger) side, adjacent to the lower crankshaft pulley, then find the tensioner operating marks (see illustration). If the indicator mark is outside the operating range, the belt should be replaced.

7   If it is necessary to adjust the belt tension on models without an automatic tensioner, either to make the belt tighter or looser, it is done by moving the belt tensioner or the alternator, depending on which belt is being adjusted.

8   If it is necessary to adjust the alternator/water pump/power steering pump belt, loosen the adjustment and pivot bolts on the alternator, then move the alternator in the required direction by placing an open-end wrench over the lug on the alternator. Hold the alternator in position and tighten the adjustment bolt, followed by the pivot bolt.

9   If it is necessary to adjust the air conditioning compressor/air pump drivebelt, loosen the adjustment and pivot bolts on the tensioner, insert a 1/2-inch drive breaker bar into the square drive hole in the tensioner and apply tension. Tighten the adjustment bolt when the desired tension is attained, followed by the pivot bolt.

**10.6 On some models the serpentine drivebelt is automatically tensioned and requires no service as long as it is in good condition and the indicator is in the proper range**

## DRIVEBELT REPLACEMENT

### Models without an automatic tensioner

10  Follow the above procedures for drivebelt adjustment but slip the belt off the pulleys and remove it. Since belts tend to wear out more or less at the same time, it's a good idea to replace both of them at the same time.

11  Take the old belts with you when purchasing new ones in order to make a direct comparison for length, width and design.

12  Adjust the belts as described earlier in this Section. mounting bolt to the Specification listed in this Chapter.

### Models with an automatic tensioner

13  To replace the belt, lift the tensioner arm with a ratchet or breaker bar (see illustration).

14  Remove the belt from the auxiliary components and carefully release the tensioner.

15  Route the new belt over the various pulleys, again rotating the tensioner to allow the belt to be installed, then release the belt tensioner. Make sure the belt fits properly into the pulley grooves - it must be completely engaged.

➡**Note: Most models have a drivebelt routing decal on the upper radiator panel to help during drivebelt installation (see illustration).**

**10.13  Place a socket over the tensioner bolt and lift up to release the belt tension**

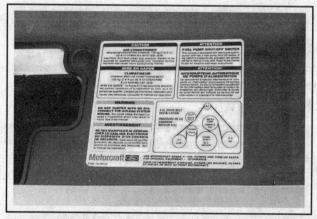

**10.15  The routing schematic for the serpentine belt is usually found on the fan shroud**

## DRIVEBELT TENSIONER REPLACEMENT

▶ **Refer to illustration 10.17**

16  Remove the drivebelt (see Steps 13 and 14).
17  Remove the tensioner mounting bolt (see illustration).
18  Remove the tensioner from the engine.
19  Installation is the reverse of removal. Torque the tensioner

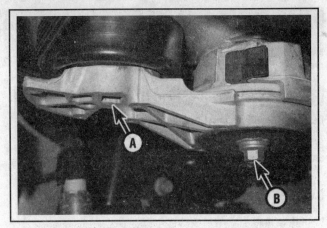

**10.17 Drivebelt tensioner details**

A    Square hole for ratchet or breaker bar (to release tension)
B    Mounting bolt

## 11  Tire rotation (every 7500 miles or 6 months)

▶ **Refer to illustration 11.2**

❋❋ **WARNING:**

**On models with air suspension, turn the air suspension switch to Off before raising the vehicle.**

1    The tires should be rotated at the specified intervals and whenever uneven wear is noticed. Since the vehicle will be raised and the tires removed anyway, check the brakes also (see Section 21).

2    Radial tires must be rotated in a specific pattern (see illustration). If your vehicle has a compact spare tire, don't include it in the rotation pattern.

3    Refer to the information in *Jacking and towing* at the front of this manual for the proper procedure to follow when raising the vehicle and changing a tire. If the brakes must be checked, don't apply the parking brake as stated.

4    The vehicle must be raised on a hoist or supported on jackstands to get all four wheels off the ground. Make sure the vehicle is safely supported!

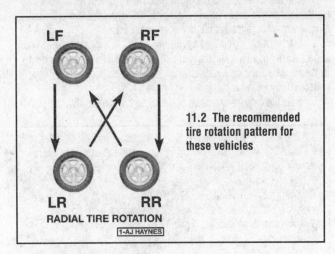

**11.2 The recommended tire rotation pattern for these vehicles**

5    After the rotation procedure is finished, check and adjust the tire pressures as necessary and be sure to check the lug nut tightness.

## 12  Seat belt check (every 7500 miles or 6 months)

1    Check seat belts, buckles, latch plates and guide loops for obvious damage and signs of wear.

2    See if the seat belt reminder light comes on when the key is turned to the Run or Start position. A chime should also sound. On passive restraint systems, the shoulder belt should move into position in the A-pillar.

3    The seat belts are designed to lock up during a sudden stop or impact, yet allow free movement during normal driving. Make sure the retractors return the belt against your chest while driving and rewind the belt fully when the buckle is unlatched.

4    If any of the above checks reveal problems with the seat belt system, replace parts as necessary.

## 13 Battery check, maintenance and charging (every 7500 miles or 6 months)

**Refer to illustrations 13.1, 13.6a, 13.6b, 13.7a, 13.7b and 13.8**

**WARNING:**

**Certain precautions must be followed when checking and servicing the battery. Hydrogen gas, which is highly flammable, is always present in the battery cells, so keep lighted tobacco and all other open flames and sparks away from the battery. The electrolyte inside the battery is actually dilute sulfuric acid, which will cause injury if splashed on your skin or in your eyes. It will also ruin clothes and painted surfaces. When removing the battery cables, always detach the negative cable first and hook it up last!**

1 A routine preventive maintenance program for the battery in your vehicle is the only way to ensure quick and reliable starts. But before performing any battery maintenance, make sure that you have the proper equipment necessary to work safely around the battery (see illustration).

2 There are also several precautions that should be taken whenever battery maintenance is performed. Before servicing the battery, always turn the engine and all accessories off and disconnect the cable from the negative terminal of the battery.

3 The battery produces hydrogen gas, which is both flammable and explosive. Never create a spark, smoke or light a match around the battery. Always charge the battery in a ventilated area.

4 Electrolyte contains poisonous and corrosive sulfuric acid. Do not allow it to get in your eyes, on your skin on your clothes. Never ingest it. Wear protective safety glasses when working near the battery. Keep children away from the battery.

5 Note the external condition of the battery. If the positive terminal and cable clamp on your vehicle's battery is equipped with a rubber protector, make sure that it's not torn or damaged. It should completely cover the terminal. Look for any corroded or loose connections, cracks in the case or cover or loose hold-down clamps. Also check the entire length of each cable for cracks and frayed conductors.

6 If corrosion, which looks like white, fluffy deposits (see illustration) is evident, particularly around the terminals, the battery should be removed for cleaning. Loosen the cable clamp bolts with a wrench, being careful to remove the ground cable first, and slide them off the terminals (see illustration). Then disconnect the hold-down clamp bolt and nut, remove the clamp and lift the battery from the engine compartment.

7 Clean the cable clamps thoroughly with a battery brush or a terminal cleaner and a solution of warm water and baking soda (see illustration). Wash the terminals and the top of the battery case with the same solution but make sure that the solution doesn't get into the battery When cleaning the cables, terminals and battery top, wear safety goggles and rubber gloves to prevent any solution from coming in contact with your eyes or hands. Wear old clothes too - even diluted, sulfuric acid splashed onto clothes will burn holes in them. If the terminals have been extensively corroded, clean them up with a terminal cleaner (see illustration). Thoroughly wash all cleaned areas with plain water.

8 Make sure that the battery tray is in good condition and the hold-down clamp bolts are tight (see illustration). If the battery is removed from the tray, make sure no parts remain in the bottom of the tray when the battery is reinstalled. When reinstalling the hold-down clamp bolts, do not overtighten them.

9 Information on removing and installing the battery can be found in Chapter 5. Information on jump starting can be found at the front of this manual.

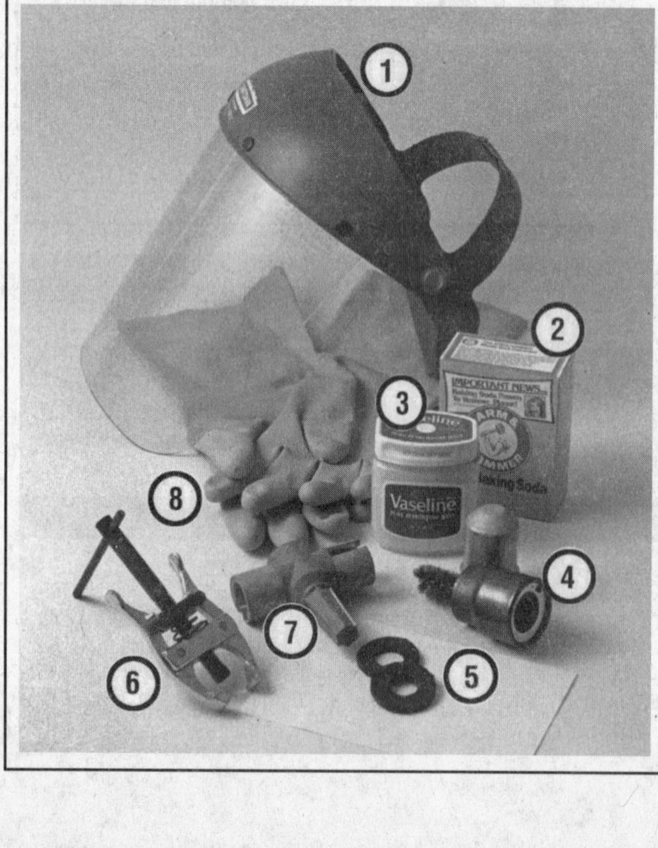


**13.1 Tools and materials required for battery maintenance**

1 ***Face shield/safety goggles*** *- When removing corrosion with a brush, the acidic particles can easily fly up into your eyes*
2 ***Baking soda*** *- A solution of baking soda and water can be used to neutralize corrosion*
3 ***Petroleum jelly*** *- A layer of this on the battery posts will help prevent corrosion*
4 ***Battery post/cable cleaner*** *- This wire brush cleaning tool will remove all traces of corrosion from the battery posts and cable clamps*
5 ***Treated felt washers*** *- Placing one of these on each post, directly under the cable clamps, will help prevent corrosion*
6 ***Puller*** *- Sometimes the cable clamps are very difficult to pull off the posts, even after the nut/bolt has been completely loosened. This tool pulls the clamp straight up and off the post without damage*
7 ***Battery post/cable cleaner*** *- Here is another cleaning tool which is a slightly different version of Number 4 above, but it does the same thing*
8 ***Rubber gloves*** *- Another safety item to consider when servicing the battery; remember that's acid inside the battery!*

## CLEANING

10 Corrosion on the hold-down components, battery case and surrounding areas can be removed with a solution of water and baking soda. Thoroughly rinse all cleaned areas with plain water.

11 Any metal parts of the vehicle damaged by corrosion should be covered with a zinc-based primer, then painted.

## CHARGING

**❋❋ WARNING:**

**When batteries are being charged, hydrogen gas, which is very explosive and flammable, is produced. Do not smoke or allow open flames near a charging or a recently charged battery. Wear eye protection when near the battery during charging. Also, make sure the charger is unplugged before connecting or disconnecting the battery from the charger.**

12 Slow-rate charging is the best way to restore a battery that's discharged to the point where it will not start the engine. It's also a good way to maintain the battery charge in a vehicle that's only driven a few miles between starts. Maintaining the battery charge is particularly important in the winter when the battery must work harder to start the engine and electrical accessories that drain the battery are in greater use.

13 It's best to use a one or two-amp battery charger (sometimes called a "trickle" charger). They are the safest and put the least strain on the battery. They are also the least expensive. For a faster charge, you can use a higher amperage charger, but don't use one rated more than 1/10th the amp/hour rating of the battery. Rapid boost charges that claim to restore the power of the battery in one to two hours are hardest on the battery and can damage batteries not in good condition. This type of charging should only be used in emergency situations.

14 The average time necessary to charge a battery should be listed in the instructions that come with the charger. As a general rule, a trickle charger will charge a battery in 12 to 16 hours.

**13.6a  Battery terminal corrosion usually appears as light, fluffy powder**

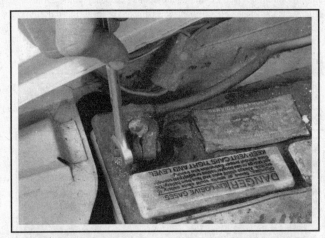

**13.6b  Removing the cable from a battery post with a wrench - sometimes special battery pliers are required for this procedure if corrosion has caused deterioration of the nut hex (always remove the ground cable first and hook it up last!)**

**13.7a  When cleaning the cable clamps, all corrosion must be removed (the inside of the clamp is tapered to match the taper on the post, so don't remove too much material)**

**13.7b  Regardless of the type of tool used on the battery posts, a clean, shiny surface should be the result**

**13.8  Make sure the battery hold-down nut and the bolt on the other side are tight (arrows)**

## 14  Windshield wiper blade check and replacement (every 15,000 miles or 12 months)

▶ **Refer to illustrations 14.4 and 14.8**

1    Road film can build up on the wiper blades and affect their efficiency, so they should be washed regularly with a mild detergent solution.

### CHECK

2    The windshield wiper and blade assembly should be inspected periodically. Even if you don't use your wipers, the sun and elements will dry out the rubber portions, causing them to crack and break apart. If inspection reveals hardened or cracked rubber, replace the wiper blades. If inspection reveals nothing unusual, wet the windshield, turn the wipers on, allow them to cycle several times, then shut them off. An uneven wiper pattern across the glass or streaks over clean glass indicate that the blades should be replaced.

3    The operation of the wiper mechanism can loosen the fasteners, so they should be checked and tightened, as necessary, at the same time the wiper blades are checked (see Chapter 12 for further information regarding the wiper mechanism).

### BLADE ASSEMBLY REPLACEMENT

4    Cycle the wiper assembly to a position on the windshield where

removal of the blade assembly can be performed without difficulty. Turn the ignition key off at the desired position. With the blade assembly resting on the windshield, insert a small screwdriver into the release spring at the center of the blade and push down on the spring (see illustration). While pressing down with the screwdriver, pull the wiper blade off the wiper arm pin.

5    To install the blade assembly, push it onto the pin until it snaps into place. Be sure that the blade assembly is securely attached to the wiper arm.

### BLADE ELEMENT REPLACEMENT

6    At one end of the rubber blade element, insert a small screwdriver between the blade and the metal backing strip. Press down and in, then twist the screwdriver clockwise to release the element from the retaining claw.

7    Slide the blade element out of the retaining claws until the element is completely detached from the frame.

8    To install the element, slide the metal backing strip into the retaining claws starting with the second claw from either end. Continue sliding the element up to the element stops, then secure the element by twisting the backing strip into the end claws (see illustration).

9    Make sure that all the claws are locked onto the metal backing strip before installing the blade on the wiper arm.

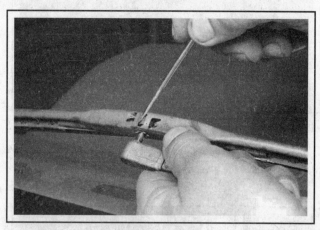

**14.4  Press down on the spring with a screwdriver to release the blade assembly from the wiper arm**

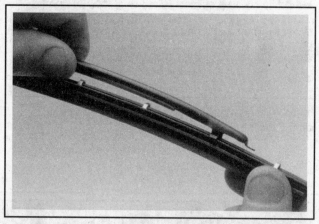

**14.8  Lock the end of the element backing strip into place by twisting it into the end claw**

## 15  Air filter replacement (every 15,000 miles or 12 months)

▶ **Refer to illustrations 15.2a, 15.2b and 15.3**

1    Purchase a new filter element for your specific engine type.

2    Detach the clips and lift the filter housing cover off (see illustrations).

3    Remove the filter element (see illustration).

4    Wipe the inside of the air cleaner housing with a clean cloth.

5    Place the new air filter element in the housing. If the element is marked TOP be sure the marked side faces up.

6    Seat the tabs, rotate the cover into place and secure it with the clips.

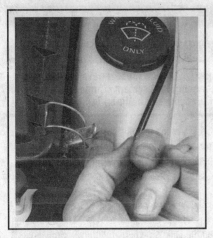

**15.2a Lift up on the ends of the clips to release them**

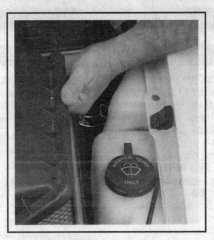

**15.2b Raise the housing cover**

**15.3 Lift the filter out of the housing**

## 16 Positive Crankcase Ventilation (PCV) valve check (every 15,000 miles or 12 months)

▶ Refer to illustrations 16.2a and 16.2b

➡ **Note: To maintain efficient operation of the PCV system, clean the hoses and check the PCV valve at the intervals recommended in the maintenance schedule. For additional information on the PCV system, refer to Chapter 6.**

1   The PCV valve is located in the right (passenger's side) valve cover.

2   Check the valve by first pulling it out of the valve cover (see illustrations). Shake it - if it rattles, reinstall it in the cover.

3   Start the engine and allow it to idle, then disconnect the PCV hose from the air cleaner housing and feel for vacuum at the hose. If vacuum is felt, the PCV valve/system is working properly (see Chapter 6 for additional PCV system information).

4   If no vacuum is felt, the oil filler cap, hoses or valve cover gasket may be leaking or the PCV valve may be bad. Check for vacuum leaks at the valve, filler cap and all hoses.

5   Pull straight up on the valve to remove it. Check the rubber grommet in the rocker arm cover for cracks and distortion. If it's damaged, replace it.

6   If the valve is clogged, the hose is also probably plugged. Remove the hose between the valve and the intake manifold and clean it with solvent.

7   After cleaning the hose, inspect it for damage, wear and deterioration. Make sure it fits snugly on the fittings.

8   If necessary, install a new PCV valve.

9   Install the clean PCV system hose. Make sure that the PCV valve and hose are secure.

**16.2a Pull the PCV valve out of the valve cover to check it**

**16.2b Late models are equipped with push-connect fittings on the PCV hoses - rotate the tab to unlock the fitting**

## 17 Fuel system check (every 15,000 miles or 12 months)

### ✵✵ WARNING 1:

Gasoline is extremely flammable, so take extra precautions when you work on any part of the fuel system. Don't smoke or allow open flames or bare light bulbs near the work area, and don't work in a garage where a gas-type appliance (such as a water heater or clothes dryer) is present. Since gasoline is carcinogenic, wear latex gloves when there's a possibility of being exposed to fuel, and, if you spill any fuel on your skin, rinse it off immediately with soap and water. Mop up any spills immediately and do not store fuel-soaked rags where they could ignite. When you perform any kind of work on the fuel system, wear safety glasses and have a Class B type fire extinguisher on hand. The fuel system is under constant pressure, so, before any lines are disconnected, the fuel system pressure must be relieved. See Chapter 4.

### ✵✵ WARNING 2:

On models with air suspension, turn the air suspension switch to Off before raising the vehicle.

1   If you smell gasoline while driving or after the vehicle has been sitting in the sun, inspect the fuel system immediately.

2   Remove the gas filler cap and inspect if for damage and corrosion. The gasket should have an unbroken sealing imprint. If the gasket is damaged or corroded, install a new cap.

3   Inspect the fuel feed and return lines for cracks. Make sure that the connections between the fuel lines and the fuel injection system and between the fuel lines and the inline fuel filter are tight.

### ✵✵ WARNING:

Your vehicle is fuel injected, so you must relieve the fuel system pressure before servicing fuel system components. The fuel system pressure relief procedure is outlined in Chapter 4.

4   Since some components of the fuel system - the fuel tank and part of the fuel feed and return lines, for example - are underneath the vehicle, they can be inspected more easily with the vehicle raised on a hoist. If that's not possible, raise the vehicle and support it on jackstands.

5   With the vehicle raised and safely supported, inspect the gas tank and filler neck for punctures, cracks and other damage. The connection between the filler neck and the tank is particularly critical. Sometimes a rubber filler neck will leak because of loose clamps or deteriorated rubber. Inspect all fuel tank mounting brackets and straps to be sure that the tank is securely attached to the vehicle.

### ✵✵ WARNING:

Do not, under any circumstances, try to repair a fuel tank (except rubber components). A welding torch or any open flame can easily cause fuel vapors inside the tank to explode.

6   Carefully check all rubber hoses and metal lines leading away from the fuel tank. Check for loose connections, deteriorated hoses, crimped lines and other damage. Repair or replace damaged sections as necessary (see Chapter 4).

## 18 Cooling system check (every 15,000 miles or 12 months)

▶ Refer to illustrations 18.4a and 18.4b

1   Many major engine failures can be attributed to a faulty cooling system. The cooling system also plays an important role in prolonging transmission life because it cools the fluid.

2   The engine should be cold for the cooling system check, so perform the following procedure before the vehicle is driven for the day or after it has been shut off for at least three hours.

3   If you're working on a 1991 or earlier model, remove the cap from the radiator. If you're working on a 1992 or later model, remove the cap from the expansion tank. Clean the cap thoroughly, inside and out, with clean water. Also clean the filler neck on the radiator or expansion tank. The presence of rust or corrosion in the filler neck means the coolant should be changed (see Section 28). The coolant inside the radiator should be relatively clean and transparent. If it's rust colored, drain the system and refill it with new coolant.

4   Carefully check the radiator hoses and the smaller diameter heater hoses (see illustration). Inspect each coolant hose along its entire

Check for a chafed area that could fail prematurely.

Check for a soft area indicating the hose has deteriorated inside.

Overtightening the clamp on a hardened hose will damage the hose and cause a leak.

Check each hose for swelling and oil-soaked ends. Cracks and breaks can be located by squeezing the hose.

18.4a  Hoses, like drivebelts, have a habit of failing at the worst possible time - to prevent the inconvenience of a blown radiator or heater hose, inspect them carefully as shown here

length, replacing any hose which is cracked, swollen or deteriorated. Cracks will show up better if the hose is squeezed. Pay close attention to hose clamps that secure the hoses to cooling system components. Hose clamps can pinch and puncture hoses, resulting in coolant leaks. Some hoses are hidden from view so sometimes you'll have to trace a coolant leak. For example, on the 4.6L V8 engine the heater hose connects to the water pump under the intake manifold. If it leaks, coolant will run down the rear of the engine (see illustration).

5   Make sure that all hose connections are tight. A leak in the cooling system will usually show up as white or rust colored deposits on the area adjoining the leak. If wire-type clamps are used on the hoses, it may be a good idea to replace them with screw-type clamps.

6   Clean the front of the radiator and air conditioning condenser with compressed air, if available, or a soft brush. Remove all bugs, leaves, etc. embedded in the radiator fins. Be extremely careful not to damage the cooling fins or cut your fingers on them.

7   If the coolant level has been dropping consistently and no leaks are detectable, have the radiator cap and cooling system pressure checked at a service station.

**18.4b  A leak in the 4.6L V8 engine heater hose means the intake manifold will have to be removed for hose replacement - coolant coming out the back of the engine is the symptom**

## 19  Exhaust system check (every 15,000 miles or 12 months)

### ※※ WARNING 1:

On models with air suspension, turn the air suspension switch to Off before raising the vehicle.

### ※※ WARNING 2:

On models with a fire suppression system, disable the system before raising the rear of the vehicle by disconnecting the cable from the negative battery terminal and waiting at least three minutes.

1   With the engine cold (at least three hours after the vehicle has been driven), check the complete exhaust system from the engine to the end of the tailpipe. Ideally, the inspection should be done with the vehicle on a hoist to permit unrestricted access. If a hoist isn't available, raise the vehicle and support it securely on jackstands.

2   Check the exhaust pipes and connections for evidence of leaks, severe corrosion and damage. Make sure that all brackets and hangers are in good condition and tight.

3   At the same time, inspect the underside of the body for holes, corrosion, open seams, etc. which may allow exhaust gases to enter the passenger compartment. Seal all body openings with silicone or body putty.

4   Rattles and other noises can often be traced to the exhaust system, especially the mounts and hangers. Try to move the pipes, muffler and catalytic converter. If the components can come in contact with the body or suspension parts, secure the exhaust system with new mounts.

5   Check the running condition of the engine by inspecting inside the end of the tailpipe. The exhaust deposits here are an indication of engine state-of-tune. If the pipe is black and sooty or coated with white deposits, the engine may need a tune-up, including a thorough fuel system inspection and adjustment.

## 20  Steering and suspension check (every 15,000 miles or 12 months)

▶ Refer to illustrations 20.10 and 20.11

### ※※ WARNING 1:

On models with air suspension, turn the air suspension switch to Off before raising the vehicle.

### ※※ WARNING 2:

On models with a fire suppression system, disable the system before raising the rear of the vehicle by disconnecting the cable from the negative battery terminal and waiting at least three minutes.

➡Note: The steering linkage and suspension components should be checked periodically. Worn or damaged suspension and steering linkage components can result in excessive and abnormal tire wear, poor ride quality and vehicle handling and reduced fuel economy. For detailed illustrations of the steering and suspension components, refer to Chapter 10.

### SHOCK ABSORBER CHECK

1   Park the vehicle on level ground, turn the engine off and set the parking brake. Check the tire pressures.

2   Push down at one corner of the vehicle, then release it while not-

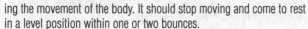

**20.10  Check the suspension balljoints by trying to move the lower edge of each tire in-and-out while watching/feeling for movement at the top of the tire and balljoints**

**20.11  Grasp each front tire as shown and try to move it back-and-forth - if any play is noted, check the steering gear mounts and make sure that they're tight; if either tie-rod is worn or bent, replace it**

ing the movement of the body. It should stop moving and come to rest in a level position within one or two bounces.

3   If the vehicle continues to move up-and-down or if it fails to return to its original position, a worn or weak shock absorber is probably the reason.

4   Repeat the above check at each of the three remaining corners of the vehicle.

5   Raise the vehicle and support it securely on jackstands.

6   Check the shock absorbers for evidence of fluid leakage. A light film of fluid is no cause for concern. Make sure that any fluid noted is from the shocks and not from some other source. If leakage is noted, replace the shocks as a set.

7   Check the shock absorbers to be sure that they are securely mounted and undamaged. Check the upper mounts for damage and wear. If damage or wear is noted, replace the shock absorbers as a set (front or rear).

8   If the shock absorbers must be replaced, refer to Chapter 10 for the procedure.

## STEERING AND SUSPENSION CHECK

9   Visually inspect the steering system components for damage and distortion. Look for leaks and damaged seals, boots and fittings.

10   Clean the lower end of the steering knuckle. Have an assistant grasp the lower edge of the tire and move the wheel in-and-out (see illustration) while you look for movement at the steering knuckle-to-control arm balljoint. If there is any movement the suspension balljoint(s) must be replaced.

11   Grasp each front tire at the front and rear edges, push in at the front, pull out at the rear and feel for play in the steering system components (see illustration). If any freeplay is noted, check the steering gear mounts and the tie-rod ends for looseness.

12   Check the steering gear mount bolt tightness. If the tie-rods are loose, the balljoints may be worn (check to make sure the nuts are tight). Additional steering and suspension system information and illustrations can be found in Chapter 10.

## 21  Brake system check (every 15,000 miles or 12 months)

### ✳✳ WARNING 1:

Brake system dust is harmful to your health. Never blow it out with compressed air and don't inhale any of it. An approved filtering mask should be worn when working on the brakes. Do not, under any circumstances, use petroleum-based solvents to clean brake parts. Use brake system cleaner only!

### ✳✳ WARNING 2:

On models with air suspension, turn the air suspension switch to Off before raising the vehicle.

### ✳✳ WARNING 3:

On models with a fire suppression system, disable the system before raising the rear of the vehicle by disconnecting the cable from the negative battery terminal and waiting at least three minutes.

➡Note: For detailed photographs of the brake system, refer to Chapter 9.

1   In addition to the specified intervals, the brake system should be inspected each time the wheels are removed or a malfunction is suspected. Raise the vehicle and support it securely on jackstands. Remove the wheels (see *Jacking and towing* at the front of this book, or refer to your owner's manual, if necessary).

## DISC BRAKES

⬧ **Refer to illustration 21.4**

2   Disc brakes are used at the front of these vehicles, and on some models at the rear as well. Extensive disc damage can occur if the pads are not replaced when needed.

3   The disc brake calipers, which contain the pads, are now visible. Each caliper has an outer and an inner pad - all pads should be checked.

4   Each caliper has an opening to inspect the pads (see illustration). If the pad material has worn to about 1/8-inch thick or less, the pads should be replaced.

5   If you're unsure about the exact thickness of the remaining lining material, remove the pads for further inspection or replacement (refer to

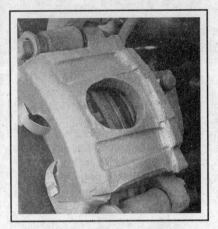

21.4 You will find an inspection hole like this in each caliper - placing a ruler across the hole should enable you to determine the thickness of remaining pad material for both inner and outer pads

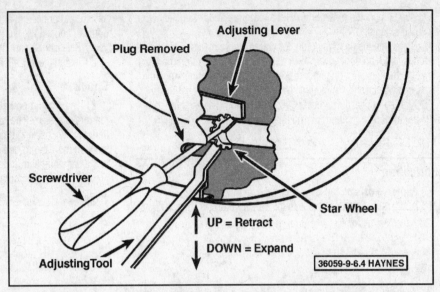

21.10 Turn the star wheel to adjust the brake shoe away from the drum

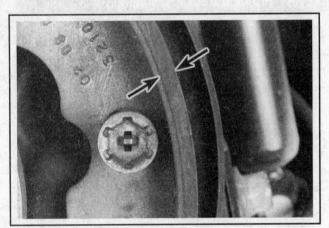

21.11 If the lining is bonded to the brake shoe, measure the lining thickness from the outer surface to the metal shoe, as shown here; if the lining is riveted to the shoe, measure from the lining outer surface to the rivet head

21.13 Carefully peel back the rubber cup on each end of the wheel cylinder - if brake fluid is evident, the wheel cylinder must be overhauled or replaced

Chapter 9).

6　Before installing the wheels, check for leakage and/or damage at the brake hoses and connections. Replace the hose or fittings as necessary, referring to Chapter 9.

7　Check the condition of the brake disc. Look for score marks, deep scratches and overheated areas (they will appear blue or discolored). If damage or wear is noted, the disc can be removed and resurfaced by an automotive machine shop or replaced with a new one. Refer to Chapter 9 for more detailed inspection and repair procedures.

## DRUM BRAKES

▶ **Refer to illustrations 21.10, 21.11 and 21.13**

8　Using a scribe or chalk, mark the drums and hub so the drum can be reinstalled in the same position on the hub.

9　Pull the brake drum off the hub and brake assembly. If this proves difficult, make sure the parking brake is released, then squirt some penetrating oil around the center hub area. Allow the oil to soak

in and try to pull the drum off again.

10　If the drum still cannot be pulled off, the brake shoes will have to be retracted. This is done by first removing the rubber plug in the backing plate. Pull the self-adjusting lever off the star wheel and use a small screwdriver to turn the adjuster wheel, which will move the shoes away from the drum (see illustration). With the drum removed, carefully wash off the accumulations of dirt and dust with brake system cleaner (see **Warning** above).

11　Note the thickness of the lining material on the brake shoes. If the material is worn to within 1/16-inch of the recessed rivets or metal backing, the shoes should be replaced (see illustration). The shoes should also be replaced if they are cracked, glazed, (shiny surface) or contaminated with brake fluid.

12　Check to make sure all the brake assembly springs are connected and in good condition.

13　Check the brake components for signs of fluid leakage. Carefully pry back the rubber cups on the wheel cylinder, located on the top of the backing plate (see illustration). Any leakage is an indication that the wheel cylinders should be replaced or overhauled immediately (see Chapter 9). Also check the hoses and connections for signs of leakage.

14 Wipe the inside of the drum with a clean rag and brake cleaner or denatured alcohol.

15 Check the inside of the drum for cracks, score marks, deep scratches and hard spots, which will appear as small discolored areas. If imperfections cannot be removed with emery cloth or sandpaper, the drums must be taken to an automotive machine shop for resurfacing.

16 After the inspection process is complete, and if all the components are in good condition, reinstall the brake drums.

## PARKING BRAKE

### Lubrication

17 Apply the parking brake.

18 Apply multi-purpose grease to the parking brake linkage, adjuster assembly, connectors and the areas of the parking brake cable that come in contact with other parts of the vehicle.

19 Release the parking brake and repeat the lubrication procedure.

20 Install the wheels and lower the vehicle to the ground.

### Check

21 The parking brake is operated by a foot pedal and locks the rear brake system. The easiest, and perhaps most obvious, method of periodically checking the parking brake is to park the vehicle on a steep hill with the parking brake set and the transmission in Neutral (remain in the car while performing this check). If the parking brake doesn't prevent the vehicle from rolling, it is in need of adjustment (see Chapter 9).

## 22  Automatic transmission control linkage lubrication (every 15,000 miles or 12 months)

### ✳✳ WARNING 1:

On models with air suspension, turn the air suspension switch to Off before raising the vehicle.

### ✳✳ WARNING 2:

On models with a fire suppression system, disable the system before raising the rear of the vehicle by disconnecting the cable from the negative battery terminal and waiting at least three minutes.

1 Raise the front of the vehicle and support it securely on jackstands.

2 Clean the linkage pivot points and lubricate them with multi-purpose grease.

## 23  Rear axle (differential) lubricant level check (every 15,000 miles or 12 months)

▶ Refer to illustration 23.2

### ✳✳ WARNING 1:

On models with air suspension, turn the air suspension switch to Off before raising the vehicle.

### ✳✳ WARNING 2:

On models with a fire suppression system, disable the system before raising the rear of the vehicle by disconnecting the cable from the negative battery terminal and waiting at least three minutes.

1 The differential has a check/fill plug which must be removed to check the lubricant level. If the vehicle is raised to gain access to the plug, be sure to support it safely on jackstands - DO NOT crawl under the vehicle when it's supported only by the jack!

2 Remove the check/fill plug from the differential (see illustration).

3 Use your little finger as a dipstick to make sure the lubricant level is even with the bottom of the plug hole. If not, use a syringe to add the

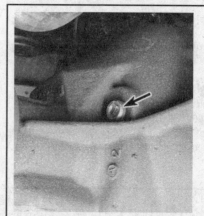

23.2 Use a 3/8-inch drive ratchet or breaker bar and an extension to remove the differential fill plug (arrow)

recommended lubricant until it just starts to run out of the opening. On some models a tag is located in the area of the plug which gives information regarding lubricant type, particularly on models equipped with a limited slip differential.

4 Install the plug and tighten it securely.

## 24  Spark plug check and replacement (every 30,000 miles or 24 months)

▶ Refer to illustrations 24.2, 24.5a, 24.5b, 24.6a, 24.6b, 24.6c, 24.8, 24.9, 24.10a and 24.10b

➡**Note: On 1997 and later models, spark plugs are replaced at 100,000 mile intervals.**

1   The spark plugs are located on the sides of the engine.

2   In most cases, the tools necessary for spark plug replacement include a spark plug socket which fits onto a ratchet (spark plug sockets are padded inside to prevent damage to the porcelain insulators on the new plugs), various extensions and a gap gauge to check and adjust the gaps on the new plugs (see illustration). A special plug wire removal tool is available for separating the wire boots from the spark plugs, but it isn't absolutely necessary. A torque wrench should be used to tighten the new plugs.

3   The best approach when replacing the spark plugs is to purchase the new ones in advance, adjust them to the proper gap and replace the plugs one at a time. When buying the new spark plugs, be sure to obtain the correct plug type for your particular engine. This information can be found in the Specifications Section at the end of this Chapter, on the Emission Control Information label located under the hood or in the factory owner's manual. If differences exist between the plug specified on the emissions label, Specifications Section or in the owner's manual, assume that the emissions label is correct.

4   Allow the engine to cool completely before attempting to remove any of the plugs. 1991 and later models engines have aluminum cylinder heads, which can be damaged if the spark plugs are removed when the engine is hot. While you are waiting for the engine to cool, check the new plugs for defects and adjust the gaps.

5   The gap is checked by inserting the proper thickness gauge between the electrodes at the tip of the plug (see illustration). The gap between the electrodes should be the same as the one specified on the Emissions Control Information label. The wire should just slide between the electrodes with a slight amount of drag. If the gap is incorrect, use the adjuster on the gauge body to bend the curved side electrode slightly until the specified gap is obtained (see illustration). If the side electrode is not exactly over the center electrode, bend it with the adjuster until it is. Check for cracks in the porcelain insulator (if any are found, the plug should not be used).

6   With the engine cool, remove the spark plug wire from one spark plug. Pull only on the boot at the end of the wire - do not pull on the wire (see illustration). A plug wire removal tool should be used if available (see illustration). On 1998 and later models it will be necessary to remove the screw retaining the ignition coil, then remove the coil assembly to access the spark plug (see illustration).  For left-bank plugs on 1998 and later models, it will also be necessary to remove the air cleaner inlet duct.

7   If compressed air is available, use it to blow any dirt or foreign material away from the spark plug hole. The idea here is to eliminate the possibility of debris falling into the cylinder as the spark plug is removed.

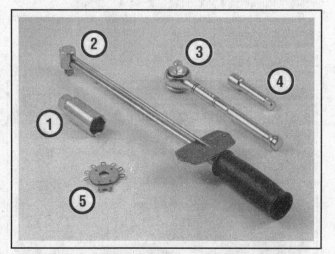

**24.2  Tools required for changing spark plugs**

1   *Spark plug socket* - This will have special padding inside to protect the spark plug's porcelain insulator
2   *Torque wrench* - Although not mandatory, using this tool is the best way to ensure the plugs are tightened properly
3   *Ratchet* - Standard hand tool to fit the spark plug socket
4   *Extension* - Depending on model and accessories, you may need special extensions and universal joints to reach one or more of the plugs
5   *Spark plug gap gauge* - This gauge for checking the gap comes in a variety of styles. Make sure the gap for your engine is included

**24.5a  Spark plug manufacturers recommend using a wire-type gauge when checking the gap - if the wire does not slide between the electrodes with a slight drag, adjustment is required**

**24.5b  To change the gap, bend the side electrode only, as indicated by the arrows, and be very careful not to crack or chip the porcelain insulator surrounding the center electrode**

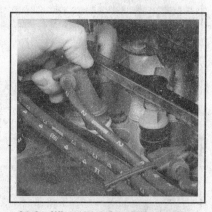

**24.6a  When removing the spark plug wires, pull only on the boot and twist it back-and-forth**

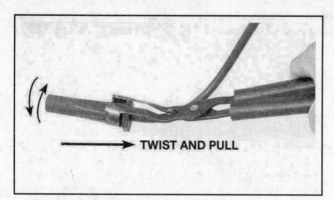

**24.6b A spark plug wire removal tool makes the job easier**

8   Place the spark plug socket over the plug and remove it from the engine by turning it in a counterclockwise direction (see illustration).

9   Compare the spark plug to those shown in this chart to get an indication of the general running condition of the engine.

10   Apply a small amount of anti-seize compound to the spark plug threads (see illustration). Install one of the new plugs into the hole until you can no longer turn it with your fingers, then tighten it with a torque wrench (if available) or the ratchet. It is a good idea to slip a short length of rubber hose over the end of the plug to use as a tool to thread it into place (see illustration). The hose will grip the plug well enough to turn it, but will start to slip if the plug begins to cross-thread in the hole - this will prevent damaged threads and the accompanying repair costs.

11   Before pushing the spark plug wire onto the end of the plug, inspect it following the procedures outlined in Section 25.

12   Attach the plug wire to the new spark plug, again using a twisting motion on the boot until it is seated on the spark plug.

13   Repeat the procedure for the remaining spark plugs, replacing them one at a time to prevent mixing up the spark plug wires.

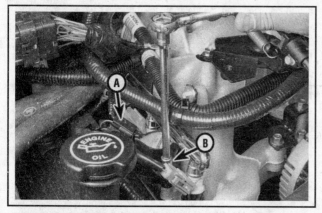

**24.6c On later 4.6L engines, each ignition coil must be removed to access each spark plug - disconnect the electrical connector (A) and remove the coil retaining screw (B) - pull straight up and out to remove the coil pack**

**24.8 Use a spark plug socket wrench with a long extension to unscrew the spark plug**

A normally worn spark plug should have light tan or gray deposits on the firing tip.

A carbon fouled plug, identified by soft, sooty, black deposits, may indicate an improperly tuned vehicle. Check the air cleaner, ignition components and engine control system.

An oil fouled spark plug indicates an engine with worn piston rings and/or bad valve seals allowing excessive oil to enter the chamber.

This spark plug has been left in the engine too long, as evidenced by the extreme gap- Plugs with such an extreme gap can cause misfiring and stumbling accompanied by a noticeable lack of power.

A physically damaged spark plug may be evidence of severe detonation in that cylinder. Watch that cylinder carefully between services, as a continued detonation will not only damage the plug, but could also damage the engine.

A bridged or almost bridged spark plug, identified by a build up between the electrodes caused by excessive carbon or oil build-up on the plug.

**24.9 Inspect the spark plug to determine engine running conditions**

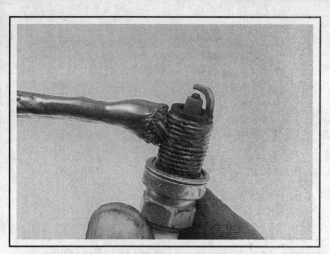

**24.10a  Apply a thin film of anti-seize compound to the spark plug threads to prevent damage to the cylinder head**

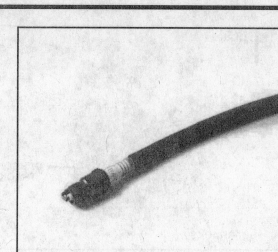

**24.10b  A length of snug-fitting rubber hose will save time and prevent damaged threads when installing the spark plugs**

## 25  Spark plug wire, distributor cap and rotor check and replacement (every 30,000 miles or 24 months)

♦ Refer to illustrations 25.11 and 25.12

### SPARK PLUG WIRES

➡Note: Every time a spark plug wire is detached from a spark plug, the distributor cap or the coil, silicone dielectric compound (a white grease available at auto parts stores) must be applied to the inside of each boot before reconnection. Use a small standard screwdriver to coat the entire inside surface of each boot with a thin layer of the compound.

1  The spark plug wires should be checked and, if necessary, replaced at the same time new spark plugs are installed.

2  The easiest way to identify bad wires is to make a visual check while the engine is running. In a dark, well-ventilated garage, start the engine and look at each plug wire. Be careful not to come into contact with any moving engine parts. If there is a break in the wire, you will see arcing or a small spark at the damaged area. If arcing is noticed, make a note to obtain new wires.

3  The spark plug wires should be inspected one at a time, beginning with the spark plug for the number one cylinder, (the cylinder closest to the radiator on the right bank), to prevent confusion. Clearly label each original plug wire with a piece of tape marked with the correct number. The plug wires must be reinstalled in the correct order to ensure proper engine operation.

4  Disconnect the plug wire from the first spark plug. A removal tool can be used, or you can grab the wire boot, twist it slightly and pull the wire free. Do not pull on the wire itself, only on the rubber boot.

5  Push the wire and boot back onto the end of the spark plug. It should fit snugly. If it doesn't, detach the wire and boot once more and use a pair of pliers to carefully crimp the metal connector inside the wire boot until it does.

6  Using a clean rag, wipe the entire length of the wire to remove built-up dirt and grease.

7  Once the wire is clean, check for burns, cracks and other damage. Do not bend the wire sharply or you might break the conductor.

8  Disconnect the wire from the distributor (1991 and earlier models). Pull only on the rubber boot. Check for corrosion and a tight fit. Reinstall the wire in the distributor.

9  Inspect each of the remaining spark plug wires, making sure that each one is securely fastened at the distributor and spark plug when the check is complete.

10  If new spark plug wires are required, purchase a set for your specific engine model. Pre-cut wire sets with the boots already installed are available. Remove and replace the wires one at a time to avoid mixups in the firing order.

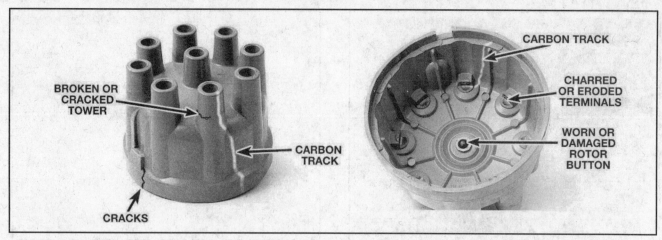

**25.11 Shown here are some the common defects to look for when inspecting the distributor cap (if in doubt about its condition, install a new one)**

## DISTRIBUTOR CAP AND ROTOR
## (1991 AND EARLIER MODELS)

→Note: It's common practice to install a new distributor cap and rotor each time new spark plug wires are installed. If you're planning to install new wires, install a new cap and rotor also. But if you're planning to reuse the existing wires, be sure to inspect the cap and rotor to make sure that they are in good condition. Models equipped with the EDIS ignition system do not have a distributor.

11 Remove the mounting screws and detach the cap from the distributor. Check it for cracks, carbon tracks and worn, burned or loose terminals (see illustration).

12 Check the rotor for cracks and carbon tracks. Make sure the center terminal spring tension is adequate and look for corrosion and wear on the rotor tip (see illustration).

13 Replace the cap and rotor if damage or defects are found. Note that the rotor is indexed so it can only be installed one way. Before installing the cap, apply silicone dielectric compound to the rotor tip (see **Note** at beginning of this Section).

14 When installing a new cap, remove the wires from the old cap one at a time and attach them to the new cap in the exact same location - do not simultaneously remove all the wires from the old cap or firing order mix-ups may occur.

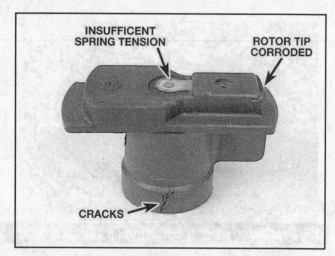

**25.12 The ignition rotor should be checked for wear and corrosion as indicated here (if in doubt about its condition, buy a new one)**

## 26  Automatic transmission fluid and filter change (every 30,000 miles or 24 months)

♦ **Refer to illustrations 26.7, 26.10, 26.11a, 26.11b and 26.12**

❊❊ **WARNING:**

On models with air suspension, turn the air suspension switch to Off before raising the vehicle.

1 At the specified intervals, the transmission fluid should be drained and replaced. Since the fluid will remain hot long after driving, perform this procedure only after the engine has cooled down completely.

2 Before beginning work, purchase the transmission fluid specified in *Recommended lubricants and fluids* at the end of this Chapter, a new filter and gaskets. Never reuse the old filter or gasket!

3 Other tools necessary for this job include jackstands to support the vehicle in a raised position, a drain pan capable of holding at least eight quarts, newspapers and clean rags.

4 Raise the vehicle and support it securely on jackstands.

5 With the drain pan in place, remove the front and side transmission pan mounting bolts.

6 Loosen the rear pan bolts approximately four turns.

7 Carefully pry the transmission pan loose with a screwdriver, allowing the fluid to drain (see illustration). Don't damage the pan or transmission gasket surfaces or leaks could develop.

8 Remove the remaining bolts, pan and gasket. Carefully clean the gasket surface of the transmission to remove all traces of the old gasket and sealant.

9 Drain the fluid from the transmission pan, clean it with solvent

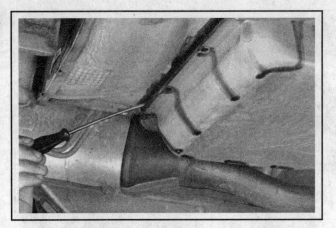

**26.7  Pry the pan free of the gasket and allow the fluid to drain**

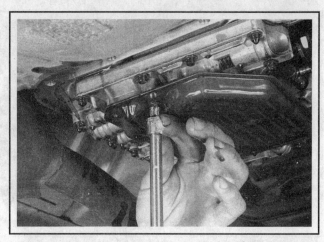

**26.10  Use a socket and extension to remove the filter bolts**

**26.11a  Install a new filter seal on the transmission . . .**

**26.11b  . . . and a gasket on the filter itself (not all models)**

**26.12  Be sure to clean all traces of the old gasket from the pan before installing a new one**

and dry it with compressed air.

10  Remove the filter from the mount inside the transmission (see illustration).

11  Install a new seal, gasket and filter (see illustrations). Tighten the mounting bolts securely.

12  Make sure the gasket surface on the transmission pan is clean, then install a new gasket (see illustration). Put the pan in place against the transmission and install the bolts. Working around the pan, tighten each bolt a little at a time until the final torque figure is reached. Don't

overtighten the bolts!

13  Lower the vehicle and add about four or five pints of automatic transmission fluid through the filler tube (see Section 7).

14  With the transmission in Park and the parking brake set, run the engine at a fast idle, but don't race it.

15  Move the gear selector through each range and back to Park. Check the fluid level. Add fluid if needed to reach the correct level.

16  Check under the vehicle for leaks during the first few trips.

## 27  Rear axle (differential) lubricant change (every 30,000 miles or 24 months)

◆ **Refer to illustrations 27.4a, 27.4b, 27.4c and 27.6**

### ✳ WARNING:

**On models with air suspension, turn the air suspension switch to Off before raising the vehicle.**

1  On these models there is no drain plug, so a hand suction pump will be required to remove the differential lubricant through the filler

hole. If a suction pump isn't available, or the gasket is leaking, be sure to obtain a new gasket at the same time the gear lubricant is purchased because it will be necessary to remove the cover plate.

2  Raise the vehicle and support it securely on jackstands. Move a drain pan, rags, newspapers and wrenches under the vehicle.

3  Remove the fill plug from the differential (see Section 23). If a suction pump is being used, insert the flexible hose. Work the hose down to the bottom of the differential housing and pump the lubricant out.

27.4a  Remove the bolts from the lower edge of the cover . . .

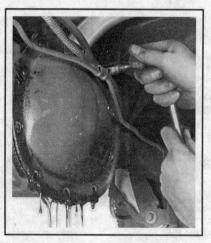

27.4b  . . . then loosen the top bolts and let the lubricant drain

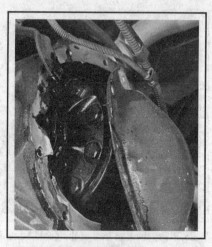

27.4c  Once the lubricant has drained, remove the cover

4   If the differential is being drained by removing the cover plate, remove the bolts on the lower half of the plate (see illustration). Loosen the bolts on the upper half and use them to keep the cover loosely attached (see illustration). Allow the oil to drain into the pan, then completely remove the cover (see illustration).

5   Using a lint-free rag, clean the inside of the cover and the accessible areas of the differential housing. As this is done, check for chipped gears and metal particles in the lubricant, indicating that the differential should be more thoroughly inspected and/or repaired.

6   Thoroughly clean the gasket mating surfaces of the differential housing and the cover plate. Use a gasket scraper or putty knife to remove all traces of the old gasket (see illustration).

7   Apply a thin layer of RTV sealant to the cover flange, then press a new gasket into position on the cover. Make sure the bolt holes align properly.

8   Place the cover on the differential housing and install the bolts. Tighten the bolts securely.

9   Use a hand pump, syringe or funnel to fill the differential housing with the specified lubricant until it's level with the bottom of the plug hole.

10  Install the filler plug and make sure it is secure.

27.6  Carefully scrape off the old material to ensure a leak-free seal

## 28  Cooling system servicing (draining, flushing and refilling) (every 30,000 miles or 24 months)

♦ Refer to illustration 28.4

### ✳✳ WARNING 1:

Do not allow antifreeze to come in contact with your skin or painted surfaces of the vehicle. Rinse off spills immediately with plenty of water. Antifreeze is highly toxic if ingested. Never leave antifreeze lying around in an open container or in puddles on the floor; children and pets are attracted by it's sweet smell and may drink it. Check with local authorities about disposing of used antifreeze. Many communities have collection centers which will see that antifreeze is disposed of safely.

### ✳✳ WARNING 2:

On models with air suspension, turn the air suspension switch to Off before raising the vehicle.

### ✳✳ CAUTION:

Some later models may have been factory-filled with orange-colored Dex-Cool coolant, which will normally be identified by a label near the radiator. Dex-Cool coolant has a 100,000 mile replacement interval.

1   Periodically, the cooling system should be drained, flushed and refilled to replenish the antifreeze mixture and prevent formation of rust and corrosion, which can impair the performance of the cooling system and cause engine damage. When the cooling system is serviced, all hoses and the radiator cap should be checked and replaced if necessary.

## DRAINING

2    Apply the parking brake and block the wheels. If the vehicle has just been driven, wait several hours to allow the engine to cool down before beginning this procedure.

3    Once the engine is completely cool, remove the cap from the radiator (1991 and earlier models) or expansion tank (1992 and later models).

4    Move a large container under the radiator drain to catch the coolant. Attach a 3/8-inch diameter hose to the drain fitting to direct the coolant into the container, then open the drain fitting (a pair of pliers may be required to turn it) (see illustration).

5    After the coolant stops flowing out of the radiator, move the container under the engine block drain plugs (5.0L engine only) and allow the coolant in the block to drain.

6    While the coolant is draining, check the condition of the radiator hoses, heater hoses and clamps (refer to Section 18 if necessary).

7    Replace any damaged clamps or hoses (refer to Chapter 3 for detailed replacement procedures).

## FLUSHING

8    Once the system is completely drained, flush the radiator with fresh water from a garden hose until water runs clear at the drain. The flushing action of the water will remove sediments from the radiator but will not remove rust and scale from the engine and cooling tube surfaces.

9    These deposits can be removed by the chemical action of a cleaner available at auto parts stores. Follow the procedure outlined in the manufacturer's instructions. If the radiator is severely corroded, damaged or leaking, it should be removed (see Chapter 3) and taken to a radiator repair shop.

10  Remove the overflow hose from the coolant recovery reservoir. Drain the reservoir and flush it with clean water, then reconnect the hose.

## REFILLING

11  Close and tighten the radiator drain. Install and tighten the block

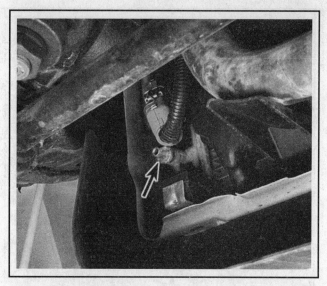

**28.4  The radiator drain fitting is located at the lower corner of the radiator (arrow)**

drain plugs.

12  Place the heater temperature control in the maximum heat position.

13  Slowly add the recommended coolant (a 50/50 mixture) to the radiator until it is full. Add coolant to the reservoir or expansion tank up to the Full Hot mark.

14  Leave the radiator or expansion tank cap off and run the engine in a well-ventilated area until the thermostat opens (coolant will begin flowing through the radiator and the upper radiator hose will become hot).

15  Turn the engine off and let it cool. Add more coolant mixture to bring the level back up to the lip on the radiator or expansion tank filler neck.

16  Squeeze the upper radiator hose to expel air, then add more coolant mixture if necessary. Replace the radiator or expansion tank cap.

17  Start the engine, allow it to reach normal operating temperature and check for leaks.

---

## 29  Front wheel bearing check, repack and adjustment (1991 and earlier models) (every 30,000 miles or 24 months)

▶ **Refer to illustrations 29.1, 29.6, 29.7, 29.8, 29.11 and 29.15**

### ❋❋ WARNING:

**On models with air suspension, turn the air suspension switch to Off before raising the vehicle.**

1    In most cases the front wheel bearings will not need servicing until the brake pads are changed. However, the bearings should be checked whenever the front of the vehicle is raised for any reason. Several items, including a torque wrench and special grease, are required

for this procedure (see illustration).

2    With the vehicle securely supported on jackstands, spin each wheel and check for noise, rolling resistance and freeplay.

3    Grasp the top of each tire with one hand and the bottom with the other. Move the wheel in-and-out on the spindle. If there's any noticeable movement, the bearings should be checked and then repacked with grease or replaced if necessary.

4    Remove the wheel.

5    Remove the brake caliper (see Chapter 9) and hang it out of the way on a piece of wire. A wood block of the appropriate width can be slid between the brake pads to keep them separated, if necessary.

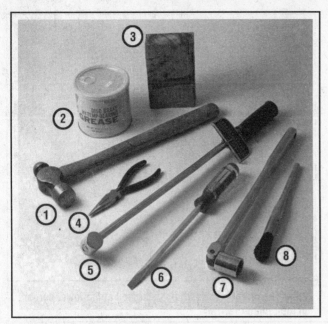

**29.1 Tools and materials needed for front wheel bearing maintenance**

1   *Hammer* - A common hammer will do just fine
2   *Grease* - High-temperature grease that is formulated for front wheel bearings should be used
3   *Wood block* - If you have a scrap piece of 2x4, it can be used to drive the new seal into the hub
4   *Needle-nose pliers* - Used to straighten and remove the cotter pin in the spindle
5   *Torque wrench* - This is very important in this procedure; if the bearing is too tight, the wheel won't turn freely - if it's too loose, the wheel will "wobble" on the spindle. Either way, it could mean extensive damage
6   *Screwdriver* - Used to remove the seal from the hub (a long screwdriver is preferred)
7   *Socket/breaker bar* - Needed to loosen the nut on the spindle if it's extremely tight
8   *Brush* - Together with some clean solvent, this will be used to remove old grease from the hub and spindle

**29.6 Dislodge the dust cap by working around the outer circumference with a hammer and chisel**

**29.7 Remove the cotter pin and discard it - use a new one when the hub is reinstalled**

6   Pry the dust cap out of the hub using a screwdriver or hammer and chisel (see illustration).

7   Straighten the bent ends of the cotter pin, then pull the cotter pin out of the nut lock (see illustration). Discard the cotter pin and use a new one during reassembly.

8   Remove the nut lock, nut and washer from the end of the spindle (see illustration).

9   Pull the hub/disc assembly out slightly, then push it back into its original position. This should force the outer bearing off the spindle enough so it can be removed.

10   Pull the hub/disc assembly off the spindle.

11   Use a screwdriver to pry the seal out of the rear of the hub (see illustration). As this is done, note how the seal is installed.

12   Remove the inner wheel bearing from the hub.

13   Use solvent to remove all traces of the old grease from the bearings, hub and spindle. A small brush may prove helpful; however make sure no bristles from the brush embed themselves inside the bearing rollers. Allow the parts to air dry.

14   Carefully inspect the bearings for cracks, heat discoloration, worn rollers, etc. Check the bearing races inside the hub for wear and damage. If the bearing races are defective, the hubs should be taken to a machine shop with the facilities to remove the old races and press new ones in. Note that the bearings and races come as matched sets and old bearings should never be installed on new races.

15   Use high-temperature front wheel bearing grease to pack the bearings. Work the grease completely into the bearings, forcing it between the rollers, cone and cage from the back side (see illustration).

16   Apply a thin coat of grease to the spindle at the outer bearing seat, inner bearing seat, shoulder and seal seat.

17   Put a small quantity of grease inboard of each bearing race inside the hub. Using your finger, form a dam at these points to provide extra grease availability and to keep thinned grease from flowing out of the bearing.

18   Place the grease-packed inner bearing into the rear of the hub and put a little more grease outboard of the bearing.

19   Place a new seal over the inner bearing and tap the seal evenly into place with a hammer and blunt punch until it's flush with the hub.

20   Carefully place the hub assembly onto the spindle and push the

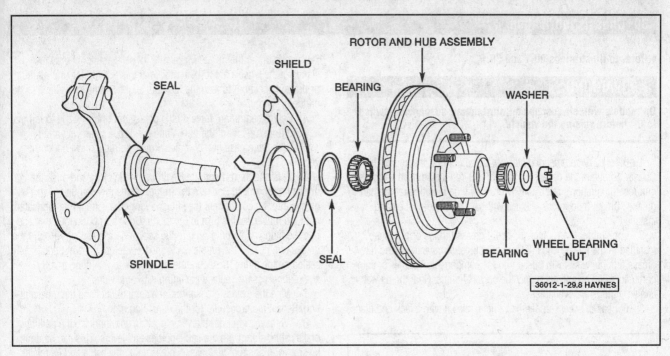

**29.8  Typical front hub and bearing components**

**29.11  Use a large screwdriver to pry the grease seal out of the rear of the hub**

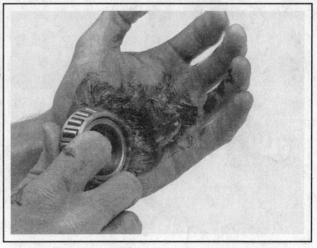

**29.15  Work the grease completely into the bearing rollers**

grease-packed outer bearing into position.

21  Install the washer and spindle nut. Tighten the nut only slightly (no more than 12 ft-lbs of torque).

22  Spin the hub in a forward direction while tightening the spindle nut to approximately 20 ft-lbs to seat the bearings and remove any grease or burrs which could cause excessive bearing play later.

23  Loosen the spindle nut 1/4-turn, then using your hand (not a wrench of any kind), tighten the nut until it's snug. Install the nut lock and a new cotter pin through the hole in the spindle and the slots in the nut lock. If the nut lock slots don't line up, remove the nut lock and turn

it slightly until they do.

24  Bend the ends of the cotter pin until they're flat against the nut. Cut off any extra length which could interfere with the dust cap.

25  Install the dust cap, tapping it into place with a hammer.

26  Place the brake caliper near the rotor and carefully remove the wood spacer. Install the caliper (see Chapter 9).

27  Install the wheel on the hub and tighten the lug nuts.

28  Grasp the top and bottom of the tire and check the bearings in the manner described earlier in this Section.

29  Lower the vehicle.

## 30 Chassis lubrication

▶ Refer to illustrations 30.1 and 30.6

### ✳✳ WARNING:

**On models with air suspension, turn the air suspension switch to Off before raising the vehicle.**

1  Refer to *Recommended lubricants and fluids* at the end of this Chapter to obtain the necessary grease, etc. You'll also need a grease gun (see illustration). Occasionally plugs will be installed rather than grease fittings. If so, grease fittings will have to be purchased and installed.

2  Look under the vehicle and see if grease fittings or plugs are installed in the tie-rod ends. If there are plugs, remove them and buy grease fittings, which will thread into the component. A dealer or auto parts store will be able to supply the correct fittings. Straight, as well as angled, fittings are available.

3  For easier access under the vehicle, raise it with a jack and place jackstands under the frame. Make sure it's safely supported by the stands. If the wheels are to be removed at this interval for tire rotation or brake inspection, loosen the lug nuts slightly while the vehicle is still on the ground.

4  Before beginning, force a little grease out of the nozzle to remove any dirt from the end of the gun. Wipe the nozzle clean with a rag.

5  With the grease gun and plenty of clean rags, crawl under the vehicle.

6  Wipe the tie-rod end grease fitting nipple clean and push the nozzle firmly over it. Squeeze the trigger on the grease gun to force grease into the component (see illustration). They should be lubricated until the rubber seal is firm to the touch. Don't pump too much grease into the fitting as it could rupture the seal. If grease escapes around the grease gun nozzle, the nipple is clogged or the nozzle is not completely seated on the fitting. Resecure the gun nozzle to the fitting and try again. If necessary, replace the fitting with a new one.

7  Wipe the excess grease from the components and the grease fitting. Repeat the procedure for the remaining fitting.

8  While you're under the vehicle, clean and lubricate the parking brake cable, along with the cable guides and levers. This can be done by smearing some of the chassis grease onto the cable and its related parts with your fingers.

9  Open the hood and smear a little chassis grease on the hood latch mechanism. Have an assistant pull the hood release lever from inside the vehicle as you lubricate the cable at the latch.

10  Lubricate all the hinges (door, hood, etc.) with engine oil to keep them in proper working order.

11  The key lock cylinders can be lubricated with spray graphite or silicone lubricant, which is available at auto parts stores.

12  Lubricate the door weatherstripping with silicone spray. This will reduce chafing and retard wear.

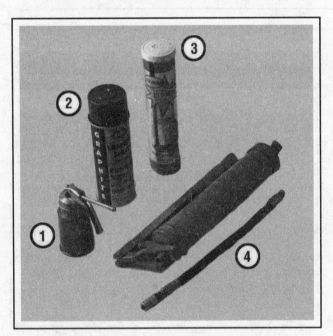

**30.1  Materials required for chassis and body lubrication**

1  *Engine oil* - Light engine oil in a can like this can be used for door and hood hinges
2  *Graphite spray* - Used to lubricate lock cylinders
3  *Grease* - Grease, in a variety of types and weights, is available for use in a grease gun. Check the Specification for your requirements
4  *Grease gun* - A common grease gun, shown here with a detachable hose and nozzle, is needed for chassis lubrication. After use, clean it thoroughly!

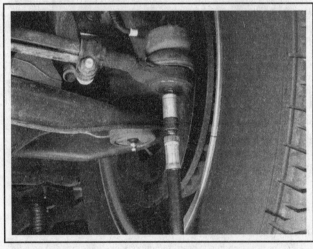

**30.6  Pump the grease into the fitting until the rubber seal is firm to the touch**

## 31  Fuel filter replacement (every 30,000 miles or 24 months)

▶ **Refer to illustration 31.3**

### ⁂ WARNING 1:

Gasoline is extremely flammable, so take extra precautions when you work on any part of the fuel system. Don't smoke or allow open flames or bare light bulbs near the work area, and don't work in a garage where a gas-type appliance (such as a water heater or clothes dryer) is present. Since gasoline is carcinogenic, wear fuel-resistant gloves when there's a possibility of being exposed to fuel, and, if you spill any fuel on your skin, rinse it off immediately with soap and water. Mop up any spills immediately and do not store fuel-soaked rags where they could ignite. When you perform any kind of work on the fuel system, wear safety glasses and have a Class B type fire extinguisher on hand.

### ⁂ WARNING 2:

The fuel system is under constant pressure, so, before removing the fuel filter, the fuel system pressure must be relieved. See Chapter 4.

### ⁂ WARNING 3:

On models with air suspension, turn the air suspension switch to Off before raising the vehicle.

**31.3  Use a small screwdriver to pry the fuel filter line clip off**

1   On 1996 and earlier models the fuel filter is located under the vehicle on the inside of the left frame rail. On 1997 and later models it is located under the vehicle on the inside of the right frame rail.

2   Inspect the hose fittings at both ends of the filter to see if they're clean. If more than a light coating of dust is present, clean the fittings before proceeding.

3   Relieve the fuel system pressure (see Chapter 4). Removal of the hairpin clip from each fitting is a two-stage procedure. First, spread the two clip legs apart about 1/8-inch to disengage them, then push in on them. Pull on the other end of the clip to detach it from the fitting (see illustration).

### ⁂ CAUTION:

If the new filter doesn't include new clips, don't use any tools or you may damage the plastic clips, which will have to be reused. Use your fingers only.

4   Once both hairpin clips are released, grasp the fuel hoses, one at a time, and pull them straight off the filter. Be prepared for fuel spillage.

5   After the hoses have been detached, check the clips for damage and distortion. If they were damaged in any way during removal, new ones must be used when the hoses are reattached to the new filter (if new clips are packaged with the filter, be sure to use them in place of the originals).

6   Remove the bolts and detach the filter and bracket assembly. On 1988 through 1994 models, note which way the arrow is pointing - the new filter must be installed the same way. On 1988 through 1994 models, use a screwdriver to loosen the clamp and remove the filter from the bracket. On 1995 and later models, the filter and bracket are a one-piece unit and cannot be separated.

7   On 1988 through 1994 models, install the new filter with the arrow pointing in the right direction and tighten the clamp. On all models, install the filter/bracket assembly and tighten the bolts securely.

8   Carefully push each hose onto the filter until it's seated against the collar on the fitting, then install the hairpin clips. Make sure the clips are securely attached to the hose fittings - if they come off, the hoses could back off the filter and a fire could result!

9   Start the engine and check for fuel leaks.

## Specifications

### Recommended lubricants and fluids

➡Note: Listed Listed here are manufacturer recommendations at the time this manual was written. Manufacturers occasionally upgrade their fluid and lubricant specifications, so check with your local auto parts store for current recommendations.

| | |
|---|---|
| Engine oil | |
|    Type | API "certified for gasoline engines" |
|    Viscosity | See accompanying chart |
| Brake fluid type | DOT 3 heavy duty brake fluid |
| Power steering fluid type | |
|    1995 and earlier models | Type F automatic transmission fluid |
|    1996 through 2008 models | MERCON automatic transmission fluid |
|    2009 and later models | MERCON V automatic transmission fluid |
| Automatic transmission fluid type | |
|    1997 and earlier models | MERCON automatic transmission fluid |
|    1998 through 2008 models | MERCON V automatic transmission fluid |
|    2009 and later models | MERCON LV automatic transmission fluid |
| Coolant type | |
|    2001 and earlier models | 50/50 mixture of ethylene glycol-based antifreeze and water |
|    2002 and later | |
|       USA models | 50/50 mixture of VC-7-B Motorcraft Premium Gold (yellow) engine coolant and water |
|       Canada models | 50/50 mixture of VC-7-A Motorcraft Premium Gold (yellow) engine coolant and water |
| Chassis grease | SAE NLGI no. 2 chassis grease |
| Differential lubricant type | SAE 80W-90 GL-5 gear lubricant* |

*\* Trak-Lok axles add 4 oz. of friction modifier (manufacturer part no. C8AZ-19B546-A) when oil is changed.*

---

❋❋ **CAUTION:**

Do not mix coolants of different colors. Doing so might damage the cooling system and/or the engine. Some 2002 models were filled with standard green, ethylene glycol-based coolant, while others were filled with Premium Gold engine coolant. When replacing coolant in a 2003 model, refill the system with the same type that was drained out.

---

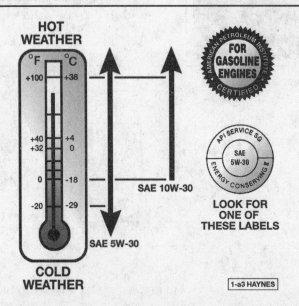

Engine oil viscosity chart

For best fuel economy and cold starting, select the lowest SAE viscosity grade for the expected temperature range

## Capacities*

Cooling system

| | |
|---|---|
| 1996 and earlier | 14.1 qts |
| 1997 through 2002 | 15.8 qts |
| 2003 and 2004 | 19.0 qts |
| 2005 and later | 18.6 qts |

Engine oil (all)

| | |
|---|---|
| 2002 and earlier | 5.0 qts |
| 2003 and later | 6.0 qts |

Automatic transmission (dry fill)**

| | |
|---|---|
| 1996 and earlier | 12.3 qts |
| 1997 and later | 13.9 qts |

\* All capacities approximate. Add as necessary to bring to appropriate level.

\*\* Since this is a dry-fill specification, the amount required during a routine fluid change will be substantially less. The best way to determine the amount of fluid to add during a routine fluid change is to measure the amount drained. It's important to not overfill the transmission.

## Radiator cap pressure

| | |
|---|---|
| Standard | 16 psi |
| Lower limit (must hold pressure) | 13 psi |
| Upper limit (must relieve pressure) | 18 psi |

## Brakes

| | |
|---|---|
| Disc brake pad thickness (minimum) | 1/8 inch |
| Drum brake shoe lining thickness (minimum) | 1/16 inch |

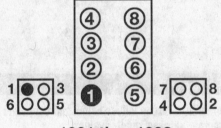

**1991 thru 1993**

36012-spec2Ba HAYNES

**Cylinder and coil terminal locations (4.6L engine)**

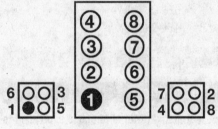

**1994 thru 1997**

36012-spec2Bb HAYNES

**Cylinder and coil terminal locations**

**1998 and later**

36012-spec2Bc HAYNES

**Cylinder location (coil-on-plug)**

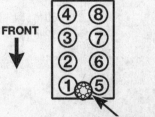

FRONT

DISTRIBUTOR

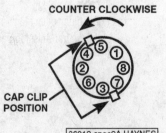

COUNTER CLOCKWISE

CAP CLIP POSITION

36012-spec2A HAYNES

**Cylinder locations and distributor rotation diagram (5.0L engine)**

## Ignition system

Spark plug type and gap

    1991 and earlier

| | |
|---|---|
| Type | Champion RS14LC or equivalent |
| Gap | 0.050 inch |

    1992 through 1996

| | |
|---|---|
| Type | Champion RS14YC6 or equivalent |
| Gap | 0.054 inch |

    1997 through 2002

| | |
|---|---|
| Type | Motorcraft AWSF-32P |
| Gap | 0.054 inch |

    2003 and 2004

        2V engine

| | |
|---|---|
| Type | Motorcraft AWSF-32EM |
| Gap | 0.054 inch |

        4V engine

| | |
|---|---|
| Type | AWSF32EM |
| Gap | 0.054 inch |

    2005

| | |
|---|---|
| Type | Motorcraft AGSF-32PM |
| Gap | 0.054 inch |

    2006 and later

        Type

| | |
|---|---|
| Flexible fuel models | Motorcraft AGSF-22FM1 |
| All other models | Motorcraft AGSF-32N |
| Gap | 0.054 inch |

Firing order

| | |
|---|---|
| 5.0L OHV V8 | 1-5-4-2-6-3-7-8 |
| 4.6L OHC V8 | 1-3-7-2-6-5-4-8 |

## Torque specifications         Ft-lbs (unless otherwise indicated)

➞ Note: One foot-pound (ft-lb) of torque is equivalent to 12 inch-pounds (in-lbs) of torque. Torque values below approximately 15 ft-lbs are expressed in inch-pounds, since most foot-pound torque wrenches are not accurate at these smaller values.

Drivebelt tensior mounting bolt

| | |
|---|---|
| Step 1 | 89 in-lbs |
| Step 2 | Tighten an additional 90 degrees |
| Wheel lug nuts | 85 to 105 |
| Spark plugs | 84 to 180 in-lbs |
| Oil pan drain plug | 15 |
| Engine block drain plug | 60 to 96 in-lbs |
| Automatic transmission pan bolts | 12 to 16 |

## 2A
## 5.0L V8 ENGINE

**Section**

**Reference to other Chapters**

CHECK ENGINE light - See Chapter 6

## 1   General information

This Part of Chapter 2 is devoted to in-vehicle repair procedures for the Overhead Valve (OHV), 5.0L V8 engine. This engine was installed in the vehicles covered by this manual from 1988 through 1991. From 1992 on, the 4.6 liter overhead cam (OHC) engine was the only engine available (see Chapter 2B). All information concerning engine removal and installation and engine block and cylinder head overhaul can be found in Part C of this Chapter.

The following repair procedures are based on the assumption that the engine is installed in the vehicle. If the engine has been removed from the vehicle and mounted on a stand, many of the steps outlined in this Part of Chapter 2 will not apply.

The Specifications included in this Part of Chapter 2 apply only to the procedures contained in this Part. Part C of Chapter 2 contains the Specifications necessary for cylinder head and engine block rebuilding.

## 2   Repair operations possible with the engine in the vehicle

Many major repair operations can be accomplished without removing the engine from the vehicle.

Clean the engine compartment and the exterior of the engine with some type of pressure washer before any work is done. It will make the job easier and help keep dirt out of the internal areas of the engine.

It may help to remove the hood to improve access to the engine as repairs are performed (see Chapter 11 if necessary).

If vacuum, exhaust, oil or coolant leaks develop, indicating a need for gasket or seal replacement, the repairs can generally be made with the engine in the vehicle. The intake and exhaust manifold gaskets, timing cover gasket, oil pan gasket, crankshaft oil seals and cylinder head gaskets are all accessible with the engine in place.

Exterior engine components, such as the intake and exhaust mani-

folds, the oil pan (and the oil pump), the water pump, the starter motor, the alternator, the distributor and the fuel system components can be removed for repair with the engine in place.

Since the cylinder heads can be removed without pulling the engine, valve component servicing can also be accomplished with the engine in the vehicle. Replacement of the timing chain and sprockets is also possible with the engine in the vehicle.

In extreme cases caused by a lack of necessary equipment, repair or replacement of piston rings, pistons, connecting rods and rod bearings is possible with the engine in the vehicle. However, this practice is not recommended because of the cleaning and preparation work that must be done to the components involved.

## 3   Top Dead Center (TDC) for number one piston - locating

◆ **Refer to illustration 3.6**

1   Top Dead Center (TDC) is the highest point in the cylinder that each piston reaches as it travels up-and-down when the crankshaft turns. Each piston reaches TDC on the compression stroke and again on the exhaust stroke, but TDC generally refers to piston position on the compression stroke. The timing marks on the vibration damper installed on the front of the crankshaft are referenced to the number one piston at TDC on the compression stroke.

2   Positioning the piston(s) at TDC is an essential part of many procedures such as rocker arm removal, valve adjustment, timing chain and sprocket replacement and distributor removal.

3   In order to bring any piston to TDC, the crankshaft must be turned using one of the methods outlined below. When looking at the front of the engine, normal crankshaft rotation is clockwise.

❋❋ **WARNING:**

**Before beginning this procedure, be sure to place the transmission in Neutral and ground the coil wire attached to the center terminal of the distributor cap to disable the ignition system. Also disable the fuel pump (see Chapter 4, Section 2).**

a)  *The preferred method is to turn the crankshaft with a large socket and breaker bar attached to the vibration damper bolt threaded into the front of the crankshaft.*

b)  *A remote starter switch, which may save some time, can also be used. Attach the switch leads to the S (switch) and B (battery) terminals on the starter motor. Once the piston is close to TDC, use a socket and breaker bar as described in the previous paragraph.*

c)  *If an assistant is available to turn the ignition switch to the Start*

*position in short bursts, you can get the piston close to TDC without a remote starter switch. Use a socket and breaker bar as described in Paragraph a) to complete the procedure.*

4   Using a felt pen, make a mark on the distributor housing directly below the number one spark plug wire terminal on the distributor cap.

➡**Note: The terminal numbers are marked on the spark plug wires near the distributor.**

5   Remove the distributor cap as described in Chapter 1.

6   Turn the crankshaft (see Paragraph 3 above) until the zero or groove on the vibration damper is aligned with the pointer or TDC mark (see illustration). The pointer or TDC mark and vibration damper are

**3.6 Turn the crankshaft until the zero on the vibration damper scale is lined up with the pointer**

located low on the front of the engine, near the pulley that turns the drivebelt.

7   The rotor should now be pointing directly at the mark on the distributor housing. If it isn't, the piston is at TDC on the exhaust stroke.

8   To get the piston to TDC on the compression stroke, turn the crankshaft one complete turn (360-degrees) clockwise. The rotor should now be pointing at the mark. When the rotor is pointing at the

number one spark plug wire terminal in the distributor cap (which is indicated by the mark on the housing) and the ignition timing marks are aligned, the number one piston is at TDC on the compression stroke.

9   After the number one piston has been positioned at TDC on the compression stroke, TDC for any of the remaining cylinders can be located by turning the crankshaft and following the firing order (refer to the Specifications).

## 4   Valve covers - removal and installation

### REMOVAL

♦ **Refer to illustrations 4.2, 4.6 and 4.7**

1   Disconnect the negative cable from the battery.

2   Note their locations, then detach the spark plug wire clips from the valve cover studs (see illustration).

3   Refer to Chapter 1 and detach the spark plug wires from the plugs. Position the wires out of the way.

4   If so equipped, detach the diverter valve and hoses from the valve cover.

5   On vehicles with cruise control, disconnect the servo linkage at the throttle body and remove the servo bracket.

6   Remove the valve cover bolts/nuts (see illustration), then detach the cover from the head.

➡**Note: If the cover is stuck to the head, bump one end with a block of wood and a hammer to jar it loose. If that doesn't work, try to slip a flexible putty knife between the head and cover to break the gasket seal. Don't pry at the cover-to-head joint or damage to the sealing surfaces may occur (leading to oil leaks in the future). Some valve covers are made of plastic - be extra careful when tapping or pulling on them.**

### INSTALLATION

7   The mating surfaces of each cylinder head and valve cover must be perfectly clean when the covers are installed. Use a gasket scraper to remove all traces of sealant and old gasket material (see illustration), then clean the mating surfaces with lacquer thinner or acetone. If there's sealant or oil on the mating surfaces when the cover is installed, oil leaks may develop.

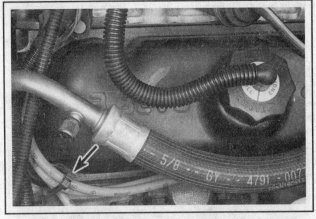

**4.2   The spark plug wire routing clips (arrow) pull off the studs**

8   Clean the mounting bolt threads with a die to remove any corrosion and restore damaged threads. Make sure the threaded holes in the head are clean - run a tap into them to remove corrosion and restore damaged threads. Apply a small amount of light oil to the bolt threads.

9   The gaskets should be mated to the covers before the covers are installed. Make sure the tabs on the gasket(s) engage in the slots in the cover(s).

10  Carefully position the cover on the head and install the bolts/nuts.

11  Tighten the bolts in two steps to the torque listed in this Chapter's Specifications. Wait two minutes between the first and the second round of tightening.

**4.6   Location of the valve cover bolts (arrows)**

**4.7   Being careful not to damage the mating surface of the cylinder head, carefully remove the valve cover gasket with a gasket scraper or putty knife**

---

⁂⁂ **CAUTION:**

Be careful with plastic valve covers, if equipped, they are easily damaged, so don't over tighten the bolts!

---

**5 Rocker arms and pushrods - removal, inspection and installation**

## REMOVAL

♦ **Refer to illustration 5.4**

1 Remove the valve cover(s) from the cylinder head(s) (see Section 4).

2 Beginning at the front of one cylinder head, remove the rocker arm fulcrum bolts. Store them separately in marked containers to ensure that they will be reinstalled in their original locations.

➡ **Note: If the pushrods are the only items being removed, loosen each bolt just enough to allow the rocker arms to be rotated to the side so the pushrods can be lifted out.**

**5.4 A perforated cardboard box provides ideal pushrod storage to ensure that they are reinstalled in their original locations**

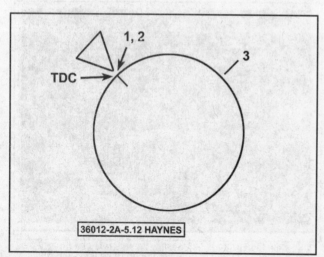

**5.12 Crankshaft positions for checking and adjusting valve clearances**

12 The remaining installation steps are the reverse of removal.

13 Start the engine and check carefully for oil leaks as the engine warms up.

3 Lift off the rocker arms, fulcrums and fulcrum guides (if used). Store them in the marked containers with the bolts (they must be reinstalled in their original locations).

4 Remove the pushrods and store them separately to make sure they don't get mixed up during installation (see illustration).

## INSPECTION

5 Check each rocker arm for wear, cracks and other damage, especially where the pushrods and valve stems contact the rocker arm faces.

6 Make sure the hole at the pushrod end of each rocker arm is open.

7 Check each rocker arm pivot area and fulcrum for wear, cracks and galling. If the rocker arms are worn or damaged, replace them with new ones and use new fulcrums as well.

8 Inspect the pushrods for cracks and excessive wear at the ends. Roll each pushrod across a piece of plate glass to see if it's bent (if it wobbles, it's bent).

## INSTALLATION

⁂⁂ **CAUTION:**

Make sure that both lifters for each cylinder are on the base circle of the cam lobe (both valves closed) before tightening the rocker arm bolts.

---

9 Lubricate the lower end of each pushrod with clean engine oil or moly-base grease and install them in their original locations. Make sure each pushrod seats completely in the lifter.

10 Apply moly-base grease to the ends of the valve stems and the upper ends of the pushrods before positioning the rocker arms, fulcrums and guides.

11 Apply moly-base grease to the fulcrums to prevent damage to the mating surfaces before engine oil pressure builds up. Set the rocker arms and guides in place, then install the fulcrums and bolts.

### Valve adjustment

♦ **Refer to illustration 5.12**

**Positive stop rocker arms**

➡ **Note: Adjustment is normally only needed after valve train components have been replaced or the valves and/or seats have been ground a considerable amount.**

12 Using a lifter bleed-down tool, press on the rocker arm until the lifter leaks down. Check the clearance between the valve stem and rocker arm with a feeler gauge. Compare the results to the Specifications and write it down for future reference. Repeat the procedure for each valve in the order shown below.

➡ **Note: The arrangement of intake and exhaust valves is as follows:**

With the crankshaft in position 1, check the valves as follows (see illustration):

*Intake - no. 1, 7 and 8*
*Exhaust - no. 1, 4 and 5*

13 Rotate the crankshaft one complete revolution (360-degrees) clockwise to position 2 and check the following valves:

*Intake - no. 4 and 5*
*Exhaust - no. 2 and 6*

14 Rotate the crankshaft 1/4-turn (90-degrees) clockwise to position 3 and check the following valves:

*Intake - no. 2, 3 and 6*
*Exhaust - no. 3, 7 and 8*

15 Clearance can be changed by using different length pushrods, available from your dealer parts department. If there isn't enough clearance, use a shorter pushrod; too much clearance, use a longer one.

## 6  Valve springs, retainers and seals - replacement

▶ **Refer to illustrations 6.4, 6.9, 6.10a and 6.10b**

➡**Note: Broken valve springs and defective valve stem seals can be replaced without removing the cylinder heads. Two special tools and a compressed air source are normally required to perform this operation, so read through this Section carefully and rent or buy the tools before beginning the job. If compressed air isn't available, a length of nylon rope can be used to keep the valves from falling into the cylinder during this procedure.**

1  Remove the valve cover from the cylinder head(s) (see Section 4). If all of the valve stem seals are being replaced, remove both valve covers.

2  Remove the spark plug from the cylinder which has the defective component. If all of the valve stem seals are being replaced, all of the spark plugs should be removed.

3  Turn the crankshaft until the piston in the affected cylinder is at Top Dead Center on the compression stroke (see Section 3). If you're replacing all of the valve stem seals, begin with cylinder number one and work on the valves for one cylinder at a time. Move from cylinder-to-cylinder following the firing order sequence (see this Chapter's Specifications).

4  Thread an adapter into the spark plug hole (see illustration) and connect an air hose from a compressed air source to it. Most auto parts stores can supply the air hose adapter.

➡**Note: Many cylinder compression gauges utilize a screw-in fitting that may work with your air hose quick-disconnect fitting.**

5  Remove the bolt, fulcrum and rocker arm for the valve with the defective part and pull out the pushrod. If all of the valve stem seals are being replaced, all of the rocker arms and pushrods should be removed (see Section 5).

6  Apply compressed air to the cylinder.

## ✳✳ WARNING:

**The piston may be forced down by compressed air, causing the crankshaft to turn suddenly. If the wrench used when positioning the number one piston at TDC is still attached to the bolt in the crankshaft nose, it could cause damage or injury when the crankshaft moves.**

7  The valves should be held in place by the air pressure. If the valve faces or seats are in poor condition, leaks may prevent air pressure from retaining the valves - refer to the alternative procedure below.

8  If you don't have access to compressed air, an alternative method can be used. Position the piston at a point approximately 45-degrees before TDC on the compression stroke, then feed a long piece of nylon rope through the spark plug hole until it fills the combustion chamber. Be sure to leave the end of the rope hanging out of the engine so it can be removed easily. Use a large ratchet and socket to rotate the crank-

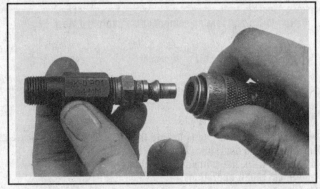

**6.4  This is what the air hose adapter that threads into the spark plug hole looks like - they're commonly available from auto parts stores**

shaft in the normal direction of rotation until slight resistance is felt.

9  Stuff shop rags into the cylinder head holes above and below the valves to prevent parts and tools from falling into the engine, then use a valve spring compressor to compress the spring. Remove the keepers with small needle-nose pliers or a magnet (see illustration).

➡**Note: A couple of different types of tools are available for compressing the valve springs with the head in place. One type, shown here, grips the lower spring coils and presses on the retainer as the knob is turned, while the other type utilizes the rocker arm bolt for leverage. Both types work very well, although the lever type is usually less expensive.**

**6.9  Once the spring is depressed, the keepers can be removed with a small magnet or needle-nose pliers (a magnet is preferred to prevent dropping the keepers)**

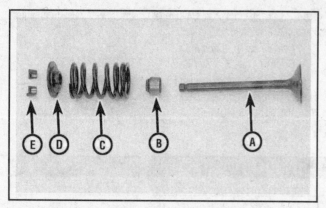

**6.10a Valve and related components - exploded view**

| | | |
|---|---|---|
| A | Valve | C | Valve spring | E | Keepers |
| B | Valve stem seal | D | Retainer | | |

10 Remove the spring retainer or rotator, sleeve (used on some intake valves) and valve spring assembly, then remove the umbrella-type guide seal (see illustrations).

➡Note: If air pressure fails to hold the valve in the closed position during this operation, the valve face or seat is probably damaged. If so, the cylinder head will have to be removed for additional repair operations.

11 Wrap a rubber band or tape around the top of the valve stem so the valve won't fall into the combustion chamber, then release the air pressure.

➡Note: If a rope was used instead of air pressure, turn the crankshaft slightly in the direction opposite normal rotation.

12 Inspect the valve stem for damage. Rotate the valve in the guide and check the end for eccentric movement, which would indicate that the valve is bent.

13 Move the valve up-and-down in the guide and make sure it doesn't bind. If the valve stem binds, either the valve is bent or the guide is damaged. In either case, the head will have to be removed for repair.

**6.10b The seal can be pulled off the guide with a pair of pliers**

14 Reapply air pressure to the cylinder to retain the valve in the closed position, then remove the tape or rubber band from the valve stem. If a rope was used instead of air pressure, rotate the crankshaft in the normal direction of rotation until slight resistance is felt.

15 Lubricate the valve stem with engine oil and the valve stem tip with polyethylene grease, then install a new guide seal.

16 Install the spring in position over the valve.

17 Install the valve spring retainer or rotator. Some intake valves also have a sleeve that fits inside the retainer. Compress the valve spring and carefully position the keepers in the groove. Apply a small dab of grease to the inside of each keeper to hold it in place.

18 Remove the pressure from the spring tool and make sure the keepers are seated.

19 Disconnect the air hose and remove the adapter from the spark plug hole. If a rope was used in place of air pressure, pull it out of the cylinder.

20 Install the rocker arm(s) and pushrod(s) (see Section 5).

21 Install the spark plug(s) and hook up the wire(s) (see Chapter 1).

22 Install the valve cover(s) (see Section 4).

23 Start and run the engine, then check for oil leaks and unusual sounds coming from the valve cover area.

## 7 Intake manifold - removal and installation

### REMOVAL

**⁂ WARNING:**

The intake manifold is heavy. It is highly recommended to have an assistant help you lift it off the engine to avoid injury.

1 Drain the cooling system (see Chapter 1).

2 Remove the PCV and canister purge hoses.

3 Disconnect the accelerator cable, speed control linkage and automatic transmission cable. Remove the accelerator cable bracket (see Chapter 4).

4 Label and disconnect the all vacuum lines connected to the intake manifold.

5 Remove the distributor (see Chapter 5).

6 Relieve the fuel system pressure (see Chapter 4) and disconnect the fuel supply and return lines.

7 Disconnect the radiator, heater and water pump bypass hoses from the water outlet (see Chapter 3). Disconnect the throttle body cooler hoses.

➡Note: The heater outlet and coolant bypass tubes are pressed in and cannot be removed.

8 Disconnect the electrical connectors from the coolant temperature sending unit, air charge temperature sensor, throttle positioner, idle speed control solenoid, EGR sensors, fuel injectors and fuel charging assembly (see Chapter 4).

9 Remove the air intake plenum (see Chapter 4).

10 Loosen the lower intake manifold bolts and nuts in 1/4-turn increments until they can be removed by hand.

11 The manifold will probably be stuck to the cylinder heads and force may be required to break the gasket seal. A prybar can be used to pry up the manifold, but make sure all bolts and nuts have been removed first!

**7.16  Align the new intake manifold gaskets by seating them over the dowel pins or studs in the cylinder head (arrows)**

**✳✳ CAUTION:**

Don't pry between the block and manifold or the heads and manifold or damage to the gasket sealing surfaces may occur, leading to vacuum and oil leaks. Pry only at a manifold casting protrusion.

## INSTALLATION

♦ Refer to illustration 7.16 and 7.20

**✳✳ CAUTION:**

The mating surfaces of the cylinder heads, block and manifold must be perfectly clean when the manifold is installed. Gasket removal solvents in aerosol cans are available at most auto parts stores and may be helpful when removing old gasket material that's stuck to the heads and manifold (since the manifold is made of aluminum, aggressive scraping can cause damage!) Be sure to follow directions printed on the container.

➥Note: The manufacturer recommends the use of guide pins when installing the manifold. To make these, buy four extra manifold bolts. Cut the heads off the bolts, then grind a taper and cut a screwdriver slot in the cut ends.

12  If the manifold was disassembled, reassemble it. Use electrically conductive sealant on the temperature sending unit threads. Use a new EGR valve gasket.

13  Use a gasket scraper to remove all traces of sealant and old gasket material, then clean the mating surfaces with lacquer thinner or acetone. If there's old sealant or oil on the mating surfaces when the manifold is installed, oil or vacuum leaks may develop. When working on the heads and block, cover the lifter valley with shop rags to keep debris out of the engine. Use a vacuum cleaner to remove any gasket material that falls into the intake ports in the heads.

14  Use a tap of the correct size to chase the threads in the bolt holes, then use compressed air (if available) to remove the debris from the holes.

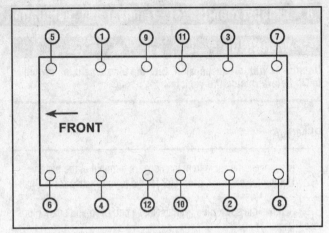

**7.20  Intake manifold bolt tightening sequence**

**✳✳ WARNING:**

Wear safety glasses or a face shield to protect your eyes when using compressed air!

Remove excessive carbon deposits and corrosion from the exhaust and coolant passages in the heads and manifold.

15  Apply a 1/8-inch wide bead of RTV sealant to the four corners where the manifold, block and heads converge.

➥Note: This sealant sets up in 10 minutes. Do not take longer to install and tighten the manifold once the sealant is applied, or leaks may occur.

16  Apply a small dab of contact adhesive  or equivalent to the manifold gasket mating surface on each cylinder head. Position the gaskets on the cylinder heads (see illustration). The upper side of each gasket will have a TOP or THIS SIDE UP label stamped into it to ensure correct installation.

17  Position the end seals on the block, then apply a 1/8-inch wide bead of RTV sealant to the four points where the end seals meet the heads.

18  Make sure all intake port openings, coolant passage holes and bolt holes are aligned correctly.

19  Carefully set the manifold in place while the sealant is still wet.

**✳✳ CAUTION:**

Don't disturb the gaskets and don't move the manifold fore-and-aft after it contacts the seals on the block. Make sure the end seals haven't been disturbed.

20  Install the bolts and tighten them to the torque listed in this Chapter's Specifications (see illustration).

21  The remaining installation steps are the reverse of removal.

22  Change the engine oil and refill the cooling system (see Chapter 1).

23  Start the engine and check carefully for oil and coolant leaks at the intake manifold joints.

24  Recheck the mounting bolt torque.

## 8   Exhaust manifold(s) - removal and installation

## REMOVAL

1   Disconnect the cable from the negative terminal of the battery.
2   Unplug the electrical connector for the oxygen sensor (see Chapter 4)
3   Remove the spark plug heat shields, if equipped and spark plugs (see Chapter 1).
4   Raise the vehicle and support it securely on jackstands.
5   Working under the vehicle, apply penetrating oil to the exhaust pipe-to-manifold studs and nuts.

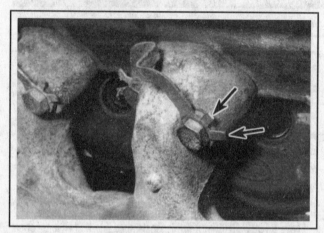

**8.11   Some models are equipped with manifold bolt locking tabs - bend these down before removing the bolts - use new locking assemblies on installation, bending the tabs up to lock the bolts in place**

6   Remove the air cleaner assembly and heat stove tube (if equipped).

### Right side manifold

7   Remove the Thermactor hardware, if equipped.
8   Remove the automatic transmission fluid dipstick tube, if necessary.
9   Remove the exhaust manifold heat shield, if equipped.

### Left side manifold

10   If it's in the way, remove the engine oil dipstick and tube.

### Both manifolds

▶ **Refer to illustration 8.11**

11   Bend back the locking tabs (if equipped). Remove the mounting bolts and separate the manifold from the head (see illustration). Note the locations of the pilot bolts.

### Installation

12   Check the manifold for cracks and make sure the bolt threads are clean and undamaged. The manifold and cylinder head mating surfaces must be clean before the manifolds are reinstalled - use a gasket scraper to remove all carbon deposits and old gasket material.
13   Position the manifold and gasket (if used) on the head and install the mounting bolts.
14   When tightening the mounting bolts, work from the center to the ends and be sure to use a torque wrench. Tighten the bolts in three equal steps until the torque listed in this Chapter's Specifications is reached.
15   The remaining installation steps are the reverse of removal.
16   Start the engine and check for exhaust leaks.

## 9   Cylinder head(s) - removal and installation

## REMOVAL

### Both cylinder heads

1   Remove the valve cover(s) (see Section 4).
2   Remove the pushrods (see Section 5).

3   Remove the intake manifold (see Section 7).
4   Remove the drivebelts (see Chapter 1) and idler pulley bracket.
5   Remove the thermactor diverter valve and pump and the crossover tube from the rear of the head (if applicable).

### Left (driver's side) cylinder head

6   Unbolt the power steering pump and tie it aside in an upright position. Leave the hoses connected (see Chapter 10).
7   Remove the air conditioning compressor and position it out of the way (see Chapter 3). DO NOT disconnect the hoses!
8   Remove the exhaust manifold(s) (see Section 8).
9   Proceed to Step 12.

### Right cylinder head

10   Detach the fuel line from the clip at the front of the head, if applicable.
11   Remove the exhaust manifold(s) (see Section 8).

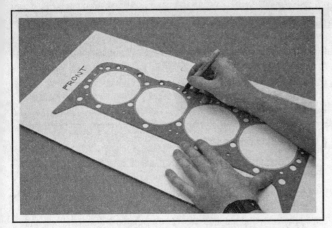

9.12  To avoid mixing up the head bolts, use a new gasket to transfer the bolt pattern to a piece of cardboard, then punch holes to accept the bolts

### Both cylinder heads

▶ **Refer to illustration 9.12**

12  Using a new head gasket, outline the cylinders and bolt pattern on a piece of cardboard (see illustration). Be sure to indicate the front of the engine for reference. Punch holes at the bolt locations.

13  Loosen the head bolts in 1/4-turn increments until they can be removed by hand. Work from bolt-to-bolt in a pattern that's the reverse of the tightening sequence (see illustration 9.22). Store the bolts in the cardboard holder as they're removed; this will ensure that the bolts are reinstalled in their original holes.

14  Lift the head(s) off the engine. If resistance is felt, DO NOT pry between the head and block as damage to the mating surfaces will result. To dislodge the head, place a block of wood against the end of it and strike the wood block with a hammer. Store the heads on blocks of wood to prevent damage to the gasket sealing surfaces.

15  Cylinder head disassembly and inspection procedures are covered in detail in Chapter 2, Part C.

## INSTALLATION

▶ **Refer to illustrations 9.19 and 9.22**

16  The mating surfaces of the cylinder heads and block must be perfectly clean when the heads are installed. Use a gasket scraper to remove all traces of carbon and old gasket material, then clean the mating surfaces with lacquer thinner or acetone. If there's oil on the mating surfaces when the heads are installed, the gaskets may not seal correctly and leaks may develop. When working on the block, cover the lifter valley with shop rags to keep debris out of the engine. Use a vacuum cleaner to remove any debris that falls into the cylinders.

17  Check the block and head mating surfaces for nicks, deep scratches and other damage. If damage is slight, it can be removed with a file - if it's excessive, machining may be the only alternative.

18  Use a tap of the correct size to chase the threads in the head bolt holes. Mount each bolt in a vise and run a die down the threads to remove corrosion and restore the threads. Dirt, corrosion, sealant and damaged threads will affect torque readings.

9.19  Be certain that the cylinder head gaskets are positioned with the correct side up (note the Front mark on the type used here)

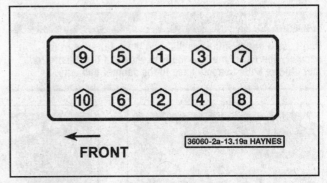

9.22  Cylinder head bolt tightening sequence

19  Position the new gasket(s) over the locating dowels in the block. Make sure it's facing the correct direction and that all bolt and coolant passage holes are aligned.

➡**Note: Most gaskets will either be marked FRONT or TOP to be sure the gasket is positioned correctly (see illustration).**

20  Carefully position the head(s) on the block without disturbing the gasket(s).

21  Before installing the head bolts, lightly oil the threads on all of the bolts.

22  Install the bolts in their original locations and tighten them finger tight. Follow the recommended sequence and tighten the bolts, in two or three steps, to the torque listed in this Chapter's Specifications (see illustration).

➡**Note: Once the bolts have been tightened to the correct final torque it is not necessary to re tighten the bolts after extended operation. However, the bolts may be checked and re-tightened if desired.**

23  The remaining installation steps are the reverse of removal.

24  Change the engine oil and filter (see Chapter 1), then start the engine and check carefully for oil and coolant leaks.

## 10  Crankshaft pulley/vibration damper - removal and installation

### REMOVAL

♦ **Refer to illustrations 10.4 and 10.5**

1   Remove the bolts attaching the fan shroud to the radiator and position the shroud back over the fan.

2   Remove the fan/clutch assembly and the shroud (see Chapter 3).

3   Remove the drivebelts (see Chapter 1).

4   Mark the crankshaft pulley and vibration damper so they can be reassembled in the same relative position. This is important, since the damper and pulley are initially balanced as a unit. Unbolt and remove the pulley (see illustration).

5   Remove the bolt from the front of the crankshaft. You'll most likely have to prevent the crankshaft from turning. Remove the torque converter access cover and wedge a large screwdriver between the teeth of the starter ring gear, allowing the screwdriver to rest against the transmission housing. Use a puller to detach the vibration damper (see illustration).

### ✱✱ CAUTION:

Don't use a puller with jaws that grip the outer edge of the damper. The puller must be the type shown in the illustration that utilizes bolts to apply force to the damper hub only.

Clean the crankshaft nose and the seal contact surface on the vibration damper with lacquer thinner or acetone. Leave the Woodruff key in place in the crankshaft keyway.

### INSTALLATION

♦ **Refer to illustration 10.6**

6   Lubricate the oil seal contact surface of the vibration damper hub with multi-purpose grease or clean engine oil, then install the damper on the end of the crankshaft. The keyway in the damper must be aligned with the Woodruff key in the crankshaft nose. If the damper cannot be seated by hand, slip the large washer over the bolt, install the bolt and tighten it to pull the damper into place. An alternative method that can be used is to use a soft face/dead blow hammer (see illustration) or a block of wood and a steel hammer to drive the damper into place.

### ✱✱ CAUTION:

Never use a steel hammer directly on the damper.

Tighten the bolt to the torque listed in this Chapter's Specifications.

7   The remaining installation steps are the reverse of removal.

8   Add coolant and check the oil level. Run the engine and check for oil and coolant leaks.

10.4  Mark the pulley and vibration damper before removing the four bolts - the large vibration damper bolt (arrow) is usually very tight, so use a six-point socket and a breaker bar to loosen it

10.5  Use the recommended puller to remove the vibration damper - if a puller that applies force to the outer edge is used, the damper will be damaged

10.6  A soft-face hammer can be used to tap the vibration damper onto the crankshaft - DON'T use a steel hammer

## 11  Timing chain cover - removal and installation

### ✱✱ WARNING:

On models with air suspension, turn the air suspension switch to Off before raising the vehicle.

### REMOVAL

♦ **Refer to illustrations 11.5 and 11.7**

1   Perform all water pump removal steps except actual removal of the pump. The pump may be removed or left attached to the timing chain cover during removal (see Chapter 3).

**11.5  When removing the timing chain cover, remove only those bolts from the oil pan that attach directly to the cover**

**11.7  Gently tap the timing chain cover loose with a soft face hammer**

2  Drain the engine oil and remove the oil filter (see Chapter 1).

3  Remove the crankshaft vibration damper (see Section 10).

4  Unbolt and remove all accessory brackets attached to the timing chain cover.

5  Remove the oil pan-to-timing chain cover bolts (see illustration).

6  Use a razor knife (thin blade) or razor blade to cut the oil pan gasket flush with the engine block face before separating the cover from the engine block.

### ✳✳ CAUTION:

**Cover the front of the oil pan opening while the chain cover is off to prevent foreign material from entering the oil pan.**

7  Remove the bolts and separate the timing chain cover from the block. If it's stuck, tap it gently with a soft-face hammer (see illustration).

### ✳✳ CAUTION:

**DO NOT use excessive force or you may crack the cover. If the cover is difficult to remove, double check to make sure all of the bolts are out.**

## INSTALLATION

▶ **Refer to illustration 11.15**

8  Remove the circular rubber seal from the front of the oil pan and stuff a shop rag into the oil pan opening to keep debris out of the engine. Use a gasket scraper to remove all traces of old gasket material and sealant from the cover, oil pan and engine block, then clean them with lacquer thinner or acetone.

9  Cut two sections out of a new oil pan gasket to install between the oil pan and timing chain cover.

10  Attach the gasket sections to the oil pan with contact adhesive or equivalent.

11  Apply a 1/8-inch bead of RTV sealant to the oil pan-to-block joints.

12  Install a new circular rubber seal in the oil pan cutout (use con-tact adhesive to hold it in place).

13  Lubricate the timing chain and crankshaft front oil seal lips with engine oil.

14  Apply a thin coat of RTV sealant to the block side of the new cover gasket, then position it on the engine. The dowel pins will hold it in place as the cover is installed.

15  Before positioning the pan gasket pieces, apply a bead of RTV sealant at the junction of the oil pan, block and timing chain cover (see illustration).

16  Apply a thin coat of RTV sealant to the gasket surface of the cover and attach it to the engine. Don't dislodge the circular rubber seal or the gaskets.

17  It may be necessary to compress the rubber seal by forcing the cover down before installing the bolts. Temporarily slip the vibration damper onto the crankshaft to align the cover.

18  Apply pipe sealant with Teflon to the threads, then install the bolts. Tighten the oil pan-to-cover bolts to the torque listed in this Chapter's Specifications while aligning the cover with the damper. Make sure the gaskets and seal stay in place.

19  Tighten the cover-to-block bolts to the torque listed in this Chapter's Specifications, then remove the vibration damper.

20  Install the remaining parts in the reverse order of removal.

21  Add engine oil and coolant (see Chapter 1).

22  Run the engine and check for leaks.

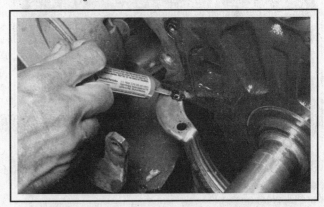

**11.15  Before positioning the new pan gasket pieces, apply a bead of RTV-type sealant at the junction of the oil pan and block as shown**

## 12 Timing chain and sprockets - inspection, removal and installation

### TIMING CHAIN INSPECTION (COVER ON ENGINE)

♦ **Refer to illustration 12.5**

1 Disconnect the negative battery cable from the battery.

2 Place the engine at Top Dead Center (TDC) compression for the number one cylinder (see Chapter 2C).

3 Rotate the crankshaft 360-degrees. Place the number one piston several degrees before TDC (BTDC).

4 Remove the right valve cover (see Section 4).

5 Attach a dial indicator to the cylinder head with the plunger in-line with and resting on the number one rocker arm at the end contacting the pushrod (see illustration).

6 Turn the crankshaft clockwise until the number one piston is at TDC. This will take up the slack on the right side of the timing chain.

7 Zero the dial indicator.

8 Slowly turn the crankshaft counterclockwise until the slightest movement is seen on the dial indicator. Stop and note how far the number one piston has moved away from the TDC mark by looking at the ignition marks.

9 If the mark has moved more than 10-degrees, install a new timing chain and sprockets.

### TIMING CHAIN INSPECTION (COVER REMOVED FROM ENGINE)

10 Disconnect the negative battery cable from the battery.

11 Detach any accessories such as the power steering pump, alternator and air conditioning compressor that block access to the timing chain cover. Leave the hoses/wires connected and tie the units aside. Refer to Chapters 3, 5 and 10 for additional information. Unbolt the accessory brackets from the front of the engine.

12 Position the number one piston at TDC on the compression stroke (see Chapter 2C).

### ✳✳ CAUTION:

**Once this has been done, do not turn the crankshaft until the timing chain and sprockets have been reinstalled (if they are removed for replacement).**

13 Remove the vibration damper (see Section 10).

14 Remove the mounting bolts and separate the timing chain cover from the block and oil pan (see Section 11).

### ✳✳ CAUTION:

**The cover is easily damaged, so DO NOT attempt to pry it off.**

15 Rotate the crankshaft in a counterclockwise direction to take up the slack in the left side (drivers side) of the chain.

16 Establish a reference point on the block and measure from that point to the chain (see illustration).

17 Reinstall the vibration damper bolt. Using this bolt, turn the crankshaft clockwise with a wrench until the slack is taken up on the right side of the chain.

18 Force the left side of the chain out with your fingers and measure the distance between the reference point and the chain. The difference between the two measurements is the deflection.

19 If the deflection exceeds 1/2-inch, install a new timing chain and sprockets.

➡**Note: Whenever a new timing chain is required, the entire set (chain, camshaft and crankshaft sprockets) must be replaced as an assembly.**

### GEAR INSPECTION

20 Inspect the camshaft gear for damage or wear, the teeth can be grooved or worn enough to cause a poor meshing of the gear and the chain and cause timing chain failure.

### ✳✳ CAUTION:

**The camshaft gear on early models may have been an aluminum gear with a nylon coating on the teeth. This nylon coating may be cracked or flaking off in small pieces. These pieces tend to end up in the oil pan and may eventually plug the oil pump pick-up screen. If the pieces have come off the camshaft gear, the oil pan should be removed to properly clean or replace the oil pump pick-up screen.**

**12.5 A dial indicator installed to measure timing chain deflection (this setup can also be used to check camshaft lobe lift)**

**12.16 Timing chain deflection check - timing chain cover removed**

21  Inspect the crankshaft gear for damage or wear. The crankshaft gear is a steel gear, but the teeth can be grooved or worn enough to also cause a poor meshing of the gear and the chain which can lead to chain failure.

## TIMING CHAIN AND SPROCKET REMOVAL

▶ **Refer to illustrations 12.24 and 12.26**

22  Make sure the number one piston is at TDC (see Section 3).

23  Remove the timing chain cover (see Section 11). Try to avoid turning the crankshaft during vibration damper removal.

24  Make sure the crankshaft and camshaft sprocket timing marks are aligned (see illustration). If they aren't, install the vibration damper bolt and use it to turn the crankshaft clockwise until the two marks are aligned.

25  Remove the camshaft sprocket mounting bolt(s).

26  Pull the sprocket/chain off the camshaft and detach the chain from the crankshaft sprocket (see illustration). Don't lose the pin in the end of the camshaft.

27  The crankshaft sprocket can be levered off with two large screwdrivers or a prybar.

## TIMING CHAIN AND SPROCKET INSTALLATION

▶ **Refer to illustrations 12.31, 12.32 and 12.33**

28  Use a gasket scraper to remove all traces of old gasket material and sealant from the cover and engine block. Stuff a shop rag into the opening at the front of the oil pan to keep debris out of the engine. Wipe the cover and block sealing surfaces with a cloth saturated with lacquer thinner or acetone.

29  Check the cover flange for distortion, particularly around the bolt holes.

➡**Note: If the timing chain cover oil seal has been leaking, refer to Section 18 and install a new one.**

30  Align the keyway in the crankshaft sprocket with the Woodruff key in the end of the crankshaft. Press the sprocket onto the crankshaft with

**12.24  Align the timing marks on the crankshaft and camshaft sprockets (arrows) as shown here before removing the sprockets from the shafts**

the vibration damper bolt, a large socket and some washers or tap it gently into place until it's completely seated.

## ✳✳ CAUTION:

**If resistance is encountered, DO NOT hammer the sprocket onto the shaft. It may eventually move into place, but it may be cracked in the process and fail later, causing extensive engine damage.**

31  Turn the crankshaft until the key is facing up (12 o'clock position) (see illustration).

32  Drape the chain over the camshaft sprocket and turn the sprocket until the timing mark faces down (6 o'clock position). Mesh the chain with the crankshaft sprocket and position the camshaft sprocket on the end of the camshaft (see illustration). If necessary, turn the camshaft so the dowel pin fits into the sprocket hole.

**12.26  Remove both timing gears and the chain as a unit (be sure to align the timing gear marks first)**

**12.31  Position the crankshaft with the key facing up (12 o'clock), then . . .**

**12.32  . . . slip the chain over the crankshaft sprocket and attach the camshaft sprocket to the camshaft**

33  When correctly installed, a straight line should pass through the center of the camshaft, the camshaft timing mark (in the 6 o'clock position), the crankshaft timing mark (in the 12 o'clock position) and the center of the crankshaft (see illustration). DO NOT proceed until the valve timing is correct!

34  Apply Loc-Tite to the threads and install the camshaft sprocket bolt(s). Tighten the bolt(s) to the torque listed in this Chapter's Specifications.

35  Reinstall the timing chain (see Section 11).

36  Lubricate the oil seal contact surface of the vibration damper hub with moly-base grease or clean engine oil, then install the damper on the end of the crankshaft. The keyway in the damper must be aligned with the Woodruff key in the crankshaft nose. If the damper cannot be seated by hand, slip the large washer over the bolt, install the bolt and tighten it to pull the damper into place. Tighten the bolt to the torque listed in this Chapter's Specifications.

37  Reinstall the remaining parts in the reverse order of removal.

38  Add coolant and check the oil level. Run the engine and check for oil and coolant leaks.

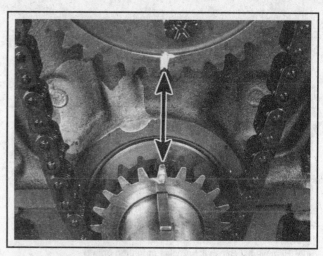

**12.33  Correctly aligned timing marks**

## 13  Valve lifters - removal, inspection and installation

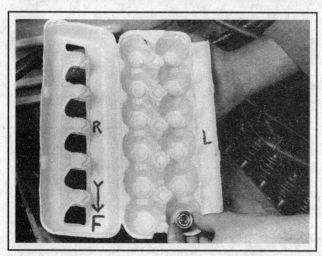

**13.4  Be sure to store the lifters in an organized manner to make sure they're reinstalled in their original locations**

**13.7a  If the bottom of any lifter is worn concave, scratched or galled, replace the entire set with the new ones**

### REMOVAL

▶ **Refer to illustration 13.4**

1  Remove the intake manifold (see Section 7).

2  Remove the rocker arms and pushrods (see Section 5).

3  There are several ways to extract the lifters from the bores. Special tools designed to grip and remove lifters are manufactured by many tool companies and are widely available, but may not be needed in every case. On newer engines without a lot of varnish buildup, the lifters can often be removed with a small magnet or even with your fingers. A machinist's scribe with a bent end can be used to pull the lifters out by positioning the point under the retainer ring in the top of each lifter.

### ❊❊ CAUTION:

**Don't use pliers to remove the lifters unless you intend to replace them with new ones (along with the camshaft). The pliers may damage the precision machined and hardened lifters, rendering them useless. On engines with a lot of sludge and varnish, work the lifters up and down, using carburetor cleaner spray to loosen the deposits.**

4  Before removing the lifters, arrange to store them in a clearly labeled box to ensure that they're reinstalled in their original locations (see illustration).

5  On engines equipped with roller lifters, the guide retainer and guide plates must be removed before the lifters are withdrawn. Remove the lifters and store them where they won't get dirty.

### INSPECTION

#### Conventional lifters

▶ **Refer to illustrations 13.7a and 13.7b**

6  Clean the lifters with solvent and dry them thoroughly without mixing them up.

7  Each lifter foot (the surface that rides on the cam lobe) must be

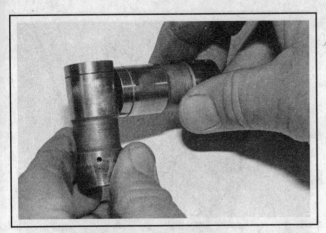

**13.7b  The foot of each lifter should be slightly convex - the side of another lifter can be used as a straightedge to check it; if it appears flat, it's worn and must be replaced**

**13.9  The roller on roller lifters must turn freely - check for wear and excessive play as well**

slightly convex, although this can be difficult to determine by eye. If the base of the lifter is concave (see illustrations), the lifters and camshaft must be replaced. If the lifter walls are damaged or worn (which is not very likely), inspect the lifter bores in the engine block as well. If the pushrod seats are worn, check the pushrod ends.

8   If new lifters are being installed, a new camshaft must also be installed. If a new camshaft is installed, then use new lifters as well. Never install used lifters unless the original camshaft is used and the lifters can be installed in their original locations.

### Roller lifters

♦ **Refer to illustration 13.9**

9   Check the rollers carefully for wear and damage and make sure they turn freely without excessive play (see illustration).
10   Check each lifter wall and pushrod seat for scuffing, score marks

and uneven wear.
11   Unlike conventional lifters, used roller lifters can be reinstalled with a new camshaft and the original camshaft can be used if new lifters are installed, provided the used parts are in good condition.

## INSTALLATION

12   Before installing the lifter(s) the air should be bled out of them as much a possible. Stand the lifter(s) upright in a container with enough oil to cover them. Use one of the pushrods to work the plunger to "prime" (fill with oil) the lifter and remove all the air.
13   The original lifters, if they're being reinstalled, must be returned to their original locations. Coat them with moly-base grease or engine assembly lube.
14   Install the lifters in the bores.
15   Install the guide plates and retainer (roller lifters only).
16   Install the pushrods and rocker arms.
17   Install the intake manifold and valve covers.
18   Reinstall the remaining parts in the reverse order of removal.

## 14  Camshaft - removal, inspection and installation

### CAMSHAFT LOBE LIFT CHECK

1   In order to determine the extent of cam lobe wear, the lobe lift should be checked prior to camshaft removal. Remove the valve covers (see Section 4).
2   Position the number one piston at TDC on the compression stroke (see Section 3).
3   Beginning with the number one cylinder, mount a dial indicator on the engine and position the plunger in-line with and resting on the first rocker arm (see illustration 12.5).
4   Zero the dial indicator, then very slowly turn the crankshaft in the normal direction of rotation until the indicator needle stops and begins to move in the opposite direction. The point at which it stops indicates maximum cam lobe lift.
5   Record this figure for future reference, then reposition the piston at TDC on the compression stroke.
6   Move the dial indicator to the remaining number one cylinder pushrod and repeat the check. Be sure to record the results for each valve.

7   Repeat the check for the remaining valves. Since each piston must be at TDC on the compression stroke for this procedure, work from cylinder-to-cylinder following the firing order sequence.
8   After the check is complete, compare the results to this Chapter's Specifications. If camshaft lobe lift is less than specified, cam lobe wear has occurred and a new camshaft should be installed.

### REMOVAL

♦ **Refer to illustrations 14.12a and 14.12b**

9   Refer to the appropriate Sections and remove the pushrods, the valve lifters and the timing chain and camshaft sprocket. The radiator should be removed as well (see Chapter 3). You also may have to remove the air conditioning condenser and the grille, but wait and see if the camshaft can be pulled out of the engine.
10   Check the camshaft endplay with a dial indicator. If it's greater than specified, replace the thrust plate with a new one when the camshaft is reinstalled.

**14.12a  Thread a long bolt into the camshaft sprocket bolt hole to use as a handle**

11  Remove the camshaft thrust plate bolts.

12  Thread a long bolt into the camshaft that can be used to pull the cam from the block and also provide leverage to support the cam so the lobes don't get nicked or gouged on the bearings as it's withdrawn (see illustrations).

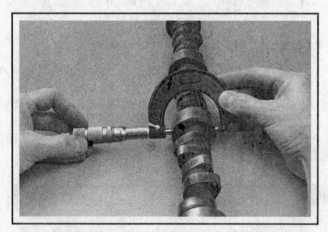

**14.14  Check the diameter of each camshaft bearing journal to pinpoint excessive wear and out-of-round conditions**

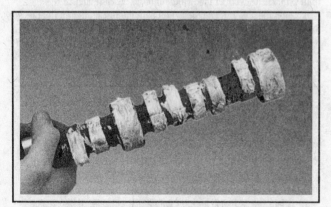

**14.17  Apply an engine assembly grease or camshaft installation lube to the camshaft lobes and journals prior to installation**

**14.12b Remove the camshaft carefully to avoid damaging the bearings (note that in this case the lifters aren't stored in a box because they will be discarded along with the camshaft)**

## INSPECTION

▶ **Refer to illustration 14.14**

13  After the camshaft has been removed from the engine, cleaned with solvent and dried, inspect the bearing journals for uneven wear, pitting and evidence of seizure. If the journals are damaged, the bearing inserts in the block are probably damaged as well. Both the camshaft and bearings will have to be replaced.

➡**Note: Camshaft bearing replacement requires special tools and expertise that make it a difficult job to do at home. However, the special tool required for bearing removal/installation is available at many stores that carry automotive tools, possibly even found at a tool rental company. It is advisable though, if the bearings are bad, that the engine be removed and the block taken to an automotive machine shop to ensure that the job is done correctly.**

14  Measure the bearing journals with a micrometer to determine if they are excessively worn or out-of-round (see illustration).

15  Check the camshaft lobes for heat discoloration, score marks, chipped areas, pitting and uneven wear. If the lobes are in good condition and if the lobe lift measurements are as specified in this Chapter, the camshaft can be reused.

## BEARING REPLACEMENT

16  Camshaft bearing replacement requires special tools and expertise that place it outside the scope of the home mechanic. Take the block to an automotive machine shop to ensure that the job is done correctly.

## INSTALLATION

▶ **Refer to illustration 14.17**

17  Lubricate the camshaft bearing journals and cam lobes with engine assembly grease or camshaft installation lube (see illustration).

18  Slide the camshaft into the engine. Support the cam near the block and be careful not to scrape or nick the bearings.

19  Apply moly-base grease or engine assembly lube to both sides

of the thrust plate, then position it on the block. Install the bolts and tighten them to the torque listed in this Chapter's Specifications.

20 Refer to the appropriate Sections and install the lifters, push-rods, rocker arms, timing chain/sprocket, timing chain cover and valve covers.

21 The remaining installation steps are the reverse of removal.

22 Before starting and running the engine, change the oil and install a new oil filter (see Chapter 1).

## 15 Oil pan - removal and installation

**✳✳ WARNING:**

**On models with air suspension, turn the air suspension switch to Off before raising the vehicle.**

## REMOVAL

▶ **Refer to illustrations 15.17 and 15.21**

1  Relieve the fuel system pressure (see Chapter 4). Disconnect the negative battery cable from the battery.

2  Remove the air cleaner assembly (see Chapter 4).

3  Remove the fan shroud mounting bolts and position the shroud back over the fan (see Chapter 3).

4  Remove the oil level dipstick and disconnect the oil level sensor switch on the side of the oil pan (if equipped).

5  If so equipped, remove the screws attaching the vacuum solenoids to the firewall behind the engine. Position the solenoids out of the way without disconnecting them.

6  Disconnect and lower the exhaust crossover pipe from the manifolds (see Section 8).

7  Carefully unbolt the exhaust pipe-to-catalytic converter connection (remember - it's already unbolted from the engine) and remove the exhaust pipe(s) section.

8  Drain the engine oil and remove the oil filter (see Chapter 1).

➡ **Note: If the vehicle being worked on has a dual-sump pan be sure to drain oil from both plugs before removing the pan.**

9  Disconnect the shift linkage where it goes from the body to the transmission (see Chapter 7).

10  Disconnect the transmission cooler lines at the radiator (see Chapter 3).

11  Remove the four torque converter cover retaining bolts and detach the cover.

12  Remove the starter motor (see Chapter 5).

13  Disconnect the fuel lines.

**✳✳ WARNING:**

**The pressure must be relieved at the Schrader valve on the fuel charging assembly before disconnecting fuel supply and return lines (see Chapter 4).**

14  Disconnect the steering flex coupling and remove the two bolts attaching the steering gear to the subframe (see Chapter 10). Let the steering gear rest on the subframe away from the oil pan.

15  Loosen the nuts holding the transmission mount to the crossmember, but don't remove them completely.

16  Remove the through bolts from the front engine mounts. Place a block of wood under the oil pan and lift the engine slightly with a jack.

**✳✳ CAUTION:**

**When raising the engine on models with an automatic transmission, watch the clearance between the transmission dipstick tube and the Thermactor downstream air tube going to the catalytic converter. If the tubes contact before adequate mount-to-sub frame clearance is achieved, lower the engine and remove the dipstick tube and downstream air tube.**

15.17 Place a block of wood between the mount and subframe

15.21 Slip the oil pan out, turning it slightly to clear the driveplate

17  Place wooden blocks between the mounts and sub frame (see illustration).

18  Remove the oil pan mounting bolts. Most models are equipped with a reinforcement strip on each side of the pan which may come loose as the bolts are removed.

19  Carefully separate the pan from the block. Don't pry between the block and pan or damage to the sealing surfaces may result and oil leaks could develop. Instead, dislodge the pan with a large rubber mallet or a block of wood and a hammer.

20  Reach in and remove the oil pump pick-up tube fasteners (see Section 16) and allow the pick-up to drop into the oil pan (the pan can't be removed with it bolted to the block - there's not enough room).

21  Rotate the crankshaft as required for clearance and remove the oil pan from the vehicle (see illustration).

## INSTALLATION

▶ Refer to illustration 15.22

➡Note: Several different oil pan gasket configurations are found on engines covered by this manual. Early model engines are equipped with rubber seals at the rear main bearing cap and timing chain cover, while conventional gaskets are used to seal the sides of the pan. Later model engines use a one-piece oil pan gasket. RTV is needed at the junctions of engine components regardless of the style of gasket being used. Be sure to follow the installation instructions included with an OEM or aftermarket gasket set - they supersede the information included here.

22 Remove the gasket(s) using a gasket scraper or putty knife, if necessary. Remove all traces of old gasket material and sealant from the pan and block (see illustration).

23 Clean the mating surfaces with lacquer thinner or acetone. Make sure the bolt holes in the block are clean.

24 Check the oil pan flange for distortion, particularly around the bolt holes. If necessary, place the pan on a block of wood and use a hammer to flatten and restore the gasket surface.

25 On the four-piece style gasket, remove the old rubber seals from the rear main bearing cap and timing chain cover, then clean the grooves and install new seals. Use RTV sealant or gasket contact adhesive to hold the new seals in place, then apply a bead of RTV sealant to the block-to-seal junctions. Use the contact adhesive to attach the new gaskets to the block.

26 Install the oil pump pick-up tube along with the pan. Tighten the pick-up tube bolts to the torque listed in this Chapter's Specifications.

27 Carefully position the pan against the block and install the bolts

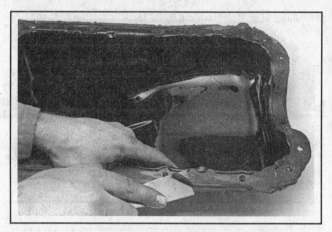

**15.22 Scrape away all traces of gasket material and sealant, then clean the gasket surfaces with lacquer thinner or acetone**

finger tight (don't forget the reinforcement strips, if used). Make sure the seal(s)/gasket(s) haven't shifted, then tighten the bolts in three steps to the torque listed in this Chapter's Specifications. Start at the center of the pan and work out toward the ends in a spiral pattern.

28 The remaining steps are the reverse of removal.

⁂ **CAUTION:**

**Don't forget to refill the engine with oil and replace the filter before starting it (see Chapter 1).**

29 Start the engine and check carefully for oil leaks at the oil pan.

## 16 Oil pump - removal and installation

▶ Refer to illustrations 16.2 and 16.3

⁂ **WARNING:**

**On models with air suspension, turn the air suspension switch to Off before raising the vehicle.**

1 Unbolt and lower the oil pan (see Section 15).

2 Remove the oil pick-up tube-to-main bearing cap nut (see illustration).

3 Remove the oil pump pick-up tube mounting bolts (see illustration).

4 Remove the oil pump mounting bolts and lower the oil pump

**16.2 Remove the nut (arrow) . . .**

**16.3 . . . and the two bolts to detach the oil pick-up tube**

assembly into the oil pan. Lift them all out together. If the pump is faulty, or you suspect that it's faulty, install a new one - do not attempt to repair the original.

5   Prime the oil pump prior to installation. Pour clean oil into the pick-up and turn the pump shaft by hand.

6   If you separate the pump from the pick-up tube, use a new gasket

and tighten the bolts securely when reattaching them.

7   As the pump is reinstalled, fit the oil pump driveshaft into the pump. It must seat all the way. DO NOT try to force it. If it doesn't align, turn the pump slightly and try again.

8   Install the mounting bolts/nut and tighten them to the torque listed in this Chapter's Specifications.

## 17  Driveplate - removal and installation

### ✳✳ WARNING:

**On models with air suspension, turn the air suspension switch to Off before raising the vehicle.**

1   Disconnect the negative battery cable from the battery.

2   Raise the vehicle and support it securely on jackstands, then refer to Chapter 7 and remove the transmission. If it's leaking, now would be a very good time to have the front pump seal/O-ring replaced.

3   Look for factory paint marks that indicate driveplate-to-crankshaft alignment. If they aren't there, use paint or a center-punch to make alignment marks on the driveplate and crankshaft to ensure correct alignment during reinstallation.

4   Remove the bolts that secure the driveplate to the crankshaft. If the crankshaft turns, wedge a screwdriver through the starter opening to jam the driveplate.

5   Remove the driveplate from the crankshaft. Since the driveplate is

fairly heavy, be sure to support it while removing the last bolt.

6   Clean the driveplate to remove grease and oil. Check for cracked and broken ring gear teeth. Lay the driveplate on a flat surface and use a straightedge to check for warpage.

7   Clean and inspect the mating surfaces of the driveplate and the crankshaft. If the crankshaft rear seal is leaking, replace it before reinstalling the driveplate.

8   Position the driveplate against the crankshaft. Be sure to align the marks made during removal. Note that some engines have an alignment dowel or staggered bolt holes to ensure correct installation. Before installing the bolts, apply sealant with Teflon to the threads.

9   Wedge a screwdriver through the starter motor opening to keep the driveplate from turning as you tighten the bolts to the torque listed in this Chapter's Specifications.

10  The remainder of installation is the reverse of the removal procedure.

## 18  Crankshaft oil seals - replacement

### FRONT SEAL

#### Timing chain cover in place

▶ **Refer to illustrations 18.5 and 18.7**

1   Remove the bolts attaching the fan shroud to the radiator and position the shroud back over the fan.

2   Remove the fan/clutch assembly and the shroud (Chapter 3).

3   Remove the drivebelts (see Chapter 1).

4   Remove the bolt from the front of the crankshaft, then use a puller to detach the vibration damper (see Section 10).

### ✳✳ CAUTION:

**Don't use a puller with jaws that grip the outer edge of the damper. The puller must be the type shown in the illustration that utilizes bolts to apply force to the damper hub only. Clean the crankshaft nose and the seal contact surface on the vibration damper with lacquer thinner or acetone. Leave the Woodruff key in place in the crankshaft keyway.**

5   The crankshaft front oil seal can be removed with the use of a special tool such as the one the manufacturer uses or it can be removed from the cover with the careful use of a small chisel and hammer (see illustration). Be careful not to damage the cover or scratch the wall of the seal bore. If the engine has accumulated a lot of miles, apply penetrating oil to the seal-to-cover joint and allow it to soak in before

**18.5  A small chisel and hammer can be used to work the seal out of the timing chain cover - be very careful not to damage the cover or nick the crankshaft!**

attempting to remove the seal.

6   Check the seal bore and crankshaft, as well as the seal contact surface on the vibration damper for nicks and burrs. Position the new seal in the bore with the open end of the seal facing IN. A small amount of oil applied to the outer edge of the new seal will make installation easier.

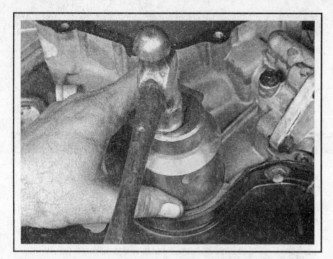

**18.7  You can drive the seal squarely into the opening with a large socket and a hammer - don't damage the seal in the process and make sure it's completely seated**

**18.17  If you're very careful not to damage the crankshaft or the seal bore, the rear seal can be pried out with a screwdriver**

7  The seal can be reinstalled in either of two ways. Either use a special tool such as the one used by the manufacturer or the seal can be driven into the bore with a large socket and hammer until it's completely seated (see illustration). Select a socket that's the same outside diameter as the seal (a section of pipe can be used if a socket isn't available).

8  **Note: If a new vibration damper is being installed, balance pins must be located in the new damper in the same relative positions as the original. Also, the pulley must be attached to the damper with the same orientation to the pins as on the original. Apply clean engine oil to the seal contact surface of the vibration damper and coat the keyway (groove) with a thin layer of RTV sealant.**

9  Install the damper on the end of the crankshaft. The keyway in the damper bore must be aligned with the Woodruff key in the crankshaft nose. If the damper can't be seated by hand, tap it into place with a soft-face hammer or slip a large washer over the bolt, install the bolt and tighten it to push the damper into place. Remove the large washer, then install the bolt and tighten it to the torque listed in this Chapter's Specifications.

10  Install the remaining parts removed for access to the seal.

11  Start the engine and check for leaks at the seal-to-cover joint.

## Timing chain cover removed

12  Remove the timing chain cover (see Section 11).

13  Use a punch or screwdriver and hammer to drive the seal out of the cover from the back side. Support the cover as close to the seal bore as possible. Be careful not to distort the cover or scratch the wall of the seal bore. If the engine has accumulated a lot of miles, apply penetrating oil to the seal-to-cover joint on each side and allow it to soak in before attempting to drive the seal out.

14  Clean the bore to remove any old seal material and corrosion. Support the cover on blocks of wood and position the new seal in the bore with the open end of the seal facing IN. A small amount of oil applied to the outer edge of the new seal will make installation easier.

15  Drive the seal into the bore with a large socket and hammer until it's completely seated. Select a socket that's the same outside diameter as the seal (a section of pipe can be used if a socket isn't available).

## REAR MAIN OIL SEAL

▶ **Refer to illustrations 18.17 and 18.19**

16  Refer to Chapter 7 and remove the transmission, then detach the driveplate and the rear cover plate from the engine (see Section 17).

17  The old seal can be removed by prying it out with a screwdriver (see illustration). Be sure to note how far it is recessed into the bore before removing it; the new seal will have to be recessed an equal amount.

**✳✳ CAUTION:**

**Be very careful not to scratch or otherwise damage the crankshaft or the bore in the housing or oil leaks could develop!**

18  Clean the crankshaft and seal bore with lacquer thinner or acetone. Check the seal contact surface very carefully for scratches and nicks that could damage the new seal lip and cause oil leaks.

**✳✳ CAUTION:**

**If the crankshaft is damaged, the only alternative is a new or different crankshaft.**

19  Make sure the bore is clean, then apply a thin coat of engine oil to the outer edge of the new seal. Apply moly-based grease to the seal lips. The seal must be pressed squarely into the bore, so hammering it into place is not recommended. If you don't have access to the special tool used for this purpose, you may be able to tap the seal in with a large section of pipe and a hammer. If you must use this method, be very careful not to damage the seal or crankshaft! And work the seal lip carefully over the end of the crankshaft with a blunt tool such as the rounded end of a socket extension.

20  Reinstall the engine rear cover plate, the driveplate and the transmission.

## 19  Engine mounts - check and replacement

1  Engine mounts seldom require attention, but broken or deteriorated mounts should be replaced immediately or the added strain placed on the driveline components may cause damage or wear.

### CHECK

2  During the check, the engine must be raised slightly to remove the weight from the mounts.

3  Raise the vehicle and support it securely on jackstands, then position a jack under the engine oil pan. Place a large block of wood between the jack head and the oil pan, then carefully raise the engine just enough to take the weight off the mounts.

4  Check the mounts to see if the rubber is cracked, hardened or separated from the metal plates. Sometimes the rubber will split right down the center.

5  Check for relative movement between the mount plates and the engine or frame (use a large screwdriver or prybar to attempt to move the mounts). If movement is noted, lower the engine and tighten the mount fasteners.

6  Rubber preservative should be applied to the mounts to slow deterioration.

### REPLACEMENT

7  Disconnect the negative battery cable from the battery, then raise the vehicle and support it securely on jackstands (if not already done).

8  Remove the nut to disconnect the mount from the frame. Disconnect the automatic transmission shift linkage (see Chapter 7).

9  Raise the engine slightly with a jack or hoist (make sure the fan doesn't hit the radiator or shroud). Remove the mount-to-block bolts and detach the mount.

10  Installation is the reverse of removal. Use thread locking compound on the mount bolts and tighten them to the torque listed in this Chapter's Specifications.

## Specifications

### General

| | |
|---|---|
| Displacement | 5.0 liters (302 cubic inches) |
| Bore and stroke | 4.00 inches x 3.00 inches |
| Cylinder numbers (front to rear) | |
|    Right side | 1-2-3-4 |
|    Left (driver's) side | 5-6-7-8 |
| Firing order | 1-5-4-2-6-3-7-8 |

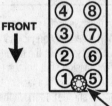

Cylinder locations and distributor rotation diagram (5.0L engine)

36012-spec2A HAYNES

### Camshaft

| | |
|---|---|
| Lobe lift | |
|    Intake | 0.2375 inch |
|    Exhaust | 0.2474 inch |
| Theoretical valve lift @ zero lash | |
|    Intake | 0.3776 inch |
|    Exhaust | 0.3934 inch |
| Endplay | |
|    Standard | 0.0005 to 0.0055 inch |
|    Service limit | 0.009 inch |
| Journal diameter | |
|    No. 1 | 2.0805 to 2.0815 inches |
|    No. 2 | 2.0655 to 2.0665 inches |
|    No. 3 | 2.0505 to 2.0515 inches |
|    No. 4 | 2.0355 to 2.0365 inches |
|    No. 5 | 2.0205 to 2.0215 inches |
| Out-of-round limit | 0.0005 inch (total indicator reading) |
| Runout limit | 0.005 inch (total indicator reading) |
| Bearing inside diameter | |
|    No. 1 | 2.0825 to 2.0835 inches |
|    No. 2 | 2.0675 to 2.0685 inches |
|    No. 3 | 2.0525 to 2.0535 inches |
|    No. 4 | 2.0375 to 2.0385 inches |
|    No. 5 | 2.0225 to 2.0235 inches |
| Journal-to-bearing (oil) clearance | |
|    Standard | 0.001 to 0.003 inch |
|    Service limit | 0.006 inch |
| Camshaft gear backlash | 0.006 to 0.011 inch |
| Front bearing location | 0.005 to 0.020 inch below front face of block |

## Oil pump

| | |
|---|---|
| Relief valve spring tension (Lbs @ specified length) | 10.6 to 12.2 @ 1.704 inches |
| Oil pressure | |
| Hot at 2000 rpm | 40 to 60 psi |
| Normal operating temperature at curb idle | 6 to 8 psi |

## Timing chain

| | |
|---|---|
| Timing chain deflection | 1/2 inch maximum |

## Valve train

| | |
|---|---|
| Valve face angle | 44 degrees |
| Valve head diameter | |
| Intake | 1.770 to 1.794 inches |
| Exhaust | 1.453 to 1.468 inches |
| Valve guide bore diameter | 0.3433 to 0.3443 inch |
| Valve stem-to-guide clearance | |
| Intake | 0.0010 to 0.0027 inch |
| Exhaust | 0.0015 to 0.0032 inch |
| Service limit | 0.0055 inch |
| Valve stem-to-rocker arm clearance (collapsed lifter) | |
| Desired | 0.096 to 0.146 inch |
| Allowable | 0.071 to 0.171 inch |
| Valve stem diameter - standard | |
| Intake | 0.3416 to 0.3423 inch |
| Exhaust | 0.3411 to 0.3418 inch |
| Out of square | 5/64 inch |
| Free length | |
| Intake | 2.04 inches |
| Exhaust | 1.88 inches |
| Compression pressure (Lbs @ specified spring height) | |
| Intake | 74 to 82 @ 1.78 inches - 194 to 214 @ 1.36 inches |
| Exhaust | 76 to 84 @ 1.60 inches - 190 to 210 @ 1.20 inches |
| Assembled height | |
| Intake | 1.75 to 1.80 inches |
| Exhaust | 1.58 to 1.65 inches |
| Rocker arm ratio | 1.59 : 1 |

## Torque specifications — Ft-lbs (unless otherwise indicated)

➡ Note: One foot-pound (ft-lb) of torque is equivalent to 12 inch-pounds (in-lbs) of torque. Torque values below approximately 15 ft-lbs are expressed in inch-pounds, since most foot-pound torque wrenches are not accurate at these smaller values.

| | |
|---|---|
| Camshaft sprocket bolt | 40 to 45 |
| Camshaft thrust plate-to-engine block bolts | 108 to 144 in-lbs |
| Cylinder head bolts (in sequence - see illustration 9.22) | |
| Step 1 | 55 to 65 |
| Step 2 | 65 to 72 |
| Drivebelt pulley-to-vibration damper bolts | 35 to 50 |
| Engine mount-to-frame bolts | 26 to 38 |
| Engine mount through bolts | 40 to 46 |
| Exhaust manifold bolts | 18 to 24 |

## Torque specifications (continued)    Ft-lbs (unless otherwise indicated)

→ **Note: One foot-pound (ft-lb) of torque is equivalent to 12 inch-pounds (in-lbs) of torque. Torque values below approximately 15 ft-lbs are expressed in inch-pounds, since most foot-pound torque wrenches are not accurate at these smaller values.**

| | |
|---|---|
| Flywheel/driveplate mounting bolts | 75 to 85 |
| Intake manifold-to-cylinder head bolts | 23 to 25* |
| Oil filter insert-to-engine block adapter bolt | 20 to 30 |
| Oil pan drain plug | 15 to 25 |
| Oil pan mounting bolts | 72 to 108 in-lbs |
| Oil pick-up tube-to-main bearing cap nut | 22 to 32 |
| Oil pick-up tube-to-oil pump bolts | 12 to 18 |
| Oil pump mounting bolts | 22 to 32 |
| Rocker arm fulcrum bolts | 18 to 25 |
| Timing chain cover bolts | 12 to 18 |
| Valve cover bolts | |
|     1990 and earlier | 72 to 108 in-lbs |
|     1991 | 144 to 180 in-lbs |
| Vibration damper-to-crankshaft bolt | 70 to 90 |

**\* After assembly, re-tighten to the specified torque with the engine hot**

## Section

## Reference to other Chapters

2B

4.6L V8 ENGINE

## 1   General information

This Part of Chapter 2 is devoted to in-vehicle repair procedures for the 4.6L Single Overhead Cam (OHC) V8 engine. All information concerning engine removal and installation and engine block and cylinder head overhaul can be found in Part C of this Chapter.

The following repair procedures are based on the assumption that the engine is installed in the vehicle. If the engine has been removed from the vehicle and mounted on a stand, many of the steps outlined in this Part of Chapter 2 will not apply.

The Specifications included in this Part of Chapter 2 apply only to the procedures contained in this Part. Part C of Chapter 2 contains the Specifications necessary for cylinder head and engine block rebuilding.

## 2   Repair operations possible with the engine in the vehicle

Many major repair operations can be accomplished without removing the engine from the vehicle.

If possible, clean the engine compartment and the exterior of the engine with some type of pressure washer before any work is started. It will make the job easier and help keep dirt out of the internal areas of the engine.

It may help to remove the hood to improve access to the engine as repairs are performed (refer to Chapter 11 if necessary).

If vacuum, exhaust, oil or coolant leaks develop, indicating a need for gasket or seal replacement, the repairs can generally be made with the engine in the vehicle. The intake and exhaust manifold gaskets, timing cover gasket, oil pan gasket, crankshaft oil seals and cylinder head gaskets are all accessible with the engine in place.

Exterior engine components, such as the intake and exhaust manifolds, the oil pan, the water pump, the starter motor, the alternator and the fuel system components can be removed for repair with the engine in place.

Since the cylinder heads can be removed without pulling the engine, valve component servicing can also be accomplished with the engine in the vehicle. Replacement of the timing chain and sprockets and oil pump is also possible with the engine in the vehicle.

In extreme cases caused by a lack of necessary equipment, repair or replacement of piston rings, pistons, connecting rods and rod bearings is also possible with the engine in the vehicle. However, this practice is not recommended because of the cleaning and preparation work that must be done to the components involved.

## 3   Top Dead Center (TDC) for number one piston - locating

▶ **Refer to illustration 3.1**

Refer to Chapter 2, Part A for the TDC locating procedure, but use the illustration provided with this Section for the appropriate reference marks and the following exceptions:

a) *Disable the ignition system by disconnecting the primary electrical connectors at the ignition coil pack/modules (see Chapter 5). Also, disable the fuel pump (see Chapter 4, Section 2).*

b) *Install a compression gauge in the number one spark plug hole. Turn the crankshaft clockwise with a socket and breaker bar as described in Chapter 2, Part A.*

c) *When the piston approaches TDC, pressure will register on the gauge. Continue turning the crankshaft until the notch in the crankshaft damper is aligned with the TDC mark on the front cover (see illustration). At this point number one cylinder is at TDC on the compression stroke.*

**3.1 When placing the engine at Top Dead Center (TDC), be sure to align the notch in the crankshaft damper (arrow) with the correct indicator on the timing chain cover**

## 4   Valve covers - removal and installation

### REMOVAL

▶ **Refer to illustrations 4.2, 4.5, 4.7a, 4.7b and 4.10**

1   Disconnect the cable from the negative battery terminal.

2   Note their locations, then detach the spark plug wire clips from the rocker arm cover studs (see illustration).

3   Detach the spark plug boots and wires from the plugs (see Chapter 1). Position the wires out of the way.

4   Disconnect the hose from the breather fitting on the left valve cover (see illustration 4.2).

5   Remove the PCV valve from the right valve cover (see illustration).

6   Remove the left (driver's side) DIS module by removing the two

**4.2  Remove the spark plug wires and clips from the valve cover studs (arrows) and remove the breather hose from the fitting (arrow)**

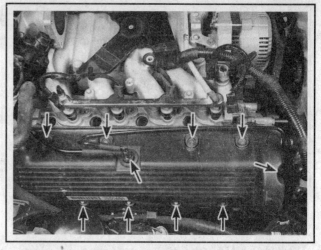

**4.5  The valve cover can be removed after removing the PCV valve and the bolts around the perimeter**

nuts and one bolt that hold it to the timing chain cover (see Chapter 5). This will provide enough clearance for the valve cover to be moved forward, as it is lifted, for removal.

7   Remove the three bolts attaching the wiper module support bracket and remove the bracket (see illustrations).

8   Remove the valve cover bolts (see illustration 4.5).

9   Remove the right valve cover from the cylinder head.

➡Note: If the cover is stuck to the head, bump one end with a wood block and a hammer to jar it loose. If that doesn't work, try to slip a flexible putty knife between the head and cover to break the gasket seal. Don't pry at the cover-to-head joint or damage to the sealing surfaces may occur (leading to oil leaks in the future). Some valve covers are made of plastic - be extra careful when tapping or pulling on them.

10  To remove the left valve cover, LIGHTLY pry up the wiper module (see illustration). Lift the valve cover over the camshaft and off the cylinder head.

➡Note: The fuel lines running over the left valve cover DO NOT have to be disconnected for the valve to be removed.

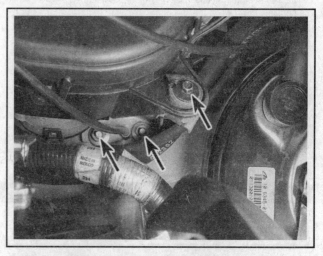

**4.7a  Remove three attaching bolts (arrows) . . .**

**4.7b  . . . and remove the wiper module support bracket**

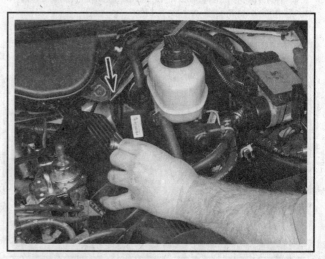

**4.10  By prying up very slightly on the wiper module, the valve cover on the driver's side can be removed from the cylinder head**

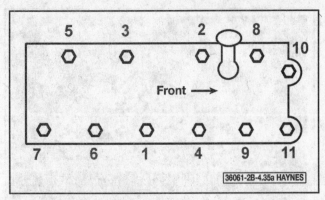

**4.15a** Valve cover bolt tightening sequence on the right side valve cover on 1998 and later models

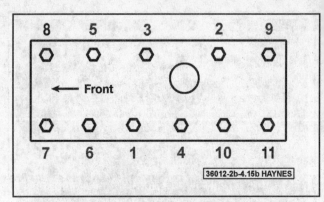

**4.15b** Valve cover bolt tightening sequence on the left side valve cover on 1998 and later models

## INSTALLATION

▶ **Refer to illustrations 4.15a and 4.15b**

11 The mating surfaces of each cylinder head and valve cover must be perfectly clean when the covers are installed. Remove all traces of sealant, and clean the mating surfaces with lacquer thinner or acetone. If there's sealant or oil on the mating surfaces when the cover is installed, oil leaks may develop.

12 Clean the mounting stud threads with a die to remove any corrosion and restore damaged threads. Apply a small amount of light oil to the stud threads.

13 The gaskets should be mated to the covers before the covers are installed. Make sure the gasket is pushed all the way into the groove in the valve cover.

14 Carefully position the cover on the head and install the nuts.

15 Tighten the nuts in two steps to the torque listed in this Chapter's Specifications. Wait two minutes between the first and the second round of tightening.

※※ **CAUTION:**

**Be careful with plastic valve covers, don't over tighten the bolts!**

➡**Note: On 1998 and later models, tighten the valve cover bolts, using the correct sequence, to the torque listed in this Chapter's Specifications (see illustrations).**

16 The remaining installation steps are the reverse of removal.

17 Start the engine and check for oil leaks as the engine warms up.

---

**5   Crankshaft pulley/vibration damper - removal and installation**

## REMOVAL

▶ **Refer to illustration 5.4**

1 Remove the bolts attaching the fan shroud to the radiator and position the shroud back over the fan (see Chapter 3).

2 Remove the fan/clutch assembly and the shroud (see Chapter 3).

3 Remove the accessory drivebelt (see Chapter 1).

4 Remove the bolt from the front of the crankshaft, and using a suitable puller, detach the vibration damper (see illustration). Leave the Woodruff key in place in the crankshaft keyway.

※※ **CAUTION:**

**Don't use a puller with jaws that grip the outer edge of the damper. The puller must be the type shown in the illustration that utilizes bolts to apply force to the damper hub only.**

**5.4** After the bolt has been removed, use a puller that bolts to the damper to remove the damper from the end of the crankshaft

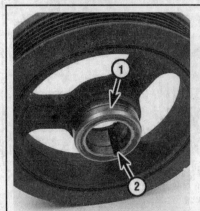

**5.5 Inspect the damper for signs of damage or excessive wear**

*1   Oil seal surface*
*2   Woodruff keyway*

## INSTALLATION

▶ **Refer to illustration 5.5**

5   Lubricate the oil seal contact surface of the vibration damper hub (see illustration) with moly-base grease or clean engine oil. Apply a silicone based sealer to the crankshaft keyway before installing the damper.

6   Install the damper on the end of the crankshaft. The keyway in the damper must be aligned with the Woodruff key in the crankshaft nose. If the damper cannot be seated by hand, slip the large washer over the bolt, install the bolt and tighten it to pull the damper into place. Tighten the bolt to the torque listed in this Chapter's Specifications.

7   The remaining installation steps are the reverse of removal.

8   Check the oil level. Run the engine and check for oil leaks.

## 6   Timing chain cover - removal and installation

### ✳✳ WARNING:

**On models with air suspension, turn the air suspension switch to Off before raising the vehicle.**

## REMOVAL

▶ **Refer to illustrations 6.5, 6.6 and 6.7**

1   Disconnect the cable from the negative battery terminal.

2   Drain the engine oil and remove the oil filter (see Chapter 1).

3   Remove the drive belt and the water pump pulley. Remove the crankshaft pulley/vibration damper (see Section 5).

4   Disconnect the electrical connector to the camshaft sensor. Disconnect the electrical connector to the crankshaft sensor. Disconnect, unbolt and remove both ignition coil packs (one is attached to each side of the timing chain cover) (see Chapter 5).

5   Remove the bolts securing the power steering pump to the engine.

➡ **Note: The front lower bolt on the power steering pump will not come all the way out.**

Position the pump aside and secure it out of the way. Remove the accessory drivebelt idler from the timing chain cover (see illustration) to gain access to one of the cover bolts.

6   Remove both valve covers (see Section 4). Remove the timing chain cover-to-block bolts.

➡ **Note: Be sure to remove the four oil pan-to-timing chain cover bolts from underneath.**

**6.5  Remove the bolt (arrow) and accessory drivebelt idler pulley from the timing chain cover**

7   Separate the timing chain cover from the block (see illustration). If it's stuck, tap it gently with a soft-face hammer just enough to break the gasket's bond.

### ✳✳ CAUTION:

**DO NOT use excessive force or you may crack the cover. If the cover is difficult to remove, double check to make sure all of the bolts have been removed.**

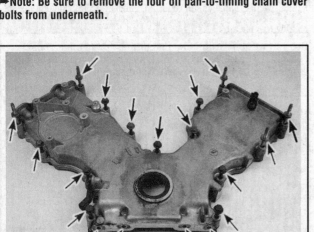

**6.6  There are nineteen bolts to be removed (note the locations of special studded bolts) before the timing chain cover can be removed**

**6.7  Separate the timing chain cover from the engine, using a soft-faced hammer if necessary to break the gasket seal**

## INSTALLATION

▶ **Refer to illustration 6.10**

8    Apply a 1/8-inch bead of RTV sealant to the junctions of the oil pan, timing chain cover and engine block.

9    Lubricate the timing chains and the lip of the front crankshaft oil seal with clean engine oil.

10   Install the front cover on the engine. Tighten the cover-to-block bolts to the torque listed in this Chapter's Specifications (see illliustration).

11   Install the remaining parts in the reverse order of removal.

12   Add the proper type and quantity of engine oil (see Chapter 1). Run the engine and check for leaks.

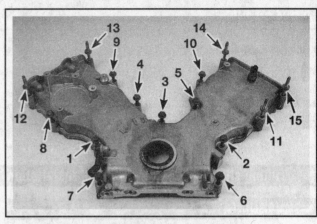

**6.10  Timing chain cover bolt tightening sequence for 1999 and later models**

---

## 7    Timing chains, tensioners and sprockets - inspection, removal and installation

### ✳ WARNING:

**On models with air suspension, turn the air suspension switch to Off before raising the vehicle.**

### ✳ CAUTION:

**At no time, once the timing chain(s) have been removed, can the crankshaft or the camshafts be rotated. If moved, damage to the valves and/or pistons can occur. Special tools are necessary to prevent the camshafts from moving when the timing chain is removed.**

➡Note: Because this engine is not a "freewheeling" engine, if it has "jumped time," there will be damage to the valves and/or pistons and will require removal of the cylinder heads.

### REMOVAL

▶ **Refer to illustrations 7.3, 7.5, 7.6a, 7.6b, 7.7 and 7.9**

### ✳ CAUTION:

**The timing system is complex. Severe engine damage will occur if you make any mistakes. Do not attempt this procedure unless you are highly experienced with this type of repair. If you are at all unsure of your abilities, consult an expert. Double-check all your work and be sure everything is correct before you attempt to start the engine.**

1    Disconnect the cable from the negative battery terminal.

2    Because of the interference design of these engines, the rocker arms must be removed before the timing chains and camshafts are removed. This will be accomplished in two stages. In the first stage, certain valve springs on the designated cylinders must be compressed and the rocker arms removed from the cylinder head to prevent any valve-to-piston contact during the repair procedure. Position the number one cylinder on the TDC number 1 position. Use the special tool to compress the valve springs and remove the rocker arms from cylinders

with the camshaft lobes up (closed valves) on Bank 1 and Bank 2. In the second stage, the engine will be rotated 360-degrees to remove the rocker arms from the remaining cylinders.

3    Stage 1: Position the engine at TDC number 1 (see Section 3). Remove the rocker arms from the cylinders with the closed valves. The camshaft lobes will be located away from valve contact (up position). Use a special valve spring compressing tool (see illustration). Compress the springs and remove the rocker arms.

### ✳ CAUTION:

**Do not allow the valve spring keepers to fall off the valve stems or the valves will release and drop down into the cylinders.**

4    Stage 2: Rotate the engine 360-degrees CLOCKWISE. Remove the rocker arms from the remaining cylinders using the special valve spring compressing tool. Compress the springs and remove the rocker arms. The rocker arms must be reinstalled with the same camshaft lobe that they were originally removed from. Label and store all components

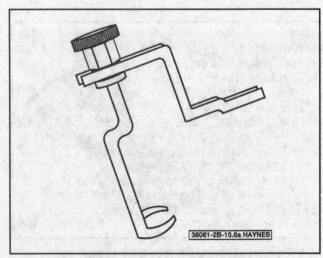

**7.3  Use a special tool to compress the valve springs and remove the rocker arms**

**7.5  The crankshaft sensor tooth wheel has a specific direction to be installed, look for the word "rear" stamped into the gear (arrow)**

**7.6a  This tool slips over the end of the crankshaft and engages with the dowel pin on the right side of the engine**

**7.6b  The special camshaft locking tools attach to the camshaft and cylinder head and prevent the camshafts from rotating - note that some models attach the tool into the notch at the rear of the camshaft**

to avoid confusion during reassembly. Rotate the engine 360 degrees CLOCKWISE back to the TDC number 1 position.

5   Remove the timing chain cover (see Section 6). Remove the crankshaft position sensor toothed wheel (see illustration) by sliding it off the crankshaft nose. Be sure to note the stamped word "rear" to be sure it is reinstalled in the correct position.

6   Install the appropriate camshaft holding tools (see illustration). The tool locks the camshaft from moving in either direction when the timing chain(s) are removed.

> ※ **CAUTION:**
>
> **The camshaft(s) MUST be kept at TDC. Any movement will cause the valve timing to be off when the timing chain(s) are reinstalled. This mis-alignment will cause severe problems when the engine is started.**

In 1991 the camshaft holding tool is installed on the "flats" of the camshaft (located at the center of the cam, between the two camshaft cluster caps). On 1992 and later models, the holding tool is installed into the rear of the camshaft and holds the cam in place by locking into the specially shaped hole in the rear of the camshaft (see illustration). This will prevent any movement of the camshafts in either direction, due to valve spring pressure, when the timing chains are removed.

7   Remove the right side timing chain tensioner(see illustration).

8   Remove the right timing chain from the crankshaft and camshaft sprockets.

9   Remove the right side stationary guide (see illustration).

10  Remove the left side timing chain tensioner. Remove the chain from the crankshaft and camshaft sprockets.

11  Remove the left side stationary guide.

12  If necessary, remove the crankshaft sprockets, camshaft sprockets and camshaft sprocket spacers, noting the position of each sprocket so it may be reinstalled in its original location. The camshaft sprockets should only be removed from the camshafts if replacement of one of the components is necessary.

**7.7  To remove the timing chain tensioner from the block, remove the two bolts from the tensioner (arrow) and detach the guide assembly from the dowel at the opposite end**

**7.9  The stationary chain guide is removed by removing the two bolts at the mount plate (arrow) and detaching the guide from the dowel at the opposite end**

**7.14a To fully retract the tensioner, release the plunger lock (arrow) and push the plunger into the tensioner body**

**7.14b Check the tensioner oil feed hole (arrow) to be sure it's not plugged by debris**

**7.17 When installing the timing chain, align one of the bright links in the timing chain with the dimple on the camshaft (arrows)**

## INSPECTION

▶ **Refer to illustrations 7.14a and 7.14b**

13 Inspect the individual sprocket teeth and keyways for wear and damage. Check the chain for cracked plates, pitted or worn rollers. Check the plastic surface of the chain guides for wear and damage. Replace any excessively worn or defective parts with new ones.

### ❊❊ CAUTION:

**If excessive plastic material is missing from the chain guides, the oil pan should be removed and cleaned of all debris. Check the oil pick-up tube and screen. Replace the assembly if it is clogged.**

14 Check the tensioner for proper operation:

a) *Release the plunger lock (see illustration) and make sure the piston moves freely.*

b) *Submerge the tensioner in a can of oil or solvent, remove from the fluid and depress the plunger to make sure the oil feed oil is not plugged (see illustration).*

➡**Note: Also inspect the oil feed hole in the block to be certain it's not plugged.**

## INSTALLATION

▶ **Refer to illustrations 7.17, 7.19 and 7.22**

### ❊❊ CAUTION:

**Before starting the engine, carefully rotate the crankshaft by hand through at least two full revolutions (use a socket and breaker bar on the crankshaft pulley centerbolt). If you feel any resistance, STOP! There is something wrong - most likely, valves are contacting the pistons. You must find the problem before proceeding. Check your work and see if any updated repair information is available.**

15 Install the stationary chain guides, for both sides, and tighten the bolts to the torque listed in this Chapter's Specifications.

16 If removed, install the crankshaft sprockets. Place the left chain crankshaft sprocket on the crankshaft with the beveled hub of the sprocket facing forward. Place the right chain sprocket on the crankshaft with the beveled hub facing towards the engine. When the two sprockets are placed correctly the hubs will be facing each other and there will be the maximum space possible between the two sprockets. The timing marks on each sprocket will also align.

17 Install the left timing chain on the camshaft sprocket, aligning the bright link with the dimple (see illustration). Loop the timing chain under the crankshaft sprocket and align the bright link with the alignment mark on the crankshaft sprocket. The timing marks on the crankshaft sprockets should be in the 6-o'clock position (see illustration 7.22).

18 Install the cam sprocket and chain on the camshaft. Install the camshaft sprocket bolt and, holding the camshaft stationary, tighten the bolt to the torque listed in this Chapter's Specifications. Install the right chain and sprocket in the same manner. Verify that all timing marks are in alignment (see illustration 7.22).

19 The steps for installing the timing chain tensioner/guide are the same for both sides, either side can be done first. Before assembling the tensioner with the chain guide, compress the tensioner and lock it in this position with a paper clip, Allen wrench or drill bit (see illustration).

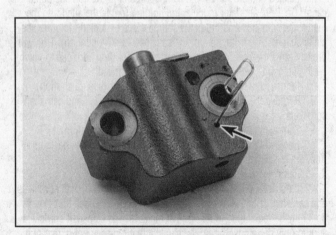

**7.19 Lock the timing chain tensioner in the fully retracted position by placing a paper clip into the hole in the tensioner body (arrow)**

20 Install the tensioner and guide assembly to the block in the retracted position. Tighten the bolts to the torque listed in this Chapter's Specifications.

21 Remove the paper clip and apply pressure against the tensioner chain guide so the tensioner fully extends against the chain guide and all slack is removed from the chain.

22 Recheck all the timing marks to make sure they are still in alignment (see illustration).

23 Slowly rotate the crankshaft in the normal direction of rotation (clockwise) at least two revolutions and again bring the engine to TDC. If you feel any resistance, stop and find out why. Check all alignment marks to verify that everything is properly assembled.

24 The remainder of installation is the reverse of removal.

7.22 Once everything is assembled, recheck all the timing chain alignment points to be certain they are properly aligned

## 8 Camshaft(s) - removal, inspection and installation

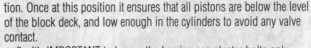

▶ Refer to illustration 8.4

1 Remove the valve cover(s) (see Section 4).

2 Remove the timing chain(s), camshaft sprocket(s) and spacers (see Section 6).

### ✳✳ CAUTION:

Don't mix up the gears, they are marked, as RB (right bank and LB (left bank), and must go back on the same camshaft.

3 Measure the thrust clearance (endplay) of the camshaft(s) with a dial indicator. If the clearance is greater than the value listed in this Chapter's Specifications, replace the camshaft and/or the cylinder head.

4 There are two camshaft cap clusters, for each camshaft. The configuration of the two cap clusters are different and must be placed in their original locations. Mark the camshaft cap clusters with a front and rear indication, for both the left and right cylinder heads.

➡ Note: Two bolts used on one of the camshaft cap clusters are different than the others (see illustration), be sure they go back in the same locations on reassembly.

5 Before removing the camshaft caps and camshafts, rotate the crankshaft 45-degrees counterclockwise (as you are facing the engine) from TDC. This will place the crankshaft keyway in the 9 'o-clock posi-

tion. Once at this position it ensures that all pistons are below the level of the block deck, and low enough in the cylinders to avoid any valve contact.

6 It's IMPORTANT to loosen the bearing cap cluster bolts only 1/4-turn at a time, following the reverse sequence of the tightening procedure (see illustration 8.16), until they can be removed by hand.

7 Remove the two cap clusters and lift the camshaft off the cylinder head. Don't mix up the camshafts or any of the components. They must all go back on the same positions, and on the same cylinder head they were removed from.

8 Repeat this procedure for removal of the other camshaft.

## INSPECTION

▶ Refer to illustrations 8.9a, 8.9b, 8.10a, 8.10b, 8.10c, 8.11a, 8.11b and 8.13

9 Visually examine the cam lobes and bearing journals for score marks, pitting, galling and evidence of overheating (blue, discolored areas). Look for flaking of the hardened surface of each lobe (see illustrations).

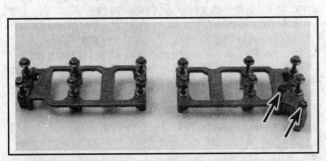

8.4 Each camshaft has two camshaft cap clusters, rather than individual bearing caps, that hold the camshaft in place on the cylinder head. Note the position of the bolts (arrows)

8.9a Areas to look for excessive wear or damage on the camshafts are; the bearing surfaces and the camshaft lobes (arrows)

**8.9b** Inspect the bearing surfaces of the camshaft cap clusters (arrow) for signs of excessive wear, damage or overheating

**8.10a** Measuring the camshaft bearing journal diameter

**8.10b** Measure the camshaft lobe at its greatest dimension . . .

**8.10c** . . . and subtract the camshaft lobe diameter at its smallest dimension to obtain the lobe lift specification

**8.11a** Lay a strip of Plastigage on each of the camshaft journals

**8.11b** Compare the width of the crushed Plastigage to the scale on the envelope to determine the oil clearance

10 Using a micrometer, measure the diameter of each camshaft journal and the lift of each camshaft lobe (see illustrations). Compare your measurements with the Specifications listed at the end of this Chapter, and if the diameter of any one of these is less than specified, replace the camshaft.

11 Check the oil clearance for each camshaft journal as follows:

a) *Clean the bearing surfaces and the camshaft journals with lacquer thinner or acetone.*

b) *Carefully lay the camshaft(s) in place in the head. Don't install the lifters and don't use any lubrication.*

c) *Lay a strip of Plastigage on each journal (see illustration).*

d) *Install the camshaft cap clusters.*

e) *Tighten the cluster cap bolts, a little at a time, to the torque listed in this Chapter's Specifications.*

→ **Note: Don't turn the camshaft while the Plastigage is in place.**

f) *Remove the bolts and detach the caps.*

g) *Compare the width of the crushed Plastigage (at its widest point) to the scale on the Plastigage envelope (see illustration).*

h) *If the clearance is greater than specified, and the diameter of any journal is less than specified, replace the camshaft. If the journal diameters are within specifications but the oil clearance is too great, the cylinder head is worn and must be replaced.*

12 Scrape off the Plastigage with your fingernail or the edge of a

credit card - don't scratch or nick the journals or bearing surfaces.

13 Finally, be sure to check the timing chain tensioner oil feed tube and reservoir (see illustration) before installing the cam cap cluster. it must be absolutely clean and free of all obstructions or it will affect the operation of the timing chain tensioner.

## INSTALLATION

▶ **Refer to illustration 8.16**

14 If the lash adjusters and/or camshaft followers have been removed, install them in their original locations (see Section 9).

15 Apply moly-base grease or camshaft installation lube to the camshaft lobes and bearing journals, then install the camshaft(s).

16 Install the camshaft cap clusters in the correct locations, and following the correct bolt tightening sequence (see illustration), tighten the bolts in 1/4 turn increments to the torque listed in this Chapter's Specifications.

17 Rotate the crankshaft 45-degrees clockwise, to bring it back to top dead center (TDC) before reinstalling the timing chain(s).

18 Install the camshaft sprockets, timing chain(s), tensioners and timing chain cover (see Section 7).

19 The remainder of installation is the reverse of the removal procedure.

**8.13 Oil is delivered to the timing chain tensioner by a feed tube and reservoir in the cylinder head**

| 1 | Tensioner oil feed tube | 2 | Reservoir |

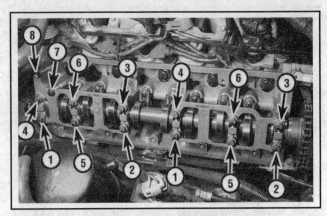

**8.16 The camshaft cap cluster bolt tightening sequence, notice that each cap is tightened separately and has its own sequence**

## 9 Valve lash adjusters and roller cam followers - removal, inspection and installation

There are two methods described in this Section. The method recommended by the manufacturer accomplishes the removal of the camshaft roller followers without the removal of the camshaft(s). Although it does require the use of two special tools specified by the manufacturer; a valve spring spacer (T91P-6565-AH) and a valve spring compressor (T91P-6565-A) which are made specifically for the overhead cam engine. The valve spring compressor uses the camshaft as a pivot point and, with a ratchet attached, pushes down on the spring to release tension on the cam follower. The spring spacer keeps the spring from collapsing too far and hitting the valve stem seal. The alternative method requires the removal of the camshaft (see Section 8) in order to remove the cam followers. Either method will achieve the same results, but it is much easier using the manufacturers recommended procedure, if the correct tools can be located.

## REMOVAL

1  Remove the valve cover(s) (see Section 4).
2  Position the cylinder being serviced so that the cam followers are on the base of each camshaft lobe. Install valve spring compressor (tool no. T91P-6565-A) and valve spring spacer (tool no. T91P-6565-AH). If the spacer isn't in place between one of the valve coils, the spring can be compressed to far and damage the valve seal will result.

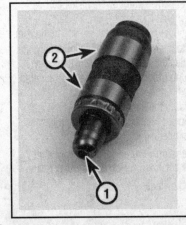

**9.8 Inspect the lash adjuster for signs of excessive wear or damage, such as pitting, scoring or signs of overheating (bluing or discoloration), where the tip contacts the camshaft follower (1) and the side surfaces that contact the lifter bore in the cylinder head (2)**

3  Compress the spring and remove the camshaft roller follower. Camshaft roller followers and hydraulic lash adjusters, MUST be reinstalled with the same camshaft lobe that they were removed from. Label and store all components to avoid confusion during reassembly.
4  Remove the hydraulic lash adjuster(s). If there are many miles on the vehicle, the adjusters may have become varnished and difficult to remove. Apply a little penetrating oil around the lash adjuster to help loosen the varnish.

### Alternative procedure

5  Remove the camshaft (see Section 8).
6  Lift the camshaft roller followers from the head. Camshaft roller followers and hydraulic lash adjusters, MUST be reinstalled with the same camshaft lobe that they were removed from. Label and store all components to avoid confusion during reassembly.
7  Remove the hydraulic lash adjusters

## INSPECTION

◆ **Refer to illustrations 9.8 and 9.10**

8  Inspect each adjuster carefully for signs of wear or damage. The areas of possible wear are the ball tip that contacts the cam follower and the sides of the adjuster that contacts the bore in the cylinder head (see illustration). Since the lash adjusters frequently become clogged as mileage increases, we recommend replacing them if you're concerned about their condition or if the engine is exhibiting valve "tapping" noises.
9  A thin wire or paper clip can be placed in the oil hole to move the plunger and make sure it's not stuck.

➡**Note: The lash adjuster must have no more than 1.5mm of total plunger travel. It's recommended that if replacement of any of the adjusters is necessary, that the entire set be replaced. This will avoid the need to repeat the repair procedure as the others require replacement in the future.**

10  Inspect the roller cam follower for signs of wear or damage. The areas of wear are the ball socket that contacts the lash adjuster and the roller where the follower contacts the camshaft (see illustration).

## INSTALLATION

11 Before installing the lash adjuster(s) as much air as possible should be bled out of them. Stand the adjuster(s) upright in a container of oil. Use a thin wire or paper clip to work the plunger up and down. This "primes" the adjuster and removes most of the air. Leave the adjusters in the oil until ready to install.

12 Lubricate the valve stem tip, roller follower and the lash adjuster bore with clean engine oil.

13 Install the lash adjuster(s) and roller cam follower(s).

14 The remainder of installation is the reverse of the removal procedures.

15 When re-starting the engine after replacing the adjusters, the adjusters will normally make some "tapping" noises, until all the air is bled from the lash adjusters. After the engine is warmed-up, raise the speed from idle to 3,000 rpm for one minute. Stop the engine and let it cool down. All of the noise should be gone when it is restarted.

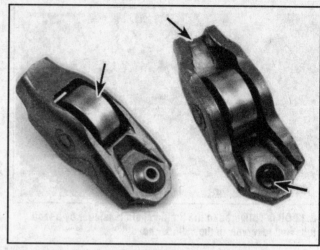

**9.10 Check the roller surface (arrow) and the areas where the valve stem and lash adjuster contact the camshaft follower (arrows) for signs of excessive wear or damage, such as pitting, scoring or signs of overheating (bluing or discoloration)**

## 10 Valve springs, retainers and seals - replacement

Broken valve springs and/or defective valve stem seals can be replaced without removing the cylinder heads. There are two methods described in this Section. The method recommended by the manufacturer accomplishes the removal of the valve springs and seals without the removal of the camshafts. Although it does require the use of two special tools specified by the manufacturer; a valve spring spacer (T91P-6565-AH) and a valve spring compressor (T91P-6565-A) which are made specifically for the overhead cam engine. The valve spring compressor uses the camshaft as a pivot point and, with a ratchet attached, pushes down on the spring to release tension on the cam follower. The spring spacer keeps the spring from collapsing too far and hitting the valve stem seal. The alternative method uses a more commonly available tool, but will require the removal of the camshaft (see Section 8) in order to remove the valve spring. Either method will achieve the same results, but it is much easier using the manufacturers recommended procedure, if the correct tools can be located.

In either repair procedure, a compressed air source is normally required to perform this operation, so read through this Section carefully and rent or buy the tools before beginning the job. If compressed air isn't available, a length of nylon rope can be used to keep the valves from falling into the cylinder during this procedure.

## REMOVAL

▶ **Refer to illustration 10.4**

1 Remove the valve cover (see Section 4).

2 Remove the spark plug from the cylinder with the defective component. If all of the valve stem seals are being replaced, remove all the spark plugs.

3 Turn the crankshaft until the piston in the affected cylinder is at Top Dead Center (TDC) on the compression stroke (see Section 3). If

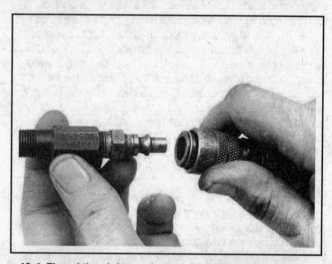

**10.4 Thread the air hose adapter into the spark plug hole - adapters are commonly available from auto parts stores**

you're replacing all of the valve stem seals, begin with cylinder number one and work on the valves for one cylinder at a time. Move from cylinder-to-cylinder following the firing order sequence (see this Chapter's Specifications).

4 Thread an air hose adapter into the spark plug hole (see illustration) and connect an air hose from a compressed air source to it. Most auto parts stores can supply the air hose adapter.

➡**Note: Many cylinder compression gauges utilize a screw-in fitting that may work with your air hose quick-disconnect fitting.**

5 Apply compressed air to the cylinder.

**10.13  Installation of a valve spring compressor more commonly available at local automotive parts stores (note the camshaft must be removed for the use of this type of valve spring compressor)**

### ✳✳ WARNING:

**The piston may be forced down by compressed air, causing the crankshaft to turn suddenly. If the wrench used when positioning the number one piston at TDC is still attached to the bolt in the crankshaft nose, it could cause damage or injury when the crankshaft moves.**

6   The valves should be held in place by the air pressure.

7   If you don't have access to compressed air, an alternative method can be used. Position the piston at a point a few degrees before TDC on the compression stroke, then feed a long piece of nylon rope through the spark plug hole until it fills the combustion chamber. Be sure to leave the end of the rope hanging out of the engine so it can be removed easily. Use a large ratchet and socket to rotate the crankshaft in the normal direction of rotation until slight resistance is felt.

8   Stuff shop rags into the cylinder head holes above and below the valves to prevent parts and tools from falling into the engine.

9   Install valve spring compressor (tool no. T91P-6565-A) and valve spring spacer (tool no. T91P-6565-AH).

**10.16  Use pliers, of any type, to firmly grasp the old seal and pull it off the valve guide**

**10.14  Once the spring is compressed remove the keepers with a needle nose pliers or a magnet, as shown here**

### ✳✳ CAUTION:

**If the spacer isn't in place between one of the valve coils, the spring can be compressed to far and damage the valve seal.**

10   Compress the spring and remove the camshaft roller follower. Camshaft roller followers and hydraulic lash adjusters, MUST be reinstalled with the same camshaft lobe that they were removed from. Label and store all components to avoid confusion during reassembly.

11   Keeping the spring compressed remove the keepers with small needle-nose pliers or a magnet (see illustration 10.14). Remove the spring retainer and valve spring. Remove the valve stem seal (see illustration 10.16). If air pressure fails to hold the valve in the closed position during this operation, the valve face and/or seat is probably damaged. If so, the cylinder head will have to be removed for additional repair operations.

### Alternative procedure

▶ **Refer to illustrations 10.13, 10.14 and 10.16**

12   Remove the camshaft and roller followers (see Section 8).

13   Install the valve spring compressor (see illustration).

14   Compress the spring and remove the keepers with small needle-nose pliers or a magnet (see illustration).

15   Remove the spring retainer and valve spring.

16   Remove the stem seal (see illustration). If air pressure is being used, and it fails to hold the valve in the closed position during this operation, the valve face and/or seat is probably damaged. If so, the cylinder head will have to be removed for additional repair operations.

### INSTALLATION

▶ **Refer to illustrations, 10.21a, 10.21b and 10.23**

17   Wrap a rubber band or tape around the top of the valve stem so the valve won't fall into the combustion chamber, then release the air pressure. If rope was used instead of air pressure, turn the crankshaft slightly in the direction opposite normal rotation.

18   Inspect the valve stem for damage. Rotate the valve in the guide and check the end for eccentric movement, which would indicate that the valve is bent.

19   Move the valve up-and-down in the guide and make sure it

**10.21a  The valve stem seals used on the OHC engines combines a seal with the valve spring seat**

**10.21b  A deep socket that fits over the seal can be used to gently tap the seal into place**

**10.23  Apply a small dab of grease to each keeper as shown here before installation - it'll hold them in place on the valve stem as the spring is released**

doesn't bind. If the valve stem binds, either the valve is bent or the guide is damaged. In either case, the head will have to be removed for repair.

20  Reapply air pressure to the cylinder to retain the valve in the closed position, then remove the tape or rubber band from the valve stem. If a rope was used instead of air pressure, rotate the crankshaft in the normal direction of rotation until slight resistance is felt.

21  Lubricate the valve stem with engine oil and install a new seal (see illustration). There is a special tool for the installation of the valve seal. If the tool isn't available, a socket that will fit over the seal make and contact with the seat (see illustration), can be used to carefully tap the new seal into place.

### ❊❊ CAUTION:

**The valve seal used on the OHC engine is a combination seal and spring seat. Never place a valve spring directly against the aluminum head, the hardened spring would damage the cylinder head.**

22  Install the spring in position over the valve.

23  Install the valve spring retainer. Compress the valve spring and carefully position the keepers in the groove. Apply a small dab of grease to the inside of each keeper to hold it in place if necessary (see illustration).

24  Remove the pressure from the spring tool and make sure the keepers are seated.

25  Disconnect the air hose and remove the adapter from the spark plug hole. If a rope was used in place of air pressure, pull it out of the cylinder.

26  If the camshaft(s) were removed, reinstall them at this time (see Section 8).

27  Install the spark plug(s) and connect the wire(s).

28  The remaining installation steps are the reverse of removal.

29  Start and run the engine, then check for oil leaks and unusual sounds coming from the valve cover area.

## 11  Intake manifold - removal and installation

➡**Note: Removal and installation of the intake manifold on the 1996 and newer models is the same as on previous years. The only difference is that it is manufactured of plastic instead of aluminum and the throttle body is now attached to a throttle body spacer that is attached to the center of the intake manifold.**

### REMOVAL

◆ **Refer to illustration 11.10, 11.16 and 11.23**

1  Relieve the fuel system pressure. Disconnect the cable from the negative battery terminal.

2  Drain the cooling system and remove the drivebelt (see Chapter 1.)

3  Disconnect the radiator, heater and water pump bypass hoses from the water outlet (see Chapter 3).

4  Remove the thermostat housing (see Chapter 3). The thermostat housing bolts also retain the intake manifold.

5  Remove the air inlet tube.

6  Label and disconnect the intake manifold vacuum lines.

7  Remove the PCV and canister purge hoses from the valve covers (see Section 4).

8  Disconnect the accelerator cable, automatic transmission cable and speed control linkage (if so equipped).

9  Disconnect the ignition wire brackets, boots and wires and set them out of the way.

10  Remove the two bolts holding the alternator to the intake manifold (see illustration).

11  Disconnect the alternator electrical connectors and remove the alternator (see Chapter 5).

**11.10  Remove the two bolts attaching the alternator bracket to the intake manifold (arrows)**

**11.16  Separate the wire loom bracket from the intake manifold extension**

12  Disconnect both ignition coils (see Chapter 5).

13  Disconnect the electrical connectors from the ignition coils and camshaft sensor, coolant temperature sending unit, air charge temperature sensor, throttle positioner, idle speed control solenoid, EGR sensors, fuel injectors and fuel charging assembly (see Chapter 5).

14  Remove the 42-pin engine harness electrical connector from the retainer bracket on the vacuum brake booster and disconnect it from the main electrical harness.

15  Remove the throttle body (see Chapter 4).

16  Separate the wire loom bracket from the intake manifold extension, at the rear of the manifold (see illustration).

17  Raise the vehicle with a jack and place it securely on jack stands.

18  Disconnect the EGR tube from the right exhaust manifold (see Chapter 4).

19  Disconnect the electrical connector at the oil pressure sending unit (see Chapter 2, Part C).

20  Lower the vehicle and position the harness out of the way.

21  Disconnect the fuel supply and return lines (see Chapter 4).

22  Loosen the lower intake manifold bolts and nuts in 1/4-turn increments, following the reverse order of the tightening sequence (see illustration 11.30), until they can be removed by hand. The injectors

and fuel rails can be left on the intake manifold during removal.

23  Lift the lower intake manifold from the cylinder heads (see illustration). The manifold may be stuck to the cylinder heads and force may be required to break the gasket seal. A prybar can be used to pry up the manifold, but make sure all bolts and nuts have been removed first!

### ✳✳ CAUTION:

The cylinder heads and the intake manifold (1988 through 1995) are aluminum. The intake manifold on 1996 models is plastic. Don't pry between the block and manifold or the cylinder heads or damage to the gasket sealing surface may occur, leading to vacuum and oil leaks. Pry only at the manifold casting protrusion.

24  Remove the intake manifold gaskets and clean all traces of gasket or sealant material from the sealing surfaces of the cylinder heads and intake manifold.

## INSTALLATION

▶ Refer to illustrations 11.30a, 11.30b, and 11.30c

### ✳✳ CAUTION:

The mating surfaces of the cylinder heads, block and manifold must be perfectly clean when the manifold is installed. Gasket removal solvents in aerosol cans are available at most auto parts stores and may be helpful when removing old gasket material that's stuck to the heads and manifold. Since the cylinder heads are aluminum and the intake manifold is aluminum or plastic, aggressive scraping can cause damage! Be sure to follow directions printed on the container.

25  If the manifold was disassembled, reassemble it or if being replaced, transfer all components to the new intake manifold. Use electrically conductive sealant on the temperature sending unit threads. Use a new EGR valve gasket.

26  Use a gasket scraper to remove all traces of sealant and old gasket material, then clean the mating surfaces with lacquer thinner or acetone. If there's old sealant or oil on the mating surfaces when the manifold is installed, oil or vacuum leaks may develop. When working

**11.23  Make sure there is nothing else attached to the manifold (fuel injector rails and injectors can stay on the intake) and remove the manifold from the engine**

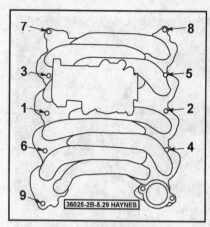

**11.30a Intake manifold bolt tightening sequence on 1995 and earlier models**

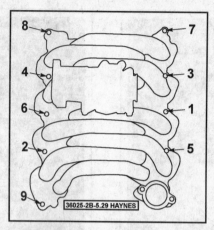

**11.30b Intake manifold bolt tightening sequence on 1996 through 2002 models**

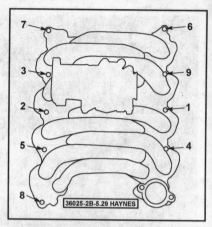

**11.30c Intake manifold bolt tightening sequence on 2003 and later models**

on the heads and block, cover the open engine areas with shop rags to keep debris out of the engine. Use a vacuum cleaner to remove any gasket material that falls into the intake ports in the heads.

27  Use a tap of the correct size to chase the threads in the bolt holes, then use compressed air (if available) to remove the debris from the holes.

### ❊❊ WARNING:

**Wear safety glasses or a face shield to protect your eyes when using compressed air!**

Remove excessive carbon deposits and corrosion from the exhaust and coolant passages in the heads and manifold.

28  Install the gaskets on the cylinder heads. Make sure all alignment tabs, intake port openings, coolant passage holes and bolt holes are aligned correctly.

29  Carefully set the manifold in place. Don't disturb the gaskets and don't move the manifold fore-and-aft after it contacts the gaskets on the block.

30  Install the nine intake manifold bolts and, following the correct tightening sequence (see illustrations), tighten them to the torque listed in this Chapter's Specifications. Replace the O-ring seal on the thermostat housing. Install the thermostat housing and tighten the bolts to the torque listed in Chapter 3 Specifications

31  The remaining installation steps are the reverse of removal. Start the engine and check carefully for oil and coolant leaks at the intake manifold joints.

## 12  Exhaust manifolds - removal and installation

### ❊❊ WARNING:

**On models with air suspension, turn the air suspension switch to Off before raising the vehicle.**

### REMOVAL

▶ **Refer to illustrations 12.4a, 12.4b and 12.8**

1  Disconnect the cable from the negative battery terminal.

2  Raise the vehicle and support it securely on jackstands.

3  Working under the vehicle, apply penetrating oil to the exhaust pipe-to-manifold studs and nuts (they're usually corroded or rusty).

4  Remove the nuts holding the exhaust pipe(s) to the manifold(s) (see illustrations). In extreme cases you may have to heat them with a propane or acetylene torch in order to loosen them.

➡**Note: There is very little room to get at the lower row of exhaust manifold bolts from the top, although it's possible. It's easier to remove the bolts from underneath at the same time that the exhaust pipes are being separated from the manifolds.**

5  Disconnect the EGR tube connector from the right side manifold

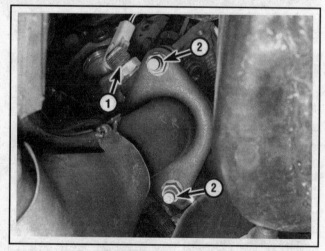

**12.4a On the right side exhaust manifold disconnect the EGR pipe (1) and remove the two manifold-to-exhaust pipe nuts (2)**

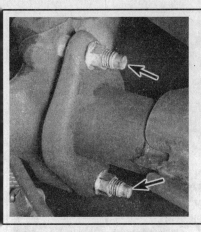

**12.4b** On the left side, only the two exhaust manifold-to-exhaust pipe nuts need to be removed (arrows)

(see illustration 12.4a).

6   Remove the through bolts for the engine mounts (see Section 18).

7   Slowly raise the engine with a floor jack, using a piece of wood between the jack and the oil pan, until the fan just touches the fan shroud.

### ✳ CAUTION:

**Since none of the coolant, air conditioning and power steering hoses or other connections are being separated from the engine, be careful that nothing is being pulled or stretched to tightly. Areas to watch for are; the wiper module at the left rear valve cover, the cooling fan and shroud and the fuel lines at the manifold connections.**

8   Remove the left side engine mount from the block (see illustration), if necessary, to get to all the manifold bolts. It isn't necessary to remove the right side engine mount.

9   Remove the exhaust manifold(s)-to-cylinder head bolts (see illustration 12.8) and separate the manifold(s) from the cylinder head(s).

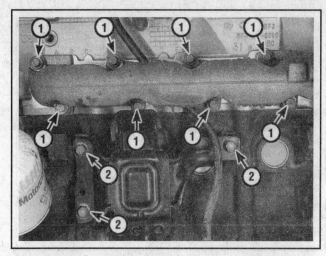

**12.8  The engine mount on the left side may have to be removed to be able to get to all the lower exhaust manifold bolts**

1   Exhaust manifold-to-cylinder head bolts

2   Engine mount-to-block bolts

## INSTALLATION

10  Check the manifold for cracks and make sure the bolt threads are clean and undamaged. The manifold and cylinder head mating surfaces must be clean before the manifolds are reinstalled - use a gasket scraper to remove all carbon deposits.

11  Position the manifold on the head and install the mounting bolts.

12  When tightening the mounting bolts, work from the center to the ends and be sure to use a torque wrench. Tighten the bolts in three equal steps to the torque listed in this Chapter's Specifications.

13  The remaining installation steps are the reverse of removal.

14  Start the engine and check for exhaust leaks.

## 13  Cylinder heads - removal and installation

### ✳ CAUTION 1:

**These engines are difficult to work on and require special tools. On any procedures involving timing chains, camshafts or cylinder head removal, the steps must be read carefully and disassembly must proceed using the special tools otherwise damage to the engine could result.**

### ✳ CAUTION 2:

**The engine must be completely cool when the cylinder heads are removed. Failure to allow the engine to cool off could result in cylinder head warpage.**

### ✳ CAUTION 3:

**The manufacturer states that the cylinder head on 2001 and later models cannot be machined in the event of warping. If the cylinder head warpage exceeds 0.001 inch, replace the cylinder head.**

## REMOVAL

▶ **Refer to illustrations 13.6, 13.7, 13.8, 13.11 and 13.12**

1   Disconnect the cable from the negative battery terminal. Remove the valve cover(s) (see Section 4).

2   Remove the intake manifold (see Section 11).

3   Remove the timing chain cover (see Section 7).

4   Remove the timing chains (see Section 7).

### ✳ CAUTION:

**Use the required camshaft holding fixture to lock the camshafts in place. Leave the holding fixtures in place until after the reassembly is complete.**

5   Separate the exhaust manifold-to-exhaust pipe(s) (see Section 12).

6   Detach the positive battery cable bracket at the rear of the cylinder head (see illustration).

**13.6 Loosen the bolt on the back of the right cylinder head and slip the battery cable bracket (arrow) up and off the cylinder head**

7   Loosen the nut and slide the positive battery cable bracket up and off the stud on the right side of the cylinder head (see illustration)

8   At the rear of the right cylinder head remove the ground strap (see illustration).

9   Disconnect the heater hose at the pipe fastened at the rear of the right side cylinder head. The pipe can remain attached to the head during removal.

10   Remove the exhaust manifold(s), if desired (see Section 12).

➡**Note: Even though the exhaust manifold adds extra weight to the removal of the cylinder head, the difficulty of getting at the bolts to remove the manifold makes leaving the manifold attached to the head during removal easier than separating the manifold from the head while in the vehicle.**

11   Remove the head bolts by loosening them 1/4 turn at a time (see illustration), following the reverse of the tightening sequence (see illustration 13.21a) until they can be removed by hand. The lower rear head bolt on the right cylinder head, once loosened, cannot be removed because of the location of the heater/air conditioning case. Use a rubber band to hold the bolt out of the block during cylinder head removal. Discard the head bolts - new bolts MUST be used when reinstalling the head(s).

**13.8 At the back of the right cylinder head, remove nut and disconnect the ground strap**

**13.7 Loosen the bolt on the side of the right cylinder head and slip the battery cable bracket (arrow) up and off the cylinder head and set the cable out of the way for cylinder head removal**

12   Lift the head(s) off the engine (see illustration). If resistance is felt, DO NOT pry between the head and block as damage to the mating surfaces will result. To dislodge the head, place a wood block against the end and strike the wood block with a hammer. Store the heads on wood blocks to prevent damage to the gasket sealing surfaces.

13   Remove the old head gasket(s). Before removing, note which gasket goes on which side, they are different and cannot be interchanged.

14   Cylinder head disassembly and inspection procedures are covered in detail in Chapter 2, Part C.

## INSTALLATION

◆ **Refer to illustrations 13.18, 13.19, 13.21a, 13.21b and 13.21c**

15   The mating surfaces of the cylinder heads and block must be perfectly clean when the heads are installed. Use a gasket scraper to remove all traces of carbon and old gasket material, then clean the mating surfaces with lacquer thinner or acetone. If there's oil on the mating surfaces when the heads are installed, the gaskets may not seal

**13.11 Use a breaker bar and deep socket to loosen the cylinder head bolts, 1/4 turn at a time until they can be removed by hand (head bolts CANNOT be reused)**

**13.12  Lift the cylinder head from the block, it may be necessary to break the gasket bond by placing a wood block on the head and striking it with a hammer (DO NOT pry between the head and the cylinder block)**

correctly and leaks may develop. When working on the block, cover the open areas of the engine with shop rags to keep debris out during repair and reassembly. Use a vacuum cleaner to remove any debris that falls into the cylinders.

**13.19  Position the gaskets on the correct cylinder banks, push them down over the alignment dowels**

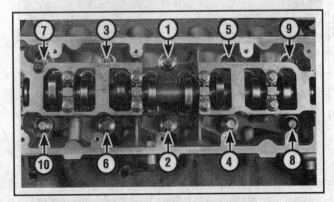

**13.21a  Cylinder head bolt tightening sequence**

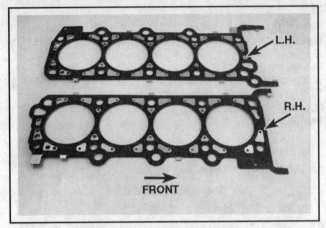

**13.18  Identify the left and right cylinder head gaskets, the shapes are different and cannot be interchanged**

16  Check the block and head mating surfaces for nicks, deep scratches and other damage. If damage is slight, it can be removed with a file - if it's excessive, machining may be the only alternative.

17  Use a tap of the correct size to chase the threads in the head bolt holes. Dirt, corrosion, sealant and damaged threads will affect torque readings.

18  Make sure the new gaskets are on the correct cylinder banks (see illustration). They are not interchangeable.

19  Position the new gasket(s) over the alignment dowels (see illustration) in the block.

20  Before placing the cylinder heads back on the block, rotate the crankshaft counterclockwise, as you are facing the engine, so the keyway is in the 9 o'clock position.

**✳✳ CAUTION:**

**If the crankshaft isn't placed in the position described, damage will occur to either pistons and/or valve train parts.**

21  Carefully position the head(s) on the block without disturbing the gasket(s). Install the NEW head bolts and follow the recommended sequence (see illustration) and tighten the bolts, in three steps, as listed in this Chapter's Specifications. Mark a stripe on each of the head bolts (see illustrations). This will help keep track of the bolts that have been

**13.21b  By marking each head bolt with a stripe (arrow) . .**

turned the additional 90 degrees.

**Note:** The method used for the head bolt tightening procedure is referred to as "torque-angle" or "torque-to-yield" method. The first tightening sequence will be to a specified torque. The second and third tightening steps use a torque-angle, which uses a predetermined angle, such as an additional 85 to 95-degrees, to get the correct bolt stretch. This has been shown to give a more uniform clamping load for better head gasket sealing.

22 The remaining installation steps are the reverse of removal.

23 Change the engine oil and filter (see Chapter 1), then start the engine and check carefully for oil and coolant leaks.

**13.21c** . . .it will be easier to keep track of the head bolts that have had the additional turn (arrows)

## 14 Oil pan - removal and installation

**✳✳ WARNING:**

On models with air suspension, turn the air suspension switch to Off before raising the vehicle.

### REMOVAL

▶ **Refer to illustrations 14.4, 14.5, 14.8, 14.9, 14.15, 14.17a and 14.17b**

1 Disconnect the cable from the negative battery terminal.
2 Drain the engine oil and remove the oil filter (see Chapter 1).
3 Disconnect the exhaust pipe from the manifolds (see Section 12).
4 Support the exhaust pipe, with a length of mechanics wire, just ahead of the catalytic converters, at the H-pipe section of the exhaust pipes (see illustration).
5 Disconnect and remove the section of exhaust pipe between the manifolds and converters (see illustration).

**✳✳ WARNING:**

When the bolts are removed, the exhaust pipe section will fall out if not supported. Be prepared to handle and remove the pipe before the bolts are taken out.

6 Remove the fan shroud mounting bolts and position the shroud back over the fan.
7 Remove the starter motor (see Chapter 5).
8 Remove the reinforcement bracket on both right and left sides of the engine block and remove the transmission line bracket bolt (see illustration).
9 Loosen the nuts holding the transmission mount to the crossmember, but don't remove them completely (see illustration). This will allow the engine/transmission assembly to be moved up, providing clearance for oil pan removal.
10 Remove the through bolts from the front engine mounts (see Section 18).

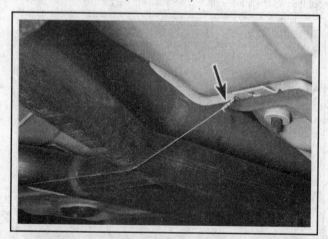

**14.4 Support the exhaust pipes, just ahead of the catalytic converters at the H-pipe, with a length of mechanics wire (arrow)**

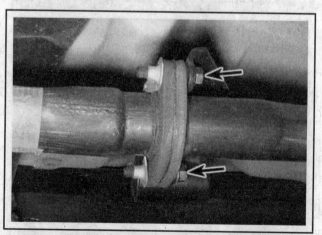

**14.5 Remove the two bolts (arrows) that connect the two exhaust pipe sections, and remove the front exhaust section from the under the vehicle**

**14.8 Remove the reinforcement brackets from each side of the block (1), and remove the transmission line bracket bolt (2)**

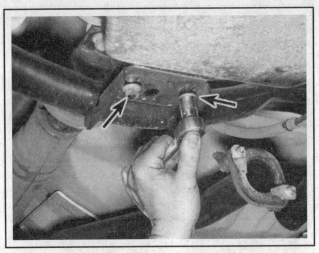

**14.9 Loosen the transmission rear mount bolts (arrows), but do not remove, this allows the rear of the transmission to be raised enough to clear the oil pan**

11  Place a jack under the oil pan, using a wood block between the jack head and the oil pan. Raise the engine until the valve cover just makes contact with the wiper module, which is located at the firewall behind the left valve cover (see Section 4). Place a wood block between the exhaust manifold and the frame (see illustration 18.9).

12  Move the jack to the right side of the engine and raise the right side of the engine, it will twist and allow the right to raise slightly higher than the left side. Raise it as far as possible.

13  Place wood block between the exhaust manifold and the frame on the right side.

14  Lower the engine onto the wood block and remove the jack.

15  Remove the oil pan mounting bolts (see illustration).

16  Carefully separate the pan from the engine block and let it hang down as far as possible.

**✳✳ CAUTION:**

**Don't pry between the block and pan or damage to the sealing surfaces may result and oil leaks could develop. Instead, dislodge the pan with a large rubber mallet or a wood block and a hammer.**

17  Reach in between the oil pan and the cylinder block, and remove the oil pump pick-up tube/screen bolts (see illustrations) and allow the pick-up to drop into the oil pan. The pan can't be removed with the pick-up tube bolted to the block - there's not enough room.

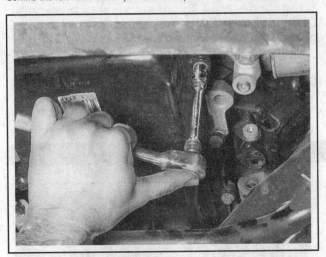

**14.15 Remove the sixteen oil pan bolts from around the perimeter of the pan and lower the pan to the frame crossmember**

**14.17a The oil pick-up tube and screen must be unbolted at the number two main cap (arrow)**

**14.17b Remove the two bolts at the oil pump body (arrows), lower the pick-up into the pan and remove the tube and screen with the oil pan (oil pan removed for clarity)**

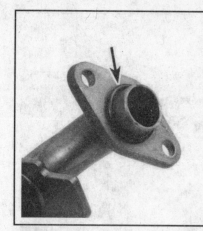

**14.22 Before the pick-up tube is reinstalled into the oil pump, inspect the O-ring (arrow) and replace it if necessary**

18 Maneuver the pan out the front, between the subframe and engine.

## INSTALLATION

▶ **Refer to illustration 14.22 and 14.23**

19 Remove all traces of old gasket material and sealant from the pan and block.

20 Clean the mating surfaces with lacquer thinner or acetone. Make sure the bolt holes in the block are clean.

21 The oil pan has a reinforcement rail welded to the oil pan, check the flange for distortion, particularly around the bolt holes. If necessary, place the pan on a wood block and use a hammer to flatten and restore the gasket surface.

22 Check the O-ring (see illustration) on the pick-up tube. Replace

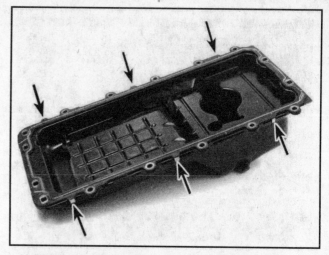

**14.23 Place the gasket on the oil pan, the locating tabs (arrows) on each side of the gasket will keep the gasket aligned during installation**

if necessary.

23 Place the oil pan gasket on the oil pan. The gasket has alignment tabs that will keep it in place on the oil pan (see illustration).

24 Place the pick-up tube in the oil pan and reinstall the oil pan and pick-up tube to the engine. Tighten the bolts to the torque listed in this Chapter's Specifications. When tightening the oil pan bolts, start at the center of the oil pan and work out toward the ends in a spiral pattern.

25 The remaining steps are the reverse of removal.

26 Fill the engine with the correct type and quantity of oil (see Chapter 1). Start the engine and check for oil leaks at the oil pan.

## 15  Oil pump - removal and installation

▶ **Refer to illustration 15.4**

### ✳✳ WARNING:

**On models with air suspension, turn the air suspension switch to Off before raising the vehicle.**

➡Note: The oil pump is available as a complete replacement unit only. No service parts or repair specifications are available from the manufacturer.

1 Unbolt and lower the oil pan as described in Section 14. It's not necessary to completely remove the oil pan.

2 Remove the two bolts that attach the oil pump pick-up tube to the oil pump (see illustration 14.17b).

3 Remove the timing cover, timing chains, chain guides and crankshaft sprockets (see Section 7).

4 Remove the four oil pump mounting bolts (see illustration) and separate the pump from the block.

5 Prime the oil pump prior to installation. Pour clean oil into the pick-up port and turn the pump by hand.

6 Inspect the O-ring gasket on the pick-up tube, if damaged replace it.

7 Install the oil pump the engine and tighten the bolts to the torque listed in this Chapter's Specifications.

**15.4 Remove the four oil pump mounting bolts (arrows) and oil pump from the engine block**

8 The remainder of installation is the reverse of removal procedure.

9 Fill the engine with the correct type and quantity of oil. Start the engine and check for leaks.

## 16  Driveplate - removal and installation

**✳✳ WARNING:**

On models with air suspension, turn the air suspension switch to Off before raising the vehicle.

## REMOVAL

▶ **Refer to illustration 16.2**

1  Disconnect the cable from the negative battery terminal. Raise the vehicle and support it securely on jackstands, refer to Chapter 7 and remove the transmission. Inspect the transmission, if it's leaking, now would be a very good time to have the transmission front pump seal/O-ring replaced.

➡**Note: The driveplate-to-torque converter bolts can be accessed for removal through the large rubber plug on the right rear of the engine block**

2  Look for factory paint marks that indicate driveplate-to-crankshaft alignment. If they aren't there, scribe or paint marks on the driveplate and crankshaft to ensure correct alignment during reassembly (see illustration).

3  Remove the bolts that secure the driveplate to the crankshaft (see illustration 16.2). If the crankshaft turns, wedge a screwdriver through the starter opening to jam the driveplate.

4  Remove the driveplate from the crankshaft. Be sure to support it

while removing the last bolt.

➡**Note: After the driveplate is removed, there is an reinforcement/mounting plate that is located between the engine block and the driveplate. It doesn't need to be removed, unless being replaced.**

## INSTALLATION

▶ **Refer to illustration 16.5**

5  If removed, be sure the reinforcement plate is installed as shown (see illustration), so it is correctly positioned for the starter installation.

6  Clean and inspect the mating surfaces of the driveplate and the crankshaft. If the crankshaft rear seal is leaking, replace it before reinstalling the driveplate.

7  Check for cracked, broken or missing ring gear teeth. If any of these conditions are found, replace the driveplate.

8  Install the driveplate to the engine aligning the marks made during removal. Note that some engines have an alignment dowel or staggered bolt holes to ensure correct installation. Before installing the bolts, apply a sealant with Teflon to the threads.

9  Wedge a screwdriver through the starter motor opening to keep the driveplate from turning as you tighten the bolts to the torque listed in this Chapter's Specifications.

10  The remainder of installation is the reverse of the removal procedure.

**16.2  Make an alignment mark (arrow), if not already on the driveplate, to reassure proper reassembly**

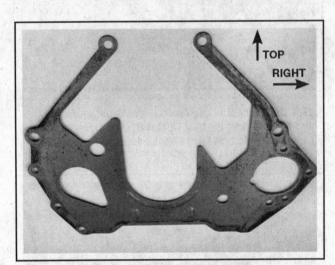

**16.5  If the reinforcement plate is removed, for any reason, it should be reinstalled in the direction shown here**

## 17 Crankshaft oil seals - replacement

### FRONT SEAL

▶ **Refer to illustrations 17.4 and 17.6**

1 Remove the fan/clutch assembly and the fan shroud (see Chapter 3).

2 Remove the drivebelt (see Chapter 1).

3 Remove the crankshaft pulley/vibration damper (see Section 5).

4 Carefully remove the seal from the cover with a seal removal tool (see illustration), a screwdriver will also work. If the timing cover is removed, use a chisel or small punch and hammer to drive the seal out of the cover from the back side. Support the cover as close to the seal bore as possible with two blocks of wood. Be careful not to damage the cover or scratch the wall of the seal bore.

5 Check the seal bore and crankshaft, as well as the seal contact surface on the vibration damper for nicks and burrs. Position the new

seal in the bore with the open end of the seal facing IN. A small amount of oil or grease applied to the outer edge of the new seal will make installation easier - but don't overdo it!

6 Drive the seal into the bore with a large socket and hammer until it's completely seated (see illustration). If the cover is removed, support the cover on blocks of wood. Select a socket that's the same outside diameter as the seal (a section of pipe can be used if a socket isn't available).

7 Lubricate the lip of the seal with clean engine oil and install the damper on the end of the crankshaft. The keyway in the damper bore must be aligned with the Woodruff key in the crankshaft nose.

8 If the damper can't be seated by hand, tap it into place with a soft-face hammer, or install the bolt and washer and tighten it to push the damper into place.

9 Tighten the damper bolt to the torque listed in this Chapter's Specifications.

10 Install the drivebelt.

11 Install the fan/clutch assembly and fan shroud.

12 Install the remaining parts removed for access to the seal.

13 Start the engine and check for leaks.

### REAR SEAL

▶ **Refer to illustrations 17.16, 17.17, 17.18 and 17.19**

14 Disconnect the cable from the negative battery terminal. Refer to Chapter 7 and remove the transmission.

15 Remove the driveplate and the rear cover plate from the engine (see Section 16).

16 Remove the bolts, detach the seal retainer (see illustration) and clean off all the old gasket and/or sealant material from both the engine block and the seal retainer.

17 Support the seal and retainer assembly on wood blocks and drive the old seal out from the back side with a chisel or a punch and hammer (see illustration).

18 Drive the new seal into the retainer with a wood block (see illustration).

19 Clean the crankshaft and seal bore with lacquer thinner or

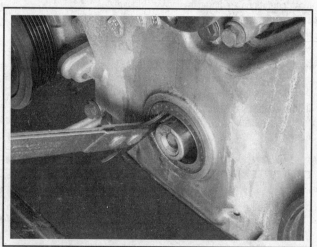

**17.4 Using a special seal removal tool, a screwdriver will also work, remove the front crankshaft oil seal, being very careful not to scratch the crankshaft during seal removal**

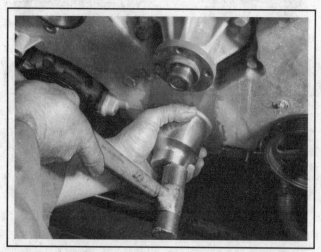

**17.6 There is special tool for installing the front oil seal into the timing chain cover, but if the tool is unavailable a large socket, the same diameter as the seal can be used to drive the seal into place**

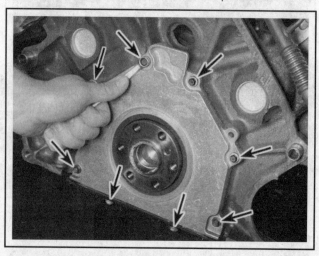

**17.16 Remove the eight bolts (arrows) and separate the seal retainer from the block**

**17.17 Support the seal retainer on two blocks of wood and drive out the old seal with a punch and hammer**

**17.18 Support the seal retainer and drive the new seal into the housing with a wood block or a section of pipe, be sure not to cock the seal in the bore while installing**

**17.19 Inspect the seal contact surface on the crankshaft (arrow) for signs of excessive wear or grooves**

acetone. Check the seal contact surface on the crankshaft very carefully for scratches or nicks that could damage the new seal lip and cause oil leaks (see illustration). If the crankshaft is damaged, the only alternative is a new or different crankshaft.

20  Lubricate the crankshaft seal journal and the lip of the new seal with engine oil.

21  Place a small bead (1.5mm wide) of RTV sealant on either the engine block or the seal retainer.

22  Install the oil seal retainer by slowly and carefully pushing the seal onto the crankshaft. The seal lip is stiff, so work it onto the crankshaft with a smooth object such as the end of a socket extension as you push the retainer against the block.

23  Install and tighten the retainer bolts to the torque listed in this Chapter's Specifications.

24  Reinstall the engine rear cover plate, driveplate and the transmission.

25  The remaining steps are the reverse of removal.

26  Check the oil level and add if necessary, run the engine and check for oil leaks.

## 18  Engine mounts - check and replacement

### ❊❊ WARNING:

**On models with air suspension, turn the air suspension switch to Off before raising the vehicle.**

## CHECK

▶ **Refer to illustration 18.4**

1  Engine mounts seldom require attention, but broken or deteriorated mounts should be replaced immediately or the added strain placed on the driveline components may cause damage or wear.

2  During the check, the engine must be raised slightly to remove the weight from the mounts.

3  Raise the vehicle and support it securely on jackstands, then position a jack under the engine oil pan. Place a large wood block between the jack head and the oil pan, then carefully raise the engine just enough to take the weight off the mounts.

4  Check the mounts to see if the rubber is cracked, hardened or separated from the metal plates (see illustration). Sometimes the rubber will split right down the center.

5  Check for relative movement between the mount plates and the engine or frame (use a large screwdriver or pry bar to attempt to move the mounts). If movement is noted, lower the engine and tighten the mount fasteners.

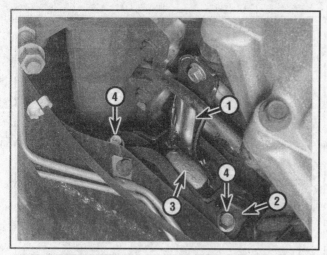

**18.4 Inspect the engine mount components for cracked rubber insulators, missing through bolts or cracked metal engine mounts**

| | | | |
|---|---|---|---|
| 1 | Engine mount (block half) | 4 | Through bolts (only one on |
| 2 | Engine mount (frame half) | | the right engine mount) |
| 3 | Rubber insulator | | |

6   Rubber preservative should be applied to the mounts to slow deterioration.

## REPLACEMENT

♦ **Refer to illustrations 18.8, 18.9, 18.10 and 18.11**

7   Disconnect the cable from the negative battery terminal. Raise the vehicle and support it securely on jackstands (if not already done). Place a large wood block between the jack head and the oil pan, then carefully raise the engine just enough to take the weight off the mounts and through bolts.

8   Remove the through bolts that connect the upper and lower motor mount halves (see illustration).

➡**Note: There are two through bolts for the left hand engine mount and one through bolts used on the right hand mount.**

**18.10  Remove the three bolts (arrows) and mount from the engine block**

**18.8  Using a flex-socket and a long extension, remove the through bolts (there are two on the left engine mount and only one on the right side mount)**

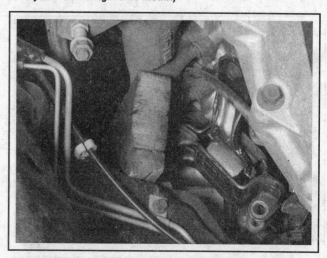

**18.9  With the engine raised, place a wood block between the frame and the exhaust manifold, on both sides, to support the engine and provide enough clearance for engine mount removal**

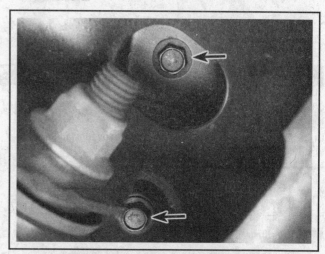

**18.11  If the lower half of the engine mount needs to be removed or replaced, unbolt the mount from the frame through access holes in the frame (arrows)**

9  Once the bolts have been removed from the mounts on both sides of the engine, raise the engine up until the fan blades just meet the fan shroud. Place a wood block between the frame and the exhaust manifold, on both sides of the engine (see illustration).

10  Remove the mount-to-block bolts and detach the mount (see illustration).

11  If the mounts are being replaced, the bolts attaching them to the frame can be reached with a socket and long extension through the access holes in the frame (see illustration).

12  Installation is the reverse of removal. Use thread locking compound on the mount bolts and tighten them to the torque listed in this Chapter's Specifications.

## Specifications

### General

| | |
|---|---|
| Displacement | 4.6 liters (281 CID) |
| Bore | |
|     2000 and earlier models | 3.5539 inches |
|     2001 and later models | 3.5512 inches |
| Stroke | |
|     2000 and earlier models | 3.5460 inches |
|     2001 and later models | 3.5433 inches |
| Cylinder numbers (front to rear) | |
|     Right side | 1-2-3-4 |
|     Left (driver's) side | 5-6-7-8 |
| Firing order | 1-3-7-2-6-5-4-8 |

### Camshaft

| | |
|---|---|
| Lobe lift | |
|   Intake | |
|     2000 and earlier models | 0.2596 inch |
|     2001 and 2002 | 0.2591 inch |
|     2003 and later models | 0.2799 inch |
|   Exhaust | |
|     2000 and earlier models | 0.2596 inch |
|     2001 and 2002 models | |
|       Right exhaust camshaft | 0.2593 inch |
|       Left exhaust camshaft | 0.2597 inch |
|     2003 and later models | |
|       Right exhaust camshaft | 0.2952 inch |
|       Left exhaust camshaft | 0.2951 inch |
| Theoretical valve lift @ zero lash | |
|   Intake | |
|     2000 and earlier models | 0.4728 inch |
|     2001 and later models | 0.4724 inch |
|   Exhaust | |
|     2000 and earlier models | 0.4728 inch |
|     2001 and later models | 0.4724 inch |

**1991 thru 1993**

36012-spec2Ba HAYNES

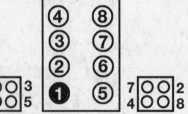

**1994 thru 1997**

36012-spec2Bb HAYNES

**1998 and later**

36012-spec2Bc HAYNES

**Cylinder and coil terminal locations**

**Cylinder location (coil-on-plug)**

Endplay
>    2000 and earlier models
>    >    Standard                     0.0010 to 0.0065 inch
>    >    Service limit                0.0075 inch maximum
>    2001 and later models
>    >    Standard                     0.0011 to 0.0075 inch
>    >    Service limit                0.0075 inch maximum

Journal diameter
>    2000 and earlier models         1.0613 to 1.0623 inches
>    2001 and later models           1.0605 to 1.0615 inches

Bearing inside diameter
>    2000 and earlier models         1.0633 to 1.0643 inches
>    2001 and later models           1.0625 to 1.0635 inches

Journal to bearing oil clearance
>    Standard          0.0010 to 0.0030 inch
>    Service limit                   0.0048 inch maximum

## Torque specifications

**Ft-lbs (unless otherwise indicated)**

➡ **Note: One foot-pound (ft-lb) of torque is equivalent to 12 inch-pounds (in-lbs) of torque. Torque values below approximately 15 foot-pounds are expressed in inch-pounds, because most foot-pound torque wrenches are not accurate at these smaller values.**

Camshaft sprocket bolt
>    1991 through 2004               81 to 95
>    2005 and later
>    >    Step 1                     30
>    >    Step 2                     Tighten an additional 90 degrees
Camshaft cap cluster bolts          72 to 96 in-lbs
Timing chain cover bolts
>    1991 through 1998               16 to 22
>    1999 through 2005 models (see illustration 6.10)
>    >    Step 1  Bolts 1 through 7          18
>    >    Step 2  Bolts 6 through 13         35
>    2006 models                     18
Cylinder head bolts
>    1991 through 2000 models
>    >    Step 1
>    >    >    1991 through 1996          15 to 22
>    >    >    1997 through 2000          27 to 32
>    >    Step 2                     Tighten an additional 85 to 95 degrees
>    >    Step 3                     Tighten an additional 85 to 95 degrees
>    2001 and later models
>    >    Step 1                     30
>    >    Step 2                     Tighten an additional 90 degrees
>    >    Step 3                     Loosen one complete turn (360 degrees)
>    >    Step 4                     30
>    >    Step 5                     Tighten an additional 90 degrees
>    >    Step 6                     Tighten an additional 90 degrees

## Torque specifications (continued)    Ft-lbs (unless otherwise indicated)

➡ Note: One foot-pound (ft-lb) of torque is equivalent to 12 inch-pounds (in-lbs) of torque. Torque values below approximately 15 foot-pounds are expressed in inch-pounds, because most foot-pound torque wrenches are not accurate at these smaller values.

| | |
|---|---|
| Vibration damper-to-crankshaft bolt | |
|    1996 and earlier | 114 to 121 |
|    1997 and later | |
|       Step 1 | 66 then loosen bolt |
|       Step 2 | 34 to 39 |
|       Step 3 | Tighten additional 85 to 90 degrees |
| Valve cover bolts | 70 to 106 in-lbs |
| Oil pan-to-engine block bolts | |
|    1991 through 1996 models | 15 to 22 |
|    1997 through 2000 models | |
|       Step 1 | 18 in-lbs |
|       Step 2 | 15 |
|       Step 3 | Tighten an additional 60 degrees |
|    2001 and later models | |
|       Step 1 | 15 |
|       Step 2 | Tighten an additional 60 degrees |
| Exhaust manifold-to-cylinder head bolts | 15 to 22 |
| Intake manifold-to-cylinder head bolts | 15 to 22* |
| Oil filter insert-to-engine block adapter bolt | 15 to 22 |
| Oil pump-to-block mounting bolts | 70 to 106 in-lbs |
| Oil pick-up tube-to-main bearing cap nut | 15 to 22 |
| Oil pick-up tube-to-oil pump bolts | 70 to 106 in-lbs |
| Driveplate mounting bolts | |
|    1996 and earlier | 75 to 85 |
|    1997 and later | 54 to 64 |
| Timing chain tensioner bolts | 15 to 22 |
| Timing chain guide bolts | 89 in-lbs |
| Engine mount-to-block bolts | |
|    1996 and earlier | 15 to 22 |
|    1997 and later | 39 to 53 |
| Engine mount through bolts | |
|    1996 and earlier | 15 to 22 |
|    1997 and later | 39 to 53 |

* After assembly, retorque with the engine warm.

## Section



# 2C

# GENERAL ENGINE OVERHAUL PROCEDURES

2C-2 GENERAL ENGINE OVERHAUL PROCEDURES

## 1   General information

Included in this portion of Chapter 2 are the general overhaul procedures for the cylinder head(s) and internal engine components.

The information ranges from advice concerning preparation for an overhaul and the purchase of replacement parts to detailed, step-by-step procedures covering removal and installation of internal engine components and the inspection of parts.

The following Sections have been written based on the assumption that the engine has been removed from the vehicle. For information concerning in-vehicle engine repair, as well as removal and installation of the external components necessary for the overhaul, see Parts A and B of this Chapter and Section 7 of this Part.

The Specifications included in this Part are only those necessary for the inspection and overhaul procedures which follow. Refer to Parts A and B for additional Specifications.

## 2   Engine overhaul - general information

▶ **Refer to illustration 2.4**

It is not always easy to determine when, or if, an engine should be completely overhauled, as a number of factors must be considered.

High mileage is not necessarily an indication that an overhaul is needed, while low mileage does not preclude the need for an overhaul. Frequency of servicing is probably the most important consideration. An engine that has had regular and frequent oil and filter changes, as well as other required maintenance, will most likely give many thousands of miles of reliable service. Conversely, a neglected engine may require an overhaul very early in its life.

Excessive oil consumption is an indication that piston rings and/or valve guides are in need of attention. Make sure that oil leaks are not responsible before deciding that the rings and/or guides are bad. Test the cylinder compression (see Section 3) or have a leak down test performed by an experienced tune-up mechanic to determine the extent of the work required.

If the engine is making obvious knocking or rumbling noises, the connecting rod and/or main bearings are probably at fault. To accurately test oil pressure, temporarily connect a mechanical oil pressure gauge in place of the oil pressure sending unit (see illustration). Compare the reading to the pressure listed in this Chapter's Specifications. If the pressure is extremely low, the bearings and/or oil pump are probably worn out.

Loss of power, rough running, excessive valve train noise and high fuel consumption rates may also point to the need for an overhaul, especially if they are all present at the same time. If a complete tune-up does not remedy the situation, major mechanical work is the only solution.

An engine overhaul involves restoring the internal parts to the specifications of a new engine. During an overhaul, the piston rings are replaced and the cylinder walls are reconditioned (rebored and/or honed). If a re-bore is done, new pistons are required. The main bearings, connecting rod bearings and camshaft bearings are generally replaced with new ones and, if necessary, the crankshaft may be reground to restore the journals. Generally, the valves are serviced as well, since they are usually in less-than-perfect condition at this point. While the engine is being overhauled, other components, such as the distributor, starter and alternator, can be rebuilt as well. The end result should be a like new engine that will give many trouble free miles.

➡**Note: Critical cooling system components such as the hoses, the drivebelts, the thermostat and the water pump MUST be replaced with new parts when an engine is overhauled. The radiator should be checked carefully to ensure that it isn't clogged or leaking. If in doubt, replace it with a new one. Also, we do not recommend overhauling the oil pump - always install a new one when an engine is rebuilt.**

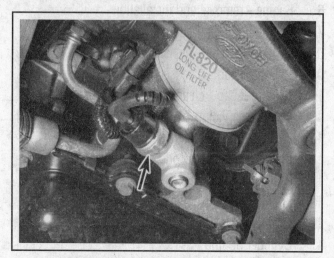

**2.4  The oil pressure sending unit is located at the lower left (driver's side) corner of the engine, near the oil filter (4.6L engine shown, 5.0L engine similar)**

Before beginning the engine overhaul, read through the entire procedure to familiarize yourself with the scope and requirements of the job. Overhauling an engine is not difficult, but it is time consuming. Plan on the vehicle being tied up for a minimum of two weeks, especially if parts must be taken to an automotive machine shop for repair or reconditioning. Check on availability of parts and make sure that any necessary special tools and equipment are obtained in advance. Most work can be done with typical hand tools, although a number of precision measuring tools are required for inspecting parts to determine if they must be replaced. Often an automotive machine shop will handle the inspection of parts and offer advice concerning reconditioning and replacement.

➡**Note: Always wait until the engine has been completely disassembled and all components, especially the engine block, have been inspected before deciding what service and repair operations must be performed by an automotive machine shop.**

Since the block's condition will be the major factor to consider when determining whether to overhaul the original engine or buy a rebuilt one, never purchase parts or have machine work done on other components until the block has been thoroughly inspected. As a general rule, time is the primary cost of an overhaul, so it does not pay to install worn or substandard parts.

As a final note, to ensure maximum life and minimum trouble from a rebuilt engine, everything must be assembled with care in a spotlessly clean environment.

## 3   Cylinder compression check

♦ **Refer to illustration 3.6**

1   A compression check will tell you what mechanical condition the upper end (pistons, rings, valves, head gaskets) of your engine is in. Specifically, it can tell you if the compression is down due to leakage caused by worn piston rings, defective valves and seats or a blown head gasket.

➡**Note: The engine must be at normal operating temperature for this check and the battery must be fully charged.**

2   Begin by cleaning the area around the spark plugs before you remove them (compressed air works best for this). This will prevent dirt from getting into the cylinders as the compression check is being done.

3   Remove all of the spark plugs from the engine (see Chapter 1).

4   Block the throttle wide open.

5   Disconnect the primary wires from the coil(s). Disable the fuel system (see Chapter 4, Section 2).

6   With the compression gauge in the number one spark plug hole, crank the engine over at least four compression strokes and watch the gauge (see illustration). The compression should build up quickly in a healthy engine. Low compression on the first stroke, followed by gradually increasing pressure on successive strokes, indicates worn piston rings. A low compression reading on the first stroke, which does not build up during successive strokes, indicates leaking valves or a blown head gasket (a cracked head could also be the cause). Record the highest gauge reading obtained.

7   Repeat the procedure for the remaining cylinders and compare the results to the Specifications.

8   Add some engine oil (about three squirts from a plunger-type oil can) to each cylinder, through the spark plug hole, and repeat the test.

9   If the compression increases after the oil is added, the piston rings are definitely worn. If the compression does not increase significantly, the leakage is occurring at the valves or head gasket. Leakage past the valves may be caused by burned valve seats and/or faces or warped, cracked or bent valves.

**3.6  A compression gauge with a threaded fitting for the spark plug hole is preferred over the type that requires hand pressure to maintain the seal - be sure to open the throttle valve as far as possible during the compression check**

10   If two adjacent cylinders have equally low compression, there is a strong possibility that the head gasket between them is blown. The appearance of coolant in the combustion chambers or the crankcase would verify this condition.

11   If the compression is unusually high, the combustion chambers are probably coated with carbon deposits. If that is the case, the cylinder heads should be removed and decarbonized.

12   If compression is way down or varies greatly between cylinders, it would be a good idea to have a leak-down test performed by an automotive repair shop. This test will pinpoint exactly where the leakage is occurring and how severe it is.

## 4   Vacuum gauge diagnostic checks

A vacuum gauge provides valuable information about what is going on in the engine at a low-cost. You can check for worn rings or cylinder walls, leaking head or intake manifold gaskets, incorrect carburetor adjustments, restricted exhaust, stuck or burned valves, weak valve springs, improper ignition or valve timing and ignition problems.

Unfortunately, vacuum gauge readings are easy to misinterpret, so they should be used in conjunction with other tests to confirm the diagnosis.

Both the absolute readings and the rate of needle movement are important for accurate interpretation. Most gauges measure vacuum in inches of mercury (in-Hg). The following references to vacuum assume the diagnosis is being performed at sea level. As elevation increases (or atmospheric pressure decreases), the reading will decrease. For every 1,000 foot increase in elevation above approximately 2000 feet, the gauge readings will decrease about one inch of mercury.

Connect the vacuum gauge directly to intake manifold vacuum, not to ported (throttle body) vacuum. Be sure no hoses are left disconnected during the test or false readings will result.

Before you begin the test, allow the engine to warm up completely. Block the wheels and set the parking brake. With the transmission in Park, start the engine and allow it to run at normal idle speed.

### ✳✳ WARNING:

**Carefully inspect the fan blades for cracks or damage before starting the engine. Keep your hands and the vacuum gauge clear of the fan and do not stand in front of the vehicle or in line with the fan when the engine is running.**

Read the vacuum gauge; an average, healthy engine should normally produce about 17 to 22 inches of vacuum with a fairly steady needle. Refer to the following vacuum gauge readings and what they indicate about the engine's condition:

1   A low steady reading usually indicates a leaking gasket between the intake manifold and cylinder head(s) or throttle body, a leaky vacuum hose, late ignition timing or incorrect camshaft timing. Check ignition timing with a timing light and eliminate all other possible causes, utilizing the tests provided in this Chapter before you remove the timing chain cover to check the timing marks.

2   If the reading is three to eight inches below normal and it fluctuates at that low reading, suspect an intake manifold gasket leak at an intake port or a faulty fuel injector.

3   If the needle has regular drops of about two-to-four inches at a steady rate, the valves are probably leaking. Perform a compression

check or leak-down test to confirm this.

4  An irregular drop or down-flick of the needle can be caused by a sticking valve or an ignition misfire. Perform a compression check or leak-down test and read the spark plugs.

5  A rapid vibration of about four in.-Hg vibration at idle combined with exhaust smoke indicates worn valve guides. Perform a leak-down test to confirm this. If the rapid vibration occurs with an increase in engine speed, check for a leaking intake manifold gasket or head gasket, weak valve springs, burned valves or ignition misfire.

6  A slight fluctuation, say one inch up and down, may mean ignition problems. Check all the usual tune-up items and, if necessary, run the engine on an ignition analyzer.

7  If there is a large fluctuation, perform a compression or leak-down test to look for a weak or dead cylinder or a blown head gasket.

8  If the needle moves slowly through a wide range, check for a clogged PCV system, incorrect idle fuel mixture, carburetor/throttle body or intake manifold gasket leaks.

9  Check for a slow return after revving the engine by quickly snapping the throttle open until the engine reaches about 2,500 rpm and let it shut. Normally the reading should drop to near zero, rise above normal idle reading (about 5 in.-Hg over) and then return to the previous idle reading. If the vacuum returns slowly and doesn't peak when the throttle is snapped shut, the rings may be worn. If there is a long delay, look for a restricted exhaust system (often the muffler or catalytic converter). An easy way to check this is to temporarily disconnect the exhaust ahead of the suspected part and redo the test.

## 5  Engine removal - methods and precautions

If you have decided that an engine must be removed for overhaul or major repair work, several preliminary steps should be taken.

Locating a suitable work area is extremely important. A shop is, of course, the most desirable place to work. Adequate work space, along with storage space for the vehicle, will be needed. If a shop or garage is not available, at the very least a flat, level, clean work surface made of concrete or asphalt is required.

Cleaning the engine compartment and engine before beginning the removal procedure will help keep tools clean and organized.

An engine hoist or A-frame will be needed. Make sure that the equipment is rated in excess of the combined weight of the engine and its accessories. Safety is of primary importance, considering the potential hazards involved in lifting the engine out of the vehicle.

If the engine is being removed by a novice, a helper should be available. Advice and aid from someone more experienced would also be helpful. There are many instances when one person cannot simultaneously perform all of the operations required when lifting the engine out of the vehicle.

Plan the operation ahead of time. Arrange for or obtain all of the tools and equipment you will need prior to beginning the job. Some of the equipment necessary to perform engine removal and installation safely and with relative ease are (in addition to an engine hoist) a heavy duty floor jack, complete sets of wrenches and sockets as described in the front of this manual, wooden blocks and plenty of rags and cleaning solvent for mopping up spilled oil, coolant and gasoline. If the hoist is to be rented, make sure that you arrange for it in advance and perform beforehand all of the operations possible without it. This will save you money and time.

Plan for the vehicle to be out of use for a considerable amount of time. A machine shop will be required to perform some of the work which the do-it-yourselfer cannot accomplish due to a lack of special equipment. These shops often have a busy schedule, so it would be wise to consult them before removing the engine in order to accurately estimate the amount of time required to rebuild or repair components that may need work.

Always use extreme caution when removing and installing the engine. Serious injury can result from careless actions. Plan ahead, take your time and a job of this nature, although major, can be accomplished successfully.

## 6  Engine - removal and installation

♦ Refer to illustration 6.6, 6.19, 6.21, 6.26, 6.27, 6.28 and 6.29

### ❊❊ WARNING 1:

The air conditioning system is under high pressure! Have a dealer service department or service station discharge the system before disconnecting any air conditioning system hoses or fittings.

### ❊❊ WARNING 2:

Gasoline is extremely flammable, so take extra precautions when you work on any part of the fuel system. Don't smoke or allow open flames or bare light bulbs near the work area, and don't work in a garage where a gas-type appliance (such as a water heater or a clothes dryer) is present. Since gasoline is carcinogenic, wear latex gloves when there's a possibility of being exposed to fuel, and, if you spill any fuel on your skin, rinse it off immediately with soap and water. Mop up any spills immediately and do not store fuel-soaked rags where they could ignite. The fuel system is under constant pressure, so, if any fuel lines are to be disconnected, the fuel pressure in the system must be relieved first (see Chapter 4 for more information). When you perform any kind of work on the fuel system, wear safety glasses and have a Class B type fire extinguisher on hand.

### ❊❊ WARNING 3:

On models with air suspension, turn the air suspension switch to Off before raising the vehicle.

## REMOVAL

1  Relieve the fuel system pressure (see Chapter 4).

2  Disconnect the negative cable from the battery.

3  Cover the fenders and cowl and remove the hood (see Chapter 11). Special pads are available to protect the fenders, but an old bedspread or blanket will also work.

4  Remove the air cleaner assembly.

5  Drain the cooling system (see Chapter 1).

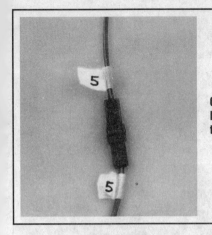

**6.6 Label each wire before unplugging the connector**

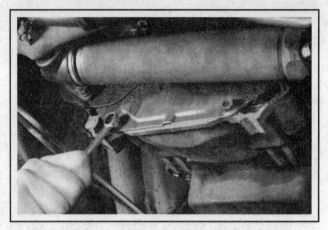

**6.19 Remove the bolts and take off the torque converter access cover**

6   Label the vacuum lines, emissions system hoses, electrical connectors, ground straps and fuel lines that would interfere with engine removal, to ensure correct reinstallation, then detach them. Pieces of masking tape with numbers or letters written on them work well (see illustration). If there's any possibility of confusion, make a sketch of the engine compartment and clearly label the lines, hoses and wires.

7   Label and detach all coolant hoses from the engine.

8   Remove the cooling fan, shroud and radiator (see Chapter 3).

9   Remove the drivebelt(s) (see Chapter 1).

10  Disconnect the accelerator cable and Throttle Valve (TV) linkage/speed control cable from the engine (see Chapter 4).

11  Unbolt the power steering pump (see Chapter 10). Leave the lines/hoses attached and make sure the pump is kept in an upright position in the engine compartment (use wire or rope to restrain it out of the way).

12  On air conditioned models, unbolt the compressor (see Chapter 3) and set it aside. Do not disconnect the hoses.

13  Remove the air inlet tube.

14  On 4.6L engine models, remove the 42-pin connector from the retaining bracket on the vacuum booster and separate the 42-pin connector from the transmission harness and position it out of the way.

15  Drain the engine oil (see Chapter 1) and remove the filter.

16  Remove the starter motor (see Chapter 5).

17  Remove the alternator (see Chapter 5).

18  Unbolt the exhaust system from the engine (see Chapter 2, Part A or B, whichever applies to the engine being worked on).

19  Remove the torque converter access cover (see illustration) and remove the torque converter-to-driveplate fasteners.

20  Support the transmission with a jack. Position a block of wood between them to prevent damage to the transmission. Special transmission jacks with safety chains are available - use one if possible.

21  Attach an engine sling or a length of chain to the engine and then to the engine hoist (see illustration).

22  Roll the hoist into position and connect the sling to it. Take up the slack in the sling or chain, but don't lift the engine.

**✳✳ WARNING:**

**DO NOT place any part of your body under the engine when it's supported only by a hoist or other lifting device.**

23  Remove the transmission-to-engine block bolts (see Chapter 7).

24  Remove the engine mount through bolts from both sides (see Chapter 2, Part A or B, depending which engine is being worked on).

25  Recheck to be sure nothing is still connecting the engine to the transmission or vehicle. Disconnect anything still remaining.

26  Raise the engine slightly. Carefully work it forward to separate it from the transmission (see illustration). If you're working on a vehicle with an automatic transmission, be sure the torque converter stays in

**6.21 Center the chain, or sling, on the engine hoist to balance the engine as well as keeping any remaining coolant from spilling out onto the floor**

**6.26 Use a prybar or a large screwdriver and pry the engine from the transmission bellhousing**

**6.27 Mark the relationship of the driveplate to the crankshaft**

**6.28 Use long high-strength bolts (arrows) to hold the engine block on the engine stand - make sure they are tight before lowering the hoist and placing the entire weight of the engine on the stand**

the transmission (clamp a pair of vise-grips to the transmission housing to keep the converter from sliding out). Slowly raise the engine out of the engine compartment. Check carefully to make sure nothing is hanging up.

27 Remove the driveplate (see illustration).

28 Mount the engine on an engine stand (see illustration).

29 Once the engine is removed, support the transmission with a

**6.29 Use a piece of pipe or chain to support the transmission once the engine has been removed, then remove the floor jack that supported the transmission during engine removal**

chain or pipe that crosses from side to side to hold the transmission as the floor jack is removed (see illustration).

## INSTALLATION

30 Check the engine and transmission mounts. If they're worn or damaged, replace them.

31 Carefully lower the engine into the engine compartment - make sure the engine mounts line up.

32 Guide the torque converter into the crankshaft following the procedure outlined in Chapter 7.

33 Install the transmission-to-engine bolts and tighten them securely.

### ❉❉ CAUTION:

**DO NOT use the bolts to force the transmission and engine together!**

34 Reinstall the remaining components in the reverse order of removal.

35 Add coolant and oil as needed. Run the engine and check for leaks and proper operation of all accessories, then install the hood and test drive the vehicle.

## 7    Engine rebuilding alternatives

The do-it-yourselfer is faced with a number of options when performing an engine overhaul. The decision to replace the engine block, piston/connecting rod assemblies and crankshaft depends on a number of factors, with the number one consideration being the condition of the block. Other considerations are cost, access to machine shop facilities, parts availability, time required to complete the project and the extent of prior mechanical experience on the part of the do-it-yourselfer.

Some of the rebuilding alternatives include:

**Individual parts** - If the inspection procedures reveal that the engine block and most engine components are in reusable condition, pur-

chasing individual parts may be the most economical alternative. The block, crankshaft and piston/connecting rod assemblies should all be inspected carefully. Even if the block shows little wear, the cylinder bores should be surface honed.

**Crankshaft kit** - This rebuild package consists of a reground crankshaft and a matched set of pistons and connecting rods. The pistons will already be installed on the connecting rods. Piston rings and the necessary bearings will be included in the kit. These kits are commonly available for standard cylinder bores, as well as for engine blocks which have been bored to a regular oversize.

**Short block** - A short block consists of an engine block with a crankshaft and piston/connecting rod assemblies already installed. All new bearings are incorporated and all clearances will be correct. The existing cylinder head(s), camshaft, valve train components and external parts can be bolted to the short block with little or no machine shop work necessary.

**Long block** - A long block consists of a short block plus an oil pump, oil pan, cylinder head(s), valve cover(s), camshaft and valve train components, timing sprockets, belt or chain and timing cover. All components are installed with new bearings, seals and gaskets incorporated throughout. The installation of manifolds and external parts is all that is necessary.

Give careful thought to which alternative is best for you and discuss the situation with local automotive machine shops, auto parts dealers or parts store countermen before ordering or purchasing replacement parts.

## 8  Engine overhaul - disassembly sequence

### ✳✳ CAUTION:

**The cylinder head bolts on the 4.6L engine are "angle torque" bolts and are NOT reusable. A predetermined stretch of the bolt gives the even clamping load needed to seal the cylinders properly. Once removed they must be replaced.**

1   It's much easier to disassemble and work on the engine if it's mounted on a portable engine stand. A stand can often be rented quite cheaply from an equipment rental yard. Before the engine is mounted on a stand, the flywheel/driveplate should be removed from the engine.

2   If a stand isn't available, it's possible to disassemble the engine with it blocked up on the floor. Be extra careful not to tip or drop the engine when working without a stand.

3   If you're going to obtain a rebuilt engine, all external components must come off first, to be transferred to the replacement engine, just as they will if you're doing a complete engine overhaul yourself. These include:

   *Alternator and brackets*
   *Emissions control components*
   *Distributor (if equipped)*
   *Spark plug wires and spark plugs*
   *Thermostat and housing cover*
   *Water pump*
   *EFI components*
   *Intake/exhaust manifolds*
   *Oil filter (replace)*
   *Engine mounts*
   *Driveplate*
   *Engine rear plate*

➡**Note: When removing the external components from the engine, pay close attention to details that may be helpful or important during installation. Note the installed position of gaskets, seals, spacers, pins, brackets, washers, bolts and other small items.**

4   If you're obtaining a short block, which consists of the engine block, crankshaft, pistons and connecting rods all assembled, then the cylinder head(s), oil pan and oil pump will have to be removed as well. See *Engine rebuilding alternatives* for additional information regarding the different possibilities to be considered.

5   If you're planning a complete overhaul, the engine must be disassembled and the internal components removed in the following order:

   *Driveplate*
   *Valve covers*
   *Intake manifold*
   *Exhaust manifolds*
   *Rocker arms and pushrods (5.0L engines)*
   *Camshafts and followers (4.6L engine)*
   *Valve lifters (5.0L engines)*
   *Vibration damper*
   *Timing chain cover*
   *Timing chain and sprockets (5.0L engines)*
   *Timing chains, sprockets, guides and tensioners (4.6L engine)*
   *Camshaft (5.0L engines)*
   *Valve lifters (4.6L engine)*
   *Cylinder heads*
   *Oil pan*
   *Oil pump (replace)*
   *Piston/connecting rod assemblies*
   *Crankshaft and main bearings ((replace)*

6   Before beginning the disassembly and overhaul procedures, make sure the following items are available. Also, refer to *Engine overhaul - reassembly sequence* for a list of tools and materials needed for engine reassembly.

   *Common hand tools*
   *Small cardboard boxes or plastic bags for storing parts*
   *Gasket scraper*
   *Ridge reamer*
   *Vibration damper puller*
   *Micrometers*
   *Telescoping gauges*
   *Dial indicator set*
   *Valve spring compressor*
   *Cylinder surfacing hone*
   *Piston ring groove cleaning tool*
   *Electric drill motor*
   *Tap and die set*
   *Wire brushes*
   *Oil gallery brushes*
   *Cleaning solvent*

## 9  Cylinder head - disassembly

♦ **Refer to illustrations 9.1, 9.2a, 9.2b and 9.3**

➡**Note: New and rebuilt cylinder heads are commonly available for most engines at dealerships and auto parts stores. Due to the fact that some specialized tools are necessary for the disassembly and inspection procedures, and replacement parts may not be readily available, it may be more practical and economical for the home mechanic to purchase replacement head(s) rather than taking the time to disassemble, inspect and recondition the original(s).**

9.1 A small plastic bag, with an appropriate label, can be used to store the valve train components so they can be kept together and reinstalled in the original position

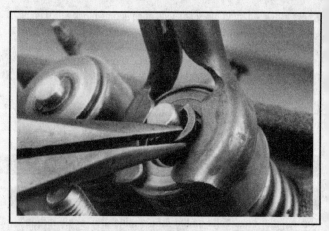

9.2a Use a valve spring compressor to compress the spring, then remove the keepers from the valve stem with a needle nose pliers . . .

9.2b . . . or use a magnet, as shown here on the 4.6L engine

9.3 If the valve won't pull through the guide, deburr the edge of the stem end and the area around the top of the keeper groove with a file or whetstone

1   Cylinder head disassembly involves removal of the intake and exhaust valves and related components. If they're still in place, remove the rocker arm nuts, pivot balls and rocker arms from the cylinder head studs. Label the parts or store them separately (see illustration) so they can be reinstalled in their original locations and in the same valve guides they are removed from.

2   Compress the springs on the first valve with a spring compressor and remove the keepers (see illustrations). Carefully release the valve spring compressor and remove the retainer, sleeve (if used), the spring and the spring seat (if used).

3   Pull the valve out of the head, then remove the oil seal from the guide. If the valve binds in the guide (won't pull through), push it back

into the head and deburr the area around the keeper groove with a fine file or whetstone (see illustration).

4   Repeat the procedure for the remaining valves. Remember to keep all the parts for each valve together so they can be reinstalled in the same locations.

5   Once the valves and related components have been removed and stored in an organized manner, the head should be thoroughly cleaned and inspected. If a complete engine overhaul is being done, finish the engine disassembly procedures before beginning the cylinder head cleaning and inspection process.

## 10  Cylinder head - cleaning and inspection

1   Thorough cleaning of the cylinder head(s) and related valve train components, followed by a detailed inspection, will enable you to decide how much valve service work must be done during the engine overhaul.

➡**Note: If the engine was severely overheated, the cylinder head is probably warped (see Step 12).**

### CLEANING

2   Scrape all traces of old gasket material and sealing compound off the head gasket, intake manifold and exhaust manifold sealing surfaces. Be very careful not to gouge the cylinder head. Special gasket removal solvents that soften gaskets and make removal much easier are avail-

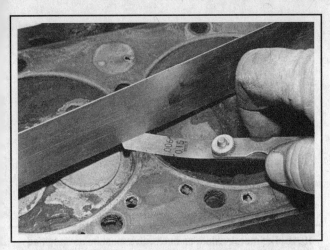

**10.12a Check the cylinder head gasket surface for warpage by trying to slip a feeler gauge under the straightedge (see this Chapter's Specifications for the maximum warpage allowed and use a feeler gauge of that thickness)**

able at auto parts stores.

3  Remove all built up scale from the coolant passages.

4  Run a stiff wire brush through the various holes to remove deposits that may have formed in them.

5  Run an appropriate size tap into each of the threaded holes to remove corrosion and thread sealant that may be present. If compressed air is available, use it to clear the holes of debris produced by this operation.

## ✶✶ WARNING:

**Wear eye protection when using compressed air!**

6  Clean the exhaust manifold stud threads, if equipped. Clean the rocker arm pivot stud threads (if applicable) with a wire brush.

7  Clean the cylinder head with solvent and dry it thoroughly. Compressed air will speed the drying process and ensure that all holes and recessed areas are clean.

➡**Note: Decarbonizing chemicals are available and may prove very useful when cleaning cylinder heads and valve train components. They are very caustic and should be used with caution. Be sure to follow the instructions on the container.**

**10.14 Lay the head on its edge, pull each valve out about 1/8 inch, set up a dial indicator with the probe touching the valve stem, wiggle the valve and measure its movement**

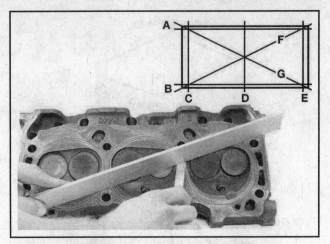

**10.12b Check for both "twist" and "bulge" warpage by positioning the straightedge diagonally as well as straight across the gasket surface**

8  Clean the rocker arms, fulcrums and bolts and pushrods with solvent and dry them thoroughly (don't mix them up during the cleaning process).

➡**Note: Compressed air will speed the drying process and can be used to clean out the oil passages.**

9  Clean all the valve springs, spring seats, keepers and retainers (or rotators) with solvent and dry them thoroughly. Work the components from one valve at a time to avoid mixing up the parts.

10  Scrape off any heavy deposits that may have formed on the valves, then use a motorized wire brush to remove deposits from the valve heads and stems. Again, make sure the valves don't get mixed up.

## INSPECTION

➡**Note: Be sure to perform all of the following inspection procedures before concluding that machine shop work is required. Make a list of the items that need attention.**

### Cylinder head

◆ **Refer to illustration 10.12a, 10.12b and 10.14**

11  Inspect the head very carefully for cracks, evidence of coolant leakage and other damage. If cracks are found, check with an automotive machine shop concerning repair. If repair isn't possible, a new cylinder head should be obtained.

12  Using a straightedge and feeler gauge, check the head gasket mating surface for warpage (see illustrations). If the warpage exceeds the limit listed in this Chapter's Specifications, it will have to be resurfaced at an automotive machine shop.

➡**Note 1: If the 5.0L cylinder heads are resurfaced, the intake manifold flanges will also require machining.**

➡**Note 2: The manufacturer states that the cylinder head on 2001 and later models cannot be machined in the event of warping. If the cylinder head warpage exceeds 0.001 inch, replace the cylinder head.**

13  Examine the valve seats in each of the combustion chambers. If they're pitted, cracked or burned, the head will require valve service that's beyond the scope of the home mechanic.

14  Check the valve stem-to-guide clearance by measuring the lateral movement of the valve stem with a dial indicator attached securely to the head (see illustration). The valve must be in the guide and approxi-

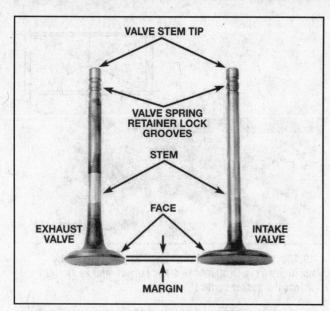

10.15 Check for valve wear at the points shown here

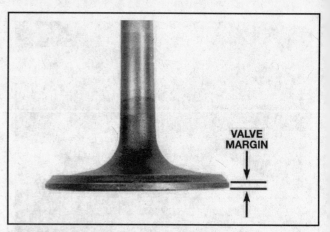

10.16 The margin width on each valve must be as specified (if no margin exists, the valve cannot be reused)

mately 1/16-inch off the seat. The total valve stem movement indicated by the gauge needle must be divided by two to obtain the actual clearance. After this is done, if there's still some doubt regarding the condition of the valve guides they should be checked by an automotive machine shop (the cost should be minimal).

## Valves

♦ Refer to illustrations 10.15 and 10.16

15 Carefully inspect each valve face for uneven wear, deformation, cracks, pits and burned areas (see illustration). Check the valve stem for scuffing and galling and the neck for cracks. Rotate the valve and check for any obvious indication that it's bent. Look for pits and excessive wear on the end of the stem. The presence of any of these conditions indicates the need for valve service by an automotive machine shop.

16 Measure the margin width on each valve (see illustration). Any valve with a margin narrower than 1/32-inch will have to be replaced with a new one.

## Valve components

♦ Refer to illustrations 10.17, 10.18 and 10.19

17 Check each valve spring for wear (on the ends) and pits. Measure the free length and compare it to the Specifications (see illustration). Any springs that are shorter than specified have sagged and should not be reused. The tension of all springs should be checked with a special fixture before deciding that they're suitable for use in a rebuilt engine (take the springs to an automotive machine shop for this check).

18 Stand each spring on a flat surface and check it for squareness (see illustration). If any of the springs are distorted or sagged, replace all of them with new parts.

19 Check the spring retainers (or rotators) and keepers for obvious wear and cracks. Any questionable parts should be replaced with new ones, as extensive damage will occur if they fail during engine operation. Make sure the rotators operate smoothly with no binding or excessive play (see illustration).

## Rocker arm components (5.0L engines)

20 Clean all the parts thoroughly. Make sure all oil passages are open.

21 Check the rocker arm faces (the areas that contact the pushrod ends and valve stems) for pits, wear, galling, score marks and rough spots.

10.17 Measure the free length of each valve spring with a dial or vernier caliper

10.18 Check each valve spring for squareness, if it is bent it should be replaced

10.19 The exhaust valve rotators can be checked by turning the inner and outer sections in opposite directions to feel for smooth movement and excessive play

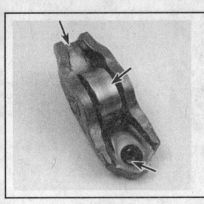

**10.28 On 4.6L engines, check the camshaft followers for signs of wear or damage to the areas that contact the cam, lifter or valve stem tip (arrows)**

22 Check the rocker arm pivot contact areas and fulcrums. Look for cracks in each rocker arm and bolt (or nut on some very early 5.0L engines).

23 Inspect the pushrod ends for scuffing and excessive wear. Roll each pushrod on a flat surface, like a piece of plate glass, to determine if it's bent.

24 Check the rocker arm studs in the cylinder heads (if applicable) for damaged threads and secure installation.

25 Any damaged or excessively worn parts must be replaced with new ones.

26 If the inspection process indicates that the valve components are in generally poor condition and worn beyond the limits specified, which is usually the case in an engine that's being overhauled, reassemble the valves in the cylinder head and refer to Section 11 for valve servicing recommendations.

## Cam followers (4.6L engine)

▶ Refer to illustration 10.28

27 Clean all the parts thoroughly. Make sure all oil passages are open.

28 Check the cam follower pads (the areas that contact the lifter and valve stems end) for pits, wear, galling, score marks and rough spots (see illustration).

29 Check the cam follower roller (the area that contacts the camshaft) for pits, wear, galling, score marks and rough spots.

30 Any damaged or excessively worn parts must be replaced with new ones.

31 If the inspection process indicates that the valve components are in generally poor condition and worn beyond the limits specified, which is usually the case in an engine that's being overhauled, reassemble the valves in the cylinder head and refer to Section 11 for valve servicing recommendations.

## 11 Valves - servicing

1 Because of the complex nature of the job and the special tools and equipment needed, servicing of the valves, the valve seats and the valve guides, commonly known as a valve job, should be done by a professional.

2 The home mechanic can remove and disassemble the head, do the initial cleaning and inspection, then reassemble and deliver it to a dealer service department or an automotive machine shop for the actual service work. Doing the inspection will enable you to see what condition the head and valve train components are in and will ensure that you know what work and new parts are required when dealing with an automotive machine shop.

3 The dealer service department or automotive machine shop will

remove the valves and springs, recondition or replace the valves and valve seats, recondition the valve guides, check and replace the valve springs, spring retainers or rotators and keepers (as necessary), replace the valve seals with new ones, reassemble the valve components and make sure the installed spring height is correct. The cylinder head gasket surface will also be resurfaced if it's warped.

4 After the valve job has been performed by a professional, the head will be in like-new condition. When the head is returned, be sure to clean it again before installation on the engine to remove any metal particles and abrasive grit that may still be present from the valve service or head resurfacing operations. Use compressed air, if available, to blow out all the oil holes and passages.

## 12 Cylinder head - reassembly

▶ Refer to illustrations 12.3a, 12.3b, 12.6, 12.7a, 12.7b and 12.9

1 Regardless of whether or not the head was sent to an automotive repair shop for valve servicing, make sure it's clean before beginning reassembly.

2 If the head was sent out for valve servicing, the valves and related components will already be in place. Begin the reassembly procedure with Step 9.

3 On all engines, lubricate and install the valves, then install new seals on each of the valve guides. Using a hammer and deep socket, gently tap each seal into place until it's seated on the guide (see illustrations). Don't twist or cock the seals during installation or they will not seat properly on the valve stems.

**12.3a On models with the type of seal shown, use a hammer and a seal installer (or a deep socket, as shown here) to drive the seal onto the valve guide/head casting boss (umbrella-type seals don't need to be driven into place)**

12.3b  Installing a valve stem seal on an 4.6L engine - the socket must contact the flange (spring seat) of the seal

12.6  4.6L engines use valve stem seals that are a valve spring seat and seal combined into one part - make sure replacement parts are the same as the ones removed earlier

12.7a  Apply a small dab of grease to each keeper as shown here before installation - it'll hold them in place on the valve stem as the spring is released

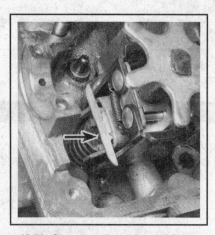

12.7b  Compress the springs with a valve spring compressor and position the keepers in the upper groove, then slowly release the compressor and make sure the keepers seat properly

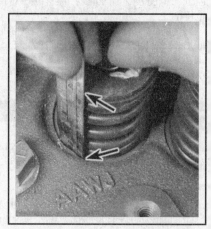

12.9  Valve spring installed height is the distance from the spring seat on the head to the bottom of the spring retainer

4    On 4.6L engines, reinstall the valve lifters.

5    Beginning at one end of the head, lubricate and install the first valve. Apply moly-base grease or clean engine oil to the valve stem.

6    Drop the spring seat or shim(s) over the valve guide and set the valve spring, retainer (or rotator) and sleeve (if used) in place.

➡Note: On 4.6L engines, the valve seal has the spring seat/shim incorporated into one piece (see illustration). A valve spring should never sit directly against an aluminum cylinder head.

7    Apply a small dab of grease to each keeper to hold it in place (see illustration). Compress the springs with a valve spring compressor and carefully install the keepers in the upper groove (see illustration), then slowly release the compressor and make sure the keepers seat properly.

8    Repeat the procedure for the remaining valves. Be sure to return the components to their original locations - don't mix them up!

9    Check the installed valve spring height with a ruler graduated in 1/32-inch increments or a dial caliper. If the head was sent out for service work, the installed height should be correct (but don't automatically assume that it is). The measurement is taken from the top of each spring seat or shim(s) to the bottom of the retainer (see illustration). If the height is greater than the figure listed in this Chapter's Specifications, shims can be added under the springs to correct it.

**✳✳ CAUTION:**

Don't, under any circumstances, shim the springs to the point where the installed height is less than specified.

10   Apply moly-base grease to the rocker arm faces and the fulcrums, then install the rocker arms and fulcrums on the cylinder head studs.

## 13 Pistons/connecting rods - removal

▶ Refer to illustrations 13.1, 13.3a, 13.3b, 13.4, 13.6a, 13.6b, 13.7 and 13.8

➡Note: Prior to removing the piston/connecting rod assemblies, remove the cylinder head(s), the oil pan and the oil pump (on 5.0L engines) by referring to the appropriate Sections in Chapter 2, Part A or Part B, depending which engine is being overhauled.

1   Use your fingernail to feel if a ridge has formed at the upper limit of ring travel (about 1/4-inch down from the top of each cylinder). If carbon deposits or cylinder wear have produced ridges, they must be completely removed with a special tool (see illustration). Follow the manufacturer's instructions provided with the tool. Failure to remove the ridges before attempting to remove the piston/connecting rod assemblies may result in piston breakage.

➡Note: Do not let the tool cut into the ring travel area more than 1/32-inch.

2   After the cylinder ridges have been removed, turn the engine upside-down so the crankshaft is facing up.

3   Before the connecting rods are removed, check the endplay with a dial indicator (see illustration) or with feeler gauges (see illustration). Slide them between the first connecting rod and the crankshaft throw until the play is removed. The endplay is equal to the thickness of the feeler gauge(s). If the endplay exceeds the service limit, new connecting rods will be required. If new rods (or a new crankshaft) are installed, the endplay may fall under the specified minimum (if it does, the rods will have to be machined to restore it - consult an automotive machine shop for advice if necessary). Repeat the procedure for the remaining connecting rods.

4   Check the connecting rods and caps for identification marks. If they aren't plainly marked, use a small center-punch, number stamping die (see illustration), or scribe, to make the appropriate number of indentations, or marks, on each rod and cap (1, 2, 3, etc., depending on the engine type and cylinder they're associated with).

5   Loosen each of the connecting rod cap nuts 1/2-turn at a time until they can be removed by hand.

6   Remove the connecting rod cap and bearing insert (see illustrations). Don't drop the bearing insert out of the cap.

13.1  A ridge reamer is required to remove the ridge from the top of each cylinder - do this before removing the pistons!

13.3a  Check the connecting rod side clearance (endplay) with a dial indicator . . .

13.4  Mark the rod bearing caps in order from the front of the engine to the rear (numbers can be used or use one mark for the front cap, two for the second one and so on)

13.3b  . . . or with a feeler gauge

**13.6a  Remove the rod and bearing insert together**

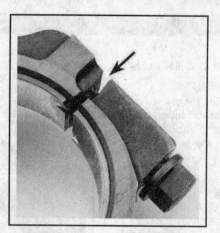

**13.6b  On 4.6L engine connecting rods the method used to manufacture and machine the rod cap is unique; they "fracture" (break) the cap from the rod to give a perfect match upon reassembly**

**13.7  To prevent damage to the crankshaft journals and cylinder walls, slip sections of hose over the rod bolts (if assembled with this type of rod nut and bolt) before removing the piston/rod assemblies**

**13.8  Use a hammer handle to drive the piston and connecting assembly down and out of the cylinder block, being very careful not to nick the crankshaft on the way out**

➥Note: The 4.6L engine uses a different method, referred to as fractured cap method, to more accurately match the rod cap to the connecting rod. The mating line of the rod and cap (see illustration) is made by breaking ("fracturing") the cap from the rod. This is supposed to ensure a perfect match once reassembled with its corresponding rod.

7  If the connecting rod has studs with attaching nuts (rather than cap bolts as shown in illustration 13.6a) slip a short length of plastic or rubber hose over each connecting rod cap bolt to protect the crankshaft journal and cylinder wall as the piston is removed (see illustration).

8  Remove the bearing insert and push the connecting rod/piston assembly out through the top of the engine. Use a wooden or plastic hammer handle to push on the upper bearing surface in the connecting rod (see illustration). If resistance is felt, double-check to make sure that all of the ridge was removed from the cylinder.

9  Repeat the procedure for the remaining cylinders.

10  After removal, reassemble the connecting rod caps and bearing inserts in their respective connecting rods and install the cap nuts finger tight. Leaving the old bearing inserts in place until reassembly will help prevent the connecting rod bearing surfaces from being accidentally nicked or gouged.

11  Don't separate the pistons from the connecting rods (see Section 18 for additional information).

## 14  Crankshaft - removal

▶ Refer to illustrations 14.1, 14.3, 14.4a and 14.4b

➥Note: The crankshaft can be removed only after the engine has been removed from the vehicle. It's assumed that the flywheel or driveplate, vibration damper, timing chain(s) or gears, oil pan, oil pump and piston/connecting rod assemblies have already been removed.

1  Before the crankshaft removal procedure is started, check the endplay. Mount a dial indicator with the stem in line with the crankshaft and just touching the end of the crankshaft (see illustration).

2  Push the crankshaft all the way to the rear and zero the dial indicator. Next, pry the crankshaft to the front as far as possible and check the reading on the dial indicator. The distance that it moves is the endplay. If it's greater than limit listed in this Chapter's Specifications, check the crankshaft thrust surfaces for wear. If no wear is evident, new main bearings should correct the endplay.

3  If a dial indicator isn't available, feeler gauges can be used. Gently pry or push the crankshaft all the way to the front of the engine. Slip

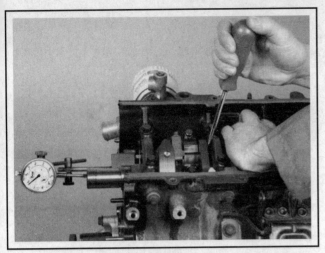

**14.1 Checking crankshaft endplay with a dial indicator**

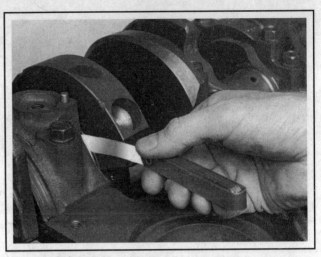

**14.3 Checking crankshaft endplay with a feeler gauge**

**14.4a The main bearing caps are usually marked to indicate their locations (arrows). They should be numbered consecutively from the front of the engine to the rear**

**14.4b Mark the main bearing caps with number stamping dies or a center punch if they aren't numbered**

feeler gauges between the crankshaft and the front face of the thrust main bearing to determine the clearance (see illustration).

4   Check the main bearing caps to see if they're marked to indicate their locations (see illustration). They should be numbered consecutively from the front of the engine to the rear. If they aren't, mark them with number stamping dies or a center-punch (see illustration). Main bearing caps generally have a cast-in arrow, which points to the front of the engine.

## 5.0L ENGINES

➡️Note: The thrust bearing on the 5.0L engines is the number three main bearing cap location. It has an upper and lower thrust bearing shell.

5   Loosen the main bearing cap bolts 1/4-turn at a time each, until they can be removed by hand. Note if any stud bolts are used and make sure they're returned to their original locations when the crankshaft is reinstalled.

## 4.6L ENGINES

▶ **Refer to illustrations 14.6, 14.7 and 14.9**

6   The 4.6L engines have a more complex crankshaft removal and assembly procedure than 5.0L engines because of the number of bolts

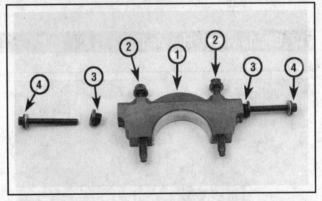

**14.6  4.6L engines used main bearing caps that are fastened to the block through the use of a set of bolts and specific adjustment procedures**

1   Main bearing cap
2   Main bearing cap bolts
3   Jack screws (left handed thread)
4   Side bolts

used to fasten the main cap to the cylinder block (see illustration). There are two main cap bolts, two jack screws and two side bolts on each of the number one through number four main caps.

➡️Note: The number five main bearing cap is the thrust bearing location and has upper and lower thrust bearing halves. It is

14.7 Remove the side bolts

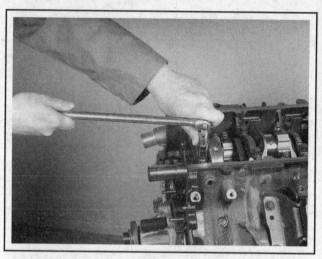

14.9 Following the reverse order of the tightening sequence (see illustration 23.27), remove the main bearing cap bolts, loosening them 1/4 turn at a time until they can be removed by hand

bolted to the block with two main cap bolts; no jack screws or side bolts are used, although it is drilled for jack screws.

It is extremely important to follow the removal and the installation procedure to ensure correct assembly and operation.

7 Remove all side bolts (see illustration).

8 Bottom all jack screws (which are 8 mm, Allen head screw, with left hand threads) against the main bearing caps (see illustration 14.6).

9 Remove the main bearing cap bolts (see illustration).

## ※※ CAUTION:

**The main bearing cap bolts are "angle torque" bolts and are NOT reusable. A pre-determined stretch of the bolt, calculated by the manufacturer, gives the added rigidity required with this cylinder block. Once removed they must be replaced. The side bolts and jack screws are reusable.**

## ALL ENGINES

10 Gently tap the caps with a soft-face hammer, then separate them from the engine block. If necessary, use the bolts as levers to remove the caps. Try not to drop the bearing inserts if they come out with the caps.

11 Carefully lift the crankshaft out of the engine. It may be a good idea to have an assistant available, since the crankshaft is quite heavy. With the bearing inserts in place in the engine block and main bearing caps, return the caps to their respective locations on the engine block and tighten the bolts finger tight.

## 15 Engine block - cleaning

15.1a A hammer and a large punch can be used to knock the core plugs sideways in their bores

◆ Refer to illustrations 15.1a, 15.1b, 15.8 and 15.10

## ※※ CAUTION:

**The core plugs (also known as freeze plugs or soft plugs) may be difficult or impossible to retrieve if they're driven into the block coolant passages.**

1 Using the wide end of a punch (see illustration) tap in on the outer edge of the core plug to turn the plug sideways in the bore. Then, using a pair of pliers, pull the core plug from the engine block (see illustration). Don't worry about the condition of the old core plugs as they are being removed because they will be replaced on reassembly with new plugs.

2 Using a gasket scraper, remove all traces of gasket material from

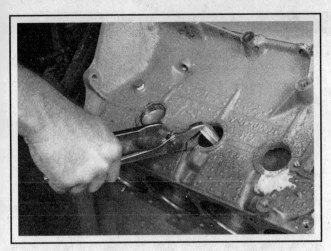

**15.1b  Pull the core plugs from the block with pliers**

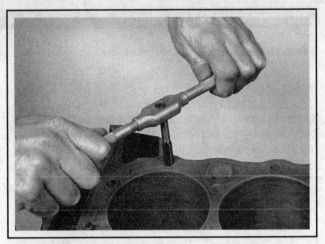

**15.8  All bolt holes in the block - particularly the main bearing cap and head bolt holes - should be cleaned and restored with a tap (be sure to remove debris from the holes after this is done)**

the engine block. Be very careful not to nick or gouge the gasket sealing surfaces.

3   Remove the main bearing caps and separate the bearing inserts from the caps and the engine block (see Section 14). Tag the bearings, indicating which cylinder they were removed from and whether they were in the cap or the block, then set them aside.

4   Remove all of the threaded oil gallery plugs from the block. The plugs are usually very tight - they may have to be drilled out and the holes re-tapped. Use new plugs when the engine is reassembled.

5   If the engine is extremely dirty it should be taken to an automotive machine shop to be steam cleaned or hot tanked.

6   After the block is returned, clean all oil holes and oil galleries one more time. Brushes specifically designed for this purpose are available at most auto parts stores. Flush the passages with warm water until the water runs clear, dry the block thoroughly and wipe all machined surfaces with a light, rust preventive oil. If you have access to compressed air, use it to speed the drying process and to blow out all the oil holes and galleries.

### ❊❊ WARNING:

**Wear eye protection when using compressed air!**

7   If the block isn't extremely dirty or sludged up, you can do an adequate cleaning job with hot soapy water and a stiff brush. Take plenty of time and do a thorough job. Regardless of the cleaning method used, be sure to clean all oil holes and galleries very thoroughly, dry the block completely and coat all machined surfaces with light oil.

8   The threaded holes in the block must be clean to ensure accurate torque readings during reassembly. Run the proper size tap into each of the holes to remove rust, corrosion, thread sealant or sludge and restore damaged threads (see illustration). If possible, use compressed air to clear the holes of debris produced by this operation. Now is a good time to clean the threads on the head bolts and the main bearing

**15.10  A large socket on an extension can be used to drive the new core plugs into the bores**

cap bolts as well.

9   Reinstall the main bearing caps and tighten all bolts finger tight.

10   After coating the sealing surfaces of the new core plugs with core plug sealant, install them in the engine block (see illustration). Make sure they're driven in straight and seated properly or leakage could result. Special tools are available for this purpose, but a large socket, with an outside diameter that will just slip into the core plug, a 1/2-inch drive extension and a hammer will work just as well.

11   Apply non-hardening sealant (such as Permatex no. 2 or Teflon pipe sealant) to the new oil gallery plugs and thread them into the holes in the block. Make sure they're tightened securely.

12   If the engine isn't going to be reassembled right away, cover it with a large plastic trash bag to keep it clean.

## 16 Engine block - inspection

▸ **Refer to illustrations 16.4a, 16.4b and 16.4c**

1   Before the block is inspected, it should be cleaned as described in Section 15.

2   Visually check the block for cracks, rust and corrosion. Look for stripped threads in the threaded holes. It's also a good idea to have the block checked for hidden cracks by an automotive machine shop that has the special equipment to do this type of work. If defects are found, have the block repaired, if possible, or replaced.

3   Check the cylinder bores for scuffing and scoring.

4   Measure the diameter of each cylinder at the top (just under the ridge area), center and bottom of the cylinder bore, parallel to the crankshaft axis (see illustrations).

5   Next, measure each cylinder's diameter at the same three locations across the crankshaft axis. Compare the results to this Chapter's Specifications.

6   If the required precision measuring tools aren't available, the piston-to-cylinder clearances can be obtained, though not quite as accurately, using feeler gauge stock. Feeler gauge stock comes in 12-inch lengths and various thicknesses and is generally available at auto parts stores.

7   To check the clearance, select a feeler gauge and slip it into the cylinder along with the matching piston. The piston must be positioned exactly as it normally would be. The feeler gauge must be between the piston and cylinder on one of the thrust faces (90-degrees to the piston pin bore).

8   The piston should slip through the cylinder (with the feeler gauge in place) with moderate pressure.

9   If it falls through or slides through easily, the clearance is excessive and a new piston will be required. If the piston binds at the lower end of the cylinder and is loose toward the top, the cylinder is tapered. If tight spots are encountered as the piston/feeler gauge is rotated in the cylinder, the cylinder is out-of-round.

10  Repeat the procedure for the remaining pistons and cylinders.

11  If the cylinder walls are badly scuffed or scored, or if they're out-of-round or tapered beyond the limits given in this Chapter's Specifications, have the engine block rebored and honed at an automotive machine shop. If a rebore is done, oversize pistons and rings will be required.

12  If the cylinders are in reasonably good condition and not worn to the outside of the limits, and if the piston-to-cylinder clearances can be maintained properly, then they don't have to be rebored. Honing is all that's necessary (see Section 17).

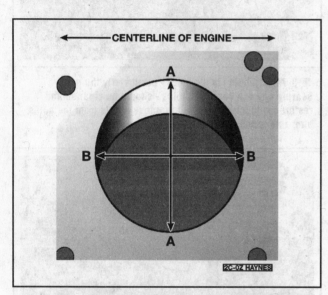

**16.4a  Measure the diameter of each cylinder at a right angle to the engine centerline (A), and parallel to engine centerline (B) - out-of-round is the difference between A and B, taper is the difference between A and B at the top of the cylinder and A and B at the bottom of the cylinder**

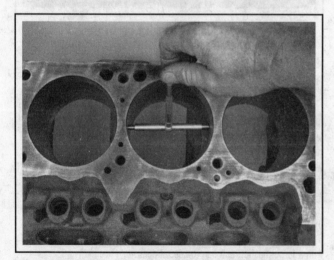

**16.4b  The ability to "feel" when the telescoping gauge is at the correct point will be developed over time, so work slowly and repeat the check until you're satisfied the bore measurement is accurate**

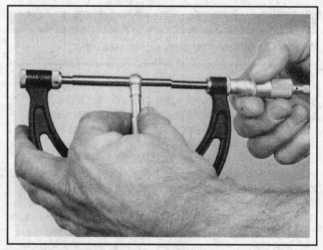

**16.4c  The gauge is then measured with a micrometer to determine the bore size**

## 17 Cylinder honing

▶ **Refer to illustrations 17.3a and 17.3b**

1   Prior to engine reassembly, the cylinder bores must be honed so the new piston rings will seat correctly and provide the best possible combustion chamber seal.

➡**Note: If you don't have the tools or don't want to tackle the honing operation, most automotive machine shops will do it for a reasonable fee.**

2   Before honing the cylinders, install the main bearing caps and tighten the bolts to the torque listed in this Chapter's Specifications.

3   Two types of cylinder hones are commonly available - the flex hone or "bottle brush" type and the more traditional surfacing hone with spring-loaded stones. Both will do the job, but for the less experienced mechanic the "bottle brush" hone will probably be easier to use. You'll also need some kerosene or honing oil, rags and an electric drill motor. Proceed as follows:

a) *Mount the hone in the drill motor, compress the stones and slip it into the first cylinder (see illustration). Be sure to wear safety goggles or a face shield!*

b) *Lubricate the cylinder with plenty of honing oil, turn on the drill and move the hone up-and-down in the cylinder at a pace that will produce a fine crosshatch pattern on the cylinder walls. Ideally, the crosshatch lines should intersect at approximately a 60-degree angle (see illustration). Be sure to use plenty of lubricant and don't take off any more material than is absolutely necessary to produce the desired finish.*

➡**Note: Piston ring manufacturers may specify a smaller cross-hatch angle than the traditional 60-degrees - read and follow any instructions included with the new rings.**

c) *Don't withdraw the hone from the cylinder while it's running. Instead, shut off the drill and continue moving the hone up-and-down in the cylinder until it comes to a complete stop, then compress the stones and withdraw the hone. If you're using a "bottle brush" type hone, stop the drill motor, then turn the chuck in the normal direction of rotation while withdrawing the hone from the cylinder.*

d) *Wipe the oil out of the cylinder and repeat the procedure for the remaining cylinders.*

4   After the honing job is complete, chamfer the top edges of the cylinder bores with a small file so the rings won't catch when the pistons are installed. Be very careful not to nick the cylinder walls with the end of the file.

5   The entire engine block must be washed again very thoroughly with warm, soapy water to remove all traces of the abrasive grit produced during the honing operation.

➡**Note: The bores can be considered clean when a lint-free white cloth - dampened with clean engine oil - used to wipe them out doesn't pick-up any more honing residue, which will**

**17.3a  A "bottle brush" hone is the easiest type of hone to use**

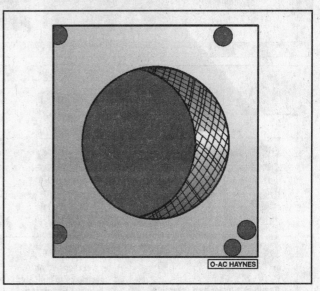

**17.3b  The cylinder hone should leave a smooth, crosshatch pattern with the lines intersecting at approximately a 60-degree angle**

**show up as gray areas on the cloth. Be sure to run a brush through all oil holes and galleries and flush them with running water.**

6   After rinsing, dry the block and apply a coat of light rust preventive oil to all machined surfaces. Wrap the block in a plastic trash bag to keep it clean and set it aside until reassembly.

# ENGINE BEARING ANALYSIS

## Debris

Babbitt bearing embedded with debris from machinings

Microscopic detail of debris

Microscopic detail of gouges

Overplated copper alloy bearing gouged by cast iron debris

Aluminum bearing embedded with glass beads

Microscopic detail of glass beads

Damaged lining caused by dirt left on the bearing back

## Misassembly

Result of a lower half assembled as an upper - blocking the oil flow

Excessive oil clearance is indicated by a short contact arc

Polished and oil-stained backs are a result of a poor fit in the housing bore

Result of a wrong, reversed, or shifted cap

## Overloading

Damage from excessive idling which resulted in an oil film unable to support the load imposed

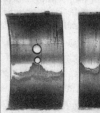

Damaged upper connecting rod bearings caused by engine lugging; the lower main bearings (not shown) were similarly affected

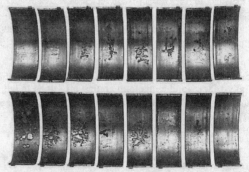

The damage shown in these upper and lower connecting rod bearings was caused by engine operation at a higher-than-rated speed under load

# Misalignment

A warped crankshaft caused this pattern of severe wear in the center, diminishing toward the ends

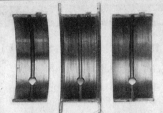

A poorly finished crankshaft caused the equally spaced scoring shown

A tapered housing bore caused the damage along one edge of this pair

A bent connecting rod led to the damage in the "V" pattern

# Corrosion

Microscopic detail of corrosion

Corrosion is an acid attack on the bearing lining generally caused by inadequate maintenance, extremely hot or cold operation, or inferior oils or fuels

# Lubrication

Result of dry start: The bearings on the left, farthest from the oil pump, show more damage

Result of a low oil supply or oil starvation

Severe wear as a result of inadequate oil clearance

Microscopic detail of cavitation

Example of cavitation - a surface erosion caused by pressure changes in the oil film

Damage from excessive thrust or insufficient axial clearance

Bearing affected by oil dilution caused by excessive blow-by or a rich mixture

## 18 Pistons/connecting rods - inspection

♦ **Refer to illustrations 18.4a, 18.4b, 18.10 and 18.11**

1   Before the inspection process can be carried out, the piston/connecting rod assemblies must be cleaned and the original piston rings removed from the pistons.

➡ **Note: Always use new piston rings when the engine is reassembled.**

2   Using a piston ring installation tool, carefully remove the rings from the pistons (see illustration 22.11). Be careful not to nick or gouge the pistons in the process.

3   Scrape all traces of carbon from the top of the piston. A hand-held wire brush or a piece of fine emery cloth can be used once the majority of the deposits have been scraped away. Do not, under any circumstances, use a wire brush mounted in a drill motor to remove deposits from the pistons. The piston material is soft and may be eroded away by the wire brush.

4   Use a piston ring groove cleaning tool to remove carbon deposits from the ring grooves. If a tool isn't available, a piece broken off the old ring will do the job (see illustrations). Be very careful to remove only the carbon deposits - don't remove any metal and do not nick or scratch the sides of the ring grooves.

5   Once the deposits have been removed, clean the piston/rod assemblies with solvent and dry them with compressed air (if avail-

able). Make sure the oil return holes in the back sides of the ring grooves are clear.

6   If the pistons and cylinder walls aren't damaged or worn excessively, and if the engine block is not rebored, new pistons won't be necessary. Normal piston wear appears as even vertical wear on the piston thrust surfaces and slight looseness of the top ring in its groove. New piston rings, however, should always be used when an engine is rebuilt.

7   Carefully inspect each piston for cracks around the skirt, at the pin bosses and at the ring lands.

8   Look for scoring and scuffing on the thrust faces of the skirt, holes in the piston crown and burned areas at the edge of the crown. If the skirt is scored or scuffed, the engine may have been suffering from overheating and/or abnormal combustion, which caused excessively high operating temperatures. The cooling and lubrication systems should be checked thoroughly. A hole in the piston crown is an indication that abnormal combustion (pre-ignition) was occurring. Burned areas at the edge of the piston crown are usually evidence of spark knock (detonation). If any of the above problems exist, the causes must be corrected or the damage will occur again. The causes may include intake air leaks, incorrect fuel/air mixture, incorrect ignition timing and EGR system malfunctions.

9   Corrosion of the piston, in the form of small pits, indicates that coolant is leaking into the combustion chamber and/or the crankcase. Again, the cause must be corrected or the problem may persist in the rebuilt engine.

10  Measure the piston ring side clearance by laying a new piston ring in each ring groove and slipping a feeler gauge in beside it (see illustration). Check the clearance at three or four locations around each groove. Be sure to use the correct ring for each groove - they are different. If the side clearance is greater than the figure listed in this Chapter's Specifications, new pistons will have to be used.

11  Check the piston-to-bore clearance by measuring the bore (see Section 16) and the piston diameter. Make sure the pistons and bores are correctly matched. Measure the piston across the skirt, at a 90-degree angle to, and in line with, the piston pin (see illustration). Subtract the piston diameter from the bore diameter to obtain the clearance. If it's greater than specified, the block will have to be rebored and new pistons and rings installed.

12  Check the piston-to-rod clearance by twisting the piston and rod in opposite directions. Any noticeable play indicates excessive wear,

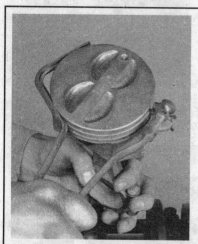

**18.4a  The piston ring grooves can be cleaned with a special tool, as shown here . . .**

**18.4b . . . or a section of a broken ring**

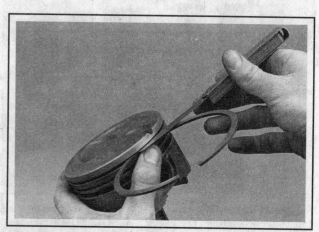

**18.10  Check the ring side clearance with a feeler gauge at several points around the groove**

which must be corrected. The piston/connecting rod assemblies should be taken to an automotive machine shop to have the pistons and rods resized and new pins installed.

13  If the pistons must be removed from the connecting rods for any reason, they should be taken to an automotive machine shop. While they are there have the connecting rods checked for bend and twist, since automotive machine shops have special equipment for this purpose.

➡**Note: Unless new pistons and/or connecting rods must be installed, do not disassemble the pistons and connecting rods.**

14  Check the connecting rods for cracks and other damage. Temporarily remove the rod caps, lift out the old bearing inserts, wipe the rod and cap bearing surfaces clean and inspect them for nicks, gouges and scratches. After checking the rods, replace the old bearings, slip the caps into place and tighten the nuts finger tight.

➡**Note: If the engine is being rebuilt because of a connecting rod knock, be sure to install new rods.**

18.11  Measure the piston diameter at a 90-degree angle to the piston pin and in line with it

## 19  Crankshaft - inspection

▶ **Refer to illustrations 19.1, 19.2, 19.3, 19.6 and 19.8**

1   Remove all burrs from the crankshaft oil holes with a stone, file or scraper (see illustration).

2   Clean the crankshaft with solvent and dry it with compressed air (if available). Be sure to clean the oil holes with a stiff brush (see illustration) and flush them with solvent.

3   Rub a penny across each journal several times (see illustration). If a journal picks up copper from the penny, it's too rough and must be reground.

4   Check the main and connecting rod bearing journals for uneven wear, scoring, pits and cracks.

5   Check the rest of the crankshaft for cracks and other damage. It should be magnafluxed to reveal hidden cracks - an automotive machine shop will handle the procedure.

6   Using a micrometer, measure the diameter of the main and connecting rod journals and compare the results to this Chapter's Speci-

19.1  The oil holes should be chamfered so sharp edges don't gouge or scratch the new bearings

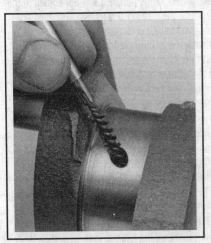

19.2  Use a wire or stiff plastic bristle brush to clean the oil passages in the crankshaft

19.3  Rubbing a penny lengthwise on each journal will reveal its condition - if copper rubs off and is embedded in the crankshaft, the journals should be reground

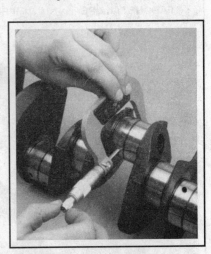

19.6  Measure the diameter of each crankshaft journal at several points to detect taper and out-of-round conditions

**19.8 If the seals have worn grooves in the crankshaft journals, or if the seal contact surfaces are nicked or scratched, the new seals will leak**

fications (see illustration). By measuring the diameter at a number of points around each journal's circumference, you'll be able to determine whether or not the journal is out-of-round. Take the measurement at each end of the journal, near the crank throws, to determine if the journal is tapered.

7   If the crankshaft journals are damaged, tapered, out-of-round or worn beyond the limits given in the Specifications, have the crankshaft reground by an automotive machine shop. Be sure to use the correct size bearing inserts if the crankshaft is reconditioned.

8   Check the oil seal journals at each end of the crankshaft for wear and damage. If the seal has worn a groove in the journal, or if it's nicked or scratched (see illustration), the new seal may leak when the engine is reassembled. In some cases, an automotive machine shop may be able to repair the journal by pressing on a thin sleeve. If repair isn't feasible, a new or different crankshaft should be installed.

9   Refer to Section 20 and examine the main and rod bearing inserts.

## 20   Main and connecting rod bearings - inspection

▶ **Refer to illustration 20.1**

1   Even though the main and connecting rod bearings should be replaced with new ones during the engine overhaul, the old bearings should be retained for close examination, as they may reveal valuable information about the condition of the engine (see illustration).

2   Bearing failure occurs because of lack of lubrication, the presence of dirt or other foreign particles, overloading the engine and cor-

rosion. Regardless of the cause of bearing failure, it must be corrected before the engine is reassembled to prevent it from happening again.

3   When examining the bearings, remove them from the engine block, the main bearing caps, the connecting rods and the rod caps and lay them out on a clean surface in the same general position as their location in the engine. This will enable you to match any bearing problems with the corresponding crankshaft journal.

4   Dirt and other foreign particles get into the engine in a variety of ways. It may be left in the engine during assembly, or it may pass through filters or the PCV system. It may get into the oil, and from there into the bearings. Metal chips from machining operations and normal engine wear are often present. Abrasives are sometimes left in engine components after reconditioning, especially when parts are not thoroughly cleaned using the proper cleaning methods. Whatever the source, these foreign objects often end up embedded in the soft bearing material and are easily recognized. Large particles will not embed in the bearing and will score or gouge the bearing and journal. The best prevention for this cause of bearing failure is to clean all parts thoroughly and keep everything spotlessly clean during engine assembly. Frequent and regular engine oil and filter changes are also recommended.

5   Lack of lubrication (or lubrication breakdown) has a number of interrelated causes. Excessive heat (which thins the oil), overloading (which squeezes the oil from the bearing face) and oil leakage or throw off (from excessive bearing clearances, worn oil pump or high engine speeds) all contribute to lubrication breakdown. Blocked oil passages, which usually are the result of misaligned oil holes in a bearing shell, will also oil starve a bearing and destroy it. When lack of lubrication is the cause of bearing failure, the bearing material is wiped or extruded from the steel backing of the bearing. Temperatures may increase to the point where the steel backing turns blue from overheating.

6   Driving habits can have a definite effect on bearing life. Full throttle, low speed operation (lugging the engine) puts very high loads on bearings, which tends to squeeze out the oil film. These loads cause the bearings to flex, which produces fine cracks in the bearing face (fatigue failure). Eventually the bearing material will loosen in pieces and tear away from the steel backing. Short trip driving leads to corrosion of bearings because insufficient engine heat is produced to drive

**CRATERS OR POCKETS**

**FATIGUE FAILURE**

**BRIGHT (POLISHED) SECTIONS**

**IMPROPER SEATING**

**SCRATCHES**

**DIRT IMBEDDED INTO BEARING MATERIAL**

**SCRATCHED BY DIRT**

**OVERLAY WIPED OUT**

**LACK OF OIL**

**OVERLAY GONE FROM ENTIRE SURFACE**

**EXCESSIVE WEAR**

**RADIUS RIDE**

**TAPERED JOURNAL**

**20.1 Typical bearing failures**

off the condensed water and corrosive gases. These products collect in the engine oil, forming acid and sludge. As the oil is carried to the engine bearings, the acid attacks and corrodes the bearing material.

7   Incorrect bearing installation during engine assembly will lead to bearing failure as well. Tight fitting bearings leave insufficient bearing oil clearance and will result in oil starvation. Dirt or foreign particles trapped behind a bearing insert result in high spots on the bearing which lead to failure.

## 21  Engine overhaul - reassembly sequence

1   Before beginning engine reassembly, make sure you have all the necessary new parts, gaskets and seals as well as the following items on hand:

Common hand tools
A 1/2-inch drive torque wrench
A 3/8-inch drive torque wrench (inch-lb measurement)
Piston ring installation tool
Piston ring compressor
Vibration damper installation tool
Short lengths of rubber or plastic hose to fit over connecting rod bolts
Plastigage
Feeler gauges
A fine-tooth file
New engine oil
Engine assembly lube or moly-base grease
Gasket sealant
Thread locking compound

2   In order to save time and avoid problems, engine reassembly must be done in the following general order:

### 5.0L engines

New camshaft bearings (recommended to be done by an automotive machine shop)
Piston rings
Crankshaft and main bearings
Piston/connecting rod assemblies
Oil pump
Oil pan
Camshaft
Valve lifters
Timing chain and sprockets
Timing chain cover
Cylinder heads
Rocker arms and pushrods
Intake and exhaust manifolds
Valve covers
Driveplate

### 4.6L engines

Piston rings
Crankshaft and main bearings
Piston/connecting rod assemblies
Oil pump
Oil pan
Cylinder heads
Valve lifters
Camshaft followers
Camshaft(s)
Camshaft cap cluster assemblies
Timing chain(s) and sprockets
Timing chain guides and tensioners
Timing chain cover
Intake and exhaust manifolds
Valve covers
Driveplate

## 22  Piston rings - installation

▶ **Refer to illustrations 22.3, 22.4, 22.8a, 22.8b and 22.11**

1   Before installing the new piston rings, the ring end gaps must be checked. It's assumed that the piston ring side clearance has been checked and verified correct (see Section 18).

2   Lay out the piston/connecting rod assemblies and the new ring sets so the ring sets will be matched with the same piston and cylinder during the end gap measurement and engine assembly.

3   Insert the top (number one) ring into the first cylinder and square it up with the cylinder walls by pushing it in with the top of the piston (see illustration). The ring should be near the bottom of the cylinder, at the lower limit of ring travel.

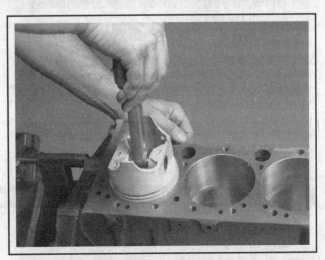

**22.3  When checking piston ring end gap, the ring must be square in the cylinder bore (this is done by pushing the ring down with the top of a piston as shown)**

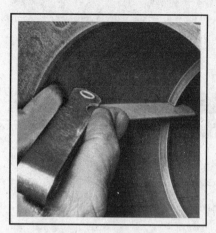

**22.4 With the ring square in the cylinder, measure the end gap with a feeler gauge**

**22.8a Installing the spacer/expander in the oil control ring groove . . .**

**22.8b . . . followed by the side rails - DO NOT use a piston ring installation tool when installing the oil ring side rails**

**22.11 Installing the compressor rings with a ring expander - the mark (arrow) must face up**

4   To measure the end gap, slip feeler gauges between the ends of the ring until a gauge equal to the gap width is found (see illustration). The feeler gauge should slide between the ring ends with a slight amount of drag. Compare the measurement to this Chapter's Specifications. If the gap is larger or smaller than specified, double-check to make sure you have the correct rings before proceeding. If there is any doubt contact the parts store where the rings were purchased, to verify that the correct ring set is being used.

5   Excess end gap isn't critical unless it's greater than 0.040-inch. Again, double-check to make sure you have the correct rings for your engine.

6   Repeat the procedure for each ring that will be installed in the first cylinder and for each ring in the remaining cylinders. Remember to keep rings, pistons and cylinders matched up.

7   Once the ring end gaps have been checked/corrected, the rings can be installed on the pistons.

8   The oil control ring (lowest one on the piston) is usually installed first. It's composed of three separate components. Slip the spacer/expander into the groove (see illustration). Next, install the lower side rail. Don't use a piston ring installation tool on the oil ring side rails, as they may be damaged. Instead, place one end of the side rail into the groove between the spacer/expander and the ring land, hold it firmly in place and slide a finger around the piston while pushing the rail into the groove (see illustration). Next, install the upper side rail in the same manner.

9   After the three oil ring components have been installed, check to make sure that both the upper and lower side rails can be turned smoothly in the ring groove.

10  The number two (middle) ring is installed next. It's usually stamped with a mark which must face up, toward the top of the piston.

➡Note: Always follow the instructions printed on the ring package or box - different manufacturers may require different approaches. Do not mix up the top and middle rings, as they have different cross sections.

11  Use a piston ring installation tool and make sure the identification mark is facing the top of the piston, then slip the ring into the middle groove on the piston (see illustration). Don't expand the ring any more than necessary to slide it over the piston.

12  Install the number one (top) ring in the same manner. Make sure the mark is facing up. Be careful not to confuse the number one and number two rings.

13  Repeat the procedure for the remaining pistons and rings.

## 23  Crankshaft - installation and main bearing oil clearance check

1   Crankshaft installation is the first step in engine reassembly. It's assumed at this point that the engine block and crankshaft have been cleaned, inspected and repaired or reconditioned.

2   Position the engine with the bottom facing up.

3   Remove the main bearing cap bolts and lift out the caps. Lay them out in the proper order to ensure correct installation.

4   If they're still in place, remove the original bearing inserts from the block and the main bearing caps. Wipe the bearing surfaces of the block and caps with a clean, lint-free cloth. They must be kept spotlessly clean.

**23.11 Lay the Plastigage strips (arrow) on the main bearing journals, parallel to the crankshaft centerline**

**23.15 Compare the width of the crushed Plastigage to the scale on the envelope to determine the main bearing oil clearance (always take the measurement at the widest point of the Plastigage); be sure to use the correct scale - standard and metric ones are included**

## MAIN BEARING OIL CLEARANCE CHECK

▶ **Refer to illustrations 23.11 and 23.15**

5   Clean the back sides of the new main bearing inserts and lay one in each main bearing saddle in the block. If one of the bearing inserts from each set has a large groove in it, make sure the grooved insert is installed in the block. Lay the other bearing from each set in the corresponding main bearing cap. Make sure the tab on the bearing insert fits into the recess in the block or cap.

### ✳✳ CAUTION:

The oil holes in the block must line up with the oil holes in the bearing insert. Do not hammer the bearing into place and don't nick or gouge the bearing faces. No lubrication should be used at this time.

6   The flanged thrust bearing must be installed in the third cap and saddle on 5.0L engines, or the fifth cap and saddle on 4.6L engines.

7   Clean the faces of the bearings in the block and the crankshaft main bearing journals with a clean, lint-free cloth.

8   Check or clean the oil holes in the crankshaft, as any dirt here can go only one way - straight through the new bearings.

9   Once you're certain the crankshaft is clean, carefully lay it in position in the main bearings.

10   Before the crankshaft can be permanently installed, the main bearing oil clearance must be checked.

11   Cut several pieces of the appropriate size Plastigage (they must be slightly shorter than the width of the main bearings) and place one piece on each crankshaft main bearing journal, parallel with the journal axis (see illustration).

12   Clean the faces of the bearings in the caps and install the caps in their respective positions (don't mix them up) with the arrows pointing toward the front of the engine (see Section 14). Don't disturb the Plastigage.

13   Starting with the center main and working out toward the ends, tighten the main bearing cap bolts, in three steps, to the torque listed in this Chapter's Specifications.

➡Note: On the 4.6L engine it is not necessary to install the jack screws or the side bolts for Plastigage measurement purposes. Don't rotate the crankshaft at any time during this operation.

14   Remove the bolts and carefully lift off the main bearing caps. Keep them in order. Don't disturb the Plastigage or rotate the crankshaft. If any of the main bearing caps are difficult to remove, tap them gently from side-to-side with a soft-face hammer to loosen them.

15   Compare the width of the crushed Plastigage on each journal to the scale printed on the Plastigage envelope to obtain the main bearing oil clearance (see illustration). Check the Specifications to make sure it's correct.

16   If the clearance is not as specified, the bearing inserts may be the wrong size (which means different ones will be required). Before deciding that different inserts are needed, make sure that no dirt or oil was between the bearing inserts and the caps or block when the clearance was measured. If the Plastigage was wider at one end than the other, the journal may be tapered (refer to Section 19).

17   Carefully scrape all traces of the Plastigage material off the main bearing journals and/or the bearing faces. Use your fingernail or the edge of a credit card - don't nick or scratch the bearing faces.

## FINAL CRANKSHAFT INSTALLATION

18   Carefully lift the crankshaft out of the engine.

19   Clean the bearing faces in the block, then apply a thin, uniform layer of moly-base grease or engine assembly lube to each of the bearing surfaces. Be sure to coat the thrust faces as well as the journal face of the thrust bearing.

20   Make sure the crankshaft journals are clean, then lay the crankshaft back in place in the block.

21   Clean the faces of the bearings in the caps, then apply lubricant to them.

22   Install the caps in their respective positions with the arrows pointing toward the front of the engine.

### 5.0L engines

▶ **Refer to illustration 23.27**

23   Install the main cap bolts.

24   Tighten all, except the thrust bearing cap bolts (number 3) to the torque listed in this Chapter's Specifications (work from the center out and approach the final torque in three steps).

25   Tighten the thrust bearing cap bolts finger tight.

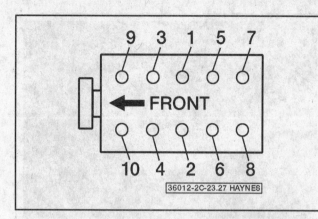

**23.27 Tighten the main bearing cap bolts in the sequence shown (5.0L engine)**

26 Pry the crankshaft forward and while holding pressure on the crankshaft, pry the thrust bearing cap backward. Forcing these two in opposite directions, against each other, will align the thrust bearing surfaces.

27 While keeping forward pressure on the crankshaft, re-tighten ALL main bearing cap bolts to the torque listed in this Chapter's Specifications, following the proper tightening sequence (see illustration).

28 Rotate the crankshaft a number of times by hand to check for any obvious binding.

29 The final step is to check the crankshaft endplay with a feeler gauge or a dial indicator (see Section 13) The endplay should be correct if the crankshaft thrust faces aren't worn or damaged and new bearings have been installed.

30 Install the rear main oil seal (see Chapter 2, Part A).

### 4.6L engines

▶ Refer to illustrations 23.35, 23.36a, 23.36b, 23.36c, 23.37a, 23.37b and 23.37c

31 Install the jack screws into the main caps and bottom them lightly against the caps, this must be done before the caps are placed into the block.

32 Place the main caps on their correct journals and tap the caps into place with a brass or soft-face hammer.

### ✳✳ CAUTION:

**All main bearing caps MUST be tapped into position prior to tightening. Failure to do so may result in improper torque.**

**23.36a Place the Allen wrench through the side bolt hole and tighten the jack screw against the cylinder block . . .**

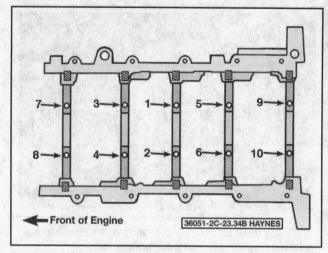

**23.35 Tighten the main bearing cap bolts in the sequence shown (4.6L engine)**

33 Install the main cap bolts and tighten them to 10-to-12 ft-lbs.

➡**Note: The crankshaft main bearing cap bolts must be replaced with new bolts. These bolts are designed as torque-to-yield bolts and they cannot be reused once they are removed.**

34 Push the crankshaft forward using a screwdriver or prybar to seat the thrust bearing.

### ✳✳ CAUTION:

**Once the crankshaft is pushed fully forward, to seat the thrust bearing, leave the screwdriver in position so that pressure stays placed on the crankshaft until after all main bearing cap bolts have been tightened.**

35 Tighten the main bearing cap bolts in two steps in the sequence shown (see illustration) and to the torque and angle indicated in the Specifications listed at the end of this Chapter.

36 Tighten all jack screws in two steps and in the sequence shown (see illustrations) to the Specifications listed at the beginning of this Chapter.

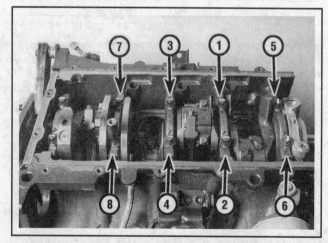

**23.36b . . . in two steps following the sequence shown and using the torque specifications found at the end of this Chapter - 1991 through 1994 models shown**

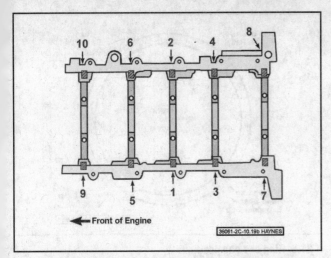

**23.36c** Jack screw tightening sequence on 1995 and later 4.6L models

**23.37a** Tighten the side bolts . . .

**23.37b** . . . in two steps following the sequence shown and using the torque specifications found at the end of this Chapter - 1991 through 1994 moedls shown

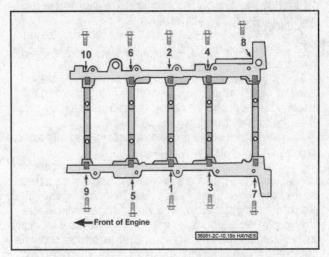

**23.37c** Side bolt tightening sequence on 1995 and later 4.6L models

37  Tighten all side bolts in two steps and in the sequence shown (see illustrations) to the Specifications listed at the end of this Chapter.

38  Check crankshaft endplay again and verify that it is correct (see Section 14).

39  Rotate the crankshaft a number of times by hand to check for any obvious binding.

40  Install the rear main oil seal (see Chapter 2, Part B).

## 24  Pistons/connecting rods - installation and rod bearing oil clearance check

1  Before installing the piston/connecting rod assemblies, the cylinder walls must be perfectly clean, the top edge of each cylinder must be chamfered, and the crankshaft must be in place.

2  Remove the cap from the end of the number one connecting rod (refer to the marks made during removal). Remove the original bearing inserts and wipe the bearing surfaces of the connecting rod and cap with a clean, lint-free cloth. They must be kept spotlessly clean.

### CONNECTING ROD BEARING OIL CLEARANCE CHECK

▶ Refer to illustrations 24.3, 24.5, 24.9, 24.11, 24.13 and 24.17

3  Clean the back side of the new upper bearing insert, then lay it in place in the connecting rod (see illustration). Make sure the tab on the

bearing fits into the recess in the rod. Don't hammer the bearing insert into place and be very careful not to nick or gouge the bearing face. Don't lubricate the bearing at this time.

4  Clean the back side of the other bearing insert and install it in the rod cap (see illustration 24.3). Again, make sure the tab on the bearing fits into the recess in the cap, and don't apply any lubricant. It's critically important that the mating surfaces of the bearing and connecting rod are perfectly clean and oil free when they're assembled.

5  Position the piston ring gaps at intervals around the piston (see illustration).

6  On 5.0L engines, slip a section of plastic or rubber hose over each connecting rod bolt (see illustration 13.7).

➡**Note: 4.6L engines use cap bolts that are screwed into the rod after the rod and cap are assembled on the crankshaft.**

**24.3 Insert the connecting rod bearing halves, making sure the bearing tab (arrows) are in the notches in the rod and cap**

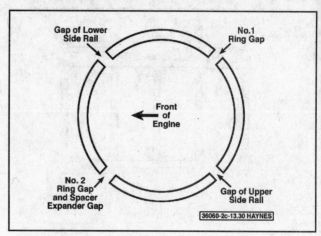

**24.5 Ring end gap positions**

7   Lubricate the piston and rings with clean engine oil and attach a piston ring compressor to the piston. Leave the skirt protruding about 1/4-inch to guide the piston into the cylinder. The rings must be compressed until they're flush with the piston.

8   Rotate the crankshaft until the number one connecting rod journal is at BDC (bottom dead center) and apply a coat of engine oil to the cylinder walls.

9   With the arrow or notches on top of the piston (see illustration) facing the front of the engine, gently insert the piston/connecting rod assembly into the number one cylinder bore and rest the bottom edge of the ring compressor on the engine block.

10   Tap the top edge of the ring compressor to make sure it's contacting the block around its entire circumference.

11   Gently tap on the top of the piston with the end of a wooden hammer handle (see illustration) while guiding the end of the connecting rod into place on the crankshaft journal. The piston rings may try to pop out of the ring compressor just before entering the cylinder bore, so keep some downward pressure on the ring compressor. Work slowly, and if any resistance is felt as the piston enters the cylinder, stop immediately. Find out what's hanging up and fix it before proceeding. Do not, for any reason, force the piston into the cylinder - you might break a ring and/or the piston.

12   Once the piston/connecting rod assembly is installed, the connecting rod bearing oil clearance must be checked before the rod cap is permanently bolted in place.

13   Cut a piece of the appropriate size Plastigage slightly shorter than the width of the connecting rod bearing and lay it in place on the number one connecting rod journal, parallel with the journal axis (see illustration).

14   Clean the connecting rod cap bearing face, remove the protective hoses from the connecting rod bolts and install the rod cap. Make sure the mating mark on the cap is on the same side as the mark on the connecting rod.

15   Install the nuts and tighten them to the torque listed in this Chapter's Specifications, working up to it in three steps.

➡**Note: Use a thin-wall socket to avoid erroneous torque readings that can result if the socket is wedged between the rod cap and nut/bolt. If the socket tends to wedge itself between the nut and the cap, lift up on it slightly until it no longer contacts the cap. Do not rotate the crankshaft at any time during this operation.**

16   Remove the nuts/bolts and detach the rod cap, being very careful not to disturb the Plastigage.

17   Compare the width of the crushed Plastigage to the scale printed on the Plastigage envelope to obtain the oil clearance (see illustration). Compare it to the Specifications to make sure the clearance is correct.

18   If the clearance is not as specified, the bearing inserts may be the wrong size (which means different ones will be required). Before deciding that different inserts are needed, make sure that no dirt or oil was between the bearing inserts and the connecting rod or cap when the clearance was measured. Also, recheck the journal diameter. If the Plastigage was wider at one end than the other, the journal may be tapered (refer to Section 18).

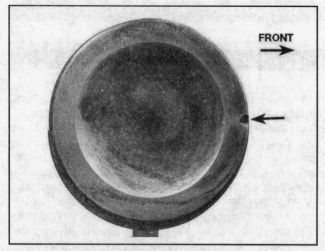

**FRONT** →

**24.9 Turn the piston when installing it to make sure the mark/notch in the piston faces the front of the engine as they are installed**

**24.11 The piston can be driven gently into the cylinder bore with the end of a wooden or plastic hammer handle**

**24.13 Lay the Plastigage strips on each rod bearing journal, parallel to the crankshaft centerline**

## FINAL CONNECTING ROD INSTALLATION

19  Carefully scrape all traces of the Plastigage material off the rod journal and/or bearing face. Be very careful not to scratch the bearing - use your fingernail or the edge of a credit card.

20  Make sure the bearing faces are perfectly clean, then apply a uniform layer of clean moly-base grease or engine assembly lube to both of them. You'll have to push the piston into the cylinder to expose the face of the bearing insert in the connecting rod - be sure to slip the protective hoses over the rod bolts first (5.0L engines only).

21  Slide the connecting rod back into place on the journal, remove the protective hoses from the rod cap bolts, install the rod cap and tighten the nuts or bolts to the torque listed in this Chapter's Specifications. Again, work up to the torque in three steps.

### ✳✳ CAUTION:

**On 4.6L engines, new rod bolts must be used.**

**24.17 Measuring the width of the crushed Plastigage to determine the rod bearing oil clearance (be sure to use the correct scale - standard and metric ones are included)**

22  Repeat the entire procedure for the remaining pistons/connecting rods.

23  The important points to remember are:
   a)  *Keep the back sides of the bearing inserts and the insides of the connecting rods and caps perfectly clean when assembling them.*
   b)  *Make sure you have the correct piston/rod assembly for each cylinder.*
   c)  *The notches or mark on the piston must face the FRONT of the engine.*
   d)  *Lubricate the cylinder walls with clean oil.*
   e)  *Lubricate the bearing faces when installing the rod caps after the oil clearance has been checked.*

24  After all the piston/connecting rod assemblies have been properly installed, rotate the crankshaft a number of times by hand to check for any obvious binding.

25  As a final step, the connecting rod endplay must be checked. Refer to Section 13 for this procedure.

26  Compare the measured endplay to the Specifications to make sure it's correct. If it was correct before disassembly and the original crankshaft and rods were reinstalled, it should still be right. If new rods or a new crankshaft were installed, the endplay may be inadequate. If so, the rods will have to be removed and taken to an automotive machine shop for resizing.

## 25  Initial start-up and break-in after overhaul

### ✳✳ WARNING:

**Have a fire extinguisher handy when starting the engine for the first time.**

1  Once the engine has been installed in the vehicle, double-check the engine oil and coolant levels.

2  With the spark plugs out of the engine and the ignition system disabled (see Chapter 1), crank the engine until oil pressure registers on the gauge or the light goes out.

3  Install the spark plugs, hook up the plug wires and restore the ignition system functions.

4  Start the engine. It may take a few moments for the fuel system to build up pressure, but the engine should start without a great deal of effort.

➡ **Note: If backfiring occurs through the throttle body, recheck the valve timing and ignition timing.**

5  After the engine starts, it should be allowed to warm up to normal operating temperature. While the engine is warming up, make a thorough check for fuel, oil and coolant leaks.

6  Shut the engine off and recheck the engine oil and coolant levels.

7  Drive the vehicle to an area with minimum traffic, accelerate from 30 to 50 mph, then allow the vehicle to slow to 30 mph with the throttle closed. Repeat the procedure 10 or 12 times. This will load the piston rings and cause them to seat properly against the cylinder walls. Check again for oil and coolant leaks.

8  Drive the vehicle gently for the first 500 miles (no sustained high speeds) and keep a constant check on the oil level. It is not unusual for an engine to use oil during the break-in period.

9  At approximately 500 to 600 miles, change the oil and filter.

10  For the next few hundred miles, drive the vehicle normally. Do not pamper it or abuse it.

11  After 2000 miles, change the oil and filter again and consider the engine broken in.

# GLOSSARY

## B

**Backlash** - The amount of play between two parts. Usually refers to how much one gear can be moved back and forth without moving gear with which it's meshed.

**Bearing Caps** - The caps held in place by nuts or bolts which, in turn, hold the bearing surface. This space is for lubricating oil to enter.

**Bearing clearance** - The amount of space left between shaft and bearing surface. This space is for lubricating oil to enter.

**Bearing crush** - The additional height which is purposely manufactured into each bearing half to ensure complete contact of the bearing back with the housing bore when the engine is assembled.

**Bearing knock** - The noise created by movement of a part in a loose or worn bearing.

**Blueprinting** - Dismantling an engine and reassembling it to EXACT specifications.

**Bore** - An engine cylinder, or any cylindrical hole; also used to describe the process of enlarging or accurately refinishing a hole with a cutting tool, as to bore an engine cylinder. The bore size is the diameter of the hole.

**Boring** - Renewing the cylinders by cutting them out to a specified size. A boring bar is used to make the cut.

**Bottom end** - A term which refers collectively to the engine block, crankshaft, main bearings and the big ends of the connecting rods.

**Break-in** - The period of operation between installation of new or rebuilt parts and time in which parts are worn to the correct fit. Driving at reduced and varying speed for a specified mileage to permit parts to wear to the correct fit.

**Bushing** - A one-piece sleeve placed in a bore to serve as a bearing surface for shaft, piston pin, etc. Usually replaceable.

## C

**Camshaft** - The shaft in the engine, on which a series of lobes are located for operating the valve mechanisms. The camshaft is driven by gears or sprockets and a timing chain. Usually referred to simply as the cam.

**Carbon** - Hard, or soft, black deposits found in combustion chamber, on plugs, under rings, on and under valve heads.

**Cast iron** - An alloy of iron and more than two percent carbon, used for engine blocks and heads because it's relatively inexpensive and easy to mold into complex shapes.

**Chamfer** - To bevel across (or a bevel on) the sharp edge of an object.

**Chase** - To repair damaged threads with a tap or die.

**Combustion chamber** - The space between the piston and the cylinder head, with the piston at top dead center, in which air-fuel mixture is burned.

**Compression ratio** - The relationship between cylinder volume (clearance volume) when the piston is at top dead center and cylinder volume when the piston is at bottom dead center.

**Connecting rod** - The rod that connects the crank on the crankshaft with the piston. Sometimes called a con rod.

**Connecting rod cap** - The part of the connecting rod assembly that attaches the rod to the crankpin.

**Core plug** - Soft metal plug used to plug the casting holes for the coolant passages in the block.

**Crankcase** - The lower part of the engine in which the crankshaft rotates; includes the lower section of the cylinder block and the oil pan.

**Crank kit** - A reground or reconditioned crankshaft and new main and connecting rod bearings.

**Crankpin** - The part of a crankshaft to which a connecting rod is attached.

**Crankshaft** - The main rotating member, or shaft, running the length of the crankcase, with offset throws to which the connecting rods are attached; changes the reciprocating motion of the pistons into rotating motion.

**Cylinder sleeve** - A replaceable sleeve, or liner, pressed into the cylinder block to form the cylinder bore.

## D

**Deburring** - Removing the burrs (rough edges or areas) from a bearing.

**Deglazer** - A tool, rotated by an electric motor, used to remove glaze from cylinder walls so a new set of rings will seat.

## E

**Endplay** - The amount of lengthwise movement between two parts. As applied to a crankshaft, the distance that the crankshaft can move forward and back in the cylinder block.

## F

**Face** - A machinist's term that refers to removing metal from the end of a shaft or the face of a larger part, such as a flywheel.

**Fatigue** - A breakdown of material through a large number of loading and unloading cycles. The first signs are cracks followed shortly by breaks.

**Feeler gauge** - A thin strip of hardened steel, ground to an exact thickness, used to check clearances between parts.

**Free height** - The unloaded length or height of a spring.

**Freeplay** - The looseness in a linkage, or an assembly of parts, between the initial application of force and actual movement. Usually perceived as slop or slight delay.

**Freeze plug** - See Core plug.

## G

**Gallery** - A large passage in the block that forms a reservoir for engine oil pressure.

**Glaze** - The very smooth, glassy finish that develops on cylinder walls while an engine is in service.

## H

**Heli-Coil** - A rethreading device used when threads are worn or damaged. The device is installed in a retapped hole to reduce the thread size to the original size.

## I

**Installed height** - The spring's measured length or height, as installed on the cylinder head. Installed height is measured from the spring seat to the underside of the spring retainer.

## J

**Journal** - The surface of a rotating shaft which turns in a bearing.

## K

**Keeper** - The split lock that holds the valve spring retainer in position on the valve stem.

**Key** - A small piece of metal inserted into matching grooves machined into two parts fitted together - such as a gear pressed onto a shaft - which prevents slippage between the two parts.

**Knock** - The heavy metallic engine sound, produced in the combustion chamber as a result of abnormal combustion - usually detonation. Knock is usually caused by a loose or worn bearing. Also referred to as detonation, pinging and spark knock. Connecting rod or main bearing knocks are created by too much oil clearance or insufficient lubrication.

## L

**Lands** - The portions of metal between the piston ring grooves.

**Lapping the valves** - Grinding a valve face and its seat together with lapping compound.

**Lash** - The amount of free motion in a gear train, between gears, or in a mechanical assembly, that occurs before movement can begin. Usually refers to the lash in a valve train.

**Lifter** - The part that rides against the cam to transfer motion to the rest of the valve train.

## M

**Machining** - The process of using a machine to remove metal from a metal part.

**Main bearings** - The plain, or babbitt, bearings that support the crankshaft.

**Main bearing caps** - The cast iron caps, bolted to the bottom of the block, that support the main bearings.

## O

**O.D.** - Outside diameter.

**Oil gallery** - A pipe or drilled passageway in the engine used to carry engine oil from one area to another.

**Oil ring** - The lower ring, or rings, of a piston; designed to prevent excessive amounts of oil from working up the cylinder walls and into the combustion chamber. Also called an oil-control ring.

**Oil seal** - A seal which keeps oil from leaking out of a compartment. Usually refers to a dynamic seal around a rotating shaft or other moving part.

**O-ring** - A type of sealing ring made of a special rubberlike material; in use, the O-ring is compressed into a groove to provide the sealing action.

**Overhaul** - To completely disassemble a unit, clean and inspect all parts, reassemble it with the original or new parts and make all adjustments necessary for proper operation.

## P

**Pilot bearing** - A small bearing installed in the center of the flywheel (or the rear end of the crankshaft) to support the front end of the input shaft of the transmission.

**Pip mark** - A little dot or indentation which indicates the top side of a compression ring.

**Piston** - The cylindrical part, attached to the connecting rod, that moves up and down in the cylinder as the crankshaft rotates. When the fuel charge is fired, the piston transfers the force of the explosion to the connecting rod, then to the crankshaft.

**Piston pin (or wrist pin)** - The cylindrical and usually hollow steel pin that passes through the piston. The piston pin fastens the piston to the upper end of the connecting rod.

**Piston ring** - The split ring fitted to the groove in a piston. The ring contacts the sides of the ring groove and also rubs against the cylinder wall, thus sealing space between piston and wall. There are two types of rings: Compression rings seal the compression pressure in the combustion chamber; oil rings scrape excessive oil off the cylinder wall.

**Piston ring groove** - The slots or grooves cut in piston heads to hold piston rings in position.

**Piston skirt** - The portion of the piston below the rings and the piston pin hole.

**Plastigage** - A thin strip of plastic thread, available in different sizes, used for measuring clearances. For example, a strip of plastigage is laid across a bearing journal and mashed as parts are assembled. Then parts are disassembled and the width of the strip is measured to determine clearance between journal and bearing. Commonly used to measure crankshaft main-bearing and connecting rod bearing clearances.

**Press-fit** - A tight fit between two parts that requires pressure to force the parts together. Also referred to as drive, or force, fit.

**Prussian blue** - A blue pigment; in solution, useful in determining the area of contact between two surfaces. Prussian blue is commonly used to determine the width and location of the contact area between the valve face and the valve seat.

## R

**Race (bearing)** - The inner or outer ring that provides a contact surface for balls or rollers in bearing.

**Ream** - To size, enlarge or smooth a hole by using a round cutting tool with fluted edges.

**Ring job** - The process of reconditioning the cylinders and installing new rings.

**Runout** - Wobble. The amount a shaft rotates out-of-true.

## S

**Saddle** - The upper main bearing seat.

**Scored** - Scratched or grooved, as a cylinder wall may be scored by abrasive particles moved up and down by the piston rings.

**Scuffing** - A type of wear in which there's a transfer of material between parts moving against each other; shows up as pits or grooves in the mating surfaces.

**Seat** - The surface upon which another part rests or seats. For example, the valve seat is the matched surface upon which the valve face rests. Also used to refer to wearing into a good fit; for example, piston rings seat after a few miles of driving.

**Short block** - An engine block complete with crankshaft and piston and, usually, camshaft assemblies.

**Static balance** - The balance of an object while it's stationary.

**Step** - The wear on the lower portion of a ring land caused by excessive side and back-clearance. The height of the step indicates the ring's extra side clearance and the length of the step projecting from the back wall of the groove represents the ring's back clearance.

**Stroke** - The distance the piston moves when traveling from top dead center to bottom dead center, or from bottom dead center to top dead center.

**Stud** - A metal rod with threads on both ends.

## T

**Tang** - A lip on the end of a plain bearing used to align the bearing during assembly.

**Tap** - To cut threads in a hole. Also refers to the fluted tool used to cut threads.

**Taper** - A gradual reduction in the width of a shaft or hole; in an engine cylinder, taper usually takes the form of uneven wear, more pronounced at the top than at the bottom.

**Throws** - The offset portions of the crankshaft to which the connecting rods are affixed.

**Thrust bearing** - The main bearing that has thrust faces to prevent excessive end-play, or forward and backward movement of the crankshaft.

**Thrust washer** - A bronze or hardened steel washer placed between two moving parts. The washer prevents longitudinal movement and provides a bearing surface for thrust surfaces of parts.

**Tolerance** - The amount of variation permitted from an exact size of measurement. Actual amount from smallest acceptable dimension to largest acceptable dimension.

## U

**Umbrella** - An oil deflector placed near the valve tip to throw oil from the valve stem area.

**Undercut** - A machined groove below the normal surface.

**Undersize bearings** - Smaller diameter bearings used with re-ground crankshaft journals.

## V

**Valve grinding** - Refacing a valve in a valve-refacing machine.

**Valve train** - The valve-operating mechanism of an engine; includes all components from the camshaft to the valve.

**Vibration damper** - A cylindrical weight attached to the front of the crankshaft to minimize torsional vibration (the twist-untwist actions of the crankshaft caused by the cylinder firing impulses). Also called a harmonic balancer.

## W

**Water jacket** - The spaces around the cylinders, between the inner and outer shells of the cylinder block or head, through which coolant circulates.

**Web** - A supporting structure across a cavity.

**Woodruff key** - A key with a radiused backside (viewed from the side).

## Specifications

### General

Oil pressure
| | |
|---|---|
| 5.0L (engine hot at 2,000 rpm) | 40 to 60 psi |

4.6L
| | |
|---|---|
| 1991 through 1998 (engine hot at 1,500 rpm) | 20 to 45 psi |
| 1999 and later (engine hot at 2,500 rpm) | 40 to 70 psi |

Cylinder head warpage limit*
| | |
|---|---|
| 5.0L | 0.003 (in any 6 inches) 0.006 inch overall |

4.6L
| | |
|---|---|
| 1991 through 2000 | 0.003 (in any 6 inches) 0.006 inch overall |
| 2001 and later* | 0.001 inch |
| Compression pressure | Lowest reading cylinder must be within 75 psi of highest reading cylinder (100 psi minimum) |

*The manufacturer states that the cylinder head on 2001 and later models cannot be machined in the event of warping. If the cylinder head warpage exceeds 0.001 inch, replace the cylinder head.

### Cylinder bore

**5.0L engine**

Diameter ..................................................... 4.000 to 4.0048 inches

Out-of-round
| | |
|---|---|
| Standard | 0.0015 inch |
| Service limit | 0.005 inch |
| Taper | 0.010 inch maximum |

**4.6L engine**

Diameter

1991 through 2002
| | |
|---|---|
| Coded red 1 | 3.5539 to 3.5544 inches |
| Coded blue 2 | 3.5544 to 3.5549 inches |
| Coded yellow 3 | 3.5549 to 3.5554 inches |
| 2003 and later | 3.5544 to 3.5550 inches |

Out of round
| | |
|---|---|
| Standard | 0.0006 inch |
| Service limit | 0.0008 inch |
| Taper | 0.0002 inch maximum |

### Valves and related components
### Valve arrangement (front-to-rear)

**4.6L and 5.0L engine**
| | |
|---|---|
| Left cylinder head | E-I-E-I-E-I-E-I |
| Right cylinder head | I-E-I-E-I-E-I-E |

## Intake valve

### 5.0L engine

| | |
|---|---|
| Seat angle | 45-degrees |
| Seat width | 0.060 to 0.080 inch |
| Seat runout limit | 0.002 inch maximum (total indicator reading) |
| Stem diameter | |
| Standard | 0.3416 to 0.3423 inch |
| 0.015 oversize | 0.3566 to 0.3573 inch |
| 0.030 oversize | 0.3716 to 0.3723 inch |
| Valve stem-to-guide clearance | |
| Standard | 0.0010 to 0.0027 inch |
| Service limit | 0.0055 inch maximum |
| Valve face angle | 44-degrees |
| Valve face runout limit | 0.002 inch maximum |

### 4.6L engine

| | |
|---|---|
| Seat angle | 45 degrees |
| Seat width | 0.0748 to 0.0827 inch |
| Seat runout limit | 0.0010 inch maximum (total indicator reading) |
| Stem diameter | 0.2746 to 0.2753 inch |
| Valve stem to guide clearance | 0.0007 to 0.0027 inch |
| Valve face angle | 45.5 degrees |
| Valve face runout limit | 0.0020 inch maximum |

## Exhaust valve

### 5.0L engine

| | |
|---|---|
| Seat angle | 45-degrees |
| Seat width | 0.060 to 0.080 inch |
| Seat runout limit | 0.002 inch maximum (total indicator reading) |
| Stem diameter | |
| Standard | 0.3411 to 0.3418 inch |
| 0.015 oversize | 0.3561 to 0.3568 inch |
| 0.030 oversize | 0.3711 to 0.3718 inch |
| Valve stem-to-guide clearance | |
| Standard | 0.0015 to 0.0032 inch |
| Service limit | 0.0055 inch maximum |
| Valve face angle | 44-degrees |
| Valve face runout limit | 0.002 inch maximum |

### 4.6L engine

| | |
|---|---|
| Seat angle | 45 degrees |
| Seat width | 0.0748 to 0.0827 inch |
| Seat runout limit | 0.0010 inch maximum (total indicator reading) |
| Stem diameter | 0.2735 to 0.2744 inch |
| Valve stem to guide clearance | 0.0018 to 0.0037 inch |
| Valve face angle | 45.5 degrees |
| Valve face runout limit | 0.0020 inch maximum |

## Valve spring

### 5.0L engine
Free length
    Intake                               2.02 inches
    Exhaust                          1.79 inch
Installed height
    Intake                               1-3/4 to 1-13/16 inches
    Exhaust                          1-37/64 to 1-41/64 inches
Out-of-square limit                 5/64 inch
Pressure
Intake
    Valve open                       211 to 230 lbs at 1.36 inches
    Valve closed                    74 to 82 lbs at 1.78 inches
Exhaust
    Valve open                       200 to 226 lbs at 1.15 inches
    Valve closed                    77 to 85 lbs at 1.60 inches
Valve spring pressure service limit     10-percent pressure loss at specified length

### 4.6L engine
Free length
    1991 through 1996
        Intake                       1.9523 inches
        Exhaust                  1.9523 inches
    1997 through 2000
        Intake                       1.9764 inches
        Exhaust                  1.9764 inches
    2001 and later
        Intake                       1.9763 inches
        Exhaust                  1.9763 inches
Out of square limit                 2.5 degrees maximum
Installed height
    1991 through 2002
        Intake                       1.5748 inches
        Exhaust                  1.5748 inches
    2003 and later
        Intake                       1.5984 to 1.7165 inches
        Exhaust                  1.5984 to 1.7165 inches
Pressure
    1991 through 1996
        Intake
            Valve open              131.9 lbs at 1.103 inches
            Valve closed            54.9 lbs at 1.575 inches
        Exhaust
            Valve open              131.9 lbs at 1.103 inches
            Valve closed            54.9 lbs at 1.575 inches
        Service limit               10 percent pressure loss at 1.103 inches
    1997 and later
        Intake
            Valve open              142.3 to 158.3 lbs at 1.103 inches
            Valve closed            61.0 to 68.8 lbs at 1.575 inches

Exhaust
    Valve open                        142.3 to 158.3 lbs at 1.103 inches
    Valve closed                  61.0 to 68.8 lbs at 1.575 inches

## Hydraulic lash adjuster (lifter)

### 5.0L engine

Diameter
    Standard                      0.8740 to 0.8745
Lifter-to-bore clearance
    Standard                      0.0007 to 0.0027 inch
    Service limit                0.005 inch maximum
Collapsed tappet gap
    Desired                      0.096 to 0.146 inch
    Allowable                   0.071 to 0.0171 inch
Rocker arm ratio                 1.59:1

### 4.6L engine

Diameter                            0.6294 to 0.6299 inch
Lifter-to-bore clearance
    Standard                      0.0007 to 0.0027 inch
    Service limit                0.0006 inch maximum
Collapsed tappet gap - desired       0.0177 to 0.0335 inch
Rocker arm ratio (roller cam followers)    1.75:1

## Crankshaft and connecting rods

## Crankshaft

### 5.0L engine

Endplay
    Standard                      0.004 to 0.008 inch
    Service limit                0.012 inch maximum
Runout to rear face of block       0.005 inch maximum (total indicator reading)

### 4.6L engine

Endplay                           0.0051 to 0.0118 inch
Runout to rear face of block
    Standard                      0.002 inch
    Service limit                0.005 inch maximum

## Connecting rods

### 5.0L engine

Connecting rod journal
Diameter                            2.1228 to 2.1236 inches
Out-of-round/taper limit          0.0006 inch per inch maximum
Bearing oil clearance
    Desired                      0.0008 to 0.0015 inch
    Allowable                   0.0008 to 0.0024 inch
Connecting rod side clearance (endplay)
Standard                        0.010 to 0.020 inch
Service limit                    0.023 inch maximum

## Connecting rods (continued)

### 4.6L engine

| | |
|---|---|
| Connecting rod journal | |
| Diameter | |
|     1991 through 2004 | 2.0874 to 2.0891 inches |
|     2005 and later | 2.0859 to 2.0867 inches |
| Bearing oil clearance | |
|     Desired | 0.0011 to 0.0027 inch |
|     Allowable | 0.0011 to 0.0027 inch |
| Connecting rod side clearance (endplay) | |
| Standard | 0.0006 to 0.0177 inch |
| Service limit | 0.0197 inch |

## Main bearing journal

### 5.0L engine

| | |
|---|---|
| Diameter | 2.2490 to 2.2482 inches |
| Out-of-round limit | 0.0006 inch |
| Taper limit | 0.0004 inch per inch |
| Bearing oil clearance | 0.0008 to 0.0015 inch |

### 4.6L engine

| | |
|---|---|
| Diameter | 2.6568 to 2.6576 inches |
| Bearing oil clearance | |
|     Desired | 0.0011 to 0.0027 inch |
|     Allowable | 0.0011 to 0.0027 inch |

## Pistons and rings

## Piston diameter

### 5.0L engine

| | |
|---|---|
| Coded red | 3.9972 to 3.9980 inch |
| Coded blue | 3.9984 to 3.9992 inch |
| Coded yellow | 3.9996 to 4.0004 inch |

### 4.6L engine

| | |
|---|---|
| 1991 through 2002 | |
|     Code red 1 | 3.5526 to 3.5531 inches |
|     Code blue 2 | 3.5531 to 3.5536 inches |
|     Code yellow 3 | 3.5536 to 3.5541 inches |
| 2003 and 2004 | |
|     Code 1 | 3.5535 to 3.5541 inches |
|     Code 2 | 3.5540 to 3.5547 inches |
|     Code 3 | 3.5545 to 3.5551 inches |
| 2005 and later | |
|     Code 1 | 3.5508 to 3.5514 inches |
|     Code 2 | 3.5513 to 3.5519 inches |
|     Code 3 | 3.5518 to 3.5524 inches |

## Piston-to-bore clearance limit

| | |
|---|---|
| 5.0L engine | 0.0030 to 0.0038 inch |
| 4.6L engine | |
|     1991 through 1996 | 0.0008 to 0.0018 inch |
|     1997 and later | 0.0002 to 0.0010 inch |

## Piston ring end gap

### 5.0L engine

| | |
|---|---|
| Compression rings | 0.010 to 0.020 inch |
| Oil ring | 0.015 to 0.055 inch |

### 4.6L engine

| | |
|---|---|
| Compression rings | |
|     1991 through 1996 | |
|         Top ring | 0.009 to 0.019 inch |
|         Second ring | 0.009 to 0.019 inch |
|     1997 and 1998 | |
|         Top ring | 0.005 to 0.010 inch |
|         Second ring | 0.012 to 0.022 inch |
|     1999 and later | 0.006 to 0.012 inch |
| Oil ring | |
|     1991 through 1998 | 0.006 to 0.026 inch |
|     1999 and later | 0.006 to 0.012 inch |

## Piston ring side clearance

### 5.0L engine

| | |
|---|---|
| Compression rings | 0.002 to 0.004 inch |
| Service limit | 0.006 inch |
| Oil ring | Snug fit |

### 4.6L engine

| | |
|---|---|
| Compression ring (top) | |
|     1991 through 1998 | |
|         Top ring | 0.0016 to 0.0036 inch |
|         Second ring | 0.0012 to 0.0032 inch |
|     1999 and later | |
|         Top ring | 0.0008 to 0.0024 inch |
|         Second ring | 0.0008 to 0.0024 inch |
| Service limit | 0.0006 inch maximum |
| Oil ring | Snug fit |

## Torque specifications*                    Ft-lbs (unless otherwise indicated)

➡ Note: One foot-pound (ft-lb) of torque is equivalent to 12 inch-pounds (in-lbs) of torque. Torque values below approximately 15 foot-pounds are expressed in inch-pounds, because most foot-pound torque wrenches are not accurate at these smaller values.

Main bearing cap bolts (on 4.6L engines, tighten first)

| | |
|---|---|
| 5.0L engine | 60 to 70 |
| 4.6L engine* | |
|     1991 through 1996 | |
|         Step 1 | 22 to 25 |
|         Step 2 | Tighten an additional 85 to 95 degrees |
|     1997 and later | |
|         Main bearing cap bolts | |
|         Step 1 | 30 |
|         Step 2 | Tighten an additional 90 degrees |
|         Jack screws | |
|         Step 1 | 44 in-lbs |
|         Step 2 | 89 in-lbs |
|         Side bolts | |
|         Step 1 | 89 in-lbs |
|         Step 2 | 15 |
| Connecting rod cap nuts/bolts | |
|     5.0L engine | 19 to 24 |
|     4.6L engine** | |
|         1996 and earlier | |
|         First step | 18 to 25 |
|         Second step | Rotate an additional 85 to 95 degrees |
|         1997 and later | |
|         Step 1 | 30 to 33 |
|         Step 2 | Rotate an additional 90 to 120 degrees |

➡ Note: Refer to Part A and B for additional torque specifications.

* The crankshaft main bearing cap bolts must be replaced with new bolts.
** On 4.6L engines, new rod bolts must be installed.

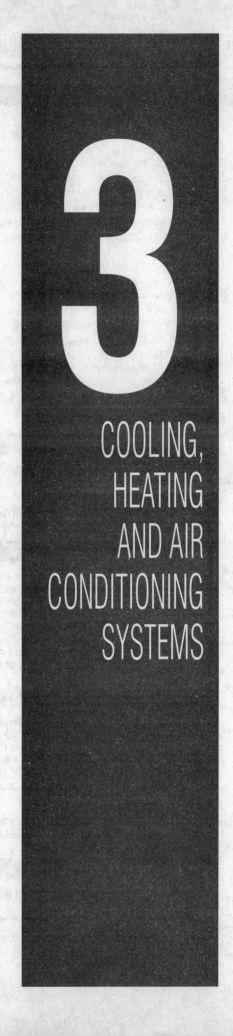

3

COOLING,
HEATING
AND AIR
CONDITIONING
SYSTEMS

**Section**

## 1  General information

The cooling system consists of a radiator, an expansion tank, a pressure cap (located on the expansion tank), a thermostat, a cooling fan and clutch, and a belt-driven water pump.

The radiator cooling fan is mounted on the front of the water pump. The fan incorporates a fluid drive fan clutch, which saves horsepower and reduces noise. When the engine is cold, the fluid in the clutch offers little resistance and allows the fan to freewheel. As the engine heats up and reaches a predetermined temperature, the fluid in the clutch thickens and drives the fan.

The expansion tank, referred to by the manufacturer as a "degas bottle," functions somewhat differently than a conventional recovery tank. Designed to separate any trapped air in the coolant, it is pressurized by the radiator and has a pressure cap on top. The radiator on these models does not have a pressure cap. When the thermostat is closed, no coolant flows in the expansion tank, but when the engine is fully warmed up, coolant flows from the top of the radiator through a small hose that enters the top of the expansion tank, where the air separates and the coolant falls into a coolant reservoir in the bottom of the tank, which is fed to the cooling system through a larger hose connected to the lower radiator hose.

### ✳✳ WARNING:

Unlike a conventional coolant recovery tank, the pressure cap on the expansion tank should never be opened after the engine has warmed up, because of the danger of severe burns caused by steam or scalding coolant.

Coolant in the right side of the radiator circulates up the lower radiator hose to the water pump, where it is forced through the water passages in the cylinder block. The coolant then travels up into the cylinder head, circulates around the combustion chambers and valve seats, travels out of the cylinder head past the open thermostat into the upper radiator hose and back into the radiator.

When the engine is cold, the thermostat restricts the circulation of coolant to the engine. When the minimum operating temperature is reached, the thermostat begins to open, allowing coolant to return to the radiator.

These models have a cooler element incorporated into the radiator to cool the transmission fluid.

The heating system works by directing air through the heater core mounted in the dash and then to the interior of the vehicle by a system of ducts. Temperature is controlled by mixing heated air with fresh air, using a system of flapper doors in the ducts, and a heater motor.

The air conditioning system consists of an evaporator core located under the dash, a condenser in front of the radiator, a receiver-drier in the engine compartment and a belt-driven compressor mounted at the front of the engine.

## 2  Antifreeze - general information

### ✳✳ WARNING:

Do not allow antifreeze to come in contact with your skin or painted surfaces of the vehicle. Rinse off spills immediately with plenty of water. Antifreeze is highly toxic if ingested. Never leave antifreeze lying around in an open container or in puddles on the floor; children and pets are attracted by it's sweet smell and may drink it. Check with local authorities about disposing of used antifreeze. Many communities have collection centers which will see that antifreeze is disposed of safely.

### ✳✳ CAUTION:

Later models are factory-filled with orange-colored Dex-Cool coolant, which will normally be identified by a label near the radiator. Add only Dex-Cool-type coolant to Dex-Cool systems, and be sure to maintain a 50-50 mixture with water to avoid damaging the cooling system.

The cooling system should be filled with the recommended antifreeze solution which will prevent freezing down to at least -20-degrees F (even lower in cold climates). It also provides protection against corrosion and increases the coolant boiling point.

The cooling system should be drained, flushed and refilled at least every other year on standard cooling systems (see Chapter 1). The use of standard-type antifreeze solutions for periods of longer than two years is likely to cause damage and encourage the formation of rust and scale in the system.

Before adding antifreeze to the system, check all hose connections. Antifreeze can leak through very minute openings.

The exact mixture of antifreeze to water which you should use depends on the relative weather conditions. The mixture on standard cooling systems should contain at least 50-percent antifreeze, but should never contain more than 70-percent antifreeze. On Dex-cool systems, cooling system damage can occur if a 50-50 mixture is not maintained.

## 3  Thermostat - check and replacement

### ✳✳ WARNING:

The engine must be completely cool when this procedure is performed.

➡Note: Don't drive the vehicle without a thermostat! The computer may stay in open loop and emissions and fuel economy will suffer.

## CHECK

1  Before condemning the thermostat, check the coolant level, drivebelt tension and temperature gauge (or light) operation.

2  If the engine takes a long time to warm up, the thermostat is probably stuck open. Replace the thermostat.

3  If the engine runs hot, check the temperature of the upper radiator hose. If the hose isn't hot, the thermostat is probably stuck shut.

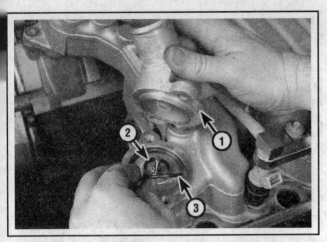

**3.9 Once the bolts are removed, separate the housing from the intake manifold in order to remove the gasket and thermostat (4.6L shown)**

| | | | |
|---|---|---|---|
| 1 | Thermostat housing cover | 3 | O-ring seal |
| 2 | Thermostat | | |

Replace the thermostat.

4 If the upper radiator hose is hot, it means the coolant is circulating and the thermostat is open. Refer to the Troubleshooting section for the cause of overheating.

5 If an engine has been overheated, you may find damage such as leaking head gaskets, scuffed pistons and warped or cracked cylinder heads.

## REPLACEMENT

▶ **Refer to illustrations 3.9 and 3.12**

6 Drain coolant (about 1 gallon) from the radiator, until the coolant level is below the thermostat housing (See Chapter 1).

7 On some models of the 5.0L engines, it may be necessary to remove the distributor cap in order to remove the thermostat housing (see Chapter 4).

8 Disconnect the upper radiator hose from the thermostat housing. Disconnect the bypass hose from the thermostat housing on 5.0L engines.

9 Remove the bolts and lift the cover off (see illustration). It may be necessary to tap the cover with a soft-face hammer to break the gasket seal on a 5.0L engine. Remove the O-ring seal on a 4.6L engine.

10 Note how it's installed, then remove the thermostat. Be sure to

**3.12 When installing the thermostat pay special attention to the direction in which it's placed in the engine, the spring will go into the intake manifold**

use a replacement thermostat with the correct opening temperature (see this Chapter's Specifications).

11 Use a scraper or putty knife to remove all traces of old gasket material and sealant from the mating surfaces.

➡**Note: On 4.6L engines the gasket has been replaced by an O-ring. Make sure no gasket material falls into the coolant passages; it is a good idea to stuff a rag in the passage. Wipe the mating surfaces with a rag saturated with lacquer thinner or acetone.**

12 Install the thermostat and make sure the correct end faces out (see illustration) - the spring is directed toward the engine.

13 On models that use a conventional paper gasket, apply a thin coat of RTV sealant to both sides of the new gasket and position it on the engine side, over the thermostat, and make sure the gasket holes line up with the bolt holes in the housing.

➡**Note: No RTV sealant should be used on the later model O-ring seal.**

14 On models that use an O-ring seal, install the new O-ring into the intake manifold.

15 Carefully position the cover and install the bolts. Tighten them to the torque listed in this Chapter's Specifications - do not over tighten them or the cover may be cracked or distorted.

16 Reattach the radiator hose to the cover and tighten the clamp - now may be a good time to check and replace the hoses and clamps (see Chapter 1).

17 Refer to Chapter 1 and refill the system, then run the engine and check carefully for leaks.

18 Repeat steps 1 through 5 to be sure the repairs corrected the previous problem(s).

## 4   Radiator and expansion tank - removal and installation

### ☀☀ WARNING:

**The engine must be completely cool when this procedure is performed.**

## RADIATOR

### Removal

▶ **Refer to illustrations 4.2, 4.3 and 4.4**

1 Disconnect the cable from the negative battery terminal.

2 Drain the cooling system as described in Chapter 1, then disconnect the overflow hose, upper radiator hose and lower radiator hose from the radiator (see illustration).

3 If equipped with an automatic transmission or engine oil cooler, remove the cooler lines from the radiator (see illustration) - be careful not to damage the lines or fittings. Plug the ends of the disconnected lines to prevent leakage and stop dirt from entering the system. Have a drip pan ready to catch any spills.

4 Remove the radiator mounting bolts (see illustration).

5 Unbolt the fan shroud and slip it back over the fan.

6 Lift the radiator from the engine compartment. Take care not to contact the fan blades.

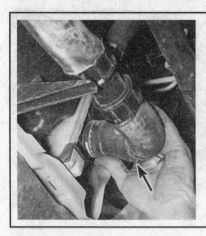

4.2  When removing the hoses, use a pliers to squeeze the tangs together and slide the clamp away from the end of the hose (arrow), then pull the hose from the radiator connection

7    Prior to installation of the radiator, replace any damaged hose clamps and radiator hoses.

## Installation

♦ Refer to illustration 4.8

8    Radiator installation is the reverse of removal. When installing the radiator, make sure it seats properly in the lower saddles and that the rubber mounts are intact (see illustration).

9    After installation, fill the system with the proper mixture of anti-freeze, and also check the automatic transmission fluid level.

## EXPANSION TANK

### Removal and installation

♦ Refer to illustration 4.10

10   Drain the engine coolant (see Chapter1). Remove the coolant overflow hoses from the tank (see illustration).

11   Remove the bolts and detach the tank.

12   Prior to installation make sure the tank is clean and free of debris which could be drawn into the radiator (wash it with soap and water if necessary).

13   Installation is the reverse of removal.

4.3  Use a flare-nut wrench on the fluid line (arrows) and a back up wrench at the radiator fitting, as shown, to prevent damage to the transmission cooler lines when removing them from the radiator

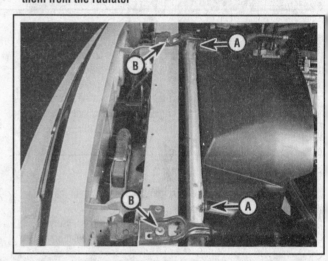

4.4  The cooling fan shroud is held in place by two bolts (A) as is the radiator support bracket (B). Both the shroud and the bracket must be removed before the radiator can be removed

4.8  Check to make sure that the rubber mounts (arrow) are in place and in good shape, if they're beginning to deteriorate, now is the time to replace them

4.10  Locate the two hoses attached to the expansion tank (arrows) and disconnect them

## 5   Engine cooling fan - check, removal and installation

### ✳✳ WARNING:

**To avoid possible injury or damage, DO NOT operate the engine with a damaged fan. Do not attempt to repair fan blades - replace a damaged fan with a new one.**

➥**Note: Late models are equipped with a hydraulically controlled electric cooling fan. This system uses hydraulic fluid that is pumped into a turbine at a precise flow to control fan speed and engine cooling capacity.**

## CHECK

### Mechanical cooling fan

1   Disconnect the cable from the negative terminal of the battery.

2   Visually inspect for substantial fluid leakage from the clutch assembly, a deformed bi-metal spring or grease leakage from the cooling fan bearing. If any of these conditions exist, replace the fan clutch.

3   Rock the fan back and forth by hand to check for excessive bearing play. If problems are noted, replace the clutch assembly.

4   With the engine cold (and not running), turn the fan blades by hand. The fan should turn freely.

5   Reconnect the cable to the negative terminal of the battery, then start the engine and allow it to reach normal operating temperature. Turn off the engine and disconnect the cable from the negative terminal of the battery. Turn the fan by hand. More drag should be evident. If the fan turns easily, replace the fan clutch.

### Electric cooling fan

6   On later models, the engine cooling fan is controlled by the engine management system's Powertrain Control Module (PCM), acting on the information received from the Engine Coolant Temperature (ECT) sensor (see Chapter 6).

7   Warm the engine up to normal operating temperature. The fan should come on. If it does not, check the cooling fan fuse and relays (see Chapter 12).

➥**Note: It's possible that the CHECK ENGINE light may come on indicating a stored diagnostic trouble code (DTC) if there is a problem with the cooling fan circuit. Refer to Chapter 6 regarding the retrieval and definition of any stored codes.**

8   To test the fan motor, unplug the fan electrical connector and use fused jumper wires to connect the fan directly to the battery.

9   If the fan does not operate, replace the motor. If the motor works, the problem is with a temperature sensor, the engine management system (see Section 6) or in the wiring (see Chapter 12).

## REMOVAL AND INSTALLATION

### Mechanical cooling fan

▶ **Refer to illustrations 5.11a, 5.11b, 5.12, 5.14a and 5.14b**

10   If you're working on a model with a 5.0L engine, remove the drivebelts (see Chapter 1).

11   If you're working on a model with a 5.0L engine, loosen the fan clutch-to-water pump bolts (see illustration). If you're working on a model with a 4.6L, engine loosen the large hex nut on the fan clutch shaft (see illustration).

➥**Note: A special spanner wrench (obtainable at most auto parts stores) may be required to hold the water pump pulley while a large wrench is used to loosen the hex nut on the fan clutch shaft.**

12   Remove the fan shroud bolts (see illustration). Detach the lower radiator hose from the guide on the bottom of the shroud.

13   Unbolt the fan/clutch assembly and detach it from the water pump. Remove the fan and shroud together, being careful not to contact the radiator.

**5.11a  Loosen the fan clutch-to-water pump bolts on a 5.0L engine**

**5.12  Fan shroud bolts (arrows)**

**5.11b  Loosen the large hex-nut on the fan clutch shaft (right hand thread) to remove the cooling fan from the water pump on a 4.6L engine**

**5.14a To separate the fan clutch from the fan blades remove the four attaching bolts (arrows)**

**5.14b When storing the fan clutch after removal, always place it with this side down, to prevent silicone fluid from leaking out or into the bearing**

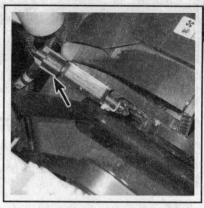

**5.17 Cooling fan electrical connector**

14 The fan clutch can be unbolted from the fan blade assembly for replacement (see illustration).

> ✳✳ **CAUTION:**
>
> **To prevent silicone fluid from draining from the clutch assembly into the bearing and ruining the lubricant, DO NOT position the drive unit with the rear of the shaft pointing down (see illustration).**

### Electric cooling fan

▶ Refer to illustration 5.17

> ✳✳ **WARNING:**
>
> **The engine must be completely cool before beginning this procedure.**

15 Drain the cooling system (see Chapter 1), then remove the coolant expansion tank (see Section 4). Detach the upper radiator hose from the radiator on models where it would interfere with removal of the shroud/fan assembly.

16 Unbolt the power steering fluid reservoir and set it aside.

17 Disconnect the electrical connector from the fan motor (see illustration).

18 Detach the transmission cooler lines from the fan shroud, then remove the fan shroud mounting bolts.

19 Lift the electric cooling fan and shroud assembly out of the engine compartment.

20 Carefully inspect the fan blades for damage and defects. Replace it if necessary.

21 Installation is the reverse of removal. Refill the cooling system (see Chapter 1).

---

## 6   Coolant temperature sending unit - check and replacement

▶ Refer to illustrations 6.1a and 6.1b

> ✳✳ **WARNING:**
>
> **Wait until the engine is completely cool before beginning this procedure.**

### CHECK

1   The coolant temperature indicator system is composed of a light or temperature gauge mounted in the dash and a coolant temperature sending unit mounted on the engine (see illustration). Some vehicles have more than one sending unit (see illustration), but only one is used for the indicator system and the other is used to send engine temperature information to the computer.

2   If an overheating indication occurs, check the coolant level in the system. Make sure the wiring between the light or gauge and the send-

ing unit is secure and all fuses are intact.

3   When the ignition switch is turned on and the starter motor is turning, the indicator light (if equipped) should glow (bulb check).

4   If the light is not on, the bulb may be burned out, the ignition switch may be faulty or the circuit may be open. Test the circuit by grounding the wire to the sending unit while the ignition is on (engine NOT running for safety). If the gauge deflects full scale or the light comes on, replace the sending unit.

5   As soon as the engine starts, the light should go out and remain out unless the engine overheats. Failure of the light to go out may be due to a grounded wire between the light and the sending unit, a defective sending unit or a faulty ignition switch. Also, check the coolant to make sure it's of the proper type and mixture.

### REPLACEMENT

6   If the sending unit must be replaced, disconnect the electrical connector and simply unscrew the sensor from the engine and install

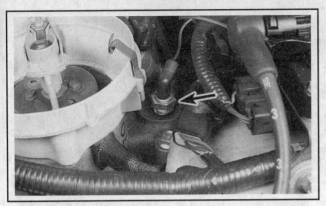

**6.1a  The coolant temperature sending unit, on 5.0L engines, is located at the front of the intake manifold near the distributor**

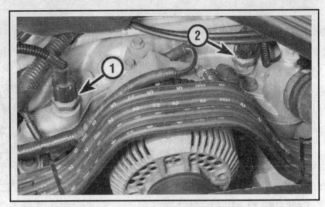

**6.1b  On the 4.6L engine, the coolant temperature sending unit is one of two at the front of the intake manifold, be sure to select the correct one for the repair procedure**

1   *Coolant temperature sending unit (gauge)*      2   *Coolant temperature sensor (computer)*

the replacement.

**✳✳ CAUTION:**

**The sending unit is made up of metal and plastic and is fragile. Use care when removing not to crack the unit.**

Use sealant on the threads. Make sure the engine is cool before removing the defective sending unit. There will be some coolant loss as the unit is removed, so be prepared to catch it. Check the coolant level after the replacement unit has been installed.

## 7  Water pump - check

▸ **Refer to illustration 7.3**

1   Water pump failure can cause overheating and serious damage to the engine. There are three ways to check the operation of the water pump while it's installed on the engine. If any one of the three following quick checks indicates water pump problems, it should be replaced immediately.

2   Start the engine and warm it up to normal operating temperature. Squeeze the upper radiator hose. If the water pump is working properly, you should feel a pressure surge as the hose is released.

3   A seal protects the water pump impeller shaft bearing from contamination by engine coolant. If this seal fails, a weep hole in the water pump snout will leak coolant (see illustration) (an inspection mirror can be used to look at the underside of the pump if the hole isn't on top). If the weep hole is leaking, shaft bearing failure will follow. Replace the water pump immediately.

4   Besides contamination by coolant after a seal failure, the water pump impeller shaft bearing can also prematurely wear out. If a noise is coming from the water pump during engine operation, the shaft bearing has failed - replace the water pump immediately.

➡**Note: Do not confuse drivebelt noise with bearing noise. Loose or glazed drivebelts may emit a high-pitched squealing noise.**

5   To identify excessive bearing wear before the bearing actually fails, grasp the water pump pulley and try to force it up-and-down or from side-to-side. If the pulley can be moved either horizontally or vertically, the bearing is nearing the end of its service life. Replace the water pump.

**7.3  If there's coolant leaking from the weep hole (arrow) the water pump should be replaced**

## 8  Water pump - removal and installation

### REMOVAL

▸ **Refer to illustration 8.9a, 8.9b and 8.9c**

1   Disconnect the cable from the negative battery terminal.
2   With the engine cold, drain the cooling system (see Chapter 1).
3   Remove the fan shroud and the fan assembly (see Section 5).
4   Remove the drivebelt(s) (see Chapter 1) and remove the water pump pulley.
5   On 5.0L engines, if the power steering pump bracket is retained at the water pump, the power steering pump should be completely removed and laid to one side to facilitate removal of the bracket.

8.9a On 5.0L engines, after the belt-driven accessory brackets have been removed, remove the hoses and the water pump retaining bolts

8.9b On 4.6L engines, remove the four bolts (arrows) . . .

8.9c . . . and remove the water pump from out of the engine block

8.11 Inspect the sealing surface (arrow) in the pump cavity for dirt or signs of pitting

8.12 On 4.6L engines, install a new O-ring seal on the water pump

6   On 5.0L engines equipped with air conditioning, remove the idler pulley and bracket assembly.

7   Remove any accessory brackets that attach to the water pump.

8   On 5.0L engines, remove the lower radiator hose, the heater hose and the by-pass hose from the water pump.

9   Remove the water pump retaining bolts and remove the water pump (see illustrations). On 5.0L engines, take note of the installed positions of the various length bolts.

## INSTALLATION

▶ Refer to illustrations 8.11 and 8.12

10  Before installation, remove and clean all gasket or sealant material from the water pump, cylinder front cover, or cylinder block.

11  On 4.6L engines, inspect the O-ring and sealing surface of water pump housing in the block for dirt and/or debris (see illustration). Clean thoroughly before reassembly.

12  On 5.0L engines, position new gaskets on the water pump and coat them on both sides with RTV sealant. On 4.6L engines, lubricate a new O-ring seal with a clean antifreeze and install it to the water pump (see illustration).

13  Install the water pump and tighten the bolts to the torque listed in this Chapter's Specifications.

14  On 5.0L engines, it may be necessary to transfer some hose ports and/or fittings from the old pump if you are replacing it with a new one.

15  On 5.0L engines, install the lower radiator hose, heater hose and by-pass hose to the water pump. Replace the hose clamps with new, if necessary.

16  Install the remaining components to the water pump and engine in the reverse order of removal.

17  Fill the cooling system with the proper coolant mixture.

18  Start the engine and make sure there are no leaks. Check the level frequently during the first few weeks of operation to ensure there are no leaks and that the level in the system is stable.

## 9   Heater and air conditioning blower motor and circuit - check and switch replacement

### CHECK

▶ Refer to illustration 9.3

➡Note: The blower motor is switched on the ground-side of the circuit. Amperage readings will increase as the blower speed is increased. Voltage readings, on ground-side switching circuits, decrease instead of increasing as the blower motor speed is increased. A maximum blower speed switch position will produce a zero voltage reading as a result of the blower speed switch bypassing the resistor assembly.

1   Check the fuse and all connections in the circuit for looseness

9.3 Unplug the electrical connector at the blower motor (arrow), and using a voltmeter, test for power at the motor

9.6 Remove the two screws (arrows) holding the blower motor resistor to the heater case, and remove for inspection

and corrosion. Make sure the battery is fully charged.

2   With the transmission in Park, the parking brake securely set, turn the ignition switch to the run position. It isn't necessary to start the vehicle.

3   Connect a voltmeter to the blower motor connector (see illustration).

4   Move the blower switch through each of its positions and note the voltage readings. Changes in voltage indicates that the motor speeds will also vary as the switch is moved to the different positions.

## Thermal limiter resistor assembly

♦ **Refer to illustration 9.6**

5   The thermal limiter relay assembly is located on the evaporator case in the engine compartment. There are three resistance elements mounted on the resistor board to provide four blower speeds. Note: The high blower setting bypasses the resistors to give the fourth blower speed. A thermal limiter resistor is integrated into the circuits to prevent heat damage to the evaporator case assembly. If the thermal limiter circuit has been opened as a result of excessive heat, it should be replaced only with the identical replacement part. A standard limiter cannot be used.

6   Remove the thermal resistor relay from the heater case mounting location (see illustration) and visually check for damage. Check the resistor block for continuity between all terminals.

## Blower motor operates at only one speed

7   If there is voltage, but the blower motor does not operate connect a jumper wire between the motor ground terminal (or case) and a good chassis ground. Connect a fused jumper wire between the battery positive terminal and the positive terminal on the motor. If the motor now works, remove the jumper wire, and if the motor stops working when the ground wire is removed, check for bad ground and re-test. If the motor still doesn't work, the blower motor is probably faulty.

8   If there's no voltage at the motor, remove the resistor block connector and check it for voltage. If there's voltage at any of the connector terminals, check the resistor block and the wiring between the resistor block and the motor for an open or short.

9   If there's no voltage at any of the terminals in the resistor block connector, remove the heater control panel (if necessary) and, with the ignition ON, check for voltage at the connector for the blower motor switch.

10  If there's no voltage, check the wiring between the fuse panel and the switch for an open or a short.

11  If there's voltage, connect one end of a jumper wire to the terminal of the switch connector with voltage. Connect the other end of the jumper to each of the terminals that carry voltage to the resistor block. If the motor now operates normally, replace the switch.

## Blower motor doesn't operate at any speed

12  Again, check the fuse, if not already done.

13  With the ignition and blower motor switch on, check for voltage at the motor positive connector. If there's no voltage, check the wiring between the fuse panel and the motor for an open or short. If there's voltage, test the motor, as described in step 5.

14  If the motor works when tested, remove the heater control panel and use a jumper wire to ground each terminal of the blower motor switch connector. Make sure the ignition switch is on. If the motor now works, check for a bad ground at the switch. If the switch ground is good, replace the switch.

## SWITCH REPLACEMENT

15  Remove the control assembly from the instrument panel (see Section 11).

16  Remove the screw, from beneath the assembly, that holds the switch to the main assembly and remove the switch.

## 10   Heater blower motor - removal and installation

## REMOVAL

♦ **Refer to illustration 10.3**

1   Disconnect the blower motor electrical connector from the motor (see illustration 9.3).

2   Remove the cooling tube from the underside of the blower motor.

3   Remove the retaining screws from the blower motor mounting plate (see illustration).

4   Turn the blower motor slightly to the right so that the bottom edge of the mounting plate aligns with the contour of the wheel-well splash panel. While still in the blower housing, lift the motor assembly

**10.3 Blower motor mounting fasteners**

up and maneuver it out of the heater housing assembly.

## INSTALLATION

➡Note: If the blower motor is being replaced, the fan wheel should be transferred to the new motor at this time. It is attached to the blower motor shaft with a push nut. Grasp the nut with a pliers and pull it off or get a small screwdriver under it and pry it off, being careful not to crack the push nut. To reinstall the nut, simply push it on to the shaft.

5   Position the motor and fan assembly so that the bottom edge (the straight portion) follows the contour of the wheel-well splash panel. Maneuver the assembly past the wheel-well splash panel and into the top portion of the housing opening, then down into position.

6   The remainder of the installation is the reverse of removal.

---

### 11   Heater and air conditioning control assembly - removal and installation

## REMOVAL

▶ Refer to illustrations 11.9 and 11.10

### ✳✳ WARNING:

Some models have airbags. Always disconnect the negative battery cable, then the positive battery cable and wait 2 minutes before working in the vicinity of the impact sensors, steering column or instrument panel to avoid the possibility of accidental deployment of the airbag, which could cause personal injury (see Chapter 12).

➡Note: The following procedure requires the removal of several interior trim parts. Refer to Chapter 11 for specific removal and installation procedures.

1   Remove left side and right side instrument panel molding assemblies. Remove cluster trim panel screws.

2   Remove the knob from headlamp switch and remove headlamp switch shaft.

3   Remove the lower insulator/knee protector panel.

4   Remove steering column upper and lower covers.

5   Remove the screws retaining the steering column trim panel reinforcement bracket and remove the bracket.

6   Position the wheels in the straight ahead position. Remove the nuts retaining the steering column. Lower the steering column and remove the PRNDL cable. Let the steering column rest on the front seat.

7   Remove the instrument cluster bezel and the center bezel.

8   Disconnect the electrical connectors to any of the accessory switches.

9   Remove four cap screws from the air conditioning control assembly (see illustration).

10  Pull the control out of the instrument panel (see illustration). The vacuum lines and electrical switch can be disconnected after the control has been removed from the dash.

11  Installation is the reverse of the removal procedure.

**11.9 After the trim is removed, remove the four screws (arrows) and pull the control assembly out of the dash**

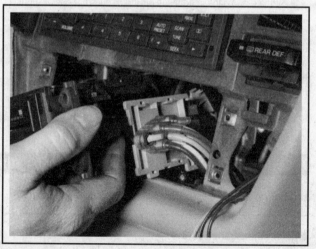

**11.10 The vacuum lines are clustered together, and removed as a single connection**

## 12  Heater core - removal and installation

### REMOVAL

▶ **Refer to illustration 12.2**

**✳✳ WARNING:**

Some models have airbags. Always disconnect the negative battery cable, then the positive battery cable and wait 2 minutes before working in the vicinity of the impact sensors, steering column or instrument panel to avoid the possibility of accidental deployment of the airbag, which could cause personal injury (see Chapter 12).

➡Note: The following procedure requires the removal of several interior trim parts. Refer to Chapter 11 for specific removal and installation procedures.

1  Disconnect the cable from the negative battery terminal.

2  Drain the cooling system and disconnect the heater hoses from the heater core inlet and outlet tubes (see illustration).

3  Plug the heater core tubes to avoid spilling any coolant during the plenum removal.

4  Remove three nuts located below the windshield wiper motor that hold the left end of the plenum to the firewall.

5  Remove one nut holding the upper left side corner of the evaporator case to the firewall.

6  Disconnect the two vacuum supply hoses from the vacuum source. Push the grommet and the vacuum supply hose into the passenger compartment.
➡Note: On late models, disconnect the left side bulkhead connector and push the assembly through the opening in the dash.

7  Remove the instrument panel trim moldings and remove the left side and right side lower instrument trim panel insulators.

8  Remove the upper and lower steering column covers, disconnect the PRNDL cable from the column and remove the reinforcement brace from under the steering column.

9  Position the wheels in the straight ahead position and remove the nuts retaining the steering column to the instrument panel. Lower the steering column as far as possible and support it securely.

10  Open the glove compartment door, depress the tabs and lower the door. Reaching through the left side of the glove compartment opening, remove the bolts retaining the instrument panel to the dash brace. Close the glove compartment door.

11  Loosen both the left and right side door sill plates and remove both left and right side cowl trim panels. Remove the bolts on each end of the instrument panel retaining the instrument panel to the A-pillars.

12  Remove the defroster grille, support the instrument panel and remove the instrument panel to cowl retaining screws.

13  Pull the instrument panel back as far as possible without disconnecting any wiring harness electrical connectors.

14  Remove the cross body brace and disconnect the wiring harness from the temperature blend door actuator and disconnect the temperature control sensor tube from the evaporator case connector.

**12.2  Squeeze and slide the clamps back on the heater hoses so they can be separated from the heater core inlet and outlet pipes**

15  Disconnect the vacuum jumper harness at the multiple vacuum connector near the floor air distribution duct.

16  Disconnect the vacuum hose from the outside-recirculating door vacuum motor.

17  Remove the plastic push fastener retaining the floor air distribution duct to the left end of the plenum.

18  Remove the left side screw and loosen the right side screw on the rear of the plenum and remove the floor air distribution duct.

19  Remove two nuts from the two studs along the lower edge of the plenum.

20  Carefully move plenum rearward to allow the heater core tubes and the stud at the top of the plenum to clear the holes in the dash panel. Remove the plenum from the vehicle by rotating the top of the plenum forward, down and out from under the instrument panel. Carefully pull the lower edge of instrument panel rearward as necessary while rolling the plenum from behind the instrument panel.

21  Remove the four retaining screws from the heater core cover and remove the cover to expose the heater core. Then pull the heater core and seal from the plenum assembly.

### INSTALLATION

22  Route the vacuum supply hose through the dash panel and seat the grommet in the opening.

23  Position the plenum under the instrument panel with the register duct opening up and the heater core tubes down. Rotate the plenum up behind the instrument panel and position the plenum to the dash panel. Insert the heater core tubes and mounting studs through their respective holes in the dash panel and the evaporator case.

24  The remainder of the installation is the reverse of removal.

## 13  Air conditioning and heating system - check and maintenance

**✳✳ WARNING:**

The air conditioning system is under high pressure. DO NOT loosen any fittings or remove any components until after the system has been discharged. Air conditioning refrigerant should be properly discharged into an EPA-approved container at a dealer service department or an automotive air conditioning repair facility. Always wear eye protection when disconnecting air conditioning system fittings.

➡Note: The 1988 through 1993 air conditioning systems use R-12 refrigerant. In 1994 the refrigerant system was changed to use the new, "environmentally friendly" R-134a refrigerant. Each system uses similar components and locations but components are NOT interchangeable. The oil each systems uses is also different and should not be mixed. R-12 systems use 525 viscosity mineral oil and R-134 systems use Polyalkylene Glycol oil (PAG). All discharging of refrigerant, for part replacement or maintenance, should be done by an approved air conditioning facility with the proper refrigerant recovery equipment.

1   The following maintenance steps should be performed on a regular basis to ensure that the air conditioner continues to operate at peak efficiency.

   a)  Check the tension of the drivebelt and adjust if necessary (see Chapter 1).
   b)  Check the condition of the hoses. Look for cracks, hardening and deterioration.

**✳✳ WARNING:**

Do not replace air conditioning hoses until the system has been discharged by a dealer or air conditioning shop.

   c)  Check the fins of the condenser for leaves, bugs and other foreign material. A soft brush and compressed air can be used to remove them.
   d)  Check the wire harness for correct routing, broken wires, damaged insulation, etc. Make sure the harness connections are clean and tight.

   e)  Maintain the correct refrigerant charge.

2   The system should be run for about 10 minutes at least once a month. This is particularly important during the winter months because long-term non-use can cause hardening of the internal seals.

3   Because of the complexity of the air conditioning system and the special equipment required to effectively work on it, accurate troubleshooting of the system should be left to a professional technician. One probable cause for poor cooling that can be determined by the home mechanic is low refrigerant charge. Should the system lose its cooling ability, the following procedure will help you pinpoint the cause.

### CHECK

4   Warm the engine up to normal operating temperature.

5   Place the air conditioning temperature selector at the coldest setting and put the blower at the highest setting. Open the doors (to make sure the air conditioning system doesn't cycle off as soon as it cools the passenger compartment).

6   With the compressor engaged - the clutch will make an audible click and the center of the clutch will rotate - inspect the sight glass, if equipped. If the refrigerant looks foamy, it's low. Charge the system as described later in this Section. If the refrigerant appears clear, the system is properly charged.

### ADDING REFRIGERANT

➡Note: Because of recent Federal regulations proposed by the Environmental Protection Agency, 14-ounce cans of R-12 refrigerant may not be available in your area. If this is the case, it will be necessary to take the vehicle to a licensed air conditioning technician for charging. If you decide to add refrigerant from one of the large 30 lb. cans available, you will need a set of manifold gauges, all the necessary fittings, adapters and hoses to hook everything up.

## 14  Air conditioning compressor - removal and installation

**✳✳ WARNING:**

The air conditioning system is under high pressure. DO NOT loosen any fittings or remove any components until after the system has been discharged. Air conditioning refrigerant should be properly discharged into an EPA-approved container at a dealer service department or an automotive air conditioning repair facility. Always wear eye protection when disconnecting air conditioning system fittings.

➡Note: Special spring lock coupling tools are required to release the connectors used on the refrigerant lines throughout the air conditioning system. There are different tools for each line size. These tools can usually be found at local auto parts stores. Many times the necessary coupling tool may be included in the kit used for parts replacement.

### REMOVAL

▶ Refer to illustrations 14.2a, 14.2b, 14.2c, 14.2d and 14.4

**✳✳ CAUTION:**

Whenever a compressor is replaced, it will be necessary to replace the suction accumulator/drier.

1   Have the system discharged by a dealer service department or an automotive air conditioning repair facility.

2   Remove the accessory drivebelt(s) (see Chapter 1). Remove the refrigerant line fitting block (coupled hose assembly) connected to the rear of the compressor (see illustrations). Some compressor models may have separate refrigerant lines threaded to connections, or the fitting block may be bolted to the side or top of the compressor.

**14.2a Unbolt the refrigerant line block from the compressor, or using a special tool, disconnect the lines at the spring lock couplings**

| | |
|---|---|
| *1  Refrigerant line fitting block* | *3  Compressor clutch electrical connection* |
| *2  Spring lock couplers* | |

3  Disconnect the electrical connection at the compressor clutch.
4  Remove the compressor mounting bolts (see illustration).
5  Remove the compressor from the mounting location.
6  Drain and measure the refrigerant oil from the compressor.

## INSTALLATION

7  If the compressor is being replaced, add the appropriate amount of refrigerant oil to maintain the correct level. Add refrigerant oil to the component being replaced based on the following guidelines:

*a) If the amount removed was between three and five ounces, add the same amount of clean refrigerant oil to the new compressor.*
*b) If the amount of oil removed was greater than five ounces, add only five ounces to the component before installation.*
*c) If the amount of oil removed was less than three ounces, add three ounces to the component before reinstallation.*

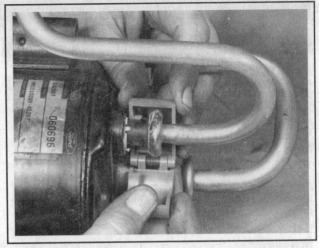

**14.2b Slip the proper size tool over the fitting with the tang facing the spring lock . . .**

This will maintain the correct oil level in the system after the repairs are completed.

### ✳✳ CAUTION:

**When replacing a compressor, the fixed orifice tube must also be replaced (see Section 17).**

➡**Note: When replacing the compressor, transfer the clutch assembly to the new compressor. A universal spanner wrench, snap ring pliers and a two jaw puller will be needed to remove the clutch from the old compressor. The compressor shaft seal should also be replaced at this time.**

8  Installation procedures are the reverse of those for removal. When installing the fitting block, use new O-rings and lubricate them with clean refrigerant oil.

9  After the compressor is installed have the system evacuated, recharged and leak tested by a dealer service department or an air conditioning repair facility.

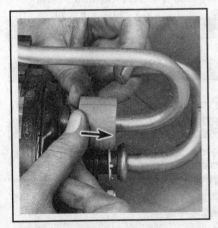

**14.2c . . . close the tool and push it in . . .**

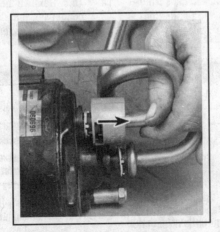

**14.2d . . . then pull the line off**

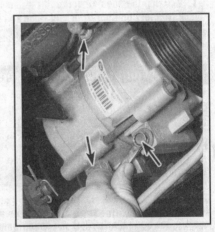

**14.4 Remove the mounting bolts (arrows) to remove the air conditioning compressor from the block**

## 15 Air conditioning condenser - removal and installation

### ✳✳ WARNING:

The air conditioning system is under high pressure. DO NOT loosen any fittings or remove any components until after the system has been discharged. Air conditioning refrigerant should be properly discharged into an EPA-approved container at a dealer service department or an automotive air conditioning repair facility. Always wear eye protection when disconnecting air conditioning system fittings.

➡Note: Special spring lock coupling tools are required to release the connectors used on the refrigerant lines throughout the air conditioning system.

### REMOVAL

▸ Refer to illustrations 15.2 and 15.4

### ✳✳ CAUTION:

Whenever a condenser is replaced, it will be necessary to replace the suction accumulator/drier.

1  Disconnect the cable at the negative battery terminal.
2  Have the system discharged by a dealer service department or an automotive air conditioning repair facility. Disconnect the coupled hose and liquid line fittings (see illustration).
3  Remove the screws retaining the top radiator shroud (see Section 4).
4  Remove the bolts holding the condenser to the top radiator support (see illustration).
5  Carefully tilt the radiator to the rear and lift the condenser out of the bottom cradle supports.
6  If the condenser is being replaced with a new one, transfer the brackets and mounts from the old unit to the new one.
7  When replacing the condenser add one ounce of refrigerant oil to the condenser before reassembly. This will maintain the correct oil level in the system after the repairs are completed.
8  Before installation, check the bracket assemblies and mounts for excessive wear or damage. Replace them if necessary.
9  The installation procedures are the reverse of those for removal. When installing the hose and fittings, use new O-rings and lubricate them with clean refrigerant oil.
10  After the condenser is installed have the system evacuated, recharged and leak tested by a dealer service department or an air conditioning repair facility.

15.2  Using the special tool required, disconnect the spring lock couplers on the refrigerant lines and separate the lines

15.4  Remove the condenser bracket bolt at the top of the condenser, there's a similar bolt location on the opposite side of the condenser

## 16 Air conditioning accumulator/drier - removal and installation

### REMOVAL

▸ Refer to illustration 16.2

### ✳✳ WARNING:

The air conditioning system is under high pressure. DO NOT loosen any fittings or remove any components until after the system has been discharged. Air conditioning refrigerant should be properly discharged into an EPA-approved container at a dealer service department or an automotive air conditioning repair facility. Always wear eye protection when disconnecting air conditioning system fittings.

1  Disconnect the cable at the negative battery terminal.
2  Disconnect the refrigerant inlet and outlet lines (see illustration). Cap or plug the open lines immediately.
➡Note: Special spring lock coupling tools are required to release the connectors used on the refrigerant lines throughout the air conditioning system.

3  Remove the mounting bolt and slide the receiver-drier assembly up and out of the mounting bracket.

### INSTALLATION

4  If you are replacing the receiver/drier, drain the refrigerant oil

from the old accumulator/drier. Add the same amount plus two ounces of clean refrigerant oil to the new accumulator. This will maintain the correct oil level in the system after the repairs are completed.

5   Place the new receiver-drier into position, tighten the mounting bracket screw securely.

6   Install the inlet and outlet lines. Lubricate the O-rings using clean refrigerant oil and tighten the through-bolt and refrigerant line connections securely.

7   Connect the cable to the negative terminal of the battery.

8   Have the system evacuated, recharged and leak tested by a dealer service department or an air conditioning repair facility.

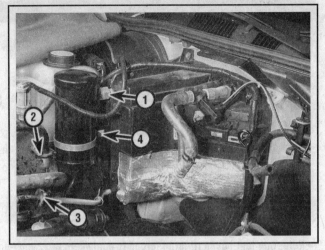

**16.2  Disconnect the two refrigerant lines at the accumulator/drier, one is a conventional nut and the other is a spring lock coupling**

*1   Accumulator/drier suction line (threaded fitting)*
*2   Accumulator/drier liquid line (spring lock coupler)*
*3   Evaporator core liquid refrigerant line (spring lock coupler)*
*4   Mounting bracket and screw*

## 17  Fixed orifice tube - replacement

The fixed orifice tube assembly is the restriction between the high-pressure and low-pressure liquid refrigerant. It meters the flow of liquid refrigerant into the evaporator core.

Evaporator temperature is controlled by sensing the pressure inside the evaporator core with a pressure operated electric switch. The switch controls compressor operation to keep the evaporator within the required pressure limits.

If, when the system is checked with the appropriate gauges, the high-pressure reads extremely high and low-pressure reads almost a vacuum, the fixed orifice tube is plugged and must be replaced.

### ✳✳ WARNING:

**The air conditioning system is under high pressure. DO NOT loosen any fittings or remove any components until after the system has been discharged. Air conditioning refrigerant should be properly discharged into an EPA-approved container at a dealer service department or an automotive air conditioning repair facility. Always eye wear protection when disconnecting air conditioning system fittings.**

### ✳✳ CAUTION:

**DON'T try to remove or install the fixed orifice tube with anything except the special tool recommended by the manufacturer, tool number T83L-19990-A. To try to remove any other way will break the fixed orifice tube inside the evaporator core tube, and may require the replacement of the evaporator core.**

### REMOVAL

1   Disconnect the liquid line from the evaporator core (see illustration 16.2).

➡**Note: Special spring lock coupling tools are required to release the connectors used on the refrigerant lines throughout the air conditioning system.**

2   Pour a small amount of refrigerant oil into the evaporator core tube to lubricate the O-rings seals on the orifice tube during removal.

3   Using the special tool, remove the fixed orifice tube.

4   Cap or plug the open refrigerant lines immediately to prevent any dirt or excessive moisture from entering the system.

### INSTALLATION

5   Lubricate the O-rings on the new fixed orifice tube with clean refrigerant oil.

6   Place the new fixed orifice tube into the special tool (the same tool is used for removal and installation) and insert it into the evaporator core tube until the orifice tube is seated at the stop.

7   Remove the tool.

8   Replace the O-ring at the refrigerant line spring lock coupling.

9   Reconnect the refrigerant lines.

10  Have the system evacuated, recharged and leak tested by a dealer service department or an air conditioning repair facility.

## Specifications

| | |
|---|---|
| Coolant capacity | See Chapter 1 |
| Thermostat | |
| Opening temperature | 188 to 200 degrees |
| Fully open temperature | 212 to 221 degrees |
| Expansion tank pressure cap | |
| Specified cap pressure | 16 psi |
| Minimum (must maintain) | 13 psi |
| Maximum (must relieve) | 18 psi |

## Torque specifications          Ft-lbs (unless otherwise indicated)

➡ **Note: One foot-pound (ft-lb) of torque is equivalent to 12 inch-pounds (in-lbs) of torque. Torque values below approximately 15 foot-pounds are expressed in inch-pounds, because most foot-pound torque wrenches are not accurate at these smaller values.**

| | |
|---|---|
| Fan-to-fan clutch bolts | |
| 5.0L engine | 12 to 18 |
| 4.6L engine | 15 to 20 |
| Fan clutch-to-water pump bolts (5.0L only) | 15 to 22 |
| Fan clutch-to-water pump hub (4.6L only) | 37 to 46 |
| Water pump-to-engine bolts | |
| 5.0L engine | 12 to 18 |
| 4.6L engine | 15 to 22 |
| Transmission oil line fitting-to-radiator | 12 to 18 |
| Fan shroud-to-radiator | 24 to 48 inch-lbs |
| Thermostat housing bolts | |
| 5.0L engine | 12 to 18 |
| 4.6L engine | 15 to 22 |

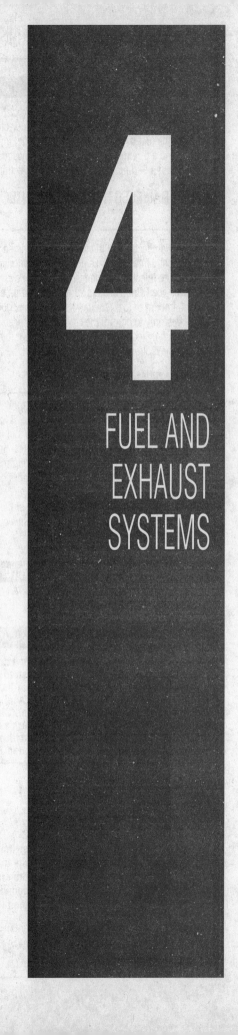

# 4

## FUEL AND EXHAUST SYSTEMS

**Section**

**Reference to other Chapters**

## 1  General information

The fuel system consists of a fuel tank, an electric fuel pump (located in the fuel tank), a fuel pump relay, fuel injectors, an air cleaner assembly and a throttle body unit. The fuel injection components are all equipped with a Sequential Electronic Fuel Injection (SEFI) system.

### SEQUENTIAL ELECTRONIC FUEL INJECTION (SEFI) SYSTEM

Sequential Electronic Fuel Injection uses timed impulses to inject the fuel directly into the intake port of each cylinder according to its firing order. The injectors are controlled by the Powertrain Control Module (PCM). The PCM monitors various engine parameters and delivers the exact amount of fuel required into the intake ports. The throttle body serves only to control the amount of air passing into the system. Because each cylinder is equipped with its own injector, much better control of the fuel/air mixture ratio is possible.

### FUEL PUMP AND LINES

#### 2002 and earlier models

Fuel is circulated from the fuel tank to the fuel injection system, and back to the fuel tank, through a pair of metal lines running along the underside of the vehicle. An electric fuel pump is located inside the fuel tank. A vapor return system routes all vapors back to the fuel tank through a separate return line.

The fuel pump will operate as long as the engine is cranking or running and the PCM is receiving ignition reference pulses from the elec

tronic ignition system. If there are no reference pulses, the fuel pump will shut off after two or three seconds.

#### 2003 and later models

Fuel is circulated from the fuel tank to the fuel injection system through a metal line running along the underside of the vehicle. An electric fuel pump/fuel level sensor is located inside the fuel tank. The fuel pump/fuel level sensor assembly consists of the pump, the fuel level sensor, an inlet filter (sometimes referred to as a sock or strainer), a check valve to maintain pressure after the pump is shut off and a pressure relief valve to protect the pump from over-pressurization in the event of a blocked fuel line. But what sets this pump apart from conventional in-tank pumps is its variable speed capability. The PCM controls fuel pressure by controlling the speed (rpm) of the pump. The PCM alters the fuel pressure by controlling the duty cycle, which in turn controls the speed of the fuel pump by modulating the voltage to the fuel pump. The fuel pump driver is built internal to the PCM on 2003 and 2004 models. 2005 and later models are equipped with an externally mounted driver module termed the Fuel Pump Driver Module (FPDM).

### EXHAUST SYSTEM

The exhaust system includes an exhaust manifold fitted with an exhaust oxygen sensor, a catalytic converter, an exhaust pipe, and a muffler.

The catalytic converter is an emission control device added to the exhaust system to reduce pollutants. A single-bed converter is used in combination with a three-way (reduction) catalyst. Refer to Chapter 6 for more information regarding the catalytic converter.

## 2  Fuel pressure relief procedure

▶ Refer to illustration 2.1 and 2.4

### ✳✳ WARNING:

Gasoline is extremely flammable, so take extra precautions when you work on any part of the fuel system. Don't smoke or allow open flames or bare light bulbs near the work area, and don't work in a garage where a gas-type appliance (such as a water heater or a clothes dryer) is present. Since gasoline is carcinogenic, wear latex gloves when there's a possibility of being exposed to fuel, and, if you spill any fuel on your skin, rinse it off immediately with soap and water. Mop up any spills

immediately and do not store fuel-soaked rags where they could ignite. The fuel system is under constant pressure, so, if any fuel lines are to be disconnected, the fuel pressure in the system must be relieved first. When you perform any kind of work on the fuel system, wear safety glasses and have a Class B type fire extinguisher on hand.

➡Note: After the fuel pressure has been relieved. it's a good idea to lay a shop towel over any fuel connection to be disassembled, to absorb the residual fuel that may leak out when servicing the fuel system.

2.1  The inertia switch is located in the trunk. Disconnect the electrical connector to disable the fuel pump

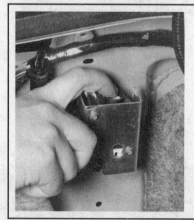

2.4  If necessary, push the reset button after connecting the inertia switch to energize the fuel pump

1   The fuel pump switch - sometimes called the "inertia switch" - which shuts off fuel to the engine in the event of a collision, affords a simple and convenient means by which fuel pressure can be relieved before servicing fuel injection components. The switch is located in the luggage compartment (see illustration) and is usually covered by the carpet which comes up the sides of the trunk.

2   Unplug the inertia switch electrical connector.

3   Start the engine and allow it to run until it stops. This should take only a few seconds.

4   The fuel system pressure is now relieved. When you're finished working on the fuel system, simply plug the electrical connector back into the switch. If the inertia switch was "popped" (activated) during this procedure, push the reset button on the top of the switch (see illustration).

## 3   Fuel pump/fuel pressure - check

### ☀ WARNING:

Gasoline is extremely flammable, so take extra precautions when you work on any part of the fuel system. Don't smoke or allow open flames or bare light bulbs near the work area, and don't work in a garage where a gas-type appliance (such as a water heater or a clothes dryer) is present. Since gasoline is carcinogenic, wear latex gloves when there's a possibility of being exposed to fuel, and, if you spill any fuel on your skin, rinse it off immediately with soap and water. Mop up any spills immediately and do not store fuel-soaked rags where they could ignite. The fuel system is under constant pressure, so, if any fuel lines are to be disconnected, the fuel pressure in the system must be relieved first (see Section 2 for more information). When you perform any kind of work on the fuel system, wear safety glasses and have a Class B type fire extinguisher on hand.

➡ Note 1: To perform the fuel pressure test, you will need to obtain a fuel pressure gauge and adapter set (fuel line fittings).

➡ Note 2: The fuel pump will operate as long as the engine is cranking or running and the PCM is receiving ignition reference pulses from the electronic ignition system. If there are no reference pulses, the fuel pump will shut off after two or three seconds.

➡ Note: 3 After the fuel pressure has been relieved. it's a good idea to lay a shop towel over any fuel connection to be disassembled, to absorb the residual fuel that may leak out when servicing the fuel system.

## PRELIMINARY INSPECTION

♦ Refer to illustrations 3.2a, 3.2b, 3.2c, 3.2d, 3.3a and 3.3b

1   Should the fuel system fail to deliver the proper amount of fuel, or any fuel at all, inspect it as follows. Remove the fuel filler cap. Have an assistant turn the ignition key to the On position (engine not running) while you listen at the fuel filler opening. You should hear a whirring sound that lasts for a couple of seconds.

2   If you don't hear anything, check the fuel pump fuse (see Chapter 12). If the fuse is blown, replace it and see if it blows again. If it does, trace the fuel pump circuit for a short. If it isn't blown, remove the fuel pump relay and install a jumper wire into the fuel pump relay terminals that power the fuel pump (see illustrations). Listen at the fuel filler opening again - if you now hear the whirring sound, the fuel pump relay or its control circuit is faulty. If there is still no whirring sound, there is a problem in the fuel pump circuit from the relay panel to the fuel pump, defective power relay or a defective fuel pump.

3   Check for battery voltage to the fuel pump relay connector and the power relay connector (see illustrations). If there is battery voltage present, have the relay(s) tested at a dealer service department or other qualified automotive repair shop.

3.2a  On models with the 4.6L engine, first lift the relay control assembly from the fuse center and press the tab on the cover . . .

3.2b . . . then slide the cover off the relay control panel

3.2c  Relay control panel

1   PCM power relay
2   Fuel pump relay
3   Air conditioning cutout relay

4   If there is no voltage present, check the fuse(s) and the wiring circuit for the fuel pump relay and/or power relay (see Chapter 12).

**3.2d  Use a jumper wire and jump
the connector to power the fuel pump
(yellow wire and green/yellow wire)**

**3.3a  Checking for battery voltage on
the fuel pump relay power
supply terminal**

**3.3b  Checking for battery voltage on
the power relaysupply terminal**

## OPERATING PRESSURE CHECK

▶ **Refer to illustrations 3.7, 3.8a and 3.8b**

5   Relieve the fuel system pressure (see Section 2).

### 2002 and earlier models

6   Detach the cable from the negative battery terminal.

7   Remove the cap from the fuel pressure test port and attach a fuel pressure gauge (see illustration). If you don't have the correct adapter for the test port, remove the Schrader valve and connect the gauge hose to the fitting. Tighten the hose clamp securely.

8   Attach the cable to the negative battery terminal. Turn the ignition

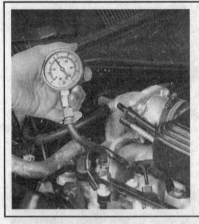

**3.7  If you don't
have the correct
adapter, it is
possible to remove
the Schrader valve
from the fitting and
install a standard
fuel pressure
gauge, using a
hose clamp**

key ON (engine not running). Locate the Diagnostic Test connector and install a jumper wire from terminal Fp (see illustrations) to ground. This will activate the fuel pump without running the engine.

9   Note the fuel pressure and compare it with the pressure listed in this Chapter's Specifications.

10  Next, remove the jumper wire from the Diagnostic Test connector and start the engine. Note the fuel pressure and compare it with the pressure listed in this Chapter's Specifications.

11  If the system fuel pressure is less than specified:

a)  *Inspect the system for a fuel leak. Repair any leaks and recheck the fuel pressure.*

b)  *If the fuel pressure is still low, replace the fuel filter (it may be clogged) and recheck the fuel pressure.*

c)  *If the pressure is still low, check the fuel pump output pressure (see below) and the fuel pressure regulator (see Section 13).*

12  If the pressure is higher than specified:

a)  *Check the fuel return line for an obstruction.*

b)  *Check the fuel pressure regulator (see Section 13).*

13  Turn the ignition switch to Off, wait five minutes and recheck the pressure on the gauge. Compare the reading with the hold pressure listed in this Chapter's Specifications. If the hold pressure is less than specified:

a)  *The fuel lines may be leaking.*

b)  *The fuel pressure regulator may be allowing the fuel pressure to bleed through to the return line (see Section 13).*

c)  *A fuel injector (or injectors) may be leaking.*

d)  *The fuel pump may be defective.*

**3.8a  With the
ignition key ON
(engine not running)
ground terminal Fp
to activate the fuel
pump**

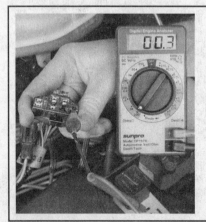

**3.8b  Double-check
for continuity from
the Fp terminal to
the fuel pump relay
connector to verify
that there are not
any damaged or
open circuits**

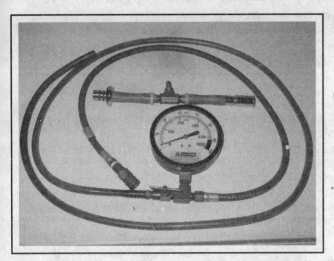

**3.14  A typical fuel pressure gauge, with hoses and fittings suitable for tee-ing into the fuel system between the fuel delivery line and the fuel rail**

## 2003 and later models

♦ Refer to illustrations 3.14 and 3.16

14  In addition to a fuel pressure gauge capable of reading fuel pressure up to 70 psi, you'll need a hose and an adapter suitable for tee-ing into the fuel system at the quick-connect fitting between the fuel delivery hose and the fuel rail (see illustration).

15  Disconnect the quick-connect fitting at the connection between the fuel delivery hose and the fuel rail (if you're unfamiliar with quick-connect fittings, refer to Section 4).

16  Tee in the fuel pressure gauge between the fuel delivery hose and the fuel rail (see illustration).

➡Note: Some models may be equipped with a fuel pressure test port built into the fuel rail.

17  Turn off all the accessories, then start the engine and let it idle. The fuel pressure should be within the operating range listed in this Chapter's Specifications. If the pressure reading is within the specified range, the system is operating correctly.

18  If the fuel pressure is higher than specified, then the pump, the Fuel Pump Driver Module (FPDM), the Powertrain Control Module (PCM) or the circuit connecting these components is probably defective. But checking this circuit is beyond the scope of the home mechanic, so have the circuit checked by a professional.

19  If the fuel pressure is lower than specified, inspect the fuel delivery lines and hoses for an obstruction or a kink. Also inspect all fuel delivery line and hose quick-connect fittings for leaks. Replace the fuel filter (see Chapter 1) and re-check the pressure. If the lines, hoses, connections and the fuel filter are all in good shape, remove the fuel pump/fuel level sensor assembly (see Section 7) and inspect the fuel pump inlet strainer for restrictions. If everything else is okay, replace the fuel pump (see Section 8).

20  Turn the ignition switch to OFF, wait five minutes and recheck the pressure on the gauge. Compare the reading with the hold pressure listed in this Chapter's Specifications. If the hold pressure is less than specified:

  a)  *The fuel delivery line or a quick-connect fitting might be leaking.*
  b)  *A fuel injector (or injectors) may be leaking.*
  c)  *The fuel pump might be defective.*

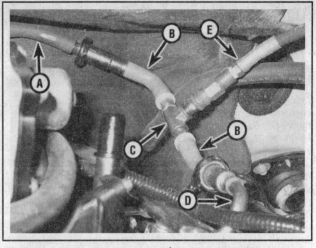

**3.13  Here's a typical setup for tee-ing into the fuel system between the fuel delivery hose and the fuel rail:**

| | |
|---|---|
| *A  Fuel delivery hose* | *D  Fuel rail delivery pipe* |
| *B  Adapter hoses* | *E  Hose to fuel pressure* |
| *C  Tee-fitting* | *    gauge* |

21  After the testing is complete, relieve the fuel pressure (see Section 2), remove the fuel pressure gauge and connect the fuel delivery line to the fuel rail (see Section 4 if you're unfamiliar with quick-connect fittings).

## FUEL PUMP OUTPUT PRESSURE CHECK (2002 AND EARLIER MODELS)

### ✳✳ WARNING:

**For this test it is necessary to use a fuel pressure gauge with a bleeder valve in order to relieve the fuel pressure after the test is completed (the normal procedure for pressure relief will not work because the gauge is connected directly to the fuel pump).**

22  Relieve the system fuel pressure (see Section 2).

23  Detach the cable from the negative battery terminal.

24  Attach a fuel pressure gauge directly to the fuel feed line at the fuel tank.

25  Attach the cable to the negative battery terminal.

26  Using a jumper wire, bridge the terminals on the Diagnostic Test connector located in the engine compartment (see illustration 3.8a).

27  Note the pressure reading on the gauge and compare the reading to the value listed in this Chapter's Specifications.

28  If the indicated pressure is less than specified, inspect the fuel line for leaks between the pump and gauge. If no leaks are found, replace the fuel pump.

29  Turn the ignition key to Off and wait five minutes. Note the reading on the gauge and compare it to the hold pressure listed in this Chapter's Specifications. If the hold pressure is less than specified, check the fuel line between the pump and gauge for leaks. If no leaks are found, replace the fuel pump.

30  Remove the jumper wire from the diagnostic test connector.

31  Open the bleeder valve on the gauge and allow the pressurized fuel drain into an approved fuel container. Remove the gauge and reconnect the fuel line.

## 4 Fuel lines and fittings - replacement

▶ Refer to illustrations 4.26a, 4.26b and 4.26c

## ✳ WARNING:

Gasoline is extremely flammable, so take extra precautions when you work on any part of the fuel system. Don't smoke or allow open flames or bare light bulbs near the work area, and don't work in a garage where a gas-type appliance (such as a water heater or a clothes dryer) is present. Since gasoline is carcinogenic, wear latex gloves when there's a possibility of being exposed to fuel, and, if you spill any fuel on your skin, rinse it off immediately with soap and water. Mop up any spills immediately and do not store fuel-soaked rags where they could ignite. The fuel system is under constant pressure, so, if any fuel lines are to be disconnected, the fuel pressure in the system must be relieved first (see Section 2 for more information). When you perform any kind of work on the fuel system, wear safety glasses and have a Class B type fire extinguisher on hand.

## PUSH-CONNECT FITTINGS - DISASSEMBLY AND REASSEMBLY

1   The manufacturer uses two different push-connect fitting designs. Fittings used with 3/8 and 5/16-inch diameter lines have a "hairpin" type clip; fittings used with 1/4-inch diameter lines have a "duck bill" type clip. The procedure used for releasing each type of fitting is different. The clips should be replaced whenever a connector is disassembled.

2   Disconnect all push-connect fittings from fuel system components such as the fuel filter, the fuel charging assembly, the fuel tank, etc. before removing the assembly.

## 3/8 AND 5/16-INCH FITTINGS (HAIRPIN CLIP)

3   Inspect the internal portion of the fitting for accumulations of dirt. If more than a light coating of dust is present, clean the fitting before disassembly.

4   Some adhesion between the seals in the fitting and the line will occur over a period of time. Twist the fitting on the line, then push and pull the fitting until it moves freely.

5   Remove the hairpin clip from the fitting by bending the shipping tab down until it clears the body. Then, using nothing but your hands, spread each leg about 1/8-inch to disengage the body and push the legs through the fitting. Finally, pull lightly on the triangular end of the clip and work it clear of the line and fitting. Remember, don't use any tools to perform this part of the procedure.

6   Grasp the fitting and hose and pull it straight off the line.

7   Do not reuse the original clip in the fitting. A new clip must be used.

8   Before reinstalling the fitting on the line, wipe the line end with a clean cloth. Inspect the inside of the fitting to ensure that it's free of dirt and/or obstructions.

9   To reinstall the fitting on the line, align them and push the fitting into place. When the fitting is engaged, a definite click will be heard. Pull on the fitting to ensure that it's completely engaged. To install the new clip, insert it into any two adjacent openings in the fitting with the triangular portion of the clip pointing away from the fitting opening. Using your index finger, push the clip in until the legs are locked on the outside of the fitting.

## 1/4-INCH FITTINGS (DUCK BILL CLIP)

10   The duck bill clip type fitting consists of a body, spacers, O-rings and the retaining clip. The clip holds the fitting securely in place on the line. One of the two following methods must be used to disconnect this type of fitting.

11   Before attempting to disconnect the fitting, check the visible internal portion of the fitting for accumulations of dirt. If more than a light coating of dust is evident, clean the fitting before disassembly.

12   Some adhesion between the seals in the fitting and line will occur over a period of time. Twist the fitting on the line, then push and pull the fitting until it moves freely.

13   The preferred method used to disconnect the fitting requires a special tool. To disengage the line from the fitting, align the slot in the push-connect disassembly tool (No. T82L-9500-AH or equivalent tool) with either tab on the clip (90-degrees from the slots on the side of the fitting) and insert the tool. This disengages the duck bill from the line.

➡Note: Some fuel lines have a secondary bead which aligns with the outer surface of the clip. The bead can make tool insertion difficult. If necessary, use the alternative disassembly method described in Step 16.

14   Holding the tool and the line with one hand, pull the fitting off.

➡Note: Only moderate effort is necessary if the clip is properly disengaged. The use of anything other than your hands should not be required.

15   After disassembly, inspect and clean the line sealing surface. Also inspect the inside of the fitting and the line for any internal parts that may have been dislodged from the fitting. Any loose internal parts should be immediately reinstalled (use the line to insert the parts).

16   The alternative disassembly procedure requires a pair of small adjustable pliers. The pliers must have a jaw width of 3/16-inch or less.

17   Align the jaws of the pliers with the openings in the side of the fitting and compress the portion of the retaining clip that engages the body. This disengages the retaining clip from the body (often one side of the clip will disengage before the other - both sides must be disengaged).

18   Pull the fitting off the line.

➡Note: Only moderate effort is required if the retaining clip has been properly disengaged. Do not use any tools for this procedure.

19   Once the fitting is removed from the line end, check the fitting and line for any internal parts that may have been dislodged from the fitting. Any loose internal parts should be immediately reinstalled (use the line to insert the parts).

20   The retaining clip will remain on the line. Disengage the clip from the line bead to remove it. Do not reuse the retaining clip - install a new one!

21   Before reinstalling the fitting, wipe the line end with a clean cloth. Check the inside of the fitting to make sure that it's free of dirt and/or obstructions.

22   To reinstall the fitting, align it with the line and push it into place. When the fitting is engaged, a definite click will be heard. Pull on the fitting to ensure that it's fully engaged.

23   Install the new replacement clip by inserting one of the serrated edges on the duck bill portion into one of the openings. Push on the other side until the clip snaps into place.

**4.26a If the spring lock couplings are equipped with safety clips, pry them off with a small screwdriver**

**4.26b Open the spring-loaded halves of the spring lock coupling tool and place it in position around the coupling, then close it**

**4.26c To disconnect the coupling, push the tool into the cage opening to expand the garter spring and release the female fitting, then pull the male and female fittings apart**

## SPRING LOCK COUPLINGS - DISASSEMBLY AND REASSEMBLY

24 The fuel supply and return lines used on SEFI engines utilize spring lock couplings at the engine fuel rail end instead of plastic push-connect fittings. The male end of the spring lock coupling, which is girded by two O-rings, is inserted into a female flared end engine fitting. The coupling is secured by a garter spring which prevents disengagement by gripping the flared end of the female fitting. On later models, a cup-tether assembly provides additional security.

25 To disconnect the 1/2-inch (12.7 mm) spring lock coupling supply fitting, you will need to obtain a spring lock coupling tool D87L-9280-B or its equivalent; for the 3/8-inch (9.52 mm) return fitting, get tool D87L-9280-A or its equivalent.

26 Study the accompanying illustrations carefully before detaching either spring lock coupling fitting (see illustrations).

## 5  Fuel tank - removal and installation

▶ Refer to illustrations 5.5, 5.6a, 5.6b, 5.6c and 5.9

### ✳✳ WARNING 1:

Gasoline is extremely flammable, so take extra precautions when you work on any part of the fuel system. Don't smoke or allow open flames or bare light bulbs near the work area, and don't work in a garage where a gas-type appliance (such as a water heater or a clothes dryer) is present. Since gasoline is carcinogenic, wear latex gloves when there's a possibility of being exposed to fuel, and, if you spill any fuel on your skin, rinse it off immediately with soap and water. Mop up any spills immediately and do not store fuel-soaked rags where they could ignite. The fuel system is under constant pressure, so, if any fuel lines are to be disconnected, the fuel pressure in the system must be relieved first (see Section 2 for more information). When you perform any kind of work on the fuel system, wear safety glasses and have a Class B type fire extinguisher on hand.

### ✳✳ WARNING 2:

On models with air suspension, turn the air suspension switch to Off before raising the vehicle.

➡Note: Don't begin this procedure until the gauge indicates that the tank is empty or nearly empty. If the tank must be removed when it's full (for example, if the fuel pump malfunctions), siphon any remaining fuel from the tank prior to removal.

1  Unless the vehicle has been driven far enough to completely empty the tank, it's a good idea to siphon the residual fuel out before removing the tank from the vehicle.

### ✳✳ WARNING:

DO NOT start the siphoning action by mouth! Use a siphoning kit (available at most auto parts stores).

2  Relieve the fuel pressure (refer to Section 2).
3  Detach the cable from the negative terminal of the battery.
4  Raise the vehicle and support it securely on jackstands.
5  Remove the fuel tank filler neck bracket bolts securing the fuel filler neck and the fuel tank filler pipe retainer (see illustration) and slide the assembly from the vehicle.
6  Disconnect the fuel lines (see illustrations) and vapor lines.
7  Remove the electric fuel pump and sending unit electrical connector with a screwdriver.

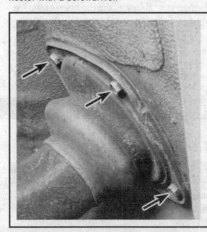

**5.5 Remove the bolts (arrows) from the fuel filler neck on the inside of the fenderwell**

5.6a  Push down to release the safety clamps (arrows) from the fuel fittings

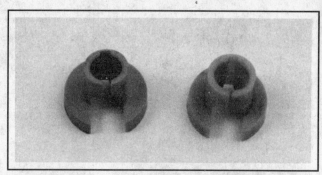

5.6b  Use special fuel line tools called "duck bill" clip fittings to separate the fuel lines. Refer to Section 3 for more detailed information on these type of fuel line removal tools

5.6c  Push the tool (arrow) into the fuel line housing to release the locking mechanism

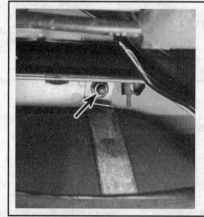

5.9  Remove the bolt (arrow) from the fuel tank strap (the other fuel tank strap is not visible in this photo)

8    Place a floor jack under the tank and position a block of wood between the jack pad and the tank. Raise the jack until it's supporting the tank.

9    Remove the bolts or nuts from the front ends of the fuel tank straps (see illustration). The straps are hinged at the other end so you can swing them out of the way.

10   Lower the tank far enough to unplug any vapor lines or wire harness brackets that may be difficult to reach when the fuel tank is in the vehicle.

11   Slowly lower the jack while steadying the tank. Remove the tank from the vehicle.

12   If you're replacing the tank, or having it cleaned or repaired, refer to Section 6.

13   Refer to Section 7 to remove and install the fuel pump/sending unit.

14   Installation is the reverse of removal. SAE 10W-40 engine oil can be used as an assembly aid when pushing the fuel filler neck back into the tank.

## 6    Fuel tank - cleaning and repair

1    Repairs to the fuel tank or filler neck should be performed by a professional with the proper training to carry out this critical and potentially dangerous work. Even after cleaning and flushing, explosive fumes can remain and could explode during repair of the tank.

2    If the fuel tank is removed from the vehicle, it should not be placed in an area where sparks or open flames could ignite the fumes coming out of the tank.

### ✳✳ WARNING:

Be especially careful inside a garage where a gas appliance is located because it could cause an explosion!

## 7    Fuel pump - removal and installation

▶ Refer to illustrations 7.7, 7.8 and 7.11

### ✳✳ WARNING 1:

Gasoline is extremely flammable, so take extra precautions when you work on any part of the fuel system. Don't smoke or allow open flames or bare light bulbs near the work area, and don't work in a garage where a gas-type appliance (such as a water heater or a clothes dryer) is present. Since gasoline is carcinogenic, wear latex gloves when there's a possibility of being exposed to fuel, and, if you spill any fuel on your skin, rinse it off immediately with soap and water. Mop up any spills immediately and do not store fuel-soaked rags where they could ignite. The fuel system is under constant pressure, so, if any fuel lines

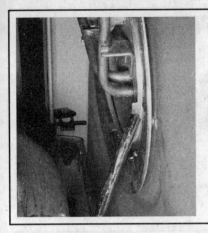

7.7 Use a brass punch to turn the locking ring on the fuel pump/sending unit assembly counterclockwise

7.8 Carefully angle the fuel pump/sending unit out of the fuel tank without damaging the fuel strainer or sending unit

are to be disconnected, the fuel pressure in the system must be relieved first (see Section 2 for more information). When you perform any kind of work on the fuel system, wear safety glasses and have a Class B type fire extinguisher on hand.

### ✳✳ WARNING 2:

On models with a fire suppression system, disable the system before raising the rear of the vehicle by disconnecting the cable from the negative battery terminal and waiting at least three minutes.

1   Unless the vehicle has been driven far enough to completely empty the tank, it's a good idea to siphon the residual fuel out before removing the fuel pump from the vehicle.

### ✳✳ WARNING:

DO NOT start the siphoning action by mouth! Use a siphoning kit (available at most auto parts stores).

2   Relieve the fuel pressure (refer to Section 2).
3   Detach the cable from the negative terminal of the battery.
4   Raise the vehicle and support it securely on jackstands.
5   Disconnect the fuel lines from the fuel pump/fuel level sender assembly (see illustration 5.6c). Follow the procedure for the duck bill clip fitting in Section 3.
6   Disconnect the fuel pump/fuel level sender electrical connector.

## 1995 AND EARLIER MODELS

7   Using a brass punch or wood dowel only, tap the lock ring counterclockwise until it's loose (see illustration).
8   Carefully pull the fuel pump/sending unit assembly from the tank (see illustration).
9   Remove the old lock ring gasket and discard it.
10   If you're planning to reinstall the original fuel pump/sending unit, remove the strainer by prying it off with a screwdriver, wash it in clean solvent, then push it back onto the metal pipe on the end of the pump. If you're installing a new pump/sending unit, the assembly will include a new strainer.
11   To separate the fuel pump from the assembly, remove the clamp (see illustration) and disconnect the electrical connector from the fuel pump.
12   Clean the fuel pump mounting flange and the tank mounting surface and seal ring groove.

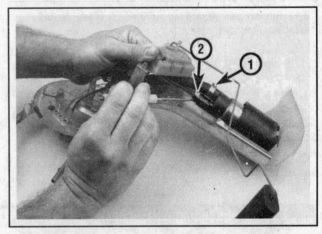

7.11 Remove the clamp (1) and disconnect the electrical connector (2) from the fuel pump, then separate the pump from the sending unit assembly

13 Installation is the reverse of removal. Apply a thin coat of heavy grease to the new seal ring to hold it in place during assembly.

## 1996 AND LATER MODELS

▶ Refer to illustrations 7.16, 7.17 and 7.18

14 Remove the fuel tank (see Section 5).
15 Remove the mounting bolts from the perimeter of the fuel pump/fuel level sensor assembly.
16 Lift up the fuel pump/fuel level sensor assembly, then carefully lift it out of the fuel tank (see illustration).

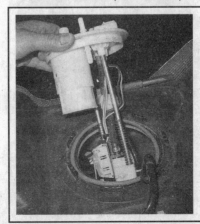

7.16 Carefully lift the fuel pump/fuel level sensor assembly from the fuel tank. Angle the pump/sending unit as necessary to protect the float arm and float from damage

**7.17 Remove and discard the old O-ring type seal for the fuel pump/fuel level sensor**

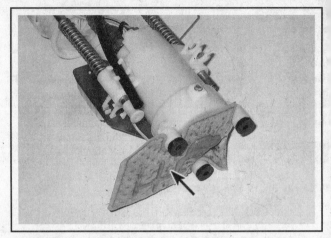

**7.18 If you're going to install the old fuel pump, inspect the fuel inlet strainer. If it's slightly dirty, scrub it gently with a small brush and rinse it off with clean solvent. If the strainer is so dirty that you can't clean it, replace the fuel pump. The strainer cannot be removed**

17 Remove the old O-ring type seal (see illustration) and discard it.

18 If you're planning to reinstall the original fuel pump unit, inspect the condition of the fuel inlet strainer (see illustration). The strainer is a permanent part of the pump and cannot be removed. If it's only slightly dirty, try scrubbing it gently with a small brush, then rinse it off with clean solvent. But if the strainer is so dirty that it's obstructed - and you're unable to clean it - you must replace the pump.

19 Clean the fuel pump mounting flange and the tank mounting sur-

face, particularly the area where the O-ring type seal is installed.

20 Be sure to use a new O-ring seal and apply a thin coat of heavy grease to the new seal ring to hold it in place while installing the fuel pump/fuel level sensor assembly.

21 Installation is otherwise the reverse of removal.

## 8   Fuel level sending unit – check and replacement

♦ Refer to illustrations 8.3 and 8.5

## CHECK

1 Raise the vehicle and support it securely on jackstands.

2 Disconnect the electrical connector for the fuel level sending unit.

3 Position the ohmmeter probes into the electrical connector (see illustration) and check the resistance. Use the 200-ohm scale on the ohmmeter.

4 With the fuel tank completely full, the resistance should be about 170.0 ohms. With the fuel tank nearly empty, the resistance of the sending unit should be about 11.0 ohms.

5 If the readings are incorrect, replace the sending unit.

➡**Note: A more accurate check of the sending unit can be made by removing it from the fuel tank and checking its resistance while manually operating the float arm (see illustration).**

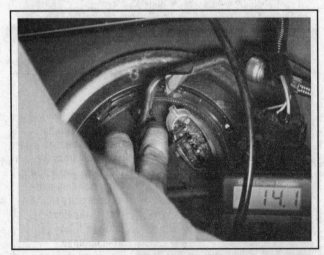

**8.3 Using an ohmmeter, probe the top two terminals of the fuel pump/sending unit assembly to check the resistance**

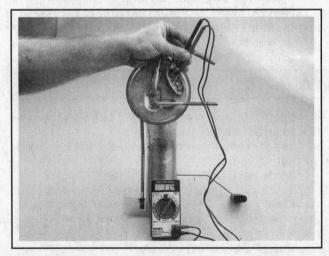

**8.5 A more accurate check of the fuel level sending unit can be performed with the assembly on the bench, the ohmmeter probes on the connector and the float positioned on "empty" (bottom) and "full" (top). Check for a smooth change in resistance between these positions**

## REPLACEMENT

6   Remove the fuel pump/sending unit assembly from the vehicle (see Section 7).

7   Carefully angle the sending unit out of the opening without damaging the fuel level float located at the bottom of the assembly.

8   Remove the sending unit electrical connector from the fuel pump assembly.

9   Remove the screws that secure the sending unit to the fuel pump assembly.

10  Installation is the reverse of removal.

11  If the float arm and float wire loop were damaged or bent during removal and installation, adjust the angle and travel distance.

12  Be sure to install a new rubber gasket.

## 9   Air cleaner housing - removal and installation

▶ **Refer to illustrations 9.2 and 9.5**

1   Detach the cable from the negative terminal of the battery.

2   Loosen the bolt(s) from the air intake assembly on the intake manifold and the clamps on the air cleaner housing and remove the air intake assembly from the engine compartment (see illustration).

3   Unclip the upper half of the air cleaner housing assembly and remove it (see Chapter 1).

4   Remove the air filter element.

5   Remove the air cleaner housing mounting nuts (see illustration) and detach the assembly.

6   Installation is the reverse of removal.

**9.2  Remove the mounting bolt and clamp (arrow) from the air intake assembly (4.6L engine shown)**

**9.5  Remove the mounting nuts (arrows) from the air cleaner housing (4.6L engine shown)**

## 10  Accelerator cable - removal, installation and adjustment

## REMOVAL

▶ **Refer to illustrations 10.2 and 10.3**

1   Remove the air intake duct from the throttle body and intake manifold area (see Section 9).

2   Detach the accelerator cable from the throttle lever (see illustration).

3   Remove the cruise control cable from the cable bracket (see illustration).

4   Separate the accelerator cable from the cable bracket.

5   Pull the cable end out from the accelerator pedal recess in the driver's compartment.

6   Disconnect the accelerator cable clips mounted on the intake manifold and valve cover.

7   Remove the cable through the firewall from the engine compartment.

**10.2  Carefully remove the accelerator cable from the throttle lever by twisting (if necessary, pry it off with a screwdriver)**

## INSTALLATION

8   Installation is the reverse of removal. Be sure the cable is routed correctly.

9   If necessary, at the engine compartment side of the firewall, apply sealant around the accelerator cable to prevent water from entering the passenger compartment.

## ADJUSTMENT

10   Measure the freeplay at the accelerator pedal. Freeplay should be 3/64 to 1/8-inch.

11   To adjust, loosen the locknut on the cable bracket and adjust the deflection until it is within the specified range.

**10.3  Remove the bolt (arrow) and separate the cruise controlcable from the bracket**

## 11  Fuel injection system - general information

### SEQUENTIAL ELECTRONIC FUEL INJECTION (SEFI)

The Sequential Electronic Fuel Injection (SEFI) system is known as a multi-point, pulse timed, speed density control fuel injection system. On the SEFI system, fuel is metered into each intake port in sequence with the engine firing order in accordance with engine demand through eight injectors mounted on a tuned intake manifold.

#### 2002 and earlier models

The two-piece air intake manifold on the 5.0L engines includes an air intake plenum. The 4.6L engine incorporates a single intake manifold (see Section 13).

This system incorporates an on-board Electronic Engine Control (EEC-IV) computer that accepts inputs from various engine sensors to compute the required fuel flow rate necessary to maintain a prescribed air/fuel ratio throughout the entire engine operational range. The computer then outputs a command to the fuel injectors to meter the approximate quantity of fuel. The system automatically senses and compensates for changes in altitude, load and speed.

➡Note: The computer terminology has changed from Electronic Control Module (ECM) to the Powertrain Control Module (PCM) due to standardization of the Self Diagnosis system within the automotive industry.

The fuel delivery systems include an electric in-tank fuel pump which forces pressurized fuel through a series of metal and plastic lines and an inline fuel filter/reservoir to the fuel charging manifold assembly. The SEFI system uses a single high-pressure pump mounted inside the tank.

The fuel charging manifold assembly incorporates electrically actuated fuel injectors directly above each intake port. When energized, the injectors spray a metered quantity of fuel into the intake air stream.

A constant fuel pressure drop is maintained across the injector nozzles by a pressure regulator. The regulator is positioned downstream from the fuel injectors. Excess fuel passes through the regulator and returns to the fuel tank through a fuel return line.

On the SEFI system, each injector is energized once every other crankshaft revolution in sequence with engine firing order. The period of time that the injectors are energized (known as "on time" or "pulse width") is controlled by the EEC-IV computer. Air entering the engine is sensed by speed, pressure and temperature sensors. The outputs of these sensors are processed by the EEC-IV computer. The computer determines the needed injector pulse width and outputs a command to the injector to meter the exact quantity of fuel.

#### 2003 and later models

##### Torque-based Electronic Throttle Control (ETC) system

In a conventional induction system with an accelerator cable, the position of the throttle plate inside the throttle body is determined by the position of the accelerator pedal, which is determined by your foot, isn't always appropriate to the prevailing operating conditions. For example, if you mash the accelerator pedal when the transmission is in high gear and the vehicle is cruising down the freeway under no load, it takes a moment for the PCM to downshift the transmission and spin up the engine speed so that it can respond to your new demand. The manufacturer claims that its Generation II (Gen II) Torque Based Electronic Throttle Control (ETC) system produces the ideal transmission output shaft torque because the position of the throttle plate inside the throttle body is no longer based solely on driver demand (the position of the accelerator pedal).

##### Electronic throttle body and Throttle Position (TP) sensors

Instead, the PCM-controlled electronic throttle body regulates the amount of air entering the intake manifold in response to driver demand and in response to the operating conditions. There is no accelerator cable or cruise control cable connected to the throttle body. Both of these functions are handled by the PCM. There is also no Idle Air Control (IAC) motor on the electronic throttle body. This function is also handled by the PCM, which opens the throttle plate slightly in response to any load imposed on the engine during idle or low-speed maneuvers.

The electronic throttle body uses two Throttle Position (TP) sensors (TP1 and TP2) because the monitor for this system requires a redundant TP sensor. TP1 has a negative slope (increasing angle, decreasing voltage) and TP2 has a positive slope (increasing angle, increasing voltage). When the engine is running, the negatively-sloped TP1 is used by the ETC system as the actual TP sensor and TP2 is used as a reference sensor by the monitor. The replacement procedure for the electronic throttle body is in this Chapter.

### Electronic Throttle Control (ETC) module and Accelerator Pedal Position Sensors (APPS)

The accelerator pedal is equipped with three Accelerator Pedal Position Sensors (APPS), all three of which are housed inside a small plastic housing, known as the Electronic Throttle Control (ETC) module, at the top of the pedal. APP1 has a negative slop (increasing angle, decreasing voltage) and APP2 and APP3 have a positive slop (increasing angle, decreasing voltage). When the engine is running, APP1 is the actual APP sensor. The PCM uses APP2 and APP3 as reference sensors to calculate where a signal should be so that it can infer whether a sensor signal makes sense or not. If any one signal is irrational (doesn't match the other two signals), the PCM is still able to compute the correct outcome. If two of the three input signals are bad, the PCM substitutes a default value and turns on the Malfunction Indicator Lamp (MIL). The ETC module and the accelerator pedal are integrated into a single assembly. Neither component can be serviced separately. If one of the APP sensors is defective, you must replace the "pedal and sensor assembly," which is the manufacturer's term for this assembly (see Chapter 6 for the replacement procedure).

Besides eliminating the accelerator and cruise control cables and the IAC motor, the torque based ETC system also results in, according to the manufacturer, an improved airflow range, a more responsive powertrain at altitude and improved shift quality.

### Electronically controlled returnless fuel system

In a conventional fuel system with a return line, a fuel pressure regulator maintains the pressure within the correct operating range. When the vehicle decelerates, intake manifold goes up and a vacuum hose between the intake manifold and the pressure regulator lifts the spring-loaded diaphragm inside the regulator, allowing excess fuel pressure to bleed off and the unused fuel to return to the fuel tank. When the vehicle accelerates again, intake manifold vacuum goes down and the spring inside the regulator closes the diaphragm, shutting off the return line and allowing fuel pressure to rise again. But all of the models covered by this manual use a returnless fuel system, i.e. there is no fuel pressure regulator and no fuel return line.

### Fuel Pump Driver Module (FPDM) (2005 and later models)

In the type of returnless fuel system used by the vehicles covered by this manual, the PCM controls the fuel pressure by controlling the duty cycle of the Fuel Pump Driver Module (FPDM), which in turn controls the speed of the fuel pump by modulating the voltage to the fuel pump. The FPDM is located underneath the vehicle, near the trunk area. To replace the FPDM, refer to Chapter 6. The fuel pump driver is built internal to the PCM on 2003 and 2004 models. 2005 and later models are equipped with an externally mounted driver module (FPDM) (see Chapter 6).

### Fuel Rail Pressure Temperature (FRPT) sensor

These engines covered by this manual are equipped with a Fuel Rail Pressure Temperature (FRPT) sensor, which measures both the pressure and the temperature of the fuel in the fuel rail. The FRPT sensor is located at the front end of the left fuel rail. The FRPT sensor uses intake manifold vacuum as a reference to determine the pressure difference between the fuel rail and the intake manifold. The relationship between fuel pressure and fuel temperature is used to determine the likelihood of the presence of fuel vapor in the fuel rail. Both the pressure and temperature signals are used to control the speed of the fuel pump. The speed of the fuel pump controls the pressure inside the fuel rail in order to keep the fuel in a liquid state. Keeping the fuel in a liquid state increases the efficiency of the injectors because the higher fuel rail pressure allows a decrease in the injector pulse width (the interval of time during which the injector is open). To replace the FRPT sensor, refer to Chapter 6.

## 12  Fuel injection system - check

### ✳✳ WARNING:

Gasoline is extremely flammable, so take extra precautions when you work on any part of the fuel system. Don't smoke or allow open flames or bare light bulbs near the work area, and don't work in a garage where a gas-type appliance (such as a water heater or a clothes dryer) is present. Since gasoline is carcinogenic, wear latex gloves when there's a possibility of being exposed to fuel, and, if you spill any fuel on your skin, rinse it off immediately with soap and water. Mop up any spills immediately and do not store fuel-soaked rags where they could ignite. The fuel system is under constant pressure, so, if any fuel lines are to be disconnected, the fuel pressure in the system must be relieved first (see Section 2 for more information). When you perform any kind of work on the fuel system, wear safety glasses and have a Class B type fire extinguisher on hand.

→Note: The following procedure is based on the assumption that the fuel pump is working and the fuel pressure is adequate (see Section 3).

### PRELIMINARY CHECKS

1  Check all electrical connectors that are related to the system. Loose electrical connectors and poor grounds can cause many problems that resemble more serious malfunctions.

2  Check to see that the battery is fully charged, as the control unit and sensors depend on an accurate supply voltage in order to properly meter the fuel.

3  Check the air filter element - a dirty or partially blocked filter will severely impede performance and economy (see Chapter 1).

4   If a blown fuse is found, replace it and see if it blows again. If it does, search for a grounded wire in the harness to the fuel pump (see Chapter 12).

## SYSTEM CHECKS

▸ **Refer to illustration 12.7, 12.8 and 12.9**

5   Check the condition of the vacuum hoses connected to the intake manifold.

6   Remove the air intake duct from the throttle body and check for dirt, carbon or other residue build-up in the throttle body, particularly around the throttle plate. If it's dirty, clean it with carburetor cleaner and a toothbrush.

7   With the engine running, place an automotive stethoscope against each injector, one at a time, and listen for a clicking sound, indicating operation (see illustration). If you don't have a stethoscope, you can place the tip of a long screwdriver against the injector and listen through the handle.

8   If an injector isn't functioning (not clicking), purchase a special injector test light (sometimes called a "noid" light) and install it into the injector electrical connector (see illustration). Start the engine and check to see if the noid light flashes. If it does, the injector is receiving proper voltage. If it doesn't flash, further diagnosis should be performed by a dealer service department or other repair shop.

9   With the engine OFF and the fuel injector electrical connectors disconnected, measure the resistance of each injector (see illustration).

**12.7  Use a stethoscope or screwdriver to determine if the injectors are working properly - they should make a steady clicking sound that rises and falls with engine speed changes**

Check the Specifications listed in this Chapter for the correct ohmmeter readings.

10   The remainder of the system checks can be found in Section 13 and Chapter 6.

**12.8  Install the noid light into the fuel injector electrical connector and confirm that it blinks when the engine is running**

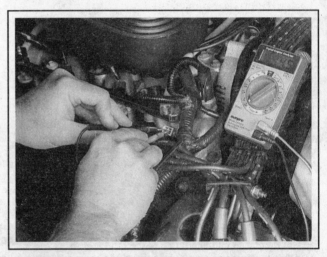

**12.9  Measure the resistance of each injector. It should be within Specifications**

## AIR INTAKE PLENUM (UPPER INTAKE MANIFOLD) (5.0L ENGINE) WITH THROTTLE BODY

### Removal

1   Detach the cable from the negative terminal of the battery.

2   Unplug the electrical connectors at the air bypass valve, throttle position sensor and EGR position sensor.

3   Detach the accelerator cable (see Section 10) and transmission linkage (see Chapter 7) from the throttle body assembly.

4   Remove the accelerator cable/throttle valve (TV) cable bracket from the intake manifold (see Section 10) and position the bracket and cables out of the way.

5   Clearly label, then detach, the vacuum lines from the upper intake manifold vacuum tree, the EGR valve and the fuel pressure regulator.

6   Detach the PCV system by disconnecting the hose from the fitting on the rear of the upper manifold.

7   If equipped, detach the canister purge line or lines from the throttle body and detach the EGR spacer coolant lines from the EGR spacer.

➡**Note: It will be necessary to drain the coolant from the radiator (see Chapter 1).**

8   Remove the six upper intake manifold retaining bolts.

9   Remove the upper intake manifold and throttle body as an assembly from the lower intake manifold.

### Installation

10  Be sure to clean and inspect the mounting faces of the lower intake manifold (see Chapter 2A) and the air intake plenum before positioning the new gasket(s) onto the lower intake mounting face. The use of alignment studs may be helpful. Install the air intake plenum and throttle body assembly onto the lower intake manifold. Ensure the gasket remains in place (if alignment studs are not used). Install the six upper intake manifold retaining bolts and tighten to the specified torque. Be sure to install the long bolts into the middle and the short bolts into the ends (see illustration 13.8). Installation is otherwise the reverse of removal.

## THROTTLE BODY (5.0L AND 4.6L ENGINES)

➡**Note: Removal and installation of the throttle body on 1996 models is the same as on previous years. The only difference is the throttle body is now attached to a throttle body spacer that is attached to the center of the plastic intake manifold. The throttle body is now positioned transversely to the engine instead of in line with it as on previous models.**

### Removal

▶ **Refer to illustration 13.15**

11  Detach the cable from the negative terminal of the battery.

12  Detach the throttle position sensor and throttle air bypass valve electrical connectors.

13  Disconnect the accelerator cable (see Section 10) and the Throttle Valve (TV) cable from the throttle body, on modlels so equipped.

14  If equipped, remove the PCV vent closure hose at the throttle body.

15  Remove the four throttle body mounting nuts (see illustration).

16  On 5.0L engines, carefully separate the throttle body from the

**13.15  Remove the four bolts (arrows) from the throttle body to intake manifold extension (1988 through 1995 4.6L engine shown)**

EGR spacer.

17  Remove and discard the gasket between the throttle body and the EGR spacer (5.0L engines only).

### Installation

18  Clean the gasket mating surfaces. If scraping is necessary, be careful not to damage the gasket surfaces or allow material to drop into the manifold. Installation is the reverse of removal. Be sure to tighten the throttle body mounting nuts to the torque listed in this Chapter's Specifications.

## THROTTLE POSITION (TP) SENSOR

19  Refer to Chapter 6, Section 4 for the check and replacement procedures for the TP sensor.

## AIR BYPASS VALVE ASSEMBLY

20  Refer to Section 14 for the check, adjustment and replacement procedures for the air bypass valve.

## FUEL RAIL ASSEMBLY

▶ **Refer to illustration 13.24a, 13.24b, 13.24c, 13.25a and 13.25b**

➡**Note: Removal and installation of the fuel rail on models since 1996 is the same as on previous years. The illustrations shown in this procedure are shown on a pre-1996 4.6L engine which is equipped with a different type of intake manifold.**

### Removal

21  Relieve the fuel pressure (see Section 2).

22  Detach the cable from the negative terminal of the battery.

23  On 5.0L engines, remove the air intake plenum assembly (see Steps 1 through 9). On 4.6L engines, remove the air intake assembly (see Section 9).

24  Using the special spring lock coupling tool, disconnect the fuel

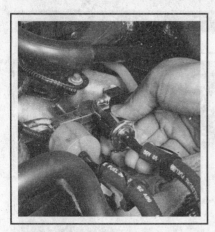

13.24a  Push down to release the safety clamp from the fuel line connectors

13.24b  Install the correct diameter spring lock coupling tool and push away from the fuel rail to release the internal locking mechanism

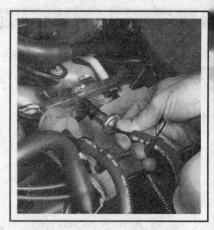

13.24c  Detach the fuel line from the fuel rail

feed and return lines from the fuel rail assembly (see illustrations).

➡️**Note: Refer to Section 4 for additional information on disconnecting fuel lines.**

25  Remove the four fuel rail assembly retaining bolts (two on each side) (see illustrations).

26  Carefully disengage the fuel rail from the fuel injectors and remove the fuel rail.

➡️**Note: It may be easier to remove the injectors with the fuel rail as an assembly.**

27  Use a rocking, side-to-side motion while lifting to remove the injectors from the fuel rail.

## Installation

➡️**Note: It's a good idea to replace the injector O-rings whenever the fuel rail is removed.**

28  Ensure that the injector caps are clean and free of contamination.

29  Place the fuel injector fuel rail assembly over each of the injectors and seat the injectors into the fuel rail. Ensure that the injectors are well seated in the fuel rail assembly.

➡️**Note: It may be easier to seat the injectors in the fuel rail and then seat the entire assembly in the lower intake manifold.**

30  Secure the fuel rail assembly with the four retaining bolts and tighten them to the torque listed in this Chapter's Specifications.

31  The remainder of installation is the reverse of removal.

## FUEL PRESSURE REGULATOR

### Check

🔸 **Refer to illustrations 13.36 and 13.41**

➡️**Note: This procedure assumes the fuel filter is in good condition.**

32  Relieve the fuel system pressure (see Section 2).

33  Detach the cable from the negative battery terminal.

34  Disconnect the fuel line and install a fuel pressure gauge (see Section 3). Reconnect the battery cable.

35  Start the engine and check for leakage around the gauge connections.

36  Disconnect the vacuum hose from the fuel pressure regulator and

13.25a  Remove the four bolts (arrows) from the fuel rail assembly (4.6L engine)

13.25b  It will be necessary to disconnect the wiring harness from all the engine components (air conditioning compressor, power steering pressure switch, oil pressure switch etc.) in order to be able to lift the fuel rail assembly as a complete unit from the 4.6L engine

**13.36  Connect a hand-held vacuum pump to the fuel pressure regulator - as vacuum is applied, fuel pressure should decrease**

**13.41  Use a vacuum gauge to check for engine vacuum to the fuel pressure regulator**

**13.45a  Remove the two fuel rail bolts (arrows) . . .**

hook up a hand-held vacuum pump (see illustration) to the port on the fuel pressure regulator.

37  Read the fuel pressure gauge with vacuum applied to the pressure regulator and also with no vacuum applied. The fuel pressure should decrease as vacuum increases (and increase as vacuum decreases).

38  Reconnect the vacuum hose to the regulator and check the fuel pressure at idle, comparing your reading with the value listed in this Chapter's Specifications. Disconnect the vacuum hose and watch the gauge – the pressure should jump up considerably as soon as the hose is disconnected. If it doesn't, proceed to Step 41.

39  If the fuel pressure is low, pinch the fuel return line shut and watch the gauge. If the pressure doesn't rise, the fuel pump is defective or there is a restriction in the fuel feed line. If the pressure rises sharply, replace the pressure regulator.

40  If the fuel pressure is too high, turn the engine off. Disconnect the fuel return line and blow through it to check for a blockage. If there is no blockage, replace the fuel pressure regulator.

41  Connect a vacuum gauge to the pressure regulator vacuum hose. Start the engine and check for vacuum (see illustration). If there isn't vacuum present, check for a clogged hose or vacuum port. If the

amount of vacuum is adequate, replace the fuel pressure regulator.

### Replacement

▶ **Refer to illustration 13.45a and 13.45b**

➡**Note: On 1999 and later models it will be necessary to remove the upper intake plenum (see Chapter 2B). The illustrations shown in this procedure are shown on a pre-1996 4.6L engine, which is equipped with the earlier type of intake manifold.**

42  Relieve the fuel pressure from the system (see Section 2). Disconnect the cable from the negative terminal of the battery.

43  Clean any dirt from around the fuel pressure regulator.

44  Detach the vacuum hose from the fuel pressure regulator.

45  On 4.6L engines, remove the bolts from one side of the fuel rail (see illustration) and carefully lift one side of the fuel rail assembly to gain access to the fuel pressure regulator mounting bolts (see illustration).

46  Remove the bolts that retain the fuel pressure regulator and detach the regulator from the fuel rail.

47  Install new O-rings on the pressure regulator and lubricate them with a light coat of oil.

48  Installation is the reverse of removal. Tighten the pressure regulator mounting bolts securely.

## FUEL INJECTOR

▶ **Refer to illustrations 13.52a, 13.52b, 13.55a and 13.55b**

### Removal

49  Relieve the system fuel pressure (see Section 2).

50  If you're working on a 5.0L engine, remove the air intake plenum assembly (see Steps 1 through 9). On 4.6L engines, remove the air intake assembly (see Section 9).

51  Remove the fuel rail assembly (see above).

52  If you're working on a 4.6L engine, remove the fuel rail bolts from the fuel rail and carefully lift the assembly to gain access to the injectors (see illustrations).

➡**Note: If all of the injectors are going to be replaced, remove the entire fuel rail.**

**13.45b  . . . and carefully lift one side to install a Torx drive tool into the fuel pressure regulator bolts**

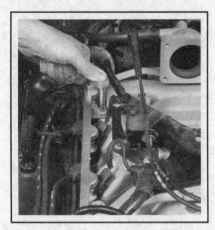

**13.52a Remove the fuel rail bolts . . .**

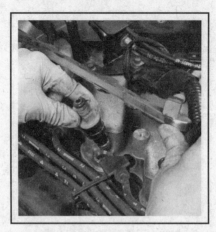

**13.52b . . . and wiggle the injector out of the manifold**

**13.55a Remove the O-ring from the top of the fuel injector . . .**

53  Carefully detach the electrical connectors from the individual injectors as required.

54  Grasping the injector body, pull up while gently rocking the injector from side-to-side.

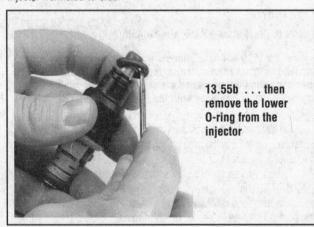

**13.55b . . . then remove the lower O-ring from the injector**

55  Inspect the injector O-rings (two per injector) for signs of deterioration (see illustrations). Replace as required.

➡Note: As long as you have the fuel rail off (or the injector(s) removed), it's a good idea to replace the O-rings.

56  Inspect the injector plastic "hat" (covering the injector pintle) and washer for signs of deterioration. Replace as required. If the hat is missing, look for it in the intake manifold.

### Installation

57  Lubricate the new O-rings with light grade oil and install two on each injector.

✳✳ **CAUTION:**

**Do not use silicone grease. It will clog the injectors.**

58  Using a light twisting motion, install the injector(s).
59  The remainder of installation is the reverse of removal.

## 14  Bypass air valve and idle speed - check, removal and adjustment

▸ **Refer to illustration 14.11**

➡Note: The minimum idle speed is pre-set at the factory and should not require adjustment under normal circumstances; however, if the throttle body has been replaced or you suspect the minimum idle speed has been tampered with (for example, if the idle stop screw was removed) follow this procedure.

### CHECK

1  The bypass air valve (BPA-ISC) controls the amount of air that bypasses the throttle body assembly throttle valve and consequently controls the engine idle speed. This output actuator is mounted on the throttle body and is controlled by voltage pulses sent from the PCM (computer). The BPA-ISC valve body moves in or out allowing more or less intake air into the system according to the engine conditions. To increase idle speed, the PCM extends the BPA-ISC valve body from the seat and allows more air to bypass the throttle bore. To decrease idle speed, the PCM retracts the BPA-ISC valve body towards the seat, reducing the air flow.

2  To check the system, first check for the voltage signal from the PCM. Turn the ignition key On (engine not running) and with a voltmeter, probe the wires of the terminals of the BPA-ISC valve electrical connector. It should be approximately 10.5 volts. This indicates that the BPA-ISC valve is receiving the proper signal from the PCM.

3  Next, remove the valve (proceed to Step 10) and check the pintle for excessive carbon deposits. If necessary, clean it with carburetor cleaner spray. Also clean the valve housing to remove any deposits.

### ADJUSTMENT (5.0L ENGINES)

4  Place the transmission in Park (automatic transmission models) and set the emergency brake for safety. Start the engine and allow it to run until it reaches normal operating temperatures.

➡Note: On 1989 through 1992 models, go to Step 6 for the adjustment procedure.

**14.11 Remove the two bolts (arrows) and lift the BPA-ISC valve from the intake manifold assembly (4.6L engine shown)**

5   On 1988 models, raise the engine speed to 1800 rpm and hold the pedal there for 30 seconds. Position the transmission selector in Drive and check idle speed. Install a tachometer according to the manufacturers specifications and set the idle speed between 550 and 600 rpm by turning the throttle plate adjusting screw clockwise and then back the screw OUT an additional 1/2 turn.

6   On 1989 through 1992 models, place the transmission in Park and set the emergency brake. With the engine off, back out the throttle plate stop screw so it does not touch the throttle lever pad. Insert a 0.010 inch feeler gauge between the throttle plate stop screw and the throttle lever pad.

7   Tighten the screw until it touches the feeler gauge. Remove the feeler gauge and turn the screw IN an additional 1-1/2 turns.

8   Start the engine and allow it to stabilize for two minutes, then depress the accelerator quickly and allow the engine rpm to settle back down to idle. The PCM and BPA-ISC valve should adjust the idle from this point. If idle quality suffers (high or low) run a complete diagnosis of the fuel injection and emission control system (see Chapter 6). Also, check the throttle valve (TV) cable adjustment (see Chapter 7).

## ADJUSTMENT (4.6L ENGINES)

9   The idle speed on the 4.6L is not adjustable. This procedure requires a special tool to extract working parameters (voltage signals) from the computerized engine control system while it is running. Have the vehicle repaired at a dealer service department or other qualified repair shop.

## REMOVAL

10   Unplug the electrical connector from the BPA-ISC valve.

11   Remove the two valve attaching screws and withdraw the assembly (see illustration).

12   Check the condition of the O-ring. If it's hardened or deteriorated, replace it.

13   Clean the sealing surface and the bore of the throttle body assembly to ensure a good seal.

> **✳✳ CAUTION:**
>
> **The BPA-ISC valve itself is an electrical component and must not be soaked in any liquid cleaner, as damage may result.**

## INSTALLATION

14   Position the new O-ring on the BPA-ISC valve. Lubricate the O-ring with a light film of engine oil.

15   Install the BPA-ISC valve and tighten the screws securely.

16   Plug in the electrical connector at the BPA-ISC valve assembly.

## 15  Exhaust system servicing - general information

▶ **Refer to illustration 15.4**

> **✳✳ WARNING 1:**
>
> **Inspection and repair of exhaust system components should be done only after enough time has elapsed after driving the vehicle to allow the system components to cool completely. Also, when working under the vehicle, make sure it is securely supported on jackstands.**

> **✳✳ WARNING 2:**
>
> **On models with air suspension, turn the air suspension switch to Off before raising the vehicle.**

> **✳✳ WARNING 3:**
>
> **On models with a fire suppression system, disable the system before raising the rear of the vehicle by disconnecting the cable from the negative battery terminal and waiting at least three minutes.**

1   The exhaust system consists of the exhaust manifold(s), the catalytic converter, the muffler, the tailpipe and all connecting pipes, brackets, hangers and clamps. The exhaust system is attached to the body with mounting brackets and rubber hangers. If any of the parts are improperly installed, excessive noise and vibration will be transmitted to the body.

2   Conduct regular inspections of the exhaust system to keep it safe and quiet. Look for any damaged or bent parts, open seams, holes, loose connections, excessive corrosion or other defects which could allow exhaust fumes to enter the vehicle. Deteriorated exhaust system components should not be repaired; they should be replaced with new parts.

3   If the exhaust system components are extremely corroded or rusted together, welding equipment will probably be required to remove them. The convenient way to accomplish this is to have a muffler repair shop remove the corroded sections with a cutting torch. If, however, you want to save money by doing it yourself (and you don't have a welding outfit with a cutting torch), simply cut off the old components with a hacksaw. If you have compressed air, special pneumatic cutting

chisels can also be used. If you do decide to tackle the job at home, be sure to wear safety goggles to protect your eyes from metal chips and work gloves to protect your hands.

4  Here are some simple guidelines to follow when repairing the exhaust system:

a) *Work from the back to the front when removing exhaust system components.*

b) *Apply penetrating oil to the exhaust system component fasteners (see illustration) to make them easier to remove.*

c) *Use new gaskets, hangers and clamps when installing exhaust systems components.*

d) *Apply anti-seize compound to the threads of all exhaust system fasteners during reassembly.*

e) *Be sure to allow sufficient clearance between newly installed parts and all points on the underbody to avoid overheating the floor pan and possibly damaging the interior carpet and insulation. Pay particularly close attention to the catalytic converter and heat shield.*

**15.4  Be sure to spray penetrating oil on exhaust system bolts (arrows) before attempting to remove them**

## Specifications

### Fuel pressure

Key on, engine off

| | |
|---|---|
| 1991 and earlier | 35 to 45 psi |
| 1992 through 1996 | 35 to 40 psi |
| 1997 through 2002 | 35 to 45 psi |
| 2003 and later | 20 to 60 psi |

Key on, engine running

| | |
|---|---|
| 1991 and earlier | 30 to 40 psi |
| 1992 through 2002 | 30 to 45 psi |
| 2003 and later | 25 to 40 psi |
| Fuel system hold pressure (after 5 minutes) | Less than 5 psi loss from indicated operating pressure |
| Fuel pump pressure (maximum) (2002 and earlier) | 65 psi |
| Fuel pump hold pressure (2002 and earlier) | 50 psi |

**Injector resistance**  13.5 to 19 ohms

## Torque specifications    Ft-lbs (unless otherwise specified)

➡ **Note: One foot-pound (ft-lb) of torque is equivalent to 12 inch-pounds (in-lbs) of torque. Torque values below approximately 15 foot-pounds are expressed in inch-pounds, because most foot-pound torque wrenches are not accurate at these smaller values.**

| | |
|---|---|
| Air intake plenum mounting bolts (5.0L engine) | 12 to 18 |
| Throttle body mounting bolts (4.6L engine) | |
| 1988 through 1995 | 12 to 18 |
| 1996 and later | 96 to 106 in-lbs |
| Throttle body mounting nuts (5.0L engine) | 12 to 18 |
| EGR valve-to-throttle body (5.0L engine) | 12 to 18 |
| Fuel rail mounting bolts | 70 to 105 in-lbs |
| Exhaust pipe-to-exhaust manifold bolts | 25 to 35 |

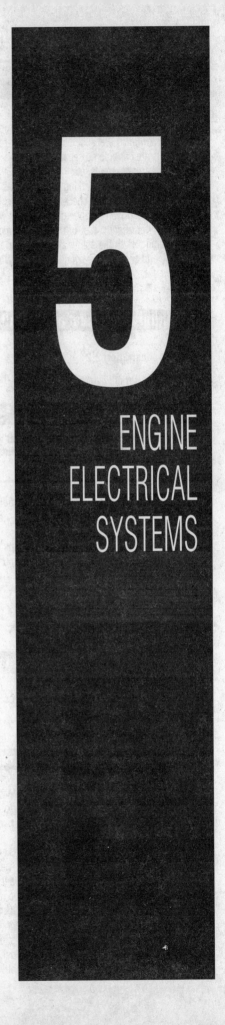

# Section

## Reference to other Chapters

# 5

# ENGINE ELECTRICAL SYSTEMS

## 1   General information

The engine electrical systems include all ignition, charging and starting components. Because of their engine-related functions, these components are considered separately from chassis electrical devices like the lights, instruments, etc.

Be very careful when working on the engine electrical components. They are easily damaged if checked, connected or handled improperly. The alternator is driven by an engine drivebelt which could cause serious injury if your hands, hair or clothes become entangled in it with the engine running. Both the starter and alternator are connected directly to the battery and could arc or even cause a fire if mishandled, overloaded or shorted out.

Never leave the ignition switch on for long periods of time with the engine off. Don't disconnect the battery cables while the engine is running. Correct polarity must be maintained when connecting battery cables from another source, such as another vehicle, during jump starting. Always disconnect the negative cable first and hook it up last or the battery may be shorted by the tool being used to loosen the cable clamps.

Additional safety related information on the engine electrical systems can be found in Safety first near the front of this manual. It should be referred to before beginning any operation included in this Chapter.

## 2   Battery - removal and installation

▶ **Refer to illustration 2.2**

1   Disconnect both cables from the battery terminals.

### ✳✳ CAUTION:

**Always disconnect the negative cable first and hook it up last or the battery may be shorted by the tool being used to loosen the cable clamps.**

2   Locate the battery hold-down clamp straddling the top of the battery. Remove the bolt and nut and the hold-down clamp (see illustration).

3   Lift out the battery. Use the special straps that attach to the battery posts - lifting and moving the battery is much easier if you use one.

4   Installation is the reverse of removal.

**2.2 Detach the battery cables (negative first) then remove the nut and bolt (arrows) from the battery hold-down clamp**

## 3   Battery - emergency jump starting

Refer to the *Booster battery (jump) starting* procedure at the front of this manual.

## 4   Battery cables - check and replacement

1   Periodically inspect the entire length of each battery cable for damage, cracked or burned insulation and corrosion. Poor battery cable connections can cause starting problems and decreased engine performance.

2   Check the cable-to-terminal connections at the ends of the cables for cracks, loose wire strands and corrosion. The presence of white, fluffy deposits under the insulation at the cable terminal connection is a sign that the cable is corroded and should be replaced. Check the terminals for distortion, missing mounting bolts and corrosion.

3   When replacing the cables, always disconnect the negative cable first and hook it up last or the battery may be shorted by the tool used to loosen the cable clamps. Even if only the positive cable is being replaced, be sure to disconnect the negative cable from the battery first.

4   Disconnect and remove the cable. Make sure the replacement cable is the same length and diameter.

5   Clean the threads of the relay or ground connection with a wire brush to remove rust and corrosion. Apply a light coat of petroleum jelly to the threads to prevent future corrosion.

6   Attach the cable to the relay or ground connection and tighten the mounting nut/bolt securely.

7   Before connecting the new cable to the battery, make sure that it reaches the battery post without having to be stretched. Clean the battery posts thoroughly and apply a light coat of petroleum jelly to prevent corrosion.

8   Connect the positive cable first, followed by the negative cable.

## DISTRIBUTOR TYPE (DURASPARK LL AND TFI-LV)

1   These ignition systems are a solid state electronic design consisting of an ignition module, coil, distributor, the spark plug wires and the spark plugs. Mechanically, the system is similar to a breaker point system, except that the distributor cam and ignition points are replaced by an armature and magnetic pick-up unit. The coil primary circuit is controlled by an amplifier module.

2   When the ignition is switched on, the ignition primary circuit is energized. When the distributor armature "teeth" or "spokes" approach the magnetic coil assembly, a voltage is induced which signals the amplifier to turn off the coil primary current. A timing circuit in the amplifier module turns the coil current back on after the coil field has collapsed.

3   When it's on, current flows from the battery through the ignition switch, the coil primary winding, the amplifier module and then to ground. When the current is interrupted, the magnetic field in the ignition coil collapses, inducing a high voltage in the coil secondary windings. The voltage is conducted to the distributor where the rotor directs it to the appropriate spark plug. This process is repeated continuously.

### Duraspark II

4   These systems are equipped with a gear driven distributor with a die cast base housing a "Hall Effect" vane switch stator assembly and a device for fixed octane adjustment.

5   Duraspark distributors have a two piece cap. When removing the cap, the upper half is removed, then the rotor is removed, then the lower half of the cap is removed. TFI-IV distributors have a conventional one-piece cap.

6   However, there are a few differences between earlier Canadian and US distributors. The distributors on earlier Canadian vehicles are equipped with centrifugal and vacuum advance mechan-isms which control the actual point of ignition based on engine speed and load. As engine speed increases, two weights move out and alter the position of the armature in relation to the distributor shaft, advancing the ignition timing. As engine load increases (when climbing hills or accelerating, for example), a drop in intake manifold vacuum causes the base plate to move slightly in the opposite direction (clockwise) under the action of the spring in the vacuum unit, retarding the timing and counteracting the centrifugal advance. Under light loads (moderate steady speeds, for example), the comparatively high intake manifold vacuum acting on the vacuum advance diaphragm causes the base plate assembly to move in a counterclockwise direction to provide a greater amount of timing advance.

### TFI-IV

7   Later models use the Thick Film Integrated IV (TFI-IV) ignition module, which is housed in a molded thermoplastic box mounted on the base of the distributor. "Thick Film" refers to the type of manufactured solid state trigger and power units in the module. The important difference between the DSII and TFI-IV modules is that the TFI-IV module is controlled by the Electronic Engine Control IV (EEC-IV), while the Duraspark II modules are not.

8   The TFI-IV/EEC-IV type distributor is similar to the Duraspark

II model but has neither a centrifugal nor a vacuum advance mechanism (advance is handled by the computer instead). The computer uses information from the Profile Ignition Pick-up (PIP) and Cylinder Identification (CID) to determine the proper point to fire the coil. The ignition control module sends the Spark Output (SPOUT) signal to the TFI module to turn the coil ON and OFF. The TFI module also generates an Ignition Diagnostic Monitor (IDM) signal so that the EEC module can check the TFI operation. These signals are important in diagnosing problems with the ignition system.

## ELECTRONIC DISTRIBUTORLESS IGNITION (EDIS) TYPE

9   The Electronic Distributorless Ignition System (EDIS) is a completely electronically controlled ignition system that does not incorporate a distributor or rotor and cap. The EDIS system consists of a crankshaft timing sensor (Variable Reluctance Sensor [VRS]), EDIS module, two ignition coil packs, the Spark Angle Word (SAW) signal from the EEC IV module, the spark plug wires and the spark plugs. This engine is equipped with an ignition coil for each pair of spark plugs. The EDIS system features a waste-spark method of spark distribution. Each cylinder is paired with its companion cylinder in the firing order (1-6, 5-3, 4-7, 2-8) so one cylinder under compression fires simultaneously with its opposing cylinder, where the piston is on the exhaust stroke. Since the cylinder on the exhaust stroke requires very little of the available voltage to fire its plug, most of the voltage is used to fire the plug under compression.

10   This ignition system does not have any moving parts (no distributor) and all engine timing and spark distribution is handled electronically. This system has fewer parts that require replacement and provides more accurate spark timing. During engine operation, the EDIS ignition module calculates spark angle and determines the turn-on and firing time of the ignition coil.

11   The crankshaft timing sensor is a variable reluctance-type sensor consisting of a 35-tooth trigger wheel with one missing tooth that is incorporated into the crankshaft front damper. The signal generated by this sensor is called a Variable Reluctance Sensor signal (VRS) and it provides the base timing and engine RPM information to the EDIS ignition modules. The main function of the EDIS module is to synchronize the ignition coils so they are turned ON an OFF in the proper sequence for accurate spark control.

## INTEGRATED ELECTRONIC IGNITION SYSTEM (COP)

12   The integrated Electronic Ignition System uses individual coils for each spark plug. These coils are directly connected to the spark plug via a short spark plug boot, thus giving it the name Coil On Plug ignition. In addition to the coils other components include the PCM, which acts as the ignition module, turning the coil primary circuit on and off as required. The Crankshaft position sensor (CKP) with reluctor ring located on the crankshaft behind the front cover, and the Camshaft position sensor (CMP). These sensors send signals to the PCM that allow the PCM to determine correct ignition firing sequence and timing.

**6 Ignition system - check**

## CALIBRATED IGNITION TESTER METHOD (DURASPARK II AND TFI-IV SYSTEMS ONLY)

▶ **Refer to illustration 6.2 and 6.6**

1   If the engine turns over but won't start, disconnect the spark plug lead from any spark plug and attach it to a calibrated ignition tester (available at most auto parts stores). Make sure the tester is designed for these ignition systems if a universal tester isn't available.

2   Connect the clip on the tester to a bolt or metal bracket on the engine (see illustration), crank the engine and watch the end of the tester to see if bright blue, well-defined sparks occur.

3   If sparks occur, sufficient voltage is reaching the plug to fire it (repeat the check at the remaining plug wires to verify that the distributor cap and rotor are OK). However, the plugs themselves may be fouled, so remove and check them as described in Chapter 1 or install new ones.

4   If no sparks or intermittent sparks occur, remove the distributor cap and check the cap and rotor as described in Chapter 1. If moisture is present, dry out the cap and rotor, then reinstall the cap and repeat the spark test.

5   If there's still no spark, detach the coil secondary wire from the distributor cap and hook it up to the tester (reattach the plug wire to the spark plug), then repeat the spark check.

6   If no sparks occur, check the primary (small) wire connections at the coil to make sure they're clean and tight. Check the ignition coil supply voltage circuit (see illustration). Make any necessary repairs, then repeat the check again.

7   If sparks now occur, the distributor cap, rotor, plug wire(s) or

spark plug(s) (or all of them) may be defective.

8   On Duraspark II systems, check the ballast resistor. Measure the resistance of the ballast resistor between the BATT terminal of the ignition coil connector and the module harness connector red wire. It will be necessary to disconnect the electrical connector and measure the resistance from the ballast resistor side. The resistance should be 0.8 to 1.6 ohms. If the test results are incorrect, replace it with a new part.

9   If there's still no spark, the coil-to-cap wire may be bad (check the resistance with an ohmmeter and compare it to the Specifications). If a known good wire doesn't make any difference in the test results, the ignition coil, module or other internal components may be defective (see Sections 7 and 10).

## ELECTRONIC DISTRIBUTORLESS IGNITION (EDIS) SYSTEM

### Calibrated ignition tester method

▶ **Refer to illustration 6.13**

10  If the engine turns over but won't start, disconnect the spark plug lead from any spark plug and attach it to a calibrated ignition tester (available at most auto parts stores). Make sure the tester is designed for these ignition systems if a universal tester isn't available.

11  Connect the clip on the tester to a bolt or metal bracket on the engine (see illustration 6.2), crank the engine and watch the end of the tester to see if bright blue, well-defined sparks occur.

12  If sparks occur, sufficient voltage is reaching the spark plug to fire it (repeat the check at the remaining plug wires to verify that all the ignition coils and wires are functioning). However, the plugs themselves may be fouled, so remove and check them as described in Chapter 1 or install new ones.

13  If no sparks or intermittent sparks occur, check for battery voltage to the ignition coil (see illustration). Check for a bad spark plug wire by swapping wires. Check the coils and EDIS ignition module (see Sections 7 and 10).

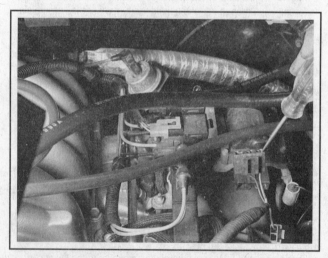

**6.2  To use a calibrated ignition tester, simply disconnect a spark plug wire, clip the tester to a convenient ground (like a valve cover bolt) and operate the starter - if there is enough power to fire the plug, sparks will be visible between the electrode tip and the tester body**

**6.6  Disconnect the electrical connector from the ignition coil and check for battery voltage to the coil with the ignition key on**

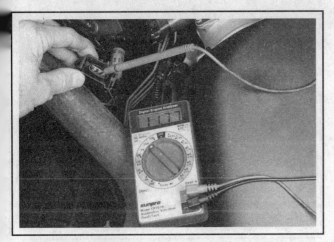

**6.13 It is better to use a voltmeter but a test light is adequate to check for battery voltage on the center terminal of the ignition coil electrical connector**

## INTEGRATED ELECTRONIC IGNITION SYSTEM (COP)

➡ Note: It may be necessary to repeat this procedure for all cylinders.

14 If the engine turns over but won't start check for spark by removing one coil and attaching a calibrated ignition tester. If there is a bright blue spark, sufficient voltage is available to fire the spark plug. However the plug may be fouled, so remove and check the plug as described in Chapter 1

15 If no spark occurs, check the 25A #7 fuse located in the central fuse box inside the passenger compartment.

16 Check the connection at the CKP sensor and the CMP sensor. They should be clean and tight fitting.

17 Disconnect one coil primary lead and, with a DVOM, check for 12V at the red wire with the light green stripe. Be careful not to damage the terminal or force the tester lead into the terminal as this can collapse the terminal and cause a poor or no contact fit when reattached to the coil. If there is no voltage check for an open wire from the fuse to the coil.

18 Connect a incandescent test light across the coil harness connec-tor, disable the fuel pump, then crank the engine. If the test light blinks while the engine is cranking the PCM is most likely not the problem. Substitute one of the other coils in place of the coil you are testing. If the substitute coil fires the spark tester, replace the original coil.

19 Further testing is not recommended. Consult with the dealer service department or other automotive professional.

## ALTERNATIVE METHOD (DURASPARK II, TFI-IV AND EDIS SYSTEMS)

➡ Note: If you're unable to obtain a calibrated ignition tester, the following method will allow you to determine if the ignition system has spark, but it won't tell you if there's enough voltage produced to actually initiate combustion in the cylinders.

20 Remove the wire from one of the spark plugs. Using an insulated tool, hold the wire about 1/4-inch from a good ground and have an assistant crank the engine.

21 If bright blue, well-defined sparks occur, sufficient voltage is reaching the plug to fire it. However, the plug(s) may be fouled, so remove and check them as described in Chapter 1 or install new ones.

22 If there's no spark, check the remaining wires in the same manner. A few sparks followed by no spark is the same condition as no spark at all.

23 If no sparks occur, remove the distributor cap and check the cap and rotor as described in Chapter 1. If moisture is present, dry out the cap and rotor, then reinstall the cap and repeat the spark test.

24 If there's still no spark, disconnect the secondary coil wire from the distributor cap, hold it about 1/4-inch from a good engine ground and crank the engine again.

25 If no sparks occur, check the primary (small) wire connections at the coil to make sure they're clean and tight.

26 If sparks now occur, the distributor cap and rotor (Duraspark II and TFI-IV systems only), plug wire(s) or spark plug(s) (or all of them) may be defective.

27 If there's still no spark, the coil-to-cap wire may be bad (check the resistance with an ohmmeter and compare it to the Specifications). If a known good wire doesn't make any difference in the test results, the ignition coil, module or other internal components may be defective. Refer further testing to a dealer service department or qualified electrical specialist.

---

## 7  Ignition coil - check and replacement

## DISTRIBUTOR TYPE IGNITION SYSTEM (DURASPARK LL AND TFI-LV)

### Check

#### Primary and secondary coil resistance

▶ Refer to illustrations 7.1 and 7.2

1  With the ignition off, disconnect the wires from the coil. Connect an ohmmeter across the coil primary (small wire) terminals (see illustration). The resistance should be as listed in this Chapter's Specifications. If not, replace the coil.

2  Connect an ohmmeter between the negative primary terminal and the secondary terminal (see illustration) (the one that the distributor cap wire connects to). The resistance should be as listed in this Chapter's Specifications. If not, replace the coil.

**7.1 Checking the coil primary resistance on a TFI-IV ignition system**

**Ignition coil primary winding-to-case resistance**

3  Measure the resistance from the positive primary terminal to the case of the ignition coil.

4  If the indicated resistance is less or more than the resistance listed in this Chapter's Specifications, replace the ignition coil.

5  Reconnect the ignition coil wires.

### Replacement

6  Detach the cable from the negative terminal of the battery.

7  Detach the wires from the primary terminals on the coil (some coils have a single electrical connector for the primary wires).

8  Unplug the coil secondary lead.

9  Remove both bracket bolts and detach the coil.

10  Installation is the reverse of removal.

## ELECTRONIC DISTRIBUTORLESS IGNITION (EDIS) SYSTEM

### Check

▸ **Refer to illustrations 7.11 and 7.12**

11  With the ignition off, disconnect the electrical connector(s) from the coil. Connect an ohmmeter across the coil primary (center terminal) terminal and the outer terminal (see illustration). The resistance should be as listed in this Chapter's Specifications. If not, replace the coil.

12  Connect an ohmmeter between the secondary terminals (see illustration) (the one that the spark plug wires connect to) of each coil pack. The resistance should be as listed in this Chapter's Specifications.

➡**Note: Each coil pack is paired 7/4, 8/2, 1/6 and 3/5. Be sure to check resistance with these designated terminals only. If not, replace the coil.**

### Replacement

13  Disconnect the negative cable from the battery.

14  Disconnect the ignition coil electrical connector(s) from each individual coil pack.

15  Disconnect the ignition wires by squeezing the locking tabs and

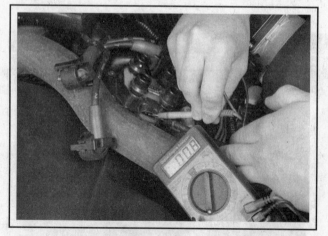

**7.11  To check the primary resistance of the EDIS coil, install the probes to the center terminal and outer terminal of the coil. Be sure to check the other coil pack (opposite terminal) and then the other coil pack assembly mounted on the right engine bank. The resistance should be the same for all four tests**

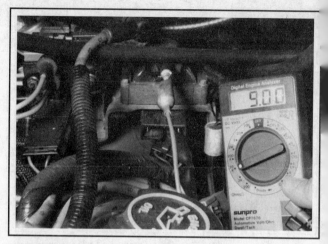

**7.2  Checking the coil secondary resistance on a TFI-IV ignition system**

twisting while pulling. DO NOT just pull on the wires to disconnect them. Disconnect all spark plug leads.

16  Remove the bolts securing the ignition coil to the mounting bracket on the engine.

17  Installation is the reverse of the removal procedure with the following additions:

a)  Prior to installing the spark plug lead into the ignition coil, coat the entire interior of the rubber boot with Silicone Dielectric Compound.

b)  Insert each spark plug wire into the proper terminal of the ignition coil. Push the wire into the terminal and make sure the boots are fully seated and both locking tabs are engaged properly.

➡**Note: Refer to the EDIS firing order schematic in Chapter 2 Specifications to correctly identify each cylinder and its corresponding coil pack terminal.**

## INTEGRATED ELECTRONIC IGNITION SYSTEM (COP)

The diagnosis outlined in section 6 should be followed. When it has been determined a coil needs replacement, unplug the coil, remove the retaining bolt, remove the coil, inspect the spark plug, check the coil harness connector terminals, then replace the coil and reconnect the harness.

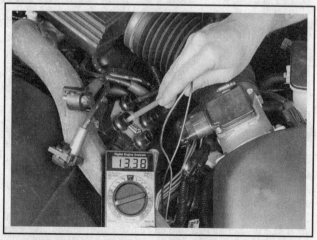

**7.12  Check the coil secondary resistance by probing the paired companion cylinders (7/4, 8/2, 1/6 and 3/5)**

## 8  Distributor - removal and installation

### REMOVAL

▶ **Refer to illustration 8.3**

1  Unplug the primary lead from the coil.
2  Unplug the electrical connector for the module. Follow the wires as they exit the distributor to find the connector.
3  Note the raised "1" on the distributor cap (see illustration). This marks the location for the number one cylinder spark plug wire terminal.
4  Remove the distributor cap (see Chap-ter 1) and turn the engine over until the rotor is pointing toward the number one spark plug terminal (see the TDC locating procedure in Chapter 2).
5  Make a mark on the edge of the distributor base directly below the rotor tip and in line with it. Also, mark the distributor base and the engine block to ensure that the distributor is installed correctly.
6  Remove the distributor hold-down bolt and clamp, then pull the distributor straight up to remove it. Be careful not to disturb the intermediate driveshaft.

### ❋ CAUTION:

**DO NOT turn the engine while the distributor is removed, or the alignment marks will be useless.**

### INSTALLATION

7  Insert the distributor into the engine in exactly the same relationship to the block that it was in when removed.
8  To mesh the helical gears on the camshaft and the distributor, it may be necessary to turn the rotor slightly. If the distributor doesn't seat completely, the hex shaped recess in the lower end of the distributor shaft is not mating properly with the oil pump shaft. Recheck the alignment marks between the distributor base and the block to verify that the

**8.3  The number "1" on the distributor cap marks the location of the spark plug wire terminal for the number 1 cylinder spark plug**

distributor is in the same position it was in before removal. Also check the rotor to see if it's aligned with the mark you made on the edge of the distributor base.

➡**Note: If the crankshaft has been moved while the distributor is out, locate Top Dead Center (TDC) for the number one piston (see Chapter 2) and position the distributor and rotor accordingly.**

9  Place the hold-down clamp in position and loosely install the bolt.
10  Install the distributor cap and tighten the cap screws securely.
11  Plug in the module electrical connector.
12  Reattach the spark plug wires to the plugs (if removed).
13  Connect the cable to the negative terminal of the battery.
14  Check and, if necessary, adjust the ignition timing (refer to Section 9) and tighten the distributor hold-down bolt securely.

## 9  Ignition timing - check and adjustment

▶ **Refer to illustration 9.4**

➡**Note 1: Ignition timing on the Electronic Distributorless (EDIS) Ignition system is preset and cannot be adjusted.**

➡**Note 2: Always check the Vehicle Emission Control Information (VECI) label on your vehicle to see if a different procedure is specified. The VECI label contains detailed information which is specific to your vehicle.**

➡**Note 3: The ignition timing procedure for the 4.6L engine is basically the same as the "computed engine timing test" performed during the code extraction procedure in Chapter 6, Section 2. Both tests check base timing only, since timing on the 4.6L EDIS systems cannot be adjusted. Any timing problems on the 4.6L engine will have to repaired by a dealer service department.**

1  Apply the parking brake and block the wheels. Place the transmission in DRIVE (emergency brake applied) on the 5.0L engines or NEUTRAL on the 4.6L engines. Turn off all accessories (heater, air conditioner, etc.).
2  Start the engine and warm it up. Once it has reached operating temperature, turn it off.
3  If you have a vehicle with a Duraspark II ignition system (see Section 5), disconnect the vacuum hoses from the distributor vacuum advance unit and plug the hoses.
4  Unplug the single wire connector or SPOUT (Spark Output) located immediately above the harness connector for the module (see illustration).

➡**Note: The SPOUT controls the ignition signal from the computer. Disconnecting the SPOUT will display only the base timing settings without any changes from the computer.**

5   Connect an inductive timing light and a tachometer in accordance with the manufacturer's instructions.

### ⁕⁕ CAUTION:

**Make sure that the timing light and tach wires don't hang anywhere near the cooling fan or they may become entangled in the fan blades when the fan begins to rotate.**

6   Locate the timing marks on the crankshaft pulley (see Chapter 2).

7   Start the engine again.

8   Point the timing light at the pulley timing marks and note whether the specified timing mark (see the VECI label) is aligned with the timing pointer on the front of the timing chain/belt cover.

9   On 5.0L engines, if the proper mark isn't aligned with the stationary pointer, loosen the distributor hold-down bolt. Turn the distributor clockwise (to retard timing) or counterclockwise (to advance timing) until the correct timing mark on the crankshaft pulley is aligned with the stationary pointer. Tighten the distributor hold-down bolt securely when the timing is correct and recheck it to make sure it didn't change when the bolt was tightened.

10  Turn off the engine.

11  Plug in the single wire connector (TFI-IV-equipped vehicles) or attach the vacuum hoses ( DS II-equipped vehicles).

12  Restart the engine and check the idle speed. The specified rpm for each vehicle is different (see your VECI Label). On vehicles with an adjustable idle speed, see Chapter 4 for adjustment procedure. On engines equipped with automatic idle speed control, idle rpm is not

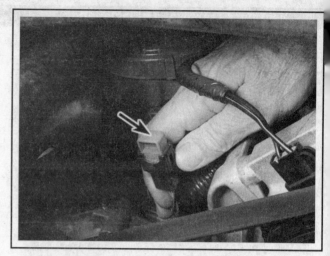

**9.4   Before adjusting the ignition timing, unplug the SPOUT (arrow) (single wire connector) attached to the ignition module wire harness (if you do not, the EEC-IV system will still be controlling the base ignition timing)**

adjustable. If the idle rpm is not within the range specified on your VECI label, take the vehicle to a dealer service department or repair shop. Adjustment requires specialized test equipment and procedures that are beyond the scope of the home mechanic.

13  Turn off the engine.

14  Remove the timing light and tachometer.

### 10   Ignition module and stator  - check and replacement

### ⁕⁕ CAUTION:

**The ignition module is a delicate and relatively expensive electronic component. Failure to follow the step-by-step procedures could result in damage to the module and/or other electronic devices, including the EEC-IV microprocessor itself. Additionally, all devices under computer control are protected by a Federally mandated extended warranty. Check with your dealer concerning this warranty before attempting to diagnose and replace the module yourself.**

## DURASPARK II IGNITION MODULE

### Check

1   Duraspark II ignition systems are equipped with either a three connector module or a two connector module. Do not be confused with these ignition modules but instead follow the same color code for all diagnostic voltage and resistance checks.

2   Check for power to the ignition module. Using a voltmeter, probe the red wire from the module. With the ignition ON (engine not running), there should be battery voltage.

3   Check the resistance of the distributor stator. Using an ohmmeter, probe the orange and purple wires at the distributor electrical connector and check the resistance. It should be between 400 and 1,000 ohms. If not, replace the stator assembly within the distributor.

4   Check the ground circuit continuity. Using a voltmeter, probe the black wire from the ignition module. With the ignition ON (engine not running), there should be approximately 0.5 volts or greater.

5   If battery voltage is not reaching the ignition module, trace the circuit to the ignition switch and battery (see Chapter 12) and check for open circuits or a damaged wire harness. If any of the other test results are incorrect, replace the ignition module with a new part.

### Replacement

#### Ignition module

6   Detach the cable from the negative terminal of the battery.

7   Unplug the electrical connectors.

8   Remove the mounting screws and detach the module.

9   Installation is the reverse of removal.

#### Stator

10  Disconnect the cable from the negative terminal of the battery. Remove the distributor cap and rotor.

11  Using a small gear puller or two screwdrivers, carefully remove the armature and roll pin from the distributor shaft. Be very careful not to damage the armature or loose the roll pin.

12  Remove the vacuum advance unit rod retaining clip from the stator and plate assembly. Remove the retaining screws, disconnect the electrical connector and lift the stator and plate assembly from the distributor.

13  Installation is the reverse of removal.

## TFI-IV IGNITION MODULE

### Check

#### Ignition coil primary circuit

▶ **Refer to illustration 10.15**

14 Unplug the ignition wiring harness connectors and inspect them for dirt, corrosion and damage, then reconnect them.

15 Attach a 12 volt test light between the coil TACH terminal and a good engine ground (see illustration).

16 Remove the coil wire from the ignition coil and use a suitable wire to ground the secondary terminal.

17 Crank the engine.

18 The test light should flash with each output signal from the coil primary circuit as the engine turns over.

#### Ignition module checks

▶ **Refer to illustrations 10.19, 10.22 and 10.27**

19 Check for power to the ignition module. Using a voltmeter, probe terminal number 3 (TFI PWR) from the module (see illustration). With the ignition ON (engine not running), there should be battery voltage.

20 Remove the distributor from the engine (see Section 8).

21 Remove the module from the distributor.

22 Using an ohmmeter, ensure that the resistance between terminals GND and PIP IN is greater than 500 ohms (see illustration).

23 Ensure resistance between terminals PIP PWR and PIP IN is less than 2,000 ohms.

24 Ensure resistance between terminals PIP PWR and TFI PWR is less than 200 ohms.

25 Ensure resistance between terminals GND and IGN GND is less than 2 ohms.

26 Ensure resistance between terminals PIP IN and PIP is less than 200 ohms.

27 Ensure resistance between terminals PIP and SPOUT is less than 7,000 ohms (see illustration).

28 If any of these test results are incorrect, replace the ignition module with a new part.

29 If all these tests are correct, replace the stator (see Steps 35 through 38).

### Replacement

#### Ignition module

▶ **Refer to illustrations 10.31, 10.32 and 10.33**

30 Remove the distributor from the engine (see Section 8) if access to the module is blocked.

31 Remove the two module mounting screws with a 1/4-inch drive 7/32-inch deep socket (see illustration).

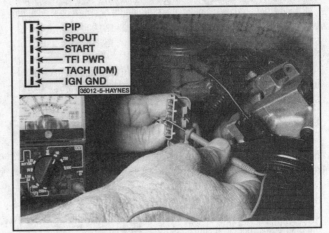

**10.19 Checking for battery voltage on terminal number 3 (TFI PWR) with the ignition key ON (engine not running). If the probes of the voltmeter do not penetrate the electrical connector, install a pin into the terminal and place the probe onto the pin**

**10.15 Checking the ignition coil primary circuit using a test light on the ignition coil TACH terminal**

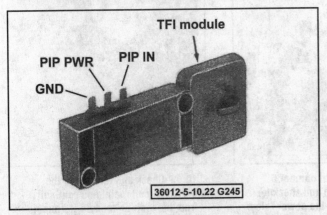

**10.22 Ignition module terminal identification (tfi-iv system)**

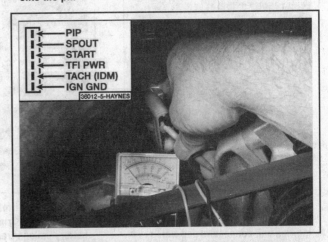

**10.27 Check the resistance of the PIP to SPOUT circuit with an ohmmeter. It should be less than 7,000 ohms**

**10.31 To remove the TFI-IV ignition module from the distributor base, remove the two screws (arrows) . . .**

**10.32 . . . then pull the module straight down to detach the spade terminals from the stator connector**

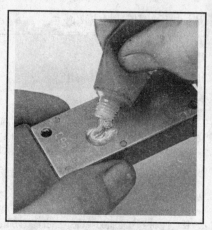

**10.33 Be sure to wipe the back side of the module clean and apply a film of dielectric grease (essential for cool operation of the module) - DO NOT use any other type of grease**

32 Pull straight down on the module to disconnect the spade connectors from the stator connector (see illustration).

33 Whether you are installing the old module or a new one, wipe the back side of the module clean with a soft, clean rag and apply a film of silicone dielectric grease to the back side of the module (see illustration).

34 Installation is the reverse of removal. When plugging in the module, make sure that the three terminals are inserted all the way into the stator connector.

### Stator

35 Disconnect the cable from the negative terminal of the battery. Remove the distributor (see Section 8). Remove the distributor cap, rotor and TFI-IV ignition module from the distributor.

36 Using an appropriate size pin punch, drive the roll pin from the distributor gear and shaft. Press the gear off the shaft and remove the shaft assembly from the distributor base. If necessary, deburr and clean the distributor shaft so it slides out of the base easily.

37 Remove the octane rod. Remove the two stator assembly screws and lift the stator from the distributor.

38 Installation is the reverse of removal with the following additions:
a) Apply a light coat of clean engine oil to the distributor shaft before installation.
b) Align the hole in the gear and shaft exactly, before pressing the gear on. DO NOT use a drift punch to align the holes.
c) Drive a NEW roll pin through the gear and shaft until it's flush with the gear.
d) Apply silicone dielectric grease to the backside of the ignition module before installation (see illustration 10.33).
e) Replace the distributor base O-ring.

## EDIS IGNITION MODULE

▶ **Refer to illustrations 10.40, 10.42 10.43 and 10.44**

### Ignition coil primary circuit

39 Unplug the ignition coil wiring harness connectors and inspect them for dirt, corrosion and damage.

40 Attach a 12 volt test light to the battery positive (+) terminal and

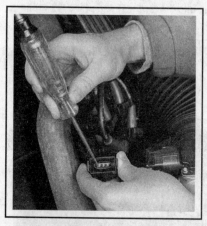

**10.40 Connect a test light between the coil outer terminals on the ignition coil connectors and watch for a blinking light when the engine is cranked**

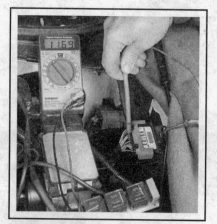

**10.42 Probe terminal number 6 (black/orange stripe) and check for battery voltage from the power relay**

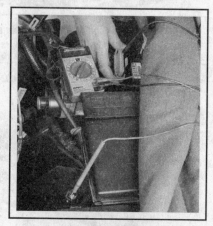

**10.43 Check and make sure the SPOUT circuit maintains continuity from the ignition module (terminal number 3) and the SPOUT connector**

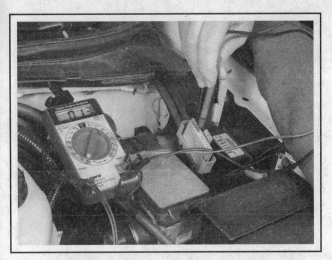

**10.44 Check the crankshaft sensor resistance on terminals number 4 and 5. It should be between 1.0 and 1.5 ohms**

the coil electrical connector (see illustration) and crank the engine.

41 The test light should flash with each output signal from the EDIS ignition module through the coil primary circuit as the engine fires.

➡**Note: It will be necessary to check each circuit that governs each coil pack. Install the test light into the opposite terminal** on the harness connector (outside terminals) and repeat the test. Follow the same procedure for the other coil assembly also.

### Ignition module checks

42 Check for power to the ignition module. Using a voltmeter, probe terminal number 6 (black/orange stripe) and check for battery voltage through the power relay (see illustration). With the ignition ON (engine not running), there should be battery voltage.

43 Check the circuit from the ignition module to the SPOUT connector (terminal number 3) for a complete circuit (see illustration). Continuity should exist.

44 Also check the resistance of the crankshaft sensor (see illustration). It should be between 1.0 and 1.5 ohms.

45 If battery voltage is not reaching the ignition module, trace the electrical circuit to the ignition and battery (see Chapter 12) and check for open circuits or a damaged wire harness. If any of the other test results are incorrect, replace the ignition module with a new one.

### Replacement

46 Disconnect the negative cable from the battery.

47 Disconnect the electrical connector from the EDIS ignition module.

48 Remove the screws securing the EDIS module to the fenderwell.

49 Installation is the reverse of the removal procedure.

## 11  Charging system - general information and precautions

The charging system includes the alternator, either an internal or an external voltage regulator, a charge indicator or warning light, the battery, a fusible link and the wiring between all the components. The charging system supplies electrical power for the ignition system, the lights, the radio, etc. The alternator is driven by a drivebelt at the front of the engine.

The purpose of the voltage regulator is to limit the alternator's voltage to a preset value. This prevents power surges, circuit overloads, etc., during peak voltage output. On EVR (external voltage regulator) systems, the regulator is mounted on the right fender apron of the vehicle. On IAR (Integral Alternator/Regulator) systems, a solid state regulator is housed inside a plastic module mounted on the alternator itself.

The fusible link is a short length of insulated wire integral with the engine compartment wiring harness. The link is several wire gauges smaller in diameter than the circuit it protects. Production fusible links and their identification flags are identified by the flag color. Refer to Chapter 12 for additional information on fusible links.

The charging system doesn't ordinarily require periodic maintenance. However, the drivebelt, battery and wires and connections should be inspected at the intervals outlined in Chapter 1.

Be very careful when making electrical circuit connections to a vehicle equipped with an alternator and note the following:

a) *When reconnecting wires to the alternator from the battery, be sure to note the polarity.*

b) *Before using arc welding equipment to repair any part of the vehicle, disconnect the wires from the alternator and the battery terminals.*

c) *Never start the engine with a battery charger connected.*

d) *Always disconnect both battery cables before using a battery charger (negative cable first, positive cable last).*

## 12  Charging system - check

▶ **Refer to illustration 12.2**

1  If a malfunction occurs in the charging circuit, do not immediately assume that the alternator is causing the problem. First check the following items:

a) *The battery cables where they connect to the battery. Make sure the connections are clean and tight.*

b) *The battery electrolyte specific gravity. If it is low, charge the battery.*

c) *Check the external alternator wiring and connections.*

d) *Check the drivebelt condition and tension (see Chapter 1).*

e) *Check the alternator mounting bolts for tightness.*

f) *Run the engine and check the alternator for abnormal noise.*

2  Using a voltmeter, check the battery voltage with the engine off. It should be at least 12.66-volts (see illustration).

3  Start the engine and check the battery voltage again. It should now be approximately 14 to 15-volts.

4   If the indicated voltage reading is less or more than the specified charging voltage, replace the voltage regulator. If replacing the regulator fails to restore the voltage to the specified range, the problem may be within the alternator.

5   Due to the special equipment necessary to test or service the alternator, it is recommended that if a fault is suspected the vehicle be taken to a dealer or a shop with the proper equipment. Because of this, the home mechanic should limit maintenance to checking connections and the inspection and replacement of the brushes.

6   Some models are equipped with an ammeter on the instrument panel that indicates charge or discharge - current passing in or out of the battery. With all electrical equipment switched ON, and the engine idling, the gauge needle may show a discharge condition. At fast idle or normal driving speeds the needle should stay on the charge side of the gauge, with the charged state of the battery determining just how far over (the lower the battery state of charge, the farther the needle should swing toward the charge side).

7   Some models are equipped with a voltmeter on the instrument panel that indicates battery voltage with the key on and engine off, and alternator output when the engine is running.

8   The charge light on the instrument panel illuminates with the key on and engine not running, and should go out when the engine runs.

9   If the gauge does not show a charge when it should or the alternator light (if equipped) remains on, there is a fault in the system.

**12.2  To measure battery voltage, attach the voltmeter leads to the battery terminals - to measure charging voltage, start the engine**

Before inspecting the brushes or replacing the alternator, the battery condition, alternator belt tension and electrical cable connections should be checked.

## 13  Alternator - removal and installation

▶ Refer to illustrations 13.2, 13.3a and 13.3b

1   Detach the cable from the negative terminal of the battery.
2   Unplug the electrical connectors from the alternator (see illustration).
3   Loosen the alternator bolts (see illustrations) and detach the drivebelt.
4   On 4.6L engines, remove the ignition wire assembly from the intake manifold area.
5   Remove the adjustment and pivot bolts and separate the alternator from the engine.
6   Installation is the reverse of removal.
7   After the alternator is installed, adjust the drivebelt tension (see Chapter 1).

**13.2  Be sure to mark each electrical connector (arrows) before unplugging them from the alternator (5.0L engine shown)**

**13.3a  Remove the bolts (arrows) from the alternator bracket and separate the bracket from the intake manifold (4.6L engine)**

**13.3b  The lower mounting bolts (arrows) can be reached without removing the fan shroud (4.6L engine)**

## 14  Alternator brushes - replacement (EVR type alternator)

➡Note: Internal replacement parts for alternators may not be readily available. Check the availability of replacement parts before proceeding.

### REAR TERMINAL ALTERNATOR

▸ Refer to illustrations 14.2, 14.5a, 14.5b and 14.7

1   Remove the alternator as described in Section 13.

2   Scribe a line across the length of the alternator housing to ensure correct reassembly (see illustration).

3   Remove the housing through-bolts and the nuts and insulators from the rear housing. Make a careful note of all insulator locations.

4   Withdraw the rear housing section from the stator, rotor and front housing assembly.

5   Remove the brushes and springs from the brush holder assembly, which is located inside the rear housing (see illustrations).

6   Check the length of the brushes against the wear dimensions given in the Specifications and replace the brushes with new ones if necessary.

7   Install the springs and brushes in the holder assembly and hold them in place by inserting a piece of stiff wire through the rear housing and brush terminal insulator (see illustration). Make sure enough wire protrudes through the rear housing so it can be withdrawn after assembly.

8   Attach the rear housing, rotor and front housing assembly to the stator, making sure the scribed marks are aligned.

9   Install the housing through-bolts and rear end insulators and nuts but do not tighten the nuts at this time.

10   Carefully extract the piece of wire from the rear housing and make sure that the brushes are seated on the slip ring. Tighten the through bolts and rear housing nuts.

11   Install the alternator as described in Section 13.

### SIDE TERMINAL ALTERNATOR

12   Remove the alternator as described in Section 13 and scribe a mark on both end housings and the stator for ease of reassembly.

13   Remove the through-bolts and separate the front housing and rotor from the rear housing and stator. Be careful that you do not separate the rear housing and stator.

14   Use a soldering iron to unsolder and disengage the brush holder from the rear housing. Remove the brushes and springs from the brush holders.

15   Remove the two brush holder attaching screws and lift the brush holder from the rear housing.

16   Remove any sealing compound from the brush holder and rear housing.

17   Inspect the brushes for damage and check their dimensions against the Specifications. If they are worn, replace them with new ones.

18   To reassemble, install the springs and brushes in the brush holders, inserting a piece of stiff wire to hold them in place.

19   Place the brush holder in position in the rear housing, using the wire to retract the brushes through the hole in the rear housing.

20   Install the brush holder attaching screws and push the holder toward the shaft opening as you tighten the screws.

#### ✳✳ CAUTION:

The rectifier can be overheated and damaged if the soldering is not done quickly. Press the brush holder lead onto the rectifier lead and solder them in place.

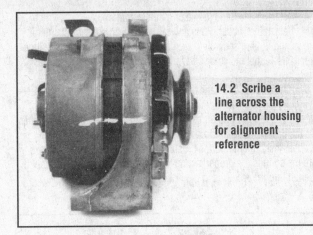

14.2  Scribe a line across the alternator housing for alignment reference

14.5a  Remove the bolts and detach the brush holder and the brush in the holder

14.5b  Remove the rear field housing nut (orange) to detach the remaining brush

14.7  Insert a paper clip through the hole in the back to retain the brushes

21 Place the rotor and front housing in position in the stator and rear housing. After aligning the scribe marks, install the through-bolts.

22 Turn the fan and pulley to check for binding in the alternator.

23 Withdraw the wire which is retracting the brushes and seal the hole with waterproof cement.

**※※ CAUTION:**

Do not use RTV-type sealer on the hole.

## 15 External Voltage Regulator (EVR) - replacement

1 Detach the cable from the negative terminal of the battery.

2 Locate the voltage regulator on the right side of the engine compartment.

3 If necessary, remove the battery or air cleaner duct to gain access to the voltage regulator.

4 Unplug the electrical connector from the voltage regulator.

5 Remove the regulator mounting bolts.

6 Remove the regulator.

7 Installation is the reverse of removal.

## 16 Voltage regulator/alternator brushes - replacement (IAR-type alternator)

◆ Refer to illustrations 16.3, 16.4, 16.5 and 16.9

1 Remove the alternator (see Section 13).

2 Set the alternator on a clean workbench.

3 Remove the four voltage regulator mounting screws (see illustration).

4 Detach the voltage regulator (see illustration).

5 Detach the rubber plugs and remove the brush lead retaining screws and nuts to separate the brush leads from the holder (see illustration). Note that the screws have Torx heads and require a special screwdriver.

6 After noting the relationship of the brushes to the brush holder assembly, remove both brushes. Don't lose the springs.

7 If you're installing a new voltage regulator, insert the old brushes into the brush holder of the new regulator. If you're installing new brushes, insert them into the brush holder of the old regulator. Make sure the springs are properly compressed and the brushes are properly inserted into the recesses in the brush holder.

16.3 To detach the voltage regulator/brush holder assembly, remove the four screws

16.4 Lift the assembly from the alternator

16.5 To remove the brushes from the voltage regulator/brush holder assembly, detach the rubber plugs from the two brush lead screws and remove both screws (arrows)

8   Install the brush lead retaining screws and nuts.

9   Insert a short section of wire, like a paper clip, through the hole in the voltage regulator (see illustration) to hold the brushes in the retracted position during regulator installation.

10   Carefully install the regulator. Make sure the brushes don't hang up on the rotor.

11   Install the voltage regulator screws and tighten them securely.

12   Remove the wire or paper clip.

13   Install the alternator (see Section 13).

16.9 Before installing the voltage regulator/ brush holder assembly, insert a paper clip as shown to hold the brushes in place during installation - after installation, simply pull the paper clip out

## 17   Starting system - general information and precautions

1   The starting system is composed of the starter motor, neutral start switch or Manual Lever Position switch/Transmission Range sensor, the Powertrain Control Module (PCM) (later models), starter relay, battery, switch and connecting wires.

2   Turning the ignition key to the Start position actuates the starter relay through the starter control circuit. The starter relay then connects the battery to the starter. The battery supplies the electrical energy to the starter motor, which does the actual work of cranking the engine.

3   Early models are equipped with an external relay mounted on the fenderwell along with a starter unit to engage the starter motor with the flywheel while later models are equipped with a starter/solenoid assembly that is mounted to the transmission bellhousing.

4   All vehicles are equipped with a Neutral start switch in the starter control circuit, which prevents operation of the starter unless the shift lever is in Neutral or Park.

5   Never operate the starter motor for more than 15 seconds at a time without pausing to allow it to cool for at least two minutes. Excessive cranking can cause overheating, which can seriously damage the starter.

## 18   Starter motor and circuit - in-vehicle check

➡Note: Before diagnosing starter problems, make sure the battery is fully charged.

1   If the starter motor doesn't turn at all when the switch is operated, make sure the shift lever is in Neutral or Park.

2   Make sure the battery is charged and that all cables at the battery and starter relay/solenoid terminals are secure.

3   If the starter motor spins but the engine doesn't turn over, then the drive assembly in the starter motor is slipping and the starter motor must be replaced (see Section 20 or 21).

4   If, when the switch is actuated, the starter motor doesn't operate at all but the starter relay/solenoid operates (clicks), then the problem lies with either the battery, the starter relay/solenoid contacts or the starter motor connections.

5   If the starter relay/solenoid doesn't click when the ignition switch is actuated, either the starter relay/solenoid circuit is open or the relay/solenoid itself is defective. Check the starter relay/solenoid circuit (see the wiring diagrams at the end of this book) or replace the relay or solenoid (see Section 20).

6   To check the starter relay/solenoid circuit, remove the push-on connector from the relay/solenoid wire. Make sure that the connection is clean and secure and the relay bracket is grounded. If the connections are good, check the operation of the relay/solenoid with a jumper wire. To do this, place the transmission in Park. Remove the push-on connector from the relay/solenoid. Connect a jumper wire between the battery positive terminal and the exposed terminal on the relay/solenoid. If the starter motor now operates, the starter relay/solenoid is okay. The problem is in the ignition switch, Neutral start switch or in the starting circuit wiring (look for open or loose connections).

7   If the starter motor still doesn't operate, replace the starter relay/ solenoid (see Section 20 and 21).

8   If the starter motor cranks the engine at an abnormally slow speed, first make sure the battery is fully charged and all terminal connections are clean and tight. Also check the connections at the starter relay/solenoid and battery ground. Eyelet terminals should not be easily rotated by hand. Also check for a short to ground. If the engine is partially seized, or has the wrong viscosity oil in it, it will crank slowly.

## 19 Starter motor - removal and installation

### RELAY TYPE STARTER

1   Detach the cable from the negative terminal of the battery.
2   Raise the vehicle and support it securely on jackstands.
3   Disconnect the large cable from the terminal on the starter motor.
4   Remove the starter motor mounting bolts and detach the starter from the engine.
5   If necessary, turn the wheels to one side to provide removal access.
6   Installation is the reverse of removal.

### SOLENOID/STARTER ASSEMBLY TYPE

▶ **Refer to illustration 19.10**

7   Detach the cable from the negative terminal of the battery.
8   Raise the vehicle and support it securely on jackstands.
9   Disconnect the large cable from the terminal on the starter motor and the solenoid terminal connections.
10  Remove the starter motor mounting bolts (see illustration) and detach the starter from the engine.

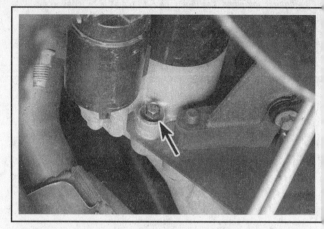

**19.10  Remove the starter/solenoid assembly bolts (arrow) and separate the assembly from the transmission bellhousing. The top bolts are hidden from view**

11  If necessary, turn the wheels to one side to provide removal access.
12  Installation is the reverse of removal.

## 20 Starter relay - removal and installation

▶ **Refer to illustration 20.2**

1   Detach the cable from the negative terminal of the battery.
2   Label the wires and the terminals then disconnect the Neutral safety switch wire, the battery cable, the fusible link and the starter cable from the relay terminals (see illustration).
3   Remove the mounting bolts and detach the relay.
4   Installation is the reverse of removal.

**20.2  To remove the starter relay, detach the Neutral safety switch wire, the fusible link, the battery positive lead and the starter motor leads (arrows), then remove the relay mounting bracket bolts (arrows)**

## 21 Starter solenoid - replacement

➡**Note: The solenoid on the 4.6L engine can only be replaced as a complete unit along with the starter assembly.**

## Specifications

### Battery voltage

| | |
|---|---|
| Engine off | 12.66-volts |
| Engine running | 14-to-15 volts |

### Firing order

See Chapter 2

### Ignition coil-to-distributor cap wire resistance

| | |
|---|---|
| Duraspark II systems | 5000 ohms per inch |
| TFI-IV system | 5000 ohms per foot |

### Ignition coil resistance

| | |
|---|---|
| Duraspark II systems | |
|     Primary resistance | 0.8 to 1.6 ohms |
|     Secondary resistance | 7.7 to 10.5 K-ohms |
| TFI-IV system | |
|     Primary resistance | 0.3 to 1.0 ohms |
|     Secondary resistance | 6.5 to 11.5 K-ohms |
| EDIS system | |
|     Primary resistance | 0.8 to 0.9 ohms |
|     Secondary resistance | 13.0 to 14.0 K-ohms |
| Ballast resistor | 0.8 to 1.6 ohms |
| Ignition coil primary winding-to-case resistance | 10-M ohms |

### Ignition timing

| | |
|---|---|
| 5.0L engines | 10 degrees BTDC with SPOUT disconnected, vehicle in DRIVE with emergency brake applied |
| 4.6L engines | Timing not adjustable |

### Alternator brush length

| | |
|---|---|
| New | 1/2 inch |
| Minimum | 1/4 inch |

**Notes**

**Section**

**Reference to other Chapters**

CHECK ENGINE light - See Chapter 6

# 6

EMISSIONS
AND ENGINE
CONTROL
SYSTEMS

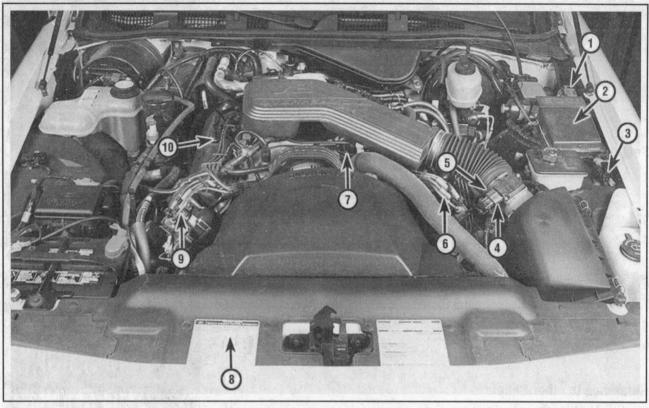

**1.1b Emission and engine control system component locations on the 4.6L engine**

| | | | | | |
|---|---|---|---|---|---|
| 1 | EDIS module | 5 | IAT sensor | 8 | VECI label |
| 2 | Relays | 6 | Coil pack | 9 | Coil pack |
| 3 | Diagnostic connector | 7 | Coolant temperature sensor | 10 | Positive Crankcase Ventilation valve |
| 4 | MAF sensor | | | | |

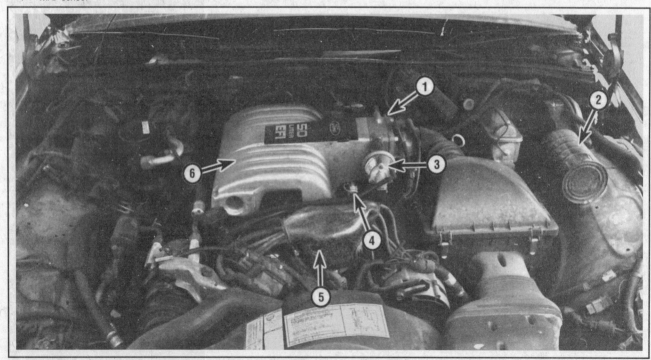

**1.1a Emission and engine control system component locations on the 5.0L engine**

| | | | | | |
|---|---|---|---|---|---|
| 1 | BPA-ISC valve | 3 | EGR valve | 5 | TFI-IV distributor |
| 2 | Vacuum canister | 4 | Coolant temperature sensor | 6 | Air intake plenum |

## 1  General information

▶ **Refer to illustrations 1.1a, 1.1b and 1.7**

To prevent pollution of the atmosphere from incompletely burned and evaporating gases, and to maintain good driveability and fuel economy, a number of emission control systems are incorporated (see illustrations). They include the:

*Electronic Engine Control system (EEC-IV)*
*Evaporative Emission Control (EECS) system*
*Positive Crankcase Ventilation (PCV) system*
*Exhaust Gas Recirculation (EGR) system*
*Catalytic converter*

All of these systems are linked, directly or indirectly, to the emission control system.

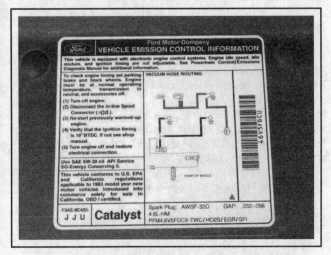

**1.7 The Vehicle Emission Control Information (VECI) label is located in the engine compartment on the radiator support and contains information on the emission devices on your vehicle, vacuum line routing, etc.**

The Sections in this Chapter include general descriptions, checking procedures within the scope of the home mechanic and component replacement procedures (when possible) for each of the systems listed above.

Before assuming that an emissions control system is malfunctioning, check the fuel and ignition systems carefully. The diagnosis of some emission control devices requires specialized tools, equipment and training. If checking and servicing become too difficult or if a procedure is beyond your ability, consult a dealer service department. Remember, the most frequent cause of emissions problems is simply a loose or broken vacuum hose or wire, so always check the hose and wiring connections first.

This doesn't mean, however, that emission control systems are particularly difficult to maintain and repair. You can quickly and easily perform many checks and do most of the regular maintenance at home with common tune-up and hand tools.

➡ **Note: Because of a Federally mandated extended warranty which covers the emission control system components, check with your dealer about warranty coverage before working on any emissions-related systems. Once the warranty has expired, you may wish to perform some of the component checks and/or replacement procedures in this Chapter to save money.**

Pay close attention to any special precautions outlined in this Chapter. It should be noted that the illustrations of the various systems may not exactly match the system installed on the vehicle you're working on because of changes made by the manufacturer during production or from year-to-year.

A Vehicle Emissions Control Information (VECI) label is located in the engine compartment (see illustration). This label contains important emissions specifications and adjustment information, as well as a vacuum hose schematic with emissions components identified. When servicing the engine or emissions systems, the VECI label in your particular vehicle should always be checked for up-to-date information.

## 2  On Board Diagnostic (OBD) system and trouble codes

### GENERAL DESCRIPTION

▶ **Refer to illustration 2.23**

1  Early models (1994 and earlier) use the Electronic Engine Control (EEC-IV) system. Late models (1995 and later) use the EEC-V system. Both of these On Board Diagnostic systems consists of an onboard computer, known as the Powertrain Control Module (PCM), and information sensors, which monitor various functions of the engine and send data to the PCM. Based on the data and the information programmed into the computer's memory, the PCM generates output signals to control various engine functions via control relays, solenoids and other output actuators.

2  The PCM, located under the instrument panel, is the "brain" of the OBD system. It receives data from a number of sensors and other electronic components (switches, relays, etc.). Based on the information it receives, the PCM generates output signals to control various relays, solenoids and other actuators. The PCM is specifically calibrated to optimize the emissions, fuel economy and driveability of the vehicle.

3  Because of a Federally-mandated extended warranty which covers the EEC-IV and EEC-V system components and because any owner-induced damage to the PCM, the sensors and/or the control devices may void the warranty, it isn't a good idea to attempt diagnosis or replacement of the PCM at home while the vehicle is under warranty. Take the vehicle to a dealer service department if the PCM or a system component malfunctions.

### INFORMATION SENSORS

4  When battery voltage is applied to the air conditioning compressor clutch, a signal is sent to the PCM, which interprets the signal as an added load created by the compressor and increases engine idle

speed accordingly to compensate.

5 The Intake Air Temperature sensor (IAT), threaded into a runner of the intake manifold (see Section 4), provides the PCM with fuel/air mixture temperature information. The PCM uses this information to control fuel flow, ignition timing and EGR system operation.

6 The Engine Coolant Temperature (ECT) sensor, which is threaded into a coolant passage in the intake manifold, monitors engine coolant temperature. The ECT sends the PCM a constantly varying voltage signal which influences PCM control of the fuel mixture, ignition timing and EGR operation.

7 The Heated Exhaust Gas Oxygen (HEGO) sensors, which are threaded into the exhaust manifolds, constantly monitor the oxygen content of the exhaust gases. A voltage signal which varies in accordance with the difference between the oxygen content of the exhaust gases and the surrounding atmosphere is sent to the PCM. The PCM converts this exhaust gas oxygen content signal to the fuel/air ratio, compares it to the ideal ratio for current engine operating conditions and alters the signal to the injectors accordingly.

8 The Throttle Position Sensor (TPS), which is mounted on the side of the throttle body (see Section 4) and connected directly to the throttle shaft, senses throttle movement and position, then transmits an electrical signal to the PCM. This signal enables the PCM to determine when the throttle is closed, in its normal cruise condition or wide open.

9 The Mass Air Flow (MAF) sensor, which is mounted in the air cleaner intake passage, measures the mass of the air entering the engine (see Section 4). Because air mass varies with air temperature (cold air is denser than warm air), measuring air mass provides the PCM with a very accurate way of determining the correct amount of fuel to obtain the ideal fuel/air mixture.

10 Accelerator Pedal Position Sensors (APPS) - 2003 and later models are equipped with the Generation II (GEN II) Torque Based Electronic Throttle Control (ETC) system. The ETC system uses an electronic throttle body instead of a conventional cable-operated throttle body. The Powertrain Control Module (PCM) controls the position of the throttle plate with a solenoid that's located in the throttle body. The PCM's commands are based on the inputs that it receives from the APPS, all three of which are located inside a small plastic module, known as the Electronic Throttle Control (ETC) module, which is located at the top of the accelerator pedal assembly. The three APP sensors are referred to as APP1, APP2 and APP3. APP1 has a negative slope (increasing angle, decreasing voltage) and APP2 and APP3 both have a positive slope (increasing angle, increasing voltage). The PCM uses APP1 as the principal sensor for pedal position. Its signal is converted into a rotary angle (degrees of pedal travel) by the PCM, and then it's converted into "counts," which is the input used by the second-generation (Gen II) torque-based ETC system.

The ETC module is an integral component of the accelerator pedal assembly. If one APP sensor fails, you must replace the pedal and sensors as a single assembly.

11 Fuel Rail Pressure Temperature (FRPT) sensor - The FRPT sensor, which is used on 2003 and later models, measures the pressure and the temperature of the fuel in the fuel rail. The FRPT sensor uses intake manifold vacuum as a reference to determine the pressure difference between the fuel rail and the intake manifold. The relationship between fuel pressure and fuel temperature is used to determine the likelihood of the presence of fuel vapor in the fuel rail. Both the pressure and temperature signals are used to control the speed of the fuel pump. The speed of the fuel pump controls the pressure inside the fuel rail in order to keep the fuel in a liquid state. Keeping the fuel in a liquid state increases the efficiency of the injectors because the higher fuel rail pressure allows a decrease in the injector pulse width (the interval

of time during which the injector is open). The FRPT sensor is located at the rear end of the left fuel rail.

12 Cylinder Head Temperature (CHT) sensor - The CHT sensor measures the temperature of the aluminum cylinder head, not the temperature of the engine coolant. But the PCM is able to infer the temperature of the coolant from the CHT sensor signal nonetheless. On late models, if the CHT indicates a cylinder head temperature of about 250 degrees F. the PCM initiates a fail-safe cooling strategy that allows you to drive home in limp-home mode. Basically, the PCM disables half of the fuel injectors. It alternates which injectors are disabled every 32 engine cycles. The cylinders that are not injected with fuel act as air pumps to help cool down the engine. If the CHT sensor indicates a temperature of about 330 degrees F. or higher, the PCM shuts down all of the injectors until the temperature goes below about 310 degrees F.

The CHT sensor is a thermistor, i.e. its resistance decreases as the temperature increases, and its resistance increases as the temperature decreases. This type of thermistor is also referred to as a Negative Temperature Coefficient (NTC) thermistor. This variable resistance produces an analogous voltage drop across the sensor terminals, thus providing an electrical signal to the PCM that accurately reflects the cylinder head temperature. The CHT sensor is a passive sensor; i.e. it's connected to a voltage divider network in which varying the resistance of the sensor produces a variation in total current flow. Voltage is dropped across a fixed resistor that's installed in series with the resistor inside the CHT sensor, and together both resistors determine the voltage signal that's provided to the PCM. This voltage signal is equal to the reference voltage minus the voltage drop across the fixed resistor.

The CHT sensor is located on the inner wall of the right cylinder head, facing in, i.e. toward the valley between the two cylinder heads.

## OUTPUT DEVICES

13 The EEC power relay, which is activated by the ignition switch, supplies battery voltage to the EEC-IV system components when the switch is in the Start or Run position.

14 The canister purge solenoid (CANP) switches manifold vacuum to operate the canister purge valve when a signal is received from the PCM. Vacuum opens the purge valve when the solenoid is energized, allowing fuel vapor to flow from the canister to the intake manifold.

15 The solenoid-operated fuel injectors are located above the intake ports (see Chapter 4). The PCM controls the length of time the injector is open. The "open" time of the injector determines the amount of fuel delivered. For information regarding injector replacement, refer to Chapter 4.

16 The fuel pump relay is activated by the PCM with the ignition switch in the On position. When the ignition switch is turned to the On position, the relay is activated to supply initial line pressure to the system. For information regarding fuel pump check and replacement, refer to Chapter 4.

17 The EDIS ignition module (see Chapter 5) installed on all 4.6L engines, mounted on a bracket between the upper intake manifold and the valve cover, triggers the ignition coils and determines dwell. The PCM uses a signal from the Profile Ignition Pick-Up (PIP) to determine crankshaft position. Ignition timing is determined by the PCM, which then signals the module to fire the coil. For further information regarding the ignition module, refer to the appropriate Section in Chapter 5.

18 Fuel Pump Driver Module (FPDM) - The fuel systems used on 2003 and later models are returnless, i.e. there is no intake-manifold-vacuum-actuated fuel pressure regulator and there is no fuel return line between the fuel rail and the fuel tank. Instead, system fuel pressure is controlled by the speed of the fuel pump. The PCM controls the duty

cycle to the FPDM (2005 and later), which modulates the voltage to the fuel pump to maintain the correct fuel pressure. The FPDM is located under the vehicle, in the vicinity of the fuel tank and the trunk. The fuel pump driver is built internal to the PCM on 2003 and 2004 models. 2005 and later models are equipped with an externally mounted driver module termed the Fuel Pump Driver Module (FPDM).

## OBTAINING CODES

➡**Note: This procedure applies to 1994 and earlier models only. 1995 and later models require a scan tool to obtain the trouble codes. The expense of a scan tool prohibits the average do-it-yourself mechanic from owning one. However, trouble-code readers are available at a fraction of the cost of scan tools and are available at auto parts stores. Codes for 1995 and later model vehicles are listed in the accompanying charts for those who purchase a scan tool or trouble-code reader. Follow the instructions included with the tool for code retrieval.**

19 The diagnostic codes for the 1994 and earlier models are arranged in such a way that a series of tests must be completed in order to extract ALL the codes from the system. If one portion of the test is performed without the others, there may be a chance the trouble code that will pinpoint a problem in your particular vehicle will remain stored in the PCM without detection. The tests start first with a Key On, Engine Off (KOEO) test followed by a computed timing test then finally a Engine Running (ER) test. Here is a brief overview of the code extracting procedures of the EEC-IV system followed by the actual test:

### Quick Test - Key On Engine Off (KOEO)

20 The following tests are all included with the key on, engine off:

**Self test codes** - These codes are accessed on the test connector by using a jumper wire and an analog voltmeter or the factory diagnostic tool called the Star tester. These codes are also called Hard Codes.

**Separator pulse codes** - After the initial Hard Codes, the system will flash a code 11 (separator pulse) (1988 through 1990) or code 111 (1991 through 1994) and then will flash a series of Soft (or Continuous Memory) Codes.

**Continuous Memory Codes** - These codes indicate a fault that may or may not be present at the time of testing. These codes usually indicate an intermittent failure. Continuous Memory codes are stored in the system and they will flash after the normal Hard Codes. These codes are either two digit (1988 through 1990) or three digit codes (1991 through 1994). These codes can indicate chronic or intermittent problems. Also called Soft Codes.

**Fast codes** - These codes are transmitted 100 times faster than normal codes and can only be read by a Star Tester at a dealer service department or an equivalent SCAN tool.

### Engine running codes (KOER) or (ER)

21 **Running tests** - These tests make it possible for the PCM to pick-up a diagnostic trouble code that cannot be set while the engine is in KOEO. These problems usually occur during driving conditions. Some codes are detected by cold or warm running conditions, some are detected at low rpm or high rpm and some are detected at closed throttle or WOT.

**I.D. Pulse codes** - These codes indicate the type of engine (4, 6 or 8 cylinder) or the correct module and Self Test mode access.

**Computed engine timing test** - This engine running test determines base timing for the engine and starts the process of allowing the

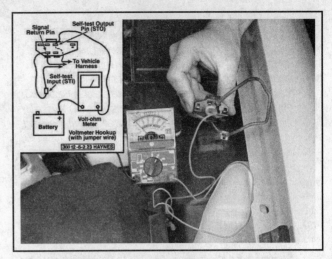

**2.23 To read any stored trouble codes, connect a voltmeter to the Diagnostic Test connector as shown, then connect a jumper wire between the self test input and pin number 2 on the larger connector - turn the ignition key ON and watch the voltmeter needle or CHECK ENGINE light on later models (4.6L engine shown)**

engine to store running codes.

**Wiggle test** - This engine running test checks the wiring system to the sensors and output actuators as the engine performs

**Cylinder balance test** - This engine running test determines injector balance as well as cylinder compression balance.

➡**Note: This test should be performed by a dealer service department.**

## BEGINNING THE TEST

22 Position the parking brake ON, Shift lever in PARK, block the drive wheels and turn off all electrical loads (air conditioning, radio, heater fan blower etc.). Make sure the engine is warmed to normal operating temperature (if possible).

23 Perform the KOEO tests:

a) *Turn the ignition key off for at least 10 seconds*

b) *Locate the Diagnostic Test connector inside the engine compartment. Install the voltmeter leads onto the battery and pin number 4 (STO) of the test connector (see illustration). Install a jumper wire from the test terminal to pin number 2 of the Diagnostic Test terminal (STI).*

c) *Turn the ignition key ON (engine not running) and observe the needle sweeps on the voltmeter. For example code 23, the voltmeter will sweep once, pause 1/2 second and sweep again. There will be a two second pause between digits and then there will be three distinct sweeps of the needle to indicate the second digit of the code number. On three digit codes, the sequence is the same except there will be an additional sequence of numbers (sweeps) to indicate the third digit in the code. Additional codes will be separated by a four second pause and then the indicated sweeps on the voltmeter. Be aware that the code sequence may continue into the continuous memory codes (read further).*

➡**Note: Later models will flash the CHECK ENGINE light on the dash in place of the voltmeter.**

24 Interpreting the continuous memory codes:

a) *After the KOEO codes are reported, there will be a short pause and any stored Continuous Memory codes will appear in order. Remember that the "Separator" code is 11, or 111 on 1991 through 1994 models. The computer will not enter the Continuous Memory mode without flashing the separator pulse code. The Continuous Memory codes are read the same as the initial codes or "Hard Codes". Record these codes onto a piece of paper and continue the test.*

25 Perform the Engine Running (ER) tests.

a) *Remove the jumper wires from the Diagnostic Test connector to start the test.*

b) *Run engine until it reaches normal operating temperature.*

c) *Turn the engine OFF for at least 10 seconds.*

d) *Install the jumper wire onto Diagnostic Test connector (see illustration 2.19) and start the engine.*

e) *Observe that the voltmeter or CHECK ENGINE light will flash the engine identification code. This code indicates 1/2 the number of cylinders of the engine. For example, 4 flashes represent an 8 cylinder engine, or 3 flashes represent a six cylinder engine.*

f) *Within 1 to 2 seconds of the I.D. code, turn the steering wheel at least 1/2 turn and release. This will store any power steering pressure switch trouble codes.*

g) *Depress the brake pedal and release.*

➡**Note: Perform the steering wheel and brake pedal procedure in succession immediately (1 to 2 seconds) after the I.D. codes are flashed.**

h) *Observe all the codes and record them on a piece of paper. Be sure to count the sweeps or flashes very carefully as you jot them down.*

26 On some models the PCM will request a Dynamic Response check. This test quickly checks the operation of the TPS, MAF or MAP sensors in action. This will be indicated by a code 1 or a single sweep of the voltmeter needle (one flash on CHECK ENGINE light). This test will require the operator to simply full throttle ("goose") the accelerator pedal for one second. DO NOT throttle the accelerator pedal unless it is requested.

27 The next part of this test makes sure the system can advance the timing. This is called the Computed Timing test. After the last ER code has been displayed, the PCM will advance the ignition timing a fixed amount and hold it there for approximately 2 minutes. Use a timing light to check the amount of advance. The computed timing should equal the base timing plus 20 BTDC. The total advance should equal 27 to 33 degrees advance. If the timing is out of specification, have the system checked at a dealer service department.

➡**Note: Remember to remove the SPOUT from the connector as described in the ignition timing procedure in Chapter 5. This will remove the computer from the loop and give base timing.**

28 Finally perform the Wiggle Test. This test can be used to recreate a possible intermittent fault in the harness wiring system.

a) *Use a jumper wire to ground the STI lead on the Diagnostic Test connector (see illustration 2.23).*

b) *Turn the ignition key ON (engine not running).*

c) *Now deactivate the self test mode (remove the jumper wire) and then immediately reactivate the self-test mode. Now the system has entered Continuous Monitor Test Mode.*

d) *Carefully wiggle, tap or remove any suspect wiring to a sensor or output actuator. If a problem exists, a trouble code will be stored that indicates a problem with the circuit that governs the particular component. Record the codes that are indicated.*

e) *Next, enter Engine Running Continuous Monitor Test Mode to check for wiring problems only when the engine is running. Start first by deactivating the Diagnostic Test connector and turning the ignition key OFF. Now start the engine and allow it to idle.*

f) *Use a jumper wire to ground the STI lead on the Diagnostic Test connector (see illustration 2.23). Wait ten seconds and then deactivate the test mode and reactivate it again (install jumper wire). This will enter Engine Running Continuous Monitor Test Mode.*

g) *Carefully wiggle, tap or remove any suspect wiring to a sensor or output actuator. If a problem exists, a trouble code will be stored that indicates a problem with the circuit that governs the particular component. Record the codes that are indicated.*

29 If necessary, perform the Cylinder Balance Test. This test must be performed by a dealer service department.

## CLEARING CODES

To clear the codes from the PCM memory, start the KOEO self test diagnostic procedure (see illustration 2.23) and install the jumper wire into the Diagnostic Test connector. When the codes start to display themselves on the voltmeter or CHECK ENGINE light, remove the jumper wire from the Diagnostic Test connector. This will erase any stored codes within the system.

**✳✳ CAUTION:**

**Do not disconnect the battery from the vehicle to clear the codes. This will erase stored operating parameters from the KAM (Keep Alive Memory) and cause the engine to run rough for a period of time while the computer relearns the information.**

## 2 Digit Trouble Codes

| Code | Test Condition* | Probable Cause |
| --- | --- | --- |
| 11 | O,C,R | Pass (separator code) |
| 12 | R | RPM not within Self-test upper limit |
| 13 | R | RPM not within Self-test lower limit |
| 14 | C | Profile Ignition Pick-up circuit fault |
| 15 | O | Read Only Memory test failed |
| 15 | C | Keep Alive Memory test failed |
| 16 | R | RPM too low to perform Oxygen Sensor/fuel test |
| 18 | C | Loss of TACH input to PCM; SPOUT circuit grounded |
| 18 | R | SPOUT circuit open |
| 19 | O | Failure in EEC reference voltage |
| 21 | O,R | Coolant Temperature Sensor out of range |
| 22 | O,C | Manifold Absolute/Baro Pressure Sensor out of range |
| 23 | O,R | Throttle Position Sensor out of range |
| 24 | O,R | Intake Air Temperature sensor out of range |
| 26 | O,R | Mass Air Flow Sensor out of range |
| 29 | C | No input from Vehicle Speed Sensor |
| 31 | O,C,R | EGR Valve Position Sensor out of range (low) |
| 32 | O,C,R | EGR valve not seated; closed voltage low |
| 33 | C,R | EGR valve not opening; Insufficient flow detected |
| 34 | O,C,R | EGR Valve Pressure Transducer/Position Sensor sonic voltage above closed limit |
| 35 | O,C,R | EGR Valve Pressure Transducer/Position Sensor voltage out of range (high) |
| 41 | R | Heated Oxygen Sensor circuit indicates system lean, right side |
| 41 | C | No Heated Oxygen Sensor switch detected, right side |
| 42 | R | Heated Oxygen Sensor circuit indicates system rich, right side |
| 44 | R | Thermactor Air system inoperative, right side |
| 45 | R | Thermactor Air upstream during Self-test (5.0L only) |
| 46 | R | Thermactor Air not by-passed during Self-test (5.0L only) |
| 51 | O,C | Coolant Temperature sensor circuit open |
| 53 | O,C | Throttle Position sensor out of range (high) |
| 54 | O,C | Intake Air Temperature sensor circuit open |
| 56 | O,C | Mass Air Flow sensor out of range (high) |
| 61 | O,C | Coolant Temperature sensor circuit grounded |
| 63 | O,C | Throttle Position sensor circuit out of range (low) |
| 64 | O,C | Intake Air Temperature sensor circuit grounded |
| 66 | C | Mass Air Flow sensor circuit out-of-range (low) |
| 67 | O | Neutral Drive Switch circuit open |
| 72 | R | Insufficient Mass Air Flow change during Dynamic Response Test |
| 73 | R | Insufficient Throttle Position output during Dynamic Response Test |
| 74 | R | Brake On/Off switch failure |
| 75 | R | Brake On/Off circuit failure |
| 77 | R | Wide Open Throttle not sensed during Self-test |
| 79 | O | Air conditioning on during self-test |
| 81 | O | Air Management 2 circuit failure (5.0L only) |
| 82 | O | Air Management 1 circuit failure (5.0L only) |
| 84 | O | EGR Vacuum Regulator circuit failure |

*  O = Key On, Engine Off;  C = Continuous Memory;  R = Engine Running

## 2 Digit Trouble Codes (continued)

| | | |
|---|---|---|
| 85 | O | Canister Purge circuit failure |
| 87 | O,C | Primary Fuel Pump circuit failure |
| 91 | R | Heated oxygen sensor indicates system lean, left side |
| 91 | C | No heated oxygen sensor switching indicated, left side |
| 92 | R | Heated oxygen sensor indicates system rich, left side |
| 94 | R | Thermactor Air system inoperative, left side (5.0L only) |
| 95 | O,C | Fuel Pump circuit open, PCM to motor |
| 96 | O,C | Fuel Pump circuit open, Battery to PCM |
| 98 | R | Hard Fault present |

## 3 and 4 Digit Trouble Codes

➡Note: These codes may be preceded by the letter and number P0 for 3 digit codes or just the letter P for 4 digit codes.

| Code | Test Condition* | Probable Cause |
|---|---|---|
| 102 | O,C,R | MAF sensor circuits open or sensor defective |
| 103 | O,C,R | MAF sensor screen blocked or sensor defective |
| 104 | C | MAF sensor circuit erratic |
| 106 | O,C,R | BARO sensor slow responding |
| 107 | O,C,R | BARO sensor low voltage, open sensor circuits or defective sensor. |
| 108 | O,C,R | BARO sensor high voltage detected. BARO circuit shorted to power or defective sensor. |
| 109 | O,C,R | BARO sensor intermittent. Check for loose connections. |
| 111 | O,C,R | Pass |
| 112 | O,C,R | Intake Air Temperature sensor circuit indicates circuit grounded/above 245 degrees F |
| 113 | O,C,R | Intake Air Temperature sensor circuit indicates open circuit/below -40 degrees F |
| 114 | O,C,R | Intake Air Temperature sensor out of self-test range |
| 116 | O,R | Coolant Temperature sensor out of self-test range |
| 117 | O,C | Coolant Temperature circuit below minimum voltage or indicates above 245 degrees F |
| 118 | O,C | Coolant Temperature sensor circuit above maximum voltage or indicates below -40 degrees F |
| 119 | C | Coolant Temperature sensor circuit erratic |
| 121 | O,C,R | Throttle Position sensor out of self-test range |
| 121 | C | Electronic Throttle Control circuit performance problem |
| 122 | O,C | Throttle Position sensor below minimum voltage |
| 122 | C | Electronic Throttle Control circuit low input |
| 123 | O,C | Throttle Position sensor above maximum voltage |
| 123 | C | Electronic Throttle Control circuit high input |
| 124 | C | Throttle Position Sensor voltage higher than expected |
| 125 | C | Throttle Position Sensor voltage lower than expected |
| 125** | O,C,R | Coolant Temp sensor slow response. Check coolant level |
| 126 | O,C,R | MAP/BARO sensor higher than expected (1993 and 1994 only) |
| 128 | C | MAP sensor vacuum hose damaged or disconnected (1993 and 1994 only) |
| 129 | R | Insufficient Manifold Absolute Pressure/Mass Air Flow change during Dynamic Response Check |
| 131 | O,C,R | Heated oxygen sensor out of range |
| 133 | O,C,R | Heated oxygen sensor slow response |
| 135 | O,C,R | Heated oxygen sensor circuits open, shorted or grounded |
| 136** | O,C,R | Heated oxygen sensor circuits open, shorted or have corroded connections |
| 136 | R | Heated oxygen sensor indicates lean condition, left side |
| 137 | R | Heated oxygen sensor indicates rich condition, left side |

\* O = Key On, Engine Off; C = Continuous Memory; R = Engine Running
\** 1995 and later models

| Code | Test Condition* | Probable Cause |
| --- | --- | --- |
| 139 | C | No heated oxygen sensor switching detected, left side |
| 141 | O,C,R | Heated oxygen sensor circuits open shorted or grounded |
| 144 | C | No heated oxygen sensor switching detected, right side |
| 151 | O,C,R | Heated oxygen sensor out of range |
| 153 | O,C,R | Heated oxygen sensor slow response |
| 155 | O,C,R | Heated oxygen sensor circuits open, shorted or grounded |
| 156 | O,C,R | Heated oxygen sensor circuits open, shorted or have corroded connections |
| 157 | R,C | Mass Air Flow Sensor below minimum voltage |
| 158 | O,R,C | Mass Air Flow Sensor above maximum voltage |
| 159 | O,R | Mass Air Flow Sensor out of self-test range |
| 161 | O,C,R | Heated oxygen sensor circuits open shorted or grounded |
| 167 | R | Insufficient Throttle Position Sensor change during Dynamic Response Check |
| 171 | C | Heated oxygen sensor unable to switch, right side |
| 171** | C,R | Heated oxygen sensor indicates lean condition, left side |
| 172 | C,R | Heated oxygen sensor indicates lean condition, right side |
| 172** | C,R | Heated oxygen sensor indicates rich condition, left side |
| 173 | C,R | Heated oxygen sensor indicates rich condition, right side |
| 174 | C | Heated oxygen sensor switching slow, right side |
| 174** | C,R | Heated oxygen sensor indicates lean condition, right side |
| 175 | C | Heated oxygen sensor unable to switch, left side |
| 175** | C,R | Heated oxygen sensor indicates rich condition, right side |
| 176 | C | Heated oxygen sensor indicates lean condition, left side |
| 176** | O,C,R | Flexible fuel sensor malfunction |
| 177 | C | Heated oxygen sensor indicates rich condition, left side |
| 178 | C | Heated oxygen sensor switching slow, left side |
| 179 | C | Adaptive Fuel lean limit reached at part throttle, system rich, right side |
| 180 | O,C,R | Engine fuel temperature sensor circuit open, shorted or grounded |
| 181 | C | Adaptive Fuel rich limit reached at part throttle, right side |
| 181** | O,C,R | Engine fuel temperature sensor circuit open, shorted or grounded |
| 182** | O,C,R | Engine fuel temperature sensor circuit open, shorted or grounded |
| 182 | C | Adaptive Fuel lean limit reached at idle, right side |
| 183 | C | Adaptive Fuel rich limit reached at idle, right side |
| 183** | O,C,R | Engine fuel temperature sensor circuit open, shorted or grounded |
| 184 | C | Mass Air Flow higher than expected |
| 185 | C | Mass Air Flow lower than expected |
| 186 | C | Injector Pulse-width higher than expected |
| 186** | O,C,R | Engine fuel temperature sensor circuit open, shorted or grounded |
| 187 | C | Injector Pulse-width lower than expected |
| 187** | O,C,R | Engine fuel temperature sensor circuit open, shorted or grounded |
| 188 | C | Adaptive Fuel lean limit reached, left side |
| 188** | O,C,R | Engine fuel temperature sensor circuit open, shorted or grounded |
| 189 | C | Adaptive Fuel rich limit reached, left side |
| 190 | O,C,R | Fuel rail pressure sensor circuit open |
| 191 | C | Adaptive Fuel lean limit reached at idle, left side |
| 191** | O,C,R | Fuel rail pressure sensor circuit performance |
| 192 | C | Adaptive Fuel rich limit reached at idle, left side |

\* O = Key On, Engine Off;  C = Continuous Memory;  R = Engine Running
\*\* 1995 and later models

## 3 and 4 Digit Trouble Codes (continued)

➡Note: These codes may be preceded by the letter and number P0 for 3 digit codes or just the letter P for 4 digit codes.

| Code | Test Condition* | Probable Cause |
|---|---|---|
| 192** | O,C,R | Fuel rail pressure sensor circuit low input |
| 193 | O | Flexible Fuel (FF) sensor circuit failure (1993 and 1994) |
| 193** | O,C,R | Fuel rail pressure sensor circuit high input |
| 201 | C | Injector number 1 circuit malfunction |
| 202 | C | Injector number 2 circuit malfunction |
| 203 | C | Injector number 3 circuit malfunction |
| 204 | C | Injector number 4 circuit malfunction |
| 205 | C | Injector number 5 circuit malfunction |
| 206 | C | Injector number 6 circuit malfunction |
| 207 | C | Injector number 7 circuit malfunction |
| 208 | C | Injector number 8 circuit malfunction |
| 211 | C | Profile Ignition Pick-up circuit fault |
| 212 | C | Ignition module circuit failure/SPOUT circuit grounded |
| 213 | R | SPOUT circuit open |
| 214 | C | Cylinder identification (CID) circuit failure |
| 215 | C | PCM detected coil 1 primary circuit failure |
| 216 | C | PCM detected coil 2 primary circuit failure |
| 217 | C | PCM detected coil 3 primary circuit failure |
| 217 | C | Engine coolant over-temperature condition |
| 218 | C | Transmission Fluid Temperature (TFT) over-temperature condition |
| 219 | C | Spark timing defaulted to 10 degrees SPOUT circuit open (EI) |
| 221 | C | Spark timing error (1993 and 1994 only) |
| 221 | C | Throttle Position (TP) sensor 2 circuit, range performance problem |
| 222 | C | Throttle Position (TP) sensor 2 circuit, low input |
| 223 | C | Throttle Position (TP) sensor 2 circuit, high input |
| 225 | C | Knock sensor not detected during dynamic response test KOER |
| 226 | O | Ignition Diagnostic Module (IDM) signal not received (EI) (1993 and 1994) |
| 230 | O,R | Fuel pump primary circuit malfunction. Check fuel pump relay and for open, shorted or grounded wiring |
| 231 | O,R | Fuel pump primary circuit low. Check fuel pump relay and for open, shorted or grounded wiring |
| 232 | C | PCM detected coil 1,2,3 or 4 primary circuit failure (EI) (1993 and 1994 only) |
| 232** | O,C,R | Fuel pump primary circuit high. Check fuel pump relay and for open, shorted or grounded wiring. Also, inertia switch may be open |
| 238 | C | PCM detected coil 4 primary circuit failure (EI) (1993 and 1994 only) |
| 241 | C | ICM to PCM - IDM pulse width transmission error (EI) (1993 and 1994 only) |
| 244 | R | CID circuit fault present when cylinder balance test requested (1993 and 1994 only) |
| 298 | O,R | Engine oil overheat. Check oil level |
| 300 | O,C,R | Random misfire. Check ignition and fuel system |
| 301 ñ308 | O,C,R | Misfire in the corresponding cylinder. Check ignition and fuel system |
| 310 | C | Misfire detection monitor |
| 311 | R | Thermactor Air System inoperative, right side |
| 313 | R | Thermactor Air not by-passed |
| 314 | R | Thermactor Air inoperative, left side |

\* O = Key On, Engine Off; C = Continuous Memory; R = Engine Running
\*\* 1995 and later models

| Code | Test Condition* | Probable Cause |
| --- | --- | --- |
| 320 | O,C,R | Engine ignition speed input circuit malfunction |
| 325 | O,C,R | knock sensor circuit bank 1 |
| 326 | C,R | EGR circuit voltage lower than expected |
| 326** | O,C,R | Knock sensor circuit bank 1 |
| 327 | O,C,R | EGR Valve Pressure Transducer/Position Sensor circuit below minimum voltage |
| 328 | O,C,R | EGR Valve Position Sensor voltage below closed limit |
| 330 | O,C,R | Knock sensor circuit bank 2 |
| 331 | O,C,R | Knock sensor circuit bank 2 |
| 332 | C,R | EGR valve opening not detected |
| 334 | O,C,R | EGR valve position sensor voltage above closed limit |
| 335 | O | EGR Sensor voltage out-of-range |
| 336 | R | EGR circuit higher than expected |
| 337 | O,C,R | EGR Valve Pressure Transducer/Position Sensor circuit above maximum voltage |
| 340 | O,C,R | Camshaft position sensor circuit. Check wiring for opens, shorts and grounds |
| 341 | O | Octane adjust service pin open (1993 and 1994 only) |
| 350 | O,C,R | Ignition coil primary circuit malfunction. Check each coil primary circuit |
| 351-358 | O,C,R | Ignition coil primary circuit malfunction. Check the corresponding coil primary circuit |
| 381 | C | Frequent air conditioning clutch cycling (1993 and 1994 only) |
| 400 | C | EGR flow failure - outside the minimum or maximum flow standards |
| 401 | O,C,R | EGR low flow. Check vacuum supply and valve operation |
| 402 | O,C,R | EGR flow at idle. Check for a stuck-open valve |
| 403 | C | EGR vacuum regulator solenoid circuit malfunction |
| 405 | C | Differential Pressure Feedback (DPF) circuit low voltage detected |
| 406 | C | Differential Pressure Feedback (DPF) circuit high voltage detected |
| 411 | R | Unable to control RPM during Low RPM Self-test |
| 411** | O,C,R | Secondary Air System no or low flow |
| 412 | R | Unable to control RPM during High RPM Self-test |
| 412** | O,C,R | Secondary Air System circuit open |
| 415 | R | Idle Air Control (IAC) system at maximum adaptive lower limit |
| 416 | C | Idle Air Control (IAC) system at upper adaptive learning limit |
| 420 | O,C,R | Catalyst system low efficiency, left bank |
| 430 | O,C,R | Catalyst system low efficiency, right bank |
| 442 | O,C,R | Evaporative control system - small leak detected |
| 443 | O,C,R | Evaporative control system canister purge valve circuit malfunction |
| 446 | O,C,R | Evaporative control system canister vent solenoid control circuit malfunction |
| 451 | C | EVAP system Fuel Tank Pressure (FTP) sensor system circuit malfunction |
| 452 | C | No input from Vehicle Speed Sensor |
| 452** | O,C,R | FTP sensor circuit |
| 453 | R | Servo leaking down (KOER IVSC test) (1993 and 1994 only) |
| 453** | O,C,R | FTP sensor circuit high voltage |
| 454 | R | Servo leaking up (KOER IVSC test) (1993 and 1994 only) |
| 454** | O,C,R | FTP sensor circuit noisy |
| 455 | R | Insufficient rpm increase (KOER IVSC test) (1993 and 1994 only) |
| 455** | O,C,R | Evaporative control system large leak detected |
| 456 | R | Insufficient rpm decrease (KOER IVSC test) (1993 and 1994 only) |
| 457 | O | Speed control command switch(s) circuit not functioning (KOEO IVSC test) (1993 and 1994 only) |

* *O = Key On, Engine Off; C = Continuous Memory; R = Engine Running*
** *1995 and later models*

## 3 and 4 Digit Trouble Codes (continued)

➡Note: These codes may be preceded by the letter and number P0 for 3 digit codes or just the letter P for 4 digit codes.

| Code | Test Condition* | Probable Cause |
|---|---|---|
| 458 | O | Speed control command switch(s) stuck/circuit grounded (KOEO IVSC test) (1993 and 1994 only) |
| 459 | O | Speed control ground circuit open (KOEO IVSC test) |
| 460 | C | Fuel level sensor circuit |
| 461 | C | Fuel level sensor circuit, range or performance problem |
| 462 | C | Fuel level sensor circuit, low input |
| 463 | C | Fuel level sensor circuit, high input |
| 480 | C | Cooling electrical malfunction |
| 480 | C | Low Fan Control (LFC) Fan Control Number 1 (FC 1), primary circuit malfunction |
| 481 | C | High Fan Control (LFC) Fan Control Number 3 (FC 3), primary circuit malfunction |
| 482 | C | Medium Fan Control (MFC), primary circuit malfunction |
| 500 | O,C,R | Vehicle speed sensor. Check for opens, shorts and grounds in the VSS circuits |
| 501 | O,C,R | Vehicle speed sensor. Check for opens, shorts and grounds in the VSS circuits |
| 503 | O,C,R | Vehicle speed sensor signal intermittent. Check for opens, shorts and grounds in the VSS circuits |
| 505 | O,C | Idle Air Control (IAC) fail during self test |
| 506 | C | Idle Air Control (IAC) rpm lower than expected |
| 507 | C | Idle Air Control (IAC) rpm higher than expected |
| 511 | C | Idle Air Control (IAC) circuit malfunction |
| 511 | O | Read Only Memory test failed - replace PCM |
| 512 | C | Keep Alive Memory test failed |
| 513 | O | Internal voltage failure in PCM |
| 519 | O | Power steering pressure switch (PSP) circuit open (1993 and 1994 only) |
| 521 | R | Power steering pressure switch (PSP) circuit did not change states (1993 and 1994 only) |
| 522 | O | Manual Lever Position (MLP) sensor circuit open/vehicle in gear |
| 525 | O | Indicates vehicle in gear, air conditioning on |
| 527 | O | Manual Lever Position (MLP) sensor circuit open, air conditioning on during KOEO (1993 and 1994 only) |
| 529 | C | Data Communication link (DCL) or PCM circuit failure (1993 and 1994 only) |
| 532 | C | Cluster Control Assembly (CCA) circuit failure |
| 532 | C | Air Conditioning Pressure (ACP) sensor, high voltage detected |
| 533 | C | Data Communications Link (DCL) or Electronic Instrument Cluster (EIC) circuit failure |
| 533 | C | Air Conditioning Pressure (ACP) sensor, low voltage detected |
| 534 | C | Low air conditioning cycling period, frequent A/C clutch cycling |
| 536 | C,R | Brake ON/Off (BOO) circuit failure/not activated during the KOER |
| 537 | C | Air Conditioning Evaporator Temperature (ACET) circuit, low input |
| 538 | C | Air Conditioning Evaporator Temperature (ACET) circuit, high input |
| 538 | R | Insufficient change in RPM/operator error in Dynamic Response Check |
| 539 | O | Air conditioning on during Self-test |
| 542 | O,C | Fuel Pump circuit open; PCM to motor |
| 543 | O,C | Fuel Pump circuit open; Battery to PCM |
| 551 | O | Idle Air Control (IAC) circuit failure KOEO |
| 552 | O | Air Management 1 circuit failure |
| 552** | O,C,R | Power steering pressure sensor open or shorted to ground |
| 552 | O | Secondary Air Injection Bypass (AIRB) circuit failure (1993 and 1994 only) |

* O = Key On, Engine Off;  C = Continuous Memory;  R = Engine Running
** 1995 and later models

| Code | Test Condition* | Probable Cause |
|------|-----------------|----------------|
| 553 | O | Secondary Air Injection Diverter (AIRB) circuit failure (1993 and 1994 only) |
| 553** | O,C,R | Power steering pressure sensor shorted to power |
| 554 | O | Fuel Pressure Regulator Control (FPRC) circuit failure |
| 556 | O,C | Primary Fuel Pump circuit failure |
| 557 | O,C | Low speed fuel pump primary circuit failure (1993 and 1994 only) |
| 558 | O | EGR Vacuum Regulator circuit failure |
| 559 | O | Air Conditioning On (ACON) relay circuit failure (1993 and 1994) |
| 563 | O | High fan control (HFC) circuit failure (1993 and 1994 only) |
| 564 | O | Fan control (FC) circuit failure (1993 and 1994 only) |
| 565 | O | Canister Purge circuit failure |
| 567 | O | Speed Control Vent (SCVNT) circuit failure (KOEO IVSC test) |
| 568 | O | Speed Control Vacuum (SCVAC) circuit failure (KOEO IVSC test) |
| 569 | O | Auxiliary Canister Purge (CANP2) circuit failure KOEO |
| 571 | O | EGRA solenoid circuit failure KOEO |
| 572 | O | EGRV solenoid circuit failure KOEO |
| 578 | C | A / C pressure sensor circuit shorted |
| 579 | C | Insufficient AIR CONDITIONING pressure change |
| 581 | C | Power to Fan circuit over current |
| 582 | O | Fan circuit open |
| 583 | C | Power to Fuel pump over current |
| 584 | C | VCRM Power ground circuit open (VCRM Pin 1) |
| 585 | C | Power to A / C clutch over current |
| 586 | C | A / C clutch circuit open |
| 587 | O,C | Variable Control Relay Module (VCRM) communication failure |
| 602 | O,C,R | Control module programming error |
| 603 | O,C,R | Powertrain control module test error |
| 605 | C | Powertrain control module read only memory PCM error |
| 606 | C | Powertrain control module internal communication error |
| 617 | C | 1-2 shift error |
| 618 | C | 2-3 shift error |
| 619 | C | 3-4 shift error |
| 621 | O,C | Shift Solenoid 1 (SS 1) circuit failure KOEO |
| 622 | O | Shift Solenoid 2 (SS2) circuit failure KOEO |
| 623 | O | Transmission Control Indicator Light (TCIL) circuit failure |
| 624 | O,C | Electronic Pressure Control (EPC) circuit failure |
| 625 | O,C | Electronic Pressure Control (EPC) driver open in PCM |
| 626 | O | Coast Clutch Solenoid (CCS) circuit failure KOEO |
| 627 | O | Torque Converter Clutch (TCC) solenoid circuit failure |
| 628 | C | Excessive converter clutch slippage |
| 629 | O,C | Torque Converter Clutch (TCC) solenoid circuit failure |
| 631 | O | Transmission Control Indicator Lamp (TCIL) circuit failure KOEO |
| 632 | R | Transmission Control Switch (TCS) circuit did not change states during KOER |
| 634 | O,C,R | Manual Lever Position (MLP) sensor voltage higher or lower than expected |
| 636 | O,R | Transmission Fluid Temp (TFT) higher or lower than expected |
| 637 | O,C | Transmission Fluid Temp (TFT) sensor circuit above maximum voltage/ -40°F (-40°C) indicated / circuit open |

\* O = Key On, Engine Off;  C = Continuous Memory;  R = Engine Running
\*\* 1995 and later models

## 3 and 4 Digit Trouble Codes (continued)

➡Note: These codes may be preceded by the letter and number PO for 3 digit codes or just the letter P for 4 digit codes.

| Code | Test Condition* | Probable Cause |
|------|-----------------|----------------|
| 638 | O,C | Transmission Fluid Temp (TFT) sensor circuit below minimum voltage/ 290°F (143°C) indicated / circuit shorted |
| 639 | R,C | Insufficient input from Transmission Speed Sensor (TSS) |
| 641 | O,C | Shift Solenoid 3 (SS3) circuit failure |
| 643 | O,C | Torque Converter Clutch (TCC) circuit failure |
| 645 | C | Incorrect gear ratio obtained for first gear |
| 645 relay | C | Open or shorted wide open throttle (WOT) A/C cutoff, circuit open, shorted or damaged WAC |
| 646 | C | Incorrect gear ratio obtained for second gear |
| 647 | C | Incorrect gear ratio obtained for third gear |
| 648 | C | Incorrect gear ratio obtained for fourth gear |
| 649 | C | Electronic Pressure Control (EPC) higher or lower than expected |
| 651 | C | Electronic Pressure Control (EPC) circuit failure |
| 652 | O | Torque Converter Clutch (TCC) solenoid circuit failure |
| 653 | R | Transmission Control Switch (TCS) did not change states during KOER |
| 654 | O | Transmission Range (TR) sensor not indicating PARK during KOEO |
| 656 | C | Torque Converter Clutch continuous slip error |
| 657 | C | Transmission over temperature condition occurred |
| 659 | C | High vehicle speed in park indicated |
| 660 | C | intake Manifold Tuning Valve (IMTV) control circuit open (Bank 1) |
| 663 | C | intake Manifold Tuning Valve (IMTV) control circuit open (Bank 2) |
| 667 | C | Transmission Range sensor circuit voltage below minimum |
| 668 | C | Transmission Range circuit voltage above maximum |
| 675 | C | Transmission Range sensor circuit voltage out of range |
| 703 | O,C,R | Brake switch input, check for open switch |
| 704 | O,C,R | Clutch pedal position switch, check for opens, shorts and grounds |
| 720 | O,C,R | Insufficient input from output shaft speed sensor |
| 721 | O,C,R | Noise interference on output shaft speed sensor signal |
| 722 | O,C,R | No signal from output shaft speed sensor |
| 723 | O,C,R | Output shaft speed sensor circuit intermittent signal |
| 812 | O,C,R | Reverse switch input circuit |
| 998 | O | Hard fault present |
| 1000 | O,C,R | Monitor testing not complete |
| 1001 | O,C,R | KOER not able to complete |
| 1100 | O,C,R | MAF sensor intermittent |
| 1101 | O,C,R | MAF sensor out of self test range |
| 1109 | O,C,R | IAT sensor intermittent signal |
| 1112 | O,C,R | IAT sensor intermittent signal |
| 1114 | O,C,R | IAT sensor low input |
| 1115 | O,C,R | IAT sensor high input |
| 1116 | O,C,R | ECT sensor out of range |
| 1117 | O,C,R | ECT sensor out intermittent |
| 1120 | O,C,R | TPS out of range |
| 1121 | O,C,R | TPS sensor |

\* O = Key On, Engine Off; C = Continuous Memory; R = Engine Running
\*\* 1995 and later models

| Code | Test Condition* | Probable Cause |
|------|-----------------|----------------|
| 1124 | O,C,R | TPS sensor out of self test range |
| 1125 | O,C,R | TPS sensor intermittent |
| 1127 | O,C,R | Exhaust not warm enough to test sensor |
| 1128 | O,C,R | Oxygen sensors swapped from bank to bank, check O2 sensor for correct connection |
| 1129 | O,C,R | Oxygen sensors swapped from bank to bank, check O2 sensor for correct connection |
| 1130 | O,C,R | Lack of O2 sensor switch, left bank sensor 1(1/1) |
| 1131 | O,C,R | Lack of O2 sensor switch, lean(1/1) |
| 1132 | O,C,R | Lack of O2 sensor switch, rich 91/1) |
| 1137 | O,C,R | Lack of O2 sensor switch, lean, left bank sensor 2(1/2) |
| 1138 | O,C,R | Lack of O2 sensor switch, rich, left bank sensor 2(1/2) |
| 1150 | O,C,R | Lack of O2 sensor switch, right bank sensor 1 (2/1) |
| 1151 | O,C,R | Lack of O2 sensor switch, right bank sensor 1 (2/1) lean |
| 1152 | O,C,R | Lack of O2 sensor switch, right bank sensor 1 (2/1) rich |
| 1157 | O,C,R | Lack of O2 sensor switch, right bank sensor 1 (2/2) lean |
| 1158 | O,C,R | Lack of O2 sensor switch, right bank sensor 1 (2/2) rich |
| 1168 | O,C,R | Fuel rail pressure sensor, low pressure indicated |
| 1169 | O,C,R | Fuel rail pressure sensor, high pressure indicated |
| 1180 | O,C,R | Fuel delivery system low, check fuel filter |
| 1181 | O,C,R | Fuel delivery system high |
| 1183 | O,C,R | Engine oil temperature sensor circuit |
| 1184 | O,C,R | Engine oil temperature sensor self test fail |
| 1233 | O,C,R | Fuel system disabled, check inertia switch |
| 1234 | O,C,R | Fuel system disabled, check inertia switch |
| 1235 | O,C,R | Fuel pump control out of range |
| 1236 | O,C,R | Fuel pump control out of range |
| 1237 | O,C,R | Fuel pump secondary circuit malfunction |
| 1238 | O,C,R | Fuel pump secondary circuit malfunction |
| 1244 | O,C,R | Generator load input low, check charging system |
| 1245 | O,C,R | Generator load input high, check charging system |
| 1246 | O,C,R | Generator load input failed, check charging system |
| 1260 | O,C,R | Theft detected vehicle immobilized |
| 1270 | O,C,R | Engine RPM vehicle speed limiter |
| 1285 | O,C,R | Cylinder head over temperature sensed |
| 1288 | O,C,R | Cylinder head temperature sensor circuit out of self test range |
| 1289 | O,C,R | Cylinder head temperature sensor circuit high input |
| 1290 | O,C,R | Cylinder head temperature sensor circuit low input |
| 1299 | O,C,R | Cylinder head over temperature protection active |
| 1309 | O,C,R | Misfire monitor disabled |
| 1400 | O,C,R | DPF-EGR sensor circuit low voltage, check EGR circuits for shorts, opens and grounds |
| 1401 | O,C,R | DPF-EGR sensor circuit high voltage, check EGR circuits for shorts, opens and grounds |
| 1405 | O,C,R | DPF-EGR sensor upstream hose off or plugged |
| 1406 | O,C,R | DPF-EGR sensor downstream hose off or plugged |
| 1408 | O,C,R | EGR flow out of self test range |
| 1409 | O,C,R | EGR vacuum regulator solenoid circuit malfunction |
| 1411 | O,C,R | Secondary Air Injection system downstream flow |
| 1413 | O,C,R | Secondary Air Injection system monitor circuit high |

\* O = Key On, Engine Off;  C = Continuous Memory;  R = Engine Running
\*\* 1995 and later models

## 3 and 4 Digit Trouble Codes (continued)

➡Note: These codes may be preceded by the letter and number PO for 3 digit codes or just the letter P for 4 digit codes.

| Code | Test Condition* | Probable Cause |
|------|-----------------|----------------|
| 1414 | O,C,R | Secondary Air Injection system monitor circuit low |
| 1443 | O,C,R | EVAP control system canister purge valve malfunction |
| 1450 | O,C,R | Unable to bleed up fuel tank vacuum |
| 1451 | O,C,R | EVAP control system canister vent solenoid circuit malfunction |
| 1460 | O,C,R | Wide Open Throttle A/C cutout primary circuit malfunction |
| 1461 | O,C,R | Air Conditioning pressure sensor (ACP) high voltage |
| 1462 | O,C,R | Air Conditioning pressure sensor (ACP) low voltage |
| 1463 | O,C,R | Air Conditioning pressure sensor (ACP) insufficient pressure change |
| 1464 | O,C,R | A/C demand out of self test range |
| 1469 | O,C,R | Low A/C cycling period |
| 1500 | O,C,R | Vehicle speed sensor intermittent (VSS) |
| 1501 | O,C,R | Vehicle speed sensor (VSS) out of self test range |
| 1502 | O,C,R | Vehicle speed sensor intermittent (VSS) |
| 1504 | O,C,R | Idle Air Control (IAC) circuit malfunction |
| 1506 | O,C,R | Idle Air Control (IAC) overspeed error |
| 1507 | O,C,R | Idle Air Control (IAC) underspeed error |
| 1550 | O,C,R | Power steering pressure (PSP) sensor malfunction |
| 1605 | O,C,R | Keep Alive Memory test failure |
| 1633 | O,C,R | Keep Alive power voltage too low |
| 1635 | O,C,R | Tire/Axle ratio out of acceptable range |
| 1650 | O,C,R | Power steering pressure (PSP) switch malfunction |
| 1651 | O,C,R | Power steering pressure (PSP) switch signal malfunction |
| 1705 | O,C,R | Transmission range sensor out of self test range |
| 1709 | O,C,R | Park/Neutral switch out of self test range |
| 1780 | O,C,R | Transmission control switch out of self test range |
| 1900 | O,C,R | Output shaft speed sensor circuit intermittent failure |

\* *O = Key On, Engine Off;  C = Continuous Memory;  R = Engine Running*
\*\* *1995 and later models*

## 3  Powertrain Control Module (PCM)

▸ Refer to illustrations 3.3, 3.4 and 3.5

1  The Powertrain Control Module (PCM) is located inside the passenger compartment under the driver's side dashboard, tucked into the corner. The retaining bracket and bolts must be removed from the engine compartment and the module must be removed inside the driver's compartment. The PCM is easily distinguished by the aluminum casing surrounding the module.

2  Disconnect the negative battery cable from the battery.

### ✷✷ WARNING:

**Some models have airbags. Always disconnect the negative battery cable, then the positive battery cable and wait 2 minutes before working in the vicinity of the impact sensors, steering column or instrument panel to avoid the possibility of accidental deployment of the airbag, which could cause personal injury (see Chapter 12).**

**3.3 Working in the engine compartment, remove the bolt that retains the electrical connector to the PCM**

**3.4 Remove the nuts (arrows) from the PCM brackets**

**3.5 Remove the PCM from under the dash area on the driver's side**

3  Working in the engine compartment, remove the bolt that retains the electrical connector to the PCM (see illustration).

## ☀☀ CAUTION:

The ignition switch must be turned OFF when pulling out or plugging in the electrical connectors to prevent damage to the PCM.

4  Remove the retaining nuts (see illustration) from the PCM studs.
5  Working inside the driver's compartment, carefully slide the PCM out far enough to clear the kick panel (see illustration).

➡ Note: Avoid any static electricity damage to the computer by using gloves and a special anti-static pad to store the PCM on once it is removed.

## 4   Information sensors

### ENGINE COOLANT TEMPERATURE SENSOR

➡ Note: The check procedure applies only to 1994 and earlier models. The OBD-II system on 1995 and later models requires special diagnostic tools.

▸ Refer to illustrations 4.2, 4.3 and 4.4

#### General description

1  The coolant sensor is a thermistor (a resistor which varies the value of its voltage output in accordance with temperature changes). The change in the resistance values will directly affect the voltage signal from the coolant sensor. As the sensor temperature DECREASES, the resistance values will INCREASE. As the sensor temperature INCREASES, the resistance values will DECREASE. A failure in the coolant sensor circuit should set a trouble code. These codes indicate a failure in the coolant temperature circuit, so in most cases the appropriate solution to the problem will be either repair of a wire or replacement of the sensor.

#### Check

2  Check the resistance value of the coolant temperature sensor while it is completely cold (50 to 65-degrees F = 58,750 to 40,500 ohms). Next, start the engine and warm it up until it reaches operating temperature (see illustration). The resistance should be lower (180 to 220-degrees F = 3,600 to 1,840 ohms).

**4.2 Check the resistance of the coolant temperature sensor with the engine completely cold and then with the engine at operating temperature. Resistance should decrease as temperature increases.**

➡ Note: Access to the coolant temperature sensor makes it difficult to position electrical probes on the terminals. If necessary, remove the sensor and perform the tests in a pan of heated water to simulate the conditions.

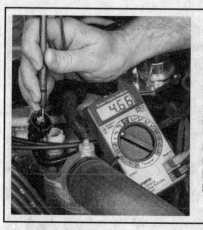

4.3 Working on the harness side, check the voltage from the PCM to the coolant temperature sensor with the ignition key ON and the engine not running. It should be approximately 5.0 volts

4.4 To prevent leakage, wrap the threads of the coolant temperature sensor with Teflon tape before installing it

3   If the resistance values on the sensor are correct, check the signal voltage to the sensor from the PCM (see illustration). It should be approximately 5.0 volts.

### Replacement

4   Before installing the new sensor, wrap the threads with Teflon sealing tape to prevent leakage and thread corrosion (see illustration).

5   To remove the sensor, unplug the electrical connector, then carefully unscrew it.

### ✳✳ CAUTION:

Handle the coolant sensor with care. Damage to this sensor will affect the operation of the entire fuel injection system. Install the sensor and tighten it securely.

## MANIFOLD ABSOLUTE PRESSURE (MAP) SENSOR

➡Note: The check procedure applies only to 1994 and earlier models. The OBD-II system on 1995 and later models requires special diagnostic tools.

▸ Refer to illustration 4.9

### General description

6   The Manifold Absolute Pressure (MAP) sensor monitors the intake manifold pressure changes resulting from changes in engine load and speed and converts the information into a voltage output. The PCM uses the MAP sensor to control fuel delivery and ignition timing. The PCM will receive information as a frequency generated voltage signal. This signal can be detected using a tachometer. The frequency will vary from 200 "rpm" at closed throttle (high vacuum) to 310 "rpm" at wide open throttle (low vacuum).

7   A failure in the MAP sensor circuit should set a trouble code.

### Check

8   Disconnect the electrical connector from the MAP sensor. Using a voltmeter, check for reference voltage to the MAP sensor on the VREF wire (see illustration 4.9). With the ignition key ON (engine not running), the reference voltage should be approximately 4.0 to 6.0 volts.

9   Connect the electrical connector to the MAP sensor and back-probe the harness with a tachometer. With the ignition key ON (engine not running) check the signal from the MAP/BP Signal wire (middle terminal) to the signal return wire (ground) (see illustration). Install a tachometer to the signal wire and set the meter to the six-cylinder scale.

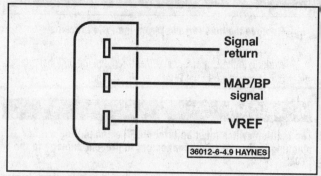

Signal return

MAP/BP signal

VREF

36012-6-4.9 HAYNES

4.9  Using a tachometer set on the 6-cylinder scale, probe the backside of the MAP electrical sensor MAP/BP SIGNAL wire and SIGNAL RETURN (ground wire) and check for a frequency voltage. It should be between 300 and 320 rpm with no vacuum, depending on the altitude. It is possible to place the negative probe of the voltmeter onto another more convenient ground (valve cover bolt). Now apply a vacuum of 20 in-Hg. and confirm that the reading decreases to 200 to 230 rpm. There should be a smooth transition between the readings

10  Use a hand-held vacuum pump and apply 10 in-Hg of vacuum to the MAP sensor and observe the tachometer readings. Without vacuum, the tachometer should read approximately 310 rpm. With 20 in-Hg of vacuum applied, the tachometer should read about 200 rpm. Look for a smooth transition between these two readings.

11  If the test results are incorrect, replace the MAP sensor.

## OXYGEN SENSOR

➡Note: The check procedure applies only to 1994 and earlier models. The OBD-II system on 1995 and later models requires special diagnostic tools.

▸ Refer to illustrations 4.14 and 4.16

### General description and check

12  The heated oxygen sensors (HEGO), which are located in the exhaust manifolds, monitor the oxygen content of the exhaust gas stream. The oxygen content in the exhaust reacts with the oxygen sensor to produce a voltage output which varies from 0.1-volt (high oxygen, lean mixture) to 0.9-volts (low oxygen, rich mixture). The PCM constantly monitors this variable voltage output to determine the ratio of oxygen to fuel in the mixture. The PCM alters the air/fuel mixture ratio by controlling the pulse width (open time) of the fuel injectors.

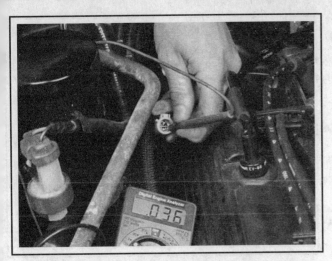

4.14 The oxygen sensor creates a very small voltage signal when the sensor is warmed up. A quick oxygen sensor check is to immediately disconnect the sensor connector when it is warmed up and probe the signal wire (sensor side of connector) and check for a millivolt reading.

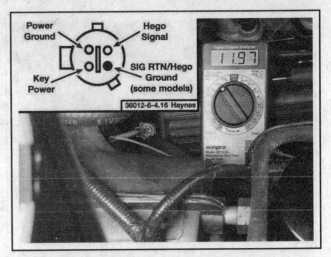

4.16 Working on the harness side, probe the electrical connector with key power ON and check for reference voltage. It should be approximately 12.0 volts with the ignition key on and the engine not running

A mixture ratio of 14.7 parts air to 1 part fuel is the ideal mixture ratio for minimizing exhaust emissions, thus allowing the catalytic converter to operate at maximum efficiency. It is this ratio of 14.7 to 1 which the PCM and the oxygen sensor attempt to maintain at all times.

13 The oxygen sensor produces no voltage when it is below its normal operating temperature of about 600-degrees F. During this initial period before warm-up, the PCM operates in open loop mode.

14 Allow the engine to reach normal operating temperature and check that the oxygen sensor is producing a steady signal voltage between 0.35 and 0.55-volts (see illustration).

15 A delay of two minutes or more between engine start-up and normal operation of the sensor, followed by a low or a high voltage signal or a short in the sensor circuit, will cause the PCM to also set a code. Codes that indicate problems in the oxygen sensor system are 41, 42, 91 and 92 for the two digit code system.

16 Also check to make sure the oxygen sensor heater(s) is supplied with battery voltage (see illustration).

17 When any of the above codes occur, the PCM operates in the open loop mode - that is, it controls fuel delivery in accordance with a programmed default value instead of feedback information from the oxygen sensor.

18 The proper operation of the oxygen sensor depends on four conditions:

a) *Electrical - The low voltages generated by the sensor depend upon good, clean connections which should be checked whenever a malfunction of the sensor is suspected or indicated.*

b) *Outside air supply - The sensor is designed to allow air circulation to the internal portion of the sensor. Whenever the sensor is removed and installed or replaced, make sure the air passages are not restricted.*

c) *Proper operating temperature - The PCM will not react to the sensor signal until the sensor reaches approximately 600-degrees F. This factor must be taken into consideration when evaluating the performance of the sensor.*

d) *Unleaded fuel - The use of unleaded fuel is essential for proper operation of the sensor. Make sure the fuel you are using is of this type.*

19 In addition to observing the above conditions, special care must be taken whenever the sensor is serviced.

a) *The oxygen sensor has a permanently attached pigtail and electrical connector which should not be removed from the sensor. Damage or removal of the pigtail or electrical connector can adversely affect operation of the sensor.*

b) *Grease, dirt and other contaminants should be kept away from the electrical connector and the louvered end of the sensor.*

c) *Do not use cleaning solvents of any kind on the oxygen sensor.*

d) *Do not drop or roughly handle the sensor.*

e) *The silicone boot must be installed in the correct position to prevent the boot from being melted and to allow the sensor to operate properly.*

## Replacement

➡Note: Because it is installed in the exhaust manifold or pipe, which contracts when cool, the oxygen sensor may be very difficult to loosen when the engine is cold. Rather than risk damage to the sensor (assuming you are planning to reuse it in another manifold or pipe), start and run the engine for a minute or two, then shut it off. Be careful not to burn yourself during the following procedure.

20 Disconnect the cable from the negative terminal of the battery.

21 Raise the vehicle and place it securely on jackstands.

22 Carefully disconnect the electrical connector from the sensor.

23 Carefully unscrew the sensor from the exhaust manifold.

**✷✷ CAUTION:**

**Excessive force may damage the threads.**

24 Anti-seize compound must be used on the threads of the sensor to facilitate future removal. The threads of new sensors will already be coated with this compound, but if an old sensor is removed and reinstalled, recoat the threads.

25 Install the sensor and tighten it securely.

26 Reconnect the electrical connector of the pigtail lead to the main engine wiring harness.

27 Lower the vehicle and reconnect the cable to the negative terminal of the battery.

**4.31 Check the reference voltage to the TPS with a voltmeter. Backprobe terminal VOLT REF with the positive (+) probe of the voltmeter and make sure the reference voltage is approximately 5.0 volts**

## THROTTLE POSITION SENSOR (TPS)

➡Note: The check procedure applies only to 1994 and earlier models. The OBD-II system on 1995 and later models requires special diagnostic tools.

### General description

♦ Refer to illustrations 4.31, 4.32 and 4.33

28 The Throttle Position Sensor (TPS) is located on the end of the throttle shaft on the throttle body. By monitoring the output voltage from the TPS, the PCM can determine fuel delivery based on throttle valve angle (driver demand). A broken or loose TPS can cause intermittent bursts of fuel from the injector and an unstable idle because the PCM thinks the throttle is moving. Any problems in the TPS or circuit will set a trouble code.

### Check

29 To check the TPS, turn the ignition switch to ON (engine not running) and install the probes of the voltmeter into the ground wire and

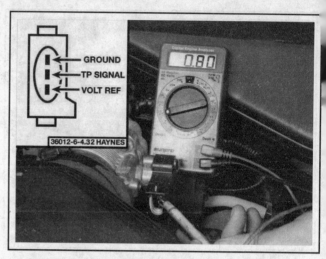

**4.32 Use sharp-tipped electrical probes on TPS terminals GROUND and TP SIGNAL and, with the throttle completely closed, check the resistance of the sensor. It should be 0.8 to 1.0 ohm**

signal wire on the backside of the electrical connector. This test checks for the proper signal voltage from the TPS.

➡Note: Be careful when backprobing the electrical connector. Do not damage the wiring harness or pull on any connectors to make clean contact. Be sure the probes are placed in the correct position by referring to illustration 4.32.

30 The sensor should read 0.50 to 1.0-volt at idle. Have an assistant depress the accelerator pedal to simulate full throttle and the sensor should increase voltage to 4.0 to 5.0-volts. If the TPS voltage readings are incorrect, replace it with a new unit.

31 Also, check the TPS reference voltage. With the ignition key ON (engine not running), install the positive (+) probe of the voltmeter (see illustration) onto the voltage reference wire. There should be approximately 5.0 volts sent from the PCM to the TPS.

32 Also, check the resistance of the potentiometer within the TPS. Disconnect the TPS electrical connector and working on the sensor side, connect the probes of the ohmmeter onto the ground wire and the TPS signal wire. With the throttle valve fully closed, the TPS should read between 0.8 and 1.0 ohm (see illustration)

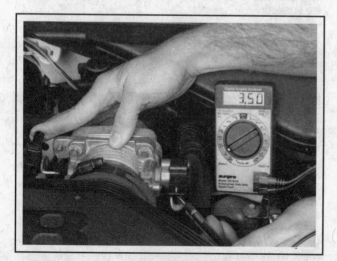

**4.33 The resistance should INCREASE to approximately 3.5 K-ohms with the throttle completely open**

**4.34 Remove the two screws (arrows) from the TPS and separate it from the throttle body**

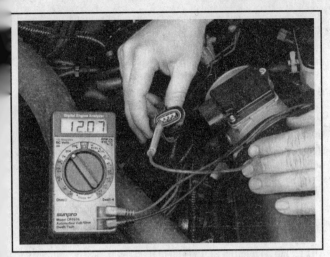

**4.37 Probe the VPWR terminal on the harness side of the MAF sensor and check for battery voltage to the MAF sensor**

33 Now open the throttle with one hand (see illustration) and check the resistance again. Slowly advance the throttle until fully open. The resistance should be approximately 3.0 to 4.0 K-ohms. The potentiometer should exhibit a smooth change in resistance as it travels from fully closed to wide open throttle. Any deviations indicate a possible worn or damaged TPS.

## Replacement

▶ Refer to illustration 4.34

34 The TPS is a non-adjustable unit. Remove the two retaining screws (see illustration) and separate the TPS from the throttle body.
35 Installation is the reverse of removal.

## MASS AIRFLOW SENSOR (MAF)

➡Note: The check procedure applies only to 1994 and earlier models. The OBD-II system on 1995 and later models requires special diagnostic tools.

### General Information

▶ Refer to illustrations 4.37, 4.38a, 4.38b and 4.44

36 The Mass Airflow Sensor (MAF) is located on the air intake duct. This sensor uses a hot wire sensing element to measure the amount of air entering the engine. The air passing over the hot wire causes it to cool. Consequently, this change in temperature can be converted into an analog voltage signal to the PCM which in turn calculates the required fuel injector pulse width.

### Check

37 Check for power to the MAF sensor. Disconnect the MAF sensor electrical connector, work on the harness side and probe the connector to check for battery voltage (see illustration). Use the VPWR terminal indicated in illustration 4.38a and 4.38b.
38 Reconnect the electrical connector and backprobe the MAF SIGNAL and MAF SIG RTN (see illustration) with the voltmeter and check for the voltage. The voltage should be 0.2 to 1.5 volts at idle.
39 Raise the engine rpm. The signal voltage from the MAF sensor should increase to about 2.0 volts at 60 mph. It is impossible to simulate these conditions in the driveway at home but it is necessary to

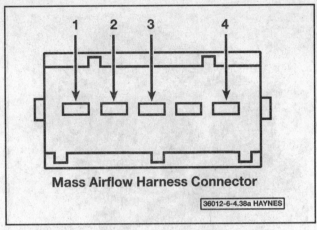

**Mass Airflow Harness Connector**

**4.38a Use a voltmeter and probe MAF SIGNAL and MAF SIG RTN for signal voltage (0.2 to 1.5 volts at idle) (5.0L engine shown)**

| 1 | MAF SIGNAL | 3 | GROUND |
| 2 | MAF SIGNAL RTN | 4 | VPWR |

observe the voltmeter for a fluctuation in voltage as the engine speed is raised. The vehicle will not be under load conditions but it should manage to vary slightly.
40 Disconnect the MAF harness connector and use an ohmmeter and probe the terminals MAF SIGNAL and MAF SIG RTN. If the hot wire element inside the sensor has been damaged it will be indicated by an open circuit (infinite resistance).
41 If the voltage readings are correct, check the wiring harness for open circuits or a damaged harness (see Chapter 12).

### Replacement

42 Disconnect the electrical connector from the MAF sensor.
43 Remove the upper section of the air cleaner assembly (see Chapter 4).
44 Remove the four bolts (see illustration) and lift the MAF sensor from the engine compartment.
45 Installation is the reverse of removal.

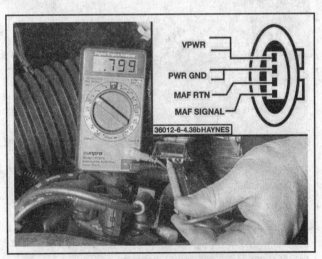

**4.38b Use a voltmeter and probe MAF SIGNAL and MAF SIG RTN for signal voltage (0.2 to 1.5 volts at idle) (4.6L engine shown)**

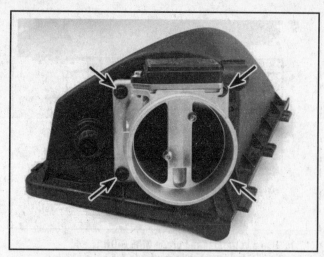

**4.44 Remove the four bolts (arrows) and separate the MAF sensor from the air cleaner housing**

## MANUAL LEVER POSITION (MLP) SENSOR

### General description

▶ Refer to illustration 4.48

➡**Note: The manual lever position (MLP) sensor has been renamed to the Transmission Range (TR) sensor on 1995 and later models. The TR sensor operates exactly the same as the MPL sensor - only the name has been changed.**

46 The Manual Lever Position (MLP) sensor located on the transmission indicates to the PCM when the transmission is in Park, Neutral, Drive or Reverse. This information is used for starting, Transmission Converter Clutch (TCC), Exhaust Gas Recirculation (EGR) and Idle Speed Control (ISC) valve operation. For example, if the signal wire(s) become grounded, it may be difficult to start the engine in Park or Neutral. A problem with the Manual Lever Position (MLP) sensor should set a trouble code.

47 In the event there is a problem with the Manual Lever Position

(MLP) sensor, first check the terminal connectors for proper attachment.

48 Use a voltmeter and with the ignition key ON (engine not running), check for power to each of the signal wires (see illustration) of the switch. There should be voltage present.

49 Check the adjustment of the switch (see Chapter 7). If the switch is out of adjustment, perform the procedure and clear the codes. Recheck the system for any other problems.

50 Any further diagnostics of the Manual Lever Position (MLP) sensor must be performed by a dealer service department or other repair shop because this system requires a special SCAN tool to access the working parameters from the PCM.

### Adjustment

51 To adjust the Manual Lever Position (MLP) sensor or to replace the switch, refer to Chapter 7.

## AIR CONDITIONING CLUTCH CONTROL

▶ Refer to illustration 4.54

➡**Note: Refer to Chapter 12, Section 6 for additional information on the location of the relays.**

52 During air conditioning operation, the PCM controls the application of the air conditioning compressor clutch. The PCM controls the air conditioning clutch control relay to delay clutch engagement after the air conditioning is turned ON to allow the BPA-ISC valve to adjust the idle speed of the engine to compensate for the additional load. The PCM also controls the relay to disengage the clutch in the event of an excessively high or low pressure within the system or an overheating problem.

53 In most cases, if the air conditioning does not function, the problem is probably related to the air conditioning system relays and switches and not the PCM.

54 To determine if a defective relay is the cause of the system not working, remove it and bridge the battery feed and compressor clutch terminals (see illustration). If the clutch engages, replace the relay.

55 If the air conditioning is operating properly and idle is too low when the air conditioning compressor turns on or is too high when the air conditioning compressor turns off, check for an open circuit between the air conditioning control relay and the PCM.

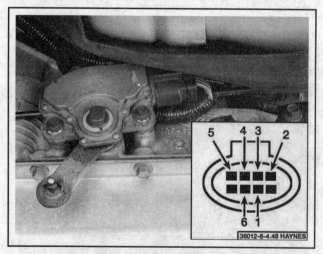

**4.48 Manual Lever Position (MLP) sensor terminal designations (1994 and earlier models)**

| | | | |
|---|---|---|---|
| 1 | PCM signal return | 4 | Accessory feed |
| 2 | Start | 5 | Start |
| 3 | Back-up lamps | 6 | Sensor signal to PCM |

**4.54 An easy check to find out if the air conditioning compressor clutch is working is to remove the air conditioning relay (near fuel pump relay and power relay) and install a jumper wire from the battery (+) supply to the compressor clutch wire**

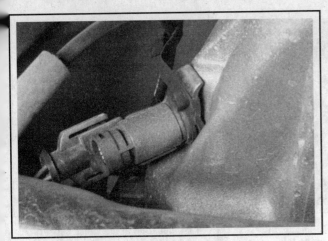

**4.56 Location of the vehicle speed sensor on the transmission**

## VEHICLE SPEED SENSOR (VSS)

▶ Refer to illustration 4.56

### General description

56 The Vehicle Speed Sensor (VSS) is located near the rear section of the transmission (see illustration). This sensor is a permanent magnetic variable reluctance sensor that produces a pulsing voltage whenever vehicle speed is over 3 mph. These pulses are translated by the PCM and provided for other systems for fuel and transmission shift control. The VSS is part of the Transmission Converter Clutch (TCC) system. Any problems with the VSS will usually set a trouble code.

### Check

57 To check the vehicle speed sensor, remove the electrical connector in the wiring harness near the sensor. Using a voltmeter, check for signal voltage to the sensor. The signal wire should have 10 volts or more available. If there is no voltage available, have the PCM diagnosed by a dealer service department or other qualified repair shop.

### Replacement

58 To replace the VSS, disconnect the electrical connector from the VSS.
59 Remove the retaining bolt and lift the VSS from the transmission.
60 Installation is the reverse of removal.

## INTAKE AIR TEMPERATURE (IAT) SENSOR

➡ Note: The check procedure applies only to 1994 and earlier models. The OBD-II system on 1995 and later models requires special diagnostic tools.

▶ Refer to illustration 4.65

### General description

61 The Intake Air Temperature (IAT) sensor is located inside the air intake duct. This sensor acts as a resistor which changes value according to the temperature of the air entering the engine. Low temperatures produce a high resistance value (for example, at 68 degrees F the resistance is 27.30K ohms) while high temperatures produce low resistance values (at 212-degrees F the resistance is 2.07K ohms). The PCM supplies approximately 5-volts (reference voltage) to the IAT sensor. The voltage will change according to the temperature of the incoming air.

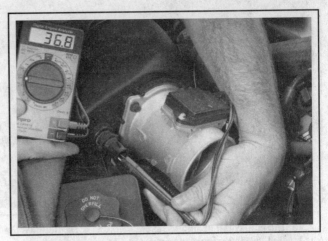

**4.65 Remove the electrical connector from the IAT sensor (located in air cleaner housing), then check the resistance of the IAT sensor cold and warm. It may be necessary to use simulated conditions to obtain accurate results**

The voltage will be high when the air temperature is cold and low when the air temperature is warm. Any problems with the IAT sensor will usually set a trouble code.

### Check

62 To check the IAT sensor, disconnect the two prong electrical connector and turn the ignition key ON but do not start the engine.
63 Measure the voltage (reference voltage). The VOM should read approximately 5-volts.
64 If the voltage signal is not correct, have the PCM diagnosed by a dealer service department or other repair shop.
65 Measure the resistance across the sensor terminals (see illustration). The resistance should be HIGH when the air temperature is LOW. Next, start the engine and let it idle (cold). Wait awhile and let the engine reach operating temperature. Turn the ignition OFF, disconnect the IAT sensor and measure the resistance across the terminals. The resistance should be LOW when the air temperature is HIGH. If the sensor does not exhibit this change in resistance, replace it with a new part.

## POWER STEERING PRESSURE SWITCH

▶ Refer to illustration 4.66

66 Turning the steering wheel increases power steering fluid pressure and engine load. The pressure switch (see illustration) will close

**4.66 The power steering pressure switch (arrow) is located under the power steering pump**

4.70  The crankshaft position sensor is located on the timing chain cover (4.6L engine)

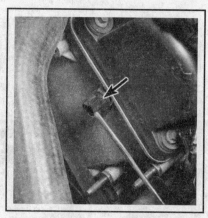

4.75  Remove the camshaft position sensor from the front of the left (driver's side) cylinder head

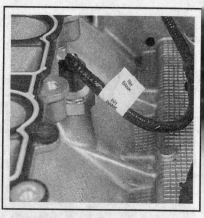

4.84  Location of the knock sensor used on later 4.6L engines

before the load can cause an idle problem. A problem in the power steering pressure switch circuit will set a trouble code.

67  A pressure switch that will not open or an open circuit from the PCM will cause timing to retard at idle and this will affect idle quality.

68  A pressure switch that will not close or an open circuit may cause the engine to die when the power steering system is used heavily.

69  Any problems with the power steering pressure switch or circuit should be repaired by a dealer service department or other qualified repair shop.

## CRANKSHAFT POSITION SENSOR

▶ **Refer to illustration 4.70**

### General information

70  The crankshaft position sensor (see illustration) defines the engine position to the PCM. A crankshaft position pulse occurs at each TDC.

### Check

71  Any problems with the crankshaft position sensor should be diagnosed by a dealer service department or other qualified repair shop.

### Replacement

➡**Note: On 2003 and later models, move the air conditioning compressor away from the engine about an inch or more for clearance to remove the crankshaft position sensor.**

72  Remove the electrical connector and the retaining bolt and lift the assembly from the engine block.

73  Installation is the reverse of removal.

## CAMSHAFT POSITION SENSOR

### General information

74  The camshaft position sensor is a variable reluctance sensor triggered by the high point mark on the camshaft sprocket. Any diagnostic work should be performed by a dealer service department or other repair shop.

### Replacement

▶ **Refer to illustration 4.75**

75  Remove the retaining screw and separate the camshaft sensor from the cylinder head (see illustration).

76  Installation is the reverse of removal.

## BRAKE ON/OFF (BOO) SWITCH

➡**Note: The check procedure applies only to 1994 and earlier models. The OBD-II system on 1995 and later models requires special diagnostic tools.**

### General information

77  The brake On/Off switch (BOO) tells the PCM when the brakes are being applied. The switch closes when brakes are applied and opens when the brakes are released. The BOO switch is located on the brake pedal assembly.

78  The brake light circuit and bulbs are wired into the BOO circuit so it is important in diagnosing any driveability problems to make sure all the brake light bulbs are working properly (not burned out) or the driver may feel poor idle quality.

### Check

79  Disconnect the electrical connector from the BOO switch and using a 12 volt test light, check for battery voltage to the BOO switch.

80  Also, check continuity from the BOO switch to the brake light bulbs. Change any burned out bulbs or damaged wire looms.

### Replacement

81  Refer to Chapter 9, Section 15 for the replacement procedure

## KNOCK SENSOR

▶ **Refer to illustration 4.84**

### General information

82  The knock sensor is used by the PCM to detect engine spark knock and adjust timing accordingly.
The knock sensor is located under the intake manifold.

### Check

83  Any problems with the Knock sensor should be diagnosed by a dealer service department or other qualified repair shop.

### Replacement

84  Remove the Intake manifold (see Chapter 2B). Remove the Knock sensor electrical connector and the retaining nut, then remove the sensor from the engine block (see illustration).

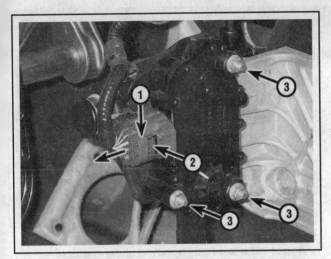

4.91 To remove the Electronic Throttle Control (ETC) module (the "pedal and sensor assembly"), slide the lock (1) away from the electrical connector, depress the release tabs (2) and pull off the connector, then remove these three nuts (3) and bolts and remove the ETC module and accelerator pedal as a single assembly (no further disassembly is possible)

85 Installation is the reverse of removal. Torque the sensor to 15 to 22 ft-lbs.

## CYLINDER HEAD TEMPERATURE SENSOR (CHT)

### General information

86 The Cylinder Head Temperature sensor, located in the left cylinder bank, provides the PCM with cylinder head temperature. The sensor once removed, should not be reused and must be replaced.

### Check

87 Any problems with the CHT sensor should be diagnosed by a dealer service department or other qualified repair shop.

### Replacement

88 Remove the intake manifold (see Chapter 2B). Disconnect the CHT electrical connector and unscrew the sensor.

Installation is the reverse of removal. Torque the sensor to 19 to 22 ft-lbs.

## ACCELERATOR PEDAL POSITION SENSORS (APPS)

➡Note: The APPS are located on the right side of the upper end of the accelerator pedal, where they're housed inside the Electronic Throttle Control (ETC) module, which is an integral component of the accelerator pedal. If the APPS must be replaced, you must replace the accelerator "pedal and sensor assembly" (the manufacturer's term for this assembly).

### Replacement

◗ Refer to illustration 4.91

89 Disconnect the cable from the negative battery terminal (see Chapter 5).

90 Remove the knee bolster (see Chapter 11).

91 Disconnect the electrical connector from the ETC module (see illustration).

92 Remove the ETC module mounting nuts and bolts, then remove

4.96 To detach the FRPT sensor from the fuel rail, depress this release tab (1) and disconnect the electrical connector, then disconnect the vacuum hose (2) from the sensor and remove the sensor mounting bolts (3)

4.99 Remove the old O-rings from the FRPT sensor and replace them with new ones

the ETC module and accelerator pedal (the "pedal and sensor assembly") from the rest of the accelerator pedal assembly.

93 Installation is the reverse of removal.

## FUEL RAIL PRESSURE TEMPERATURE (FRPT) SENSOR

### Replacement

◗ Refer to illustrations 4.96 and 4.99

94 Relieve the fuel pressure in the fuel system (see Chapter 4).

95 Disconnect the cable from the negative battery terminal (see Chapter 5).

96 Disconnect the electrical connector from the FRPT sensor (see illustration).

97 Disconnect the vacuum hose from the IPR/FRPT sensor.

98 Remove the FRPT sensor mounting bolts and remove the sensor from the fuel rail.

99 Remove the old O-ring from the FRPT sensor (see illustration).

100 Carefully clean off the mating surfaces of the FRPT sensor and the fuel rail and install a new O-ring on the FRPT sensor.

101 Installation is the reverse of removal. When you're done start the engine and check for fuel leaks in the vicinity of the FRPT sensor.

## 5  Fuel Pump Driver Module (FPDM) - replacement

♦ Refer to illustration 5.3

**✳✳ WARNING 1:**

On models with air suspension, turn the air suspension switch to Off before raising the vehicle.

**✳✳ WARNING 2:**

On models with a fire suppression system, disable the system before raising the rear of the vehicle by disconnecting the cable from the negative battery terminal and waiting at least three minutes.

➡**Note:** The fuel pump driver is built internal to the PCM on 2003 and 2004 models. 2005 and 2006 models are equipped with an externally mounted driver module termed the Fuel Pump Driver Module (FPDM). The FPDM is located underneath the vehicle, just in front of the trunk area or behind the luggage compartment panel shelf trim panel.

## 2005 THROUGH 2007 MODELS

1   Raise the rear of the vehicle and place it securely on jackstands.
2   Remove the splash shield from under the vehicle.
3   Disconnect the electrical connector from the FPDM (see illustration).
4   Remove the FPDM mounting bolts and remove the FPDM.

5.3  To remove the Fuel Pump Driver Module (FPDM), depress this release tab (1) and pull off the electrical connector, then remove the FPDM mounting bolts (2) and remove the FPDM

5   Installation is the reverse of removal.

## 2008 AND LATER MODELS

6   Open the trunk, remove the three pin retainers from the parcel shelf trim panel at the rear section and lift the trim panel from the trunk.
7   Disconnect the FPDM electrical connector, remove the mounting bolts and lift the FPDM from the trunk.
8   Installation is the reverse of removal.

## 6  Exhaust Gas Recirculation (EGR) system

➡**Note:** The EGR system on 2002 and later models is complex and cannot be diagnosed without the use of specialized scan tools and other diagnostic equipment. Have the EGR system checked by a dealer service department or other qualified automotive repair facility.

## GENERAL DESCRIPTION

♦ Refer to illustrations 6.2a, 6.2b and 6.2c

1   The EGR system is used to lower NOx (oxides of nitrogen) emission levels caused by high combustion temperatures. The EGR recirculates a small amount of exhaust gases into the intake manifold. The additional mixture lowers the temperature of combustion thereby reducing the formation of NOx compounds.
2   These vehicles are equipped with two different systems:

a)  *5.0L engines are equipped with the Electronic Exhaust Gas Recirculation (EEGR) system. This system relies upon the PCM for EGR control. The control module (PCM) calculates the desired flow of exhaust gases into the combustion chamber and subsequently controls the EGR valve position with the EGR vacuum regulator. The EGR Valve Position (EVP) sensor detects the exact position of the EGR valve pintle and relays the information to the PCM. The PCM in turn, uses this information to regulate the duty cycle (On/Off time) of the EGR vacuum regulator. A duty cycle of 50-percent would hold the EGR valve half way open. The EEGR system uses "electronic" components to control the EGR valve.*

b)  *4.6L engines are equipped with the Pressure Feedback EGR (PFE) system (see illustration). This system controls the EGR flow rate by monitoring the pressure drop across a remotely located sharp-edged orifice. This system uses a pressure transducer to receive pressure (feedback) and then vary the vacuum to the EGR vacuum regulator and consequently the EGR valve. This type of system serves only as a pressure regulator rather than a flow metering device. Some models are equipped with a Differential Pressure Feedback EGR (DPFE) system (see illustration). This operates in the same way as the PFE except it monitors the pressure drop across the orifice allowing for a more precise measurement of the exhaust gas pressures.*

## CHECK

3   Too much EGR flow tends to weaken combustion, causing the engine to run rough or stop. When EGR flow is excessive, the engine can stop after a cold start or at idle after deceleration, the vehicle can surge at cruising speeds or the idle may be rough. If the EGR valve remains constantly open, the engine may not idle at all.
4   Too little or no EGR flow allows combustion temperatures to get too high during acceleration and load conditions. This can cause spark knock (detonation), engine overheating or emission test failure.
5   The following checks will help you pinpoint problems in the EGR system. Where the procedure says to lift up on the EGR valve diaphragm, it's a good idea to wear a heat-resistant glove to prevent burns.

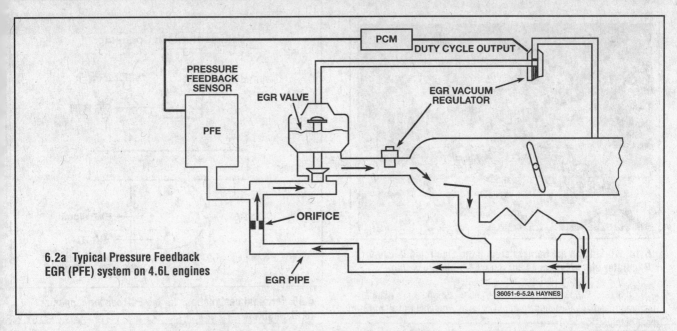

6.2a  Typical Pressure Feedback
EGR (PFE) system on 4.6L engines

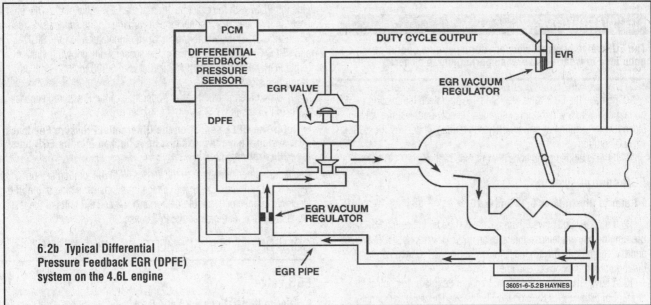

6.2b  Typical Differential
Pressure Feedback EGR (DPFE)
system on the 4.6L engine

## EGR valve

▶ Refer to illustration 6.8

6   The EGR valve is controlled by a normally open solenoid which
allows vacuum to pass when energized. The PCM energizes the solenoid to turn on the EGR. The PCM controls the EGR when three conditions are present: engine coolant is above 113-degrees F, the TPS is at
part throttle and the MAF sensor is in its mid-range.

7   Make sure the vacuum hoses are in good condition and hooked
up correctly.

8   To perform a leakage test, hook up a vacuum pump to the EGR
valve (see illustration). Apply a vacuum of 5 to 6 in-Hg to the valve.
The vacuum pump should hold vacuum.

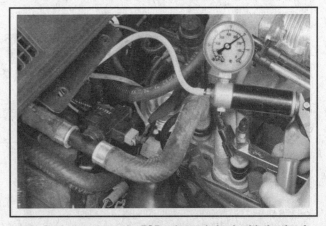

6.8  Apply vacuum to the EGR valve and check with the tip of
your finger for movement of the diaphragm. It should move
smoothly without any binding when vacuum is applied

**6.14 Working on the harness side of the Electronic Vacuum Regulator electrical connector, check for battery voltage**

9  If access is possible, position your finger tip under the vacuum diaphragm and apply vacuum to the EGR valve. You should feel movement of the EGR diaphragm.

### ※※ WARNING:

**The EGR valve becomes very hot during engine operation - it's a good idea to wear a glove when performing this check.**

10  Remove the EGR valve (see Step 19) and clean the inlet and outlet ports with a wire brush or scraper. Do not sandblast the valve or clean it with gasoline or solvents. These liquids will destroy the EGR valve diaphragm.

11  If the specified conditions are not met, replace the EGR valve.

## EGR control system

▶ **Refer to illustrations 6.14 and 6.16**

12  If a code is displayed there are several possibilities for EGR failure. Engine coolant temperature sensor, TPS, MAF sensor, TCC system and the engine rpm govern the parameters the EGR system use for distinguishing the correct ON time.

13  All systems use an Electronic Vacuum Regulator to control the amount of exhaust gas through the EGR valve. The valve is normally open (engine at operating temperature) and the vacuum source is a ported signal. The PCM uses a controlled "pulse width" or electronic signal to turn the EGR ON and OFF (the "duty cycle"). The duty cycle should be zero percent (no EGR) when in Park or Neutral, when the TPS input is below the specified value or when Wide Open Throttle (WOT) is indicated.

14  To check the EGR vacuum regulator, disconnect the electrical connector to the EGR vacuum regulator, turn the ignition key ON (engine not running) and check for battery voltage to the solenoid (see illustration). Battery voltage should be present.

15  Next, use an ohmmeter and check the resistance of the EGR vacuum regulator. It should be between 30 and 70 ohms.

16  On 5.0L engines, check for reference voltage to the sensor. With the ignition key on (engine not running), check for voltage on the harness side of the EVP electrical connector (see illustration) on terminal VREF. It should be between 4.0 and 6.0 volts. If the test results are incorrect, replace the EVP sensor.

17  Also, on 5.0L engines, check the operation of the EGR valve position (EVP) sensor. This sensor is attached to the EGR valve to pro-

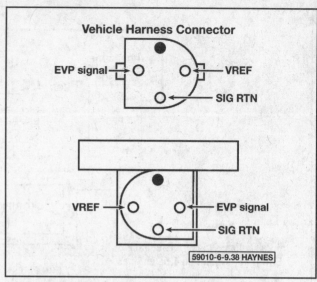

**6.16  Terminal designations for the EVP sensor connector (5.0L engine)**

vide the PCM with the exact position of the EGR valve pintle. Disconnect the EVP electrical connector and working on the sensor side (see illustration 5.16) install the probes of an ohmmeter into EVP SIGNAL and VREF. Check the resistance of the sensor while applying vacuum to the EGR valve. It should fluctuate between 5,500 to 100 ohms as vacuum is slowly applied.

18  On 4.6L engines, check the operation of the Pressure Feedback EGR (PFE) sensor.

➡**Note: The DPFE sensor on the Differential Pressure Feedback EGR systems have two exhaust lines hooked into the EGR tube (see illustration 5.2c).**

Check for reference voltage to the sensor. With the ignition key on (engine not running), check for voltage on the harness side of the PFE electrical connector. It should be between 4.0 and 6.0 volts. If the test results are incorrect, replace the PFE sensor.

## COMPONENT REPLACEMENT

### EGR valve

▶ **Refer to illustrations 6.23 and 6.24**

19  When buying a new EGR valve, make sure that you have the right EGR valve. Use the stamped code located on the top of the EGR valve.

20  Detach the cable from the negative terminal of the battery.

21  Remove the air cleaner housing assembly (see Chapter 4).

22  Detach the vacuum line from the EGR valve.

23  Raise the vehicle and support it securely on jackstands. Remove the EGR pipe from the exhaust manifold (see illustration). Lower the vehicle.

24  On 1996 4.6L engines, remove the mounting bolts securing the EGR valve to the throttle body spacer. On all other 4.6L engines and all 5.0L engines, remove the bolts securing the EGR valve to the intake manifold (see illustration).

25  Remove the EGR valve and gasket from the manifold. Discard the gasket.

26  With a wire wheel, buff the exhaust deposits from the EGR valve mounting surface on the manifold and, if you plan to use the same valve, the mounting surface of the valve itself. Look for exhaust deposits in the valve outlet. Remove deposit build-up with a screwdriver.

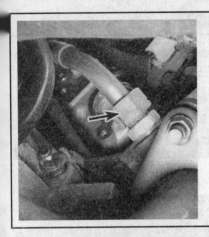

6.23 Unscrew the tube nut (arrow) to detach the EGR pipe from the manifold

6.24 Remove the two bolts (arrows) from the EGR valve (intake manifold removed for clarity)

### ❈❈ CAUTION:

**Never wash the valve in solvents or degreaser - both agents will permanently damage the diaphragm. Sand blasting is also not recommended because it will affect the operation of the valve.**

27  If the EGR passage contains an excessive build-up of deposits, clean it out with a wire wheel. Make sure that all loose particles are completely removed to prevent them from clogging the EGR valve or from being ingested into the engine.

28  Installation is the reverse of removal.

### EGR vacuum regulator

29  Detach the cable from the negative terminal of the battery.

30  Remove the air intake duct from the air cleaner assembly (see Chapter 4).

31  Unplug the electrical connector from the solenoid.

32  Clearly label and detach both vacuum hoses.

33  Remove the solenoid mounting screw and remove the solenoid.

34  Installation is the reverse of removal.

## 7  Evaporative Emissions Control System (EECS)

### ❈❈ WARNING 1:

**On models with air suspension, turn the air suspension switch to Off before raising the vehicle.**

### ❈❈ WARNING 2:

**On models with a fire suppression system, disable the system before raising the rear of the vehicle by disconnecting the cable from the negative battery terminal and waiting at least three minutes.**

➡Note: The EVAP system on 2002 and later models is complex and cannot be diagnosed without the use of a specialized scan tool and other diagnostic equipment. Have the EVAP system checked by a dealer service department or other qualified automotive repair facility.

### GENERAL DESCRIPTION

1  This system is designed to trap and store fuel vapors that evaporate from the fuel tank, throttle body and intake manifold.

2  The Evaporative Emission Control System (EECS) consists of a charcoal-filled canister and the lines connecting the canister to the fuel tank, ported vacuum and intake manifold vacuum.

3  Fuel vapors are transferred from the fuel tank, throttle body and intake manifold to a canister where they are stored when the engine is not operating. When the engine is running, the fuel vapors are purged from the canister by a purge control solenoid which is PCM controlled and consumed in the normal combustion process.

### CHECK

➡Note: 1996 and later models conform to OBD II emission standards. The PCM monitors the Evaporative emission system through a system of solenoids and pressure sensors. If, while retrieving codes, you have a three or four digit code that relates to the Evap system, you should make visual checks for leaks in the system including a loose fuel cap, and a thorough check for good electrical connections. Any further diagnosis will require taking the vehicle to a properly equipped shop.

4  Poor idle, stalling and poor driveability can be caused by an inoperative purge control solenoid, a damaged canister, split or cracked hoses or hoses connected to the wrong tubes.

5  Evidence of fuel loss or fuel odor can be caused by fuel leaking from fuel lines or the TBI, a cracked or damaged canister, an inoperative bowl vent valve, an inoperative purge valve, disconnected, misrouted, kinked, deteriorated or damaged vapor or control hoses or an improperly seated air cleaner or air cleaner gasket.

6  Inspect each hose attached to the canister for kinks, leaks and breaks along its entire length. Repair or replace as necessary.

7  Inspect the canister. If it is cracked or damaged, replace it.

8  Look for fuel leaking from the bottom of the canister. If fuel is leaking, replace the canister and check the hoses and hose routing.

9  Apply a short length of hose to the lower tube of the purge valve assembly and attempt to blow through it. Little or no air should pass into the canister (a small amount of air will pass because the canister has a constant purge hole).

10  With a hand-held vacuum pump, apply vacuum through the control vacuum signal tube near the throttle body to the purge control solenoid diaphragm.

11 If the purge control solenoid does not hold vacuum for at least 20 seconds, the purge control solenoid is leaking and must be replaced.

12 If the diaphragm holds vacuum, apply battery voltage to the purge control solenoid and observe that vacuum (vapors) are allowed to pass through to the intake system.

## COMPONENT REPLACEMENT

13 Clearly label, then detach, all vacuum lines from the canister.

14 Loosen the canister mounting clamp bolt and pull the canister out.

15 Installation is the reverse of removal.

## 8 Positive Crankcase Ventilation (PCV) system

▶ **Refer to illustration 8.1**

1 The Positive Crankcase Ventilation (PCV) system reduces hydrocarbon emissions by scavenging crankcase vapors. It does this by circulating fresh air from the air cleaner through the crankcase, where it mixes with blow-by gases and is then rerouted through a PCV valve to the intake manifold (see illustration).

2 The main components of the PCV system are the PCV valve, a fresh air filtered inlet and the vacuum hoses connecting these two components with the engine and the EECS system.

3 To maintain idle quality, the PCV valve restricts the flow when the intake manifold vacuum is high. If abnormal operating conditions arise, the system is designed to allow excessive amounts of blow-by gases to flow back through the crankcase vent tube into the air cleaner to be consumed by normal combustion.

4 Checking and replacement of the PCV valve and filter is covered in Chapter 1.

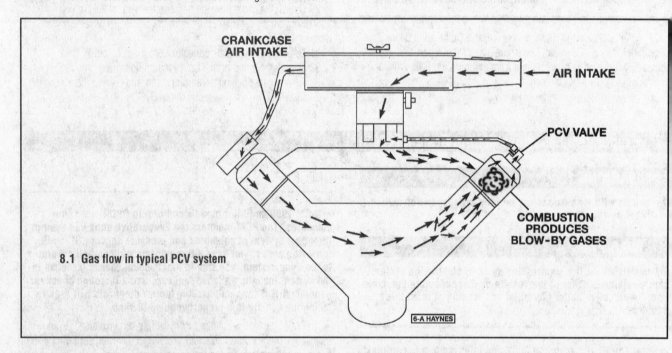

8.1 Gas flow in typical PCV system

## 9 Catalytic converter

### GENERAL DESCRIPTION

1 The catalytic converter is an emission control device added to the exhaust system to reduce pollutants from the exhaust gas stream. A single-bed converter design is used in combination with a three-way (reduction) catalyst. The catalytic coating on the three-way catalyst contains platinum and rhodium, which lowers the levels of oxides of nitrogen (NOx) as well as hydrocarbons (HC) and carbon monoxide (CO).

### CHECK

2 The test equipment for a catalytic converter is expensive and highly sophisticated. If you suspect that the converter on your vehicle is malfunctioning, take it to a dealer or authorized emissions inspection facility for diagnosis and repair.

3 Whenever the vehicle is raised for servicing of underbody components, check the converter for leaks, corrosion and other damage. If damage is discovered, the converter should be replaced.

### REPLACEMENT

4 Because the converter part of the exhaust system, converter replacement requires removal of the exhaust pipe assembly (see Chapter 4). Take the vehicle, or the exhaust system, to a dealer or a muffler shop.

**Section**

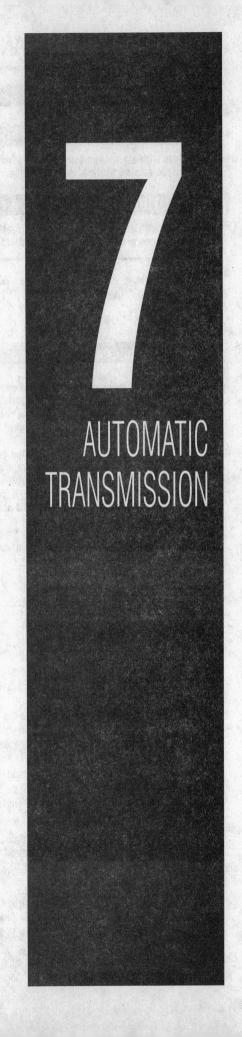

7

AUTOMATIC
TRANSMISSION

## 1 General information

The vehicles covered in this manual come equipped with either an AOD (overdrive four-speed), an AODE (overdrive electronic four-speed) or 4R70W (overdrive electronic four-speed) automatic transmission.

Due to the complexity of the automatic transmissions covered in this manual and the need for specialized equipment to perform most service operations, this Chapter contains only general diagnosis, routine maintenance, adjustment and removal and installation procedures. For information regarding the diagnostic trouble codes for AODE transmissions, refer to Chapter 6.

If the transmission requires major repair work, it should be left to a dealer service department or an automotive or transmission repair shop. You can, however, remove and install the transmission yourself and save the expense, even if the repair work is done by a transmission shop.

## 2 Diagnosis - general

➡Note: Automatic transmission malfunctions may be caused by five general conditions: poor engine performance, improper adjustments, hydraulic malfunctions, mechanical malfunctions or malfunctions in the computer or its signal network. Diagnosis of these problems should always begin with a check of the easily repaired items: fluid level and condition (see Chapter 1), shift linkage adjustment and throttle linkage adjustment. Next, perform a road test to determine if the problem has been corrected or if more diagnosis is necessary. If the problem persists after the preliminary tests and corrections are completed, additional diagnosis should be done by a dealer service department or transmission repair shop. Refer to the troubleshooting Section at the front of this manual for information on symptoms of transmission problems.

### PRELIMINARY CHECKS

1  Drive the vehicle to warm the transmission to normal operating temperature.

2  Check the fluid level as described in Chapter 1:

a) *If the fluid level is unusually low, add enough fluid to bring the level within the designated area of the dipstick, then check for external leaks (see below).*

b) *If the fluid level is abnormally high, drain off the excess, then check the drained fluid for contamination by coolant. The presence of engine coolant in the automatic transmission fluid indicates that a failure has occurred in the internal radiator walls that separate the coolant from the transmission fluid (see Chapter 3).*

c) *If the fluid is foaming, drain it and refill the transmission, then check for coolant in the fluid or a high fluid level.*

3  Check the engine idle speed.

➡Note: If the engine is malfunctioning, do not proceed with the preliminary checks until it has been repaired and runs normally.

4  Check the throttle valve cable for freedom of movement. Adjust it if necessary (see Section 4).

➡Note: The throttle cable may function properly when the engine is shut off and cold, but it may malfunction once the engine is hot. Check it cold and at normal engine operating temperature.

5  Inspect the shift control linkage (see Section 3). Make sure that it's properly adjusted and that the linkage operates smoothly.

### FLUID LEAK DIAGNOSIS

6  Most fluid leaks are easy to locate visually. Repair usually consists of replacing a seal or gasket. If a leak is difficult to find, the following procedure may help.

7  Identify the fluid. Make sure it's transmission fluid and not engine oil or brake fluid (automatic transmission fluid is a deep red color).

8  Try to pinpoint the source of the leak. Drive the vehicle several miles, then park it over a large sheet of cardboard. After a minute or two, you should be able to locate the leak by determining the source of the fluid dripping onto the cardboard.

9  Make a careful visual inspection of the suspected component and the area immediately around it. Pay particular attention to gasket mating surfaces. A mirror is often helpful for finding leaks in areas that are hard to see.

10  If the leak still cannot be found, clean the suspected area thoroughly with a degreaser or solvent, then dry it.

11  Drive the vehicle for several miles at normal operating temperature and varying speeds. After driving the vehicle, visually inspect the suspected component again.

12  Once the leak has been located, the cause must be determined before it can be properly repaired. If a gasket is replaced but the sealing flange is bent, the new gasket will not stop the leak. The bent flange must be straightened.

13  Before attempting to repair a leak, check to make sure that the following conditions are corrected or they may cause another leak.

➡Note: Some of the following conditions cannot be fixed without highly specialized tools and expertise. Such problems must be referred to a transmission repair shop or a dealer service department.

### GASKET LEAKS

14  Check the pan periodically. Make sure the bolts are tight, no bolts are missing, the gasket is in good condition and the pan is flat (dents in the pan may indicate damage to the valve body inside).

15  If the pan gasket is leaking, the fluid level or the fluid pressure may be too high, the vent may be plugged, the pan bolts may be too tight, the pan sealing flange may be warped, the sealing surface of the transmission housing may be damaged, the gasket may be damaged or the transmission casting may be cracked or porous. If sealant instead of

gasket material has been used to form a seal between the pan and the transmission housing, it may be the wrong sealant.

## SEAL LEAKS

16  If a transmission seal is leaking, the fluid level or pressure may be too high, the vent may be plugged, the seal bore may be damaged, the seal itself may be damaged or improperly installed, the surface of the shaft protruding through the seal may be damaged or a loose bearing may be causing excessive shaft movement.

17  Make sure the dipstick tube seal is in good condition and the tube is properly seated. Periodically check the area around the speedometer gear or sensor for leakage. If transmission fluid is evident, check the O-ring for damage.

## CASE LEAKS

18  If the case itself appears to be leaking, the casting is porous and will have to be repaired or replaced.

19  Make sure the oil cooler hose fittings are tight and in good condition.

## FLUID COMES OUT VENT PIPE OR FILL TUBE

20  If this condition occurs, the transmission is overfilled, there is coolant in the fluid, the case is porous, the dipstick is incorrect, the vent is plugged or the drain-back holes are plugged.

## VEHICLES WITH ELECTRONIC TRANSMISSIONS (SOME 1992 MODELS, ALL 1993 AND LATER VEHICLES)

21  The Powertrain Control Modules in vehicles with AODE (electronic) transmissions have special diagnostic trouble codes for the transmission. For information on these codes, refer to Chapter 6.

---

## 3   Shift linkage - check and adjustment

### ☀ WARNING:

**On models with air suspension, turn the air suspension switch to Off before raising the vehicle.**

## CHECK

1  Try to start the engine in each shift lever position; the starter should operate in Park and Neutral only. If the starter does not operate in Park or Neutral or operates in any position other than Park and Neutral, the shift linkage is in need of adjustment or the Neutral start switch is defective (see Section 5).

## ADJUSTMENT

### Rod-type linkage (1988 and 1989 models)

2  Have an assistant place the selector lever in Overdrive and hold it there during the following procedure.

3  Raise the vehicle and support it securely on jackstands.

4  Loosen the shift rod adjusting bolt.

5  Move the transmission lever to the Overdrive position by pushing the column shift rod down to the lowest position, then pulling it up three detents.

6  With both the selector and transmission levers now in the same positions, tighten the shift rod adjusting bolt to the torque listed in this Chapter's Specifications.

7  After adjustment, check the shift selector for proper operation.

### Cable-type linkage with adjusting nut (most later models)

8  Loosen the adjusting stud nut at the transmission shift lever.

9  Have an assistant place the steering column selector lever in Overdrive and hold it there during the following procedure.

10  Rotate the transmission manual lever clockwise to the lowest position, then rotate it counterclockwise two detent positions to the Overdrive position.

3.14a  To open the shift linkage slide adjuster (the white plastic piece), push it down (1992 models with AODE transmission and 1993 models)

11  Align the flats of the adjusting stud with the flats of the cable slot and install the cable on the stud.

➡Note: Don't push or pull on the rod while assembling the rod to the stud.

12  Tighten the adjusting stud nut to the torque listed in this Chapter's Specifications.

### Cable-type linkage with slide adjuster (some 1992 and 1993 models)

♦ Refer to illustration 3.14a, 3.14b and 3.16

13  Have an assistant place the steering column selector lever in the Overdrive position and hold it there during the following procedure.

14  Open the slide adjuster (see illustrations).

15  Move the transmission manual shift lever to the Overdrive position (the second detent from the most rearward position).

16  Push the slide adjuster closed (see illustration).

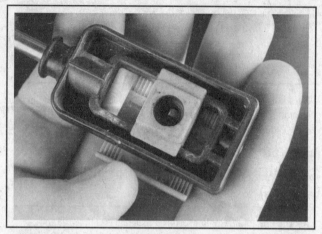

**3.14b  The slide adjuster (the white part) must be in the released position before the linkage can be adjusted properly (adjuster removed from the transmission for clarity)**

**3.16  The slide adjuster must be in the locked position (pushed up all the way) after the linkage is adjusted**

17  Check the operation of the transmission in each selector lever position. Verify that the Park and Neutral start switch is functioning properly.

## 4    Throttle valve (TV) cable (AOD transmission) - adjustment

1    The Throttle Valve (TV) cable and linkage controls transmission line pressure, shift points, shift feel, part throttle downshifts and detent downshifts. If the TV linkage is broken, sticky or misadjusted, the vehicle will experience a number of problems such as early and/or soft upshifts and no downshift or a harsh downshift function.

2    The engine should not be running and the shift lever must be in Neutral during this adjustment.

3    Remove the air cleaner assembly and inlet tube for access to the TV cable at the throttle lever.

4    Pry the grooved pin on the cable assembly out of the grommet on the throttle body lever with a wide bladed screwdriver.

5    Push the white locking tab out with a small screwdriver.

6    Make sure the plastic block with the pin and tab slides freely on the notched rod. If it doesn't, the white tab may not be pushed out far enough.

7    Hold the throttle lever firmly against the idle stop and push the grooved pin into the grommet on the throttle lever as far as it will go. Don't move the throttle lever away from the idle stop during this procedure.

8    Install the air cleaner assembly.

## 5    Neutral start switch - check and replacement (earlier models)

### ✳✳ WARNING:

**On models with air suspension, turn the air suspension switch to Off before raising the vehicle.**

### 1988 THROUGH 1991 MODELS AND 1992 MODELS WITH AOD TRANSMISSION

#### Check

1    To check the operation of the neutral start switch, apply the parking brake and try to start the engine in each position of the selector lever. The engine should start only in Park and Neutral. If it starts in any other position, adjust the shift linkage (see Section 3) and retest. If the engine still starts in any position other than Park or Neutral, replace the switch.

#### Replacement

2    Disconnect the cable from the negative battery terminal, place the shift lever in Low and apply the parking brake.

3    Raise the vehicle and place it securely on jackstands.

4    Unplug the electrical connector from the neutral start switch.

5    Carefully remove the switch and O-ring.

6    Install the switch and new O-ring and tighten it to the torque listed in this Chapter's Specifications.

### ✳✳ CAUTION:

**It is easy to crush or puncture the walls of the switch, so be careful.**

7    Install the electrical connector.

8    Connect the negative battery cable.

9    Verify that the engine starts only when the selector is in the Neutral and Park positions. This switch does not require adjustment.

### 1992 MODELS WITH AODE TRANSMISSION AND ALL 1993 AND LATER MODELS

10    The AODE and 4R70W transmissions used on these vehicles do not have a neutral switch. That function had been incorporated into an information sensor known as the Manual Lever Position (MLP) sensor or, on 1995 and later models, the Transmission Range (TR) sensor. For more information on the MLP or TR sensor, refer to Section 4 in Chapter 6. For adjustment, see Section 7 of this Chapter.

## 6   Transmission mount - check and replacement

### ✳✳ WARNING:

On models with air suspension, turn the air suspension switch to Off before raising the vehicle.

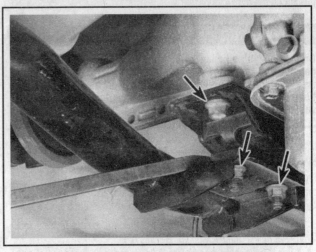

▶ **Refer to illustration 6.1**

1   Insert a large screwdriver or prybar into the space between the transmission extension housing and the crossmember and try to pry the transmission up slightly (see illustration). The transmission should not move away from the mount much at all. If it does, replace the mount.

2   To replace the mount, remove the nuts attaching the mount to the crossmember, then remove the bolts attaching the mount to the transmission extension housing (see illustration 6.1).

3   Raise the transmission slightly with a jack and remove the mount.

4   Installation is the reverse of the removal procedure. Be sure to tighten the nuts/bolts securely.

**6.1  To check the transmission mount, pry between the crossmember and the mount - there should be very little movement; to replace a mount, remove the nuts (lower arrows) that attach the mount to the crossmember, then remove the bolts (upper arrow points to right bolt, left bolt not visible)**

## 7   Manual Lever Position (MLP) or Transmission Range (TR) sensor - description, adjustment and replacement (later models)

### ✳✳ WARNING:

On models with air suspension, turn the air suspension switch to Off before raising the vehicle.

➡ **Note: This procedure applies to 1992 models with the AODE transmission and all 1993 and later models.**

### DESCRIPTION

1   The Transmission Range (TR) sensor, which is located at the manual lever on the transmission, is an information sensor for the powertrain control module (PCM). Among its functions are those normally handled by a conventional Park/Neutral switch: it prevents the engine from starting in any gear other than Park or Neutral, and closes the circuit for the back-up lights when the shift lever is moved to Reverse. For information on the TR sensor's other functions, refer to Chapter 6.

### ADJUSTMENT

**7.5  To adjust the TR sensor without the special tools: detach the shift cable, loosen the sensor retaining bolts, move the sensor slightly until the back-up lights come on, then tighten the sensor retaining bolts to the torque listed in this Chapter's Specifications and reattach the shift cable**

▶ **Refer to illustration 7.5**

2   Follow the transmission shift control cable adjustment (see Section 3) and check for a distinct "click" when the shift lever selects each gear (Park, Reverse, Neutral, Drive etc.)

3   If the engine starts in any position other Park or Neutral, the TR sensor is either out of adjustment or defective. First, perform a quick functional check to verify that the sensor is operating properly.

4   If the vehicle is equipped with air suspension, deactivate the air suspension system by turning off the air suspension switch, which is located on the right kick panel.

**❋❋ WARNING:**

**On models with air suspension, electrical power to the air suspension system must be turned off before raising the vehicle (see Chapter 10). Failure to do so can result in a sudden inflation or deflation of the air springs, causing instability of the vehicle while it's off the ground.**

5   Raise the vehicle and support it securely on jackstands. The factory recommends a special transmission range (TR) sensor alignment tool, available at most auto parts stores, but there's a quick and easy method to verify whether the sensor is adjusted, and to adjust it if it isn't:

a) *Turn the ignition switch to On, put the shift lever in Reverse and verify that the back-up lights come on:*
b) *If they do, but the engine can't be started in Park or Neutral, or it can be started in any gear other than Park or Neutral, then the sensor is probably defective. The complete sensor check procedure is in Chapter 6.*
c) *If they don't, detach the shift cable from the manual lever (see Section 6), loosen the sensor retaining bolts (see illustration) and move the sensor slightly until the back-up lights come on. Tighten the sensor retaining bolts to the torque listed in this Chapter's Specifications and reattach the shift cable.*
d) *If you can't get the back-up lights to come on by moving the sensor slightly, verify that the back-up lights and the back-up light circuit are okay (see Chapter 12 and the Wiring Diagrams at the end of Chapter 12). If the back-up lights and circuit are okay, the sensor is probably bad. Refer to Chapter 6.*

6   Remove the jackstands and lower the vehicle. If the vehicle is equipped with air suspension, reactivate the air suspension system by turning on the switch.

## REPLACEMENT

7   If the vehicle is equipped with air suspension, deactivate the air suspension system by turning off the air suspension switch, which is located on the right kick panel.

**❋❋ WARNING:**

**On models with air suspension, electrical power to the air suspension system must be turned off before raising the vehicle (see Chapter 10). Failure to do so can result in a sudden inflation or deflation of the air springs, causing instability of the vehicle while it's off the ground.**

8   Raise the vehicle and place it securely on jackstands.
9   Unplug the electrical connector from the TR sensor.
10  Detach the shift cable from the manual lever (see Section 3).
11  Remove the manual lever.
12  Remove the TR sensor retaining bolts (see illustration 7.5).
13  Remove the TR sensor.
14  Installation is the reverse of removal. Be sure to tighten the sensor retaining screws securely and adjust the sensor (see Step 5). Remove the jackstands and lower the vehicle. If the vehicle is equipped with air suspension, reactivate the air suspension system by turning on the switch.

## 8   Shift interlock system - description, check and actuator replacement

## DESCRIPTION

1   The shift interlock system prevents the shift lever from being moved out of the Park position unless the brake pedal is depressed. The system consists of a shift lock actuator mounted on the steering column. When the ignition key is turned to the Run position, the actuator is energized unless the brake pedal is depressed. If the shift lever cannot be moved out of the Park position when the brake pedal is applied, the following series of simple checks will help you quickly pinpoint the problem:

## CHECK

2   The shift lock actuator receives voltage when the ignition key is in the Run position. This circuit energizes the actuator and it prevents you from moving the shift lever out of the Park position. The actuator also receives voltage from another circuit, through the brake light switch, that is closed only when the brake pedal is depressed. It's this second circuit that de-energizes the solid state actuator when the brake pedal is depressed. So first, try to verify that the actuator is working.
3   Get inside the vehicle, close the doors and windows, start the engine, let it settle down to a fully warmed-up idle, put your head under the dash so that your ear is close to the actuator (it's mounted on the steering column), then depress the brake pedal and listen carefully for the sound of the actuator clicking.
4   If you don't hear the actuator click when you depress the brake pedal, check the 5A fuse for the actuator and the 15A fuse for the brake light switch (see Chapter 12). Replace either fuse if it's bad and recheck the actuator.
5   If the actuator and brake light switch fuses are good but the actuator still doesn't click when the brake pedal is depressed, verify that the actuator is getting battery voltage through both circuits (one is hot in the Run position, one is hot only when the brake light switch is closed).
6   If the actuator isn't getting voltage through the first "hot-in-Run-only" circuit, repair that circuit and retest.
7   If the actuator isn't getting voltage through the brake light switch circuit, apply the brake pedal and verify that the brake lights come on.

a) *If the brake lights don't come on, troubleshoot the brake light circuit and determine whether the circuit itself or the brake light switch is defective (see Chapter 9), make the necessary repairs or component replacement, then retest the actuator.*
b) *If the brake lights come on, the brake light switch and circuit are okay. Repair the circuit between the brake light switch and the actuator and retest.*
c) *If the actuator still doesn't work, replace it (see below).*

## ACTUATOR REPLACEMENT

8  Remove the steering column (see Chapter 10).
9  Remove the three shift lock actuator bolts.
10  Remove the insert plate and shift lock actuator.

11 Remove and discard the shift lock actuator clip. (The shift lock actuator clip is an assembly aid and doesn't need to be replaced). Separate the insert plate from the shift lock actuator.
12 Installation is the reverse of removal.

---

## 9  Transmission control switch - description, check and component replacement

### DESCRIPTION

1  Normally, the powertrain control module (PCM) allows automatic shifts from first through fourth gear. When the transmission control switch (TCS) is pressed, overdrive is overridden, and the PCM allows shifts from first through third only. (The PCM also turns on the transmission control indicator lamp (TCIL), an LED which indicates that "overdrive cancel mode" has been activated. If the TCIL flashes instead, there's either a sensor failure or a short in the electronic pressure control circuit (EPC); in either event, take the vehicle to a dealer to have the system serviced.) When the switch is pressed again, normal operation is resumed.

### CHECK

2  The TCS circuit can be fully tested only at the dealer. However, there are some simple tests you can do to determine whether the switch itself is bad:

a) *Check the fuse first.*
b) *Remove the TCS (see below) and check the resistance of the switch. When the TCS button is pressed and held down (it's a momentary-contact switch, so you have to hold it down to measure the resistance), the resistance should be less than 5 ohms; when the button is released, resistance should be more than 10 K-ohms. If the TCS doesn't perform as described, replace it. If the indicated resistance is within the specified range, go to the next test.*
c) *Apply battery voltage to the TCS and verify that the TCIL comes on. If it doesn't, replace the TCS. If it does come on, the switch is okay. Take the vehicle to a dealer to have the remainder of the system checked out.*

### COMPONENT REPLACEMENT

3  Remove the TCS cover.
4  Remove the TCS.
5  Installation is the reverse of removal.

---

## 10  Oil seal replacement

### ✳✳ WARNING:

**On models with air suspension, turn the air suspension switch to Off before raising the vehicle.**

### EXTENSION HOUSING SEAL

⬥ **Refer to illustrations 10.3 and 10.5**

1  Oil leaks frequently occur due to wear of the extension housing oil seal and bushing (if equipped), and/or the speedometer drive gear oil seal and O-ring. Replacement of these seals is relatively easy, since the repairs can usually be performed without removing the transmission from the vehicle.
2  The extension housing oil seal is located at the extreme rear of the transmission, where the driveshaft is attached. If leakage at the seal is suspected, raise the vehicle and support it securely on jackstands. If the seal is leaking, transmission lubricant will be built up on the front of the driveshaft and may be dripping from the rear of the transmission.
3  Remove the driveshaft (see Chapter 8). Using a screwdriver or pry bar, carefully pry the oil seal out of the rear of the transmission (see illustration). Do not damage the splines on the transmission output shaft.

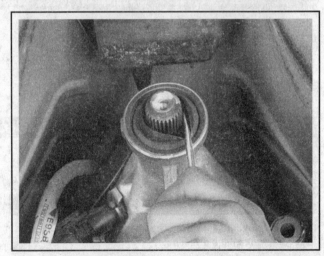

**10.3  Use a large screwdriver (shown) or a seal removal tool to pry the seal out of the transmission extension housing**

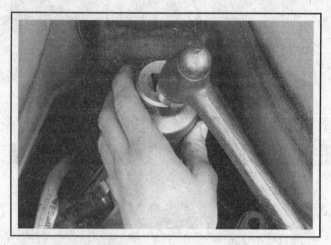

10.5 A large socket and hammer can be used to tap the new seal evenly into the bore

4    If the oil seal cannot be removed with a screwdriver or pry bar, a special oil seal removal tool (available at auto parts stores) will be required.

5    Using a large section of pipe or a very large deep socket as a drift, install the new oil seal. Drive it into the bore squarely and make sure it's completely seated (see illustration).

6    Lubricate the splines of the transmission output shaft and the outside of the driveshaft sleeve yoke with lightweight grease, then install the driveshaft. Be careful not to damage the lip of the new seal.

## SPEEDOMETER DRIVEN GEAR HOUSING/VEHICLE SPEED SENSOR O-RING

♦ Refer to illustrations 10.7 and 10.9

7    The speedometer cable and driven gear housing (1988 through 1991 models and 1992 models with AOD transmission) or the vehicle speed sensor (1992 models with AODE transmission and all 1993 and later models) is located on the side of the extension housing (see illustration). Look for transmission oil around the cable housing to determine if the seal and O-ring are leaking.

8    Disconnect the speedometer cable or electrical connector.

9    Using a hook, remove the seal (see illustration).

10.7 The speedometer driven gear housing, or vehicle speed sensor (shown), is located on the left side of the extension housing. To remove a driven gear housing or a speed sensor, simply remove the speedometer cable (speedo driven gear only) or unplug the electrical connector (some electric speedometers and all vehicle speed sensors), then remove the hold-down bolt (all models)

10.9 To replace the O-ring on a speedometer driven gear housing, or on a vehicle speed sensor (shown), simply pull it off with a hooked removal tool

10    Install a new O-ring in the driven gear housing and reinstall the driven gear housing and cable assembly on the extension housing.

## 11  Automatic transmission - removal and installation

♦ Refer to illustrations 11.3, 11.4a, 11.4b, 11.5, 11.14a, 11.14b and 11.19

### ✳✳ WARNING:

On models with air suspension, turn the air suspension switch to Off before raising the vehicle.

## REMOVAL

1    Disconnect the cable from the negative terminal of the battery.

2    Raise the vehicle and support it securely on jackstands.

3    Drain the transmission fluid (see Chapter 1), then reinstall the pan. Disconnect the oil cooler line fittings (see illustration) and plug the lines to prevent contamination.

4    Remove the torque converter cover, and on later models, the rubber plug behind the cover (see illustrations).

5    Mark the torque converter and one of the studs with white paint so they can be installed in the same position (see illustration).

6    Remove the torque converter-to-driveplate nuts. Turn the crankshaft for access to each nut. Turn the crankshaft in a clockwise direction only (as viewed from the front).

7    Rotate the torque converter until the drain plug is at its lowest point. Place the pan under the torque converter, remove the drain plug and allow the fluid to drain. Install the drain plug and tighten it securely.

8    Remove the starter motor (see Chapter 5).

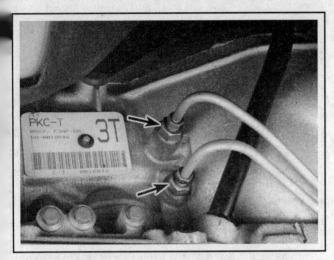

**11.3  Unscrew the oil cooler line fittings (arrows), pull the lines away from the transmission and plug them to keep out dirt and moisture**

**11.4a  To remove the torque converter cover, remove these bolts (arrows)**

**11.4b  On later models, remove both the metal inspection cover and remove this plastic plug from the access hole in the left rear part of the block**

9  Remove the driveshaft (see Chapter 8).

10  Disconnect the speedometer cable or speed sensor electrical connector (see Section 7).

11  Detach all electrical connectors from the transmission.

12  Remove any exhaust components which will interfere with transmission removal (see Chapter 4).

13  On AOD units, disconnect the TV cable (see Section 4).

14  Disconnect the shift cable from the manual lever and from the transmission cable bracket (see illustrations).

15  Support the engine with a jack. Use a block of wood under the oil pan to spread the load.

16  Support the transmission with a jack - preferably a jack made for this purpose. Safety chains will help steady the transmission on the jack.

17  Remove the two mount-to-transmission extension housing bolts (see Section 6).

18  Raise the transmission enough to allow removal, remove the crossmember-to-frame bolts, then lower the crossmember.

19  Remove the two upper transmission-to-engine bolts and the upper transmission-to-engine stud (to the right of the two upper

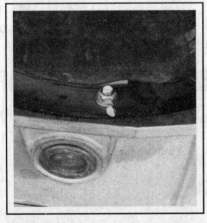

**11.5  Mark a torque converter stud to the driveplate to ensure that they're still in dynamic balance when reassembled**

**11.14a  To disconnect the shift cable from the manual lever, simply pop it loose with a screwdriver**

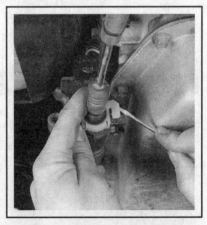

**11.14b  To disconnect the shift cable from this bracket, pop the retainer clip positioning pin loose with a small screwdriver, then pry off the retainer clip**

bolts). Remove the bolts securing the lower part of the transmission bellhousing to the engine (see illustration).

20  Lower the transmission slightly and disconnect and plug the transmission fluid cooler lines.

21  Remove the transmission dipstick tube.

22  Move the transmission to the rear to disengage it from the engine block dowel pins and make sure the torque converter is detached from the driveplate. Secure the torque converter to the transmission so it won't fall out during removal.

## INSTALLATION

23  Prior to installation, make sure the torque converter hub is securely engaged in the pump. This can be done by turning the torque converter while pushing it in toward the transmission. If the converter was not fully engaged, it will "clunk" into place (it may even "clunk" more than once).

24  With the transmission secured to the jack, raise it into position. Be sure to keep it level so the torque converter does not slide forward.

25  Turn the torque converter to line up the studs with the holes in the driveplate. The white paint mark on the torque converter and the stud made in Step 5 must line up.

26  Move the transmission forward carefully until the dowel pins and the torque converter are engaged.

27  Install the transmission-to-engine bolts. Tighten them to the torque listed in this Chapter's Specifications.

28  Install the torque converter-to-driveplate nuts. Tighten the nuts to the torque listed in this Chapter's Specifications.

29  Connect the transmission fluid cooler lines.

30  Install the transmission mount and crossmember through-bolts. Tighten the bolts and nuts securely.

31  Remove the jacks supporting the transmission and the engine.

32  Install the dipstick tube. Install the oil cooler line fittings and

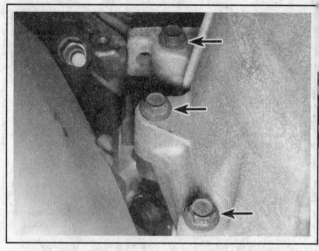

**11.19  Left side lower transmission-to-engine bolts (arrows)**

tighten them to the torque listed in this Chapter's Specifications.

33  Install the starter motor (see Chapter 5).

34  Connect the vacuum hose(s) (if equipped).

35  Connect the shift and TV linkage (see Sections 3 and 4).

36  Plug in the transmission wire harness connectors.

37  Install the torque converter cover.

38  Install the driveshaft (see Chapter 8).

39  Connect the speedometer cable or speed sensor connector.

40  Adjust the shift linkage (see Section 3).

41  Install any exhaust system components that were removed or disconnected (see Chapter 4).

42  Lower the vehicle.

43  Fill the transmission with the specified fluid (see Chapter 1), run the engine and check for fluid leaks.

## Specifications

### General

| Transmission type | |
|---|---|
| 1988 through 1991 | AOD overdrive 4-speed |
| 1992 | AOD or AODE electronic 4-speed |
| 1993 and 1994 | AODE |
| 1995 on | 4R70W |

## Torque specifications                Ft-lbs (unless otherwise indicated)

➡**Note: One foot-pound (ft-lb) of torque is equivalent to 12 inch-pounds (in-lbs) of torque. Torque values below approximately 15 foot-pounds are expressed in inch-pounds, because most foot-pound torque wrenches are not accurate at these smaller values.**

| | |
|---|---|
| Adjusting stud nut at transmission shift lever | |
| (1990 through 1992) | 9 to 18 |
| Neutral start switch | 96 to 132 in-lbs |
| Oil cooler line fittings at transmission | 12 to 18 |
| Shift rod adjusting bolt (1988 and 1989) | 14 to 23 |
| Transmission-to-engine bolts | |
| 1988 to 1998 | 40 to 50 |
| 1999 and later | 30 to 40 |
| Torque converter-to-driveplate nuts | 20 to 34 |

# 8

## DRIVELINE

**Section**

## 1 General information

**※※ WARNING:**

On models with air suspension, turn the air suspension switch to Off before raising the vehicle with a jack.

**※※ CAUTION:**

If a vehicle with an automatic transmission is disabled, do NOT tow it at speeds greater than 30 mph or distances over 50 miles.

The information in this Chapter deals with the components from the rear of the transmission to the rear wheels. For the purposes of this Chapter, these components are grouped into two categories: driveshaft and rear axle assembly. Separate Sections within this Chapter offer general descriptions and checking procedures for components in each of the two groups.

Since nearly all the procedures covered in this Chapter involve working under the vehicle, make sure it's securely supported on sturdy jackstands or on a hoist where the vehicle can be easily raised and lowered.

## 2 Driveshaft - inspection

**※※ WARNING 1:**

On models with air suspension, turn the air suspension switch to Off before raising the vehicle.

**※※ WARNING 2:**

On models with a fire suppression system, disable the system before raising the rear of the vehicle by disconnecting the cable from the negative battery terminal and waiting at least three minutes.

1   Raise the rear of the vehicle and support it securely on jackstands.

2   Crawl under the vehicle and visually inspect the driveshaft. Look for any dents or cracks in the tubing. If any are found, the driveshaft

must be replaced.

3   Check for any oil leakage at the front and rear of the driveshaft. Leakage where the driveshaft enters the transmission indicates a defective transmission rear seal. Leakage where the driveshaft enters the differential indicates a defective pinion seal.

4   While under the vehicle, have an assistant turn the rear wheel so the driveshaft will rotate. As it does, make sure the universal joints are operating properly without binding, noise or looseness.

5   The universal joints can also be checked with the driveshaft motionless, by gripping your hands on either side of the joint and attempting to twist the joint. Any movement at all in the joint is a sign of considerable wear. Lifting up on the shaft will also indicate movement in the universal joints.

6   Finally, check the driveshaft mounting bolts at the ends to make sure they are tight.

## 3 Driveshaft - removal and installation

▸ Refer to illustrations 3.2 and 3.3

**※※ WARNING 1:**

On models with air suspension, turn the air suspension switch to Off before raising the vehicle.

**※※ WARNING 2:**

On models with a fire suppression system, disable the system before raising the rear of the vehicle by disconnecting the cable from the negative battery terminal and waiting at least three minutes.

1   Raise the rear of the vehicle an support it securely on jackstands.

2   Mark the relationship of the driveshaft to the differential companion flange (see illustration).

3   Remove the bolts and separate the driveshaft from the differential

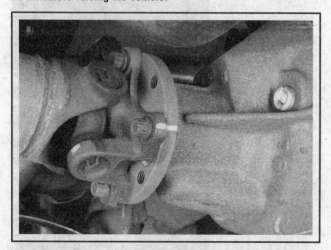

3.2 Mark the relationship of the driveshaft to the differential companion flange to ensure that the driveshaft retains its dynamic balance after reinstalling it

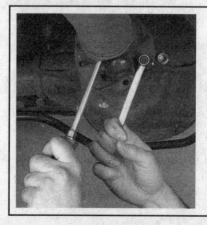

3.3 To remove the bolts that attach the driveshaft to the differential companion flange, insert a small prybar or large screwdriver through the rear U-joint and hold the driveshaft while you break loose the four flange bolts

companion flange (a 12-point socket or box end wrench will be necessary) (see illustration). Pull the driveshaft toward the rear to remove it.

4   Wrap a plastic bag tightly around the extension housing of the transmission to prevent fluid loss.

5   Installation is the reverse of removal. Be sure to align the reference marks made during removal.

➡**Note: The factory recommends using new bolts when the driveshaft is reinstalled. If new bolts are not available, use a suitable thread-locking compound on the original bolts.**

## 4   Universal joints - replacement

◆ **Refer to illustrations 4.2a, 4.2b, 4.4 and 4.9**

➡**Note: A press or large vise will be required for this procedure. It may be advisable to take the driveshaft to a local dealer service department, service station or machine shop where the universal joints can be replaced for you, normally at a reasonable charge.**

1   Remove the driveshaft as outlined in the previous Section.

2   Using a small pair of pliers, remove the snap-rings from the spider (see illustrations).

3   Supporting the driveshaft, place it in position on a workbench equipped with a vise.

4   Place a piece of pipe or a large socket with the same inside diameter over one of the bearing caps. Position a socket which is of slightly smaller diameter than the cap on the opposite bearing cap (see illustration) and use the vise or press to force the cap out (inside the pipe or large socket), stopping just before it comes completely out of the yoke. Use the vise or large pliers to work the cap the rest of the way out.

5   Transfer the sockets to the other side and press the opposite bearing cap out in the same manner.

6   Pack the new universal joint bearings with grease. Ordinarily, specific instructions for lubrication will be included with the universal joint servicing kit and should be followed carefully.

7   Position the spider in the yoke and partially install one bearing cap in the yoke.

8   Start the spider into the bearing cap and then partially install the other cap. Align the spider and press the bearing caps into position, being careful not to damage the dust seals.

9   Install the snap-rings. If difficulty is encountered in seating the snap-rings, strike the driveshaft yoke sharply with a hammer. This will spring the yoke ears slightly and allow the snap-rings to seat in the groove (see illustration).

10  Install the grease fitting and fill the joint with grease. Be careful not to overfill the joint, as this could blow out the grease seals.

11  Install the driveshaft, tightening the companion flange bolts to the torque listed in this Chapter's Specifications.

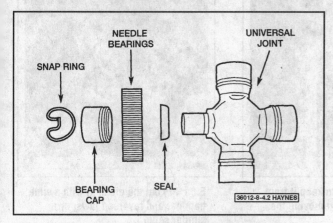

**4.2a  Exploded view of the universal joint components**

**4.2b  A pair of needle-nose pliers can be used to remove the universal joint snap-rings**

**4.4  To press the universal joint out of the driveshaft yoke, set it up in a vise with the small socket pushing the joint and bearing cap into the large socket**

**4.9  If the snap-ring will not seat in the groove, strike the yoke with a brass hammer - this will relieve the tension that has set up in the yoke, and slightly spring the yoke ears (this should also be done if the joint feels tight when assembled)**

## 5 Differential pinion oil seal - replacement

▶ Refer to illustrations 5.4, 5.5, 5.6a, 5.6b and 5.8

**✳✳ WARNING 1:**

**On models with air suspension, turn the air suspension switch to Off before raising the vehicle.**

**✳✳ WARNING 2:**

**On models with a fire suppression system, disable the system before raising the rear of the vehicle by disconnecting the cable from the negative battery terminal and waiting at least three minutes.**

1   Raise the rear of the vehicle and place it securely on jackstands.
2   Remove the rear wheels and brake drums (see Chapter 9).
3   Mark the driveshaft and companion flange for ease of realignment during reassembly, then remove the driveshaft (see Section 3).
4   Mark the relationship between the pinion and companion flange (see illustration).
5   Using an inch-pound torque wrench, measure and record the torque required to turn the pinion nut through several revolutions (pinion bearing preload). Using a suitable tool, hold the companion flange and remove the pinion nut (see illustration). Using a suitable puller, remove the companion flange.
6   Pry out the old seal with a slide hammer and reversed jaws or other appropriate tool as shown (see illustration). It may also be removed with a hammer and chisel (see illustration).
7   Clean the oil seal mounting surface.
8   Tap the new seal into place, taking care to insert it squarely as shown (see illustration).
9   Inspect the splines on the pinion shaft for burrs and nicks. Remove any rough areas with a crocus cloth. Wipe the splines clean.
10  Install the companion flange, aligning it with the marks made during removal. Gently tap the flange on with a soft-faced hammer until you can start the pinion nut on the pinion shaft.
11  Using a suitable tool, hold the companion flange while tightening the pinion nut to the minimum torque listed in this Chapter's Specifications. While tightening, take frequent rotational torque measurements, using the inch-pound torque wrench, until the measurement recorded in Step four is reached.

**5.4  Mark the relationship between the pinion and flange as shown**

**5.5  Hold the flange to keep it from turning while you're removing the pinion nut**

**5.6a  Pry out the old seal with a slide hammer and reversed jaws, or a similar setup**

**5.6b  You can also remove the old seal with a hammer and chisel or screwdriver (but make sure you don't damage the seal bore)**

**5.8  Tap the new pinion seal into place with the seal square to the bore**

**CAUTION:**

If the measurement recorded in Step four was less than the pinion bearing preload torque listed in this Chapter's Specifications, continue tightening until the specified torque is reached. If it was more than specified, stop when the specified torque is reached. Under no circumstances should the pinion nut be backed off to reduce pinion bearing preload. Increase the nut torque in small increments and check the preload after each increase.

12  Reinstall the driveshaft, brake drums and wheels.
13  Check the differential oil level and fill as necessary.
14  Lower the vehicle and take a test drive to check for leaks.

## 6   Axleshaft - removal and installation

▶ Refer to illustrations 6.3a, 6.3b, 6.4 and 6.5

**WARNING 1:**

On models with air suspension, turn the air suspension switch to Off before raising the vehicle.

**WARNING 2:**

On models with a fire suppression system, disable the system before raising the rear of the vehicle by disconnecting the cable from the negative battery terminal and waiting at least three minutes.

1  Loosen the wheel lug nuts, raise the rear of the vehicle, support it securely on jackstands and remove the wheel. Also remove the brake drum, or the caliper and disc (see Chapter 9).
2  Remove the cover from the differential carrier and allow the lubricant to drain into a container.
3  Remove the lock bolt from the differential pinion shaft. Slide the notched end of the pinion shaft out of the differential case as far as it will go (see illustrations).
4  Push the outer (flanged) end of the axleshaft in and remove the C-lock from the inner end of the shaft (see illustration).

**6.3a  Position a large screwdriver between the rear axle case and a ring gear bolt to keep the differential case from turning when removing the pinion shaft lock bolt**

**CAUTION:**

Take care to not damage the O-rings in the axleshaft grooves when removing the C-clips.

**6.3b  Rotate the differential case 180-degrees and slide the pinion shaft out of the case until the stepped part of the shaft contacts the ring gear**

**6.4  Push in on the axle flange and remove the C-lock (arrow) from the inner end of the axleshaft**

**6.5 Pull the axle out of the housing, supporting it with one hand to prevent damage to the seal**

5   Withdraw the axleshaft, taking care not to damage the oil seal in the end of the axle housing as the splined end of the axleshaft passes through it (see illustration).

---

**❋❋ CAUTION:**

**Do not rotate the differential while the pinion shaft is out, or the pinion gears could fall out.**

---

6   Installation is the reverse of removal. Tighten the differential pinion shaft lock bolt to the torque listed in this Chapter's Specifications.
7   Install the differential cover (see Chapter 1).
8   Refill the axle with the correct quantity and grade of lubricant (see Chapter 1).

## 7   Axleshaft oil seal - replacement

**7.2a Use a seal removal tool to remove the old seal from the axle housing**

◗ **Refer to illustrations 7.2a, 7.2b and 7.3**

1   Remove the axleshaft as described in the preceding Section.
2   Pry the old oil seal out of the end of the axle housing, using a seal removal tool or the inner end of the axleshaft itself as a lever (see illustrations).
3   Using a seal driver or a large socket, tap the seal into position so that the lips are facing in and the metal face is visible from the end of the axle housing (see illustration). When correctly installed, the face of the oil seal should be flush with the end of the axle housing. Lubricate the lips of the seal with gear oil.
4   Install the axleshaft (see Section 6).

**7.3 Using a seal driver to install the new axleshaft oil seal**

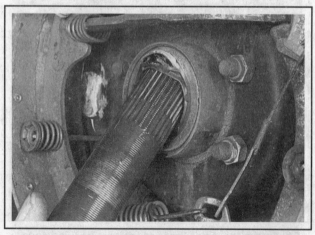

**7.2b If a seal removal tool isn't available, a prybar or even the end of the axle can be used to pop the seal out of the housing**

## 8  Axleshaft bearing - replacement

**Refer to illustrations 8.2 and 8.4**

1  Remove the axleshaft (see Section 6) and the oil seal (see Section 7).

2  A bearing puller will be required or a tool which will engage behind the bearing will have to be fabricated (see illustration).

3  Attach a slide hammer and pull the bearing out of the axle housing.

4  Clean out the bearing recess and drive in the new bearing with a bearing driver (see illustration). Lubricate the new bearing with gear lubricant. Make sure that the bearing is tapped into the full depth of its recess.

5  Discard the old oil seal and install a new one (see Section 7), then install the axleshaft.

**8.2  To remove the axle bearing, insert a bearing removal tool attached to a slide hammer through the center, pull the tool up against the back side and use the slide hammer to yank the bearing from the axle housing**

**8.4  A correctly-sized bearing driver must be used to drive the bearing into the housing**

## 9  Rear axle assembly - removal and installation

### REMOVAL

**Refer to illustration 9.8**

**⁜⁜ WARNING 1:**

On models with air suspension, turn the air suspension switch to Off before raising the vehicle.

**⁜⁜ WARNING 2:**

On models with a fire suppression system, disable the system before raising the rear of the vehicle by disconnecting the cable from the negative battery terminal and waiting at least three minutes.

1  Disconnect the cable from the negative battery terminal.

2  Loosen, but do not remove the rear wheel lug nuts. Block the front wheels and raise the rear of the vehicle. Support it securely on jackstands placed under the frame. Remove the rear wheels.

3  Remove the brake drums, or the calipers and discs (see Chapter 9).

4  Remove the rear axle cover and allow the lubricant to drain (see Chapter 1).

5  If the vehicle is equipped with ABS, remove the sensors from the torque plates (see Chapter 9).

6  Remove both rear axleshafts (see Section 6).

7  Free the ABS sensor wires, parking brake cables and brake lines from their clips on the axle housing.

8  Remove the four bolts that attach the brake drum backing plates (drum brake models) or torque plates (disc brake models) to the axle housing (see illustration). Detach the brake backing plate or torque plate assemblies from the housing and wire them out of the way.

**9.8  To remove the torque plate or brake backing plate from the axle assembly, remove these four bolts (arrows)**

9  Unbolt the driveshaft from the differential companion flange (see Section 3) and wire it out of the way.

10  Place a floor jack under the differential and raise the rear axle slightly.

11  Place a safety chain through the coil springs or disconnect the air springs (see Chapter 10).

12  Remove the shock absorber lower mounting bolts (see Chapter 10).

13  Remove the upper suspension arm-to-rear axle housing nuts and bolts (see Chapter 10).

14  On 1998 and later models, there are four axle-locating arms (upper and lower at each side), plus a Watts-linkage assembly mounted above the differential, all of which must be disconnected. If the vehicle is equipped with air suspension, disconnect the height sensor (see Chapter 10).

15  Lower the axle housing until the coil springs are fully extended, then remove them. Or remove the air springs, if equipped.

16  Remove the lower suspension arm-to-axle housing nuts and bolts (see Chapter 10).

17  Lower the axle housing and guide it out from underneath the vehicle.

## INSTALLATION

18  Raise the rear axle assembly into place and install the upper suspension arm-to-axle housing bolts and nuts. Don't completely tighten the nuts at this time.

19  Install the coil springs or air springs (see Chapter 10) and connect the lower suspension arms to the rear axle assembly.

20  Raise the axle housing to simulate normal ride height and tighten the upper and lower suspension arm-to-axle housing nuts to the torque listed in the Chapter 10 Specifications. If the vehicle is equipped with air springs, attach the height sensor (see Chapter 10).

21  Connect the lower ends of the shock absorbers to the rear axle housing and tighten the bolts to the torque listed in the Chapter 10 Specifications.

22  Connect the driveshaft to the differential companion flange, align the matchmarks and tighten the companion flange bolts to the torque listed in this Chapter's Specifications.

23  Attach the brake backing plates or torque plates to the axle housing and tighten the bolts securely.

24  Connect the brake sensor wires, the brake lines and the parking brake cables to their clips on the axle housing.

25  Install the axleshafts (see Section 6).

26  Install the brake drums, or the disc and calipers (see Chapter 10).

27  Install the rear axle cover and fill the differential with the recommended oil (see Chapter 1).

28  Install the wheels and lug nuts. Lower the vehicle and tighten the lug nuts to the torque listed in the Chapter 1 Specifications.

## Torque specifications                    Ft-lbs (unless otherwise noted)

➡**Note: One foot-pound (ft-lb) of torque is equivalent to 12 inch-pounds (in-lbs) of torque. Torque values below approximately 15 foot-pounds are expressed in inch-pounds, because most foot-pound torque wrenches are not accurate at these smaller values.**

| | |
|---|---|
| Driveshaft companion flange bolts | 71 to 95 |
| Differential pinion shaft lock bolt | 15 to 30 |
| Differential cover bolts | |
| Metal cover | 25 to 35 |
| Plastic cover | 15 to 20 |
| Companion flange/pinion nut (minimum) | 140 |
| Pinion bearing preload | |
| Used bearings | 8 to 14 in-lbs |
| New bearings | 16 to 29 in-lbs |

**Section**

**Reference to other Chapters**

9

BRAKES

## GENERAL DESCRIPTION

> ※※ **WARNING:**
>
> **On models with air suspension, turn the air suspension switch to Off before raising the vehicle with a jack.**

All models covered by this manual are equipped with hydraulically-operated, power-assisted brake systems. All front brake systems are disc type, while the rear brakes are either disc or drum type. Some models are equipped with an Anti-lock Brake System (ABS), which is described in Section 2.

All brakes are self-adjusting. The front and rear disc brakes automatically compen-sate for pad wear, while the rear drum brakes incorporate an adjustment mechanism which is activated as the brakes are applied.

The hydraulic system is a split design, meaning there are separate circuits for the front and rear brakes. If one circuit fails, the other circuit will remain functional and a warning indicator will light up on the dashboard, showing that a failure has occurred.

## MASTER CYLINDER

The master cylinder is located under the hood, mounted to the power brake booster, and is best recognized by the large fluid reservoir on top. The removable plastic reservoir is partitioned to prevent total fluid loss in the event of a front or rear brake hydraulic system failure.

The master cylinder is designed for the "split system" mentioned earlier and has separate primary and secondary piston assemblies, the piston nearest the firewall being the primary piston, which applies hydraulic pressure to the front brakes.

## BRAKE PRESSURE CONTROL VALVE

On non-ABS models, the brake pressure control valve is located in the master cylinder between the brake lines and the master cylinder body. On ABS models, the brake pressure control valve is on the underside of the ABS hydraulic control unit. Earlier non-ABS control-valve assemblies contain a proportioning valve and a pressure switch. On later non-ABS systems, pressure control is handled inside the master cylinder, but the proportioning valve is in a junction block on the frame.

The proportioning valve regulates the hydraulic pressure in the rear brake system. When the brake pedal is applied, the rear brake fluid pressure passes through the proportioning valve to the rear brake system until the valve's split point is reached. Above its split point, the proportioning valve begins to reduce the hydraulic pressure to the rear brakes thereby balancing the braking condition between the front and rear brakes. This condition will prevent the rear wheel from locking up and the vehicle from skidding out of control.

The brake pressure control valve is not serviceable - if a problem develops with the valve, it must be replaced as an assembly.

## PARKING BRAKE

The parking brake mechanically operates the rear brakes only.

On drum brake models the parking brake cables pull on a lever attached to the brake shoe assembly, causing the shoes to expand against the drum. On models with rear disc brakes, the cables operate small parking brake shoes inside the brake disc hub.

## PRECAUTIONS

There are some general cautions and warnings involving the brake system on this vehicle:

a) *Use only brake fluid conforming to DOT 3 specifications.*
b) *The brake pads and linings create dust which is hazardous to your health if inhaled. Whenever you work on brake system components, clean all parts with brake system cleaner or denatured alcohol. Do not allow the fine dust to become airborne.*
c) *Safety should be paramount whenever any servicing of the brake components is performed. Do not use parts or fasteners which are not in perfect condition, and be sure that all clearances and torque specifications are adhered to. If you are at all unsure about a certain procedure, seek professional advice. Upon completion of any brake system work, test the brakes carefully in a controlled area before putting the vehicle into normal service.*

If a problem is suspected in the brake system, don't drive the vehicle until it's fixed.

Some 1992 and 1993 and all 1994 and later models are equipped with an Anti-lock Brake System (ABS). The ABS system is designed to maintain vehicle steerability, directional stability and optimum deceleration under severe braking conditions and on most road surfaces. It does so by monitoring the rotational speed of each wheel and controlling the brake line pressure to each wheel during braking. This prevents the wheel from locking-up and provides maximum vehicle controllability. Some of these models are also equipped with an optional Traction Assist (TA) system which is designed to control wheel spin when accelerating on slippery or loose surfaces.

## ANTI-LOCK BRAKE SYSTEM

### Hydraulic control unit (HCU)

▶ **Refer to illustration 2.2**

The hydraulic control unit is located in the left (driver's side) front corner of the engine compartment, below the air cleaner. It consists of a brake pressure control valve block, a pump motor and a hydraulic control unit reservoir with a fluid level indicator assembly (see illustration).

**2.2 The ABS hydraulic control unit is located on the left side of the engine compartment, under the air cleaner housing**

During normal braking conditions, brake hydraulic fluid from the master cylinder enters the hydraulic control unit through two inlet ports and passes through four normally open inlet valves, one to each wheel.

When the anti-lock brake control module senses that a wheel is about to lock up, the anti-lock brake control module closes the appropriate inlet. This prevents any more fluid from entering the affected brake. If the module determines that the wheel is still decelerating, the module opens the outlet valve, which bleeds off pressure in the affected brake.

## Wheel sensors

▶ **Refer to illustrations 2.6a and 2.6b**

The ABS system uses four "variable-reluctance" sensors to monitor wheel speed ("reluctance" is a term used to indicate the amount of resistance to the passage of flux lines - lines of force in a magnetic field - through a given material). Each sensor contains a small inductive coil that generates an electromagnetic field. When paired with a toothed sensor ring which interrupts this field as the wheels turn, each sensor generates a low-voltage analog (continuous) signal. This voltage signal, which rises and falls in proportion to wheel rotation speed, is continuously sampled (monitored) by the control module, converted into digital data inside the module and processed (interpreted).

The front wheel sensors (see illustration) are mounted in the steering knuckle in close proximity to the toothed sensor rings, which are pressed onto the wheel hubs. The rear wheel sensors (see illustra-

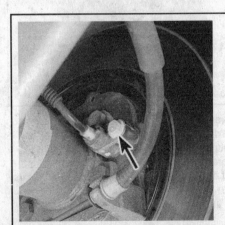

**2.6b ABS rear wheel sensor (arrow)**

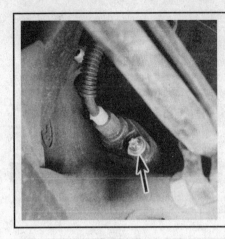

**2.6a ABS front wheel sensor (arrow)**

tion) are mounted in the caliper torque plate and the sensor rings are pressed onto the axleshafts.

### Brake control module

▶ **Refer to illustration 2.7**

The brake control module (see illustration), which is mounted in the engine compartment on a bracket attached to the radiator support, is the "brain" of the ABS system. The module (referred to as an Electronic Control Unit or ECU on 1992 models, ABS module on 1993 models and anti-lock brake control module on 1994 and later models) constantly monitors the incoming analog voltage signals from the four ABS wheel sensors, converts these signals to digital form, processes this digital data by comparing it to the map (program), makes decisions, converts these (digital) decisions to analog form and sends them to the hydraulic control unit, which opens and closes the front and/or rear circuits as necessary.

The module also has a self-diagnostic capability which operates during both normal driving as well as ABS system operation. If a malfunction occurs, a red "BRAKE" warning indicator or an amber "CHECK ANTI-LOCK BRAKES" warning indicator will light up on the dash.

   a) *If the red BRAKE light glows, the brake fluid level in the master cylinder reservoir has fallen below the level established by the fluid level switch. Top up the reservoir and verify that the light goes out.*

   b) *If the amber CHECK ANTI-LOCK BRAKES light glows, the ABS and, if equipped, Traction Assist, have been turned off because of*

**2.7 The ABS brake control module is attached to the radiator support (plastic trim piece removed)**

*a symptom detected by the module. Normal power-assisted braking is still operational, but the wheels can now lock up if you're involved in a panic-stop situation. A diagnostic code is also stored in the module when a warning indicator light comes on; when retrieved by a service technician, the code indicates the area or component where the problem is located. Once the problem is fixed, the code is cleared. These procedures, however, are beyond the scope of the home mechanic.*

## Diagnosis and repair

### ✳✳ WARNING:

**If a dashboard warning light comes on and stays on while the vehicle is in operation, the ABS system requires immediate attention!**

Although a special electronic ABS diagnostic tester is necessary to properly diagnose the system, the home mechanic can perform a few preliminary checks before taking the vehicle to a dealer who is equipped with this tester.

a) *Check the brake fluid level in the reservoir.*
b) *Verify that the control module electrical connector is securely connected.*

c) *Check the electrical connectors at the hydraulic control unit.*
d) *Check the fuses.*
e) *Follow the wiring harness to each wheel and check that all connections are secure and that the wiring is not damaged.*

If the above preliminary checks do not rectify the problem, the vehicle should be diagnosed by a dealer service department or other qualified repair shop. Due to the rather complex nature of this system, all actual repair work must be done by the dealer service department or repair shop.

## TRACTION ASSIST SYSTEM

The traction assist (TA) system, which operates at speeds up to about 34 mph, operates as follows: During acceleration, if one or both of the rear wheels lose traction and begin to spin, the ABS pump motor rapidly applies and releases the appropriate rear brake(s). An isolation valve blocks hydraulic pressure to the front brakes, directing pressure to the rear brakes. The ABS brake control module monitors TA system cycling to prevent overheating of the rear brakes. If the TA system is used continually on slippery roads, the module may shut off the system to allow the rear brakes to cool. If the driver applies the brakes, the system is shut off.

## 3   Brake pads - replacement

◆ Refer to illustrations 3.6a through 3.6k, 3.6l through 3.6r and 3.6s through 3.6x

### ✳✳ WARNING 1:

**Disc brake pads must be replaced on both front wheels or both rear wheels at the same time - never replace the pads on only one wheel. Also, the dust created by the brake system is harmful to your health. Never blow it out with compressed air and don't inhale any of it. An approved filtering mask should be worn when working on the brakes. Do not, under any circumstances, use petroleum-based solvents to clean brake parts. Use brake system cleaner only!**

### ✳✳ WARNING 2:

**On models with air suspension, turn the air suspension switch to Off before raising the vehicle.**

### ✳✳ WARNING 3:

**On models with a fire suppression system, disable the system before raising the rear of the vehicle by disconnecting the cable from the negative battery terminal and waiting at least three minutes.**

**3.6a  Remove the caliper mounting bolts (arrows)**

**3.6b  If the disc is worn down, it's impossible to pull the caliper and old pads off the disc without depressing the caliper piston into its bore far enough to allow the pads to clear the ridge around the circumference of the disc - insert a screwdriver into the cooling vanes of the disc, then pry the caliper outward - this will move the caliper out (away from the vehicle), pushing on the inner brake pad and depressing the piston**

3.6c Remove the caliper and brake pad assembly

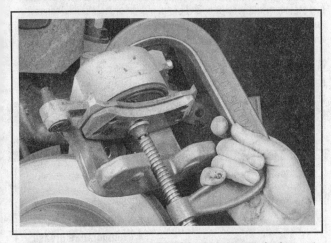

3.6e Before you can slide the caliper and two new brake pads over the disc, you'll need to depress the caliper piston all the way into its bore with a C-clamp (use the old brake pad); as the piston is depressed to the bottom of the bore, the fluid in the master cylinder will rise. Make sure it doesn't overflow. If necessary, siphon off some fluid.

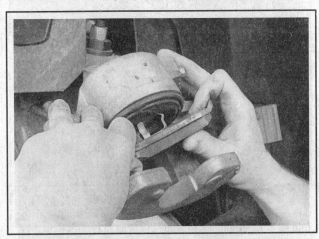

3.6f On 1988 through 1994 models, pull the inner brake pad retaining clips out of the piston and remove the inner pad. On 1995 and later models, slide the inner pad away from the piston, disengage it from the anchor plate and remove the inner pad.

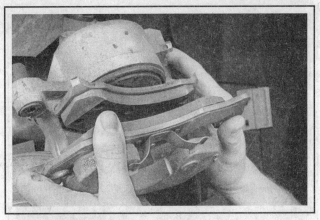

3.6d On 1988 through 1994 models, remove the outer brake pad. On 1995 and later models, slide the outer pad away from the outer leg of the anchor plate, disengage it from the anchor plate and remove the outer pad

➡ Note 1: On 1995 and later models, the front brake caliper and brake pads have been modified slightly. The brake pads are no longer held in place in the caliper assembly by retaining clips but by indexing the pads out of and into the caliper anchor plate.

➡ Note 2: On 1998 and later models, there is a new, two-piston front caliper. Follow the general pad replacement advice in the Section below, and see the captions for specific details (see illustrations 3.6l through 3.6r).

1   Remove the cover from the brake fluid reservoir and siphon out about 1/2 of the brake fluid.

2   Loosen the wheel lug nuts, raise the vehicle and support it securely on jackstands.

3   Remove the wheels. Work on one brake assembly at a time, using the assembled brake for reference if necessary.

4   Inspect the brake disc carefully as outlined in Section 5.

5   If machining is necessary, follow the information in that Section to remove the disc, at which time the pads can be removed from the caliper as well.

6   Follow the accompanying photos, beginning with illustra-

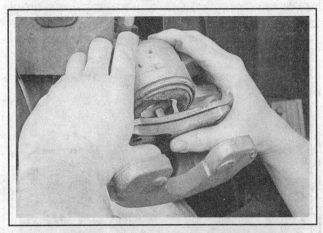

3.6g On 1988 through 1994 models, push the new inner brake pad into place - make sure it's fully seated. On 1995 and later models, make sure the anti-rattle spring is still in place in the caliper. First locate the new inner pad onto the caliper anchor plate, then push the inner pad up against the anti-rattle spring - make sure the pad is fully seated

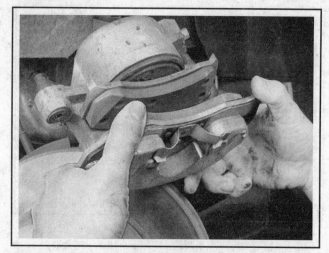

3.6h On 1988 through 1994 models, to install the new outer pad, push it down until the clip snaps it into place below the two bosses on the caliper housing; there are also a couple of locating pins on the pad backing plate that must engage a pair of matching holes in the caliper itself. On 1995 and later models, locate the new outer pad onto the caliper anchor plate, then push the inner pad up against the anti-rattle spring - make sure the pad is fully seated

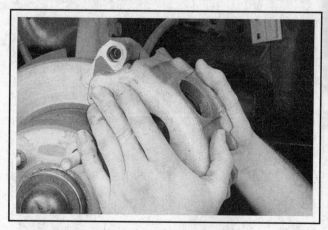

3.6i Install the caliper

tion 3.6a (1997 and earlier) or 3.6L (1998 and later), for the front brake pad replacement procedure. Be sure to stay in order and read the caption under each illustration. If you're replacing the rear brake pads, follow the photos beginning with illustration 3.6s.

7   When reinstalling the caliper, be sure to tighten the caliper bolts to the torque listed in this Chapter's Specifications. After the job has been completed, firmly depress the brake pedal a few times to bring the pads into contact with the disc.

8   Check the brake fluid level and add some, if neessary, to bring it to the appropriate level (see Chapter 1).

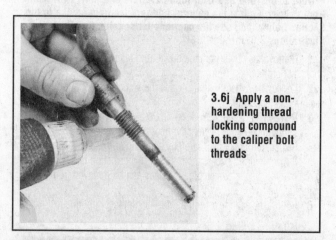

3.6j Apply a non-hardening thread locking compound to the caliper bolt threads

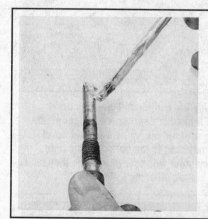

3.6k Apply high temperature grease to the sliding-surface portion of the caliper bolts

3.6l On the 1998 and later dual-piston front calipers, use a large C-clamp to slide the caliper on its bolts so the pistons will be fully retracted

3.6m Remove the two caliper mounting bolts (arrow indicates lower bolt)

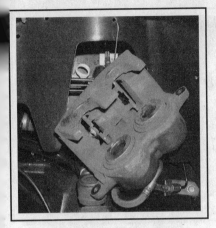

3.6n  Remove the caliper and hang it from the upper control arm with a strong wire - do NOT allow the caliper to hang by the brake hose!

3.6o  Remove the outer pad

3.6p  Remove the inner brake pad

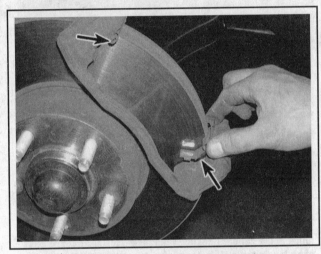

3.6q  Check that the upper and lower anti-rattle clips (arrows) are intact and snugly in place against the caliper anchor plate

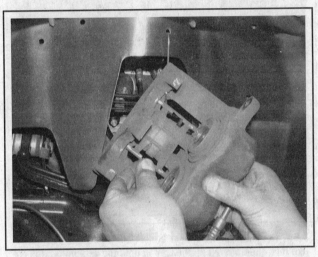

3.6r  Make sure the big anti-rattle clip inside the caliper is in good condition and fully seated. Then press the new inner and outer pads into place, making sure they are completely seated.

3.6s  Remove the two rear caliper bolts (upper and lower arrows) with a Torx Drive bit - DO NOT remove the brake hose banjo bolt (middle arrow) unless you're planning to overhaul the caliper

3.6t  Depress the caliper piston by squeezing the old pad with a pair of large water pump pliers

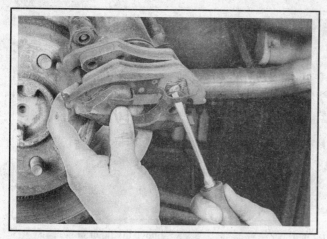

3.6u  Pry off the old outer brake pad with a screwdriver

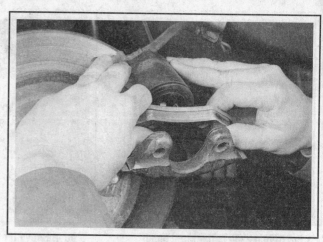

3.6v  Remove the old inner brake pad by pulling the retaining clips out of the piston

3.6w  To install the new inner brake pad, place it in position like this, then push it all the way in until the retaining clips are fully seated

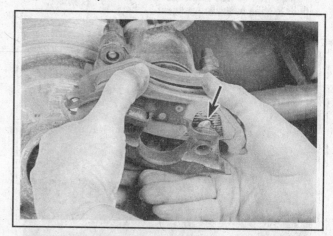

3.6x  To install the new outer brake pad, slide it down like this until the locating pins (arrow) are fully engaged with the holes in the caliper housing; then install the caliper and pads over the disc, install the caliper bolts and tighten them to the torque listed in this Chapter's Specifications

## 4   Brake caliper - removal, overhaul and installation

### ❋❋ WARNING 1:

Dust created by the brake system is harmful to your health. Never blow it out with compressed air and don't inhale any of it. An approved filtering mask should be worn when working on the brakes. Do not, under any circumstances, use petroleum-based solvents to clean brake parts. Use brake system cleaner only!

### ❋❋ WARNING 2:

If the vehicle is equipped with ABS, make sure you plug the brake hose immediately after disconnecting it from the brake caliper, to prevent the fluid from draining out of the line and air entering the HCU. The HCU on an ABS system cannot be bled without a very expensive tool.

### ❋❋ WARNING 3:

On models with air suspension, turn the air suspension switch to Off before raising the vehicle.

### ❋❋ WARNING 4:

On models with a fire suppression system, disable the system before raising the rear of the vehicle by disconnecting the cable from the negative battery terminal and waiting at least three minutes.

➡Note: If an overhaul is indicated (usually because of fluid leakage) explore all options before beginning the job. New and factory-rebuilt calipers are available on an exchange basis, which makes this job quite easy. If it is decided to rebuild the calipers, make sure that a rebuild kit is available before proceeding. Always rebuild the calipers in pairs- never rebuild just one of them.

### REMOVAL

♦ Refer to illustration 4.2

1   Apply the parking brake and block the wheels opposite the end being worked on. Loosen the wheel lug nuts, raise the vehicle and sup-

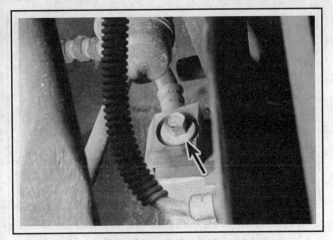

**4.2 If you're removing the caliper for overhaul, remove this banjo bolt (arrow) and detach the banjo fitting - shove a piece of rubber hose through the banjo fitting to plug the hose (front caliper shown; rear caliper banjo bolt shown in illustration 3.6l)**

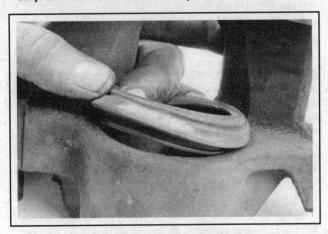

**4.6 Remove the dust boot from the caliper bore groove**

port it securely on jackstands. Remove the wheel.

2   Unscrew the brake hose banjo bolt (see illustration) and detach the hose from the caliper - remove the sealing washers from each side of the hose fitting and discard them. New sealing washers must be installed.

> ※※ **CAUTION:**
>
> On ABS-equipped models, plug the brake hose immediately to prevent air from getting into the hydraulic control unit (HCU). If air gets into the HCU, you will not be able to bleed the brakes properly at home. On non-ABS models, wrap a plastic bag around the end of the hose to prevent fluid loss and contamination.

➡ **Note: If the caliper will not be completely removed from the vehicle - as for pad inspection or disc removal - leave the hose connected and suspend the caliper with a length of wire. This will save the trouble of bleeding the brake system.**

3   Refer to the first six steps in Section 3 to separate the caliper from the steering knuckle (front) or the torque plate (rear) - it's part of the brake pad replacement procedure.

**4.5 With the caliper padded to catch the piston, use compressed air to force the piston out of its bore - make sure your hands and fingers are not between the piston and the caliper!**

**4.7 To remove the seal from the caliper bore, use a plastic or wooden tool, such as a pencil**

## OVERHAUL

▶ **Refer to illustrations 4.5, 4.6, 4.7, 4.12, 4.17, 4.18, 4.19a, 4.19b, 4.20 and 4.21**

4   Clean the exterior of the caliper with brake system cleaner. Never use gasoline, kerosene or other petroleum-based cleaning solvents. Place the caliper on a clean workbench.

5   Position a wood block or rags in the center of the caliper as a cushion, then use compressed air to remove the piston from the caliper (see illustration). Use only enough air to ease the piston out of the bore. If the piston is blown out, even with the cushion in place, it may be damaged.

> ※※ **WARNING:**
>
> Never place your fingers in front of the piston in an attempt to catch or protect it when applying compressed air, as serious injury could occur.

6   Pull the dust boot out of the caliper bore (see illustration).

7   Using a wood or plastic tool, remove the piston seal from the caliper bore (see illustration). Metal tools may cause bore damage.

**4.12 Grab the ends of the caliper bolt insulators and, using a twisting motion, push them through the caliper ears**

8   Carefully examine the piston for nicks, burrs, cracks, loss of plating, corrosion or any signs of damage. If surface defects are present, the parts must be replaced.

9   Check the caliper bore in a similar way. Light polishing with crocus cloth is permissible to remove light corrosion and stains.

**4.18 Install the dust boot in the upper groove in the caliper bore, making sure it's completely seated**

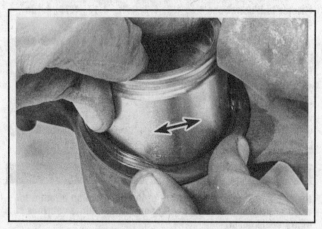

**4.19a Lubricate the piston and bore with clean brake fluid, insert the piston into the dust boot (NOT the bore) at an angle, then, using a rotating motion, work the piston completely into the dust boot . . .**

**4.17 Push the new seal into the groove with your fingers, then check to see that it isn't twisted or kinked**

10   Remove the bleeder valve and rubber cap.

11   Inspect the caliper bolts for corrosion and damage. Replace them with new ones if necessary.

12   Remove the caliper bolt insulators from the caliper ears (see illustration).

13   Use brake system cleaner to clean all the parts.

### ❊❊ WARNING:

**Do not, under any circumstances, use petroleum-based solvents to clean brake parts. Allow all parts to dry, preferably using compressed air to blow out all passages. Make sure the compressed air is filtered, as a harmful lubricant residue or moisture may be present in unfiltered systems.**

14   Push the new caliper bolt insulators into place, making sure they're installed all the way.

15   Check the fit of the piston in the bore by sliding it into the caliper. The piston should move easily (don't install it yet).

16   Thread the bleeder valve into the caliper and tighten it securely. Install the rubber cap.

17   Lubricate the new piston seal and caliper bore with clean brake fluid. Position the seal in the caliper bore groove, making sure it doesn't twist (see illustration).

18   Fit the new dust boot in the caliper bore upper groove, making sure it's seated (see illustration).

19   Lubricate the caliper piston with clean brake fluid. Push the piston into the caliper, using a turning motion to roll the lip of the dust

**4.19b . . . and push it straight into the caliper as far as possible by hand**

**4.20 Use a C-clamp and a block of wood to bottom the piston in the caliper bore - make sure it goes in perfectly straight, or the sides of the piston may be damaged, rendering it useless**

boot over the piston (see illustrations). Push the piston into the caliper by hand as far as possible.

20  Using a C-clamp and a block of wood, push the piston all the way to the bottom of the bore. Work slowly, keeping an eye on the side of the piston, making sure it enters the bore perfectly straight with no resistance (see illustration).

21  Seat the lip of the dust boot in the groove on the piston (see illustration).

**4.21 Install the lip of the dust boot in the groove on the caliper piston**

## INSTALLATION

22  Refer to Section 3 for the caliper installation procedure, as it is part of the brake pad replacement procedure.

23  Connect the brake hose to the caliper, using new sealing washers. Tighten the banjo bolt to the torque listed in this Chapter's Specifications.

24  Bleed the brakes as outlined in Section 10. This is not necessary if the banjo bolt was not loosened or removed (if the caliper was removed for access to other components, for example).

25  Install the wheel and lower the vehicle. Tighten the lug nuts to the torque listed in the Chapter 1 Specifications. Pump the brake pedal several times to bring the pads into contact with the disc.

26  Test the operation of the brakes before placing the vehicle into normal service.

## 5   Brake disc - inspection, removal and installation

## INSPECTION

▶ Refer to illustrations 5.5a, 5.5b, 5.6a and 5.6b

### ※※ WARNING 1:

On models with air suspension, turn the air suspension switch to Off before raising the vehicle.

### ※※ WARNING 2:

On models with a fire suppression system, disable the system before raising the rear of the vehicle by disconnecting the cable from the negative battery terminal and waiting at least three minutes.

**5.5a To check disc runout, mount a dial indicator as shown and rotate the disc**

➡Note: This procedure applies to both front and rear disc brake assemblies.

1   Loosen the wheel lug nuts, raise the vehicle and support it securely on jackstands. Remove the wheel.

2   Remove the brake caliper as outlined in Section 4. It's not necessary to disconnect the brake hose for this procedure. After removing the caliper bolts, suspend the caliper out of the way with a piece of wire. Don't let the caliper hang by the hose and don't stretch or twist the hose.

3   Reinstall three lug nuts (inverted) to hold the disc against the hub. It may be necessary to install washers between the disc and the lug nuts to take up space.

4   Visually check the disc surface for score marks and other damage. Light scratches and shallow grooves are normal after use and may not always be detrimental to brake operation, but deep score marks - over 0.015-inch - require disc removal and refinishing by an automotive machine shop. Be sure to check both sides of the disc. If pulsating has been noticed during application of the brakes, suspect disc runout.

5   To check disc runout, place a dial indicator at a point about 1/2-inch from the outer edge of the disc (see illustration). Set the indicator to zero and turn the disc. The indicator reading should not exceed the

**5.5b  Using a swirling motion, remove the glaze from the disc with sandpaper or emery cloth**

**5.6a  The minimum thickness limit is cast into the inside of the disc**

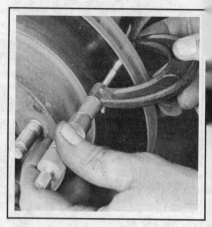

**5.6b  Use a micrometer to measure disc thickness at several points, about 1/2-inch from the edge**

specified allowable runout limit. If it does, the disc should be refinished by an automotive machine shop.

→Note: Professionals recommend resurfacing of brake discs regardless of the dial indicator reading (to produce a smooth, flat surface that will eliminate brake pedal pulsations and other undesirable symptoms related to questionable discs).

At the very least, if you elect not to have the discs resurfaced, deglaze the brake pad surface with emery cloth or sandpaper (use a swirling motion to ensure a non-directional finish) (see illustration).

**5.7  Lift the disc off the hub assembly**

6   The disc must not be machined to a thickness less than the specified minimum refinish thickness. The minimum wear (or discard) thickness is cast into the inside of the disc (see illustration). The disc thickness can be checked with a micrometer (see illustration).

## REMOVAL

▶ **Refer to illustration 5.7**

7   Mark the relationship between the disc and the hub, then lift the disc off the hub assembly. On 1998 and 1999 models, the disc is secured to the hub with two rivets. Drive the center mandrels out of the rivets with a punch, then use a 3/8-inch drill to remove the heads of the rivets for disc removal. The rivets should not be replaced on reassembly.

## INSTALLATION

8   Install the disc onto the hub assembly.
9   Install the caliper and brake pad assembly over the disc and position it on the steering knuckle (front), or on the torque plate (rear) (see Section 4). Install the caliper bolts and tighten them to the torque listed in this Chapter's Specifications.
10   Install the wheel, then lower the vehicle to the ground. Depress the brake pedal a few times to bring the brake pads into contact with the rotor. Bleeding of the system will not be necessary unless the brake hose was disconnected from the caliper. Check the operation of the brakes carefully before placing the vehicle into normal service.

## 6   Brake shoes (rear) - replacement

▶ **Refer to illustrations 6.4a through 6.4v and 6.5**

**✳✳ WARNING 1:**

Drum brake shoes must be replaced on both wheels at the same time - never replace the shoes on only one wheel. Also, the dust created by the brake system is harmful to your health. Never blow it out with compressed air and don't inhale any of it. An approved filtering mask should be worn when working on the brakes. Do not, under any circumstances, use petroleum-based solvents to clean brake parts. Use brake system cleaner only!

**✳✳ WARNING 2:**

On models with air suspension, turn the air suspension switch to Off before raising the vehicle.

**✳✳ WARNING 3:**

On models with a fire suppression system, disable the system before raising the rear of the vehicle by disconnecting the cable from the negative battery terminal and waiting at least three minutes.

6.4a Remove the brake drum

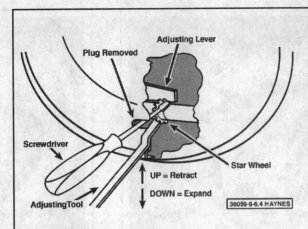

**6.4b** If the drum is difficult to remove, you may have to retract the brake shoes: Remove the rubber plug from the backing plate, insert a screwdriver through the hole, raise the adjusting lever off the star wheel and rotate the star adjuster with a brake adjustment tool or another screwdriver as shown

## ❊❊ CAUTION:

Whenever the brake shoes are replaced, the retractor and hold-down springs should also be replaced. Due to the continuous heating/cooling cycle that the springs are subjected to, they lose their tension over a period of time and may allow the shoes to drag on the drum and wear at a much faster rate than normal.

1   Loosen the wheel lug nuts, raise the rear of the vehicle and support it securely on jackstands. Block the front wheels to keep the vehicle from rolling.
2   Release the parking brake.
3   Remove the wheel.

**6.4c  Details of a typical rear drum brake assembly**

| | | |
|---|---|---|
| 1   Secondary brake shoe return spring | 6   Adjusting screw and wheel assembly | 10   Primary brake shoe return spring |
| 2   Automatic adjuster cable and guide | 7   Primary brake shoe | 11   Anchor pin |
| 3   Hold-down spring and pin | 8   Adjusting lever return spring | 12   Shoe guide |
| 4   Secondary brake shoe | 9   Wheel cylinder | 13   Parking brake link and spring |
| 5   Adjusting lever | | |

**6.4d  Remove the primary and secondary return springs with a spring removal tool**

➡Note: All four rear brake shoes must be replaced at the same time, but to avoid mixing up parts, work on only one brake assembly at a time.

4  Follow the accompanying photos (illustrations 6.4a through 6.4v)

**6.4e  Unhook the adjusting cable eye from the anchor pin**

for the inspection and replacement of the brake shoes. Be sure to stay in order and read the caption under each illustration.

➡Note: If the brake drum cannot be easily pulled off, pry the rubber plug from the backing plate inspection hole and insert a

**6.4f  Remove the shoe guide**

**6.4g  Remove the shoe retaining springs and pins - this is done by pushing the retainer in, turning it 90-degrees, then pulling it off the pin**

**6.4h  While separating the shoes, extract the adjusting screw and star wheel**

**6.4i  Remove the primary shoe and the parking brake strut and spring assembly**

**6.4j  Take out the adjusting lever. . .**

6.4k . . . and remove the secondary shoe from the backing plate

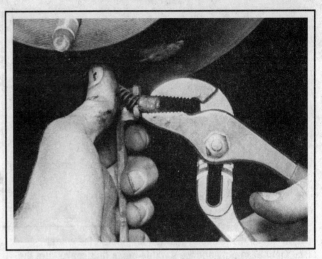

6.4l Separate the parking brake cable and spring from the actuating lever

screwdriver and a brake adjusting tool to lift the adjusting lever and rotate the adjusting screw. This will cause the brake shoes to pull together. Spray the assembly with penetrating oil and allow the oil to soak in if the mechanism is difficult to turn. The drum should now come off.

5   Before reinstalling the drum it should be checked for cracks, score marks, deep scratches and hard spots, which will appear as small discolored areas. If the hard spots cannot be removed with fine emery cloth or if any of the other conditions listed above exist, the drum must be taken to an automotive machine shop to have it turned.

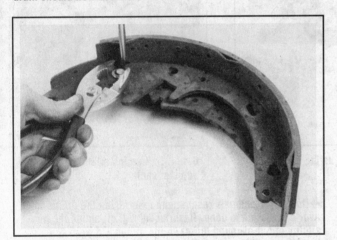

6.4m Remove the E-clip which attaches the parking brake lever to the shoe

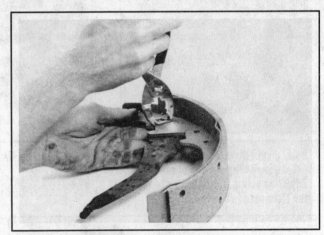

6.4n Attach the parking brake lever to the new brake shoe, using a new E-clip

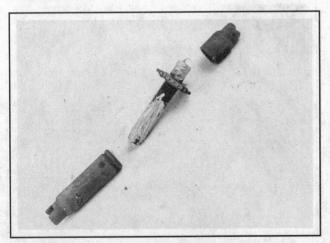

6.4o Disassemble, clean and lubricate the moving parts of the adjusting screw and wheel assembly

6.4p Lightly coat the shoe guide pads, wheel cylinder ends and anchor pin with high-temperature grease

6.4q Place the shoes in position and install the wheel cylinder assembly and the parking brake link; make sure the slots on the wheel cylinder links (A) and the parking brake link (B) are correctly engaged with the brake shoes

6.4r Install the hold-down springs; make sure the shoe retaining pins and springs are properly engaged

6.4s Install the adjusting screw - make sure the long end of the adjusting screw is pointing toward the front of the vehicle

6.4t Install the adjusting lever. . .

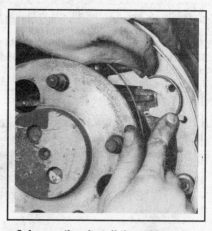

6.4u . . . then install the guide and adjuster cable

→Note: Professionals recommend resurfacing the drums whenever a brake job is done. Resurfacing will eliminate the possibility of out-of-round drums. If the drums are worn so much that they can't be resurfaced without exceeding the maximum

6.4v Connect the spring to the adjusting lever - that's it! You're done! Now go back and compare your work to illustration 6.4c and make sure everything is installed correctly, then adjust the brake shoes so the drum just slips over them. Once the drum is in place, adjust the shoes out so they drag slightly as the drum is turned, then back off the adjustment a few clicks

6.5 The maximum permissible diameter specification is cast into the brake drum

allowable diameter, which is stamped into the drum (see illustration), then new ones will be required. At the very least, if you elect not to have the drums resurfaced, remove the glazing from the surface with medium-grit emery cloth using a swirling motion.

6  Install the brake drum on the hub.
7  Mount the wheel, install the lug nuts, then lower the vehicle.
8  Make a number of forward and reverse stops to adjust the brakes until satisfactory pedal action is obtained.

## 7   Wheel cylinder - removal, overhaul and installation

### ❊❊ WARNING 1:

On models with air suspension, turn the air suspension switch to Off before raising the vehicle.

### ❊❊ WARNING 2:

On models with a fire suppression system, disable the system before raising the rear of the vehicle by disconnecting the cable from the negative battery terminal and waiting at least three minutes.

➡Note: If an overhaul is indicated (usually because of fluid leakage or sticky operation) explore all options before beginning the job. New wheel cylinders are available, which makes this job quite easy. If it's decided to rebuild the wheel cylinder, make sure that a rebuild kit is available before proceeding. Never overhaul only one wheel cylinder - always rebuild both of them at the same time.

### REMOVAL

▶ Refer to illustration 7.4

1  Raise the rear of the vehicle and support it securely on jackstands. Block the front wheels to keep the vehicle from rolling.
2  Remove the brake shoe assembly (see Section 6).
3  Remove all dirt and foreign material from around the wheel cylinder.
4  Disconnect the brake line (see illustration). Don't pull the brake line away from the wheel cylinder.
5  Remove the wheel cylinder mounting bolts.
6  Detach the wheel cylinder from the brake backing plate and place

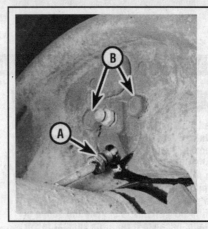

7.4  To remove the wheel cylinder, disconnect the brake line fitting (A) and remove the two mounting bolts (B)

it on a clean workbench. Immediately plug the brake line to prevent fluid loss and contamination.

### OVERHAUL

▶ Refer to illustration 7.7

7  Remove the bleeder screw, cups, pistons, boots and spring assembly from the wheel cylinder body (see illustration).
8  Clean the wheel cylinder with brake fluid, denatured alcohol or brake system cleaner.

### ❊❊ WARNING:

Do not, under any circumstances, use petroleum-based solvents to clean brake parts!

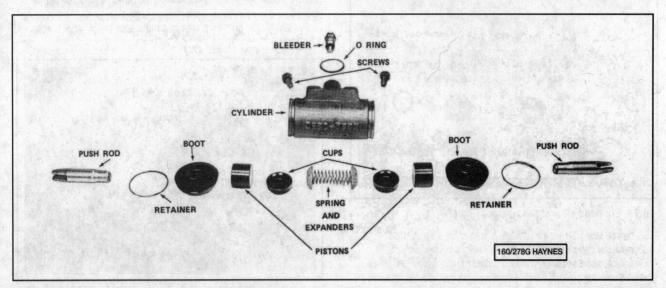

7.7  An exploded view of a typical wheel cylinder assembly

9  Use compressed air to remove excess fluid from the wheel cylinder and to blow out the passages. Make sure the compressed air is filtered and unlubricated.

10  Check the cylinder bore for corrosion and score marks. Crocus cloth can be used to remove light corrosion and stains, but the cylinder must be replaced with a new one if the defects cannot be removed easily, or if the bore is scored.

11  Lubricate the new cups with brake fluid.

12  Assemble the brake cylinder components. Make sure the cup lips face in.

## 8  Master cylinder - removal, overhaul and installation

### ✳✳ WARNING:

**If the vehicle is equipped with an Anti-lock Brake System (ABS), do not attempt to remove or overhaul the master cylinder. Have the master cylinder removed, rebuilt and installed at a dealer service department or other qualified repair shop. Removing a master cylinder from an ABS system can allow air to get into the ABS hydraulic control unit, which requires a special bleeding procedure impossible to perform at home. And overhauling a master cylinder used with ABS systems is beyond the scope of the average home mechanic because it requires special factory tools.**

➡Note: **Before deciding to overhaul the master cylinder, check on the availability and cost of a new or factory rebuilt unit and also the availability of a rebuild kit.**

### REMOVAL

1  Place rags under the brake line fittings and prepare caps or plastic bags to cover the ends of the lines once they are disconnected.

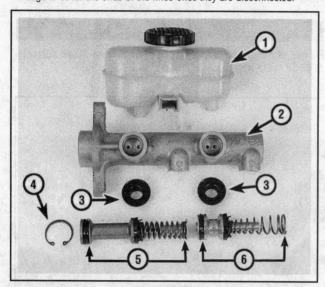

**8.7a  Exploded view of the master cylinder**

1    *Reservoir*
2    *Master cylinder body*
3    *Reservoir-to-master cylinder grommets*
4    *Snap-ring*
5    *Primary piston assembly*
6    *Secondary piston assembly*

### INSTALLATION

13  Place the wheel cylinder in position, install the mounting bolts and tighten them to the torque listed in this Chapter's Specifications.

14  Connect the brake line and install the brake shoe assembly.

15  Bleed the brakes (see Section 10).

### ✳✳ CAUTION:

**Brake fluid will damage paint. Cover all body parts and be careful not to spill fluid during this procedure.**

2  Unscrew the tube nuts at the ends of the brake lines where they enter the master cylinder. To prevent rounding off the flats on these nuts, a flare-nut wrench, which wraps around the fitting, should be used.

3  Pull the brake lines away from the master cylinder slightly and plug the ends to prevent contamination.

4  Disconnect the brake warning light electrical connector, remove the two master cylinder mounting nuts, and detach the master cylinder from the vehicle.

5  Remove the reservoir cap, then discard any fluid remaining in the reservoir.

### OVERHAUL

◗ **Refer to illustrations 8.7a, 8.7b, 8.8, 8.9, 8.10 and 8.14**

6  Mount the master cylinder in a vise with the vise jaws clamping on the mounting flange.

7  Remove the pressure control valve. On 1989 and later models, remove the stop bolt from the side of the cylinder body. Remove the primary piston snap-ring by depressing the piston and extracting the ring with a pair of snap-ring pliers. (see illustrations).

8  Remove the primary piston assembly from the cylinder bore (see illustration).

**8.7b  Use a Phillips head screwdriver to push the primary piston into the cylinder, then remove the snap-ring**

**8.8  Remove the primary piston assembly from the cylinder**

**8.9  Tap the master cylinder against a block of wood to eject the secondary piston assembly**

9   Remove the secondary piston assembly from the cylinder bore. It may be necessary to remove the master cylinder from the vise and invert it, carefully tapping it against a block of wood to expel the piston (see illustration).

10  If fluid has been leaking past the reservoir grommets, pry the reservoir from the cylinder body with a screwdriver (see illustration). Remove the grommets. Clean the master cylinder body and components with brake system cleaner.

**✳✳ WARNING:**

**DO NOT use petroleum-based solvents to clean brake parts - use brake system cleaner only.**

11  Inspect the cylinder bore for corrosion and damage. If any corrosion or damage is found, replace the master cylinder body with a new one, as abrasives cannot be used on the bore.

12  Lubricate the new reservoir grommets with silicone grease and press them into the master cylinder body. Make sure they're properly seated.

➡Note: If silicone grease is not available, use clean brake fluid.

13  Lay the reservoir on a hard surface and press the master cylinder body onto the reservoir, using a rocking motion.

14  Lubricate the cylinder bore and primary and secondary piston assemblies with clean brake fluid. Insert the secondary piston assembly into the cylinder (see illustration).

15  Install the primary piston assembly in the cylinder bore, depress it and install the snap-ring. If equipped with a stop bolt, install it now, using a new sealing washer and tightening it securely.

16  Inspect the reservoir cap and diaphragm for cracks and deformation. Replace any damaged parts with new ones and attach the diaphragm to the cap.

➡Note: Whenever the master cylinder is removed, the complete hydraulic system must be bled. The time required to bleed the system can be reduced if the master cylinder is filled with fluid and bench bled (refer to Steps 18 through 22) before the master cylinder is installed on the vehicle.

17  Insert threaded plugs of the correct size into the cylinder outlet holes and fill the reservoirs with brake fluid. The master cylinder should be supported in such a manner that brake fluid will not spill during the bench bleeding procedure.

18  Loosen one plug at a time, starting with the secondary outlet port first, and push the piston assembly into the bore to force air from the

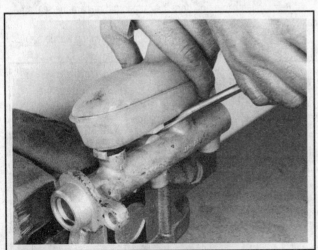

**8.10  If you must remove the fluid reservoir to replace leaking seals or a broken reservoir, gently pry it off with a screwdriver or small prybar**

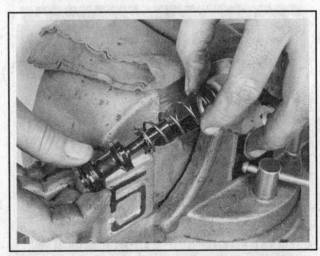

**8.14  Coat the secondary piston with clean brake fluid and install it in the master cylinder, spring end first**

master cylinder. To prevent air from being drawn back into the cylinder, the appropriate plug must be replaced before allowing the piston to return to its original position.

19 Stroke the piston three or four times for each outlet to ensure that all air has been expelled.

20 Since high pressure is not involved in the bench bleeding procedure, an alternative to the removal and replacement of the plugs with each stroke of the piston assembly is available. Before pushing in on the piston assembly, remove one of the plugs completely. Before releasing the piston, however, instead of replacing the plug, simply put your finger tightly over the hole to keep air from being drawn back into the master cylinder. Wait several seconds for the brake fluid to be drawn from the reservoir to the piston bore, then repeat the procedure. When you push down on the piston it will force your finger off the hole, allowing the air inside to be expelled. When only brake fluid is being ejected from the hole, replace the plug and go on to the other port.

21 Refill the master cylinder reservoirs and install the diaphragm and cap assembly.

## INSTALLATION

22 Carefully install the master cylinder by reversing the removal steps, then bleed the brakes (see Section 10).

## 9   Brake hoses and lines - inspection and replacement

### ❊❊ WARNING 1:

**On models with air suspension, turn the air suspension switch to Off before raising the vehicle.**

### ❊❊ WARNING 2:

**On models with a fire suppression system, disable the system before raising the rear of the vehicle by disconnecting the cable from the negative battery terminal and waiting at least three minutes.**

### ❊❊ CAUTION:

**If the vehicle is equipped with ABS, make sure you plug the brake line immediately after disconnecting it from the brake hose, to prevent the fluid from draining out of the line and air entering the HCU. The HCU on an ABS system cannot be bled without a very expensive tool.**

## INSPECTION

1   About every six months, with the vehicle raised and supported securely on jackstands, the rubber hoses which connect the steel brake lines with the front and rear brake assemblies should be inspected for cracks, chafing of the outer cover, leaks, blisters and other damage. These are important and vulnerable parts of the brake system and inspection should be complete. A light and mirror will be helpful for a thorough check. If a hose exhibits any of the above conditions, replace it with a new one.

## REPLACEMENT

### Flexible hose

▶ **Refer to illustrations 9.2 and 9.3**

2   Using a flare nut wrench, disconnect the brake line from the hose fitting, being careful not to bend the frame bracket or brake line. Hold the fitting on the hose with a wrench to prevent the metal line from twisting and the frame bracket from bending (see illustration).

3   Remove the large retaining clip (see illustration) and detach the hose from the bracket and the body.

### ❊❊ CAUTION:

**Plug the metal brake line immediately to prevent air from getting into the hydraulic control unit (HCU). If air gets into the HCU, you will not be able to bleed the brakes properly at home.**

4   Remove the banjo bolt from the caliper and discard the sealing washers.

5   Connect the hose to the caliper, using new sealing washers.

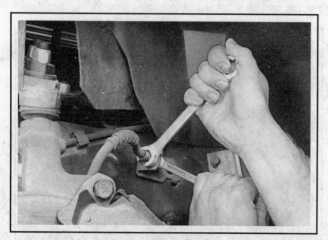

9.2 To disconnect the fitting that attaches the flexible brake hose to the metal brake line at the bracket in the wheel well, use a backup wrench on the hose fitting to ensure that the metal line doesn't get twisted

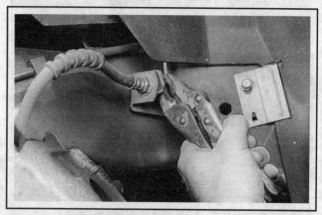

9.3 Once the fitting has been unscrewed, remove this large retainer clip and separate the hose from the bracket

Tighten the banjo bolt to the torque listed in this Chapter's Specifications.

6   Without twisting the hose, connect the other end of the line to the bracket on the chassis.

7   Connect the metal brake line to the hose fitting by hand, then, using a flare nut wrench, tighten the fitting securely. Be sure to use a wrench on the hose fitting to prevent the bracket from bending or the metal line from twisting.

8   When the brake hose installation is complete, there should be no kinks in the hose. Make sure the hose doesn't contact any part of the suspension. Check this by turning the wheels to the extreme left and right positions. If the hose makes contact, remove it and correct the installation as necessary.

## 10  Brake hydraulic system - bleeding

▶ **Refer to illustration 10.8**

### ✳✳ WARNING 1:

**Wear eye protection when bleeding the brake system. If the fluid comes in contact with your eyes, immediately rinse them with water and seek medical attention.**

### ✳✳ WARNING 2:

**On models with air suspension, turn the air suspension switch to Off before raising the vehicle.**

### ✳✳ WARNING 3:

**On models with a fire suppression system, disable the system before raising the rear of the vehicle by disconnecting the cable from the negative battery terminal and waiting at least three minutes.**

➡**Note: Bleeding the hydraulic system is necessary to remove any air that manages to find its way into the system when it's been opened during removal and installation of a hose, line, caliper or master cylinder.**

### CONVENTIONAL BRAKES (NON-ABS)

1   It will probably be necessary to bleed the system at all four brakes if air has entered the system due to low fluid level, or if the brake lines have been disconnected at the master cylinder.

2   If a brake line was disconnected only at a wheel, then only that caliper or wheel cylinder must be bled.

3   If a brake line is disconnected at a fitting located between the master cylinder and any of the brakes, that part of the system served by the disconnected line must be bled.

4   Remove any residual vacuum from the brake power booster by applying the brake several times with the engine off.

5   Remove the master cylinder reservoir cover and fill the reservoir with brake fluid. Reinstall the cover.

➡**Note: Check the fluid level often during the bleeding operation and add fluid as necessary to prevent the fluid level from falling low enough to allow air bubbles into the master cylinder.**

6   Have an assistant on hand, as well as a supply of new brake fluid, an empty clear plastic container, a length of 3/16-inch plastic, rubber or vinyl tubing to fit over the bleeder valve and a wrench to open and close the bleeder valve.

### Metal brake line

9   When replacing brake lines be sure to use the correct parts. Don't use copper tubing for any brake system components. Purchase steel brake lines from a dealer or auto parts store.

10  Prefabricated brake line, with the tube ends already flared and fittings installed, is available at auto parts stores and dealers. These lines are also sometimes bent to the proper shapes.

11  When installing the new line make sure it's securely supported in the brackets and has plenty of clearance between moving or hot components.

12  After installation, check the master cylinder fluid level and add fluid as necessary. Bleed the brake system as outlined in the next Section and test the brakes carefully before driving the vehicle in traffic.

**10.8  When bleeding the brakes, a hose is connected to the bleed screw at the caliper or wheel cylinder and then submerged in brake fluid - air will be seen as bubbles in the tube and container (all air must be expelled before moving to the next wheel)**

7   Beginning at the right rear wheel, loosen the bleeder valve slightly, then tighten it to a point where it is snug but can still be loosened quickly and easily.

8   Place one end of the tubing over the bleeder valve and submerge the other end in brake fluid in the container (see illustration).

9   Have the assistant pump the brakes slowly a few times to get pressure in the system, then hold the pedal firmly depressed.

10  While the pedal is held depressed, open the bleeder valve just enough to allow a flow of fluid to leave the valve. Watch for air bubbles to exit the submerged end of the tube. When the fluid flow slows after a couple of seconds, close the valve and have your assistant release the pedal.

11  Repeat Steps 9 and 10 until no more air is seen leaving the tube, then tighten the bleeder valve and proceed to the left rear wheel, the right front wheel and the left front wheel, in that order, and perform the same procedure. Be sure to check the fluid in the master cylinder reservoir frequently.

12  Never use old brake fluid. It contains moisture which will deteriorate the brake system components.

13  Refill the master cylinder with fluid at the end of the operation.

14  Check the operation of the brakes. The pedal should feel solid when depressed, with no sponginess. If necessary, repeat the entire process.

## ANTI-LOCK BRAKE SYSTEM (ABS)

15  ABS-equipped models cannot be bled at home if air gets into the master cylinder and/or the hydraulic control unit (HCU). The first step in the bleeding procedure for these two components requires a special anti-lock test adapter which must be plugged into the control module. Any attempt to bleed the master cylinder and HCU without this special device will trap air in the HCU, which will result in a spongy brake pedal.

16  However, as long as no air has gotten into the master cylinder or the HCU, the brake lines and the calipers can be bled in the conventional manner. Refer to Steps 1 through 14 above.

## 11  Parking brake - adjustment

### 1989 AND EARLIER MODELS

1  Place the transmission in Neutral and fully release the parking brake.

2  Raise the vehicle and support it securely on jackstands. Block the front wheels to prevent the vehicle from rolling.

3  Tighten the adjusting nut against the adjuster bracket until the rear drums drag against the shoes (see illustration 12.1). Then loosen the adjusting nut until the rear brakes are fully released. There should be no brake drag.

4  If the brake cables are replaced, stroke the parking brake forcefully a few times (to stretch the cable), release it and repeat the previous Step.

5  Lower the vehicle and check the operation of the parking brake.

### 1990 THROUGH 1996 MODELS

6  These models use a parking brake control assembly with an automatic tensioning device. No adjustment is necessary.

### 1997 AND LATER MODELS

7  On these models, an adjustment can be made at the tensioner assembly, where the cable from the foot control joins the rear cable.

8  Apply the parking brake foot control and release it, then repeat.

9  With the vehicle in Neutral, raise the vehicle and suitably support it with jackstands.

10  Pull down on the wire clip at the tensioner. The spring around the cable will apply tension to the cable automatically. Push up on the clip to lock it into place. If the clip will not engage, pull back on the spring assembly slightly until the clip aligns with the grooves in the housing.

## 12  Parking brake cables - replacement

### 1988 AND 1989 MODELS

**Front cable**

1  Raise the vehicle and support it securely on jackstands. Release the parking brake completely, then loosen the adjusting nut at the adjuster.

2  Disconnect the cable from the adjuster bracket and remove the clip retaining the cable to the body.

3  From inside the vehicle, disconnect the cable from the pedal assembly.

4  Remove the cable down trough the floorpan.

5  To install, insert the cable through the floorpan holes and attach it to the control assembly inside the vehicle. Make sure the grommet is properly seated.

6  From underneath the vehicle, fasten the cable to the adjuster bracket.

**Intermediate cable**

7  From under the vehicle, remove the cable adjusting nut.

8  Disconnect the intermediate cable ends at the left rear and at the transverse cable.

9  Remove the cable and adjuster bracket assembly, keeping track of the order in which the cotter pin, washer and spring were removed for ease of reassembly.

10  Install the equalizer assembly onto the pin, holding it in place

**12.21a  On models with rear disc brakes, remove this retaining clip from the bracket on the torque plate . . .**

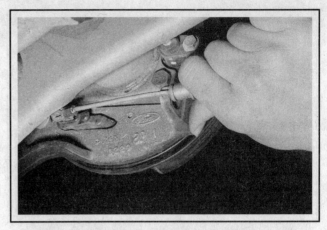

**12.21b  . . . pull the cable forward (toward the front of the vehicle) and guide it out of the bracket . . .**

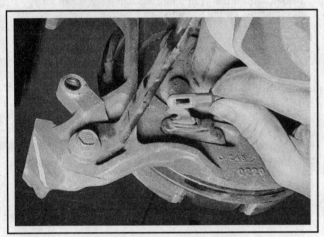

**12.21c  . . . then disconnect the cable from the parking brake lever**

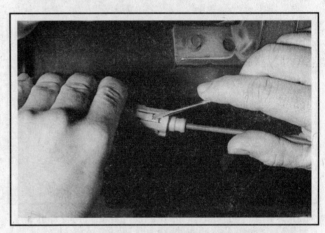

**12.22  To disconnect the left rear cable from the intermediate cable, pry open this locking tang with a small screwdriver**

while installing the spring, washer and cotter pin.

11  Connect the cable ends to the left rear and the transverse cable.

12  Install the cable adjusting nut.

## Transverse cable

13  Remove the cable adjusting nut.

14  Disconnect the cable ends at the right rear of the transverse cable and the intermediate cable.

15  Remove any retaining clips or brackets and remove the cable.

16  With the cable held in position, install the retaining clips or brackets holding the cable to the body.

17  Reconnect the cable ends.

18  Reinstall the adjusting nut.

## 1990 AND LATER MODELS

### Front cable

19  The front cable is connected to the parking brake mechanism, which is located in the extreme left corner of the area under the dash, where the firewall meets the kick panel. You need to fabricate a special tool to disconnect the front cable from the automatic spring-loaded automatic take-up reel. Unfortunately, you can't really see what you're doing until you have removed the parking brake mechanism. But a module hanging down from the dash is installed in very close proximity

to the parking brake mechanism, making removal of the parking brake assembly extremely difficult. For all these reason, we don't recommend trying to replace the front cable. If the cable breaks or the parking brake mechanism fails, take the vehicle to a dealer or other repair shop and have the cable or mechanism replaced by a professional with the right tools and know-how.

### Intermediate and rear cables

#### Removal

▶ **Refer to illustrations 12.21a, 12.21b, 12.21c, 12.22, 12.23, 12.24 and 12.25**

➡**Note: The following procedure applies to the intermediate cable (the short cable between the front cable and the two rear cables) and to either rear cable.**

20  Make sure the parking brake is released. Raise the rear of the vehicle and place it securely on jackstands.

21  Disconnect the rear cable. On models with rear drum brakes, you'll need to remove the brake drum and disassemble the brake (see Section 6) to disconnect the parking brake cable from the actuating lever (see illustration 6.4l). On models with rear disc brakes, simply follow the accompanying procedure (see illustrations)

22  Disconnect the left rear cable from the intermediate cable (see illustration).

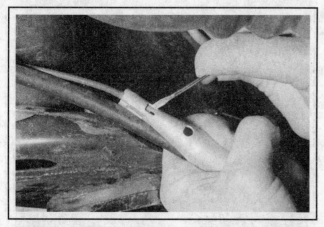

**12.23 To disconnect the right rear cable from the intermediate cable, pry open this locking tang with a small screwdriver**

**12.24 If you are replacing the intermediate cable, disconnect it from the front cable by prying it out of this connector with a small screwdriver (you'll find this connector under the crossmember for the transmission extension housing mount)**

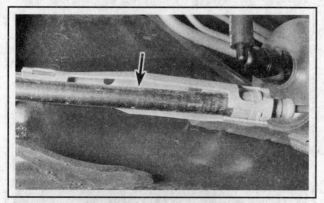

**12.25 When you reattach the two rear parking brake cables to the intermediate cable, make sure the left rear cable (arrow) is on top, and attached to the forward end of the cable connector; the right rear cable should be under the left rear cable, and should be attached to the rear end of the connector**

23 Disconnect the right rear cable from the intermediate cable (see illustration).

24 If you need to replace the intermediate cable, simply disconnect the front end of the intermediate cable from the connector at the rear end of the front cable (see illustration).

25 Installation is the reverse of removal. When you reattach the two rear cables to the intermediate cable, make sure that the left cable is on top (see illustration).

## 13 Parking brake shoes (rear disc brakes only) - inspection and replacement

◆ Refer to illustrations 13.5a through 13.5i

### ❋❋ WARNING 1:

Dust created by the brake system is hazardous to your health. Never blow it out with compressed air and don't inhale any of it. An approved filtering mask should be worn when working on the brakes. Do not, under any circumstances, use petroleum-based solvents to clean brake parts. Use brake system cleaner only!

### ❋❋ WARNING 2:

On models with air suspension, turn the air suspension switch to Off before raising the vehicle.

### ❋❋ WARNING 3:

On models with a fire suppression system, disable the system before raising the rear of the vehicle by disconnecting the cable from the negative battery terminal and waiting at least three minutes.

1  Loosen the rear wheel lug nuts. Raise the rear of the vehicle and place it securely on jackstands. Remove the rear wheels.

2  Remove the caliper (see Section 4) and the brake disc (see Section 5). It's not necessary to disconnect the brake hose from the caliper; but hang the caliper out of the way with a piece of wire to prevent damage to the hose. Remove the axleshafts (see Chapter 8).

3  Inspect the thickness of the lining material on the shoes. If the lining has worn down to 0.040 inch or less, the shoes must be replaced.

4  Disconnect the rear parking brake cable from the parking brake lever (see Section 12).

5  Follow the accompanying photos (see illustrations 13.5a through 13.5i) for the parking brake shoe replacement procedure. Be sure to stay in order and read the caption under each illustration.

6  Install the axleshaft and the brake disc. Temporarily thread three of the wheel lug nuts onto the studs to hold the disc in place.

7  Remove the rubber access plug from the backside of the brake torque plate. Adjust the parking brake shoe clearance by turning the adjuster star wheel with a brake adjusting tool or screwdriver until

**13.5a** Remove the parking brake leading shoe hold-down spring with an Allen bit . . .

**13.5b** . . . and remove the trailing shoe hold-down spring

**13.5c** Rotate the star adjuster to its shortest length, then spread the parking brake shoes apart and remove the adjuster

**13.5d** Detach the upper return spring from the parking brake shoes (it's in the back)

**13.5e** Remove the parking brake shoes, the lower return springs and the parking brake lever as a single assembly; make sure you don't damage the rubber grommet that lines the hole in the backing plate for the parking brake lever

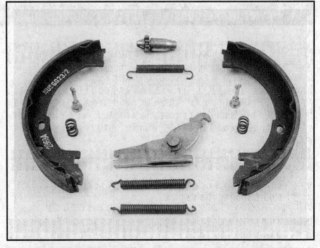

**13.5f** Finish disassembling the parking brake assembly on the bench: The two lower return springs (one in front of the shoes, one behind them) and the parking brake lever are shown bottom center

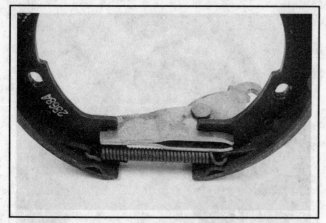

**13.5g  Here's a closeup of the correctly assembled parking brake lever and the lower return springs**

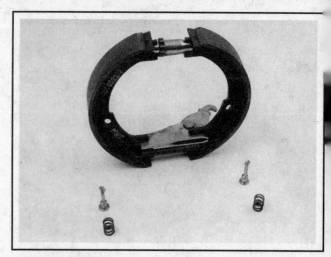

**13.5h  A correctly assembled parking brake shoe assembly (on the bench)**

**13.5i  A correctly assembled parking brake shoe assembly (on the vehicle)**

the shoes contact the disc and the disc can't be turned. Back-off the adjuster eight notches, then install the hole plug.

8   Install the brake caliper. Be sure to tighten the bolts to the torque listed in this Chapter's Specifications.

9   Install the wheel and tighten the lug nuts to the torque listed in the Chapter 1 Specifications.

10   To bed the shoes to the drum, drive the vehicle at approximately 30 mph on a dry, level road. Depress the parking brake pedal with about 20 pounds of force.

➡**Note: The vacuum release mechanism will prevent the parking brake from setting, if it is operating properly. Be sure to check the function of the vacuum release before performing the bedding-in procedure. Drive the vehicle for 1/4-mile with the parking brake applied like this.**

11   Repeat this procedure two or three times, allowing the brakes to cool between applications.

## 14   Power brake booster - check, removal, installation and adjustment

1   The power brake booster unit requires no special maintenance apart from periodic inspection of the vacuum hose and the case.

2   Dismantling of the brake booster requires special tools and is not ordinarily done by the home mechanic. If a problem develops, install a new or factory rebuilt unit.

## CHECK

3   Begin the power booster check by depressing the brake pedal several times with the engine off and make sure that there is no change in the pedal reserve distance. The reserve distance is the distance between the pedal and the floor when the pedal is fully depressed.

4   Now, depress the pedal and start the engine. If the pedal goes down slightly, operation is normal. Release the brake pedal and let the engine run for a couple of minutes.

5   Turn off the engine and depress the brake pedal several times slowly. If the pedal goes down farther the first time but gradually rises after the second or third depression, the booster is airtight.

6   Start the engine and depress the brake pedal, then stop the engine with the pedal still depressed. If there is no change in the reserve distance after holding the pedal for about 30-seconds, the booster is airtight.

7   If the pedal feels "hard" when the engine is running, the booster isn't operating properly or there is a vacuum leak in the hose to the booster.

## REMOVAL

▶ **Refer to illustration 14.11**

8   Remove the nuts attaching the master cylinder to the booster (see

**14.11  Remove the four nuts (arrows) holding the booster to the firewall**

Section 8) and carefully pull the master cylinder forward until it clears the mounting studs. Use caution so as not to bend or kink the brake lines.

9   Detach the manifold vacuum hose from the booster check valve.

10  Working in the passenger compartment under the steering col-umn, unplug the electrical connector from the brake light switch (see illustration 15.2), then remove the pushrod retaining clip and nylon washer from the brake pedal pin. Slide the pushrod off the pin.

11  Remove the nuts attaching the brake booster to the firewall (see illustration).

12  Carefully detach the booster from the firewall and lift it out of the engine compartment.

## INSTALLATION

13  Place the booster into position on the firewall and tighten the mounting nuts to the torque listed in this Chapter's Specifications. Connect the pushrod and brake light switch to the brake pedal. Install the retaining clip in the brake pedal pin.

14  Install the master cylinder to the booster, tightening the nuts to the torque listed in this Chapter's Specifications.

15  Carefully check the operation of the brakes before driving the vehicle in traffic.

## ADJUSTMENT

▶ **Refer to illustrations 14.16a, 14.16b, and 14.16c**

16  Some boosters feature an adjustable pushrod. They are matched to the booster at the factory and most likely will not require adjustment, but if a misadjusted pushrod is suspected, a gauge can be fabricated out of heavy gauge sheet metal using the accompanying templates (see ilustrations).

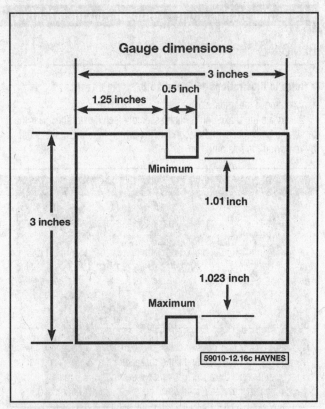

**14.16a  Power brake booster pushrod gauge template (1988, 1989, 1999 and later models)**

**14.16b  Power brake booster pushrod gauge template (1990 through 1995 models)**

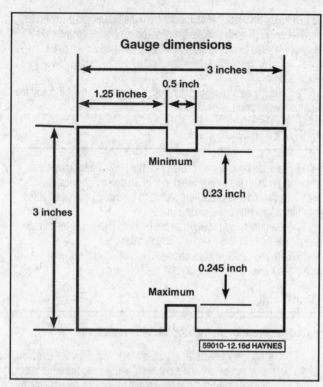

**Gauge dimensions**

3 inches

1.25 inches

0.5 inch

**Minimum**

0.23 inch

3 inches

0.245 inch

**Maximum**

59010-12.16d HAYNES

**14.16c Power brake booster pushrod gauge template (1996 through 1998 models)**

17 Some common symptoms caused by a misadjusted pushrod include dragging brakes (if the pushrod is too long) or excessive brake pedal travel accompanied by a groaning sound from the brake booster (if the pushrod is too short).

18 To check the pushrod length, unbolt the master cylinder from the booster and position it to one side. It isn't necessary to disconnect the hydraulic lines, but be careful not to bend them.

19 Block the front wheels, apply the parking brake and place the transmission in Park.

20 Start the engine and place the pushrod gauge against the end of the pushrod, exerting a force of approximately five pounds to seat the pushrod in the power unit.

➡**Note: If you have a vacuum pump, you can simply apply vacuum to the booster instead of starting the engine.**

The rod measurement should fall somewhere between the minimum and maximum cutouts on the gauge. If it doesn't, adjust it by holding the knurled portion of the pushrod with a pair of pliers and turning the end with a wrench.

21 When the adjustment is complete, reinstall the master cylinder and check for proper brake operation before driving the vehicle in traffic.

## 15 Brake light switch - removal and installation

### REMOVAL

▶ **Refer to illustrations 15.2 and 15.3**

1 Remove the under dash panel.

2 Locate the brake light switch assembly (see illustration) near the top of the brake pedal and disconnect the switch from the brake pedal by removing the retaining clip.

3 Use a small screwdriver to unlock the electrical connector, then unplug the connector from the brake light switch (see illustration).

### INSTALLATION

4 Install the switch to the electrical connector by snapping the clip into place.

5 Reconnect the assembly to the brake pedal.

6 Install the under dash panel.

7 Check the brake lights for proper operation.

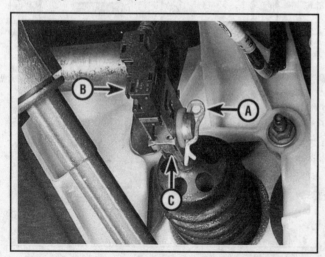

**15.2 Pull the pin (A) and disconnect the brake light switch (B) and booster pushrod (C) from the brake pedal arm - don't lose the spacers**

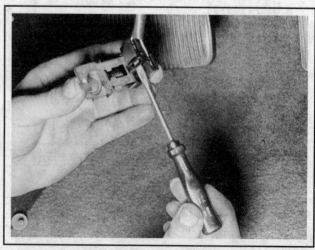

**15.3 Use a small screwdriver to disengage the clip inside the electrical connector**

## Specifications

**Brake fluid type**        See Chapter 1

## Disc brakes

| | |
|---|---|
| Minimum brake pad thickness | See Chapter 1 |
| Front brake disc | |
|   Standard thickness | |
|     1997 and earlier | 1.03 inch |
|     1998 through 2002 | 1.10 inch |
|     2003 and later | 1.06 inch |
|   Minimum thickness* | |
|     1988 through 1991 | 0.972 inch |
|     1992 on through 1997 | 0.974 inch |
|     1998 through 2002 | 1.01 inch |
|     2003 and later | 1.03 inch |
|   Runout limit | 0.003 inch |
|   Thickness variation (parallelism) | |
|     1988 through 1991 | 0.00050 inch |
|     1992 on | 0.00035 inch |
| Rear brake disc | |
|   Standard thickness | |
|     1997 and earlier | 0.50 inch |
|     1998 through 2002 | 0.56 inch |
|     2003 and later | 0.73 inch |
|   Minimum thickness* | |
|     1997 and earlier | 0.440 inch |
|     1998 through 2002 | 0.51 inch |
|     2003 and later | 0.70 inch |
|   Runout limit | 0.002 inch |
|   Thickness variation (parallelism) | 0.0005 inch |

*Refer to marks stamped on the disc (they supersede information printed here)*

## Drum brakes

| | |
|---|---|
| Drum diameter | |
|   Standard | |
|     Sedan | 10.000 inches |
|     Station wagon | 11.030 inches |
|   Maximum* | |
|     Sedan | 10.060 inches |
|     Station wagon | 11.090 inches |

*Refer to marks cast into the drum (they supersede information printed here)*

## Torque specifications — Ft-lbs (unless otherwise indicated)

➤Note: One foot-pound (ft-lb) of torque is equivalent to 12 inch-pounds (in-lbs) of torque. Torque values below approximately 15 foot-pounds are expressed in inch-pounds, because most foot-pound torque wrenches are not accurate at these smaller values.

Brake caliper (front) bolts
    1988 through 1991             40 to 60
    1992 through 1996             45 to 65
    1997 through 2002             21 to 26
    2003 through 2005             32
    2006 and later                 27
Brake caliper (rear) bolts
    1992 through 2002             20
    2003 and later                 18
Brake hose-to-brake line fittings      120 to 216 in-lbs
Brake hose-to-front caliper banjo bolts
    1988 through 1991             20 to 30
    1992 on                     30 to 40
Brake hose-to-rear caliper banjo bolts (1992 on)     30 to 40
Master cylinder to-power brake booster
    mounting nuts                 13 to 25
Power brake booster-to-firewall mounting nuts     13 to 25
Wheel cylinder-to-brake backing plate
    mounting bolts               120 to 240 in-lbs

## 10

## SUSPENSION
## AND STEERING
## SYSTEMS

**Reference to other Chapters**

## 1 General information

♦ Refer to illustrations 1.1a, 1.1b, 1.2a and 1.2b

### ✳✳ WARNING 1:

On models with air suspension, turn the air suspension switch to Off before raising the vehicle.

### ✳✳ WARNING 2:

On models with a fire suppression system, disable the system before raising the rear of the vehicle by disconnecting the cable from the negative battery terminal and waiting at least three minutes.

The front suspension (see illustrations) consists of upper and lower control arms, shock absorbers, coil springs and a stabilizer bar. The inner ends of the control arms are attached to the frame; the outer ends are attached to the steering knuckles with balljoints. The upper control arms on 1988 through 2002 models pivot on a bushing-and-shaft assembly bolted to the frame. The lower control arms pivot on two separate bolts. The shocks and springs on 1988 through 2002 models are mounted between the lower control arms and the frame. On 2003 and later models, the coil springs are integral with the shock absorber assembly. The stabilizer bar is attached to the frame with clamps. On 1988 through 1991 models, the outer ends of the stabilizer bar are attached to the lower control arms with links; on 1992 and later models, the ends of the stabilizer bar are attached to the steering knuckles with links.

The rear suspension (see illustrations) consists of shock absorbers, coil springs, upper and lower suspension arms and a stabilizer bar. The coil springs are mounted between the underside of the body and the axle housing. The shock absorbers are installed between the frame and brackets welded onto the underside of the axle assembly. The axle assembly is located by a pair of upper and lower suspension arms, attached to the frame and the axle. The stabilizer bar is attached to the axle housing and to the lower arms. On 1998 and later models, the upper control arms of the rear suspension are mounted parallel to the frame and the lower control arms. In previous years, the angle of the upper arms provided resistance to lateral movement of the rear axle housing, but the newer suspension has two additional arms mounted laterally and attached to a center pivot arm that mounts on a pivot stud located on top of the differential housing. The assembly is called a Watts linkage, and it improves vehicle ride and handling because the axle stays centered under the chassis regardless of wheel travel at

**1.1a Front suspension and steering components - early models**

| | | | | | |
|---|---|---|---|---|---|
| 1 | Pitman arm | 5 | Outer tie-rod | 9 | Lower control arm balljoint |
| 2 | Center link | 6 | Stabilizer bar clamp | 10 | Lower control arm |
| 3 | Idler arm | 7 | Front stabilizer bar | 11 | Shock absorber |
| 4 | Tie-rod adjuster | 8 | Steering knuckle | | |

either end.

1988 through 2002 models are equipped with a power steering system consisting of a power steering pump, a steering gearbox, the lines and hoses between the two components, and the steering linkage (see illustration 1.1a), which includes a Pitman arm, a center link, an idler arm, the inner and outer tie-rods and the threaded sleeves connecting them. 2003 and later models are equipped with a rack-and-pinion power steering gear.

**1.1b Front suspension and steering components - late models**

| | | | | | |
|---|---|---|---|---|---|
| 1 | Stabilizer bar | 4 | Tie-rod end | 7 | Shock absorber (lower mount) |
| 2 | Stabilizer bar clamps | 5 | Steering knuckle | 8 | Lower control arm |
| 3 | Tie-rod end jam nut | 6 | Lower balljoint nut | 9 | Power steering gear |

**1.2a Typical rear suspension components - early models**

| | | | | | |
|---|---|---|---|---|---|
| 1 | Rear stabilizer bar | 4 | Rear air spring | 6 | Rear shock absorber |
| 2 | Stabilizer bar clamp | 5 | Lower suspension arm | 7 | Upper suspension arm |
| 3 | Rear axle housing | | | | |

**1.2b Rear suspension components - late models**

| | | | | | |
|---|---|---|---|---|---|
| 1 | Coil spring | 4 | Lower suspension arm | 6 | Lateral arm (right side) |
| 2 | Shock absorber | 5 | Rear axle tube | 7 | Lateral arm (left side) |
| 3 | Upper suspension arm | | | | |

## 2 Shock absorber (front) - removal and installation

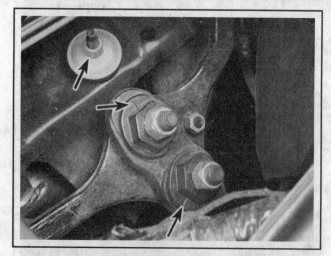

**2.1 To detach the upper end of the shock absorber from the vehicle, remove this nut (top arrow), then remove the large washer under it and the bushing under the washer. If you're replacing an upper balljoint on 1992 and later models, be sure to mark the location of the alignment marks on the adjustment cams (middle and bottom arrows) before removing the two retaining nuts**

**✳ WARNING:**

On models with air suspension, turn the air suspension switch to Off before raising the vehicle.

### REMOVAL

#### 1988 through 2002 models

⯈ Refer to illustrations 2.1 and 2.3

1    Remove the shock absorber upper attaching nut, washer and bushing (see illustration).

2    Raise the vehicle and support it securely on jackstands.

3    Remove the self-tapping bolts which attach the lower end of the shock absorber to the lower control arm (see illustration).

4    Remove the shock absorber through the hole in the lower control arm. To ensure proper reassembly, note the order in which any bushings and grommets are installed both above and below the upper control arm. Inspect these parts for cracks, tears and deterioration, and replace as necessary.

**2003 and later models**

5   Raise the vehicle and support it securely on jackstands.
6   Remove the three shock absorber upper mounting nuts.

### ✳✳ WARNING:

**Do not loosen or remove the damper rod nut located in the center of the bracket.**

7   Remove the brake caliper and the brake disc (see Chapter 9).
8   Remove the upper stabilizer bar links (see Section 3).
9   Remove the lower stabilizer bar links (see Section 3).
10  Remove the upper balljoint nut and separate the control arm from the steering knuckle (see Section 9).
11  Remove the lower mounting bolt and the shock absorber/coil spring assembly from the front end of the vehicle.
12  Inspect the shock absorber for leaking fluid, dents, cracks and other damage. Inspect the coil spring for chips and cracks which could cause premature failure. Inspect the spring seats for hardness and general deterioration. If any of the components of the assembly are worn or damaged, have the unit serviced by a qualified repair shop, or replace it with a rebuilt or new unit.

## INSTALLATION

13  Installation is the reverse of removal. Be sure you do the following:
a)  *Before installing a new shock absorber (2002 and earlier models), expel all air. Hold the shock right side up and extend it fully. Turn the shock upside down and compress it all the way. Extend and compress the shock absorber in this manner at least three times.*

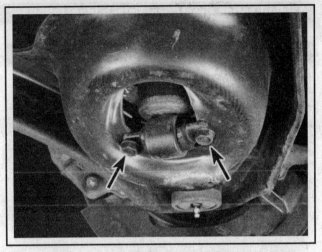

**2.3 To detach the lower end of the shock absorber from the lower A-arm, remove these two bolts (arrows)**

b)  *Install all bushings and grommets in the order in which you removed them. Also, it may be necessary to raise the lower control arm with a floor jack, after you've mounted the bottom of the shock to the lower control arm, to raise the shock rod high enough to install the upper mounting hardware.*
c)  *If the threads in the lower control arm are stripped or damaged, install 5/16-18 locknuts on the self-tapping bolts.*
d)  *ighten all fasteners to the torque listed in this Chapter's Specifications. If you had to use locknuts on the self-tapping bolts, torque them to the same specification as the bolts.*

## 3   Stabilizer bar (front) - removal and installation

▸ **Refer to illustrations 3.2 and 3.4**

### ✳✳ WARNING:

**On models with air suspension, turn the air suspension switch to Off before raising the vehicle.**

1   Raise the vehicle and place it securely on jackstands.
2   Remove the nut at each end of the stabilizer bar and disconnect

the bar from the links. On 1988 through 1991 models, the links attach the stabilizer bar to the lower control arms; on 1992 and later models, they attach it to the steering knuckles (see illustration).
3   On 2006 models, remove the shock absorber/coil spring assembly (see Section 2).
4   Remove the stabilizer bar clamp nuts (see illustration) and remove the clamps.
5   Remove the stabilizer bar.
6   Installation is the reverse of removal. Be sure to tighten all fasteners to the torque listed in this Chapter's Specifications.

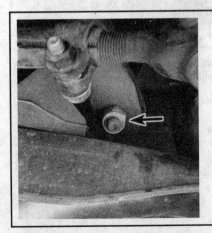

**3.2 To disconnect the stabilizer bar from the links, remove the nut (arrow) from each end (left nut on a 1993 model with link attached to the steering knuckle shown)**

**3.4 To detach the stabilizer bar from the frame, remove the nuts (arrows) that attach the bushing clamps to the frame(left bushing clamp shown)**

## 4 Coil spring (front) - removal and installation

**❊❊ WARNING:**

**On models with air suspension, turn the air suspension switch to Off before raising the vehicle.**

➡**Note: This procedure applies to 2002 and earlier models only. Coil spring removal and installation on 2003 and later models is included with the shock absorber replacement (see Section 2).**

## REMOVAL

◆ **Refer to illustrations 4.5 and 4.6**

1   Loosen the wheel lug nuts. Raise the vehicle and support it securely on jackstands. Remove the wheels.

2   On 1988 through 1991 models, disconnect the stabilizer bar from the link (see Section 3).

3   Remove the shock absorber (see Section 2).

4   Disconnect the center link from the Pitman arm (see Section 17).

5   Install a suitable spring compressor, in accordance with the manufacturer's instructions, to relieve tension on the spring (see illustration). Compress the spring.

6   Remove the nuts and bolts that secure the inner end of the lower control arm to the frame (see illustration).

7   Carefully and very slowly, lower the control arm. Remove the spring and compressor as a unit. Note how the upper insulator is installed between the upper end of the spring and the frame. If the spring is going to be replaced, loosen the spring compressor tool slowly, until all tension is removed from the spring, then remove the tool.

## INSTALLATION

8   Place the spring upper insulator on the spring and secure it with tape. Install the spring compressor in accordance with the manufacturer's instructions, then compress the spring.

9   Position the spring on the lower control arm so that the lower end is properly engaged with the seat. On 1988 through 1991 models, there are two holes in the lower control arm spring seat. The end of the spring must cover the first hole, but not the second hole.

10  Raise the lower control arm carefully while guiding the inner end to align with the bolt holes in the frame. Install the pivot bolts into the control arm and the frame. Loosely attach the nuts on the bolts.

11  Attach the center link to the Pitman arm (see Section 17).

12  Attach the lower end of the shock absorber to the lower control arm (see Section 2).

13  On 1988 through 1991 models, attach the stabilizer bar to the link (see Section 3).

14  Install the shock absorber (see Section 2).

15  Install the wheels. Remove the jackstands, lower the floor jack and lower the vehicle. Tighten the wheel lug nuts to the torque listed in the Chapter 1 Specifications.

16  After the vehicle has been lowered to the ground and is at curb height, tighten the lower control arm pivot bolt nuts to the torque listed in this Chapter's Specifications. This can also be done with the vehicle on jackstands by raising the lower control arm with a floor jack to simulate normal ride height.

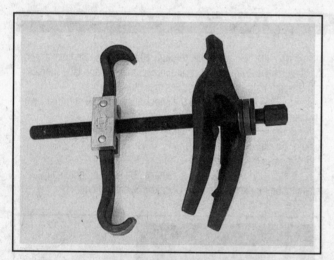

**4.5  A typical internal spring compressor tool: The hooked arms grip the upper coils of the spring, the plate is inserted below the lower coils, and when the nut on the threaded rod is turned, the spring gets compressed**

**4.6  To detach the inner end of the lower control arm from the frame, remove the pivot nuts and bolts (arrows)**

## 5  Lower control arm - removal, inspection and installation

### ✳✳ WARNING:

On models with air suspension, turn the air suspension switch to Off before raising the vehicle.

## REMOVAL

▶ **Refer to illustrations 5.5a and 5.5b**

1  Loosen the wheel lug nuts. Raise the front of the vehicle and support it securely on jackstands. Remove the front wheel.

2  Remove the shock absorber (2002 and earlier models) or shock absorber/coil spring assembly (2003 and later models) (see Section 2).

3  On 1988 through 1991 models, disconnect the stabilizer bar link from the lower control arm (see Section 3).

4  Remove the coil spring (2002 and earlier models) (see Section 4).

5  Remove and discard the cotter pin from the balljoint stud (see illustrations). Loosen the castle nut on the stud one or two turns. Rap the steering knuckle sharply in the immediate vicinity of the stud to relieve stud pressure and loosen the stud in the knuckle. If the stud won't come loose, you might have to resort to a "picklefork" type of balljoint stud separator.

### ✳✳ CAUTION:

The use of a picklefork balljoint separator will usually result in balljoint boot damage.

6  Remove the balljoint stud nut.

7  Remove the lower control arm mounting bolts and remove the lower control arm.

## INSPECTION

8  Inspect the bushings for cracks and tears. If they're damaged or worn, take the control arm to an automotive machine shop to have new bushings installed. This procedure requires a number of specialized tools, so it's not worth tackling at home.

## INSTALLATION

9  Install the lower control arm and mounting bolts. Don't fully tighten the nuts at this time.

10  If you're working on a 2002 or earlier model, install the spring compressor in accordance with the manufacturer's instructions and place the spring in position on its seat in the lower control arm. Make sure the spring is properly seated (see Section 4).

11  On 2002 and earlier models, place a floor jack under the lower control arm, raise the lower control arm and guide the upper end of the spring into position. Make sure the insulator is properly installed on top of the spring (see Section 4).

12  Insert the balljoint stud into the steering knuckle, install the castle nut and tighten it to the torque listed in this Chapter's Specifications. Continue to tighten the nut, if necessary, until the hole in the stud is in line with the slot in the nut. Install a new cotter pin.

➡ **Note: The manufacturer recommends using a new nut each time the control arm is installed. The new nut comes coated with a special adhesive compound.**

13  If you're working on a 2003 or later model, install the shock absorber/coil spring assembly.

14  On 1988 through 1991 models, attach the stabilizer bar (see Section 3).

15  If you're working on a 2002 or earlier model, install the shock absorber (see Section 2).

16  Raise the lower control arm with a floor jack to simulate normal ride height, then tighten the pivot bolt nuts to the torque listed in this Chapter's Specifications.

17  Install the wheel, remove the jackstands, lower the vehicle and tighten the wheel lug nuts to the torque listed in the Chapter 1 Specifications.

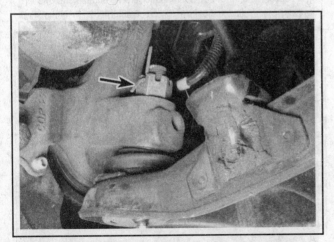

**5.5a  To separate the lower control arm from the steering knuckle, remove this cotter pin (arrow), loosen the castle nut one or two turns and give the steering knuckle a few sharp raps on the boss area adjacent to the balljoint stud to loosen the stud (2002 and earlier models)**

**5.5b  Lower balljoint nut - 2003 and later models**

## 6 Upper control arm - removal, inspection and installation

### ❋❋ WARNING:

On models with air suspension, turn the air suspension switch to Off before raising the vehicle.

## REMOVAL

1 Loosen the wheel lug nuts, raise the vehicle, support it securely on jackstands and remove the wheel.

### 1988 through 1991 models

2 Remove the cotter pin from the upper balljoint stud and loosen the stud nut one or two turns.

3 Place a floor jack under the lower control arm and raise it slightly. The jack must remain in this position during the entire operation.

4 Rap on the steering knuckle near the upper balljoint stud with a hammer to loosen the stud in the steering knuckle. If the stud won't come loose, you might have to resort to a "picklefork" type of balljoint stud separator.

### ❋❋ CAUTION:

The use of a picklefork balljoint separator will usually result in balljoint boot damage.

5 Remove the nut from the upper balljoint stud.

6 Remove the upper control arm pivot shaft attaching bolts. Remove the upper control arm and pivot shaft as an assembly.

### 1992 through 2002 models

▶ Refer to illustrations 6.8, 6.10a and 6.10b

7 Position a floor jack under the lower control arm.

8 Remove the pinch bolt and nut that retain the upper balljoint stud to the steering knuckle (see illustration).

9 Using a prybar, spread the slot in the steering knuckle far enough

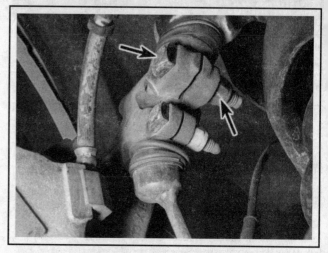

**6.8 To detach the upper control arm balljoint stud from the steering knuckle, remove the nut and pinch bolt (arrows) you'll have to drive out the pinch bolt with a drift - then insert a prybar in the gap and spread the two halves of the pinch boss apart far enough to remove the ball stud (the lower pinch bolt and nut retain the stabilizer bar link balljoint stud on 1992 and later models)**

apart to separate the balljoint stud from the knuckle.

10 Remove the upper control arm retaining bolts (see illustrations) and remove the upper control arm assembly.

### 2003 and later models

11 Remove the shock absorber/coil spring assembly (see Section 2).

12 Remove the harness retainers from the upper control arm.

13 Remove the upper control arm mounting bolts and remove the upper control arm.

## INSPECTION

14 Inspect the control arm bushings for cracks and tears. If they're damaged or worn, take the control arm to an automotive machine shop

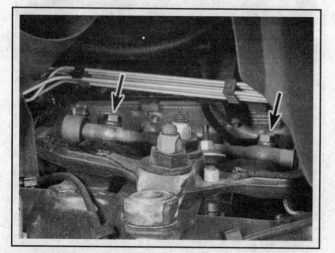

**6.10a To disconnect the upper control arm from the frame, remove these two bolts (arrows)**

**6.10b On 1997 and later models, the upper control arm is mounted to the frame with two bolts (arrows), rather than one long shaft**

to have new bushings installed. This procedure requires a number of specialized tools, so it's not worth tackling at home.

## INSTALLATION

15 Position the upper control arm pivot shaft on the frame and install the two attaching bolts and washers. Tighten the bolts to the torque listed in this Chapter's Specifications.

16 Insert the upper balljoint stud into the steering knuckle and install the ball stud nut or pinch bolt and nut. Tighten the nut to the torque listed in this Chapter's Specifications. On 1988 through 1991 models, continue to tighten the nut, if necessary, until the cotter pin hole in the stud is in line with the nut slots, then install a new cotter pin.

17 Install the wheel and tighten the lug nuts to the torque listed in this Chapter's Specifications.

18 Remove the jackstands and lower the vehicle.

19 Drive the vehicle to an alignment shop and have the caster, camber and toe-in adjusted as required.

---

## 7 Hub and bearing assembly (1992 and later models) - removal and installation

### ✳✳ WARNING:

**On models with air suspension, turn the air suspension switch to Off before raising the vehicle.**

➡ **Note: The manufacturer recommends replacing the hub retaining nut anytime it is removed.**

1 Remove the wheel cover (if applicable). Remove the dust cap and break loose the hub and bearing assembly retaining nut with a 1/2-inch drive breaker bar and socket. Use a "cheater" bar or pipe if necessary. Don't remove the nut yet.

2 Loosen the wheel lug nuts. Raise the vehicle and place it securely on jackstands. Remove the wheel.

3 Remove the brake caliper and the disc (see Chapter 9).

4 On 1988 through 2002 models, remove the hub and bearing assembly retaining nut and remove the hub and bearing assembly. If the assembly cannot be removed by hand, use a suitable hub puller.

### ✳✳ CAUTION:

**On models equipped with ABS brakes, be careful not to damage the ABS sensor or sensor ring when removing the hub.**

5 On 2003 and later models, remove the hub and bearing assembly mounting bolts on the backside of the steering knuckle and remove the hub assembly. If the hub assembly is seized to the steering knuckle, use a suitable hub puller.

6 Installation is the reverse of removal. After the vehicle is back on the ground, be sure to tighten the wheel lug nuts to the torque listed in the Chapter 1 Specifications and the hub and bearing assembly retaining nut/bolts to the torque listed in this Chapter's Specifications.

### ✳✳ WARNING:

**Do NOT attempt to tighten the hub retaining nut while the vehicle is on jackstands - do it with the vehicle on the ground, with the transmission in Park and the parking brake applied.**

---

## 8 Steering knuckle - removal and installation

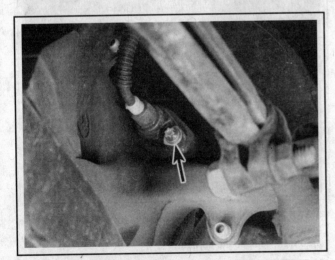

**8.6 To remove the ABS sensor, you'll need a Torx socket for the retaining bolt (arrow)**

▶ **Refer to illustration 8.6**

### ✳✳ WARNING:

**On models with air suspension, turn the air suspension switch to Off before raising the vehicle.**

1 On 1992 and later models, break loose the hub and bearing assembly retaining nut (see Section 7).

2 Loosen the wheel lug nuts. Raise the vehicle and support it securely on jackstands. Remove the wheel.

3 Remove the disc brake caliper (see Chapter 9). Wire the caliper to the underbody to prevent damage to the brake hose.

4 On 1988 through 1991 models, remove the grease cap from the hub, then remove the cotter pin, nut lock, adjusting nut, washer and outer bearing cone and roller assembly (see Chapter 1).

5 Remove the brake disc (see Chapter 9).

6 Remove the ABS sensor (see illustration), if equipped, then remove the dust shield from the steering knuckle.

7   Disconnect the tie-rod end from the steering knuckle (see Section 17).

8   Place a jack under the lower arm of the balljoint area. Raise the jack until it supports the spring load on the lower arm. The jack must remain in this position throughout the remainder of this procedure.

## ✳✳ WARNING:

**Failure to perform this step could result in serious injury.**

## 9   Balljoint - check and replacement

## ✳✳ WARNING:

**On models with air suspension, turn the air suspension switch to Off before raising the vehicle.**

## CHECK

▶ **Refer to illustration 9.2 and 9.4**

1   On 1988 through 1991 models, be sure to adjust the front wheel bearings (see Chapter 1) before checking the balljoints.

2   To do a quick visual inspection of the lower balljoints, wipe the grease fitting and checking surfaces so they're free of dirt and grease. The checking surface (see illustration) is the round boss into which the grease fitting is threaded. The checking surface should project outside the cover. If the checking surface is inside the cover, replace the lower control arm assembly (see Section 5).

➥**Note: On 1998 and later models, there are no grease fittings in the lower balljoint for the above inspection procedure. Refer to Steps 4 and 5 for other methods of checking balljoint wear.**

3   Raise the vehicle and place floor jacks under the lower control arms.

4   Axial movement is up-and-down movement. Check axial movement by using a short prybar under the tire to move the wheel up and down (see illustration). Replace the balljoints when axial movement exceeds 3/64-inch.

5   Radial movement is in-and-out play. Check for it by moving the tire toward and away from the vehicle by grasping the top and bottom of the wheel by hand. Replace the balljoints when radial movement exceeds 1/64-inch.

## REPLACEMENT

### Lower balljoints

6   On 1997 through 2002 models, the lower balljoint is replaceable. Remove the lower control arm (see Section 5); the balljoint is press fit in the lower control arm, which necessitates the use of a special press tool and receiver cup to remove and install the balljoint. Equipment rental yards and some auto parts stores have these tools available for rent. If you don't have access to this tool, take the vehicle to an automotive machine shop or other qualified repair facility to have the balljoint replaced.

➥**Note: Some balljoint replacement tools are similar to a big, heavy-duty C-clamp. With this type of tool it is only necessary to separate the balljoint from the steering knuckle.**

9   Disconnect the lower and upper balljoint studs from the steering knuckle (see Sections 5 and 6).

10   On 1992 and later models, remove the pinch bolt and nut that retain the stabilizer bar link balljoint stud to the steering knuckle (see illustration 6.8).

11   Remove the steering knuckle.

12   Installation is the reverse of removal. Be sure to tighten all fasteners to the torque values listed in this Chapter's Specifications.

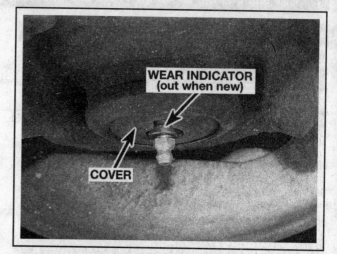

**9.2   To do a quick visual inspection of the lower balljoints, look at the checking surface (the round boss into which the grease fitting is threaded) and note whether the checking surface projects outside the cover; if it doesn't, replace the lower control arm assembly**

**9.4   To check axial movement, use a prybar under the tire to move the wheel up and down - if axial movement exceeds 3/64-inch, replace the balljoints**

7   On all other models the balljoints on lower control arms are not removable or serviceable. If a lower balljoint is damaged or worn, replace the lower control arm (see Section 5). .

## Upper balljoints

### 1988 through 1991 models

8   The upper balljoints on these models are not removable or serviceable. If an upper balljoint is damaged or worn, replace the upper control arm (see Section 6).

### 1992 through 2002 models

9   Loosen the wheel lug nuts. Raise the vehicle and place it securely on jackstands. Remove the wheel.

10   Position a floor jack under the lower control arm directly below the lower balljoint. Use a block of wood between the jack lifting pad and the balljoint to protect the balljoint. Raise the jack until it supports the spring load on the lower arm.

11   Remove the pinch bolt and nut from the upper balljoint stud (see illustration 6.8).

12   Mark the position of the caster and camber adjustment cams (see illustration 2.1).

13   Remove the two nuts which attach the upper balljoint to the upper control arm (see illustration 2.1).

14   Remove the upper balljoint assembly.

15   Installation is the reverse of removal. Be sure to align the index marks on the adjustment cams with the reference marks you made before disassembly, then hold the cams in these positions as you tighten each balljoint retaining nut to the torque listed in this Chapter's Specifications. And be sure to tighten all other fasteners to the torque listed in this Chapter's Specifications.

### 2003 and later models

16   The upper balljoints on these models are not removable or serviceable. If an upper balljoint is damaged or worn, replace the upper control arm (see Section 6).

---

## 10  Shock absorber (rear) - removal and installation

### ❋❋ WARNING 1:

On models with air suspension, turn the air suspension switch to Off before raising the vehicle.  On most models, the switch is located in the trunk, accessible either through a small access door or by pulling back the interior trunk paneling on the left side. Also, disconnect the height sensor connector link before allowing the rear suspension to hang past its normal point of full rebound.

### ❋❋ WARNING 2:

On models with a fire suppression system, disable the system before raising the rear of the vehicle by disconnecting the cable from the negative battery terminal and waiting at least three minutes.

## REMOVAL

▸ **Refer to illustrations 10.3 and 10.4**

1   Raise the rear of the vehicle and support it securely on

jackstands. If the vehicle is a 1991 or earlier model with automatic leveling rear suspension and coil springs (not air springs) allow the rear axle to hang free (be sure the ignition is in the Off position) until the shock absorbers are finished venting through the compressor (which will be evidenced by a hissing sound at the compressor).

2   Support the rear axle with a floor jack to prevent it from dropping when the shock absorber is disconnected. If you're removing an air-assisted shock absorber, detach the air line by depressing the retainer ring(s) and pulling the lines free.

3   Locate the upper retaining nut for the shock absorber on top of the frame (see illustration). It may be necessary to prevent the piston rod from turning by holding it with a wrench or locking pliers while you break loose the nut. Remove the nut, washer and insulator from the stud on the upper side of the frame. Discard the nut. Compress the shock absorber to clear the hole in the frame and remove the inner insulator and washer from the upper retaining stud. Some models have shocks with a plastic dust tube. To loosen the upper nut, a hex area at the metal cap of the dust tube can be held with an open wrench.

4   Remove the lower retaining nut (see illustration) and remove the shock absorber from the vehicle.

10.3  Locate the upper retaining nut (arrow) for the shock absorber on top of the frame. It may be necessary to prevent the piston rod from turning by holding it with a wrench or locking pliers while you break loose the nut

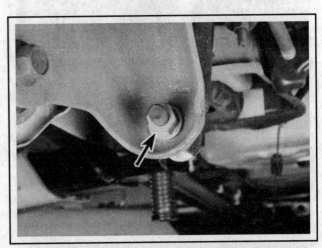

10.4  Remove the lower retaining nut (arrow) and pull the lower shock absorber mounting stud out of the mounting bracket

## INSTALLATION

5   Before installing a new shock absorber, expel all air. Hold the shock right side up and extend it fully. Turn the shock upside down and compress it all the way. Extend and compress the shock absorber in this manner at least three times.

6   Place the inner washer and rubber insulator on the shock piston rod and insert the rod through the upper mounting hole in the frame. Hold the shock in this position and install the outer insulator, washer and a new stud retaining nut on the upper side of the frame. Make sure the insulator "pilots" are properly engaged in the frame attaching holes.

Tighten the nut to the torque listed in this Chapter's Specifications.

7   Extend the shock absorber, insert the lower shock stud through the hole in the bracket on the axle tube, install a new self-locking retaining nut and tighten it to the torque listed in this Chapter's Specifications.

8   Attach the air line(s), if equipped.

9   Remove the jackstands and lower the vehicle.

10   Before attempting to drive a vehicle equipped with air suspension, turn the air suspension switch to On, start the engine and allow the compressor to inflate the air suspension springs (they deflate automatically when the rear of the vehicle is raised).

## 11  Stabilizer bar (rear) - removal and installation

▶ **Refer to illustrations 11.3 and 11.4**

### ✳✳ WARNING:

**On models with air suspension, turn the air suspension switch to Off before raising the vehicle.**

### ✳✳ WARNING:

**On models with a fire suppression system, disable the system before raising the rear of the vehicle by disconnecting the cable from the negative battery terminal and waiting at least three minutes.**

1   Raise the rear of the vehicle and support it securely on jackstands. Place the jackstands under the frame, not under the axle housing. The axle housing must be free to hang down so that the shock absorbers are fully extended.

2   On 1988 through 1991 models, remove the four (two on each arm) stabilizer bar-to-lower suspension arm bolts and remove the bar.

3   On 1992 and later models, remove the nuts that attach the stabilizer bar ends to their links (see illustration).

4   On 1992 and later models, remove the bushing clamp bolts that attach the stabilizer to the axle housing (see illustration).

5   Installation is the reverse of the removal procedure. On 1988 through 1991 models, be sure to install the bar with the paint mark on the right hand side of the vehicle. On all models, be sure to tighten all fasteners to the torque values listed in this Chapter's Specifications.

6   Before attempting to drive a vehicle equipped with air suspension, turn the air suspension switch to On, start the engine and allow the compressor to inflate the air suspension springs (they deflate automatically when the rear of the vehicle is raised).

**11.3  On 1992 and later models, remove this nut (arrow) that attaches the end of the stabilizer bar to the link (left link shown), then remove the other link nut**

**11.4  On 1992 and later models, remove this bushing clamp bolt (arrow) which attaches the stabilizer to the axle housing (left clamp bolt shown), then remove the other clamp bolt**

## 12 Coil spring (rear) - removal and installation

### REMOVAL

### ❄❄ WARNING 1:

**On models with air suspension, turn the air suspension switch to Off before raising the vehicle.**

### ❄❄ WARNING 2:

**On models with a fire suppression system, disable the system before raising the rear of the vehicle by disconnecting the cable from the negative battery terminal and waiting at least three minutes.**

➡**Note: Rear coil springs should always be replaced in pairs.**

1  Loosen the wheel lug nuts, raise the rear of the vehicle and support it securely on jackstands placed under the frame. Remove the wheel and block the front wheels.

2  Remove the rear stabilizer bar (see Section 11).

3  Support the rear axle assembly with a jack placed under the axle housing. Position a safety chain through one of the spring coils and around a convenient frame member. This will prevent the spring from flying out before it's fully extended.

4  Unsnap the right parking brake cable clip from the right upper suspension arm.

5  Disconnect the lower studs of the two rear shock absorbers from their mounting brackets on the axle tube (see Section 10). Detach the height sensor connector link from the upper control arm. On 1998 and later models, the lateral arms that are part of the Watts linkage (see Section 13) must be disconnected at the chassis ends.

6  Slowly lower the jack until the spring is fully extended. Remove the safety chain, coil spring and insulators from between the suspension arm and the spring upper seat.

### INSTALLATION

7  Set the upper insulator on top of the spring, using tape to hold it in place, if necessary.

8  Place the spring between its seat on the axle tube and the frame seat, so that the pigtail (the lower end of the spring) is pointing toward the left side of the vehicle.

9  Raise the axle assembly with the floor jack and insert the studs on the lower ends of the shocks into their holes in the brackets on the axle tubes. Install the stud retaining nuts, but don't fully tighten them yet.

10  Snap the right parking brake cable into the upper suspension arm retainer.

11  Install the rear stabilizer bar (see Section 11). Connect the height sensor connector link to the upper control arm.

12  Remove the jackstands and lower the vehicle.

13  Before attempting to drive a vehicle equipped with air suspension, turn the air suspension switch to On, start the engine and allow the compressor to inflate the air suspension springs (they deflate automatically when the rear of the vehicle is raised).

## 13 Suspension arms (rear) - removal and installation

### ❄❄ WARNING 1:

**If you're going to remove both the upper and the lower arms at the same time, then remove the coil springs first (see Section 12) or, if the vehicle has air suspension, deflate the air springs (see Section 15).**

### ❄❄ WARNING 2:

**On models with air suspension, turn the air suspension switch to Off before raising the vehicle.**

### ❄❄ WARNING: 3

**On models with a fire suppression system, disable the system before raising the rear of the vehicle by disconnecting the cable from the negative battery terminal and waiting at least three minutes.**

### UPPER ARM

➡**Note: If one upper arm requires replacement, replace the other upper arm as well. The manufacturer recommends installing new fasteners when reassembling the rear suspension components.**

### Removal

▶ **Refer to illustrations 13.3, 13.4a and 13.4b**

1  Loosen the rear wheel lug nuts. Raise the rear of the vehicle and support it securely on jackstands placed beneath the frame rails. Block the front wheels. Remove the rear wheels.

2  Position a jack under the differential and raise it slightly.

3  Unsnap the parking brake cable from its upper arm retainer.

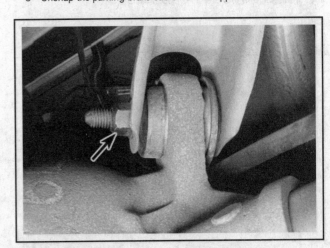

**13.3  Remove the upper arm-to-rear axle pivot bolt and nut (arrow)**

**13.4a Remove the upper arm-to-frame pivot bolt (arrow) and nut and remove the arm from the vehicle (you'll need a Torx bit to hold the bolt)**

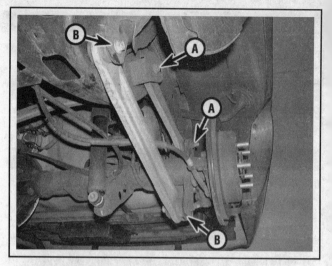

**13.4b On 1998 and later models, the upper and lower arms are both parallel to the frame (arrows at A indicate the upper arm mounting bolts and B the lower arm mounting bolts)**

Remove the upper arm-to-rear axle pivot bolt and nut (see illustration). If equipped, detach the height sensor connector link from the upper arm.

4    Remove the upper arm-to-frame pivot bolt and nut (see illustrations) and remove the arm from the vehicle. Inspect the bushings at both ends of the arm. If either bushing is damaged or worn, have it replaced by an automotive machine shop.

## Installation

5    Position the leading edge of the suspension arm in the frame bracket. Install a new pivot bolt in the same direction as originally installed (but don't tighten it yet).

➡Note: On 1998 and later models, the arms are all marked "outboard" to indicate which side faces out, and upper arms also have a "front" marking.

6    Attach the other end of the arm to the axle housing with a new pivot bolt and nut. Again, the bolt should be facing forward. It may be necessary to jack up the rear axle to align the holes. Don't fully tighten the nut yet. Attach the parking brake cable to its retainer on the upper arm.

7    Raise the axle to normal ride height and tighten the fasteners to the torque listed in this Chapter's Specifications.

## LOWER ARM

➡Note: If one lower arm requires replacement, replace the other lower arm as well. Also, the manufacturer recommends installing new fasteners when reassembling the rear suspension components.

### Removal

♦ **Refer to illustrations 13.12 and 13.13**

8    With the vehicle still on the ground, mark the rear suspension shock tube relative to the protective sleeve.

9    On 1997 and earlier models, remove the stabilizer bar (see Section 11).

10   Loosen the rear wheel lug nuts. Raise the vehicle and place it securely on jackstands (do not place the jackstands under the axle itself; the axle must be free to allow the shocks to fully extend to relieve spring pressure). Remove the wheel.

11   Place a floor jack under the differential to support the axle.

12   Remove the lower arm-to-axle pivot bolt and nut (see illustration).

13   Remove the lower arm-to-frame pivot bolt and nut (see illustration), then remove the arm from the vehicle.

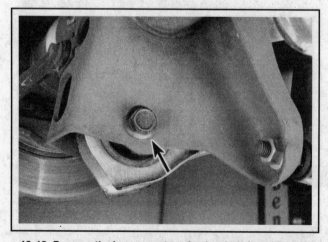

**13.12 Remove the lower arm-to-axle pivot bolt (arrow) and nut**

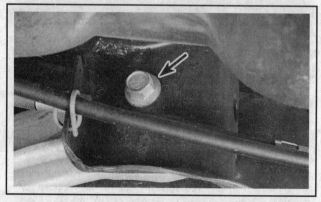

**13.13 Remove the lower arm-to-frame pivot bolt (arrow) and nut, then remove the arm from the vehicle**

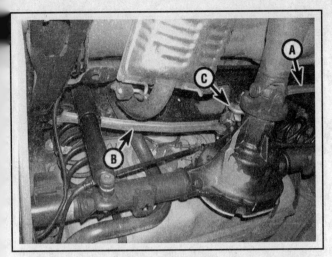

**13.19  The Watts linkage includes the left lateral arm (A), the right lateral arm (B) and the center link (C) with pivot stud**

## Installation

14  Position the lower arm in the frame mounting bracket and install a new pivot bolt and nut, with the nut facing out. Do not tighten the nut completely at this time.

15  Position the other end of the lower arm in the axle bracket and install a new bolt and nut. Do not tighten the nut at this time.

16  Raise the axle until the mark you made on the shock tube is aligned with the protective sleeve (this is the normal ride height), then tighten the pivot bolt nuts to the torque listed in this Chapter's Specifications.

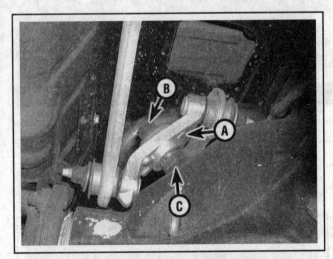

**13.24  The center link (A) is retained by the nut (B) on the pivot stud; C indicates the hex for removing the stud from the differential housing**

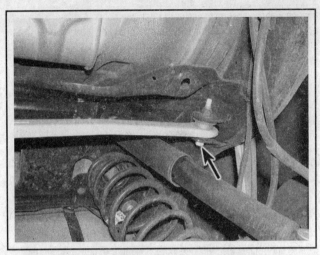

**13.22  Remove the bolts at each end of the lateral arm (arrow indicates the outboard mount at the chassis)**

17  Install the stabilizer bar (see Section 11).

18  Install the wheel and lug nuts. Remove the jackstands and floor jack, lower the vehicle and tighten the lug nuts to the torque listed in the Chapter 1 Specifications.

## WATTS LINK (1998 AND LATER MODELS ONLY)

▶ **Refer to illustrations 13.19, 13.22 and 13.24**

### Replacement

19  The rear axle is located laterally by a Watts linkage, which is made up of two lateral arms that parallel the axle, and a center link and pivot stud (see illustration).

20  With the vehicle still on the ground, mark the rear suspension shock tube relative to the protective sleeve.

21  Raise the vehicle and support it securely on jackstands placed beneath the frame rails. Block the front wheels. Raise the rear axle with a jack and remove the rear wheels. On models with air suspension, bleed the air from the air springs and disconnect the ride height sensor (see Section 15).

22  Remove the bolt at each end of the lateral arm and remove the lateral arm (see illustration).

23  While the arms are off, check the center link for any play on the pivot stud. If any play is present, replace the center link.

24  To remove the center link, remove the nut at the top of the pivot stud and lift the link off the stud (see illustration).

➡**Note: The pivot stud could come loose from the differential housing while removing the nut. If so, use an open-end wrench on the hex at the bottom of the stud to hold it.**

25  The remainder of assembly is the reverse of the removal procedure. If the pivot stud is removed, the manufacturer recommends replacing the stud and nut.

## 14  Air suspension systems - general information

### AUTOMATIC LEVELING SUSPENSION

Some models are equipped with an optional automatic leveling suspension system, which consists of an air compressor, a compressor relay, an air dryer, an exhaust solenoid, a control module, a height sensor, a pair of air adjustable rear shock absorbers and the air lines and fittings connecting the compressor to the shocks.

The adjustable air shocks used with this system are essentially conventional shock absorbers enclosed in air chambers. A rubber sleeve is attached to the dust tube and to the shock reservoir, creating a flexible chamber which can extend the shocks when air pressure is increased. When air pressure is reduced, the weight of the vehicle collapses the shocks.

As the vehicle is loaded, its weight increases, which lowers the vehicle and causes the height sensor's actuating arm to rotate up. This generates two sensor signals to the control module. After a continuous height sensor signal of 7 to 13 seconds, the control module activates the compressor through a relay. The compressor motor runs and air is sent through the system. As the shock absorbers inflate, the vehicle body moves up toward its former height and the height sensor actuating arm rotates down until the preset trim height is reached. When the body reaches the prescribed height, the control module stops the compressor.

As the vehicle is unloaded, its weight decreases, which raises the vehicle and rotates the height sensor actuating arm down. Again, this generates two sensor signals to the control module. 7 to 13 seconds later, the module activates the vent solenoid. As the body comes down, the height sensor actuating arm rotates up again until the preset trim height is reached. When the sensor arm reaches its original height above the ground, the module turns off the vent solenoid, preventing air from escaping.

Servicing this system is beyond the scope of the average home mechanic. If it malfunctions, take the vehicle to an authorized dealer to have the system serviced.

## COMPUTER-CONTROLLED SUSPENSION

Some models are equipped with an optional computer-controlled suspension system that automatically provides height control and soft spring rates to improve ride quality. This system automatically levels the rear of the vehicle and maintains the optimal vehicle attitude whether the vehicle is empty or fully loaded. The automatic air suspension system includes the following components: a compressor/air dryer assembly, a compressor relay, a pair of front air struts with integral height sensors, a pair of rear air springs, a pair of rear shocks, a control module, the air lines, a compressor, a rear height sensor (in the right rear shock absorber), a wiring harness assembly and a compressor cover.

The rear air springs, a pair of cylindrical inflatable bladders, are mounted in the same location as conventional coil springs (they even use the same upper and lower spring seats). Their main advantage over coil springs is that they allow a reduction in spring rate to soften vehicle ride quality. A pair of solenoid valves control air flow in and out of the air springs. Vehicle height is monitored and controlled by an electronic control module. A linear height sensor is located in front of the axle. The upper end of the sensor is attached to the frame crossmember and the lower end is attached to the left upper suspension arm. If vehicle height is too low (i.e. the vehicle is loaded down), the sensor gets shorter; when the ride height goes up (vehicle is unloaded), the sensor gets longer. Magnets in the lower sliding part of the sensor move up and down in relation to the sensor housing, generating a signal that is sent to the control module through two small Hall effect switches attached to the housing. The movement of these magnets determines whether the air suspension switch is open or closed. At trim (ride) height, the switches are both closed and the control module receives a "trim" signal. If the magnets move up, they open one switch to indicate a "high" condition; if the magnets move down, they open another switch to indicate a "low" condition. When the control module receives a low signal, it energizes the solenoids and activates the compressor, which pumps up the air springs until the correct vehicle height is restored; if the control module receives a high signal (vehicle is emptied), the control module activates the solenoids, which vent air from the air springs until vehicle height is correct again.

Servicing this system is beyond the scope of the average home mechanic. If it malfunctions, take the vehicle to a dealer service department or other qualified repair shop to have the system serviced. To remove an air spring, see Section 15.

## 15  Air spring (rear) - removal and installation

### REMOVAL

▶ **Refer to illustrations 15.6a and 15.6b**

### ❋❋ WARNING:

**NEVER remove an air spring when there is still air pressure in the spring. And never remove any components supporting any air spring, or supported by it, without first either exhausting the air or providing support for the air spring.**

1   Turn the air suspension switch to Off.
2   Loosen the wheel lug nuts. Raise the rear of the vehicle and support it securely on jackstands. Remove the wheel.
3   Remove the heat shield.
4   Remove the spring retainer clip.
5   To remove the air spring solenoid:

  a)  *Unplug the electrical connector and disconnect the air line.*
  b)  *Remove the solenoid clip.*
  c)  *Rotate the solenoid counterclockwise to the first stop.*
  d)  *Slowly pull the solenoid straight out to the second stop to allow any residual air to bleed from the system.*
  e)  *After all air is bled from the system, rotate the solenoid counterclockwise to the third stop and remove the solenoid from the housing.*

6   Using a prybar, dislodge the air spring from the lower spring seat (see illustrations), and remove the spring.

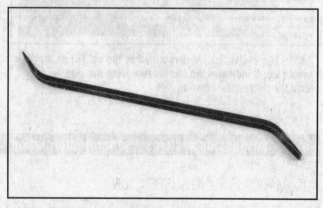

**15.6a  Using a small prybar like this . . .**

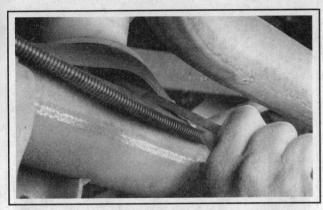

**15.6b** . . . insert the tool through the gap between the axle tube and the spring seat, position the tool so that the flat end rests on the piston knob, push down and force the piston and retainer clip off the axle spring seat

## INSTALLATION

7    Position the spring between the frame seat and the axle, then carefully pry it into place.

8    To install the air spring solenoid:

a)  *Inspect the solenoid O-rings for cracks and tears. Replace as nec-*

essary. Be sure to apply a light coat of silicone dielectric grease to the O-rings.

b)  *Insert the solenoid into the air spring end cap and rotate it clockwise to the third stop, push it into the second stop, then rotate it clockwise to the first stop.*

c)  *Install the solenoid clip.*

9    Taking care to protect the open air and electrical connection at the solenoid, install the air spring into the frame (upper) seat.

10   From the upper side of the frame, install the push-on spring retainer clip.

11   Connect the air line and plug in the electrical connector.

12   Install the heat shield.

13   Align the lower end of the air spring piston with the axle (lower) seat. Squeezing the spring to increase pressure, push down on the piston, snapping the piston into the axle seat at rebound.

14   Install the wheel. Remove the jackstands and lower the vehicle until the wheels are on the ground. Then lower the jack a little further, but do not fully lower the vehicle until the air springs have been partially inflated.

15   Turn the air suspension switch to On. Turn the ignition key to On, but don't start the vehicle. Allow the air springs to partially inflate.

16   Lower the vehicle all the way and allow the springs to fully inflate.

17   Tighten the wheel lug nuts to the torque listed in the Chapter 1 specifications.

## 16   Steering wheel - removal and installation

▶ **Refer to illustrations 16.2a, 16.2b, 16.2c, 16.3, 16.4, 16.5 and 16.8**

### ✷✷ WARNING:

**Some models have airbags. Always disconnect the negative battery cable, then the positive battery cable and wait 2 minutes before working in the vicinity of the impact sensors, steering column or instrument panel to avoid the possibility of accidental deployment of the airbag, which could cause personal injury (see Chapter 12). The steering column must not be rotated while the steering wheel is removed.**

1    Park the vehicle with the front wheels pointed straight ahead and the steering wheel centered. Disconnect the cable from the negative terminal of the battery (see Chapter 5).

2    On models without a driver's side airbag, simply pull the horn pad straight off. On models equipped with a driver's side airbag:

a)  *On models where fasteners are used to retain the airbag, remove the four (early models) or two (later models) airbag module retaining nuts, lift the module off the steering wheel and unplug the airbag connectors (see illustrations).*

b)  *On later models without any fasteners, use a long, thin screwdriver to release the internal clips inside the four recesses on the backside of the steering wheel. Work on one side of the steering wheel to release the upper and lower clips first, then release the opposite side. Insert the screwdriver into the top recess and pry the clip up to release. Once the side of the airbag module is released, secure the assembly to prevent the airbag module from locking back into position and release the clips from the opposite side.*

Store the airbag in a safe place until needed.

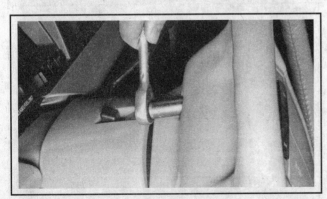

**16.2a** To remove the airbag module on models equipped with a driver's side airbag, remove the four nuts (two on each side of the steering column) from the backside of the steering wheel

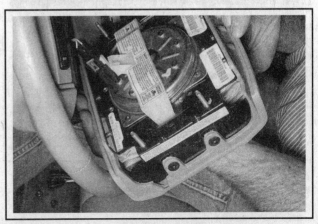

**16.2b** Pull the airbag module straight off . . .

16.2c . . . and unplug the electrical connectors

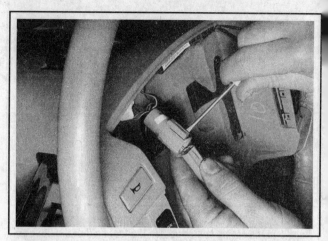

16.3 Unplug the electrical connector for the cruise control system, if equipped

### ❊❊ WARNING:

When handling the airbag module, hold it with the trim side facing away from you. Set the airbag module down in a safe location with the trim side facing up.

3   Unplug the electrical connector for the cruise control, if equipped (see illustration).

4   Unplug the electrical connector on the right side of the clockspring (see illustration 16.8)..

5   Remove the steering wheel retaining bolt (see illustration). There should already be an alignment mark on the upper edge of the steering shaft and another mark on the steering wheel hub. If not, then mark the relationship of the steering shaft to the hub (if marks don't already exist or don't line up) to simplify installation and ensure correct steering wheel alignment.

### ❊❊ WARNING:

Discard the hub bolt. Use a new one during installation.

5   Use a steering wheel puller to detach the steering wheel from the shaft (see illustration). Don't use an impact puller and don't pound on the steering wheel or shaft. Route the contact assembly wire harness through the steering wheel as the wheel is lifted off the shaft. Warning: While the steering wheel is removed, do NOT turn the steering shaft. If the steering shaft is turned, the clockspring will be uncentered and the harness may break, rendering the airbag inoperative. If the clockspring is accidentally uncentered, it must be centered before installing the steering wheel.

➡Note: On later models, a jaw-type puller is required.

6   If equipped with cruise control, make sure the slip ring grease is not contaminated. Check the slip ring contacts for wear or damage and make sure they are properly seated.

7   Make sure the clockspring is centered as follows: Verify that the front wheels are pointing straight ahead. Turn the clockspring housing counterclockwise by hand until it becomes hard to turn (don't apply too much force though, because the cable could break).

a) On 2004 and earlier models, turn the clockspring clockwise approximately three turns and align the marks (see illustration 16.8).

b) On 2005 and later models, turn the clockspring clockwise until the arrow marks are aligned. From this point, turn the clockspring two complete turns and align the marks.

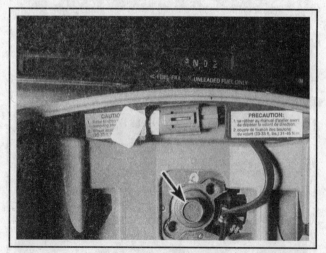

16.5 Remove the steering wheel retaining bolt (arrow) and make sure there are alignment marks on the upper edge of the steering shaft and on the steering wheel hub - if there aren't, make some

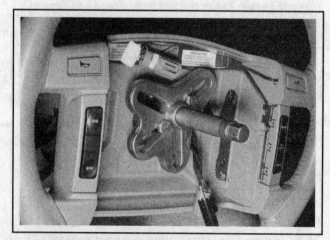

16.6 Install a steering wheel puller as shown to remove the steering wheel from the steering shaft

**16.8  After centering the clockspring, make sure the alignment marks (A) on the clockspring align with the marks on the housing. To remove the clockspring, unhook the retaining clips (B)**

8   If it's necessary to remove the clockspring from the steering column, apply two pieces of tape across the hub of the clockspring to the housing to prevent it from rotating. Release the retaining clips (see illustration) and unplug the electrical connectors, then remove it. Reverse the removal procedure to install the clockspring but make sure it is centered (as described in Step 7).

9   To install the wheel, align the mark on the steering wheel hub with the mark on the shaft and slip the wheel onto the shaft. Install a new bolt and tighten it to the torque listed in this Chapter's Specifications.

10  Plug in the cruise control connector, if equipped.

11  On models with a driver's side airbag, connect the airbag electrical connector and install the airbag module.

12  On models without a driver's side airbag, simply push the horn pad straight on to install it on the wheel. On models with a driver's side airbag, install the four airbag module retaining nuts.

13  Connect the negative battery cable.

## 17  Steering linkage (2000 and earlier models) - inspection, removal and installation

### ✻✻ WARNING:

**On models with air suspension, turn the air suspension switch to Off before raising the vehicle.**

1   The steering linkage connects the steering gear to the front wheels and keeps the wheels in proper relation to each other. The linkage consists of the Pitman (or steering gear) arm, the idler arm, the center link and two adjustable tie-rods (see illustration 1.1). The Pitman arm, which is fastened to the steering gear shaft, moves the center link back-and-forth. The center link is supported on the other end by a frame-mounted idler arm. The back-and-forth motion of the center link is transmitted to the steering knuckles through a pair of tie-rod assemblies. Each tie-rod is made up of an inner and outer tie-rod end, a threaded adjuster tube and two clamps.

**17.9  Use a two-jaw puller to separate the tie-rod end from the steering knuckle**

### INSPECTION

2   Set the wheels in the straight ahead position and lock the steering wheel.

3   Raise one side of the vehicle until the tire is approximately 1-inch off the ground.

4   Grasp the front and rear of the tire and using light pressure, wiggle the wheel back-and-forth. There should be no noticeable play. If the play in the steering system is noticeable, inspect each steering linkage pivot point and ballstud for looseness and replace parts if necessary.

5   Raise the front of the vehicle and support it on jackstands. Push up, then pull down on the center link end of the idler arm, exerting a force of approximately 25 pounds each way. If there is any looseness, replace the idler arm.

6   Check for frozen (extremely stiff) joints and bent or damaged linkage components.

### REMOVAL AND INSTALLATION

#### Tie-rod

▶ Refer to illustrations 17.9, 17.10 and 17.11

7   Loosen the wheel lug nuts, raise the vehicle and support it securely on jackstands. Apply the parking brake. Remove the wheel.

8   Remove the cotter pin and loosen, but do not remove, the castle nut from the ballstud.

9   Using a two-jaw puller, separate the tie-rod end from the steering knuckle (see illustration). Remove the nut and pull the tie-rod end from the knuckle.

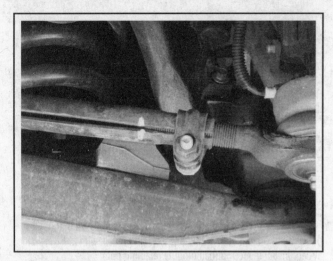

17.10 Make sure you place a mark on the threaded sleeve in line with the end of the threaded portion of the tie-rod end; thus, when you install the tie-rod end and screw it in until the inner end is aligned with this mark, front toe-in will still be the same as before

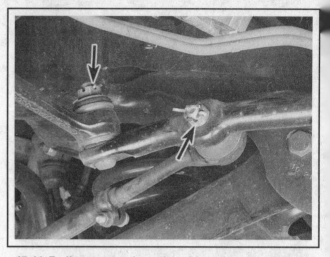

17.11 To disconnect an inner tie-rod from the center link, remove the cotter pin (lower arrow), loosen the castle nut and separate the inner tie-rod end from the center link with a small two-jaw puller like the one used in Step 9; the idler arm balljoint stud (upper arrow) is separated from the center link the same way)

10  If a tie-rod end must be replaced, mark the location of the threaded end of the outer tie-rod tube on the adjuster (see illustration), so that when the new tie-rod is screwed into the adjuster, front toe-in won't be affected. Loosen the adjuster tube clamp and unscrew the tie-rod end.

11  Remove the cotter pin and loosen the nut securing the inner tie-rod end to the center link (see illustration). Separate the inner tie-rod end from the center link in the same manner as in Step 9. Remove and discard the old nut.

12  Lubricate the threaded portion of the tie-rod with chassis grease. Screw the new tie-rod end into the adjuster sleeve until the threaded end reaches the mark you made on the adjuster sleeve. Don't tighten the clamp nut yet.

13  To install the tie-rod, connect the outer tie-rod end to the steering knuckle and install the castle nut. Tighten the nut to the torque listed in this Chapter's Specifications and install a new cotter pin. If the ballstud spins when attempting to tighten the nut, force it into the tapered hole with a large pair of pliers. If necessary, tighten the nut slightly to align a slot in the nut with the cotter pin hole in the ballstud. Install the cotter pin.

14  Insert the inner tie-rod end ballstud into the center link until it's seated. Install a new nut and tighten it to the torque listed in this Chapter's Specifications. If the ballstud spins as the nut is tightened, force the tie-rod end into the center link with a pair of large pliers.

15  Tighten the clamp nuts. The center of the bolt should be nearly horizontal and the adjuster tube slot must not line up with the gap in the clamps.

16  Install the wheel and lug nuts, lower the vehicle and tighten the lug nuts to the torque listed in the Chapter 1 Specifications. Drive the vehicle to an alignment shop to have the front end alignment checked and, if necessary, adjusted.

## Idler arm

▶ Refer to illustration 17.20

17  Raise the vehicle and support it securely on jackstands. Apply the parking brake.

18  Remove the cotter pin and loosen but do not remove the idler

17.20 To detach the idler arm assembly from the frame, simply remove these two nuts (arrows)

arm-to-center link nut (see illustration 17.11).

19  Separate the idler arm from the center link with a two-jaw puller (see illustration 17.9). Remove and discard the nut.

20  Remove the idler arm-to-frame bolts (see illustration).

21  To install the idler arm assembly, position it on the frame and install the bolts, tightening them to the torque listed in this Chapter's Specifications.

22  Insert the idler arm ballstud into the center link and install a new nut. Tighten the nut to the torque listed in this Chapter's Specifications. If the ballstud spins when attempting to tighten the nut, force it into the tapered hole with a large pair of pliers.

## Center link

▶ Refer to illustration 17.26

23  Raise the vehicle and support it securely on jackstands. Apply the parking brake.

**17.26  The Pitman arm balljoint stud (arrow) is separated from the center link the same way as shown in Step 9**

**17.33  Mark the Pitman arm and the threaded sector shaft to insure proper reassembly, then pull off the Pitman arm with a puller**

24  Separate the two inner tie-rod ends from the center link (see Illustration 17.11).

25  Separate the center link from the idler arm (see illustration 17.11).

26  Separate the center link from the Pitman arm (see illustration).

27  Installation is the reverse of the removal procedure. If the ballstuds spin when attempting to tighten the nuts, force them into the tapered holes with a large pair of pliers. Be sure to tighten all of the nuts to the torque listed in this Chapter's Specifications.

## Pitman (steering box) arm

♦ **Refer to illustration 17.33**

28  Raise the vehicle and place it securely on jackstands.

29  Remove the cotter pin and loosen the castle nut that attaches the Pitman arm ballstud to the center link.

30  Using a puller like the one in illustration 17.9, separate the center link from the Pitman arm ballstud. Discard the nut - don't reuse it.

31  Mark the Pitman arm and the steering gear shaft to ensure proper alignment at reassembly time.

32  Remove the Pitman arm nut and washer.

33  Remove the Pitman arm with a Pitman arm puller or a two-jaw puller (see illustration).

34  Inspect the ballstud threads for damage. Inspect the ballstud seals for excessive wear. Clean the threads of the ballstud.

35  Installation is the reverse of removal. Make sure the marks you made on the Pitman arm and Pitman shaft are aligned.

➡**Note: If a clamp type Pitman arm is used, spread the arm just enough, with a wedge, to slip the arm onto the Pitman shaft. Don't spread the arm more than necessary to slip it over the shaft with hand pressure. Do not hammer the arm onto the shaft or you may damage the steering gear.**

Be sure to tighten the Pitman arm nut to the torque listed in this Chapter's Specifications.

## 18  Steering gear - removal and installation

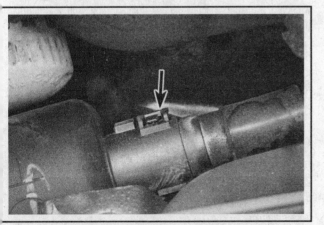

**18.1  To remove the stone shield from the steering shaft coupling, unclip this lock tab (arrow); the shield then opens into twohalves which can be separated and removed**

♦ **Refer to illustrations 18.1, 18.2 and 18.6**

### ❊❊ WARNING:

**On models with air suspension, turn the air suspension switch to Off before raising the vehicle.**

## 2002 AND EARLIER MODELS

### Removal

1  Remove the stone shield (see illustration).

2  Tag the pressure and return lines (see illustration) on the steering gear for future identification. Disconnect the lines from the steering gear. Plug the lines and ports in the gear to prevent contamination.

3  Remove the pinch bolt which secures the flexible coupling to the steering gear (see illustration 18.2).

**18.2 Before removing the steering gear, mark and disconnect the fluid line fittings (arrows) and remove the pinch bolt (arrow) that attaches the flex coupling clamp to the steering gear input shaft**

**18.6 To detach the steering gear from the frame, remove these four bolts (arrows, later models have only three bolts) inside the left wheel housing (left front wheel removed for clarity)**

4   Raise the vehicle and remove the nut that attaches the Pitman arm to the sector shaft (see Section 17)

5   Remove the Pitman arm from the sector shaft (see illustration 17.33).

6   Support the steering gear and remove the steering gear attaching bolts (see illustration).

7   Work the gear free of the flex coupling and remove the gear.

**❋❋ WARNING:**

**On models equipped with airbags, make sure that the steering shaft is not turned while the steering gear is removed or you could damage the airbag system. One way to prevent the shaft from turning is to run the seat belt through the steering wheel and clip the seat belt into place.**

### Installation

8   To install the steering gear, slide the flex coupling into place on the steering shaft assembly. Turn the steering wheel so that the spokes are in a horizontal position.

9   Center the steering gear input shaft and slide it into the flex coupling clamp and into place on the frame side rail. Install the steering gear mounting bolts and tighten them to the torque listed in this Chapter's Specifications.

10  Be sure the wheels are in the straight ahead position, then install the Pitman arm on the sector shaft (see Section 17). Install the Pitman arm nut and tighten it to the torque listed in this Chapter's Specifications.

11  Install the flex coupling-to-steering gear input shaft clamp bolt and tighten it to the torque listed in this Chapter's Specifications.

12  Connect the pressure and return lines to the steering gear. Tighten the line fittings securely. Fill the reservoir as described in Chapter I. Turn the steering wheel from stop to stop to distribute the fluid.

13  Recheck the fluid level and add fluid if necessary.

14  Start the engine and turn the steering wheel from left to right and

inspect for fluid leaks.

15  Bleed the power steering system as described in Section 20.

## 2003 AND LATER MODELS

16  Park the vehicle with the wheels pointing straight ahead.

**❋❋ WARNING:**

**Make sure that the steering shaft is not turned while the steering gear is removed or you could damage the airbag system. One way to prevent the shaft from turning is to run the seat belt through the steering wheel and clip it into its latch.**

17  Loosen the front wheel lug nuts, raise the front of the vehicle and support it securely on jackstands. Apply the parking brake. Remove the wheels.

18  Mark the relationship of the intermediate shaft coupler to the steering gear input shaft and remove the pinch bolt.

19  Position a drain pan under the steering gear. Using a flare-nut wrench, if available, unscrew the power steering pressure and return lines from the steering gear. Cap the lines to prevent leakage.

20  Detach the tie-rod ends from the steering knuckles (see illustration 17.9).

21  Remove the mounting nuts, then unscrew the studs. Lower the steering gear from the vehicle.

22  Installation is the reverse of removal, noting the following points:

a) Tighten the steering gear mounting studs and nuts, and the intermediate shaft coupler pinch bolt to the torque values listed in this Chapter's Specifications.

b) Tighten the wheel lug nuts to the torque listed in the Chapter 1 Specifications.

c) Check the power steering fluid level and add some, if necessary (see Chapter 1), then bleed the system as described in Section 20.

d) Re-check the power steering fluid level.

### 19  Power steering pump - removal and installation

▶ **Refer to illustrations 19.4 and 19.6**

#### REMOVAL

1  On 5.0L engines, relieve tension on the accessory drivebelt used to drive the power steering pump pulley; on 4.6L engines, relieve tension on the serpentine belt (see Chapter 1).

2  On 5.0L engines, the pump can be accessed from above. On 4.6L engines, raise the front of the vehicle and place it securely on jackstands (the pump is more easily accessed from underneath the vehicle on these models).

3  Locate the pump on the left (driver's) side of the engine block. Disconnect the fluid return hose from the pump and drain the fluid from the pump reservoir. Disconnect the pressure hose from the pump (but do NOT unscrew the pressure fitting itself). Plug the lines to prevent contamination.

➡ **Note: Models from 1997 on have an electrical connector (for the variable assist steering). Disconnect this electrical connector before removing the pump.**

4  On 5.0L engines, the pump is mounted on a bracket bolted to the engine. You'll have to remove the pulley before you can remove the pump-to-bracket mounting bolts. A special puller for this purpose (see illustration) is available at most auto parts stores. On 4.6L engines, the pump is mounted directly on the block, so the pulley doesn't cover up the mounting bolts. On these models, it's easier to remove the pulley on the bench after you've removed the pump assembly.

5  Remove the pump mounting bolts and remove the pump.

#### INSTALLATION

6  Installation is the reverse of the above procedure. On 5.0L engines, you'll need a special pulley installer tool (see illustration), available at most auto parts stores, to install the pulley once the pump is bolted to its mounting bracket.

7  Install the accessory drivebelt or the serpentine belt (see Chapter 1).

8  Install the pressure and return lines and fill the reservoir with an approved fluid. Start the engine and turn the steering wheel from lock to lock several times to distribute the fluid, then recheck the fluid level and top-off if necessary.

9  Bleed the power steering system as described in Section 20.

**19.4  You'll need a special puller to remove the power steering pump pulley (on 4.6L models, this can be done off the vehicle)**

**19.6  You'll also need a special pulley installer tool to push the pulley onto the pump shaft; NEVER hammer a pulley onto the shaft - you could damage the pump**

### 20  Power steering system - bleeding

1  Following any operation in which the power steering fluid lines have been disconnected, the power steering system must be bled to remove all air and obtain proper steering performance.

2  With the front wheels in the straight ahead position, check the power steering fluid level and, if low, add fluid until it reaches the Cold mark on the dipstick.

3  Start the engine and allow it to run at fast idle. Recheck the fluid level and add more if necessary to reach the Cold mark on the dipstick.

4  Bleed the system by turning the wheels from side-to-side, without hitting the stops. This will work the air out of the system. Keep the reservoir full of fluid as this is done.

5  When the air is worked out of the system, return the wheels to the straight ahead position and leave the vehicle running for several more minutes before shutting it off.

6  Road test the vehicle to be sure the steering system is functioning normally and noise free.

7  Recheck the fluid level to be sure it is up to the Hot mark on the dipstick while the engine is at normal operating temperature. Add fluid if necessary (see Chapter 1).

## 21 Wheels and tires - general information

▶ **Refer to illustration 21.1**

All models covered by this manual are equipped with metric-sized radial tires (see illustration). Use of other size or type of tires may affect the ride and handling of the vehicle. Don't mix different types of tires, such as radials and bias belted, on the same vehicle as handling may be seriously affected. It's recommended that tires be replaced in pairs on the same axle, but if only one tire is being replaced, be sure it's the same size, structure and tread design as the other.

Because tire pressure has a substantial effect on handling and wear, the pressure on all tires should be checked at least once a month or before any extended trips (see Chapter 1).

Wheels must be replaced if they are bent, dented, leak air, have elongated bolt holes, are heavily rusted, out of vertical symmetry or if the lug nuts won't stay tight. Wheel repairs that use welding or peening are not recommended.

Tire and wheel balance is important to the overall handling, braking and performance of the vehicle. Unbalanced wheels can adversely affect handling and ride characteristics as well as tire life. Whenever a tire is installed on a wheel, the tire and wheel should be balanced by a shop with the proper equipment.

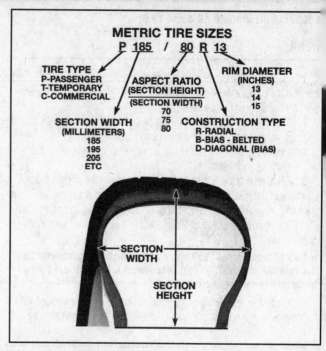

**21.1 Metric tire size code**

## 22 Front end alignment - general information

▶ **Refer to illustration 22.1**

A front end alignment refers to the adjustments made to the front wheels so they are in proper angular relationship to the suspension and the ground. Front wheels that are out of proper alignment not only affect steering control, but also increase tire wear (see illustration).

Getting the proper front wheel alignment is a very exacting process,

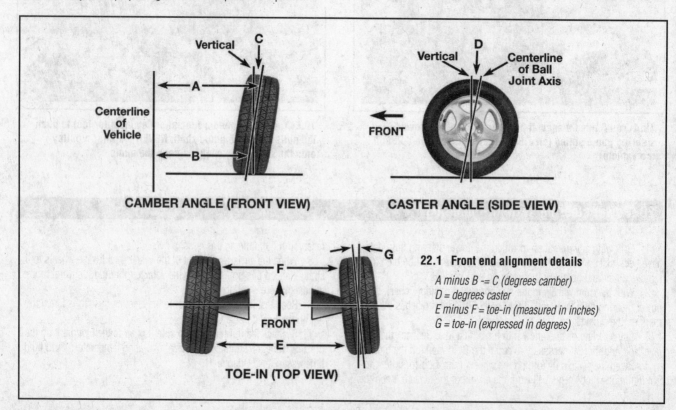

**CAMBER ANGLE (FRONT VIEW)**

**CASTER ANGLE (SIDE VIEW)**

**TOE-IN (TOP VIEW)**

**22.1  Front end alignment details**

*A minus B -= C (degrees camber)*
*D = degrees caster*
*E minus F = toe-in (measured in inches)*
*G = toe-in (expressed in degrees)*

one in which complicated and expensive machines are necessary to perform the job properly. Because of this, you should have a technician with the proper equipment perform these tasks. We will, however, use this space to give you a basic idea of what is involved with front end alignment so you can better understand the process and deal intelligently with the shop that does the work.

Toe-in is the turning in of the front wheels. The purpose of a toe specification is to ensure parallel rolling of the front wheels. In a vehicle with zero toe-in, the distance between the front edges of the wheels will be the same as the distance between the rear edges of the wheels. The actual amount of toe-in is normally only a fraction of an inch. Toe-in adjustment is controlled by the tie-rod end position on the tie-rod. Incorrect toe-in will cause the tires to wear improperly by making them scrub against the road surface.

Camber is the tilting of the front wheels from the vertical when viewed from the front of the vehicle. When the wheels tilt out at the top, the camber is said to be positive (+). When the wheels tilt in at the top the camber is negative (-). The amount of tilt is measured in degrees from the vertical and this measurement is called the camber angle. This angle affects the amount of tire tread which contacts the road and compensates for changes in the suspension geometry when the vehicle is cornering or traveling over an undulating surface.

Caster is the tilting of the top of the front steering axis from the vertical. A tilt toward the rear is positive caster and a tilt toward the front is negative caster.

**Torque specifications**                    Ft-lbs (unless otherwise indicated)

**Front suspension**

Balljoints

Lower balljoint-to-steering knuckle nut

| | |
|---|---|
| 1988 through 1996 | 80 to 119 |
| 1997 through 2002 | 129 |
| 2003 and later | 111 |

Upper balljoint-to-steering knuckle nut

| | |
|---|---|
| (1988 through 1991) | 60 to 90 |

Upper balljoint-to-upper arm retaining nuts

| | |
|---|---|
| (1992 through 2002) | 118 |

Upper balljoint-to-steering knuckle pinch bolt

| | |
|---|---|
| 1992 | 51 to 67 |
| 1993 through 2002 | 66 |

Upper balljoint-to-steering knuckle nut

| | |
|---|---|
| (2003 and later) | 111 |

Hub and bearing assembly retaining nut/bolts

| | |
|---|---|
| 1992 through 2002 | 221 |
| 2003 through 2006 | 74 |
| 2007 and later | 89 |

Lower arm-to-crossmember pivot bolt nut

| | |
|---|---|
| 1988 through 2002 | 129 |
| 2003 through 2006 | 166 |
| 2007 and later | 176 |

| | |
|---|---|
| Lower arm-to-frame bolts (2003 and later) | 66 |

Shock absorber

Upper shock mounting nut

| | |
|---|---|
| 1988 through 1991 | 22 to 30 |
| 1992 | 16 to 20 |
| 1993 through 2002 | 25 to 34 |
| 2003 and later | 22 |

Shock-to-lower control arm mounting bolts

| | |
|---|---|
| 1988 through 1991 | 12 to 18 |
| 1992 and 1993 | 13 to 16 |
| 1994 through 2002 | 11 |
| 2003 through 2006 | 166 |
| 2007 and later | 173 |

Stabilizer bar

Stabilizer bar-to-frame clamp nuts

| | |
|---|---|
| 1988 through 1990 | 14 to 26 |
| 1991 through 1995 | 44 to 59 |
| 1996 through 1998 | 14 to 26 |
| 1999 and later | 44 to 59 |

Stabilizer bar-to-link nut

| | |
|---|---|
| 1988 through 1990 | 9 to 15 |
| 1991 | 44 to 55 |
| 1992 through 1994 | 30 to 40 |
| 1995 through 1997 | 20 to 25 |
| 1998 | 34 to 46 |
| 1999 through 2002 | 41 |
| 2003 through 2005 | 46 |
| 2006 and later | 41 |

### Front suspension (continued)

| | |
|---|---|
| Stabilizer link-to-steering knuckle nut | |
| 1988 through 1990 | 9 to 15 |
| 1991 through 1994 | 30 to 40 |
| 1995 through 1998 | 20 to 25 |
| 1999 through 2002 | 22 |
| 2003 and later | 46 |
| Upper control arm | |
| Upper arm shaft retaining nuts | |
| 1988 through 1991 | 101 to 140 |
| 1992 through 1996 | 85 to 100 |
| 1997 and 1998 | 110 to 148 |
| 1999 through 2002 | 129 |
| 2003 and later | 111 |

### Rear suspension

| | |
|---|---|
| Lower arm | |
| Lower arm-to-axle nut | |
| 1988 through 1996 | 103 to 132 |
| 1997 and later | 111 |
| Lower arm-to-frame nut | |
| 1988 through 1995 | 119 to 149 |
| 1996 | 103 to 132 |
| 1997 and later | 111 |
| Shock absorber | |
| Shock absorber-to-axle bracket nut | |
| 1988 through 1991 | 52 to 85 |
| 1992 and later | 56 to 76 |
| Shock absorber-to-upper mount nut | |
| 1988 through 1991 | 19 to 27 |
| 1992 | 16 to 21 |
| 1993 and later | 25 to 34 |
| Stabilizer bar | |
| Stabilizer bar-to-lower arm nuts | |
| (1988 through 1991) | 70 to 92 |
| Stabilizer bar link-to-frame nut | 13 to 17 |
| Stabilizer bar link-to-stabilizer bar nut | 13 to 17 |
| Stabilizer bar clamp-to-axle bolts | 16 to 22 |
| Upper arm | |
| Upper arm-to-frame nut | |
| 1988 through 1995 | 119 to 149 |
| 1996 | 103 to 132 |
| 1997 | 95 to 126 |
| 1998 and later | 111 |
| Upper arm-to-axle nut | |
| 1988 through 1996 | 103 to 132 |
| 1997 | 95 to 126 |
| 1998 through 2002 | 76 |
| 2003 and later | 69 |

| Torque specifications | Ft-lbs (unless otherwise indicated) |
|---|---|
| Watts link | |
| Watts link pivot nut | 184 |
| Watts link lateral arms-to-frame | |
| 2002 and earlier | 76 |
| 2003 and later | 66 |

## Steering

| | |
|---|---|
| Tie-rods | |
| Inner tie-rod end-to-center link nuts | |
| (1988 through 2002) | 35 to 47 |
| Outer tie-rod end-to-steering knuckle nuts | |
| 1988 through 2002 | 35 to 47 |
| 2003 and later | 59 |
| Tie-rod clamp-to-adjusting sleeve nuts | |
| 1988 through 2002 | 21 |
| 2003 and later | 41 |
| Center link-to-idler arm nut | |
| 1988 through 1994 | 35 to 46 |
| 1995 through 2002 | 50 to 67 |
| Idler-arm bracket-to-frame nuts | |
| 1988 through 1994 | 73 to 97 |
| 1995 through 2002 | 56 |
| Pitman arm | |
| Pitman arm-to-center link nut | |
| 1988 through 1994 | 35 to 47 |
| 1995 through 2002 | 56 |
| Pitman arm-to-sector shaft nut | 200 to 250 |
| Steering gear to-frame mounting bolts (2002 and earlier models) | |
| 1988 through 1997 | 73 to 97 |
| 1998 through 2002 | 50 to 65 |
| Steering gear mounting nuts | |
| (2003 and later models) | 76 |
| Steering gear mounting studs | |
| (2003 and later models) | 15 |
| Steering column flex coupling pinch bolt | 31 to 41 |
| Steering wheel retaining bolt | 22 to 33 |

**Section**

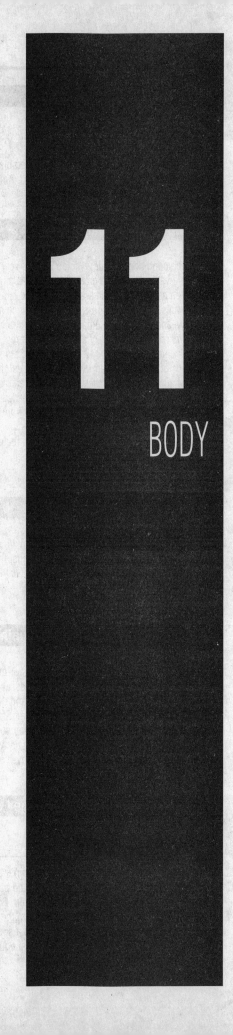

11

BODY

## 1  General information

The models covered by this manual feature a separate frame and body construction.

Certain components are particularly vulnerable to accident damage and can be unbolted and repaired or replaced. Among these parts are the body moldings, bumpers, the hood and trunk lids and all glass.

Only general body maintenance practices and body panel repair procedures within the scope of the do-it-yourselfer are included in this Chapter.

## 2  Body - maintenance

1   The condition of your vehicle's body is very important, because the resale value depends a great deal on it. It's much more difficult to repair a neglected or damaged body than it is to repair mechanical components. The hidden areas of the body, such as the wheel wells, the frame and the engine compartment, are equally important, although they don't require as frequent attention as the rest of the body.

2   Once a year, or every 12,000 miles, it's a good idea to have the underside of the body steam cleaned. All traces of dirt and oil will be removed and the area can then be inspected carefully for rust, damaged brake lines, frayed electrical wires, damaged cables and other problems. The front suspension components should be greased after completion of this job.

3   At the same time, clean the engine and the engine compartment with a steam cleaner or water soluble degreaser.

4   The wheel wells should be given close attention, since undercoating can peel away and stones and dirt thrown up by the tires can cause the paint to chip and flake, allowing rust to set in. If rust is found, clean down to the bare metal and apply an anti-rust paint.

5   The body should be washed about once a week. Wet the vehicle thoroughly to soften the dirt, then wash it down with a soft sponge and plenty of clean soapy water. If the surplus dirt is not washed off very carefully, it can wear down the paint.

6   Spots of tar or asphalt thrown up from the road should be removed with a cloth soaked in solvent.

7   Once every six months, wax the body and chrome trim. If a chrome cleaner is used to remove rust from any of the vehicle's plated parts, remember that the cleaner also removes part of the chrome, so use it sparingly.

## 3  Vinyl trim - maintenance

Don't clean vinyl trim with detergents, caustic soap or petroleum-based cleaners. Plain soap and water works just fine, with a soft brush to clean dirt that may be ingrained. Wash the vinyl as frequently as the rest of the vehicle.

After cleaning, application of a high quality rubber and vinyl protectant will help prevent oxidation and cracks. The protectant can also be applied to weatherstripping, vacuum lines and rubber hoses, which often fail as a result of chemical degradation, and to the tires.

## 4  Upholstery and carpets - maintenance

1   Every three months remove the carpets or mats and clean the interior of the vehicle (more frequently if necessary). Vacuum the upholstery and carpets to remove loose dirt and dust.

2   Leather upholstery requires special care. Stains should be removed with warm water and a very mild soap solution. Use a clean, damp cloth to remove the soap, then wipe again with a dry cloth. Never use alcohol, gasoline, nail polish remover or thinner to clean leather upholstery.

3   After cleaning, regularly treat leather upholstery with a leather wax. Never use car wax on leather upholstery.

4   In areas where the interior of the vehicle is subject to bright sunlight, cover leather seats with a sheet if the vehicle is to be left out for any length of time.

## 5  Body repair - minor damage

### PLASTIC BODY PANELS

The following repair procedures are for minor scratches and gouges. Repair of more serious damage should be left to a dealer service department or qualified auto body shop. Below is a list of the equipment and materials necessary to perform the following repair procedures on plastic body panels. Although a specific brand of material may be mentioned, it should be noted that equivalent products from other manufacturers may be used instead.

*Wax, grease and silicone removing solvent*

*Cloth-backed body tape*
*Sanding discs*
*Drill motor with three-inch disc holder*
*Hand sanding block*
*Rubber squeegees*
*Sandpaper*
*Non-porous mixing palette*
*Wood paddle or putty knife*
*Curved-tooth body file*
*Flexible parts repair material*

1   Remove the damaged panel, if necessary or desirable. In most cases, repairs can be carried out with the panel installed.

2   Clean the area(s) to be repaired with a wax, grease and silicone removing solvent applied with a water-dampened cloth.

3   If the damage is structural, that is, if it extends through the panel, clean the backside of the panel area to be repaired as well. Wipe dry.

4   Sand the rear surface about 1-1/2 inches beyond the break.

5   Cut two pieces of fiberglass cloth large enough to overlap the break by about 1-1/2 inches. Cut only to the required length.

6   Mix the adhesive from the repair kit according to the instructions included with the kit, and apply a layer of the mixture approximately 1/8-inch thick on the backside of the panel. Overlap the break by at least 1-1/2 inches.

7   Apply one piece of fiberglass cloth to the adhesive and cover the cloth with additional adhesive. Apply a second piece of fiberglass cloth to the adhesive and immediately cover the cloth with additional adhesive in sufficient quantity to fill the weave.

8   Allow the repair to cure for 20 to 30 minutes at 60-degrees to 80-degrees F.

9   If necessary, trim the excess repair material at the edge.

10  Remove all of the paint film over and around the area(s) to be repaired. The repair material should not overlap the painted surface.

11  With a drill motor and a sanding disc (or a rotary file), cut a "V" along the break line approximately 1/2-inch wide. Remove all dust and loose particles from the repair area.

12  Mix and apply the repair material. Apply a light coat first over the damaged area; then continue applying material until it reaches a level slightly higher than the surrounding finish.

13  Cure the mixture for 20 to 30 minutes at 60-degrees to 80-degrees F.

14  Roughly establish the contour of the area being repaired with a body file. If low areas or pits remain, mix and apply additional adhesive.

15  Block sand the damaged area with sandpaper to establish the actual contour of the surrounding surface.

16  If desired, the repaired area can be temporarily protected with several light coats of primer. Because of the special paints and techniques required for flexible body panels, it is recommended that the vehicle be taken to a paint shop for completion of the body repair.

## STEEL BODY PANELS

**See photo sequence**

### Repair of minor scratches

17  If the scratch is superficial and does not penetrate to the metal of the body, repair is very simple. Lightly rub the scratched area with a fine rubbing compound to remove loose paint and built up wax. Rinse the area with clean water.

18  Apply touch-up paint to the scratch, using a small brush. Continue to apply thin layers of paint until the surface of the paint in the scratch is level with the surrounding paint. Allow the new paint at least two weeks to harden, then blend it into the surrounding paint by rubbing with a very fine rubbing compound. Finally, apply a coat of wax to the scratch area.

19  If the scratch has penetrated the paint and exposed the metal of the body, causing the metal to rust, a different repair technique is required. Remove all loose rust from the bottom of the scratch with a pocketknife, then apply rust inhibiting paint to prevent the formation of rust in the future. Using a rubber or nylon applicator, coat the scratched area with glaze-type filler. If required, the filler can be mixed with thinner to provide a very thin paste, which is ideal for filling narrow scratches. Before the glaze filler in the scratch hardens, wrap a piece of smooth cotton cloth around the tip of a finger. Dip the cloth in thinner and then quickly wipe it along the surface of the scratch. This will ensure that the surface of the filler is slightly hollow. The scratch can now be painted over as described earlier in this Section.

### Repair of dents

20  When repairing dents, the first job is to pull the dent out until the affected area is as close as possible to its original shape. There is no point in trying to restore the original shape completely as the metal in the damaged area will have stretched on impact and cannot be restored to its original contours. It is better to bring the level of the dent up to a point that is about 1/8-inch below the level of the surrounding metal. In cases where the dent is very shallow, it is not worth trying to pull it out at all.

21  If the backside of the dent is accessible, it can be hammered out gently from behind using a soft-face hammer. While doing this, hold a block of wood firmly against the opposite side of the metal to absorb the hammer blows and prevent the metal from being stretched.

22  If the dent is in a section of the body which has double layers, or some other factor makes it inaccessible from behind, a different technique is required. Drill several small holes through the metal inside the damaged area, particularly in the deeper sections. Screw long, self-tapping screws into the holes just enough for them to get a good grip in the metal. Now pulling on the protruding heads of the screws with locking pliers can pull out the dent.

23  The next stage of repair is the removal of paint from the damaged area and from an inch or so of the surrounding metal. This is easily done with a wire brush or sanding disk in a drill motor, although it can be done just as effectively by hand with sandpaper. To complete the preparation for filling, score the surface of the bare metal with a screwdriver or the tang of a file or drill small holes in the affected area. This will provide a good grip for the filler material. To complete the repair, see the Section on filling and painting.

### Repair of rust holes or gashes

24  Remove all paint from the affected area and from an inch or so of the surrounding metal using a sanding disk or wire brush mounted in a drill motor. If these are not available, a few sheets of sandpaper will do the job just as effectively.

25  With the paint removed, you will be able to determine the severity of the corrosion and decide whether to replace the whole panel, if possible, or repair the affected area. New body panels are not as expensive as most people think and it is often quicker to install a new panel than to repair large areas of rust.

26  Remove all trim pieces from the affected area except those which will act as a guide to the original shape of the damaged body, such as headlight shells, etc. Using metal snips or a hacksaw blade, remove all loose metal and any other metal that is badly affected by rust. Hammer the edges of the hole in to create a slight depression for the filler material.

27  Wire-brush the affected area to remove the powdery rust from the surface of the metal. If the back of the rusted area is accessible, treat it with rust inhibiting paint.

28  Before filling is done, block the hole in some way. This can be done with sheet metal riveted or screwed into place, or by stuffing the hole with wire mesh.

29  Once the hole is blocked off, the affected area can be filled and painted. See the following subsection on filling and painting.

These photos illustrate a method of repairing simple dents. They are intended to supplement *Body repair - minor damage* in this Chapter and should not be used as the sole instructions for body repair on these vehicles.

1 If you can't access the backside of the body panel to hammer out the dent, pull it out with a slide-hammer-type dent puller. In the deepest portion of the dent or along the crease line, drill or punch hole(s) at least one inch apart . . .

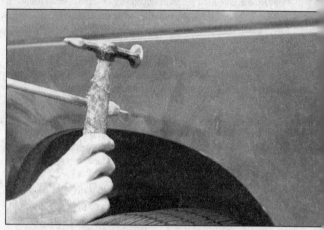

2 . . . then screw the slide-hammer into the hole and operate it. Tap with a hammer near the edge of the dent to help 'pop' the metal back to its original shape. When you're finished, the dent area should be close to its original contour and about 1/8-inch below the surface of the surrounding metal

3 Using coarse-grit sandpaper, remove the paint down to the bare metal. Hand sanding works fine, but the disc sander shown here makes the job faster. Use finer (about 320-grit) sandpaper to feather-edge the paint at least one inch around the dent area

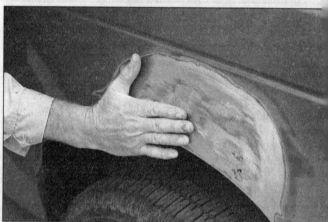

4 When the paint is removed, touch will probably be more helpful than sight for telling if the metal is straight. Hammer down the high spots or raise the low spots as necessary. Clean the repair area with wax/silicone remover

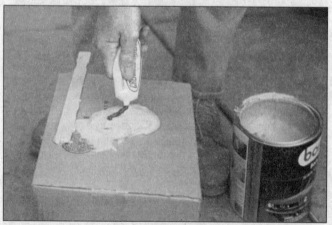

5 Following label instructions, mix up a batch of plastic filler and hardener. The ratio of filler to hardener is critical, and, if you mix it incorrectly, it will either not cure properly or cure too quickly (you won't have time to file and sand it into shape)

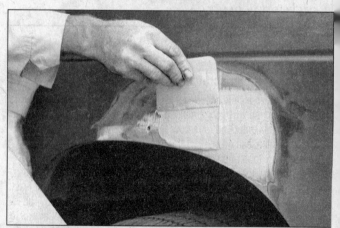

6 Working quickly so the filler doesn't harden, use a plastic applicator to press the body filler firmly into the metal, assuring it bonds completely. Work the filler until it matches the original contour and is slightly above the surrounding metal

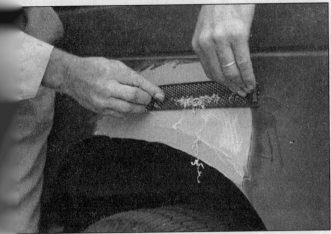

7 Let the filler harden until you can just dent it with your fingernail. Use a body file or Surform tool (shown here) to rough-shape the filler

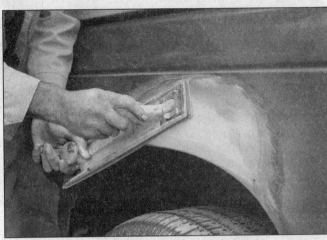

8 Use coarse-grit sandpaper and a sanding board or block to work the filler down until it's smooth and even. Work down to finer grits of sandpaper - always using a board or block - ending up with 360 or 400 grit

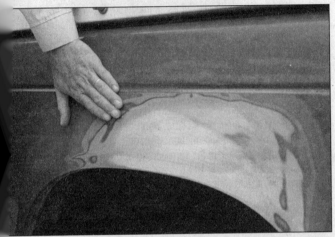

9 You shouldn't be able to feel any ridge at the transition from the filler to the bare metal or from the bare metal to the old paint. As soon as the repair is flat and uniform, remove the dust and mask off the adjacent panels or trim pieces

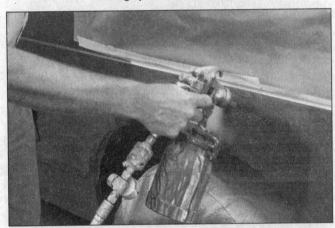

10 Apply several layers of primer to the area. Don't spray the primer on too heavy, so it sags or runs, and make sure each coat is dry before you spray on the next one. A professional-type spray gun is being used here, but aerosol spray primer is available inexpensively from auto parts stores

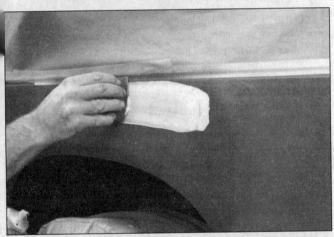

11 The primer will help reveal imperfections or scratches. Fill these with glazing compound. Follow the label instructions and sand it with 360 or 400-grit sandpaper until it's smooth. Repeat the glazing, sanding and respraying until the primer reveals a perfectly smooth surface

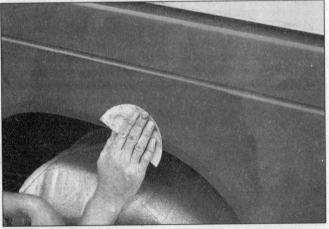

12 Finish sand the primer with very fine sandpaper (400 or 600-grit) to remove the primer overspray. Clean the area with water and allow it to dry. Use a tack rag to remove any dust, then apply the finish coat. Don't attempt to rub out or wax the repair area until the paint has dried completely (at least two weeks)

## Filling and painting

30  Many types of body fillers are available, but generally speaking, body repair kits which contain filler paste and a tube of resin hardener are best for this type of repair work. A wide, flexible plastic or nylon applicator will be necessary for imparting a smooth and contoured finish to the surface of the filler material. Mix up a small amount of filler on a clean piece of wood or cardboard (use the hardener sparingly). Follow the manufacturer's instructions on the package, otherwise the filler will set incorrectly.

31  Using the applicator, apply the filler paste to the prepared area. Draw the applicator across the surface of the filler to achieve the desired contour and to level the filler surface. As soon as a contour that approximates the original one is achieved, stop working the paste. If you continue, the paste will begin to stick to the applicator. Continue to add thin layers of paste at 20-minute intervals until the level of the filler is just above the surrounding metal.

32  Once the filler has hardened, the excess can be removed with a body file. From then on, progressively finer grades of sandpaper should be used, starting with a 180-grit paper and finishing with 600-grit wet-or-dry paper. Always wrap the sandpaper around a flat rubber or wooden block, otherwise the surface of the filler will not be completely flat. During the sanding of the filler surface, the wet-or-dry paper should be periodically rinsed in water. This will ensure that a very smooth finish is produced in the final stage.

33  At this point, the repair area should be surrounded by a ring of bare metal, which in turn should be encircled by the finely feathered edge of good paint. Rinse the repair area with clean water until all of the dust produced by the sanding operation is gone.

34  Spray the entire area with a light coat of primer. This will reveal any imperfections in the surface of the filler. Repair the imperfections with fresh filler paste or glaze filler and once more smooth the surface with sandpaper. Repeat this spray-and-repair procedure until you are satisfied that the surface of the filler and the feathered edge of the paint are perfect. Rinse the area with clean water and allow it to dry completely.

35  The repair area is now ready for painting. Spray painting must be carried out in a warm, dry, windless and dust free atmosphere. These conditions can be created if you have access to a large indoor work area, but if you are forced to work in the open, you will have to pick the day very carefully. If you are working indoors, dousing the floor in the work area with water will help settle the dust that would otherwise be in the air. If the repair area is confined to one body panel, mask off the surrounding panels. This will help minimize the effects of a slight mismatch in paint color. Trim pieces such as chrome strips, door handles, etc., will also need to be masked off or removed. Use masking tape and several thickness of newspaper for the masking operations.

36  Before spraying, shake the paint can thoroughly, then spray a test area until the spray painting technique is mastered. Cover the repair area with a thick coat of primer. The thickness should be built up using several thin layers of primer rather than one thick one. Using 600-grit wet-or-dry sandpaper, rub down the surface of the primer until it is very smooth. While doing this, the work area should be thoroughly rinsed with water and the wet-or-dry sandpaper periodically rinsed as well. Allow the primer to dry before spraying additional coats.

37  Spray on the top coat, again building up the thickness by using several thin layers of paint. Begin spraying in the center of the repair area and then, using a circular motion, work out until the whole repair area and about two inches of the surrounding original paint is covered. Remove all masking material 10 to 15 minutes after spraying on the final coat of paint. Allow the new paint at least two weeks to harden, then use a very fine rubbing compound to blend the edges of the new paint into the existing paint. Finally, apply a coat of wax.

## 6  Body repair - major damage

1  Major damage must be repaired by an auto body shop specifically equipped to perform frame and body repairs. These shops have the specialized equipment required to do the job properly.

2  If the damage is extensive, the body must be checked for proper alignment or the vehicle's handling characteristics may be adversely affected and other components may wear at an accelerated rate.

3  Due to the fact that all of the major body components (hood, fenders, etc.) are separate and replaceable units, any seriously damaged components should be replaced rather than repaired. Sometimes the components can be found in a wrecking yard that specializes in used vehicle components, often at considerable savings over the cost of new parts.

## 7  Hinges and locks - maintenance

Once every 3000 miles, or every three months, the hinges and latch assemblies on the doors, hood and trunk should be given a few drops of light oil or lock lubricant. The door latch strikers should also be lubricated with a thin coat of grease to reduce wear and ensure free movement. Lubricate the door and trunk locks with spray-on graphite lubricant.

## 8  Windshield and fixed glass - replacement

Replacement of the windshield and fixed glass requires the use of special fast-setting adhesive/caulk materials and some specialized tools and techniques. These operations should be left to a dealer service department or a shop specializing in glass work.

## 9  Hood - removal, installation and adjustment

◆ **Refer to illustrations 9.3, 9.9 and 9.10**

➡**Note: The hood is heavy and somewhat awkward to remove and install - at least two people should perform this procedure.**

## REMOVAL AND INSTALLATION

1   Use blankets or pads to cover the cowl area of the body and the fenders. This will protect the body and paint as the hood is lifted off.

2   Disconnect any cables or wire harnesses which will interfere with removal.

3   Scribe or draw alignment marks around the bolt washers to ensure proper alignment on reinstallation (see illustration). Have an assistant support the weight of the hood. Remove the hinge bracket-to-hood bolts.

4   Lift off the hood.

5   Installation is the reverse of removal.

## ADJUSTMENT

6   Fore-and-aft and side-to-side adjustment of the hood is done by moving the hinge plate in relation to the inner fender panel after loosening the bolts.

7   Scribe a line around the entire hinge plate so you can judge the amount of movement.

8   Loosen the bolts and move the hood into correct alignment. Move it only a little at a time. Tighten the hinge bolts or nuts and carefully lower the hood to check the alignment.

9   If necessary after installation, the entire hood latch assembly can be adjusted up-and-down as well as from side-to-side on the radiator support so the hood closes securely and is flush with the fenders. To do this, scribe a line around the hood latch mounting bolts to provide a reference point. Then loosen the bolts and reposition the latch assembly as necessary (see illustration). Following adjustment, retighten the mounting bolts.

10  Finally, adjust the hood bumpers on the radiator support so the hood, when closed, is flush with the fenders (see illustration).

11  The hood latch assembly, as well as the hinges, should be periodically lubricated with white lithium-based grease to prevent sticking and wear.

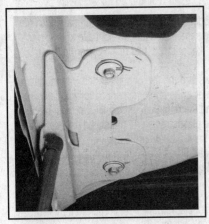
**9.3  Use a marking pen to draw a line around the hood bolts**

**9.9  Adjust the hood closed height by loosening the bolts (arrows) and moving the latch up-or-down**

**9.10  Thread the rubber bumper in-or-out to make fine adjustments to the hood closed height**

## 10  Front fender - removal and installation

### ✳✳ WARNING 1:

**Some models have airbags. Always disconnect the negative battery cable, then the positive battery cable and wait 2 minutes before working in the vicinity of the impact sensors, steering column or instrument panel to avoid the possibility of accidental deployment of the airbag, which could cause personal injury (see Chapter 12).**

### ✳✳ WARNING 2:

**On models with air suspension, turn the air suspension switch to Off before raising the vehicle.**

1   Raise the vehicle, support it securely on jackstands and remove the front wheel.

2   Remove the splash shield from the fender and body.

3   Disconnect the antenna and all light bulb wiring harness connectors and other components that would interfere with fender removal.

4   Remove the fender mounting bolts/nuts.

5   Detach the fender. It is a good idea to have an assistant support the fender while it's being moved away from the vehicle to prevent damage to the surrounding body panels.

6   Installation is the reverse of removal.

7   Tighten all nuts, bolts and screws securely.

## 11 Radiator grille - removal and installation

♦ Refer to illustration 11.4

### ❈❈ WARNING:

**Some models have airbags. Always disconnect the negative battery cable, then the positive battery cable and wait 2 minutes before working in the vicinity of the impact sensors, steering column or instrument panel to avoid the possibility of accidental deployment of the airbag, which could cause personal injury (see Chapter 12).**

## 1991 AND EARLIER MODELS

### Removal

#### Crown Victoria

1  Remove the four retaining screws and use a small screwdriver to detach the plastic locking tabs, then pull out the grille.

#### Grand Marquis

2  The grille is retained with six locking tabs. Detach the tabs with a small screwdriver and pull out the grille.

### Installation

3  Press the grille into position until it clicks in place. Install any screws that were removed.

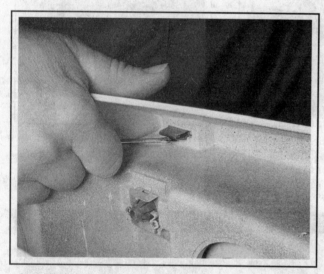

**11.4 Use a small screwdriver to detach the grille retaining clips**

## 1992 AND 1993 MODELS

### Removal

#### Crown Victoria

4  From behind the grille, use a small screwdriver to release the seven locking tabs along the top and the two locking tabs at the bottom and detach the grille (see illustration).

#### Grand Marquis

5  Remove the cover panel from behind the grille, the side marker and headlights for access.

6  Remove the eleven nuts and four screws, then remove the grille.

### Installation

7  Installation is the reverse of removal.

## 1994 AND LATER MODELS

### Removal

#### Crown Victoria

8  On 1994 to 1997 models, remove both headlight housings (see Chapter 12). On later models the headlights do not have to be removed.

9  Remove the screws, if applicable, that retain the grille to the headlight housings.

10  The number of screws and the use of clips varies with model, but all are retained to the radiator grille reinforcement panel with fasteners accessible only from behind the reinforcement panel. On most models, this requires removal of the plastic radiator sight shield that sits over the top of the radiator and the top of the grille opening. Twist the plastic fasteners one-quarter turn and lift off the sight shield, then remove the screws and release the clips as required.

#### Grand Marquis

11  On 1994 and 1995 models, remove both cornering lights and both headlight housings (see Chapter 12).

12  On 1994 and 1995 models, remove the nine retaining nuts and two screws and detach the grille.

13  On 1996 and later models, remove the four nuts and detach the grille. The grille fasteners are accessible only from behind the radiator grille reinforcement panel. On most models, this requires removal of the plastic radiator sight shield that sits over the top of the radiator and the top of the grille opening. Twist the plastic fasteners one-quarter turn and lift off the sight shield, then remove the screws and release the clips as required.

### Installation

14  Installation is the reverse of removal.

## 12 Bumpers - removal and installation

♦ Refer to illustration 12.4

✳✳ **WARNING:**

Some models have airbags. Always disconnect the negative battery cable, then the positive battery cable and wait 2 minutes before working in the vicinity of the impact sensors, steering column or instrument panel to avoid the possibility of accidental deployment of the airbag, which could cause personal injury (see Chapter 12).

**12.4 Bumper retaining nuts (arrows)**

### REMOVAL

1  To remove the bumper, the plastic bumper cover, or fascia, must be removed first. The number of bumper cover fasteners varies from year to year and model to model, but generally there are four or more front bumper cover fasteners accessible from under the vehicle (below the radiator area), several fasteners in the fenderwell securing the cover to the fender, and one fastener on each side accessible when the cornering lamps are removed (see Chapter 12). Rear bumper covers have fasteners along the bottom edge accessible from below, screws in the fenderwell, and nuts inside the trunk that are accessible when the rearmost trunk interior trim panels are removed.

2  Disconnect any wiring or other components that would interfere with bumper removal.

3  Support the bumper with a jack or jackstand.

4  Alternatively remove the retaining bolts/nuts and detach the bumper (see illustration).

### INSTALLATION

5  Installation is the reverse of removal.

6  Tighten the retaining bolts securely.

7  Install the bumper cover and any other components that were removed.

## 13 Door trim panel - removal and installation

♦ Refer to illustrations 13.2, 13.3, 13.4a, 13.4b, 13.c, 13.5 and 13.7

### REMOVAL

1  Disconnect the cable from the negative battery terminal.

2  Remove all door trim panel retaining screws and door pull/armrest assemblies (see illustration).

3  On manual window regulator equipped models, remove the window crank. On power regulator models, remove the switch housing screw, pry out the housing and unplug the switch (see illustration).

4  Dislodge the clips at the bottom edge (earlier models), grasp the trim panel and rotate the bottom edge out, then lift the panel up to detach it from the door. Unplug any wire harness connectors and remove the trim panel from the vehicle (see illustration). On 1997 and later models, there are four or more screws securing the trim panel to the door (see illustrations).

5  For access to the inner door, carefully peel back the plastic watershield (see illustration).

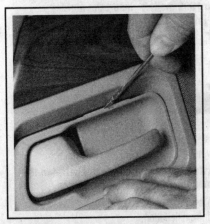

**13.2  Use a screwdriver to pry out the door trim panel screw covers**

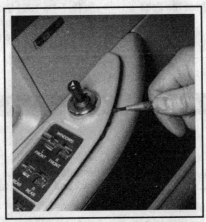

**13.3  Pry up on the power window switch housing to detach**

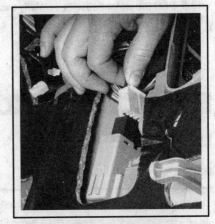

**13.4a  Pull the trim panel out and unplug the electrical connectors**

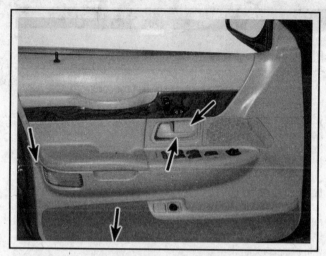

**13.4b Arrows indicate locations of front door trim screws on later models - two screws are under the handle cover**

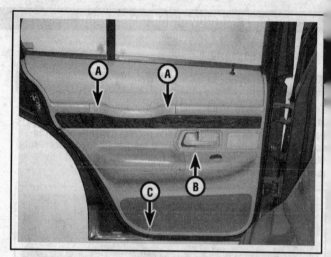

**13.4c Location of trim screws on later model rear doors; A screws are behind two plastic caps, B are under the handle cover, C at the bottom of the door panel**

## INSTALLATION

6   Prior to installation of the door panel, be sure to reinstall any clips in the panel which may have come out during the removal procedure and remain in the door itself.

7   Plug in the wire harness connectors and place the panel in

position in the window glass opening at the top of the door, then rotate it down into position and seat the clips at the bottom. Install the armrest/door pulls. On later models, insert the molded hooks into the door openings, them push straight down to seat them (see illustration). Install the manual regulator window crank or power window switch assembly.

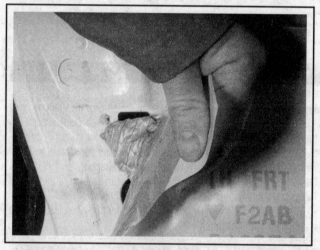

**13.5 Peel the water deflector carefully away from the door, taking care not to tear or distort it**

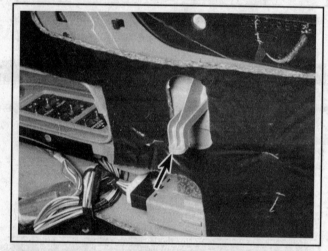

**13.7 On 1992 through 1999 models, insert the molded plastic hooks (arrow) into the door and push down to lock the trim panel in the door**

## 14  Door - removal, installation and adjustment

▶ **Refer to illustrations 14.4 and 14.6**

## REMOVAL

1   Remove the door trim panel (see Section 13). Disconnect any wire harness connectors and push them through the door opening so they won't interfere with door removal.

2   Place a jack or jackstand under the door or have an assistant on hand to support the door when the hinge bolts are removed.

➡**Note: If a jack or jackstand is used, place a rag between the jack and the door to protect the door's painted surfaces.**

3   Scribe or draw alignment marks around the door hinges to ensure proper alignment on reinstallation.

4   Remove the hinge-to-door bolts and carefully lift off the door (see illustration).

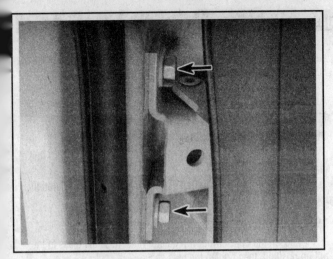

**14.4  With the door supported, remove the door hinge bolts (arrows)**

## INSTALLATION AND ADJUSTMENT

5   Installation is the reverse of removal.
6   Following installation of the door, check the alignment and adjust, if necessary, as follows:

   *a)  Up-and-down and forward-and-backward adjustments are made by loosening the hinge-to-body bolts and moving the door as necessary.*

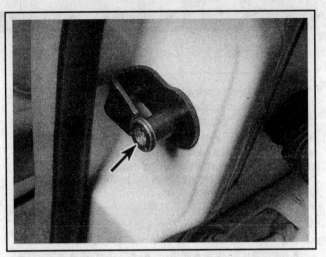

**14.6  Adjust the door closed position by loosening the Torx head screw (arrow), then moving the striker by tapping it with a mallet**

   *b)  The door lock striker can also be adjusted both up-and-down and sideways to provide positive engagement with the lock mechanism. This is done by loosening the striker pin with a Torx-bit tool, moving the pin as necessary and retightening the striker (see illustration).*

## 15  Door lock and remote controls - removal and installation

▶ **Refer to illustrations 15.2a, 15.2b and 15.4**

1   Remove the door trim panel and peel the watershield back (see Section 13).
2   Remove the remote control assembly and disconnect the rod at the control and the lock cylinder (see illustrations).

3   Disconnect the push button rod and handle from the latch.
4   Remove the screws located in the end of the door and detach the latch (see illustration).
5   Installation is the reverse of removal.

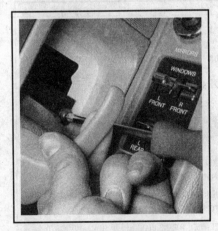

**15.2a  Remove the door remote control retaining screws**

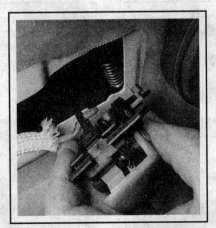

**15.2b  Pull the remote control out and disconnect it from the rod**

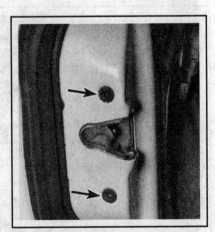

**15.4  The latch is held in place by two screws in the end of the door (arrows)**

## 16 Door window glass - removal, installation and adjustment

### REMOVAL

1   Remove the door trim panel and the watershield (see Section 13). On models with door speakers, remove the speaker mounting screws and disconnect the electrical connector.

➡**Note: On most models, the lower bolt for the front glass retainer channel must be removed to allow the window glass to be removed. It is generally about six inches from the front door jamb and about eight inches above the bottom of the door. Push the glass channel forward.**

2   Raise or lower the glass as necessary until the two retaining rivets are accessible through the holes in the inner door panel. Use a punch to remove the centers from the rivets, then drill out the rivets with a 1/4-inch drill bit. Be sure to use a block of wood to support the glass during the rivet removal process.

3   Remove the glass from the door by tipping it forward, then lifting it up and out of the opening at the top of the door, toward the outside.

### INSTALLATION

4   Lower the glass into the door, place it in position in the bracket

and install two 1/4 by 1-inch screws with washers and nuts. Tighten the nuts and screws securely.

### ADJUSTMENT

#### 1991 and earlier models

5   With the regulator run and bracket nut and bolt loose, raise the glass to the top of the door.

6   Move the glass fore-and-aft as necessary until it is centered in the tracks, then tighten the bracket and run nut and bolt.

#### 1992 and later models

7   Loosen the upper window regulator nuts, raise the glass to the full up position, then tighten the nuts securely.

8   Loosen the front glass run bolt, lower the glass to the full down position and tighten the bolt securely

#### All models

9   Cycle the glass several times to make sure it is properly adjusted.

## 17 Trunk lid - removal, installation and adjustment

♦ **Refer to illustrations 17.7a and 17.7b**

### REMOVAL

1   Open the trunk lid and cover the edges of the trunk compartment with pads or cloths to protect the painted surfaces when the lid is removed. On 1999 and later models, remove the plastic fasteners and remove the plastic trunk lid trim panel for access to the hinge bolts.

2   Disconnect any cables or wire harness connectors attached to the trunk lid that would interfere with removal.

3   Scribe or draw alignment marks around the hinge bolt mounting flanges.

4   While an assistant supports the trunk lid, remove the hinge bolts from both sides and lift it off.

### INSTALLATION AND ADJUSTMENT

5   Installation is the reverse of removal.

➡**Note: When reinstalling the trunk lid, align the hinge bolt flanges with the marks made during removal.**

6   After installation, close the lid and check to verify if it's in proper alignment with the surrounding panels. Fore-and-aft and side-to-side adjustments of the lid are controlled by the position of the hinge bolts in the slots. To adjust, loosen the hinge bolts, reposition the lid and

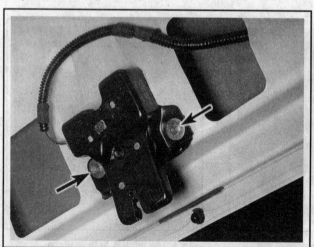

**17.7a  The trunk lid closed position can be adjusted by loosening the bolts (arrows) and moving the latch**

**17.7b  Fine adjustments of the trunk lid can be made by threading the rubber bumpers in-or-out**

retighten the bolts.

7   The height of the lid in relation to the surrounding body panels when closed can be adjusted by loosening the striker bolts, repositioning the striker and retightening the bolts. The height can also be adjusted by loosening the latch bolts, repositioning the latch and retightening the bolts (see illustration). On later models, finer adjustments of the trunk lid, when closed, can be made by threading the bumper/stops in-or-out (see illustration).

## 18   Steering column cover - removal and installation

▶ **Refer to illustrations 18.1, 18.3, 18.5a and 18.5b**

### ✳ WARNING:

**Some models have airbags. Always disconnect the negative battery cable, then the positive battery cable and wait 2 minutes before working in the vicinity of the impact sensors, steering column or instrument panel to avoid the possibility of accidental deployment of the airbag, which could cause personal injury (see Chapter 12).**

1   Remove the retaining screws (see illustration).
2   Remove the knee protector (see Section 19).
3   On tilt steering columns, use a small wrench to unscrew the tilt lever (see illustration).
4   Remove the ignition lock cylinder (see Chapter 12).
5   Remove any remaining screws, then separate the halves and remove the covers (see illustrations).
6   Installation is the reverse of the removal procedure.

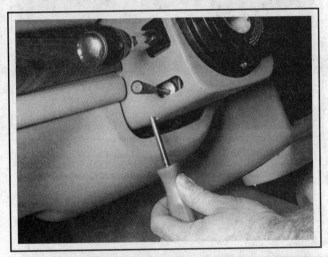

**18.1   Use a Phillips head screwdriver to remove the steering column cover screws**

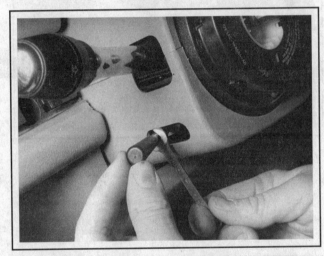

**18.3 Remove the tilt lever with a small wrench**

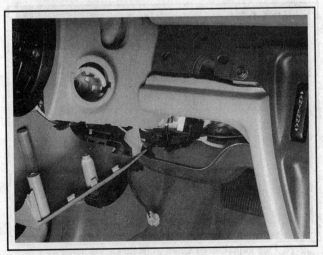

**18.5a   Detach the lower column cover**

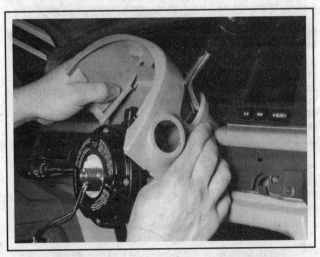

**18.5b   Lift the upper column cover up over the shift lever**

## 19 Knee protector - removal and installation

♦ Refer to illustrations 19.1 and 19.2

### ✳✳ WARNING:

Some models have airbags. Always disconnect the negative battery cable, then the positive battery cable and wait 2 minutes before working in the vicinity of the impact sensors, steering column or instrument panel to avoid the possibility of accidental deployment of the airbag, which could cause personal injury (see Chapter 12).

➡Note: The appearance of the instrument panel on models since 1996 is different. Removal and installation of the knee protector is the same, except some fasteners are in different locations.

1   Remove the retaining bolts at the lower edge of the knee protector (see illustration).

2   On models through 1998, detach the instrument cluster trim panels (around the knee protector), then remove the upper retaining bolts and lower the knee protector (see illustration). On 1999 and later models, just remove the knee protector mounting screws, remove the parking brake release lever, then pull the knee protector to release the clips at the top. On models with a courtesy light in the knee protector, disconnect the electrical connector.

3   Installation is the reverse of the removal procedure.

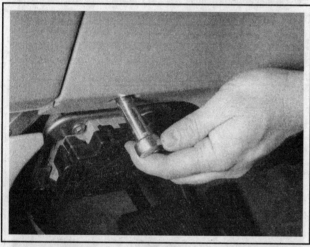

19.1  Use a socket to remove the bolts from the lower edge of the knee protector

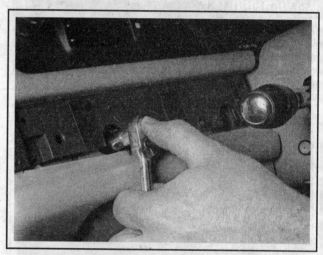

19.2  Remove the bolts from the upper edge of the knee protector

## 20 Instrument cluster bezel - removal and installation

♦ Refer to illustrations 20.2, 20.3a, 20.3b, 20.3c and 20.4

### ✳✳ WARNING:

Some models have airbags. Always disconnect the negative battery cable, then the positive battery cable and wait 2 minutes before working in the vicinity of the impact sensors, steering column or instrument panel to avoid the possibility of accidental deployment of the airbag, which could cause personal injury (see Chapter 12).

➡Note: The appearance of the instrument panel on models since 1996 is different. Removal and installation of the instrument cluster bezel is the same, except some fasteners are in different locations.

1   Remove the headlight switch knob (see Chapter 12).
2   Detach the dash trim panels (see illustration).
3   Remove to the bezel retaining screws (see illustrations).

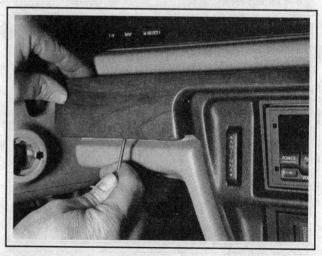

20.2  Use a small screwdriver to pry off the dash trim panels

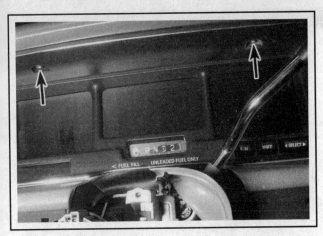

**20.3a Remove the upper cluster bezel screws (arrows) (1992 and later model shown)**

**20.3b Remove the lower left edge cluster bezel screws (arrows)**

4    Detach the bezel and remove it from the vehicle. On later models, it will be necessary to pry the left end of the bezel free and detach the retaining clips, working toward the right end until the bezel can be removed (see illustration).

5    On 1998 and later models, it is necessary to first remove the radio (see Chapter 12). When the left and right trim panels are removed, disconnect the electrical connectors behind them.

6    Installation is the reverse of the removal procedures.

**20.3c Remove the right side bezel screws**

**20.4 On 1992 and later models, detach the left side of the cluster bezel first, then work from left to right until it can be removed**

## 21   Outside mirrors- removal and installation

▶ **Refer to illustration 21.8**

1    Remove the door trim panel and watershield (see Section 13).

### CABLE-OPERATED

2    Working inside the vehicle, detach the control lever from the instrument panel or door and connect a string or thin wire to the end of the control cable, then detach any retaining clips.

3    Working outside the vehicle, remove the attaching screws, detach the mirror and pull the control cable out of the door.

4    Attach the string or wire to the control end of the new cable/mirror assembly, pull it into position in the vehicle, then install the mirror and screws.

5    Secure the cable and connect it to the door or instrument panel.

### ELECTRIC

6    Disconnect the cable from the negative battery terminal.

**21.8 Use a socket to remove the outside mirror nuts**

7    Pry off the mirror access hole cover.

8    Remove the three nuts (see illustration), detach the mirror from the door and unplug the electrical connector.

9    Installation is the reverse of the removal procedures.

**Notes**

**Section**

# 12

## CHASSIS ELECTRICAL SYSTEM

## 1  General information

The electrical system is a 12-volt, negative ground type. Power for the lights and all electrical accessories is supplied by a lead/acid-type battery which is charged by the alternator.

This Chapter covers repair and service procedures for the various electrical components not associated with the engine.

Information on the battery, alternator, distributor and starter motor can be found in Chapter 5.

It should be noted that when portions of the electrical system are serviced, the negative battery cable should be disconnected from the battery to prevent electrical shorts and/or fires.

## 2  Electrical troubleshooting - general information

A typical electrical circuit consists of an electrical component, any switches, relays, motors, fuses, fusible links or circuit breakers related to that component and the wiring and connectors that link the component to both the battery and the chassis. To help you pinpoint an electrical circuit problem, wiring diagrams are included at the end of this Chapter.

Before tackling any troublesome electrical circuit, first study the appropriate wiring diagrams to get a complete understanding of what makes up that individual circuit. Trouble spots, for instance, can often be narrowed down by noting if other components related to the circuit are operating properly. If several components or circuits fail at one time, chances are the problem is in a fuse or ground connection, because several circuits are often routed through the same fuse and ground connections.

Electrical problems usually stem from simple causes, such as loose or corroded connections, a blown fuse, a melted fusible link or a failed relay. Visually inspect the condition of all fuses, wires and connections in a problem circuit before troubleshooting the circuit.

If test equipment and instruments are going to be utilized, use the diagrams to plan ahead of time where you will make the necessary connections in order to accurately pinpoint the trouble spot.

The basic tools needed for electrical troubleshooting include a circuit tester or voltmeter (a 12-volt bulb with a set of test leads can also be used), a continuity tester, which includes a bulb, battery and set of test leads, and a jumper wire, preferably with a circuit breaker incorporated, which can be used to bypass electrical components. Before attempting to locate a problem with test instruments, use the wiring diagram(s) to decide where to make the connections.

### VOLTAGE CHECKS

Voltage checks should be performed if a circuit is not functioning properly. Connect one lead of a circuit tester to either the negative battery terminal or a known good ground. Connect the other lead to a connector in the circuit being tested, preferably nearest to the battery or fuse. If the bulb of the tester lights, voltage is present, which means that the part of the circuit between the connector and the battery is problem free. Continue checking the rest of the circuit in the same fashion. When you reach a point at which no voltage is present, the problem lies between that point and the last test point with voltage. Most of the time the problem can be traced to a loose connection.

➡**Note: Keep in mind that some circuits receive voltage only when the ignition key is in the Accessory or Run position.**

### FINDING A SHORT

One method of finding shorts in a circuit is to remove the fuse and connect a test light or voltmeter in place of the fuse terminals. There should be no voltage present in the circuit. Move the wiring harness from side-to-side while watching the test light. If the bulb goes on, there is a short to ground somewhere in that area, probably where the insulation has rubbed through. The same test can be performed on each component in the circuit, even a switch.

### GROUND CHECK

Perform a ground test to check whether a component is properly grounded. Disconnect the battery and connect one lead of a self-powered test light, known as a continuity tester, to a known good ground. Connect the other lead to the wire or ground connection being tested. If the bulb goes on, the ground is good. If the bulb does not go on, the ground is not good.

### CONTINUITY CHECK

A continuity check is done to determine if there are any breaks in a circuit - if it is passing electricity properly. With the circuit off (no power in the circuit), a self-powered continuity tester can be used to check the circuit. Connect the test leads to both ends of the circuit (or to the "power" end and a good ground), and if the test light comes on the circuit is passing current properly. If the light doesn't come on, there is a break somewhere in the circuit. The same procedure can be used to test a switch, by connecting the continuity tester to the switch terminals. With the switch turned On, the test light should come on.

### FINDING AN OPEN CIRCUIT

When diagnosing for possible open circuits, it is often difficult to locate them by sight because oxidation or terminal misalignment are hidden by the connectors. Merely wiggling a connector on a sensor or in the wiring harness may correct the open circuit condition. Remember this when an open circuit is indicated when troubleshooting a circuit. Intermittent problems may also be caused by oxidized or loose connections.

Electrical troubleshooting is simple if you keep in mind that all electrical circuits are basically electricity running from the battery, through the wires, switches, relays, fuses and fusible links to each electrical component (light bulb, motor, etc.) and to ground, from which it is passed back to the battery. Any electrical problem is an interruption in the flow of electricity to and from the battery.

## 3  Fuses - general information

▶ **Refer to illustrations 3.1a, 3.1b, 3.1c and 3.2**

The electrical circuits of the vehicle are protected by a combination of fuses, circuit breakers and fusible links. On 1991 and earlier models the fuse block is located below the left side of the dash, under a cover that is secured with two screws. 1992 and later models have two fuse blocks, one for standard fuses located under the instrument panel on the left side of the dashboard and one for high current fuses in the engine compartment, adjacent to the battery (see illustrations). Disconnect the cable to the negative battery terminal before replacing high current fuses.

Miniaturized fuses are employed in the fuse block in the passenger compartment. These compact fuses, with blade terminal design, allow fingertip removal and replacement. If an electrical component fails, always check the fuse first. The best way to check a fuse is with a test light. Check for power at the exposed terminal tips of each fuse. If power is present on one side of the fuse but not the other, the fuse is blown. A blown fuse can also be confirmed by visually inspecting it (see illustration).

Be sure to replace blown fuses with the correct type. Fuses of different ratings are physically interchangeable, but only fuses of the proper rating should be used. Replacing a fuse with one of a higher or lower value than specified is not recommended. Each electrical circuit needs a specific amount of protection. The amperage value of each fuse is molded into the fuse body.

If the replacement fuse immediately fails, don't replace it again until the cause of the problem is isolated and corrected. In most cases, the cause will be a short circuit in the wiring caused by a broken or deteriorated wire.

**3.1a  The main fuse block is located under the driver's side of the dash - release the clip by inserting a screwdriver, then pull sharply down to remove the cover**

**3.1b  Typical fuse block details**

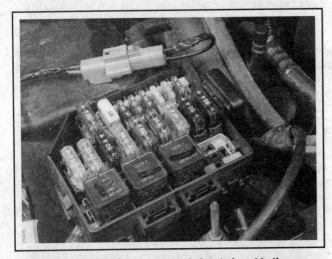

**3.1c  The underhood power center is located next to the battery in the engine compartment, and contains relays and high-amperage fuses**

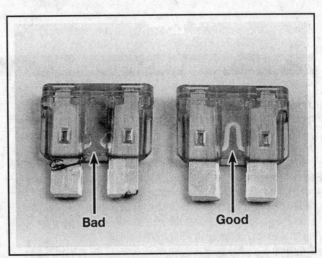

**3.2  When a fuse blows, the element between the terminals melts**

## 4　Fusible links - general information

Some circuits are protected by fusible links. The links are used in circuits which are not ordinarily fused, such as the ignition circuit.

In addition to the conventional type of fusible link described below (located in the wiring harness), cartridge fusible links, similar to large fuses, are used on some models. Cartridge fusible links are located in the engine compartment fuse block and, after disconnecting the negative battery cable, are simply unplugged and replaced by a unit of the same amperage. Some cartridge fusible links are held in place by bolts which must be loosened before removing the link.

Conventional-type fusible links cannot be repaired; a new link of the same size wire should be installed in its place. The procedure is as follows:

a) Disconnect the cable from the negative battery terminal.
b) Disconnect the fusible link from the wiring harness.
c) Cut the damaged fusible link out of the wiring just behind the connector.
d) Strip the insulation back approximately 1/2-inch.
e) Position the connector on the new fusible link and crimp it into place.
f) Use rosin core solder at each end of the new link to obtain a good solder joint.
g) Use plenty of electrical tape around the soldered joint. No wires should be exposed.
h) Connect the battery ground cable. Test the circuit for proper operation.

## 5　Circuit breakers - general information

▶ Refer to illustration 5.2

Circuit breakers protect components such as power windows, power door locks and headlights.

On some models the circuit breaker resets itself automatically, so an electrical overload in a circuit-breaker-protected system will cause the circuit to fail momentarily, then come back on. If the circuit does not come back on, check it immediately (see illustration). Once the condition is corrected, the circuit breaker will resume its normal function.

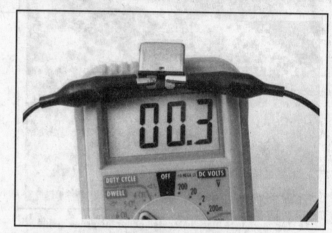

5.2　Perform a continuity test with an ohmmeter to check a circuit breaker - infinite resistance indicates a bad circuit breaker

## 6　Relays - general information and testing

### GENERAL INFORMATION

▶ Refer to illustration 6.1

1　Several electrical accessories in the vehicle, such as the fuel injection system, horns, starter, and fog lamps use relays to transmit the electrical signal to the component. Relays use a low-current circuit (the control circuit) to open and close a high-current circuit (the power circuit). If the relay is defective, that component will not operate properly. The various relays are mounted in the engine compartment (see illustration 3.1c) and several locations throughout the vehicle. Late-model vehicles have a relay center in the engine compartment, near the brake master cylinder (see illustration). In this relay center are: the air conditioning WOT cutout relay, fuel pump, PCM power relay, and PCM power diode. If a faulty relay is suspected, it can be removed and tested using the procedure below or by a dealer service department or other repair shop. Defective relays must be replaced as a unit.

### TESTING

▶ Refer to illustration 6.4

2　It's best to refer to the wiring diagram for the circuit to determine the proper hook-ups for the relay you're testing. However, if you're not able to determine the correct hook-up from the wiring diagrams, you may be able to determine the test hook-ups from the information that follows.

3　On most relays, two of the terminals are the relay's control circuit (they connect to the relay coil which, when energized, closes the large contacts to complete the circuit). The other terminals are the power circuit (they are connected together within the relay when the control-circuit coil is energized).

4　The relays are marked as an aid to help you determine which terminals are the control circuit and which are the power circuit (see illustration).

**6.1 On later models, several relays are grouped into a relay center (arrow) located underhood, near the brake master cylinder**

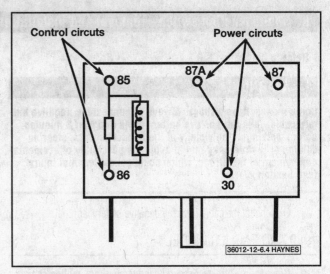

**6.4 Most relays are marked on the outside to easily identify the control and power circuits**

5   Remove the relay from the vehicle and check for continuity between the relay power circuit terminals. There should be no continuity between terminal 30 and 87.

6   Connect a fused jumper wire between one of the two control circuit terminals and the positive battery terminal. Connect another jumper wire between the other control circuit terminal and ground. When the connections are made, the relay should click. On some relays, polarity may be critical, so, if the relay doesn't click, try swapping the jumper wires on the control circuit terminals.

7   With the jumper wires connected, check for continuity between the power circuit terminals. Now, there should be continuity between terminals 30 and 87.

8   If the relay fails any of the above tests, replace it.

## 7   Turn signal/hazard flasher - check and replacement

### TURN SIGNAL FLASHER

1   On models through 1996, the turn signal flasher, located in the main interior fuse panel near the parking brake, is a small canister-shaped unit that flashes the turn signal lights when activated. On later models, the flasher function is performed by a solid-state lighting control module, located below and to the right of the steering column. On models with a lighting control module, the flasher canister can not be pulled out and replaced. The module and its circuit must be tested, a job best left to an electrical service shop.

2   When the flasher unit is functioning properly, an audible click can be heard during its operation. If the turn signals fail on one side or the other and the flasher unit does not make its characteristic clicking sound, or if it flashes much more rapidly than normal, a faulty turn signal bulb is indicated.

3   If both turn signals fail to blink, the problem may be due to a blown fuse, a faulty flasher unit, a broken switch or a loose or open connection. If a quick check of the fuse box indicates that the turn signal fuse has blown, check the wiring for a short before installing a new fuse.

4   To replace the flasher, simply pull it out of the fuse block.

5   Make sure that the replacement unit is identical to the original. Compare the old one to the new one before installing it.

6   Installation is the reverse of removal.

### HAZARD FLASHER

7   On models through 1996, the hazard flasher, located in the main interior fuse panel near the parking brake, is a small canister-shaped unit that flashes the turn signal lights when activated. On later models, the flasher function is performed by a solid-state lighting control module, located below and to the right of the steering column. On models with a lighting control module, the flasher canister can not be pulled out and replaced. The module and its circuit must be tested, a job best left to an electrical service shop.

8   The hazard flasher is checked in a fashion similar to the turn signal flasher (see Steps 2 and 3).

9   To replace the hazard flasher, pull it from the back of fuse block.

10 Make sure the replacement unit is identical to the one it replaces. Compare the old one to the new one before installing it.

11 Installation is the reverse of removal.

## 8 Multi-function switch - removal and installation

▶ Refer to illustration 8.9

**✳✳ WARNING:**

Some models have airbags. Always disconnect the negative battery cable, then the positive battery cable and wait 2 minutes before working in the vicinity of the impact sensors, steering column or instrument panel to avoid the possibility of accidental deployment of the airbag, which could cause personal injury (see Section 27).

1   Disconnect the cable from the negative battery terminal.

### 1989 AND EARLIER MODELS

2   Grasp the switch lever securely and remove it by pulling straight out.

3   Remove the steering column covers (see Chapter 11).

4   Remove the switch cover, then unplug the connector, remove the retaining screws and withdraw the switch assembly from the steering column.

5   Place the switch in position and install the screws, then plug in the electrical connector.

6   Install the steering column covers.

7   Line up the tangs on the lever with the slot in the switch and install it by pushing straight in.

### 1990 AND LATER MODELS

8   Remove the steering column covers (see Chapter 11). On most models, the ignition lock cylinder must be removed first (see Section 10), and, on models with tilt-column steering, the tilt lever must

**8.9  Remove the retaining screws and unplug the connector (arrows), then remove the multi-function switch**

also be removed before removing the covers.

9   Remove the two retaining screws, pull the switch out, unplug the connector and detach the switch assembly from the steering column (see illustration).

10  Plug in the electrical connector, insert the switch into the steering column, and install the screws.

11  Install the steering column covers, lock cylinder and tilt lever (if equipped).

### ALL MODELS

12  Connect the cable to the negative battery terminal.

## 9 Ignition switch - removal and installation

▶ Refer to illustration 9.3

**✳✳ WARNING:**

Some models have airbags. Always disconnect the negative battery cable, then the positive battery cable and wait 2 minutes before working in the vicinity of the impact sensors, steering column or instrument panel to avoid the possibility of accidental deployment of the airbag, which could cause personal injury (see Section 27).

### REMOVAL

1   Disconnect the cable from the negative battery terminal.

2   Remove the steering column covers and the knee bolster (see Chapter 11).

3   On 1996 and earlier models, remove the retaining nuts and lower the column for access to the switch screws. On 1997 through 2004 models, remove the metal reinforcement panel just behind the knee bolster for access to the switch (see illustration).

4   Unplug the ignition switch electrical connector.

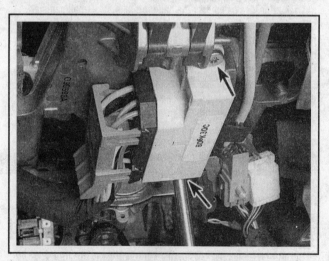

**9.3  1997 through 2004 model ignition switches are located to the right of the steering column and accessible after the knee bolster reinforcement panel is removed (arrows indicate switch mounting screws)**

5   Turn the ignition key lock cylinder to the Run position.
6   Remove the two switch retaining screws.
7   Disengage the ignition switch from the actuator pin.

## INSTALLATION

8   Make sure the actuator pin slot in the new ignition switch is in the Run position.

➡**Note: A new replacement switch assembly will be set in this position.**

9   Place the new switch in position on the actuator pin and install the retaining screws. It may be necessary to move the switch back and forth to line up the screw holes.
10 Plug the electrical connector into the switch.
11 Install the upper steering column cover.
12 Raise the steering column into position and install the retaining nuts. Tighten the nuts securely.
13 Install the steering lower column covers and lower insulator panel.
14 Connect the cable to the negative battery terminal.

## 10   Ignition lock cylinder - removal and installation

▸ **Refer to illustration 10.3**

### ✳✳ WARNING:

**Some models have airbags. Always disconnect the negative battery cable, then the positive battery cable and wait 2 minutes before working in the vicinity of the impact sensors, steering column or instrument panel to avoid the possibility of accidental deployment of the airbag, which could cause personal injury (see Section 27).**

## REMOVAL

1   Disconnect the cable from the negative battery terminal.

### 1988 through 2006 models

2   Turn the lock cylinder to the Run position.
3   Insert an 1/8-inch punch into the hole at the bottom of the casting surrounding the lock cylinder. Depress the punch while pulling out on the lock cylinder to remove it from the column housing (see illustration).

### 2007 and later models

4   Remove the tilt wheel handle and shank from the steering column.
5   Remove the steering column covers (see Chapter 11).
6   Move the gear shift selector boot up and out of the way.
7   Insert the ignition key and turn the lock cylinder to the ACC position.
8   Release the Passive Anti-Theft system locking tabs and rotate the

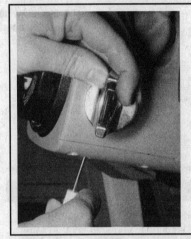

10.3  To remove the ignition lock cylinder, place the key in the "RUN" position, push in on the release tab with a screwdriver and pull the cylinder straight out

PATS transceiver until the lock cylinder release pin hole has access.
9   Insert a pin into the release hole, depress to release the lock cylinder and simultaneously slide the lock cylinder from the steering column

## INSTALLATION

10 Install the lock cylinder by turning it to the RUN or ACC position and depressing the retaining pin. Insert the lock cylinder into the lock cylinder housing. Make sure the cylinder is completely seated and aligned in the interlocking washer before turning the key to the Off position. This will permit the retaining pin to extend into the hole.
11 Turn the lock to ensure that operation is correct in all positions.
12 The remainder of installation is the reverse of removal.

## 11   Headlights - replacement

▸ **Refer to illustrations 11.10a, 11.10b and 11.11**

### ✳✳ WARNING:

**Some models have airbags. Always disconnect the negative battery cable, then the positive battery cable and wait 2 minutes before working in the vicinity of the impact sensors, steering column or instrument panel to avoid the possibility of accidental deployment of the airbag, which could cause personal injury (see Section 27).**

## SEALED BEAM

1   Disconnect the cable from the negative battery terminal.
2   Remove the retaining screws and detach the headlight bezel.
3   Remove the headlight retainer screws, taking care not to disturb the adjusting screws.
4   Remove the retainer and pull the headlight out enough to allow the connector to be unplugged.
5   Remove the headlight.

**11.10a Lift the tab to detach the headlight bulb cover**

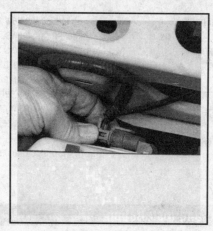

**11.10b Rotate the bulb holder counterclockwise and pull it out of the housing**

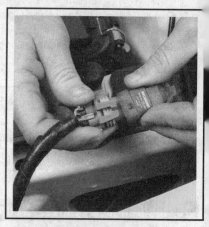

**11.11 Detach the clip and unplug the bulb assembly from the holder - when installing the new bulb, don't touch the surface; clean it with rubbing alcohol if you do**

6   To install the headlight, plug the connector in, place the headlight in position and install the retainer and screws. Tighten the screws securely.

7   Place the bezel in position and install the retaining screws.

## BULB-TYPE

### ✳ WARNING:

Halogen gas filled bulbs are under pressure and may shatter if the surface is scratched or the bulb is dropped. Wear eye protection and handle the bulbs carefully, grasping only the base whenever possible. Do not touch the surface of the bulb with your fingers because the oil from your skin could cause it to overheat and fail prematurely. If you do touch the bulb surface, clean it with rubbing alcohol.

8   Open the hood.

9   Disconnect the cable from the negative battery terminal.

10   Remove the cover (if equipped) and reach behind the headlight assembly, grasp the bulb holder and turn it counterclockwise to remove it (see illustrations). Lift the holder assembly out for access to the bulb. On later models, the bulb holder is mounted to the headlight with a retaining ring. Disconnect the electrical connector, then twist the retaining ring counterclockwise to remove it. Pull the bulb holder straight back out of the headlight housing.

11   Release the clip and unplug the bulb holder from the connector (see illustration).

12   Insert the new bulb into the connector until it clicks into place.

13   Install the bulb holder in the headlight assembly.

## 12  Headlights - adjustment

▶ Refer to illustrations 12.1 and 12.3

➡ Note: The headlights must be aimed correctly. If adjusted incorrectly they could blind the driver of an oncoming vehicle and cause a serious accident or seriously reduce your ability to see the road. The headlights should be checked for proper aim every 12 months and any time a new headlight is installed or front end body work is performed. It should be emphasized that the following procedure is only an interim step which will provide temporary adjustment until the headlights can be adjusted by a properly equipped shop.

1   Headlights have two spring-loaded adjusting screws, one on the top controlling up-and-down movement and one on the side controlling left-and-right movement. On 1991 and earlier modes these screws are accessible from the front after removing the bezel. On 1992 and later models the adjusters are reached from the rear of the headlight assembly and are turned using a small wrench or pliers (see illustration).

2   There are several methods of adjusting the headlights. The simplest method requires a blank wall 25 feet in front of the vehicle and a level floor.

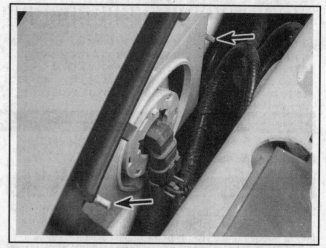

**12.1 The adjustment screws (arrows) are accessible from the back of the housing on 1992 and later models**

3   Position masking tape vertically on the wall in reference to the vehicle centerline and the centerlines of both headlights (see illustration).

4   Position a horizontal tape line in reference to the centerline of all the headlights.

➡Note: It may be easier to position the tape on the wall with the vehicle parked only a few inches away.

5   Adjustment should be made with the vehicle sitting level, the gas tank half-full and no unusually heavy load in the vehicle.

6   Starting with the low beam adjustment, position the high intensity zone so it is two inches below the horizontal line and two inches to the side of the headlight vertical line away from oncoming traffic. Adjustment is made by turning the top adjusting screw clockwise to raise the beam and counterclockwise to lower the beam. The adjusting screw on the side should be used in the same manner to move the beam left or right.

7   With the high beams on, the high intensity zone should be vertically centered with the exact center just below the horizontal line.

➡Note: It may not be possible to position the headlight aim exactly for both high and low beams. If a compromise must be made, keep in mind that the low beams are the most used and have the greatest effect on safety.

8   Have the headlights adjusted by a dealer service department or service station at the earliest opportunity.

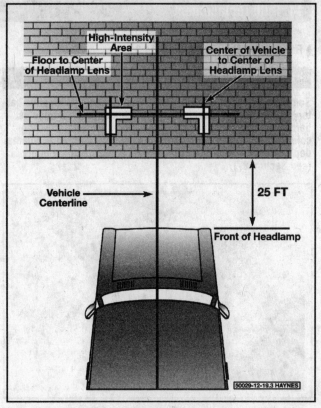

**12.3  Headlight adjustment details**

---

## 13  Headlight housing (1992 and later models) - removal and installation

▶ **Refer to illustration 13.3**

### ❊❊ WARNING:

**Some models have airbags. Always disconnect the negative battery cable, then the positive battery cable and wait 2 minutes before working in the vicinity of the impact sensors, steering column or instrument panel to avoid the possibility of accidental deployment of the airbag, which could cause personal injury (see Section 27).**

1   Disconnect the cable from the negative battery terminal.

2   Remove the headlight bulb(s) (see Section 11). On 1999 and later models, twist the three plastic retainers and remove the plastic sight shield (cover) on top of the radiator for access to the back of the headlight housings.

3   Push forward on the headlight housing while using snap-ring pliers to spread the retainer clips, then detach the housing and remove it through the grille opening (see illustration).

4   Insert the housing into the grille opening and press it into place until it seats securely in the retainers.

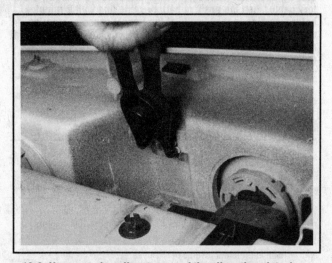

**13.3  Use snap-ring pliers to spread the clips, then detach the headlight housing**

## 14 Bulb replacement

◆ Refer to illustrations 14.2 and 14.3

### ☀ WARNING:

Some models have airbags. Always disconnect the negative battery cable, then the positive battery cable and wait 2 minutes before working in the vicinity of the impact sensors, steering column or instrument panel to avoid the possibility of accidental deployment of the airbag, which could cause personal injury (see Section 27).

1   The lenses of many lights are held in place by screws, which makes it a simple procedure to gain access to the bulbs.

2   On many lights the bulbs are held in place by clips. The bulb can be removed after detaching the clips (see illustration).

3   Several types of bulbs are used. Some are removed by pushing in and turning them counterclockwise. Others can simply be unclipped from the terminals or pulled straight out of the socket (see illustration).

4   To gain access to the instrument panel lights, the instrument cluster will have to be removed first.

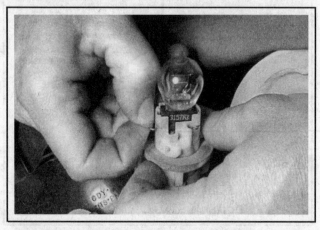

**14.2  Pull out the retaining clip, then pull the bulb out of the holder**

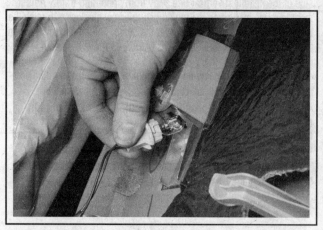

**14.3  Rotate the bulb holder counterclockwise and withdraw it from the door trim panel, then grasp the bulb and pull it straight out**

## 15 Radio/CD player and speakers - removal and installation

◆ Refer to illustrations 15.7a, 15.7b and 15.10

### ☀ WARNING:

Some models have airbags. Always disconnect the negative battery cable, then the positive battery cable and wait 2 minutes before working in the vicinity of the impact sensors, steering column or instrument panel to avoid the possibility of accidental deployment of the airbag, which could cause personal injury (see Section 27).

1   Disconnect the cable from the negative battery terminal.

### RADIO/CD PLAYER

#### 1991 and earlier models

2   Remove the screws and detach the bezel (see Chapter 11).

3   Remove the mounting screws.

4   Slide the radio/CD unit out and support it, disconnect the ground cable, antenna and electrical connectors, then remove the assembly from the instrument panel.

5   Installation is the reverse of removal.

#### 1992 and later models

6   For theft protection, the radio receiver and CD player assemblies are retained in the instrument panel by special clips. Releasing these

**15.7a  Insert the tools until they seat, then flex them out to release the clips and withdraw the radio from the dash**

clips requires a pair of radio removal tools, or two short lengths of coathanger wire bent into U-shapes. Insert the tools into the holes at the corners of the radio/CD player assembly until you feel the internal clips release.

7   With the clips released, flex out simultaneously on both tools and pull the assembly out of the instrument panel, disconnect the antenna and electrical connectors and remove the unit from the vehicle (see illustrations).

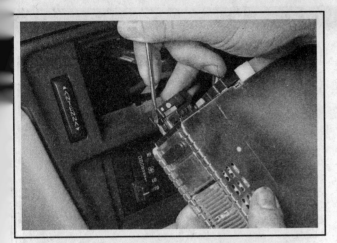

**15.7b  Use a small screwdriver to detach the electrical connector clip**

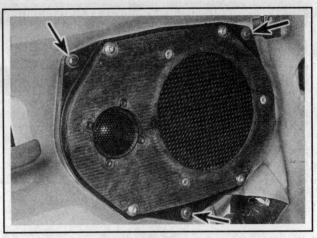

**15.10  After removing the door trim panel, the speaker retaining screws (arrows) are easy to reach**

8   Install by plugging in the electrical connectors, then sliding the radio or CD player along the track and into the instrument panel until the clips can be felt snapping in place.

## SPEAKERS

### Door mounted

9   Remove the door trim panel (see Chapter 11).
10   Remove the mounting screws, withdraw the speaker, unplug the electrical connector and remove the speaker from the vehicle (see illustration).
11   Installation is the reverse of removal.

### Rear quarter panel mounted

12   Remove the screws and pry off the speaker grille.
13   Remove the retaining screws, withdraw the speaker, unplug the electrical connector and remove the speaker from the vehicle.
14   Installation is the reverse of removal

### Package shelf mounted

15   Open the trunk lid.
16   Working under the package tray, unplug electrical connector, remove the retaining screws/nuts or detach the clips, then lower the speaker and remove it from the vehicle.
17   Installation is the reverse of removal

## 16  Radio antenna - check and replacement

▶ **Refer to illustration 16.5**

### RESISTANCE CHECK

1   With the antenna cable installed on the vehicle and the cable unplugged from the radio, check the antenna with an ohmmeter between the cable and tip. The reading should be less than 5 ohms. If not, replace the antenna and cable assembly.

➡**Note: On 1997 and later models, the antenna is a grid that is permanently bonded to the rear window. It can not be replaced like a conventional, body-mounted antenna, but it can be tested and repaired with the same procedure used for the rear window defogger grid (see Section 22).**

### REPLACEMENT

2   Disconnect the cable from the negative battery terminal.

### Power antenna

3   Lower the antenna.
4   Remove the rear screws from the right side front splash shield for access and remove the lower antenna bolt.
5   Remove the nut at the top of the antenna stanchion and remove the antenna by lowering it through the fender opening (see illustration).
6   Installation is the reverse of removal.

**16.5  Use needle nose pliers to unscrew the antenna stanchion nut**

### Manual antenna

7   Detach the antenna lead retaining clips in the engine compartment.
8   Remove the screws and detach the right cowl side trim panel.
9   Remove the radio and unplug the antenna lead cable (see Section 15).
10   Remove the radio antenna base cap, remove the mounting screws, pull the base and cable assembly through the opening in the fender and remove it into the engine compartment.
11   Installation is the reverse of removal.

## 17  Instrument cluster - removal and installation

♦ **Refer to illustration 17.3**

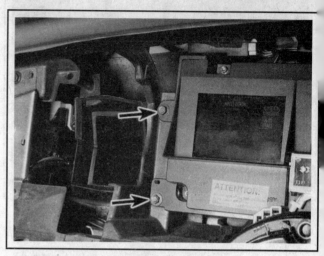

**❊❊ WARNING:**

Some models have airbags. Always disconnect the negative battery cable, then the positive battery cable and wait 2 minutes before working in the vicinity of the impact sensors, steering column or instrument panel to avoid the possibility of accidental deployment of the airbag, which could cause personal injury (see Section 27).

1  Disconnect the cable from the negative battery terminal.
2  Remove the instrument cluster bezel (see Chapter 11).
3  Remove the instrument cluster retaining screws (see illustration).
4  Pull the cluster out and unplug the electrical connectors. Disconnect the speedometer cable (see illustration 18.4) or unplug the electronic speed sensor.
5  Detach the shift indicator assembly from the cluster.
6  Remove the cluster from the instrument panel.
7  Installation is the reverse of removal.

**17.3  The instrument cluster is held in place by screws (arrows) at both sides of the housing (later electronic cluster shown)**

## 18  Speedometer cable - removal and installation

➥**Note: On later models, the speedometer is electric, with a signal provided by the Vehicle Speed Sensor (VSS). On these models there is no mechanical speedometer cable.**

**❊❊ WARNING:**

Some models have airbags. Always disconnect the negative battery cable, then the positive battery cable and wait 2 minutes before working in the vicinity of the impact sensors, steering column or instrument panel to avoid the possibility of accidental deployment of the airbag, which could cause personal injury (see Section 27).

1  Disconnect the cable from the negative battery terminal.
2  Disconnect the speedometer cable from the transmission or cruise control adapter.
3  Detach the cable from the routing clips in the engine compartment and pull the cable up to provide enough slack to allow disconnection from the speedometer.
4  Remove the instrument cluster screws, pull the cluster out, then reach behind it and disconnect the speedometer cable from the back of the cluster by pressing on the cable release clip.
5  Remove the cable from the vehicle.
6  Prior to installation, press a 3/16-inch ball of silicone or equivalent lubricant into the speedometer opening.
7  Installation is the reverse of removal.

## 19  Headlight switch - replacement

♦ **Refer to illustrations 19.5 and 19.7**

**❊❊ WARNING:**

Some models have airbags. Always disconnect the negative battery cable, then the positive battery cable and wait 2 minutes before working in the vicinity of the impact sensors, steering column or instrument panel to avoid the possibility of accidental deployment of the airbag, which could cause personal injury (see Section 27).

1  Disconnect the cable from the negative battery terminal.

### 1989 AND EARLIER MODELS

2  Reach under the dash and press the release button on the bottom of the switch, then withdraw the knob and shaft from the switch.

3  Remove the instrument cluster bezel (see Chapter 11) and use a 5/8-inch socket to remove retaining nut, then lower the switch, unplug the electrical connector and remove it.
4  Place the new switch in position on the bracket and secure it with the nut. Insert the knob and shaft into the switch. The remainder of installation is the reverse of removal.

### 1990 THROUGH 1995 MODELS

5  Detach the headlight switch knob by using a pointed tool to lift the release tab at it's base (see illustration).
6  Remove the instrument cluster bezel (see Chapter 11).
7  Remove the retaining screws and withdraw the switch from the instrument panel (see illustration).
8  Remove the nut, unplug the connector and remove the switch from the vehicle.
9  Installation is the reverse of removal.

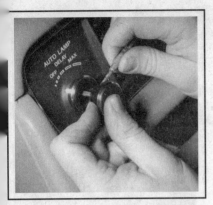

**19.5  Use a pointed hooked tool to lift the retaining clip, then pull the knob off the shaft**

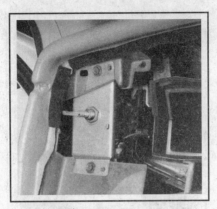

**19.7  Remove the bracket bolts and withdraw the switch**

**19.15  Use a special plastic trim panel tool to pry the switch cover from the instrument panel**

## 1996 THROUGH 2004

10  Carefully pull and detach the headlight knob from the switch shaft.

11  Remove the instrument cluster bezel (see Chapter 11).

12  Unplug the electrical wiring connector from the back side of the switch.

13  Remove the switch retaining nut and remove the switch from the bracket.

14  Installation is the reverse of removal.

## 2005 AND LATER MODELS

▶ **Refer to illustration 19.15**

15  Use a trim panel tool to carefully pry the headlight switch assembly from the instrument panel (see illustration).

16  Separate the assembly from the dash and disconnect the electrical connectors.

17  Installation is the reverse of removal.

## 20  Windshield wiper/washer switch (1989 and earlier models) - removal and installation

### ❋❋ WARNING:

Some models have airbags. Always disconnect the negative battery cable, then the positive battery cable and wait 2 minutes before working in the vicinity of the impact sensors, steering column or instrument panel to avoid the possibility of accidental deployment of the airbag, which could cause personal injury (see Section 27).

1  Disconnect the cable from the negative battery terminal.

2  Remove the screws and detach the steering column covers (see Chapter 11).

3  Remove the mounting screws and lift the wiper switch off the steering column. Unplug the electrical connector and remove the switch.

4  Installation is the reverse of removal.

## 21  Windshield wiper motor - removal and installation

▶ **Refer to illustrations 21.2a. 21.2b, 21.3 and 21.4**

### ❋❋ WARNING:

Some models have airbags. Always disconnect the negative battery cable, then the positive battery cable and wait 2 minutes before working in the vicinity of the impact sensors, steering column or instrument panel to avoid the possibility of accidental deployment of the airbag, which could cause personal injury (see Section 27).

1  Disconnect the cable from the negative battery terminal.

2  Remove the rear hood seal and the wiper motor housing cover (see illustrations).

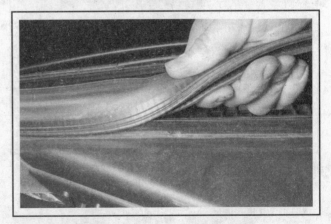

**21.2a  Pull off the rear hood seal weatherstripping**

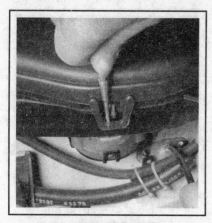

21.2b Use a small screwdriver to detach each of the wiper housing clips

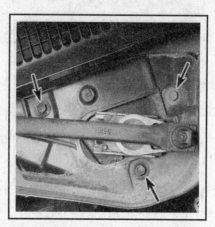

21.3 Remove the wiper motor bolts (arrows)

21.4 Use a small screwdriver to pry off the clip, then detach the wiper arm from the motor

3   Remove the wiper motor retaining bolts (see illustration).

➡**Note: On later models, the wiper motor linkage must be removed before accessing the motor mounting bolts.**

4   Remove the clip from the wiper motor and disconnect the wiper linkage drive arm from the motor (see illustration).

5   Unplug the electrical connector and lift the wiper motor from the housing.

6   Installation is the reverse of removal.

## 22  Rear window defogger - check and repair

1   The rear window defogger consists of a number of horizontal elements baked onto the glass surface.

2   Small breaks in the element can be repaired without removing the rear window.

### CHECK

▶ **Refer to illustrations 22.4, 22.5 and 22.7**

3   Turn the ignition switch and defogger system switches to the ON position.

4   When measuring voltage during the next two tests, wrap a piece of aluminum foil around the tip of the voltmeter negative probe and press the foil against the heating element with your finger (see illustration).

5   Check the voltage at the center of each heating element (see illustration). If the voltage is 6-volts, the element is okay (there is no break). If the voltage is 12-volts, the element is broken between the center of the element and the positive end. If the voltage is 0-volts the element is broken between the center of the element and ground.

6   Connect the negative lead to a good body ground. The reading should stay the same.

7   To find the break, place the voltmeter positive lead against the defogger positive terminal. Place the voltmeter negative lead with the foil strip against the heating element at the positive terminal end and slide it toward the negative terminal end. The point at which the voltmeter deflects from zero to several volts is the point at which the heating element is broken (see illustration).

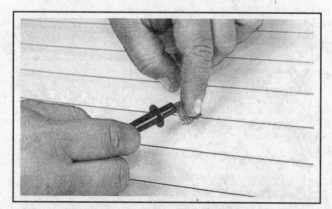

22.4  When measuring the voltage at the rear window defogger grid, wrap a piece of aluminum foil around the negative probe of the voltmeter and press the foil against the wire with your finger

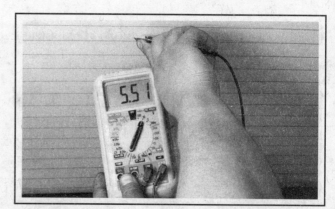

22.5  To determine if a wire has broken, check the voltage at the center of each wire. If the voltage is 6-volts, the wire is unbroken; if the voltage is 12-volts, the wire is broken between the center of the wire and the positive end; if the voltage is 0-volts, the wire is broken between the center of the wire and ground

**22.7 To find the break, place the voltmeter positive lead against the defogger positive terminal, place the voltmeter negative lead with the foil strip against the heat wire at the positive terminal end and slide it toward the negative terminal end - the point at which the voltmeter deflects from zero to several volts is the point at which the wire is broken**

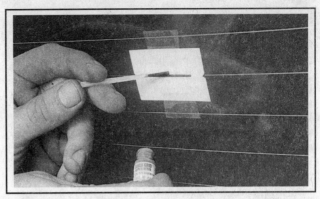

**22.13 To use a defogger repair kit, apply masking tape to the inside of the window at the damaged area, then brush on the special conductive coating**

## REPAIR

♦ **Refer to illustration 22.13**

8    Repair the break in the element using a repair kit specifically recommended for this purpose, such as Dupont paste No. 4817 (or equivalent). Included in this kit is plastic conductive epoxy.

9    Prior to repairing a break, turn off the system and allow it to cool

off for a few minutes.

10 Lightly buff the element area with fine steel wool, then clean it thoroughly with rubbing alcohol.

11 Use masking tape to mask off the area being repaired.

12 Thoroughly mix the epoxy, following the instructions provided with the repair kit.

13 Apply the epoxy material to the slit in the masking tape, overlapping the undamaged area about 3/4-inch on either end (see illustration).

14 Allow the repair to cure for 24 hours before removing the tape and using the system.

## 23  Cruise control system - description and check

♦ **Refer to illustration 23.5**

1    The cruise control system maintains vehicle speed with a servo motor located in the engine compartment on the driver's side fender-well, which is connected to the throttle linkage by a cable. The system consists of the servo motor, brake switch, control switches, speed sensors and relays. Some features of the system require special testers and diagnostic procedures which are beyond the scope of this manual. Listed below are some general procedures that may be used to locate common problems.

2    Locate and check the fuse (see Section 3).

3    Have an assistant operate the brake lights while you check their operation (voltage from the brake light switch deactivates the cruise control).

4    If the brake lights don't come on or don't shut off, correct the problem and retest the cruise control.

5    Check the control cable between the cruise control servo/amplifier and the throttle linkage and replace as necessary (see illustration).

6    The cruise control system uses a speed sensing device. The speed sensor is located in the transmission. To test the speed sensor, see Chapter 6, Section 4.

**23.5  Make sure the cruise control and accelerator linkage mounted on the throttle body are not damaged and that they operate smoothly together when the throttle is opened**

7    Test drive the vehicle to determine if the cruise control is now working. If it isn't, take it to a dealer service department or an automotive electrical specialist for further diagnosis.

## 24  Power window system - description and check

♦ **Refer to illustration 24.12**

1    The power window system operates electric motors, mounted in the doors, which lower and raise the windows. The system consists of the control switches, the motors, regulators, glass mechanisms and

associated wiring.

2    The power windows can be lowered and raised from the master control switch by the driver or by remote switches located at the individual windows. Each window has a separate motor which is reversible. The position of the control switch determines the polarity and therefore

the direction of operation.

3   The circuit is protected by a fuse and a circuit breaker. Each motor is also equipped with an internal circuit breaker, this prevents one stuck window from disabling the whole system.

4   The power window system will only operate when the ignition switch is ON. In addition, many models have a window lockout switch at the master control switch which, when activated, disables the switches at the rear windows and, sometimes, the switch at the passenger's window also. Always check these items before troubleshooting a window problem.

5   These procedures are general in nature, so if you can't find the problem using them, take the vehicle to a dealer service department or other properly equipped repair facility.

6   If the power windows won't operate, always check the fuse and circuit breaker first.

7   If only the rear windows are inoperative, or if the windows only operate from the master control switch, check the rear window lockout switch for continuity in the unlocked position. Replace it if it doesn't have continuity.

8   Check the wiring between the switches and fuse panel for continuity. Repair the wiring, if necessary.

9   If only one window is inoperative from the master control switch, try the other control switch at the window.

➡Note: This doesn't apply to the drivers door window.

10   If the same window works from one switch, but not the other, check the switch for continuity.

11   If the switch tests OK, check for a short or open in the circuit between the affected switch and the window motor.

12   If one window is inoperative from both switches, remove the trim

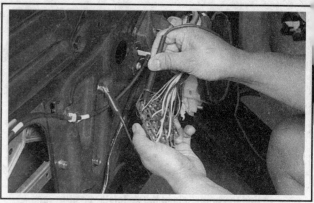

**24.12  If no voltage is found at the motor with the switch depressed, check for voltage at the switch**

panel from the affected door and check for voltage at the switch (see illustration) and at the motor while the switch is operated.

13   If voltage is reaching the motor, disconnect the glass from the regulator (see Chapter 11). Move the window up and down by hand while checking for binding and damage. Also check for binding and damage to the regulator. If the regulator is not damaged and the window moves up and down smoothly, replace the motor. If there's binding or damage, lubricate, repair or replace parts, as necessary.

14   If voltage isn't reaching the motor, check the wiring in the circuit for continuity between the switches and motors. You'll need to consult the wiring diagram for the vehicle. If the circuit is equipped with a relay, check that the relay is grounded properly and receiving voltage.

15   Test the windows after you are done to confirm proper repairs.

## 25  Power door lock and keyless entry system - description and check

▶ **Refer to illustration 25.9**

1   The power door lock system operates the door lock actuators mounted in each door. The system consists of the switches, actuators, and associated wiring. Diagnosis can usually be limited to simple checks of the wiring connections and actuators for minor faults which can be easily repaired.

2   Power door lock systems are operated by bi-directional solenoids located in the doors. The lock switches have two operating positions: Lock and Unlock. On later models with keyless entry the switches activate a module which in turn connects voltage to the door lock solenoids. Depending on which way the switch is activated, it reverses polarity, allowing the two sides of the circuit to be used alternately as the feed (positive) and ground side. On earlier models with out keyless entry the switches directly activate the door lock motors.

3   If you are unable to locate the trouble using the following general steps, consult your a dealer service department.

4   Always check the circuit protection first. On these models the battery voltage passes through the 20 amp circuit breaker located in the passenger compartment fuse block.

5   Operate the door lock switches in both directions (Lock and Unlock) with the engine off. Listen for the faint click of the door lock solenoid (motor) or relay operating.

6   If there's no click, check for voltage at the switches. If no voltage is present, check the wiring between the fuse block and the switches for shorts and opens.

7   If voltage is present but no click is heard, test the switch for continuity. Replace it if there's no continuity in both switch positions.

8   If the switch has continuity but the solenoid doesn't click, check the wiring between the switch and solenoid for continuity. Repair the wiring if there's not continuity.

9   If all but one lock solenoids operate, remove the trim panel from the affected door (see Chapter 11) and check for voltage at the solenoid while the lock switch is operated (see illustration). One of the wires should have voltage in the Lock position; the other should have voltage in the unlock position.

10   If the inoperative solenoid is receiving voltage, replace the solenoid.

➡Note: It's common for wires to break in the portion of the harness between the body and door (opening and closing the door fatigues and eventually breaks the wires).

## KEYLESS ENTRY SYSTEM

▶ **Refer to illustrations 25.13 and 25.14**

11   The keyless entry system consists of a remote control transmitter that sends a coded infrared signal to a receiver which then operates the door lock system.

12   Replace the transmitter batteries when the red LED light on the side of the case doesn't light when the button is pushed.

13   Use a small screwdriver to carefully separate the case halves (see illustration).

14   Replace the two 3-volt 2016 lithium batteries (see illustration).

15   Snap the case halves together.

**25.9 Check for voltage at the lock solenoid while the lock switch is operated**

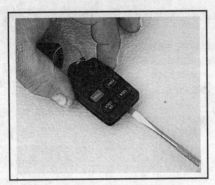

**25.13 Use a small screwdriver to separate the transmitter halves**

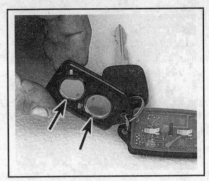

**25.14 Replace the lithium batteries (arrows)**

## 26  Electric side view mirrors - description and check

1   Most electric rear view mirrors use two motors to move the glass; one for up and down adjustments and one for left-right adjustments.

2   The control switch has a selector portion which sends voltage to the left or right side mirror. With the ignition ON but the engine OFF, roll down the windows and operate the mirror control switch through all functions (left-right and up-down) for both the left and right side mirrors.

3   Listen carefully for the sound of the electric motors running in the mirrors.

4   If the motors can be heard but the mirror glass doesn't move, there's probably a problem with the drive mechanism inside the mirror. Remove and disassemble the mirror to locate the problem.

5   If the mirrors don't operate and no sound comes from the mirrors, check the fuse (see Section 3).

6   If the fuse is OK, remove the mirror control switch from its mounting without disconnecting the wires attached to it. Turn the ignition ON and check for voltage at the switch. There should be voltage at one terminal. If there's no voltage at the switch, check for an open or

short in the wiring between the fuse panel and the switch.

7   If there's voltage at the switch, disconnect it. Check the switch for continuity in all its operating positions. If the switch does not have continuity, replace it.

8   Re-connect the switch. Locate the wire going from the switch to ground. Leaving the switch connected, connect a jumper wire between this wire and ground. If the mirror works normally with this wire in place, repair the faulty ground connection.

9   If the mirror still doesn't work, remove the mirror and check the wires at the mirror for voltage. Check with ignition ON and the mirror selector switch on the appropriate side. Operate the mirror switch in all its positions. There should be voltage at one of the switch-to-mirror wires in each switch position (except the neutral "off" position).

10  If there's not voltage in each switch position, check the wiring between the mirror and control switch for opens and shorts.

11  If there's voltage, remove the mirror and test it off the vehicle with jumper wires. Replace the mirror if it fails this test.

## 27  Airbag - general information

Later models are equipped with a Supplemental Inflatable System (SIR), more commonly known as an airbag. This system is designed to protect the driver, and on some models, front seat passenger, from serious injury in the event of a head-on or frontal collision. It consists of an airbag module in the center of the steering wheel and the right side of the instrument panel, two crash sensors mounted at the front and the interior of the vehicle and a diagnostic monitor which also contains a backup power supply located in the passenger compartment.

### AIRBAG MODULE

#### Steering wheel-mounted

The airbag inflator module contains a housing incorporating the

cushion (airbag) and inflator unit, mounted in the center of the steering wheel The inflator assembly is mounted on the back of the housing over a hole through which gas is expelled, inflating the bag almost instantaneously when an electrical signal is sent from the system. A coil assembly on the steering column under the module carries this signal to the module.

This coil assembly can transmit an electrical signal regardless of steering wheel position. The igniter in the air bag converts the electrical signal to heat and ignites the sodium azide/copper oxide powder, producing nitrogen gas, which inflates the bag.

#### Instrument panel-mounted

The airbag is mounted above the glove compartment and designated by the letters SRS (Supplemental Restraint System). It consists of an inflator containing an igniter, a bag assembly, a reaction housing and a trim cover.

The air bag is considerably larger that the steering wheel-mounted unit (8 cu ft vs. 2.3 cu ft) and is supported by the steel reaction housing. The trim cover is textured and painted to match the instrument panel and has a molded seam which splits when the bag inflates. As with the steering-wheel-mounted air bag, the igniter electrical signal converts to heat, converting sodium azide/iron oxide powder to nitrogen gas, inflating the bag.

### Side-impact airbags

Some models are equipped with side impact airbags mounted in the outer side cushions of the front seats.

### Seat belt pre-tensioners

Additionally, some models are equipped with seat belt pre-tensioners which are pyrotechnic (explosive) units in the front seat belt retracting mechanisms. During an impact of sufficient force to trigger the airbag system, the airbag control unit also triggers the seat belt retractors, which takes up any slack in the seat belts to more fully restrain the driver and front seat passenger for impact.

The airbag system should be disabled whenever work is to be done around the seats or seat belts.

## SENSORS

The system has three sensors (five on models equipped with side-impact airbags): two forward sensors at the front of the vehicle and a safing sensor on the left side of the cowl in the passenger compartment (early models) or a Restraints Control Module (RCM) mounted on the center tunnel under the instrument panel (later models). Models with side impact airbags have a side impact sensor at the bottom of each B-pillar, behind the trim panel.

These sensors are basically pressure sensitive switches that complete an electrical circuit during an impact of sufficient G force. The electrical signal from these sensors is sent to the electronic diagnostic monitor or Restraints Control Module which then completes the circuit and inflates the airbag(s).

## ELECTRONIC DIAGNOSTIC MONITOR

The electronic diagnostic monitor or Restraints Control Module supplies the current to the airbag system in the event of the collision, even if battery power is cut off. It checks this system every time the vehicle is started, causing the "AIR BAG" light to go on then off, if the system is operating properly. If there is a fault in the system, the light will go on and stay on, flash, or the dash will make a beeping sound. If this happens, the vehicle should be taken to your dealer immediately for service.

## DISABLING THE SYSTEM

Whenever working in the vicinity of the steering wheel, the impact sensors, the steering column or instrument panel or near other components of the airbag system, the system should be disarmed. To do this, perform the following steps:

### 1999 and earlier models

a) Turn the ignition switch to OFF
b) Disconnect the cable from the negative terminal of the battery, then wait 2 minutes for the electronic module backup supply to be depleted

### 2000 models

a) Turn off all vehicle accessories (radio, AC, etc.)
b) Turn the ignition switch to OFF
c) Remove the F18 fuse (10 amp) and the F10 fuse (10 amp) from the fuse box under the driver's side of the instrument panel
d) Turn the ignition switch ON (engine not running) and observe the AIRBAG light for at least 30 seconds. The light should stay ON (no flashing signals)
e) If the airbag indicator does not remain ON, make sure you pulled the correct fuses
f) Turn the ignition switch OFF, then disconnect the cable from the negative terminal of the battery

### 2001 models

a) Turn off all vehicle accessories (radio, AC, etc.)
b) Turn the ignition switch to OFF
c) Remove the F4 fuse (10 amp) from the fuse box under the driver's side of the instrument panel
d) Turn the ignition switch ON (engine not running) and observe the AIRBAG light for at least 30 seconds. The light should stay ON (no flashing signals)
e) If the airbag indicator does not remain ON, make sure you pulled the correct fuse
f) Turn the ignition switch OFF, then disconnect the cable from the negative terminal of the battery

### 2002 and later models

a) Turn off all vehicle accessories (radio, AC, etc.)
b) Turn the ignition switch to OFF
c) Remove the airbag fuse (10 amp) from the fuse box under the driver's side of the instrument panel:

### 2002 through 2004 models - remove the F2.4 fuse

*2005 models* - remove the F2.22 fuse
*2006 and later models* - remove fuse 22

d) Turn the ignition switch ON (engine not running) and observe the AIRBAG light for at least 30 seconds. The light should stay ON (no flashing signals)
e) If the airbag indicator does not remain ON, make sure you pulled the correct fuse
d) Turn the ignition switch OFF, then disconnect the cable from the negative terminal of the battery

## ENABLING THE SYSTEM

a) Turn the ignition switch to the Off position.
b) Connect the positive battery cable first, then connect the negative cable.

## 28  Wiring diagrams - general information

Since it isn't possible to include all wiring diagrams for every year covered by this manual, the following diagrams are those that are typical and most commonly needed.

Prior to troubleshooting any circuits, check the fuse and circuit breakers (if equipped) to make sure they're in good condition. Make sure the battery is properly charged and check the cable connections (see Chapter 1).

When checking a circuit, make sure that all connectors are clean, with no broken or loose terminals. When unplugging a connector, do not pull on the wires. Pull only on the connector housings themselves.

**Notes**

## INDEX OF WIRING DIAGRAMS

## SAMPLE DIAGRAM: HOW TO READ & INTERPRET WIRING DIAGRAMS

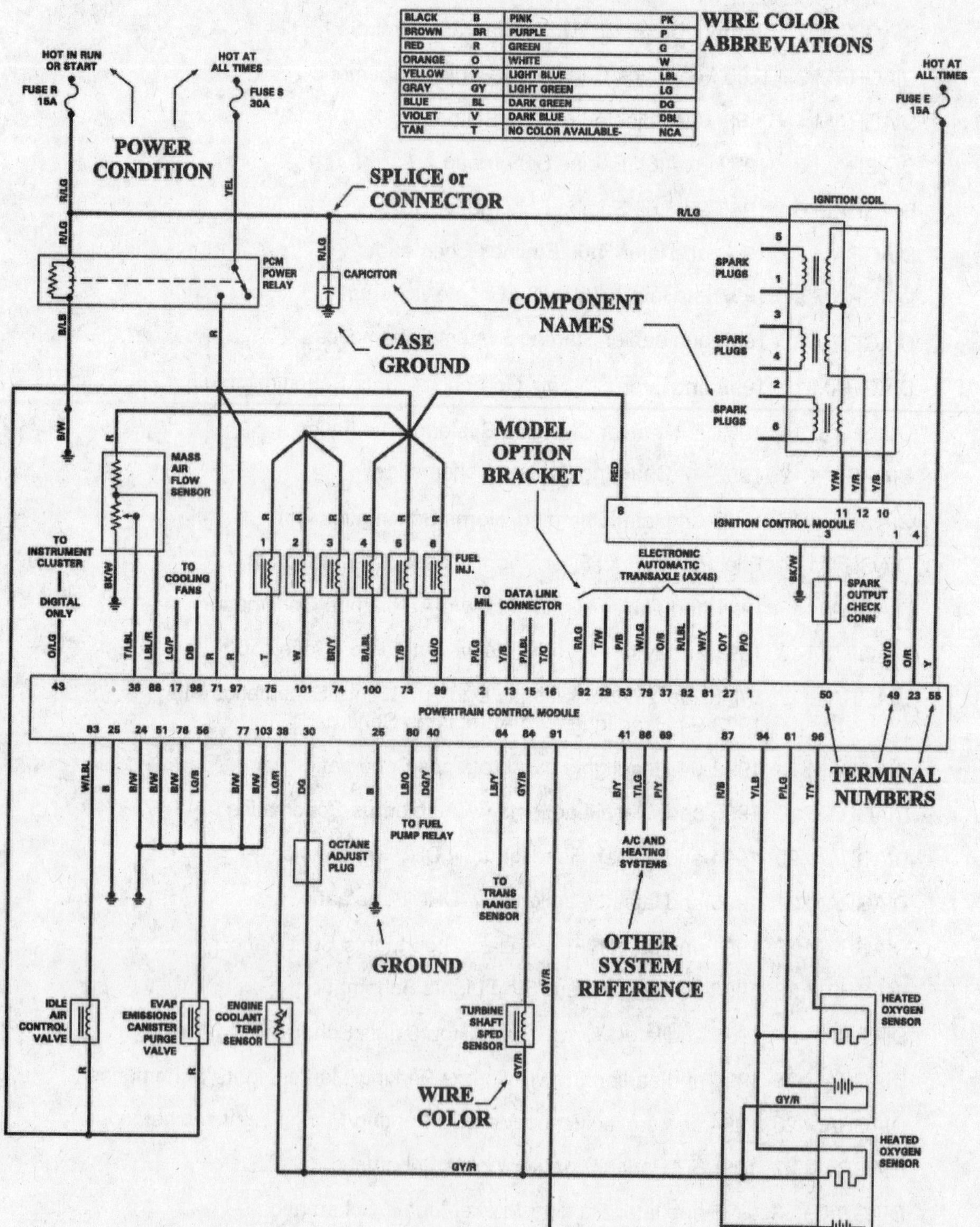

| BLACK | B | PINK | PK |
| BROWN | BR | PURPLE | P |
| RED | R | GREEN | G |
| ORANGE | O | WHITE | W |
| YELLOW | Y | LIGHT BLUE | LBL |
| GRAY | GY | LIGHT GREEN | LG |
| BLUE | BL | DARK GREEN | DG |
| VIOLET | V | DARK BLUE | DBL |
| TAN | T | NO COLOR AVAILABLE- | NCA |

**WIRE COLOR ABBREVIATIONS**

HOT IN RUN OR START
HOT AT ALL TIMES
HOT AT ALL TIMES

FUSE R 15A
FUSE S 30A
FUSE E 15A

**POWER CONDITION**

**SPLICE or CONNECTOR**

IGNITION COIL

PCM POWER RELAY

CAPICITOR

**COMPONENT NAMES**

**CASE GROUND**

SPARK PLUGS

**MODEL OPTION BRACKET**

MASS AIR FLOW SENSOR

IGNITION CONTROL MODULE

TO INSTRUMENT CLUSTER

TO COOLING FANS

FUEL INJ.

TO MIL

DATA LINK CONNECTOR

ELECTRONIC AUTOMATIC TRANSAXLE (AX4S)

SPARK OUTPUT CHECK CONN

POWERTRAIN CONTROL MODULE

**TERMINAL NUMBERS**

OCTANE ADJUST PLUG

TO FUEL PUMP RELAY

**GROUND**

TO TRANS RANGE SENSOR

A/C AND HEATING SYSTEMS

**OTHER SYSTEM REFERENCE**

IDLE AIR CONTROL VALVE

EVAP EMISSIONS CANISTER PURGE VALVE

ENGINE COOLANT TEMP SENSOR

TURBINE SHAFT SPED SENSOR

HEATED OXYGEN SENSOR

**WIRE COLOR**

HEATED OXYGEN SENSOR

**DIAGRAM 1**

# WIRING DIAGRAM SYMBOLS

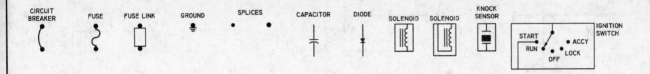

CIRCUIT BREAKER · FUSE · FUSE LINK · GROUND · SPLICES · CAPACITOR · DIODE · SOLENOID · SOLENOID · KNOCK SENSOR · IGNITION SWITCH (START, RUN, OFF, LOCK, ACCY)

NORMALLY OPEN SWITCH · NORMALLY CLOSED SWITCH · NORMALLY OPEN SWITCH · NORMALLY CLOSED SWITCH · 3 POSITION SWITCH · BATTERY · RELAY · RELAY

RESISTOR · RESISTOR · VARIABLE RESISTOR · VARIABLE RESISTOR · SPEED SENSOR · CHOICE BRACKET · MOTOR

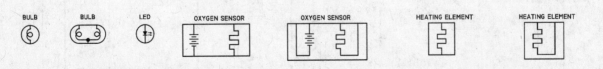

BULB · BULB · LED · OXYGEN SENSOR · OXYGEN SENSOR · HEATING ELEMENT · HEATING ELEMENT

**DIAGRAM 2**

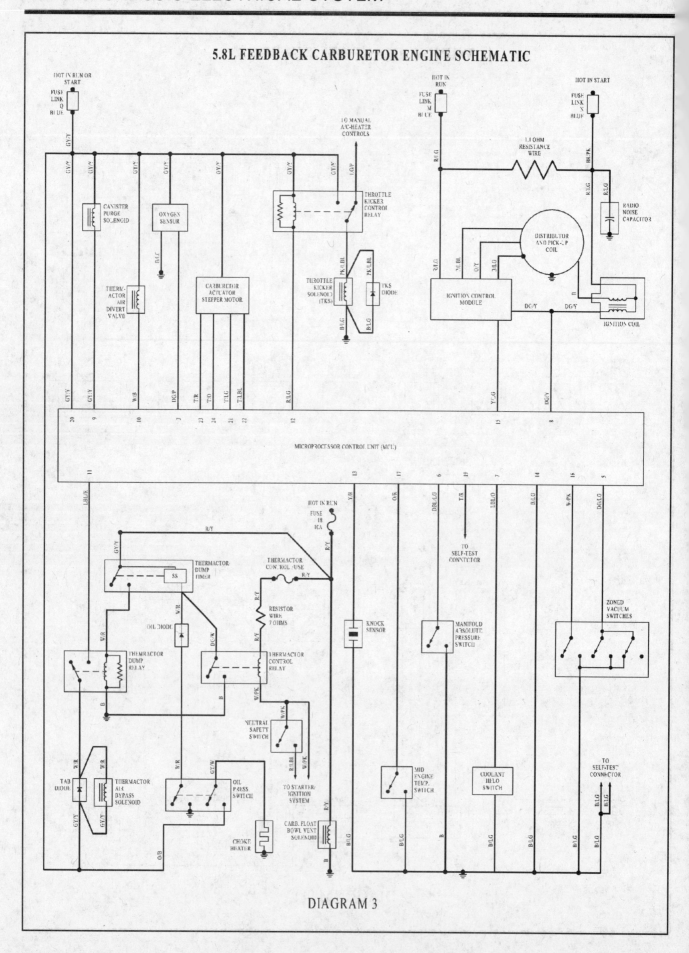

## 5.8L FEEDBACK CARBURETOR ENGINE SCHEMATIC

DIAGRAM 3

## 5.0L FUEL INJECTED ENGINE SCHEMATIC

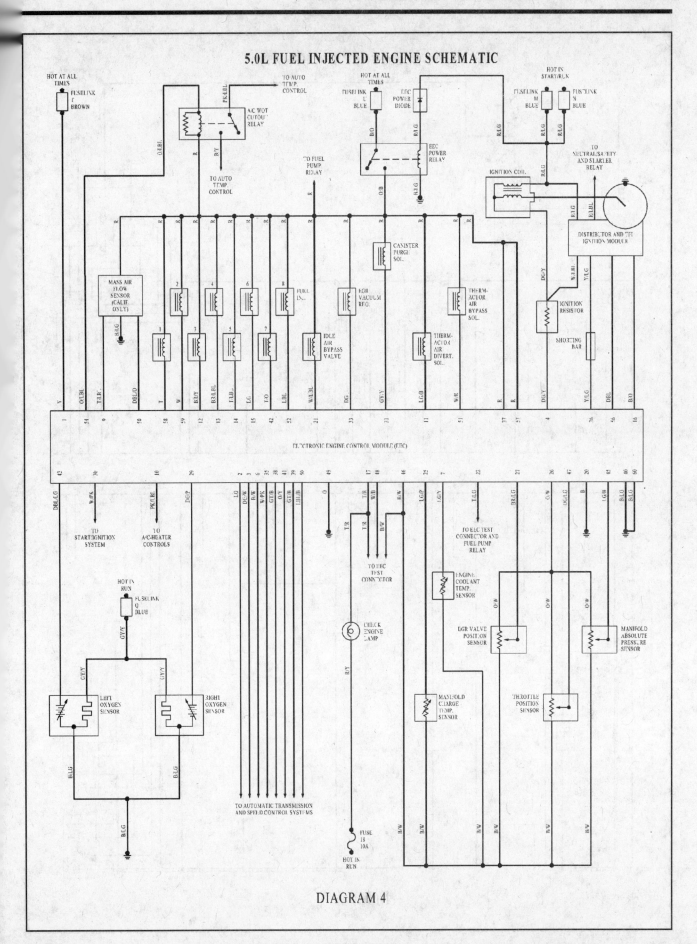

DIAGRAM 4

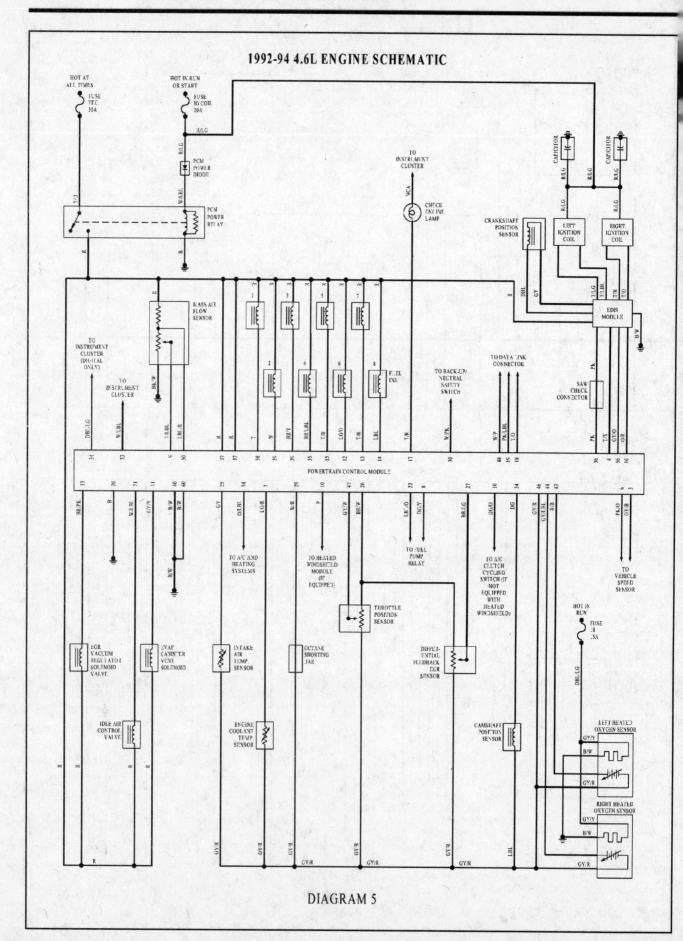

**1992-94 4.6L ENGINE SCHEMATIC**

DIAGRAM 5

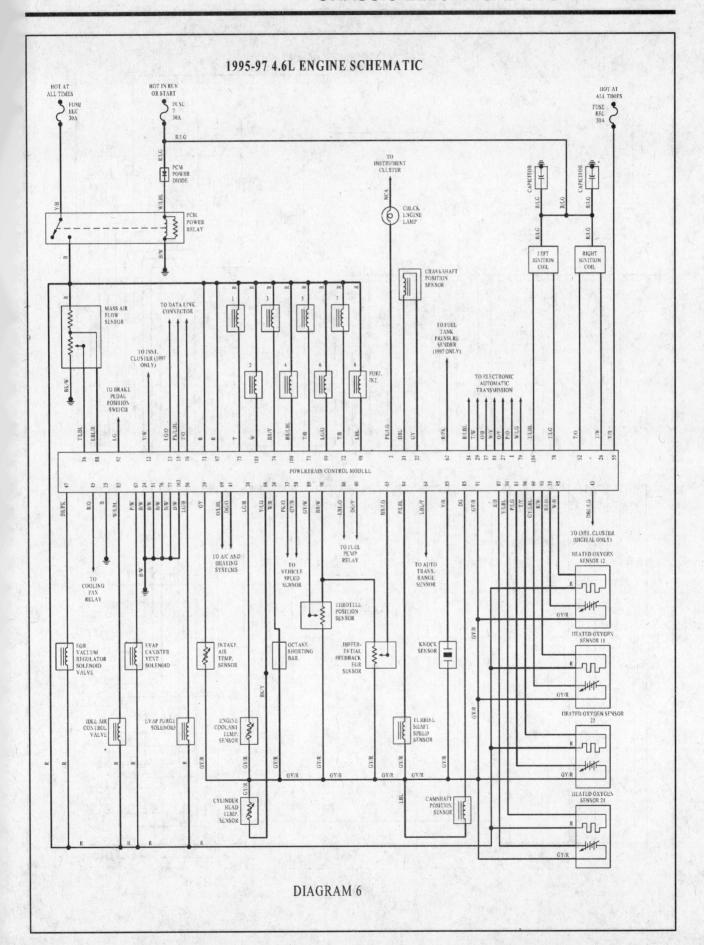

## 1995-97 4.6L ENGINE SCHEMATIC

DIAGRAM 6

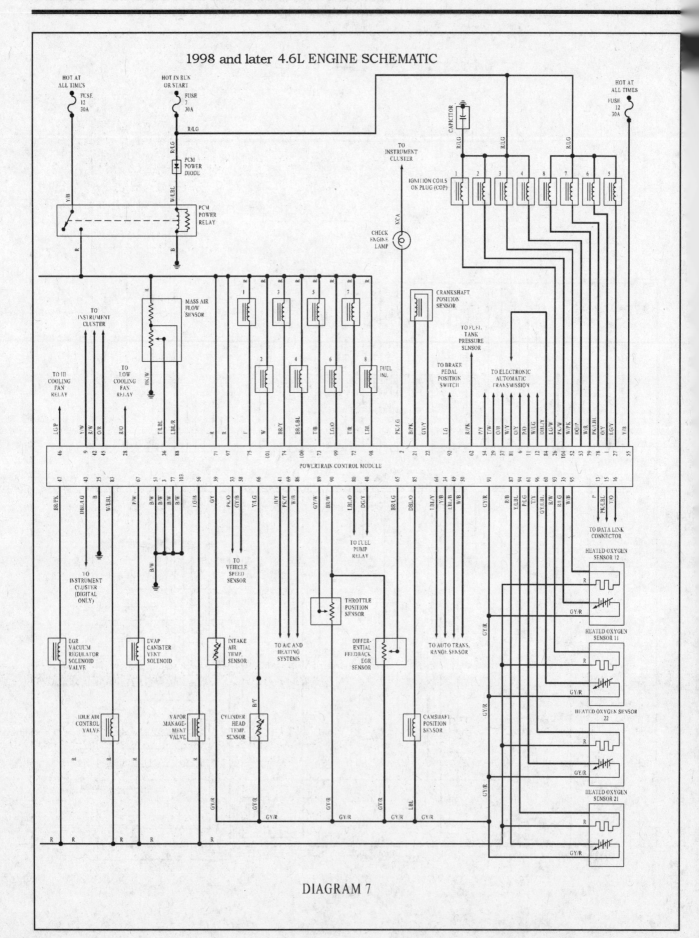

1998 and later 4.6L ENGINE SCHEMATIC

DIAGRAM 7

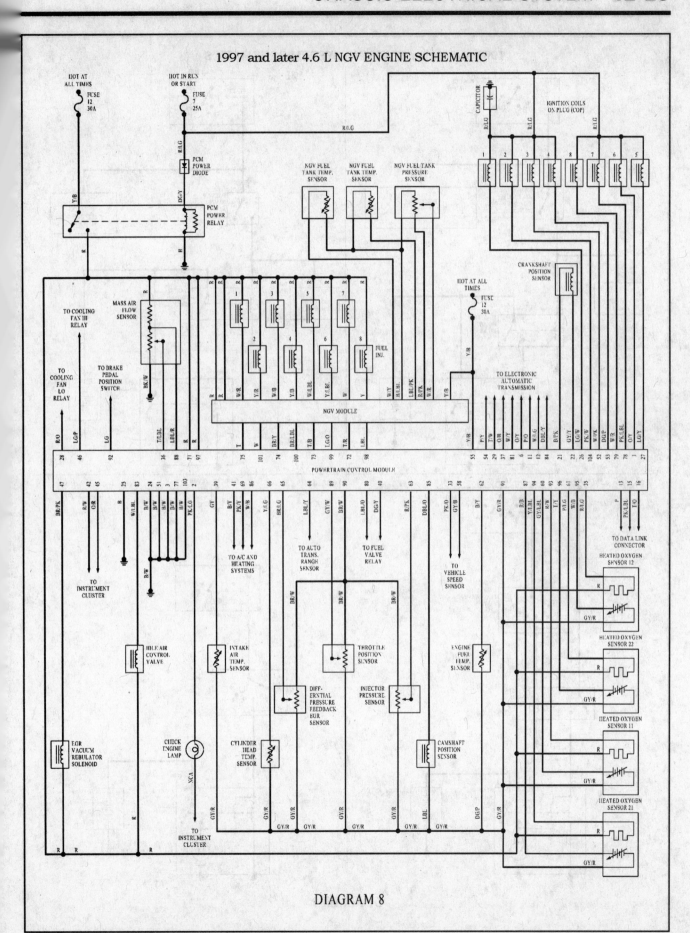

## 1997 and later 4.6 L NGV ENGINE SCHEMATIC

DIAGRAM 8

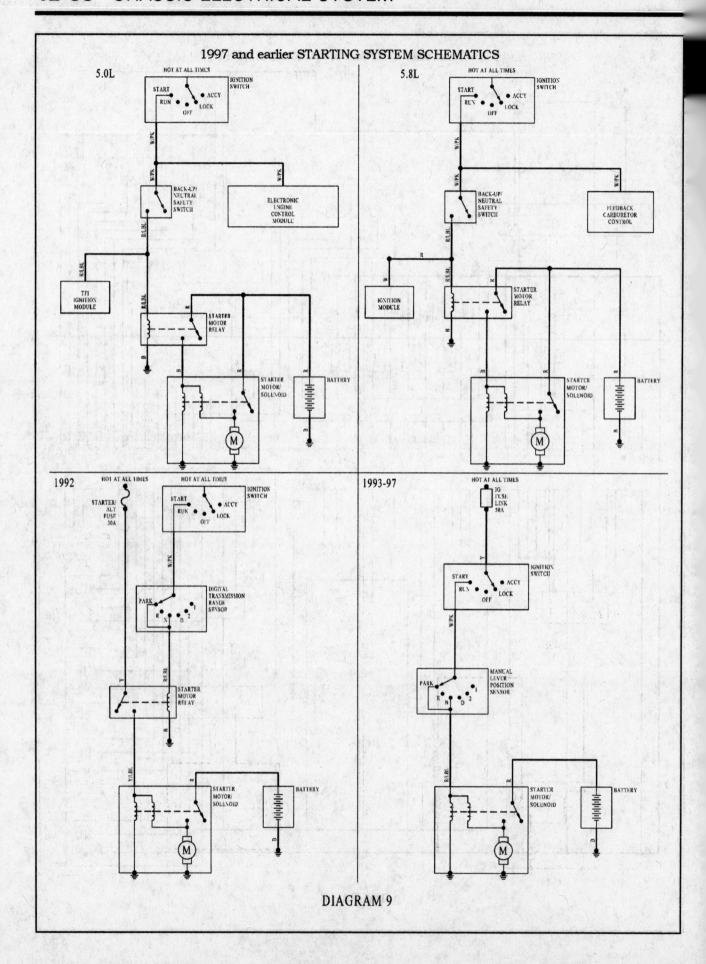

DIAGRAM 9

## 1998 and later STARTING AND CORNERING LIGHTS SCHEMATICS

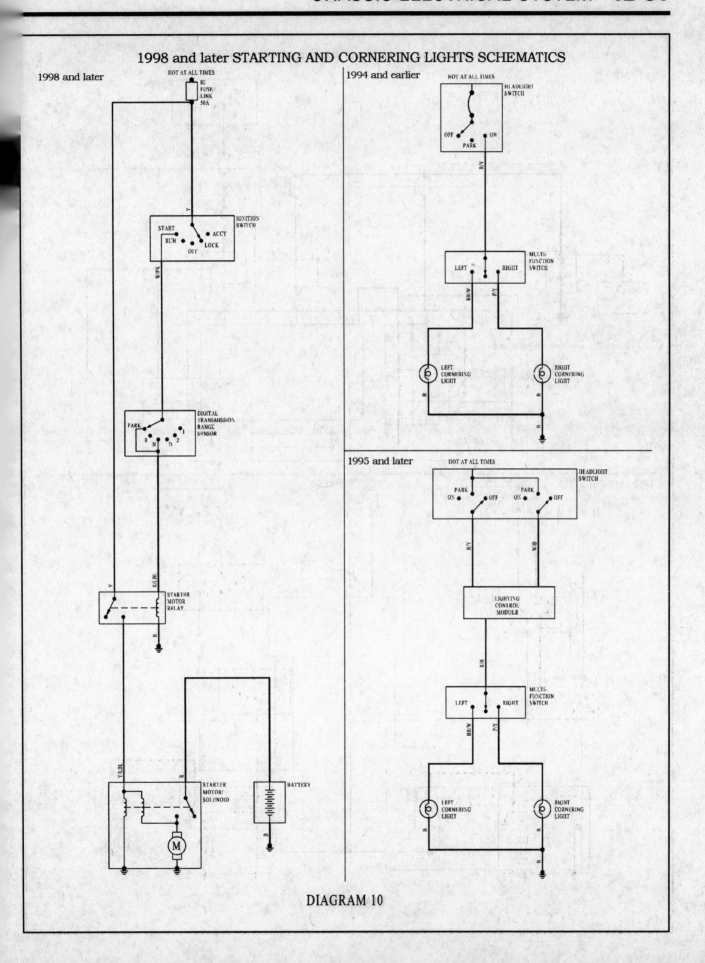

**DIAGRAM 10**

## 1991 and earlier CHARGING SYSTEM SCHEMATICS

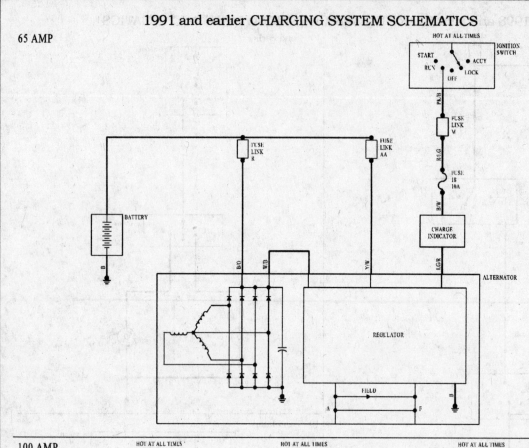

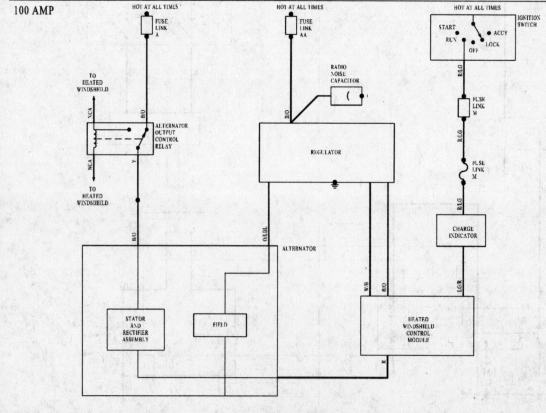

DIAGRAM 11

## 1992-97 CHARGING SYSTEM SCHEMATICS

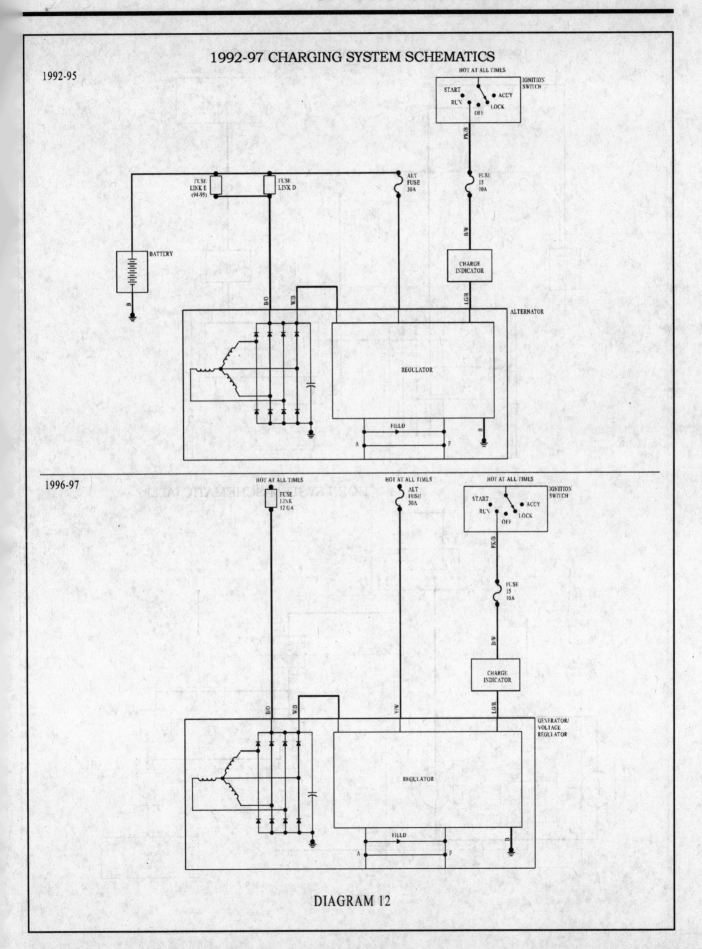

DIAGRAM 12

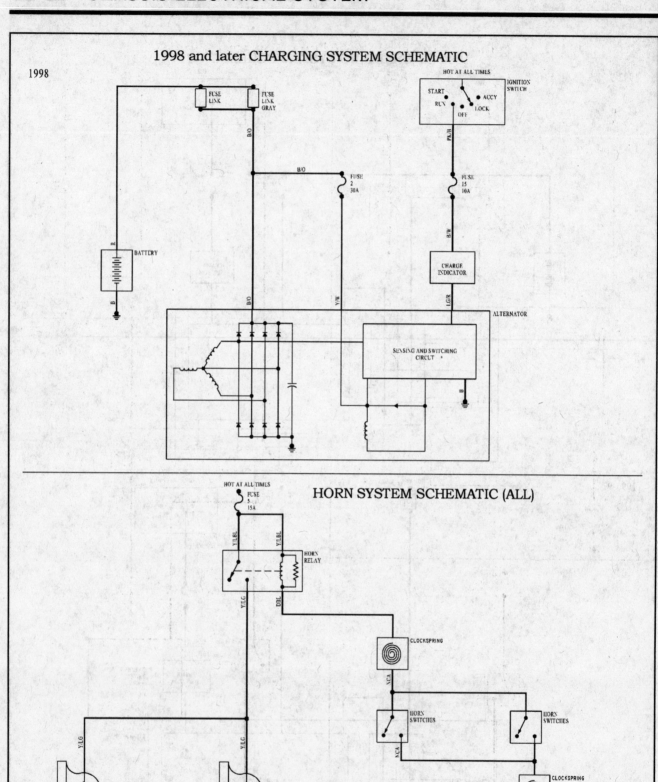

## 1998 and later CHARGING SYSTEM SCHEMATIC

## HORN SYSTEM SCHEMATIC (ALL)

DIAGRAM 13

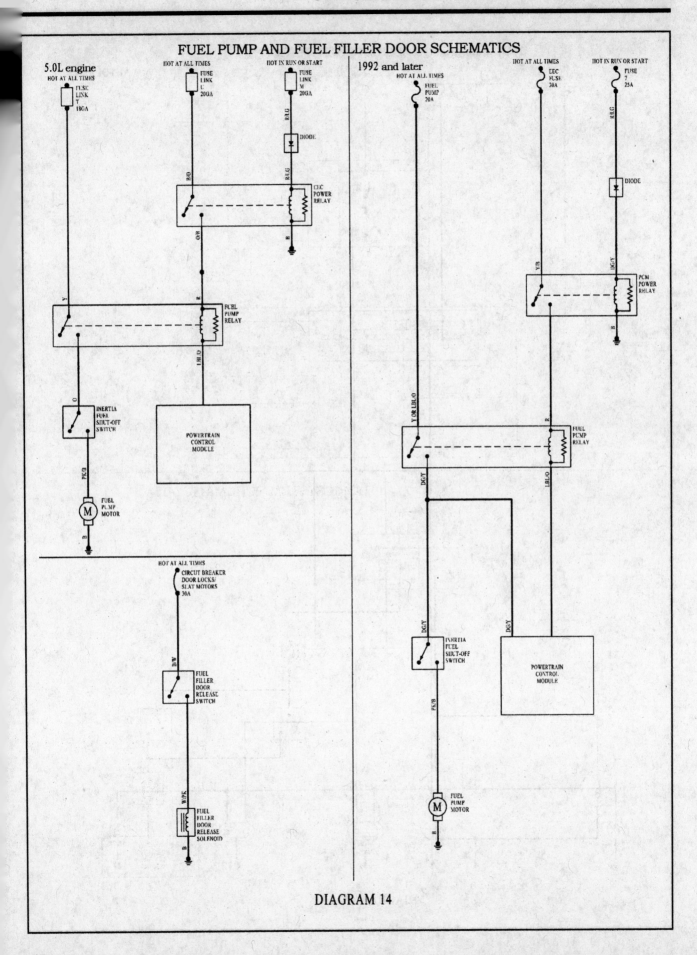

FUEL PUMP AND FUEL FILLER DOOR SCHEMATICS

DIAGRAM 14

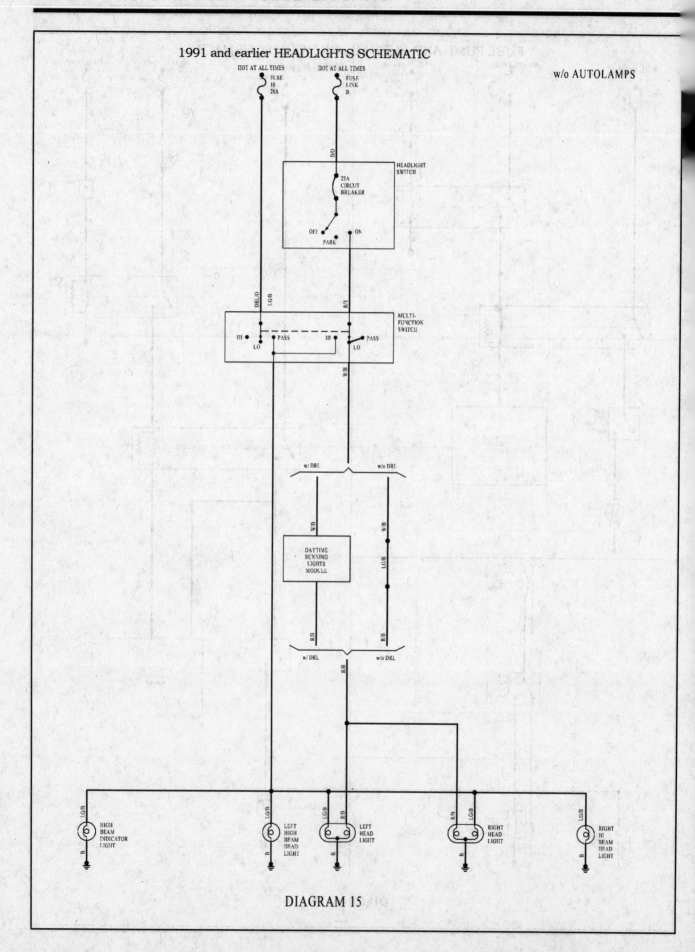

1991 and earlier HEADLIGHTS SCHEMATIC

w/o AUTOLAMPS

DIAGRAM 15

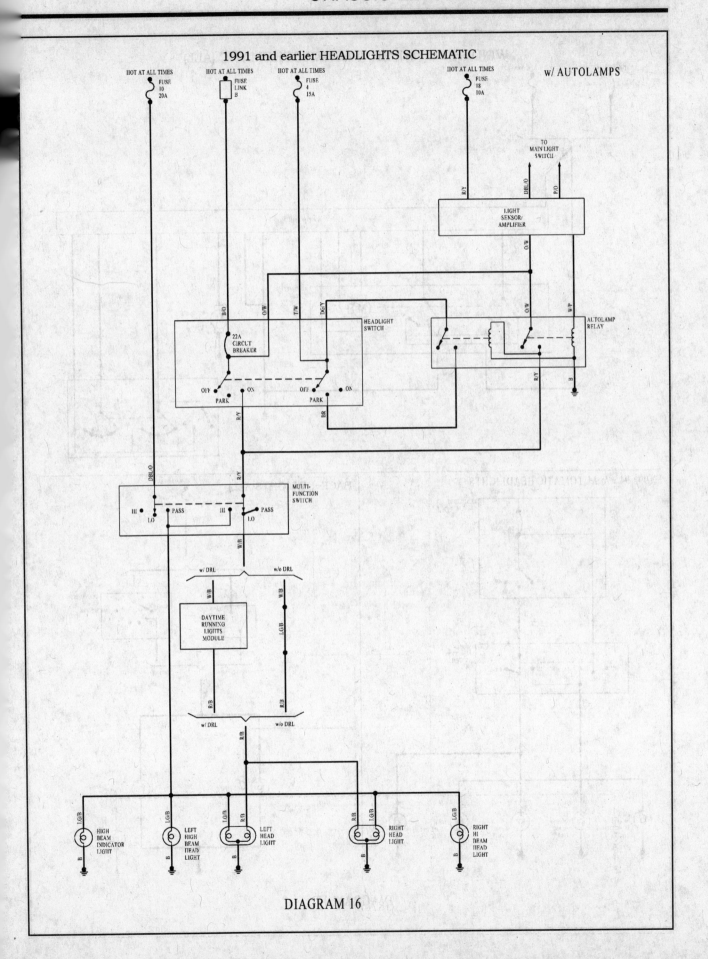

**1991 and earlier HEADLIGHTS SCHEMATIC**

DIAGRAM 16

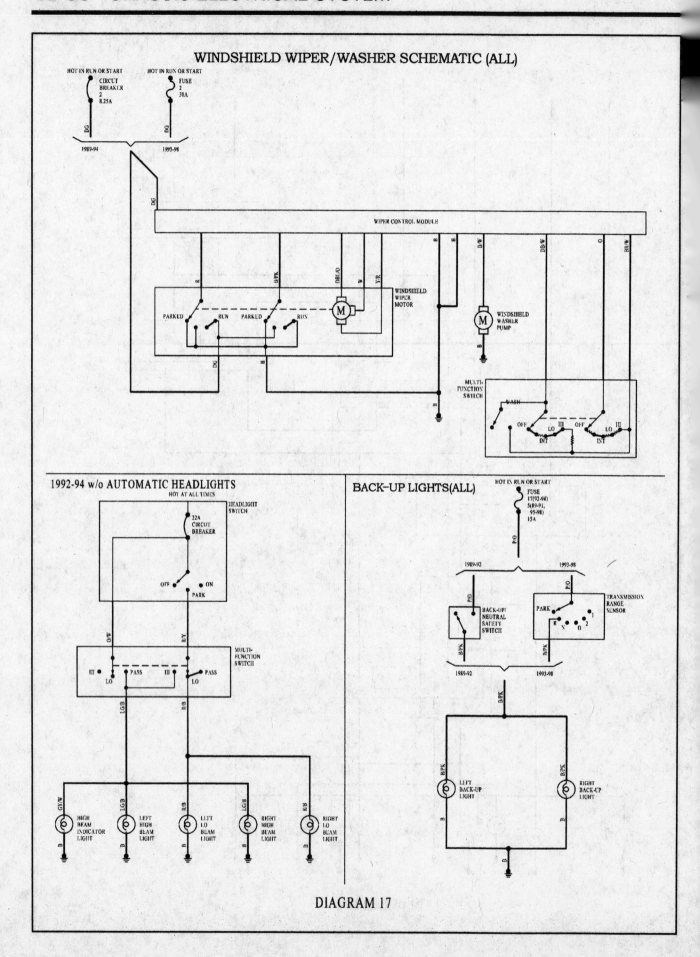

WINDSHIELD WIPER/WASHER SCHEMATIC (ALL)

1992-94 w/o AUTOMATIC HEADLIGHTS

BACK-UP LIGHTS(ALL)

DIAGRAM 17

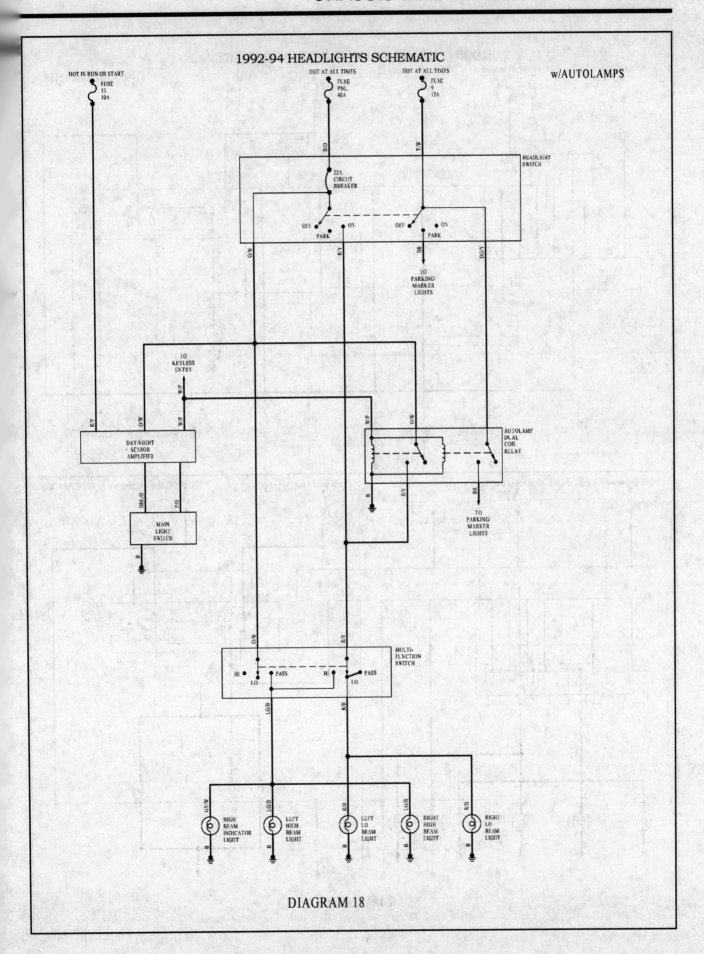

## 1992-94 HEADLIGHTS SCHEMATIC

w/AUTOLAMPS

DIAGRAM 18

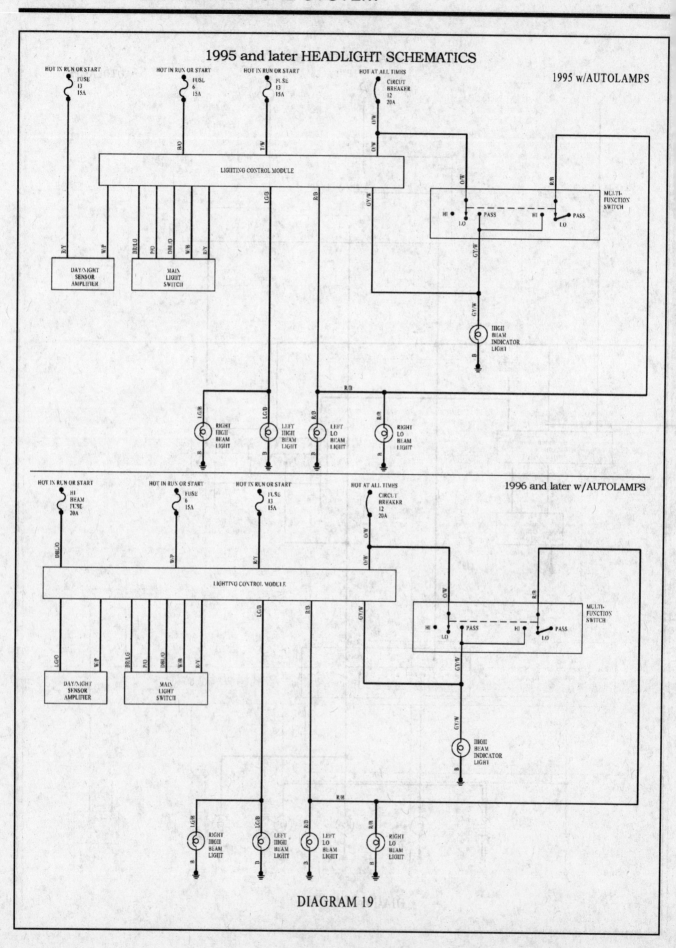

## 1995 and later HEADLIGHT SCHEMATICS

DIAGRAM 19

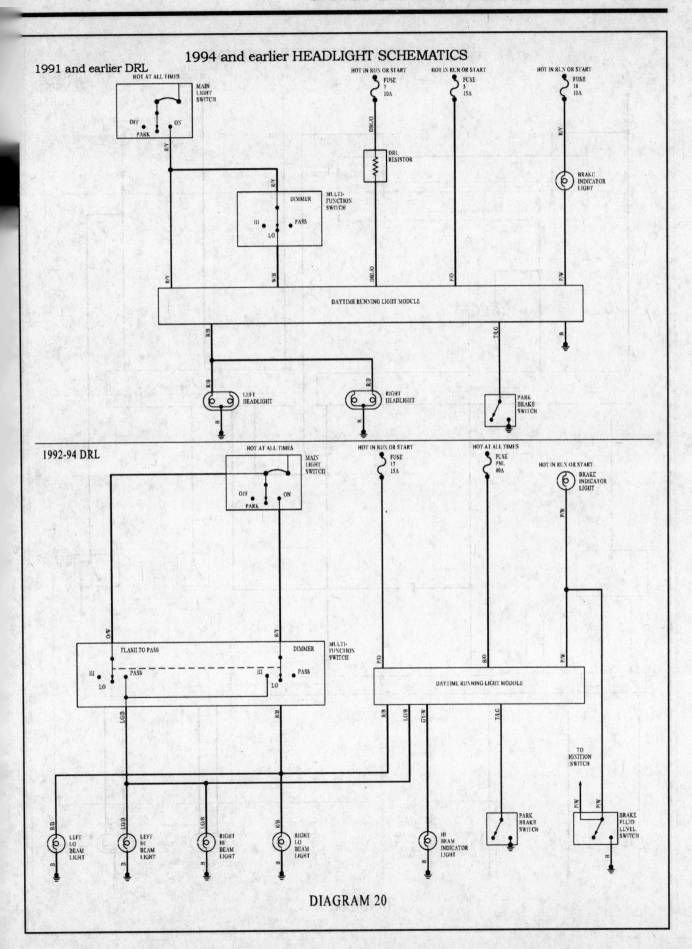

DIAGRAM 20

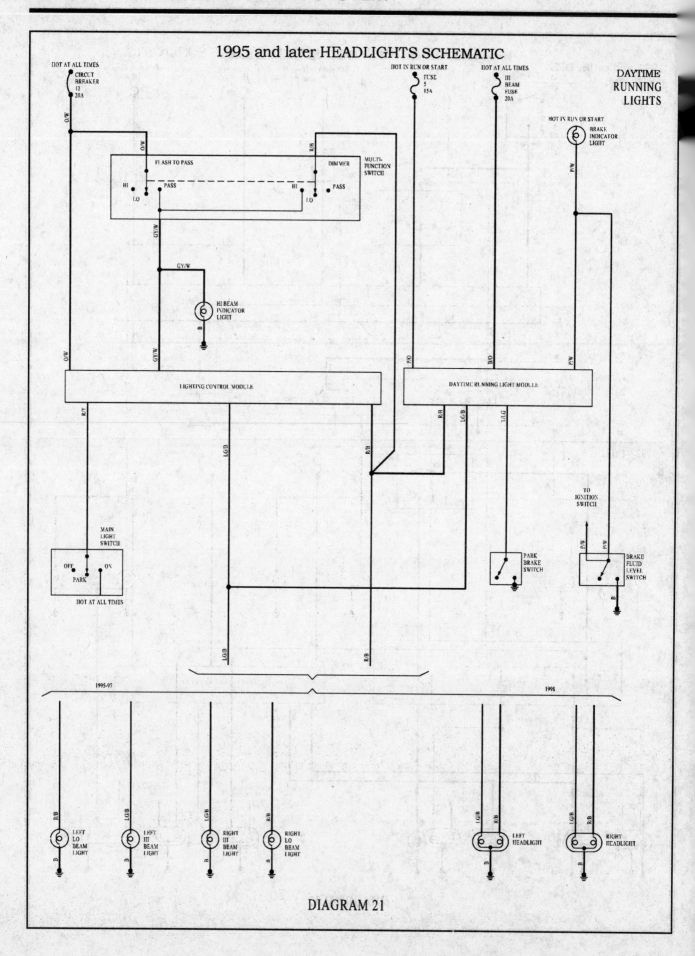

## 1995 and later HEADLIGHTS SCHEMATIC

DIAGRAM 21

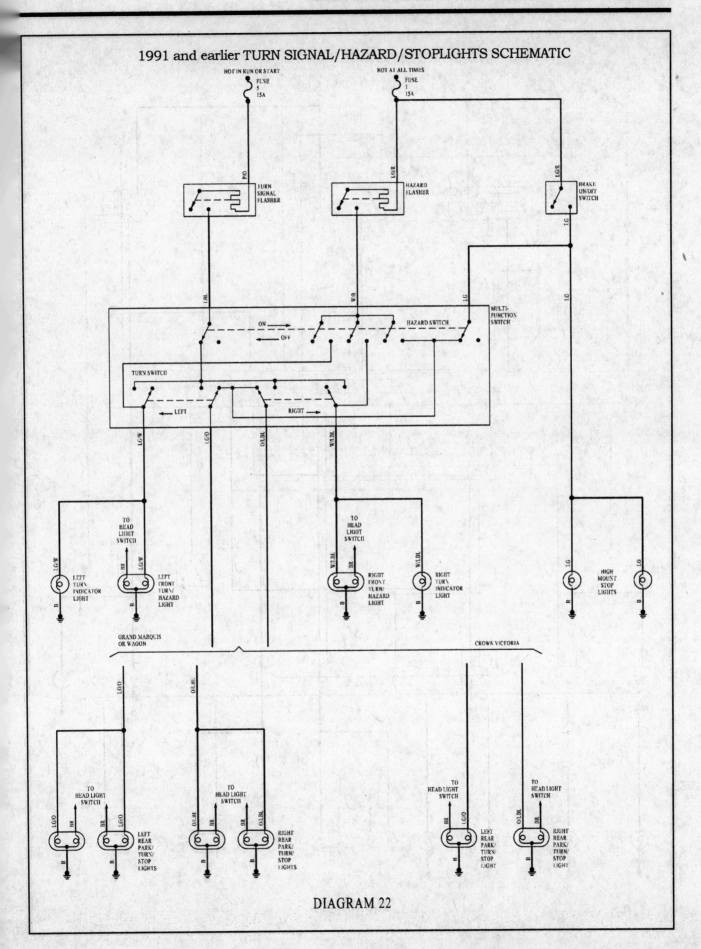

DIAGRAM 22

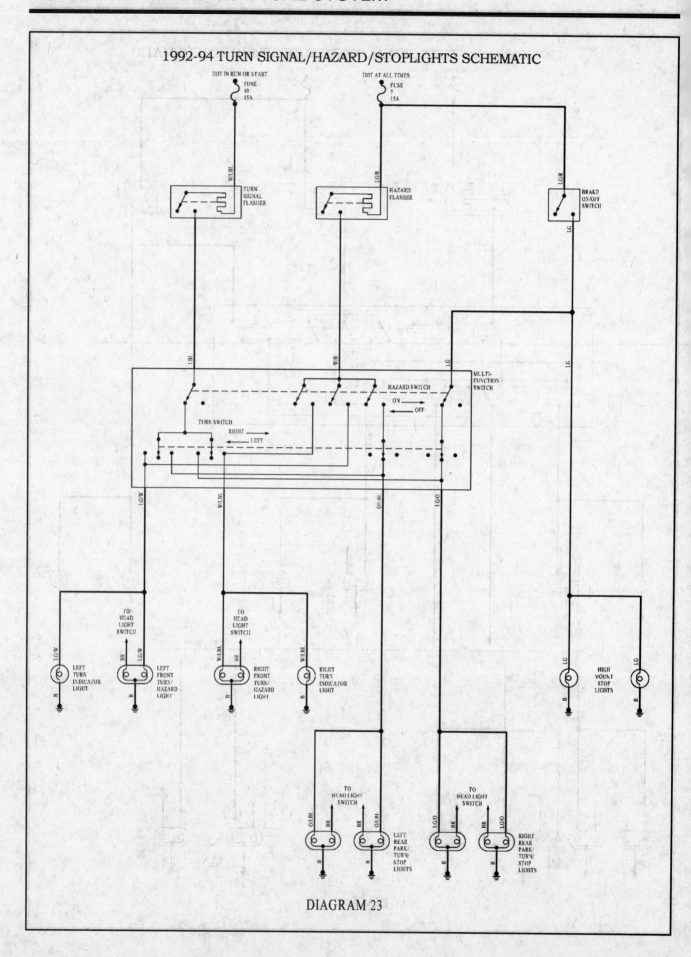

## 1992-94 TURN SIGNAL/HAZARD/STOPLIGHTS SCHEMATIC

DIAGRAM 23

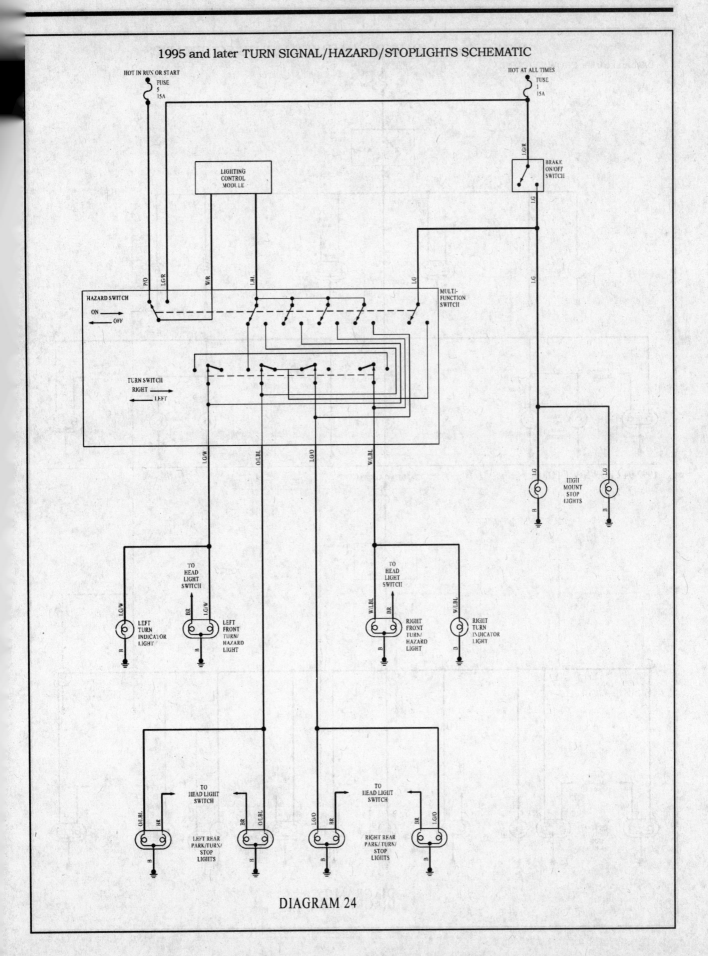

DIAGRAM 24

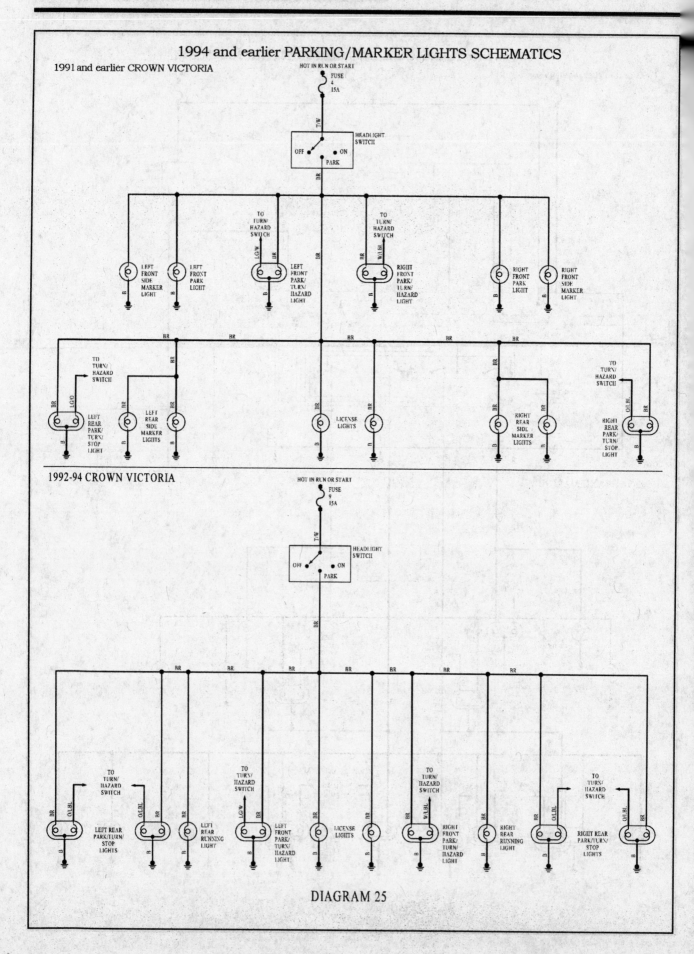

DIAGRAM 25

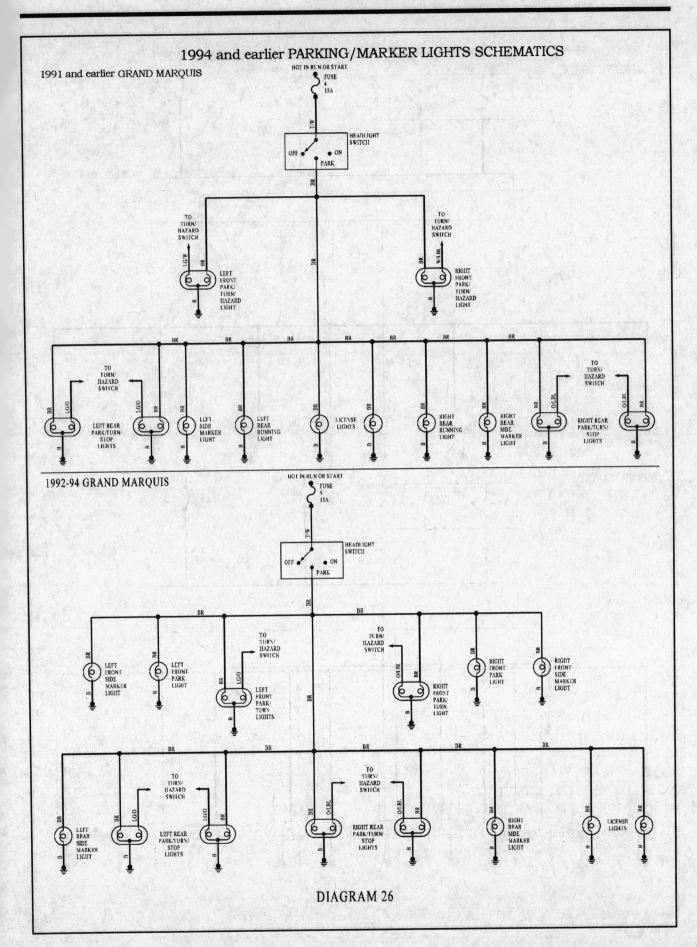

### 1994 and earlier PARKING/MARKER LIGHTS SCHEMATICS

DIAGRAM 26

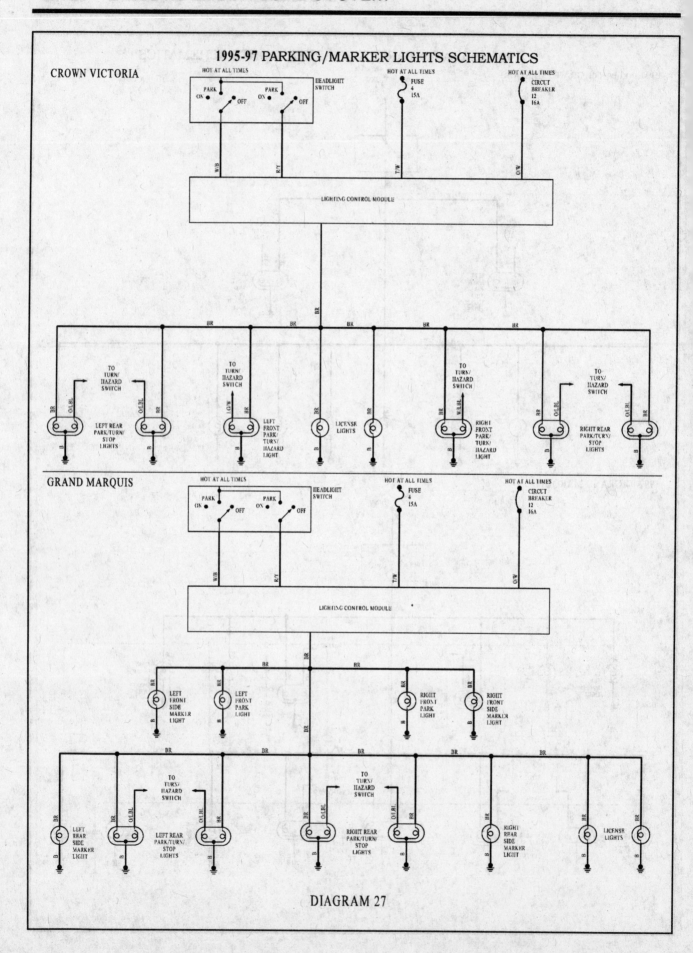

## 1995-97 PARKING/MARKER LIGHTS SCHEMATICS

DIAGRAM 27

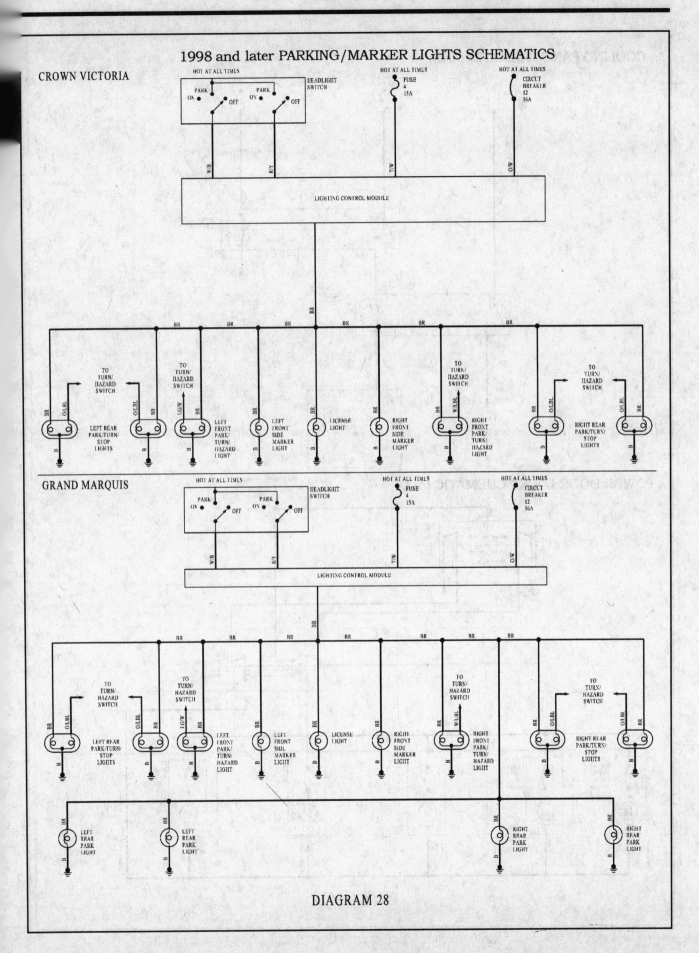

## 1998 and later PARKING/MARKER LIGHTS SCHEMATICS

DIAGRAM 28

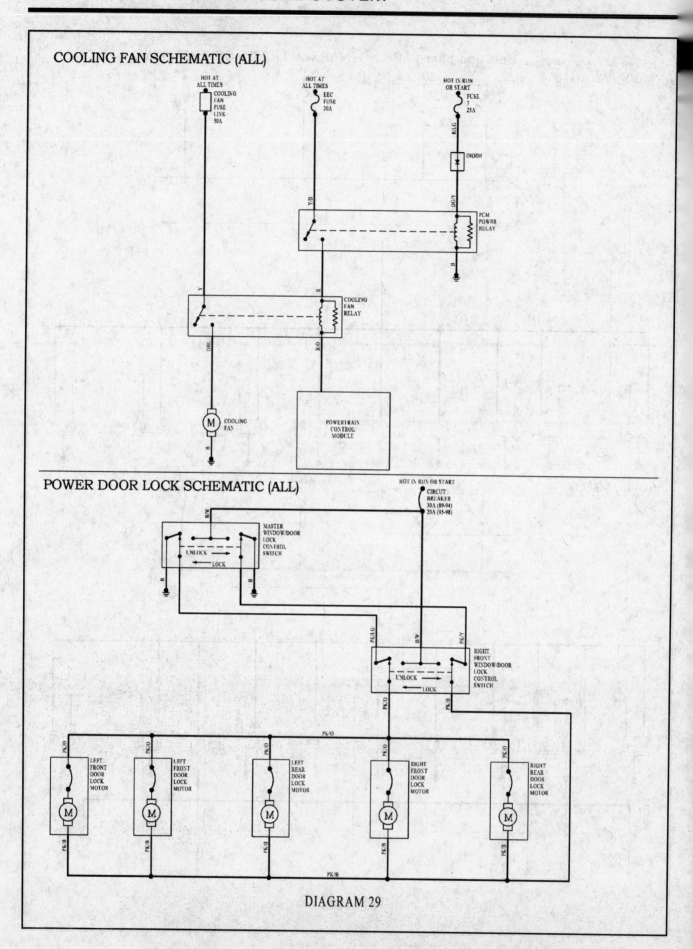

COOLING FAN SCHEMATIC (ALL)

POWER DOOR LOCK SCHEMATIC (ALL)

DIAGRAM 29

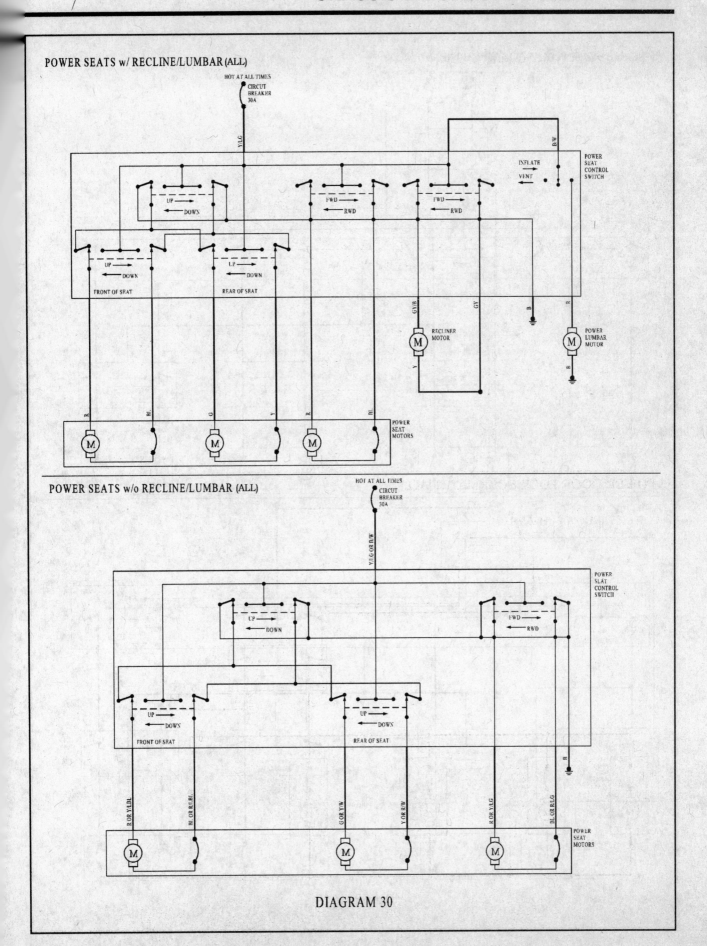

DIAGRAM 30

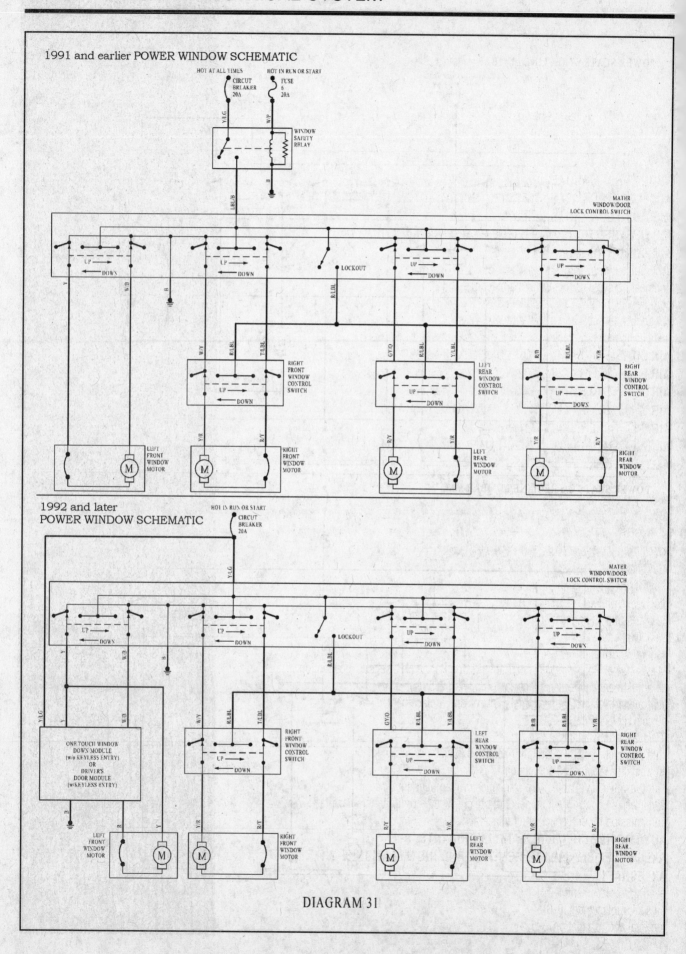

DIAGRAM 31

# A

MASTER INDEX

# G

# H

# I

# J

# K

# L